Advance [illegible]

Leadership, Equity, and Social Justice in American Higher Education

"*Leadership, Equity, and Social Justice in American Higher Education* has clearly accomplished its stated purpose '…to impact higher education preparation programs by filling the void in the literature with voices from the field.' This book is a must-read for those teaching in the academy, working in the field of higher education and especially for those seeking to be the next generation of leaders in our nation's colleges and universities. It's a crucial and timely exploration of the American higher education system, the historical and current barriers in providing access to education to those who continue to seek it in a rapidly changing democracy which has become even more divisive in our current political climate. This will be a powerful and indispensable resource for those committed to continuing to explore the concepts of diversity, equity and social justice in our institutions of higher learning."

Sonia R. Rucker, Coordinator of Institutional Equity & Diversity and Title IX Coordinator, Southeast Missouri State University

"What can be more timely and appropriate than a book on leadership, equity, and social justice as Donald Trump takes the seat in the world's most powerful chair? At the heart of the American democratic experiment there is a recognition that taking power from the monarchs, the oligarchs, the dictators, and the plutocrats and diffusing that power among a greater swath of our citizenry is a more moral, more healthy and a more sustainable way to organize social life. The more we get away from this ideal, the more fragile our democratic experiment becomes.

"As goes the nation, so goes our university system. Or, perhaps it is the other way around. First, we replaced educational leaders with business leaders and now we elect one to the highest office. Neoliberal policies and business models of leadership has shifted the power from faculty to administrators and the focus from intellectual and moral growth to the bottom line. More than ever, we need a vision of leadership that is less about career advancement and more about creating collaborative partnerships across socially constructed, yet enduring, boundaries. We need a vision of leadership that is less about technological surveillance, rubrics, and graduation rates, and more concerned with creating spaces where students can be challenged intellectually, ethically and morally.

"*Leadership, Equity, and Social Justice in American Higher Education* gives us a language of critique, ways to productively resist, and reaffirms the commitment of intellectual pursuits for a more just world. In total, the book offers a multitude of voices that are situated against and within articulations of power within various contexts. This is not a step-by-step primer on how to be an effective leader, but, rather, a collection of essays that highlight the pitfalls and promises in the modern university system. They give us hope and warnings about leadership in the academy today. The authors offer us a vision of a university based on collaboration, writing, mentoring, and praxis. They give us a vision where poetry, dialogue, and service learning can be constructed around respect and justice. *Leadership, Equity, and Social Justice in American Higher Education* is a call to save our universities from the greed and selfishness promoted by the neoliberal contexts in which our universities are enmeshed."

Daniel E. Chapman, Ph.D., Georgia Southern University

Leadership, Equity, and Social Justice in American Higher Education

Questions about the Purpose(s) of Colleges & Universities

Norman K. Denzin and Shirley R. Steinberg
General Editors

Vol. 23

The Higher Ed series is part of the Peter Lang Education list.
Every volume is peer reviewed and meets
the highest quality standards for content and production.

PETER LANG
New York • Bern • Frankfurt • Berlin
Brussels • Vienna • Oxford • Warsaw

Leadership, Equity, and Social Justice in American Higher Education

A Reader

Edited by C. P. Gause

PETER LANG
New York • Bern • Frankfurt • Berlin
Brussels • Vienna • Oxford • Warsaw

Library of Congress Cataloging-in-Publication Data

Names: Gause, C. P.
Title: Leadership, equity, and social justice in American higher education:
a reader / edited by C.P. Gause.
Description: New York: Peter Lang, 2017.
Series: Higher ed: questions about the purpose(s) of colleges and universities; vol. 23
Includes bibliographical references and index.
Identifiers: LCCN 2017001536 | ISBN 978-1-4331-2669-7 (hardcover: alk. paper)
ISBN 978-1-4331-2668-0 (paperback: alk. paper) | ISBN 978-1-4331-4002-0 (ebook pdf)
ISBN 978-1-4331-4003-7 (epub) | ISBN 978-1-4331-4004-4 (mobi)
Subjects: LCSH: Universities and colleges—United States—Administration.
Education, Higher—United States—Administration. | Educational leadership—United States.
Educational equalization—United States. | Social justice.
Classification: LCC LB2341 .L2657 2017 | DDC 378.73—dc23
LC record available at https://lccn.loc.gov/2017001536
DOI 10.3726/b11323

Bibliographic information published by **Die Deutsche Nationalbibliothek**.
Die Deutsche Nationalbibliothek lists this publication in the "Deutsche Nationalbibliografie"; detailed bibliographic data are available on the Internet at http://dnb.d-nb.de/.

The paper in this book meets the guidelines for permanence and durability of the Committee on Production Guidelines for Book Longevity of the Council of Library Resources.

© 2017 Peter Lang Publishing, Inc., New York
29 Broadway, 18th floor, New York, NY 10006
www.peterlang.com

All rights reserved.
Reprint or reproduction, even partially, in all forms such as microfilm, xerography, microfiche, microcard, and offset strictly prohibited.

Printed in the United States of America

I dedicate this volume to my friend, mentor, and colleague; Dr. Dennis Carlson. I miss you Dr. Denny. Your words of wisdom and intrigue continue to resonate as I continue to Keep the Promise.

Contents

ACKNOWLEDGEMENTS

I would like to thank Christie Wormington for her support in organizing this reader. Talha Siddiqi for his invaluable feedback and contributions and Muna Pokharel for her gift of transcription. I am incredibly grateful to the contributors for their patience, commitment, and expertise; without them, this volume would not exist. Many thanks to the team at Peter Lang. I appreciate the opportunity to work with you in bringing this reader to fruition.

INTRODUCTION

C. P. Gause

NEVER BEFORE HAS LEADERSHIP, EQUITY, AND SOCIAL JUSTICE been more important and/or critical to the mission of public universities and institutions of higher education. The 21st century has ushered in a period of instantaneous feedback, to include live newsfeeds, reviews of goods and services, and online streaming of events, as well as experiences. Anyone with a smartphone has access to millions of individuals to report their affirmation and/or dissatisfaction with individuals, products or service. Colleges and universities have not been immune to this current climate. In fact, today's students—"The Millennials" are the force behind the current state of our society. They are the largest population of "knowledge producers" and "knowledge consumers," in the United States.

The structure of higher education in the United States is derived from the German research university and the British undergraduate college. The system is influenced by several factors to include capitalism and the rationality of market competition and currently a commitment to social mobility, democracy, and equal opportunity. The latter did not come about until well into the 20th century. Historically, higher education was for the "elites." White wealthy land-owners who could send their young men to college, "for a proper education." As the United States went through social and economic change; those who were historically excluded from institutions of higher education were able to participate in the enterprise as it became a "gateway" to the middle class. This is no longer the case. The American higher education system has undergone significant change over the past 5 years.

The political disturbances and re-articulation of what it means to be a member of the White establishment in today's America is evidenced by the multiple media outlets, "talking heads," and "political pundits" who utilize the airwaves to garner support for the days of old—no Black president, no illegal immigrants, no taxes on the wealthiest Americans, no racially balanced and/or mixed public schools, no Muslims or immigrants. Ultimately, no one getting ahead of the wealthy White power elite. As I re-think American democracy and the role of education in shaping this nation, diversity, equity, and social justice are all central to our history. Democracy is an enacted daily practice through which people interact and relate through personal, social, and professional routines with a primary focus on continuing the betterment of our humanity. Democracy does not seek to embrace hegemonic practices that maintain the status quo. It does not silence individuals and, at its core foundation, is the representation of difference in society. Putnam (1991) as cited in Gause (2008) stated "democracy is not just a form of social life among other workable forms of social life; it is the precondition for the full application of intelligence to the solution of social problems" (p. 145). It is valued collaboration from all walks of life that will improve a democracy truly based on unity. We must as a society and member of this global community move away from the dichotomies that exist when we think of diversity, equity, and social justice.

Since the Great Recession of 2007 we have witnessed dramatic cuts in state funding to public universities, a significant increase in student loan debt due to ever increasing tuition, challenges to academic freedom and tenure for faculty, issues regarding access and equity to higher education by undocumented students and those in poverty, and the corporatization of higher education. Issues regarding leadership and shared governance of institutions continue to play out in the media and technology continues to impact curriculum delivery. The democratic promise of the public university has been abandoned and emptied of meaning. Severe budget cuts, divisive politics and the cultural wars has forced universities to close their doors, to shift their admissions policies to limit access, and has help to develop an underclass workforce.

The purpose and aim of this volume is to "critique" the current state of American Higher Education through the lens of critical theory and critical pedagogy. This volume seeks to impact higher education preparation programs by filling the void in the literature with voices from the field. The contributing authors are a diverse array of scholars and practitioners who are committed to moral and shared leadership, equity and access, and social justice. For specific descriptions of the enclosed chapters, please consult the introductions that precede each section.

Works Cited

Gause, C. P. (2008). *Integration matters: Navigating identity, culture and resistance.* New York, NY: Peter Lang.

Putnam, H. (1991). A reconsideration of Dewey and democracy. In M. Brint & W. Weaver (Eds.), *Pragmatism in law and society.* Boulder, CO: Westview Press.

PART ONE

The Context of Leadership

Leadership is a word that varies in meaning based upon the context in which it is used and or applied. It does connotes positional power and/or authority; however, it has moved beyond that framework. Leadership involves persuading individuals and/or or groups of individuals to pursue objectives held by the leader or shared by the leader and his or her followers. Leaders should not be thought of without the context of their appointment, position, system, and setting in which they preside. This is especially true for university leadership.

In the first chapter, C. P. Gause highlights the many challenges facing leaders of higher education institutions in the United States. He raises concerns for meeting those challenges and offers his personal and professional perspective of why leadership, equity, and social justice are so important to our democracy.

In the second chapter, John P. Elia critiques the corporatization of public higher education. He utilizes critical pedagogy and critical theory as theoretical anchors in defining corporatization and neoliberalism in the context of higher education. He concludes by "connecting the dots" and makes a case for how corporatization and neoliberalism have been detrimental to the health of institutions of higher education, as well as to the health of the individuals and communities in which they serve.

In the following chapter, Hans F. Bader asserts that "free speech" on college campuses regarding sexual issues has been undermined by Title IX, the federal law that prohibits discrimination on the basis of sex in any federally funded education program or activity. He also asserts that federal officials have seized upon this statute to issue warning to colleges to restrict sexual expression, even when it does not constitute sexual harassment.

Susan Dennison and C. P. Gause present a case study regarding a medium-size public university in North Carolina that took bold and extensive steps to redefine itself as an inclusive, diverse, collaborative, responsive and welcoming learning community for *all.* They chronicle the journey and steps through this process and ultimately share how the majority of their work over a 5 year period was dismantled due to budget cuts.

Sabrina N. Ross asserts the importance of the continued pursuit of knowledge for public good (as opposed to knowledge for profit) in higher education is vital because such efforts act as counter-hegemonic forces to resist academic capitalism and destruction to principles of democracy and equity. She also asserts that faculty of color who teach for social justice have a long history of supporting knowledge for public good and that the emergence of a supposed "post-racial" era threatens to thwart these efforts.

Jillian Volpe White and Kathy L. Guthrie explore the evolving charter between higher education and the public good. Historically, institutions of higher education existed to promote and educated and democratized citizenry that is engaged in the community through socially responsible action. They discuss the impact of declining state support and how institutions are increasingly focused on the personal and economic gains.

Angelo Letizia asserts public higher education faces unprecedented challenges to its public nature in the form of reduced funding. Although public higher education can be inclusive, democratic and the producer of radical theories, he argues that public institutions of higher education are currently being stripped of its democratic and revolutionary potential.

Andrea S. Dauber and Kim Hunt believe that higher education in the United States is at risk of devaluation owing to the dramatic increase of for-profit universities. They argue without entrance requirements, these institutions have lower academic standards, and eventually release graduates into the workforce who compete with graduates from traditional universities with corresponding higher standards in a globalizing market.

Nia I. Cantey, Cara Robinson, and Michael Harris explore the language and discourse surrounding proposed mergers between historically black colleges and universities (HBCUs) and predominately white institutions (PWIs) in contrast with their historical counterparts. They also examine the implications of these proposed mergers for HBCU students, faculty, and the Black community in their continued struggle for social, political, social control, and economic equity.

Paul Watkins discusses how university executives can deal with the wrath of parents stung by the missteps of their young students. Confronted with the pressures of anger, anxiety, and emotion how can university registrars, deans, directors or student affairs deal effectively with anger? How can they make informed, ethical decisions and effectively resolve conflict under trying conditions? How can they balance privileged power with multi-racial and multi-cultural mistrust? Most importantly, how can they strengthen university-home relations to minimize the destructive influence that anger and mistrust bring to the university? He provides five strategies, associated with the negotiating process, offer some insight.

Kathy L. Guthrie and Tessly A. Diequez argue that when examining specific emotional intelligence competencies, most notably empathy, adaptability, and organizational awareness, can lead to international leadership effectiveness. They explore using emotional intelligence competencies to teach global leader efficacy, which is critical in the twenty-first century.

Christopher Cumo, through this essay, explores the "adjunct." He argues the corporate university has simply applied lessons to academe, whereby part time faculties are as powerless as independent contract journalists. He highlights the many perils of this system. For now it suffices to say that part time faculty and the abuses that imperil them appear to be here to stay. He presents a personal narrative of Margaret Mary Vojtko from Duquesne University in Pittsburgh, Pennsylvania.

Elizabeth C. Jodoin and Christopher Gregory highlight the complexities within the intersection of residence hall design and student facility preference with issues of student success and access. They believe exploring the complexities of residence hall design with student access and success may encourage institutional administrators and housing and residence life personnel to think more holistically regarding residence hall design.

CHAPTER 1

Leadership, Equity, and Social Justice in American Higher Education

Are We Making Progress?

C. P. Gause

The United States is more ideologically, philosophically, culturally, linguistically, racially, and ethnically diverse than she has been in any given point in her history. As we view higher education through today's lens and/or the present moment. We would be led to believe that we are not making progress (Carlson & Gause, 2007). The many reports via social media that chronicles the civil unrest on today's campuses and in the streets of many cities in our nations have many to believe that we are a nation that is still experiencing slavery, the violation of due process and citizen's rights, as well as Marshall Law. If we were to believe the current 24-hour media news cycle, one would be left with this feeling of a nation that is currently under cultural and gender apartheid. The illusion of time is the context of this phenomena. This chapter highlights the many challenges facing leaders of higher education institutions in the United States. It raises concerns for meeting those challenges and offers my personal perspective of why leadership, equity, and social justice are so important to our democracy.

Leaders of today's institutions of higher learning face many challenges. The cost of receiving and/or providing an education has increased significantly. Funding issues have implications for who has access. We know institutions of higher education must have an income base to continue their existence. With the increase of tuition and the decreasing funding in state dollars, many students are being priced out of higher education.

This has become a national concern, and it impacts most heavily on individuals of color, who tend to have fewer financial assets than their white counterparts.

There are growing concerns that students no longer need a college degree to be successful. This thinking has brought about great debate and investment into new ways of credentialing and teaching students. Free online courses have been developed. A "badge" and/or certification system has been launched to acknowledge acquired skills, and many individuals are seeking ways to experience learning through YouTube videos and mediated platforms. Retention and matriculation is an issue for most universities. The national 6-year graduation rate for first-time, full-time undergraduate students who began their pursuit of a bachelor's degree at a 4-year degree-granting institution in fall 2008 was 60 percent.

University leadership are also dealing with high incidents of "under-age" drinking and sexual assaults on college campus. Students are utilizing their collective voices and social media to impact university leadership. Student protests on college and university campuses across the United States over the past two years has resulted in the departure of many university presidents, chancellors, and executive leadership. Many faculty members on campuses across the U.S. are becoming active participants in social justice education and seek reform in the academy. It is not easy. It takes hard work.

Personal Reflection

In thinking about diversity, equity and social justice and writing this chapter, I must share my own personal reflection. I am a tenured full professor of color who holds a doctoral and other advanced degrees from Tier 1 research institutions. I currently serve as a department chair at a selective regional comprehensive university in the Midwest. My department consists of 12 full equivalent faculty and I happen to be the only person of color. I am also the only Black male in the College of Education. I was mentored by highly distinguished educational scholars from diverse ethnic and gendered backgrounds. I have ample experience in leading, teaching, researching, and evaluating an array of diverse learning communities and institutions situated in a range of political, geographical and cultural contexts. The additional elements of my identities are African American, Same-affection-loving, Prophetic Christian, northerner, southerner, and Midwesterner (Cooper & Gause, 2007). My praxis is rooted in collaborative activism, social justice, political struggle, and resistance. I did not come from a privileged background. I have two other siblings and, while growing up, my father worked in another state and my mother worked in various industries. She became ill and spent many of my elementary years in the hospital. I experienced poverty and under-employment in my home. My parents communicated to us the importance of getting a "good" education to escape poverty. I had great teachers and mentors. I saw examples of exceptional leadership throughout my K-12 and university experiences. My teachers and professors cared about me and my well-being. They had open hearts, as well as high expectations.

Parker Palmer, in his work *The Courage to Teach: Exploring the Inner Landscape of a Teacher's Life*, explores this notion of courage. He asserts:

> The courage to teach is the courage to keep one's heart open in those very moments when the heart is asked to hold more than it is able so that teacher and students and subject can be woven into the fabric of community that learning, and living, require. (p. 11)

My experiences were cross-cultural, varied, and intense on so many levels. I was encouraged to excel and motivated to be the best. These experiences motivated me to receive my degrees from predominantly white institutions (PWIs). This did not come without its challenges. I spent my time in several classes being the only minority. I spent time in several programs with only a few people who "looked" like me. The terms "diversity," "equity," and "social justice" are not just buzz words for my educational lexicon. I lived those terms daily in multiple ways. I am a professor, an African American male queer professor. This narrative is a part of who I am. This narrative has been developed and re-developed through my experiences. Are we making progress? Yes, of course, we are making progress. Have we made enough progress? Well the answer depends upon who you ask.

Doing Diversity Work in Higher Education

It is difficult to do diversity work and create inclusive communities systemically. Creating such communities is not just a matter of putting into place some cultural programming or creating more committees or student groups with visible physical difference, but eliminating policies, practices, and procedures that could be perceived as barriers or discriminatory. This has not come without many challenges. While engaging in "diversity work" and "social justice activism," I have witnessed workplace bullying and decisions that were made that were not equitable. I have had conversations with individuals who have been personally attacked via email by their colleagues and students both White, Black, and Gay. Stanley (2006) provides an analysis of the literature on faculty of color at PWIs, noting that the paucity (there is a little) of empirical research mirrors the low numbers of this population at such institutions. In comparatively analyzing qualitative studies of faculty of color at PWIs, Stanley (2006) concludes they are almost universally excluded, expected to only speak about diversity issues, expected to be a minority figurehead but not to engage in service directed at assisting minorities in some way, and expected, as scholars, to device their colored identity from their professional identity. The effects of affirmative action programs on hiring practices at PWIs in research is minimal; however, the literature does emphasize the act that faculty of color, once hired, experience "cultural taxation"—additional work expectations that do not boost their chances of earning tenure and/or promotion. Roseboro and Gause (2009) argue that faculty of color face the unenviable burden of being perceived as "tokens" (e.g. unqualified for the job), being typecast (expected to only to work at certain jobs), and of conducting illegitimate research when studying issues related to diversity (the "Brown on Brown" dilemma). Some faculty on this committee have discussed that they are serving in departments that claim to be about "social justice." One in particular has discussed the mere facilitation of his move to another department created the "appearance of insensitivities" by some in leadership roles within his college. He believe the lack of courtesy and privilege of being a tenured associate professor who has worked tirelessly on behalf of diversity, equity, and inclusion has gone unnoticed and is a form of retaliation. Is it racism? Is it a lack of cultural sensitivity? Is it White privilege? Is it the continued marginalization and disenfranchisement of the "other"? I call these experiences contractual benevolence. You are welcome to come to dinner at my house and sit at my table; but you better behave while at the table. There could be numerous reasons for many of my experiences and the experiences of others who are not members of the dominant culture; however, the root of it all goes back to power and hegemony.

Theorizing about creating inclusive communities is different than actually putting theory into practice, and it can be painful in multiple ways for anyone who share this vision or mission. It requires a collective effort by members who represent as many communities as possible within the learning community. I have learned to not give the perception that I am pushing my "own" agenda. Power is continually at work within institutions regardless of membership. Creating inclusive learning communities is inherent in how individuals approach equity, access, diversity, social justice, racism, and their own biases. The majority of individuals I have encountered while conducting professional development sessions are usually operating out of a psychological view of racism. They believe if they could change what was in the heads of White people, particularly the top leadership of their institutions—who are all White and male that this would bring about a more inclusive and anti-oppressive environment. Educators often take this theoretical approach to dealing with racism. When utilizing this theoretical framework, resistance will always occur. I offer a structural analysis view of racism and diversity.

Racism is a structural construct or arrangement, if you will, among members of racial/ethnic groups. Racist institutions are controlled by the dominant culture, which develops, implements, and sustains practices, polices, and procedures that restrict the access of non-Whites to power and privilege. The evidence is clear in all institution of the United States. We see this currently regarding health care, immigration reform, access to higher education for children of undocumented workers and the killing of unarmed black men by police officers; across the nations. The debate within this country continues to grow exponentially.

Conclusion—Have We Made Enough Progress?

Leading today's institutions of higher education requires equity and diversity in all communities present within the university structure to include faculty, staff and student body. There must be ethnic-linguistic minority faculty members in the faculty ranks of PWIs (predominantly white institutions) in order for their missions and visions to be realized. All forms of segregation, self-imposed or occurring due to power and privilege must cease and desist. Opportunities to engage in social justice activism is not only welcomed but encouraged as a viable aspect of driving the curriculum.

Powell (2005) asserts

> We … find ourselves today having to defend the principles of *Brown* against arguments that segregation has been disestablished or that its persistence is merely a matter of choice. Focusing on choice misconstrues racial separation as symmetrical, as if whites and blacks choose to be exclusive in the same fashion. Segregation, however, has historically been and remains today a reality imposed with power and privilege on those without. (p. 283)

Universities must create professional learning communities where all individuals, regardless of race, ethnicity, sexual identity, sexual orientation, religion, class, and ability, both physical and cognitive can engage in knowledge production and community building. According to Roseboro and Gause (2009) this requires a greater sense of responsibility and accountability for PWIs (predominantly white institutions). They assert that

> Creating professional learning communities that attract qualified faculty members, regardless of race, should be the goal of any institution of higher education. For predominantly White institutions that are committed to creating racially inclusive professional learning communities the constructing of communities that sustain faculty of color requires an identification of what the culture of the institution is as well as the ways the institution might exclude (whether explicitly or implicitly). And, it requires recognition of the roles faculty of color might be asked to fulfill. Most important, it demands a "truth telling" process in which White faculty hear their colleagues of color, faculty of color hear their White colleagues, and both groups engage in dialogue about the institutional culture and how faculty members, administrators, staff and students might create sustainable, inclusive democratic learning communities. (p. 139)

Teaching, learning, and leading democratically requires constant participation with change. The purpose of higher education to provide opportunities and spaces for our citizenry to engage in democratic practices for the public good. Democracy is an enacted daily practice whereby people interact and relate through daily personal, social, and professional routines with a primary focus on continuing the betterment of our humanity. This is the cause of education. In order to do this, higher education must prepare critical transformative leaders who are willing and able to draw upon culturally relevant, critical, and counter-normative pedagogies. Yes, we are making progress; however, we have not made enough progress!

Works Cited

Carlson, D., & Gause, C. P. (2007). *Keeping the promise; Essays on leadership, democracy and education.* New York, NY: Peter Lang.

Cooper, C. W., & Gause, C. P. (2007). "Who's afraid of the big bad wolf?" Facing identity politics and resistance when teaching for social justice. In D. Carlson & C. P. Gause (Eds.), *Keeping the promise: Essays on leadership, democracy and education* (pp. 197–216). New York, NY: Peter Lang.

Powell, J. (2005). A new theory of integrated education: True integration. In J. Boger & G. Orfield (Eds.), *School resegregation: Must the south turn back?* (pp. 281–304). Chapel Hill, NC: University of North Carolina Press.

Roseboro, D., & Gause, C. P. (2009). Faculty of color constructing communities at predominantly White institutions. In C. A. Mullen (Ed.), *Leadership and building professional learning communities* (pp. 139–150). New York, NY: Palgrave Macmillan.

Stanley, C. (2006). *Faculty of color: Teaching in predominantly white colleges and universities.* Bolton, MA: Anker.

CHAPTER 2

U.S. Public Higher Education in Peril

The Disastrous Impacts of Corporatization

John P. Elia

Public higher education in the United States has been under assault from creeping corporatization for the past several decades. This has changed public colleges and universities at their core, and many scholars have argued that this relatively new paradigm used to run public higher education has had an extremely negative impact not only on the institution itself, but also on faculty and students. Using critical pedagogy and critical theory as theoretical anchors, this chapter begins with defining *corporatization* and *neoliberalism* in the context of higher education. Then a brief treatment of the history of corporatization in public higher education will be undertaken, including how it has gained a stronghold on everything from philosophies of education to the philosophical approach to operating public institutions of higher education. Next, this chapter turns to several ways in which corporatization and neoliberalism have manifested in U.S. public higher education. What follows is a treatment of how this corporate intensification—and its sheer number of manifestations—has affected not only the process of education, but also the individuals at the heart of the academic enterprise; namely, students and faculty. Then, this chapter boldly lays out how neoliberalism and corporatization have created ill health for, and a palpable erosion of, the once highly cherished democratic principles for which public higher education stood and that it largely achieved. In the end, corporatization has taken a terrible toll on the institution and has negatively affected the quality of life of students and faculty. The conclusion of this chapter "connects the dots" and makes a case for how corporatization and neoliberalism have been detrimental to the health of U.S. public higher education and to the health of individuals and communities. Finally, a plea is made to push back to repair and restore democratic ideals and practices of U.S. public higher education.

Corporatization and Neoliberalism: Definitions and Context

In the context of this chapter, the term *corporatization* refers to the widespread practices of colleges and universities adopting business and management methods found in the private sector. The foundations of corporatization of U.S. public higher education can be traced to neoliberalism, which promotes the ideologies and practices of free market without governmental involvement or interference. Furthermore, according to Martinez and Garcia (1997), the prominent features of neoliberalism include (1) allowing the private sector to do business without any governmental regulations or restrictions, no matter how pernicious or harmful this is to social life; (2) slashing public funding for social services such as schooling and medical care; (3) relaxing governmental regulations of anything that minimizes—or in any way interferes with—revenues and profiteering; (4) privatizing public entities, services, and possessions; and (5) jettisoning the notion of "the public good" or "community" and instead focusing on "individual responsibility." Neoliberalism, then, has given rise to—and has fueled—corporate ideologies and practices in U.S. higher education, which have been inextricably linked to elements of privatization in public colleges and universities across the nation. While some instances of corporatization (along with privatization) in higher education can be traced back to the late nineteenth and early twentieth centuries, there has been an ever-quickening escalation of corporatization ever since the early 1980s.

A Brief Historical Sketch of Corporatization and Neoliberalism in Public U.S. Higher Education

Despite romantic views that public U.S. colleges and universities of the not-too-distant past were "pure" and entirely free from corporate or commercialized interests, this is not the case. Henry Steck (2003) notes that

> beginning in the nineteenth and early twentieth centuries, there were business interests that influenced university governance, if in no other way than the presence of corporate managers as trustees and as substantial donors of buildings or chairs or programs named after themselves or their families. (p. 72)

Also tracing the early history of commercialization in higher education, Derek Bok (2003), former president of Harvard University, in his influential book *Universities in the Marketplace: The Commercialization of Higher Education*, mentions that in the early twentieth century a major university advertised to persuade students to apply for admission; in another instance there was a "Bureau of Publicity" put in place to amplify the university's prominence. Regarding the commercialization of sports, Bok reveals that "in 1905 Harvard was concerned enough about its profitable football team to hire a 26-year-old coach at a salary equal to that of its president and twice the amount paid to full professors" (p. 2). As one reads the literature on the history of corporatization and commercialization in higher education, it becomes clear that there were, indeed, precursors to the more blatant and entrenched practices we see today (see, for example, Newfield, 2003). Steck (2003) puts it best: "The process of corporatization is more extensive than prior connections to the business community in terms of both the depth and scope of the penetration to the university" (p. 75). In fact, there has been a fast-paced escalation of corporatizing public higher education over the past three plus decades.

Higher education in the United States has undergone a major shift since approximately the early 1980s. The notion that public institutions of higher learning had as their primary mission to produce well-educated citizens who would enjoy a solid liberal education and who would bring their critical sensibilities to bear on participating fully in a democratic society has been severely compromised and even crippled. Interwoven in the fabric and functioning of public colleges and universities was once a deep commitment to "teaching students to take responsibility for their future, develop unrelenting fidelity to justice, and hone their ability to discriminate between rigorous arguments and heavily charged opinions [and to enable] … young people [to] develop the values, skills, and knowledge required …" (Giroux, 2012, p. 1). Furthermore, postsecondary education for the most part once prided itself on producing critical thinkers, cultivating "leadership, social citizenship, [and preparing students for an active role in] democratic public life" (Giroux, 2001a, p. 3). While considered traditional in many North American colleges and universities, these views and aims have been largely eclipsed by the shift in priorities brought about by corporatization. There are many reasons why corporatization has gained a stronghold on public higher education. I will address only a few of the primary reasons here.

Perhaps one of the main reasons is that public colleges and universities across the nation have been steadily underfunded over several decades. Simply put, conservative politicians have worked for decades to get government out of the business of supporting social service agencies and anything remotely perceived to be part of the "welfare state," including pubic higher education. In recent history, the shrinkage of public funding is traced to the Reagan era of the 1980s, when deregulation was the order of the day, along with the widespread defunding of social services. Some politicians continue to decry that there is too much bloat and there are too many inefficiencies; they support competition that is inherent in the private sector. To shore up the lack of public funding, colleges and universities not only have had to raise tuition and student fees substantially over the past few decades, but also have taken an entrepreneurial route and formed public–private partnerships to help shore up the deficient and wholly inadequate public funding stream. This has necessarily meant that corporations and businesses have insinuated themselves into public higher education culture, which has profound implications that will be discussed later. Another reason for courting donors and corporate partners is to be able to compete with other colleges and universities to be placed on the annual *U.S. News and World Report*'s "Best Colleges" list and other college ranking lists to attract students. This is a prime example of how corporatization has taken hold. American Studies Professor Nicolaus Mills (2012) puts it best by averring that

> the most visible sign of corporatization of higher education lies in the commitment that colleges and universities have made to winning the ratings war perpetuated by the kinds of rankings *U.S. News and World Report* now offers in its annual "Best Colleges" guide (p. 6)

which had its debut in 1983.

The reduction in public funding has caused public colleges and universities to move to other, more corporate, means of funding. These institutions have *de facto* shifted their philosophies of education and their approaches to operating public institutions of higher education to be more in line with a corporation. Throughout history, the broad aims of the academy have focused heavily on fostering a learning environment that provides students with intellectual skills and an appreciation to serve the public/community. In addition, higher education has, in large part, emphasized the importance of understanding and achieving democracy in various facets of life as well as to help address social difficulties (American Council on Education & Williamson, 1949). Corporatization has eclipsed the more conventional aims of higher education. The focus is increasingly on the bottom line and on pushing students through so they can get jobs, with little emphasis on the educational journey itself. Clearly, becoming gainfully employed following graduation is important, but if the focus becomes so narrow as to foreclose a good, solid, and well-rounded educational experience, then it is highly problematic. With corporatization becoming so entrenched in the majority of public colleges and universities across the nation, some scholars of higher education have sounded an alarm about the quality of education students are receiving. The worry is that students are being "trained" as opposed to "educated." It is important to make the distinction between these terms. In his well-regarded book *The Knowledge Factory: Dismantling the Corporate University and Creating True Higher Education,* Stanley Aronowitz (2000) asserts that

> Training prepares the student in knowledges that constitute an occupation or particular set of skills … Education prepares the student to take her place in society in a manner consistent with its values in terms of her own priorities and interests. (p. 1)

Aronowitz goes on to suggest that it is progressively more difficult to find education transpiring in the academy. Put another way, *training* often transpires in the name of *education.*

Corporatization has prompted a transformation in the ways public college and university administrators manage their campuses. Most colleges and universities have been in perpetual financial crisis for many years. Such crises have become the "new normal." Given the stresses of keeping their campuses afloat, countless administrators have turned to a variety of methods of obtaining funding—from corporate donors and public–private partnerships to leaning heavily on alumni for donations—to "balance their books" and be able to compete with other schools. That many administrators have gone along with, and have been fully engaged in, corporate practices—which have become part of their philosophical schema as a way of doing business—does not necessarily indicate that they are "sellouts" per se. I would argue, as others have, that corporatization has become part of the academy's DNA and is virtually inextricably interwoven in higher education. Corporatization is much larger than being at the discretion of individual chancellors, presidents, provosts, deans, and so on. Corporatization has swept through the nation and left virtually no public college or university untouched. Many administrators have been in survival mode for years and are comforted to know that a plethora of corporate possibilities will not only help "bail out" their institutions, but also put them in good stead to be fully competitive with other institutions in terms of attracting students, faculty, and additional corporate dollars to offer naming rights to buildings, research labs, endowed professorships, and a host of other possibilities. Such practices constitute a radical change from the past in public higher education.

Manifestations of Corporatization and Neoliberalism

The unmitigated starvation of public higher education due to decades of dwindling public funding has had a horrific impact on campuses and, in large part, has invited corporatization along with all of its ill effects. The tentacles of corporatization and neoliberalism have varied and far-reaching implications. In essence, corporatization—fed by neoliberal ideologies—has touched nearly every facet of campus life. While it is not possible to comment on every manifestation here, several examples will be provided. In terms of manifestations, I will focus on grants, part-time faculty, higher education administrators, student fees/tuition and student loans, pedagogy and learning (including vocationalization of education, commodification of knowledge, and proliferation of online/distance education), corporate entities on campuses, development professionals, corporate sponsorships, and the corporate physical plant. As we will see, even with this limited list of corporate manifestations, the implications of corporate infiltration have changed the very landscape of public higher education in the United States.

Grant Funding

While Research I universities have highly encouraged—and some have required—tenure-track faculty members to obtain grant funding for their research, it is now common (particularly in the sciences and social sciences) for permanent faculty at comprehensive and teaching universities to be pressured to obtain grant funding for their research. In some cases, departments and programs have institutionalized grant-getting expectations in their retention, tenure, and promotion criteria. To be clear, there is nothing inherently wrong with obtaining grant funding for one's research. It becomes problematic when faculty members become pressured, even forced, to produce grant money for their research projects. That not being bad enough, some college and university administrators "turn their noses up" to grants that do not generate enough indirect costs (IDCs), those costs that provide monies to colleges and universities for administration of grants, overhead, and so forth. It is clearly part of the corporatization of public higher education.

There are other problems as well. Since there is such a push for, and emphasis on, obtaining grant money, the grant-getting process favors those researchers and disciplines in which grant activity is likely to occur; namely, in the sciences and social sciences. Other fields of study such as the arts and humanities are not nearly as likely to attract grant funding. In an era that focuses so heavily on external funding, it is quite easy to see how some research (i.e., scientific or social scientific grant-funded work that relies on the empirical, positivistic research paradigm) is valued more highly than other research (i.e., art studies; historical, literary, philosophical research; etc., which have usually neither attracted nor relied on grants; Williams, 2001). In fact, "95 percent of federal research funds that go to universities are concentrated in STEM [science, technology, engineering, and mathematics] fields" (Slaughter, 2012, p. 18). This creates a hierarchy of research with potential rewards for some faculty members and their departments and fallout for others. For example, could it be that departments and programs that have a track record of getting grants would be permitted to hire more tenure-track professors than departments that are virtually grantless? Is it possible that tenure-track hiring could be linked to disciplines and/or areas of research that are "hot" in terms of attracting large grants? One can see how inequities and morale issues could dominate campuses.

Speaking from personal experience, I once had a friendship with a colleague in the social sciences who kept urging me to get grants. I explained to her that the kind of work I do—history and philosophy of education focusing on school-based sexuality education and critical work in LGBT studies, queer studies, and sexuality studies—is not readily fundable. She exclaimed that it was all very sad and that she felt bad for me. I looked at her with what must have been a contorted face complete with a perplexed expression. She then had the bad sense to say that "being at the university and not having grants is like being on welfare." She then went on to say how nice it was to be able to afford assistants, get new furniture for her office, and buy herself out of as much teaching as possible. I was speechless (not a condition from which I usually suffer). Of course, I recount this story here to illustrate only one troubling example of the kind of hierarchical thinking that exists about grant funding and the perceived worth of colleagues and their work according to whether a grant is attached to them or their research.

Overreliance on Part-Time, Contingent Faculty

Yet another facet of corporatization is an escalating reliance on part-time faculty members. In the late 1960s, tenure-track and tenured faculty comprised approximately two-thirds of higher education's teaching force. Today, not even one-third of the teaching force has permanent status (Mills, 2012). Today, about 70% of faculty members are part-timers (also commonly referred to as adjunct faculty, lecturers, or contingent faculty). At its outset, one of the main purposes of hiring part-time lecturers was to fill in for sabbatical leaves. Now, it is common for lecturers to have time bases of 1.00. Many of these individuals have doctorates yet have little hope of becoming part of the tenure-track professoriate. They are teaching "work horses," often with five-course teaching loads per term. Many cobble together a full-time job by teaching at two or more campuses. Many do not have office space in which to meet students, and others hold office hours in crowded offices occupied by many other lecturers.

The main point is that lecturer faculty members are relatively inexpensive compared to permanent, full-time tenure-track professors. By hiring part-timers, colleges and universities are afforded flexibility. More so than ever before, campuses strive to reduce costs yet increase their full-time equivalent students (FTES) with efficiency (Williams, 2001), which often translates into heavily enrolled classes with fewer faculty members overall. Part-time lecturer faculty encompass the majority of those teaching classes and have the most contact with students, yet most often they are only required to teach their courses and hold a requisite number of office hours. Contractually, they are not required to (nor should they be) be engaged in faculty governance or department-wide or campus-wide service activities. It is no coincidence that the checks and balances brought about by shared faculty governance are more difficult to achieve when most campuses have only about 30% of their faculty who are expected to engage in a variety of service activities, including sitting on faculty senates and other governing bodies.

The picture is even more bleak and sinister than this. A vociferous critic of neoliberalism and a renowned education and cultural studies expert, Henry Giroux (2001b), boldly states that

> creating a permanent underclass of part-time professional workers in higher education is not only demoralizing and exploitative for many faculty who inhabit such jobs, such policies increasingly de-skill both part and full-time faculty by increasing the amount of work they have to do, while simultaneously shifting power away from the faculty to the managerial sectors of the university. (pp. 38–39)

The dwindling number of tenured faculty members constitutes a significant threat to academic freedom. The chief purposes of tenure are to afford tenured faculty the academic freedom or protection to teach content they believe is appropriate in their classes and to engage in controversial or unpopular research without the fear of losing their jobs. In addition, tenure allows tenured faculty to uphold standards in terms of assigning a range of final course grades—including low and failing grades—without fear of jeopardizing their jobs. Tenured members of the faculty are free to speak up and challenge other colleagues and administrators by offering their own points of view—however controversial—without the threat of being terminated. Although there are some cases in which it was imprudent to grant faculty members tenure, on the whole, tenure has been a very positive feature of U.S. public and private higher education. With the clear national trend of hiring lecturers (non-tenure-track) at a disproportionate rate compared to tenure-track hires (e.g., as stated earlier, today approximately 70% of faculty are lecturers and about 30% are tenured or tenure-track), one can see quite clearly that academic freedom has been eroded simply because lecturers are not protected under the tenure system. This has grim repercussions for the health of U.S. higher education. An unravelling of academic freedom means the loss of critically important protections for the majority of faculty and potential compromises to the curriculum.

Corporatization of Higher Education Administrators

High-level senior college and university administrators have become more concerned and preoccupied with fundraising than with ensuring that the educational mission is being upheld. For the past three decades, college and university administrators have become increasingly distanced from their former role as members of the faculty; while most upper administrators were once part of the professoriate, the perks and fulfillment they receive from their administrative posts offer more to them than did their former work as professors (Aronowitz, 2000). A higher percentage than ever before of presidents' duties involves fundraising. More so than ever, these upper administrators are focused on making their institutions competitive, cost effective, and efficient (Kezar, 2004). It is concerning that such administrators are focused on fundraising. Many of these administrators "have professionally benefitted the most from corporatization" (Mills, 2012, p. 8). There are many presidents who are making million-dollar salaries. Many others enjoy annual pay that is not far behind, and many of them serve on boards of directors around the country (Mills, 2012).

Exemplifying the corporatization of chief academic officers, the University of Iowa recently hired its new president, Mr. J. Bruce Harreld. While for nearly a century the majority of U.S. university presidents have come up through the academic ranks, this is not the case with Mr. Harreld. He comes directly from the corporate world with a few relatively brief stints as an adjunct faculty member. In a recent article published in *The Chronicle of Higher Education* entitled "At U. of Iowa, New President's Background is All Business," reporter Mary Ellen McIntire (2015) writes,

> Mr. Harreld's résumé is highlighted with executive positions in the corporate world. He was a senior vice president at IBM for 13 years, president and a member of the board of the Boston Market Company for two years, and chief information officer at Kraft General Foods, where he led the frozen foods unit. (p. A11)

While this article is written in a balanced fashion, it highlights that faculty members at the University of Iowa are extremely uneasy about the potential that their campus will become corporatized. Clearly, this is an example of a president who is being brought in to manage the business aspect of the University of Iowa, but given his impoverished record in the academy, to say the least, it is unclear how he will lead the academic "side of the house." Education expert David Schultz (2015) asserts that

> administrators with corporate backgrounds now make many decisions once made by faculty. Trustees, largely business leaders, select college and university presidents, often with minimal input from the faculty, and the presidents, in turn—again without faculty guidance—select deans, department heads, and other administrative personnel. (para. 8)

This is worrisome, and it fits with the current trend of corporatizing North American college and university campuses.

Spiraling Cost of Tuition and Student Loans

College tuition and fees have spiraled out of control. Over the past several years, tuition increases have outpaced the cost of living (Lerner, 2008). There are various reasons for this. One reason for such an escalation is that these costs are used, in part, to make up the shortfall of public funding for public colleges and universities (Cox, 2013). Yet another reason has to do with resourcing a variety of campus amenities. Those feeling most of the distress about rising college costs are those students from working-class backgrounds. Henry Giroux (2012) notes that "lacking adequate financial aid, students, especially poor students, will increasingly finance the high costs of their education through private corporations such as Citibank, Chase Manhattan, Marine Midland, and other sanctioned lenders" (p. 445). Paying off student loans is often daunting, and students become saddled with substantial payments for long after their college days. In some cases, college debt is on par with a mortgage for a home. The expenses to obtain a college education make it impossible for an increasing number of would-be college students to have access to higher education. This is certainly a factor in the erosion of the possibility of socioeconomic mobility, and it signals yet another blow to the middle class. Put another way, the astronomical costs of obtaining a college or university education have widened the gap between the "haves" and "have nots." It is criminal how outrageous the costs of higher education have become.

Pedagogy and Learning

While there is some innovative and creative teaching transpiring in the academy today, corporate mentalities have affected instruction and the expectations students have of the college experience. Students are progressively seen as customers in the academic marketplace in which customer satisfaction is increasingly more important. This is quite dangerous as the potential for compromising educational integrity is ever present. Another concern regarding educational integrity has to do with *vocationalizing the curriculum*, meaning that the focus of the educational experience is linked mainly to employment and how higher education can serve that purpose rather than emphasizing the broader democratic ideals, including the social and civic responsibilities, that were once integral to a college education.

Closely related to vocationalization, as discussed earlier, is the *commodification of knowledge*, which is essentially treating knowledge produced and/or obtained as commodities to be sold in the free market. This can take several forms, such as treating coursework, ideas, and ultimately college degrees as commodities to get well-paying jobs; colleges and universities selling their ideas, patents, courses of study, certificate programs, and so forth for financial gain; and even making profits from research.

Continuing with the theme of making money and operating with the greatest efficiency, there has been a *proliferation of online/distance education courses and programs.* Online course offerings have taken many forms—from the Massive Open Online Course (MOOC) in which potentially thousands of students can enroll, to the hybrid "flipped classroom" in which students are introduced to material and concepts outside of class (in an online format) interspersed with "high touch," in-person, face-to-face class meetings where students reinforce the information they learned in the online format with mini-lectures from the instructor, in-class activities, question-and-answer periods, and so on.

There are numerous forms of online instruction. This relatively new format of virtualized "education" is bitterly contested in the academy. In general, some see online instruction as the panacea, and others see it as a shameful and an outrageous sham. Some are skeptical about it while others are hopeful, and many are without a strong opinion one way or the other. There are, however, countless academics who view online education as highly problematic, especially given that it is ripe for an increasingly corporatized system of higher education that will exploit online offerings to make a profit. There are examples of colleges and universities (and even individual faculty) profiting from online instruction. Derek Bok (2003) recalls a situation in which the dean of Columbia University's Business School made a deal with "the founder and CEO of an online company interested in distance education … [This] was a collaboration that would allow Columbia professors to offer on-line courses in exchange for royalties from fees collected from subscribing students" (p. 79). Getting Columbia onboard was a surefire way of attracting other prestigious schools to this business venture (Bok, 2003). Summing up the commodification of online education, Paule Chau (2010) comments that "the online learning movement is motivated by capitalistic ideals in an increasingly knowledge-based economy whereby education is transformed into a commodity, students into consumers, faculty into entrepreneurs, and institutions of higher learning into storefronts" (p. 178). It is evident by examining (1) how the curriculum is being vocationalized, (2) how knowledge is being commodified, and (3) how online education has proliferated that corporatization has fully infiltrated pedagogy and learning in colleges and universities.

Corporate Entities on Campuses

It is quite common for colleges and universities to outsource supplies and services to corporations. For example, many campus bookstores have been privatized. Likewise, a plethora of eateries are operated by outsourced venders, and in some instances fast food franchises are on campuses. In addition, some campuses have exclusive contracts with beverage companies such as Pepsi and Coca Cola. These exclusive contracts are known as "pouring rights" and involve a beverage company having exclusive rights to sell its products in nearly every location where such products may be purchased on a college or university campus (e.g., dining and residence halls, on-campus stores, vending machines, and athletic events). In exchange for a campus entering into a contractual agreement with a particular beverage company, a campus usually receives a lump sum of up to several millions of dollars up front and then additional money is paid over multiple years in which a contract is in effect. As one can imagine, this would seem to be the ultimate "sweet" deal for cash strapped campuses looking to infuse money into their depleted coffers. However, the media and public health literature have examined this controversial practice. Those who are critical of pouring rights point out a number of difficulties including everything from the health concerns associated with pushing sugary drinks and products to the omnipresent concern about the further entrenchment of corporations into college and university life. It should be noted that while pouring rights were initially introduced in higher education in the early 1990s, there have been numerous instances in which elementary and secondary schools (e.g., middle schools and high schools) have entered into pouring rights contracts (Nestle, 2000). Perhaps the most prominent concern about pouring rights agreements is that they ultimately play a role in contributing to obesity (Almeling, 2003), diabetes, metabolic syndrome, and other chronic diseases. Beyond the health considerations, another factor is that pouring rights create yet another facet of the corporatized college or university complete with ubiquitous advertisements throughout campuses. The ability to have space on campuses to advertise is an attractive part of the deal for beverage companies (Blumenstyk, 1994). There are many faculty members and students who are concerned that pouring rights is yet another way that campuses are being sold out. The bottom line, however, is that the decisions about whether or not to pursue pouring rights agreements are about ethics, particularly given potential health concerns associated with drinking sugary sodas. To what levels will colleges and universities swoop to "be in bed" with corporations to raise money? Such financial arrangements are surely profitable for campuses and beverage companies across the nation yet such deals are fraught with difficulties.

Development Professionals

Most colleges and universities employ a team of development professionals who are responsible for securing donations from corporations, businesses, and individuals. They are also responsible for planning alumni events to secure funding. Development personnel are also instrumental in taking the leads on major campus campaign initiatives in which millions of dollars—sometimes hundreds of millions—are raised for a variety of purposes. In large part, the genesis of Offices and Divisions of Development on public campuses is to supplement dwindling public appropriations.

Corporate Sponsorships

Corporate sponsorships of universities are commonplace today. These sponsorships take many forms. However, the bulk of what is written about specifically is corporate sponsorship of research. With his usual keen and bold analysis, Henry Giroux (2001a) trenchantly writes that "as universities become increasingly strapped for money, corporations are more than willing to provide needed resources, but the costs are troubling and come with strings attached. Corporations increasingly dictate the very research they sponsor" (p. 4). There are many examples of various universities making deals with numerous corporations (see, e.g., Bok, 2003; Brownlee, 2015; Kumar, 2001; Poovey, 2001; Washburn, 2011). There is a fundamental problem with corporations sponsoring research. As Giroux says, there are strings attached. Of course, the serious issues include creating conflicts of interest, compromising academic freedom, and skewing research findings. Equally as problematic, Jamie Brownlee (2015), a legal scholar, warns that

> corporate influence has corrupted academic research, from the selection of research topics, to research secrecy, through to how conflicts of interest and research bias influence the collection and release of information … corporatization of higher education has led to systematic research bias and compromised the values that have historically defined scientific research. (p. 23)

The main reason academic freedom and tenure were put in place by the American Association of University Professors (AAUP) in 1915 was to prevent corporations and business & industry from meddling in academic affairs (Washburn, 2011). The corporation–university alliance today has reached new heights, and it is in no way hyperbolic to say that U.S. higher education has been in a very serious crisis and is getting sicker.

Corporate Physical Plant

It is not uncommon for college and university campuses to maintain well-manicured grounds with numerous amenities. Almost formulaic, one can find a bevy of dining establishments, fine-arts and performance-arts centers, megasized gyms, wellness centers (Mills, 2012), and other conveniences. These features of modern U.S. colleges and universities are elaborate and often "over the top." To be sure, many of the amenities on campuses are in some way connected to the corporate world. This is all in the name of having a pleasing atmosphere with most conveniences that are appealing to students and visitors. Having a flashy and fancy campus is particularly important in attracting potential students to select a particular college or university. The impression a campus makes on potential students during their initial campus visits is an important factor in the selection process (Strange, 2003). Ultimately, students pay a high price for such luxuries. Mills (2012) notes that "so many colleges and universities with four-year residential campuses have increased spending for student services that on a percentage basis outpace their increases in academic instruction and financial aid" (p. 7). This is contributing to making higher education difficult to afford for some and simply out of reach for others.

Intensification of Corporate Life in the Academy

While it is true that corporatization is nothing new in the academy and that its roots can be traced to the late nineteenth and early twentieth centuries, it is also true that corporatization has never played such a significant role in U.S. colleges and universities as it does today. Corporatization, born from neoliberalism, has many more tentacles now than in the past. The sheer number of corporate manifestations in the academy is overwhelming and downright frightening. As such, corporate practices in U.S.

higher education have multiplied exponentially and have badly injured the academy in a multitude of ways. The agents of corporatization do not care about the quality of education. In fact, they are more interested in *training* than in *educating*. Training individuals is akin to instructing students in such a manner that they will be prepared for jobs, and in many of those jobs, they will serve corporate interests. No one would dispute that an expectation of graduating from college is to end up being gainfully employed. That is not the issue. The issue has to do with the approach to teaching and learning. The idea of a college education has to do with exploration, with working through ideas, learning critical thinking, and assessing how one might contribute to the public good and participate in a democracy that is broadly conceived.

Regarding research, corporatization of the academy has been pernicious and is at an all-time high. Some of the implications have been discussed earlier in terms of creating conflicts of interest, compromising academic freedom, skewing research findings, and playing a large role in the selection of research topics. However, it is even more insidious and dangerous. Corporatization favors certain kinds of research that are mostly connected to biomedicine, big pharma, or other kinds of scientific research that lead to patents and so on. It also favors quantitative, empirical, positivistic research methodologies. Research in the arts and humanities, for instance, is surely seen by the corporate types as nonsense and foolishness. This fundamentally threatens higher education and specifically any semblance of liberal education. Looking down the line a decade or two, is it conceivable that we could see a higher education system that looks radically different from now with perhaps a severe reduction—or worse yet, eradication—of disciplines that do not serve corporate interests? At the risk of sounding like an alarmist or being accused of being rhetorical, I do not think any of this is beyond the realm of possibilities, and, in fact, I think it is very likely that we will see a further degradation of the academy if we do not stem the tide of corporatization.

In addition to how corporatization has negatively affected teaching and research, it stands to reason that service activities—particularly in communities—in which students and faculty engage would be entirely written off as unimportant. Corporatization is almost entirely about greed and looking out for number one. It is about making a lot of money. If service activities do not serve or benefit corporate interests, then such activities are denigrated and viewed as unimportant. This logic is very much in keeping with a corporatized philosophy of education: vocationalize instruction and get folks in the work force; there is little time to serve communities for the betterment of community/public health, social connections, democratic processes, and so on. It is a very sad commentary with extremely injurious consequences in both the short and long terms.

Ill Health of Democracy in U.S. Public Higher Education

There has been much written about the impact of neoliberalism and corporatization on U.S. higher education. An examination of the literature suggests that corporatization has affected nearly every aspect of the academy. The overarching theme, however, is how corporatization has battered and eroded the once highly cherished democratic principles and practices for which public higher education stood and which it largely achieved. Let's identify the multiple layers of the challenges and assaults to the democratic processes. They are numerous, but I will focus on a few salient points. There is a new "class" of presidents whose jobs have been morphed from tending primarily to academic matters to chasing money and making corporate deals to "save" their institutions. Some presidents are hired without track records as academics. The most recent example is the University of Iowa's president, who was hired directly from industry. To be specific, many faculty have experienced a top-down management style from some of these presidents. And many of them do not value shared, faculty governance with the checks and balances it offers. In addition, there has been by and large replacement of the tenure-track professoriate with part-time, contingent faculty, which weakens the power of the faculty. For the most part, part-timers can be replaced or simply not rehired. In addition, the ways in which online education have been rolled out are problematic on many fronts, as already discussed. Research is yet another problematic issue; corporations not only have shaped what kind of research is of value, but also have done much to control the university research they sponsor. These issues and many others pose a significant threat to the democratic health of U.S. colleges and universities. The costs and damage suffered are incalculable.

The Costs of Corporatized Public Higher Education to Individual and Community/Public Health

The lack of public funding and the rise of corporatization of U.S. public higher education have played a significant role in the exponential escalation of the costs to attend colleges and universities across the nation. These exorbitantly high costs have translated into a lack of access for many potential students. It is widely known that educational attainment is associated with positive health outcomes. According to the National Poverty Center at the University of Michigan, better educated individuals are not as likely to experience acute and chronic medical conditions as those who have a lower level of educational attainment. A longer life expectancy is also associated with those who have achieved a higher level of education (e.g., those who have a college or university education), and garnering more resources—including but not limited to annual income—as a result of having higher levels of education is positively correlated with better health outcomes (for more details, see the National Poverty Center's [NPC's] website: *www.npc.umich.edu*). With the decreased affordability of public higher education, it stands to reason that a sizeable segment of the U.S. population will be left behind and simply not have access to higher education, which in turn means that they will be a sicker segment of society compared to those with higher educational attainment. It is clear that "[t]here is a direct relationship between education and health—better educated individuals have more positive health outcomes … policies that promote college attendance would be particularly beneficial" (National Poverty Center, 2007, para. 11). Both individual and community/public health are affected by a lack of access to U.S. public higher education.

Besides the accessibility of public higher education, the quality of education is at issue regarding protecting individual and community health. Corporatization has affected the delivery of education and potentially threatens educational quality. Particularly of concern are the vocationalization of education and the commodification of knowledge. It is particularly important that a broad-based, liberal education—with an emphasis on critical thinking and democratic processes—be afforded to students. Beyond the sights of using a college education simply as a stepping stone to a job or for career advancement, it is critically important that higher education foster an environment that also stresses the importance of social justice, civic engagement, and democratic processes that would have great potential of positively affecting both individual and community/public health. The logic is that broadly educated individuals would enjoy positive health outcomes and would be positioned to serve communities in a number of different ways to increase capacity building within communities and advocate for higher education access. The object is to create a plethora of opportunities for individuals from a variety of communities to obtain higher education. Simply put, access to such higher education along with receiving a strong liberal education would be extraordinarily beneficial for individuals' and communities', not to mention the nation's health.

In summary, one of my aims of writing this chapter is to illustrate how broadly and deeply corporatization has embedded itself in U.S. public colleges and universities. Another important lesson is the magnitude of the assault by corporatization on the democratic processes in U.S. public higher education. It is more than clear that the health of U.S. public higher education is in peril and in need of serious interventions. Besides a student and faculty revolution (nothing short of a major push back), there need to be strong laws and policies that not only will focus on providing broad access to public higher education, but also will tame, if not eradicate, the corporate monster that has infiltrated and reshaped the missions, practices, and procedures of numerous public institutions of U.S. higher education. Corporatization is linked not only to the ill health of public higher education, but also to the ill health of individuals and communities. We must stem the tide of destruction and begin to repair and restore a public institution worth saving.

Work Cited

Almeling, D. S. (2003). The problems of pouring-rights contracts. *Duke Law Journal, 53*(3), 1111–1135..

American Council on Education. Committee on Student Personnel work, & Williamson, E. G. (1949). *The student personnel point of view*. Washington, D.C. American Council on Education.

Aronowitz, S. (2000). *The knowledge factory: Dismantling the corporate university and creating true higher learning*. Boston, MA: Beacon Press.

Blumenstyk, G. (1994). Campus cola wars. C*hronicle of Higher Education, 40*(23), a41.

Bok, D. (2003). *Universities in the marketplace: The commercialization of higher education*. Princeton, NJ: Princeton University Press.

Brownlee, J. (2015). The corporate corruption of academic research. *Alternate Routes: A Journal of Critical Social Research, 26*, 23–50.

Chau, P. (2010). Online higher education commodity. *Journal of Computing in Higher Education, 22*(3), 177–191.

Cox, R. W. (2013). The corporatization of higher education. *Class, Race and Corporate Power, 1*(1), 8.

Giroux, H. A. (2001a). Introduction: Critical education or training: Beyond the commodification of higher education. In H. A. Giroux & K. Myrsiades (Eds.), *Beyond the corporate university: Culture and pedagogy in the new millennium* (pp. 1–14). New York, NY: Rowman & Littlefield.

Giroux, H. A. (2001b). Vocationalizing higher education: Schooling and the politics of corporate culture. In H. A. Giroux & K. Myrsiades (Eds.), *Beyond the corporate university: Culture and pedagogy in the new millennium* (pp. 29–44). New York, NY: Rowman & Littlefield.

Giroux, H. A. (2002). Neoliberalism, corporate culture, and the promise of higher education: The university as a democratic sphere. *Harvard Educational Review, 72*(4), 425–463.

Giroux, H. A. (2012). *Education and the crisis of public values: Challenging the assault on teachers, students, & public education*. New York, NY: Peter Lang Publishers.

Kezar, A. J. (2004). Obtaining integrity? Reviewing and examining the charter between higher education and society. *The Review of Higher Education, 27*(4), 429–459.

Kumar, A. (2001). World Bank literature 101. In H. A. Giroux & K. Myrsiades (Eds.), *Beyond the corporate university: Culture and pedagogy in the new millennium* (pp. 213–226). New York, NY: Rowman & Littlefield.

Lerner, G. (2008). Corporatizing higher education. *The History Teacher, 41*(2), 219–227.

Martinez, E., & Garcia, A. (1997, January 1). What is neoliberalism? A brief definition for activists. CorpWatch. Retrieved from http://www.corpwatch.org/article.php?id=376

McIntire, M. E. (2015, September 11). At University of Iowa, new president's background is all business. *Chronicle of Higher Education*, Vol. 62, Issue 2, A11.

Mills, N. (2012). The corporatization of higher education. *Dissent, 59*(4), 6–9.

National Poverty Center. (2007, March). Policy brief: Education and health. Retrieved from www.npc.umich.edu

Nestle, M. (2000). Soft drink "pouring rights": Marketing empty calories to children. *Public Health Reports, 115*(4), 308.

Newfield, C. (2003). *Ivy and industry: Business and the making of the American university, 1880–1980*. Durham, NC: Duke University Press.

Poovey, M. (2001). The twenty-first-century university and the market: What price economic viability? *Differences: A Journal of Feminist Cultural Studies, 12*(1), 1–16.

Schultz, D. (2015). The rise and coming demise of the corporate university. *Academe, 101*(5), 21.

Slaughter, S. (2012). The research money-go-round. In J. N. Neem, B. Forster, S. Slaughter, R. Vedder, T. M. Cottom, & S. Goldrick-Rab (Eds.), *The Education Assembly Line* (p. 18). *Contexts, 11*(4). Long Island, NY: American Sociological Association.

Steck, H. (2003). Corporatization of the university: Seeking conceptual clarity. *The Annals of the American Academy of Political and Social Science, 585*(1), 66–83.

Strange, C. C. (2003). Dynamics of campus environments. *Student Services: A Handbook for the Profession, 4*, 297–316.

Washburn, J. (2011). Academic freedom and the corporate university. *Academe, 97*(1), 8–13. Retrieved from http://0-search.proquest.com.opac.sfsu.edu/docview/847665728? accountid=13802

Williams, J. J. (2001). Franchising the university. In H. A. Giroux & K. Myrsiades (Eds.), *Beyond the corporate university: Culture and pedagogy in the new millennium* (pp. 15–28). New York, NY: Rowman & Littlefield.

CHAPTER 3

Title IX
Turning Back the Clock on Free Speech and Due Process

Hans F. Bader

Introduction

Free speech on campus about sexual issues has been undermined by an ironic source: Title IX, the federal law that prohibits discrimination on the basis of sex in any federally funded education program or activity. Federal officials have seized upon this statute to issue warnings to colleges to restrict sexual expression, even when it does not constitute sexual harassment under Supreme Court precedent, and has been recognized by the courts as speech protected by the First Amendment. Such curbs on sexual speech are redolent of archaic gender stereotypes that courts rejected in striking down laws that restricted indecent or vulgar speech around women. They also violate recent federal appeals court rulings striking down overly broad sexual harassment policies. Federal officials have also seized upon Title IX to demand that colleges discard modern due process norms that promote accuracy in campus disciplinary proceedings and help guard against erroneous dismissals and expulsions. Such federal pressure violates academic freedom and institutional autonomy.

Restrictions on sexual expression used to be recognized as reactionary violations of free speech that reinforce inequality. In *Papish v. University of Missouri Curators* (1973), the Supreme Court overturned the expulsion of a student for distributing on campus a publication containing "indecent speech," ruling that the dissemination of ideas could no longer be proscribed in the name of "conventions of decency" (p. 670). And in striking down an archaic South Carolina law banning "obscene, profane, indecent, vulgar, or suggestive" communications to women, a state supreme court ruled in the *In re Joseph T.* decision that laws "based on 'old notions' such as a belief that females should be afforded special protection from 'rough talk' because of their perceived 'special sensitivities' can no longer withstand equal protection scrutiny" (p. 524).

But draconian restrictions on sexual speech are now making a comeback on campus—ironically, in the name of complying with the federal law against sex discrimination in education, Title IX. Title IX enforcers have also sought to undermine hard-won due process safeguards on campus, such as the clear and convincing standard of evidence that had become the norm in college discipline by the 1980s.

Under the impetus of Title IX, many campuses have recently become more sexually repressive, as Susan Kruth of the Foundation for Individual Rights in Education has chronicled (Kruth, 2014). For example, a letter sent to University of Missouri students by its Title IX Coordinator Linda Bennett, entitled "Welcome Back to the Fall Semester," demanded sweeping restrictions on sexual behavior on campus (University of Missouri Title IX Office, 2014).

"Examples of behavior that will not be tolerated," the letter said, include "Requesting another person to engage in a behavior with a sexual body part or enacting a sexual behavior." But as Kruth observed, "How is a student supposed to engage in any sexual activity, except by first requesting that the other person engage in it?" Other examples of forbidden behavior listed in Bennett's memo include "suggestive" sounds, "off-color jokes," and "other physical, verbal, graphic or written conduct of a sexual nature." But as Kruth noted, "millions of college students and professors engage in this sort of expression" in the course of discussing sexual issues or as part of their sex lives, and what the university had forbidden includes "a significant amount of constitutionally protected expression." Yet the University of Missouri's Title IX Office defined all these forms of expression and sexual interaction as "conduct forbidden by the Title IX policy" against sexual harassment.

Sad to say, its ban was far from unique. Many other colleges have similarly sweeping sexual harassment policies, noted Will Creeley of the Foundation for Individual Rights in Education (Creeley, 2014). For example, in June 2013, Georgia Southern University adopted a policy that defines sexual harassment as any "unwelcome conduct of a sexual nature," including "verbal or physical conduct of a sexual nature." In April 2014, the University of Louisiana at Monroe policy defined sexual harassment as "any unwelcome conduct of a sexual nature," including "offensive verbal or physical contact [sic] of a sexual nature." In August 2014, Eastern Illinois University defined sexual harassment as "unwelcome conduct of a sexual nature," which may include even "a single incident" of "offensive or inappropriate language or jokes (including electronic content)." As Creeley noted, "under such sweeping definitions, speech protected by the First Amendment is subject to investigation and punishment" (Creeley, 2014).

These colleges did not act in a vacuum. They did so in response to advice from federal officials in the Justice Department and in the Education Department's Office for Civil Rights (OCR). OCR, where I used to work, is the federal agency that enforces Title IX. As Ramesh Ponnuru of Bloomberg News noted, those officials had publicly told the University of Montana to revise its sexual harassment policy to classify *any* unwelcome sexual speech as harassment, even if it is isolated and even if it is *not* offensive to any reasonable person (Ponnuru, 2013).

The University of Montana had previously applied definitions of sexual harassment drawn from the Supreme Court's decisions in *Davis v. Monroe County Board of Education* (1999) and *Harris v. Forklift Systems* (1993)—definitions that do not reach trivially-offensive conduct or comments that are not "objectively offensive" or do not offend a "reasonable person"—in its internal sexual harassment policy. The U.S. Departments of Justice and Education took issue with this, saying that conduct should instead be classified as harassment even if it is not "objectively offensive" and does not offend a "reasonable person," in a University of Montana Letter of Findings dated May 9, 2013 (p. 9). In the course of that letter, which declared the University of Montana in violation of Title IX, they wrote that the University of Montana's sexual harassment policy *improperly suggests that the conduct does not constitute sexual harassment unless it is objectively offensive*. This policy provides examples of unwelcome conduct of a sexual nature but then states that "[w]hether conduct is sufficiently offensive to constitute sexual harassment is determined from the perspective of an objectively reasonable person of the same gender in the same situation." Whether conduct is objectively offensive is a factor used to determine if a hostile environment has been created, but it is not the standard to determine whether conduct was "unwelcome conduct of a sexual nature" and therefore constitutes "sexual harassment." … *sexual harassment should be more broadly defined as "any unwelcome conduct of a sexual nature."* (U.S. Departments of Justice & Education, 2013, p. 9) (italics added)

As education writers observed, under the federal government's logic, a professor could be classified as a sexual harasser merely for teaching sex education, if a hypersensitive student found the topic "unwelcome." If a professor discusses a sexual issue, like HIV transmission through anal sex, "making one of his 500 students uncomfortable," "he's a sexual harasser" under the Administration's proposed definition, noted education writer Joanne Jacobs. As she pointed out, it would also cover any other "expression related to sexual topics that offends any person," such as "'The Vagina Monologues,' a presentation on safe sex practices, a debate about sexual morality, a discussion of gay marriage, or a classroom lecture on Vladimir Nabokov's Lolita" (Jacobs, 2013). (Some overly sensitive students view sex education and other graphic topics as sexual harassment and file charges as a result, as a decision by the First Circuit Court of Appeals illustrates; it rejected such a lawsuit after extended analysis in *Brown v. Hot, Sexy & Safer Productions* (1995).)

As Greg Lukianoff of the Foundation for Individual Rights in Education noted in written testimony to Congress in 2015, in response to widespread outcry from civil libertarians, OCR's head backpedaled and indicated that its letter to the University of Montana merely "represents the resolution of that particular case" with the University of Montana, "and not OCR or DOJ policy" required for all colleges (Lukianoff, 2015, pp. 10–11). However, other Justice and Education Department officials have continued to suggest that this overly broad definition of harassment was a blueprint for colleges nationwide (Lukianoff, 2015, pp. 9–10). As a result of this federal pressure, he observed, colleges have radically expanded their "harassment" policies to cover constitutionally protected speech that would not previously have been treated as harassment, and "many universities—including Pennsylvania State University, the University of Connecticut, Clemson University, Colorado College, and Georgia Southern University—have revised their sexual misconduct policies to include the blueprint's broad definition of sexual harassment" (Lukianoff, 2015, p. 11).

Such colleges include Northwestern University, according to Jessica Gavora in the Wall Street Journal (Gavora, 2015). There, in early March 2015, Professor Laura Kipnis was charged with sexual harassment over an essay she wrote in the Chronicle of Higher Education (Kipnis, 2015), under a policy that expansively declared that "sexual harassment is any unwelcome conduct of a sexual nature" (Northwestern University, 2015). Such "unwelcome" verbal or visual conduct could easily encompass scholarly commentary or publications on sexual issues that a student finds offensive for idiosyncratic personal reasons.

As law professor Jonathan Adler noted in the Washington Post, Kipnis was accused of sexual harassment by students over an article she wrote in February 2015 arguing that overly broad notions of harassment under Title IX had created a climate of fear and "sexual paranoia." Then, when she wrote about the harassment complaint they filed against her based on that article, in tweets describing it as a violation of academic freedom, she was accused of retaliation in violation of Title IX, even though she had not mentioned the complainants' names (Adler, 2015).

The harassment charges were filed even though Kipnis's article was published in the Chronicle of Higher Education, which is located hundreds of miles away from her campus. Harassment guidance from the Education Department's Office for Civil Rights (OCR) contributed to her plight: OCR's October 26, 2010 Dear Colleague Letter told schools to regulate off-campus conduct, including "graphic and written statements" on "the internet" and "web sites of a sexual nature" (Office for Civil Rights, 2010, pp. 2, 6). Similarly, OCR's 2014 letter to Harvard said colleges should police "off-campus conduct" (Office for Civil Rights, 2014, p. 15). It gave these instructions even though federal appeals court rulings such as *Roe v. Saint Louis University* (2014) have rejected Title IX lawsuits over off-campus conduct, including severe misconduct—and even though courts have ruled that the First Amendment gives schools little power to restrict speech outside of school, in court rulings such as *Klein v. Smith* (1986).

Moreover, as Professor Adler notes, a Title IX complaint was also filed against the faculty-support person who accompanied her to a session with her investigators, because he had described the charges against her as a potential threat to academic freedom in discussing her situation with the faculty senate. The Title IX investigators then informed her that due to the complaint against him, he could no longer be allowed to act as her support person (Adler, 2015).

The Title IX charges against Kipnis were eventually dismissed in late May 2015, after a national outcry, as Brock Read and Robin Wilson noted in the Chronicle of Higher Education. But only after an investigation lasting more than 60 days (Adler, 2015). Other colleges, such as Mesabi Community College, have punished professors for retaliation for criticizing harassment complaints against their speech as a threat to academic freedom, as Kors and Silverglate noted in *The Shadow University* (1998). Colleges have done so even though such punishment raises serious First Amendment issues, as a First Amendment lawsuit and resulting settlement in *Osborne v. Mesabi Community College* illustrated (Kors & Silverglate, 1998, pp. 125–27).

Charges like that leveled against Professor Kipnis have occurred partly because the Education Department has effectively redefined perfectly legal speech as "sexual harassment." In its letter to the University of Montana, it defined sexual speech as harassment even when it would not offend a reasonable person (Office for Civil Rights, 2013, p. 9).

And in its published sexual harassment guidance for all schools, the Education Department defines speech and conduct as sexual harassment forbidden by Title IX even if it is not severe and pervasive, and does not occur on school grounds. For example, its April 4, 2011 Dear Colleague letter to the nation's school officials states that "a single or isolated incident of sexual harassment may create a hostile environment" if it is severe, even if it is *not* pervasive (Office for Civil Rights, 2011, p. 3). Similarly, its 2010 "Dear Colleague" letter to the nation's schools about bullying, sent to the nation's school officials, claimed that "harassment does not have to … involve repeated incidents" to be actionable, but rather need only be "severe, pervasive, *or* persistent" (Office for Civil Rights, 2010, p. 2) (italics added). That letter took aim at student speech even outside of school boundaries, arguing that harassment includes speech, such as "graphic and written statements" on the "Internet" and elsewhere (p. 2), even though the Supreme Court's *Davis* decision indicated that liability was limited to events occurring on school grounds (*Davis v. Monroe County Board of Education* (1998), pp. 645–46)).

By doing so, OCR has ignored Supreme Court rulings and other court decisions, which require that speech be offensive to a reasonable person to constitute sexual harassment (as the *Harris* decision requires), be both severe *and* pervasive to trigger Title IX liability (as the *Davis* decision requires), and occur on school grounds (*see Roe v. Saint Louis University* (2014)), and not merely be sexual in content or subject matter (*see Gallant v. Board of Trustees* (1998)).

In doing so, the Education Department has effectively mandated an unconstitutional speech code even broader than the ones struck down by federal judges in *Doe v. University of Michigan* (1989) and *DeJohn v. Temple University* (2008). Those were cases in which college students demonstrated a real possibility that they could be punished for "harassment" merely for discussing certain gender-based differences between men and women, or advocating political positions on gender issues, such as that women be banned from combat roles in the military. The danger that overly broad definitions of harassment will stifle campus debate about important political and social issues is very real, since students have been charged with racial or sexual harassment for discussing issues such as affirmative action and feminism under broadly worded campus harassment policies, as Students for Individual Liberty chronicled in a Supreme Court brief (Students for Individual Liberty, 1998).

To be classified as sexual harassment, offensive speech needs to meet a specified threshold under Supreme Court precedent. An employee must show it was "severe *or* pervasive" enough to create a hostile work environment, in a harassment lawsuit brought under Title VII of the Civil Rights Act, according to the Supreme Court's decision in *Harris v. Forklift Systems* (1993). Under Title IX, the threshold is higher still: a student must show it was "severe, pervasive, *and* objectively offensive" enough to interfere with access to an education, under the Supreme Court's *Davis* decision. (*Davis v. Monroe County Board of Education* (1998), pp. 633, 650–652, and 654). Thus, a mildly offensive racial or sexual idea does not give rise to a Title IX violation, in the eyes of the courts, merely because it is expressed by many students and thus is "pervasive" on campus, because the expression must also be "severe."

That higher threshold makes sense, because colleges and universities are the quintessential "marketplace of ideas," to quote the Supreme Court's decision in *Healy v. James* (1972) (p. 180). Meaningful debate about a sexual or racial issue (about a sexually graphic subject, or the frequency of false rape charges, or the merits of affirmative action) is impossible when a participant in that debate can be disciplined or expelled for expressing a common view in that debate, merely because that viewpoint is commonplace on campus and thus "pervasive."

In its 2000 Revised Sexual Harassment Guidance, OCR thumbed its nose at the Supreme Court's *Davis* decision by stating that speech or conduct need only be "persistent" *or* "pervasive" *or* "severe" to violate Title IX or Title VI, not "severe" *and* "pervasive," and need not necessarily interfere with a student's access to educational opportunities to violate Title IX (Office for Civil Rights, 2000, p. 66,097). People's views tend to be "persistent," and they tend to persistently express them over time in campus debates. By allowing liability for expression that is "persistent" but neither "pervasive" nor "severe," OCR has defined sexual harassment even more broadly on campus than it is defined in the workplace, disregarding the Supreme Court's *Davis* decision, which did the opposite, defining harassment more narrowly on campus.

The net result of OCR's overreaching is to pressure colleges to punish a speaker for a single instance of controversial speech that a complainant deems "severe" (even if it is not pervasive or persistent), and also, conversely, to punish a speaker for an individual comment that was only mildly offensive, but which the complainant views as collectively a "pervasive" or "persistent" phenomenon, because other students or faculty have also said something similar.

An illustration of how constitutionally-protected speech could trigger harassment charges under this overly broad definition of harassment is illustrated by its application in the parallel context of racial harassment, which also is forbidden, under to OCR's *Racial Harassment Investigative Guidance* (Office for Civil Rights, 1994). In 1994, the Education Department's general counsel refused to take a position on whether a student's criticism of affirmative action to a black student could constitute illegal racial harassment in violation of that guidance, as Stuart Taylor noted that year in the *Legal Times* (p. 27). She refused to rule out harassment liability, even though court rulings such as *Department of Corrections v. State Personnel Board* (1997) indicate that banning such criticism of affirmative action would violate the First Amendment. As Karl Jahn noted in the *Wall Street Journal,*

> In 1994, Judith Winston, overseer of the [federal] Office for Civil Rights (OCR), told American Lawyer columnist Stuart Taylor that federal laws against racial and sexual "harassment" might be violated by a student arguing against affirmative action in a college classroom … In 1993, Chico State University's award-winning historian Joseph Conlin was disciplined for "racial harassment" after he publicly criticized the university's affirmative-action policies. The university claimed that his comments created a "racially hostile" environment for minorities. After Prof. Conlin threatened a First Amendment lawsuit, the university dropped its harassment code and its action against him. But under pressure from OCR, the university subsequently imposed a new, vaguer harassment code. (Jahn, 1999)

It's not just bigots who end up being embroiled in harassment charges when the "severe and pervasive" requirement is discarded. As the Associated Press reported in 2008, a university found a student-employee guilty of racial harassment for merely reading the book, *Notre Dame vs. The Klan: How the Fighting Irish Defeated the Ku Klux Klan*, silently to himself, although it reversed this decision after a First Amendment lawsuit was threatened (Associated Press, 2008).

Getting rid of the "severe" *and* "pervasive" requirement for educational harassment claims violates federal appeals court rulings that struck down campus sexual harassment policies as overbroad. Two of those rulings, *DeJohn v. Temple University* (2008) and *Saxe v. State College Area School District* (2001), were based on the fact that the college harassment rule in question lacked the "severe" and "pervasive" requirement.

Getting rid of the severity requirement drives colleges to adopt unconstitutional zero-tolerance rules against all sexual speech that offends a listener, similar to the ones adopted by risk-averse employers in non-academic settings like factories. As law professor Eugene Volokh notes, to avoid the risk of liability for harassment, some employers have followed government officials' informal advice to ban "all sexually offensive" verbal or physical conduct (Volokh, 1997, pp. 638–42). While such restrictions may be permissible when imposed by a private employer, they are plainly unconstitutional when imposed by a public university bound be precepts of academic freedom, where people need to be able to discuss—and research—sexual issues even if some listener or reader finds the topic offensive.

Free speech is not the only casualty of the Education Department's Title IX push. Due process rights have also suffered. On April 4, 2011, the Office for Civil Rights ordered many colleges to change the burden of proof that they use in disciplinary proceedings over alleged sexual harassment, in a "Dear Colleague" letter to the nation's school officials. It also discouraged cross-examination by the accused, which could reduce accuracy in campus adjudications, violate due process in credibility contests, and result in punishment for constitutionally-protected speech in cases alleging verbal harassment (Office for Civil Rights, 2011).

By the 1980s, most colleges and universities had adopted a "clear and convincing" evidence standard of evidence in student and faculty discipline cases, to safeguard due process. As James Picozzi noted in the Yale Law Journal, "Courts, universities, and student defendants all seem to agree that the appropriate standard of proof in student disciplinary cases is one of 'clear and convincing' evidence" (Picozzi, 1987, p. 2159).

But in its "Dear Colleague" letter, OCR rejected this important protection for faculty and students, saying that in sexual harassment and assault cases, a "school's grievance procedures must use the preponderance of the evidence standard to resolve complaints of sex discrimination" (Office for Civil Rights, 2011, p. 11). As Rebecca Robbins noted in the Harvard Crimson, "preponderance of the evidence" means that if a school thinks there is as little as a 51 per chance that the accused is guilty, the accused must still be disciplined (Robbins, 2012).

OCR's position was based on a mistaken understanding of who is subject to Title IX. Title IX's requirements apply to schools, not individuals. Its reasoning for imposing this low "preponderance" standard on school disciplinary proceedings was that this "is the standard of proof established for violations of civil-rights laws" in lawsuits brought against institutions in federal court. Therefore, it claimed, preponderance must also be "the appropriate standard for" schools to use in "investigating allegations of sexual harassment or violence'" (Office for Civil Rights, 2011, p. 11).

It was completely true, but also completely irrelevant, that the preponderance of the evidence standard applies in lawsuits against colleges, including civil-rights litigation. That burden of proof applies to whether the *school* violated Title IX by behaving inappropriately, not whether *students* or staff engaged in harassment. As a federal appeals court noted in *Smith v. Metropolitan School District* (1997), only schools can violate Title IX, not individuals. Moreover, as one judge observed, students "are not agents of the school," so their actions don't count as the actions of the school (*UWM Post v. Board of Regents* (1991), p. 1177).

The mere existence of harassment is *not* enough for liability under Title IX. More is required. The school's *own* actions *in response to* the harassment must be culpable. As the Education Department admitted in its 1997 "Sexual Harassment Guidance," "Title IX does not make a school responsible for the actions of harassing students, but rather for its own discrimination in failing to remedy it once the school has notice" (Office for Civil Rights, 1997, p. 12,040). For example, the Supreme Court's dismissed a Title IX harassment lawsuit because a school had not shown indifference to harassment of a student, in *Gebser v. Lago Vista School District* (1998). So to violate Title IX, an institution's own actions must be proven culpable under a "preponderance" standard—not just the harasser's.

Since an institution itself must behave in a culpable fashion, not just the alleged harasser, courts have held that there is no violation of the civil rights laws even if harassment occurs, as long as the institution investigates in good faith in response to the allegation of harassment. That's true even if the institution ultimately refuses to discipline a harasser based on the reasonable belief that he is innocent, after applying a firm presumption of innocence. Such a refusal does not show negligence, much less indifference to harassment.

For example, in *Swenson v. Potter* (2001), the Ninth Circuit Court of Appeals reversed a jury verdict that awarded a worker $85,000 against the Postal Service for sexual harassment, even though harassment did occur, since the Postal Service had, after investigating the worker's sexual harassment complaint, reasonably, but erroneously, failed to credit plaintiff's allegations. As the court explained, "a good faith investigation of alleged harassment may satisfy the 'prompt and appropriate response' standard, even if the investigation turns up no evidence of harassment … [and] a jury later concludes that in fact harassment occurred" (*Swenson v. Potter*, 2001, p. 1196). Other appeals courts have also concluded that accused people do not have to be disciplined in the absence of convincing evidence, as I discussed several years ago (Bader, 2012). Similarly, the Supreme Court emphasized in its 1999 *Davis* decision that Title IX doesn't give complainants a "right" to second-guess a school's reasonable decisions about discipline, since there isn't any "Title IX right" to demand "particular disciplinary action," just because harassment has occurred (*Davis v. Monroe County Board of Education*, 1999, p. 648).

In its April 4, 2011 Dear Colleague Letter, the Education Department also discourages colleges from allowing accused people to cross-examine their accusers: "OCR strongly discourages schools from allowing the parties personally to question or cross-examine each other during the hearing" (Office for Civil Rights, 2011, p. 12). This attack on cross-examination was perverse, since the Supreme Court has described cross-examination as the "greatest legal engine ever invented for the discovery of truth" in cases such as *Lilly v. Virginia* (1999, p. 124). Moreover, in a few campus disciplinary cases, such as *Donohue v. Baker* (1997), judges have ruled that cross-examination *was* constitutionally required on due-process grounds to test the credibility of the accuser. The courts themselves invariably permit cross-examination in sexual and racial harassment lawsuits, and have relied upon it in dismissing weak or unfounded claims in cases such as *Newman v. Federal Express* (2001), so OCR can hardly claim that the courts view cross-examination as unfair to complainants, much less illegal. Yet OCR falsely implies that its Dear Colleague letter simply summarizes existing law, by claiming in the letter that it "does not add requirements to applicable law" (Office for Civil Rights, 2011, p. 1).

Work Cited

Adler, J. H. (2015, May 29). How Northwestern University is throwing academic freedom under the bus (and wasting money) under the guise of Title IX compliance. *Washington Post*. Retrieved from http://goo.gl/WPEIUj

Associated Press. (2008, July 15). *University says sorry to janitor over KKK book*. Retrieved from http://goo.gl/o1S42W

Bader, H. (2012, September 21). Education department illegally ordered colleges to reduce due-process safeguards. *The Examiner*. Retrieved from http://goo.gl/t4WJ97

Brown v. Hot, Sexy & Safer Productions (1995). *Federal Reporter, Third Series, 68*, 525–541. Retrieved from https://goo.gl/wEQHzB

Creeley, W. (2014, August 28). A year later, impact of Feds' "blueprint" comes into focus. *The Torch*. Retrieved from https://goo.gl/nG0Cqj

Davis v. Monroe County Board of Education. (1999). *U.S. Reports, 526*, 629–686. Retrieved from https://goo.gl/vM3bzY

DeJohn v. Temple University. (2008). *Federal Reporter, Third Series, 537*, 301–320.

Department of Corrections *v.* State Personnel *Board*. (1997). *California Appellate Reports, Fourth Series, 59*, 131–167.

Doe v. University of Michigan. (1989). *Federal Supplement, 721*, 852–869.

Donohue v. Baker. (1997). *Federal Supplement, 976*, 136–149. Retrieved from http://goo.gl/qrBaqY

Eastern Illinois Policy #175—Sexual Harassment. (2014, Aug. 4). Retrieved from http://goo.gl/lYvq48

Gallant v. Board of Trustees. (1998). *Federal Supplement, 997,* 1231–1235.

Gavora, J. (2015, June 8). How Title IX became a political weapon. *Wall Street Journal,* A13. Retrieved from http://goo.gl/1Oq3F9

Georgia Southern University Policy Prohibiting Sexual Harassment. (2014, June 1). Retrieved from http://goo.gl/HS2Q99

Harris v. Forklift Systems. (1993). *U.S. Reports, 510,* 17–26 (1993).

Healy v. James. (1972). *U.S. Reports, 408,* 169–203. Retrieved from https://goo.gl/rq0Jqr

Jacobs, J. (2013, May 11). *U.S. rule makes every student a sex harasser.* Retrieved from www.joannejacobs.com/2013/05/u-s-rule-makes-every-student-a-sex-harasser

Jahn, K. (1999, January 21). Harassment almost ruined her life. *Wall Street Journal.* Retrieved from http://goo.gl/QMNpY3

In re Joseph T. (1993). *Southeastern Reporter, second series, 430,* 523–24. Retrieved from https://goo.gl/B6ydNZ

Kipnis, L. (2015, February 27). Sexual paranoia strikes academe. *Chronicle of Higher Education.* Retrieved from http://goo.gl/M3MSvR

Klein v. Smith. (1986). *Federal Supplement, 635,* 1440–1442. Retrieved at https://goo.gl/e7S9GY

Kors, A. C., & Harvey, S. (1998). *The Shadow University.* New York, NY: Free Press.

Kruth, S. (2014, August 28). University of Missouri will tolerate teletubby, 'Will not tolerate' asking for consent. *The Torch.* Retrieved from https://goo.gl/PkuRc6.

Lilly v. Virginia. (1999). *U.S. Reports, 527,* 116–149. Retrieved from http://goo.gl/rj0I6p

Lukianoff, G. (2015). *Written testimony of Greg Lukianoff, president, foundation for individual rights in education, before the U.S. House of Representatives, Committee on the Judiciary, Subcommittee on the Judiciary, June 2, 2015. Hearing on first amendment protections on public college and university campuses.* Retrieved from http://goo.gl/a1YkBX

Newman v. Federal Express Corp. (2001). *Federal Reporter, Third Series, 266,* 401–406.

Northwestern University. (2015). *Policy on sexual harassment, Title IX statement, and additional guidance.* Retrieved from http://goo.gl/sWtIqB

Office for Civil Rights. (1994, March 10). Racial harassment investigative guidance. *Federal Register, 59,* 11448. Retrieved from http://goo.gl/MikCjJ

Office for Civil Rights. (1997, March 13). Sexual harassment guidance. *Federal Register, 62,* 12034. Retrieved from http://goo.gl/UwreqN

Office for Civil Rights. (2000, November 2). Revised sexual harassment guidance: Harassment of students by school employees, other students, or third parties. *Federal Register, 65,* 66092. Retrieved from http://goo.gl/Jfyr20

Office for Civil Rights. (2010, October 26). *Dear colleague letter on harassment and bullying.* Retrieved from http://goo.gl/GhkvKK

Office for Civil Rights. (2011, April 4). *Dear colleague letter: Sexual violence background, summary and fast facts.* Retrieved from http://goo.gl/x4pGS

Office for Civil Rights. (2014, December 30). *Harvard Law School, resolution letter re: complaint No. 01-11-2012.* Retrieved at http://goo.gl/ImLWWx

Papish v. University of Missouri Curators. (1973). *U.S. Reports, 410,* 667–678 (1973). Retrieved from http://goo.gl/f6nxXj

Picozzi, J. M. (1987). University disciplinary process: What's fair, what's due, and what you don't get. *Yale Law Journal, 96,* 2132.

Ponnuru, R. (2013, July 23). Bloomberg News: New sexual harassment rules openly defy reason. *Ames Tribune.* Retrieved from http://goo.gl/9wnvaw

Read, B. (2015, May 31). Laura Kipnis is cleared of wrongdoing in Title IX complaints. *Chronicle of Higher Education.* Retrieved from http://goo.gl/RhJgyw

Robbins, R. D. (2012, May 11). Harvard's sexual assault policy under pressure. *Harvard Crimson.* Retrieved from http://goo.gl/l9hGkJ

Saxe v. State College Area School District. (2001). *Federal Reporter, Third Series, 240,* 200–218.

Smith v. Metropolitan School District. (1997). *Federal Reporter, Third Series, 128,* 1014–1049.

Students for Individual Liberty. (1998, December 8). *Brief of Amici Curiae* filed in *Davis v. Monroe County Board of Education,* No. 97–843. Retrieved from Westlaw database at 1998 WL 847365.

Swenson v. Potter. (2001). *Federal Reporter, Third Series, 271,* 1184–1212. Retrieved from http://goo.gl/M142sp

Taylor, S., Jr. (1994, May 9). A Clintonite threat to free speech. *Legal Times,* 27.

University of Missouri Title IX Office. (2014). *Welcome back to the fall semester.* Retrieved from http://goo.gl/HrIN4T

U.S. Departments of Justice and Education. (2013, May 9). *University of Montana Letter of Findings.* Retrieved from http://goo.gl/WhDEDg

UWM Post, Inc. v. Board of Regents of University of Wisconsin System. (1991). *Federal Supplement, 774,* 1163–1181. Retrieved from http://goo.gl/9TuZAT

Volokh, E. (1997). What speech does "hostile work environment" harassment law restrict? *Georgetown Law Journal, 85,* 627–648. Retrieved from http://goo.gl/KNf7jL

Wilson, R. (2015, June 4). For northwestern, the Kipnis case is painful and personal. *Chronicle of Higher Education.* Retrieved from http://goo.gl/8LQuzT

CHAPTER 4

Funding Cuts in Higher Education Shift Priorities Away from Equity, Diversity, & Inclusivity

A Case Study

Susan Dennison and C. P. Gause

Since 2008 state cuts to higher education have been substantial and have affected almost all parts of the United States. In fact, over this five year period 48 states' spending per student has decreased for higher education costs with only North Dakota and Wyoming not following this trend (Oliff, Palacios, Johnson, & Leachman, 2013). In several of the involved states these cuts have been significant with 11 states reducing their funding per student by more than one-third and in two states, Arizona and New Hampshire; their cuts have been reduced by half per student (Oliff et al., 2013).

So what is one of the most common sources of revenue that most public universities and colleges are using to offset some of these cuts? Student tuition which has increased since the 2007/2008 academic year by 50% in seven states, more than 25% in 18 states, and in two states, Arizona and California, by more than 70% (Oliff et al., 2013). "These sharp increases in tuition have accelerated longer-term trends of reducing college affordability and shifting costs from states to students" (Oliff et al., 2013, p. 2). These tuition increases will have even more of a negative impact on minority students since often they and their families generally have less income to afford these increased costs for attending college.

These financial cuts for many public universities in this country have also resulted in the elimination of some academic programs, losses in terms of faculty lines, reductions in the number of class sections, and increased class sizes (Capaldi, 2011). In addition, during these last five years many higher education settings have been in the beginning stages of promoting and supporting diversity, equity, and inclusive community initiatives only to find that these important efforts are now also experiencing reduced budgets or, in some cases, being completely eliminated.

This chapter will focus on a case example of a medium-size public university in North Carolina that took bold and extensive steps beginning in 2008/2009 to redefine itself as an inclusive, collaborative, and responsive institution that was committed to providing transformative experiences for its students and the communities they serve. We will chronicle this Southern University's (pseudonym name for the involved university) journey from this latter beginning point to current day where most of the initial goals have been put on hold or are no longer considered priorities due to massive funding cuts and other changes regarding support of higher education from the North Carolina state legislature.

Initial Motivation to Take some Bold Steps

The initial motivation for this Southern University to become more supportive of diversity, equity, and move to being a more inclusive setting related to the lack of diversification among its faculty. Interestingly, this particular university had, for many years, the most diverse student population among the 16 campus system in North Carolina. However,

> data from the university Office of Institutional Research presented the percentages of ethnic minority faculty at this Southern University and their designated peers. Among the 11 institutions reporting these data, this university ranked 9th in overall minority representation, 3rd in Black non-Hispanic faculty, 9th (tied) in Native American faculty, 10th in Asian or Pacific Islander faculty, and 6th in Hispanic faculty. Although these numbers are low, the university has made progress in recruiting and retaining minority faculty over the last decade. (Gause, Dennison, & Perrin, 2010, p. 64)

Subcommittee on Recruitment and Retention of Ethnic Minority Faculty

The university administration realized that they needed to increase the number of ethnic-minority faculty because "diversification of faculty increases the variation of perspectives and approaches creating a richer learning environment for students" (Umbach, 2006, p. 318). So the Provost of this university established at the onset of the 2007/2008 academic year the Deans Council Subcommittee on Recruitment and Retention of Ethnic Minority Faculty. The 6-member committee was appointed with the following charge.

1. Assess the successes and challenges in recruiting and retaining minority faculty in comparison with peer institutions.
2. Review 10-year promotion and tenure data of faculty by ethnicity and include reviews and actions down to the department level.
3. Determine the extent to which ethnic minority faculty feel mentored and supported.
4. Create a set of recommendations to assist University community with recruitment and retention of ethnic minority faculty.

During the 2007/2008 academic year this subcommittee analyzed data from several sources with particular attention to other peer universities that had experienced success in their recruitment and retention of ethnic minority faculty. They also reviewed related literature to see if universities in other parts of the country had better success with recruitment and retention, attended some relevant workshops/trainings, and identified an outside consultant who could conduct fact finding interviews with groups of ethnic minority faculty and majority faculty members. These latter efforts were intended to address the first charge of this subcommittee in terms of determining other more effective methods for recruiting and retaining ethic minority faculty.

In regard to the second charge to this subcommittee, compare ten year promotion and tenure data on ethnic minority faculty with White majority faculty,

> the Office of the Provost provided promotion and tenure data to Associate Professor in the 10-year period 1997/98–2006/07. During this time period a total of 190 faculty were eligible for consideration, of which 163 (85.8% were granted tenure and promotion. Of these, 138 (84.6%) were White, 6 (3.7%) were Black, 14 (8.6%) were Asian or Pacific Islander, and 5 (3.1%) were Hispanic. For the remaining 27 cases (14.2%) tenure and promotion were not granted, either because the application was denied at any level or because the candidate elected not to come forward for consideration. There were 7 cases

(all White faculty) in which the candidate elected not to come forward. Of the remaining 20 cases that involved a denial of tenure, 17 (85%) were White and 3 (15%) were Asian; none were Black or Hispanic. Thus, the percentage of minority faculty among the successful and unsuccessful cases was almost exactly the same (15.4% and 15%, respectively). Data provided did not indicate minority faculty were awarded tenure and promotion at this university less often than their White colleagues. (Gause et al., 2010, p. 64)

Data Surfaced from Consultant on Diversity & Faculty Development

In order to address the third charge to this subcommittee, determine the extent to which ethnic minority faculty feel mentored and supported, it was decided that it would be important to elicit data regarding this issue directly from current and past ethnic minority faculty at this Southern University. Subsequently, an expert consulting firm was contracted to conduct fact finding interviews with current ethnic minority faculty and a web survey of former ethnic faculty who had left the university in the previous ten years. A total of 149 faculty members were invited to participate in these spring 2008 interviews and 60 participated. There were several responses from those interviewed whose comments were not related to ethnicity. The following five major themes were extracted from comments, related to ethnicity, made during these interviews.

1. Minority faculty find White faculty, staff and students to be insensitive to and uninformed in issues relating to diversity
2. Ethnic minorities are under-represented among faculty and administrators and feel isolated
3. Department culture is critical to minority faculty members' sense of satisfaction and belonging and the department head/chair plays a critical role in establishing that culture.
4. Minority faculty feel overwhelmed with committees and other service assignments, which they may be reluctant to refuse because of a sense of obligation to represent minority perspectives.
5. Minority faculty feel once hired they are expected to be "just like" their majority colleagues, rather than expressing diverse points of view.

Deans Council Subcommittee Recommendations

The last charge for this subcommittee was to provide recommendations for improving the recruitment and retention of ethnic minority faculty at this university. However, this group also realized that the data they surfaced in regard to this issue indicated that any new methods for recruitment and retention of ethnic minority faculty would only be successful if a set of broader concerns regarding campus diversity were addressed. Thus, the following 14 recommendations include strategies for making an impact on campus-wide diversity issues.

1. Southern University should adopt a broad statement on diversity.
2. Southern University should establish a position at the Executive staff level with special responsibility for equity and diversity.
3. A university website should have a prominent diversity section.
4. Create a search handbook focusing on strategies for increasing diversity in faculty hiring.

5. Organize annual workshops for department heads/chairs and search committee chairs to discuss strategies for more effective recruitment of minority faculty.

6. Develop a Faculty View book for use in recruitment that describes our commitment to faculty diversity.

7. Design a Diversity Fellows program.

8. Offer more opportunities for faculty awareness and training in diversity issues related to instruction.

9. Include diversity as a component of the faculty mentoring program and continue the opportunity for minority faculty to join special mentoring groups, if that proves to be a successful initiative.

10. Include diversity as a more salient component of orientation for new faculty, Staff, and students.

11. Use funds currently allocated to the Race and Gender Institute for initiatives targeted to recruitment and retention of ethnic minority faculty.

12. Include diversity training as part of orientation for new department heads/chairs and university administrators and include contributions to the recruitment and retention of a diverse faculty in their evaluation.

13. Encourage departments and programs to invite minority scholars to campus so that faculty and students become aware of the wider range of disciplinary perspectives that can be represented by a more diverse faculty.

14. Require each academic unit to establish a mechanism to ensure that issues of diversity receive authoritative and sustained attention.

The Inclusive Community Initiative

The fourteen recommendations made by the Deans' Subcommittee clearly indicated that this university was interested in more than just diversifying their faculty. After gathering data in the 2007/2008 academic year it seemed apparent to this subcommittee that a bold initiative was needed so that equity could be re-conceptualized for community members and a campus climate could be established that embraced both diversity and inclusiveness. Therefore, at the recommendation of the Faculty Senate and with full-support from the university administration, The Inclusive Community Initiative (ICI) was established at the onset of the 2008/2009 academic year with the authors serving in the initial two years as co-chairs. This was a 26 member task force that included staff, faculty, students, and community members. In August of 2008 the Faculty Senate and the Office of the Provost with support from the Office of the Chancellor gave the members of the ICI the following charge.

1. Develop a university endorsed definition of an inclusive community that is posted on the home page.

2. Conduct a campus climate assessment of the university environment.

3. Formulate a plan to better coordinate, communicate, and support all programs that contributes to campus inclusiveness.

4. Develop a rationale & position description for a Director of Equity & Inclusion.
5. Identify additional ways that this university can become a more inclusive campus and include these recommendations in the Strategic Plan.

The ICI decided at its first meeting to divide into four subgroups that could then work specifically on the first four initiative goals listed above. In regard to the fifth goal, identify ways the campus could become more inclusive, the members decided to work on this goal as a total group by conducing monthly focus groups with specific minority members of the campus. In addition, this 26 member group held an Open Microphone meeting at the onset of the 2008/2009 academic year where they invited all faculty and staff. The purpose of this session was to elicit what faculty and staff perceive as barriers to the university being more inclusive and their suggestions for making it a more inclusive community. Following are the two questions asked along with some of the responses.

What do you see as current barriers to this university being an inclusive community?

- Many on campus believe we are already inclusive
- Lack of education on campus re: diversity, similarities, and making campus more inclusive
- Caste systems still in place (lack of opportunities for some members of campus to move into higher positions)
- Lack of equal opportunities/benefits (e.g., no domestic partner benefits)
- Lack of accessibility of campus for all groups
- Few GLBT staff and faculty members are out on campus
- Lack of time and space to build an inclusive community
- Fears of addressing diversity and creating a more inclusive Community (Gause et al., 2010).

What are your suggestions for making this university a more inclusive community?

- Make this issue a priority and provide time to build an inclusive campus
- Plan more events that bring the entire campus together like a dance
- Provide domestic partner benefits
- Provide ongoing workshops on diversity and creating a more inclusive community
- Make physical plant of campus accessible to everyone
- Use student satisfaction data to inform changes on campus
- Allow staff to attend campus events without their having to use vacation time
- Increase diversity across all parts of the campus (Gause et al., 2010).

As a result of this Open Microphone meeting the ICI decided that conducting focus groups with specific minority groups on the campus would be one of the most informative ways to determine how well this Southern University was doing in regard to diversity issues and working towards being a more inclusive community. Thus, these focus groups became part of the ICI monthly meetings.

University Endorsed Definition of an Inclusive Community

The first charge given to the ICI was to develop an official statement on equity, diversity, & inclusive community that would be endorsed by the university. One subgroup of the ICI spent the first two years of the initiative working on this definition which would embrace all that this Southern University wanted to target as their new way of functioning. Following is the definition that was approved during the 2009/2010 academic year and then was posted on both the university home page and a new web page for the Office of Equity, Diversity, and Inclusion which was created at the recommendation of the ICI.

> Southern University fully supports and values an inclusive community where there is visible and meaningful representation of the diversity present in the wider community at all university levels. Diversity

is the combination of characteristics, experiences, and competencies that make each person unique, and increases the value of our community. We strive to maintain a climate of equity and respect, where we protect the rights of all in order to ensure that every member feels empowered, valued, and respected for their contributions to the mission of the university. Southern University is committed to providing all staff, faculty, and students' equitable access to services, benefits, and opportunities. (Gause et al., 2010)

Campus Climate Assessment

The second charge given to ICI was to conduct a campus climate assessment since that last one had been done three year earlier. A subgroup of ICC partnered with the Campus Unity Council which was established at this Southern University in 2000 with the task of surveying the faculty, staff and student body every three years to gather longitudinal data regarding perceptions of diversity on the campus. The campus was surveyed in 2000, 2003, 2005, and 2008. The Campus Unity Council in 2008 worked with the Inclusive Community Initiative to update the data instrument so survey items would reflect specific issues surrounding diversity and inclusiveness. Surveys were emailed to all faculty and staff, and a random sample of students. Overall survey distribution and response rate is as follows:

Faculty: 370 of 1191 = 31.1% (95% confidence interval ± 4.23)
Student: 591 of 3830 = 15.4% (95% confidence interval ± 3.71)
Staff with E-mail: 685 of 2031 = 33.7% (95% confidence interval ± 3.05)
Staff with E-mail and also others by hard copy: 703 of 2402 = 29.3%
(95% confidence interval ± 3.11) (Gause et al., 2010).

Summary of Campus Unity Council 2008 Survey Data

- The responses are overwhelmingly positive. No one area on the survey was found to have a significant percentage of respondents viewing this campus at a deficit regarding diversity.
- The responses improved for each question, almost uniformly, from 2005 to 2008. Those responses that dropped did so minimally.
- Across the board (faculty, staff, and students) agree that diversity is represented at this university, particularly among the student body. However, this is limited in two regards. One, the representation is about numbers, not the quality or how diverse populations are embraced. Second, diversity is represented in terms of ethnicity and international student populations, but not always in terms of sexual orientation, religious views, or political and ideological differences.
- The percentages of agreement are low when it comes to maintenance of diversity. All three groups seem to agree that efforts are lacking in terms of creating opportunities to strengthen and embrace diversity. They also agree that communication of such opportunities is poor.
- Staff ratings tend to be higher on many items, but the percentage is much lower when it comes to their perceived impact on creating an inclusive, learning community.
- Staff and student ratings are consistently higher than that of faculty, with students almost overwhelmingly rating each item the highest.
- Students see the faculty as more diverse than faculty and staff do. And, students see more collaboration among faculty, staff and students than faculty and staff sees (Gause et al., 2010).

Recommendations from Campus Unity Council 2008 Survey

The Campus Unity Council worked collaboratively with the ICI members to both analyze data from the 2008 survey and make recommendations to the university administration and wider campus. Following are some of the major recommendations.

1. Policies and practices related to ensuring the campus embraces diversity and students' learning benefits need to be communicated more clearly across the university.

2. Improve communication regarding events related to diversity and inclusive community building.

3. A university wide plan is needed for recruitment and retention of minority faculty that includes rewarding community engaged research and alternative research as part of standard tenure across departments.

4. Diversity across ethnic groups needs to be supported more rather than just Black/White diversity. Related to this expansion of diversity support more efforts need to be made to support religious diversity on the campus.

5. Staff members and some adjuncts specially do not feel as supported so more efforts to recognize these campus members is needed along with events that show appreciation for their contributions to the university community.

6. More efforts have to be made at the departmental level to embrace diversity, ensure students' learning benefits from this diversity, and faculty of color are provided more supports so they feel less isolated and respected for their contributions.

7. Consider the creation of a position for a Director of Diversity who could more effectively oversee, communicate, and coordinate campus wide efforts related to diversity and creating a more inclusive community (Gause et al., 2010).

Plan to Coordinate & Promote University Events related to Diversity & Inclusion

The third charge given to the ICI was to develop a plan to better coordinate, communicate, and promote all university events related to diversity and making the campus more inclusive. A subgroup from ICI work on this issue and after much discussion decided to recommend that an Office for Equity, Diversity, & Inclusion be created at the university with a Director Equity & Inclusion being in charge of this office. This latter position was the fourth charge given to ICI. This subgroup worked with university resources over the period of two years and subsequently were able to get this office established, designed and implemented a web page for this office, and assisted with the physical set up of this office which was placed under the office of the Chancellor.

Position for a Director of Equity & Inclusion

The fourth charge to the ICI was to provide a rationale statement and job description for the Director of Equity & Inclusion which was addressed by a subgroup. This latter group worked for two years gathering job descriptions of comparable positions at other universities and then developing a position description for this new Director. All necessary approvals at this Southern University for this new positions were obtained so that at the end of the 2009/2010 academic year the Chancellor was able to begin identifying a chair and the membership for a search committee.

Identify Ways This University Can Be More Inclusive

The fifth and final charge given to the ICI was to identify other ways this university could become a more inclusive community and work on making this goal with related plans part of the strategic plan. The ICI decided to work on this charge as a total group by spending an hour of each monthly meeting interviewing a minority group on campus. Subsequently, during the 2008/2009 year the ICI members met with Gay, Lesbian, Bisexual, Transgender, Intersecting, Questioning, and Queer students (GLBTIQQ), housekeeping staff members, international students, minority students, male students, and minority faculty members. Then in the 2009/2010 academic year the ICI met with new faculty members, students with disabilities, non-traditional students, office support staff, maintenance staff, and Human Resource liaisons. Important and informative data were surfaced from posing the following four questions to these twelve groups.

1. How inclusive is the UNCG campus?
2. What contributes to UNCG being an inclusive community?
3. What are current barriers to UNCG being a more inclusive community?
4. What are your suggestions for ways UNCG could become a more inclusive community?

A tremendous amount of data was surfaced after the ICI interviewed the twelve minority groups on the campus. Following are just a few samples of direct quotes related to the four questions posed to each group.

How Inclusive Is the UNCG Community from Your Perspective?

"The department is quite diverse across faculty and student lines. The department established statement of commitments that govern them. I feel like I am in a place that is wonderful, beautiful and creative; however, I am finding that this is different in other parts of the campus."

"UNCG is not inclusive at all, particularly with GLBT faculty."

What Are Barriers to Making UNCG a More Inclusive Community?

"I am a South-Asian Lesbian who believes this community has not reached out to the GLBT community."

"No support system for GLBT faculty."

"African Americans are promoted in leadership positions but are not allowed to stay."

"A culture and history exist around framing diversity around gender; particularly around white women and placing them in leadership."

"Faculty in my department think I am a fornicator and I find that quite problematic."

"We have attended Latino events and many Latino students are dissatisfied with their experiences."

"Not enough tenured faculty of color, particularly black faculty."

What Are Your Suggestions for Making UNCG a More Inclusive Community?

"Provide same-sex partner benefits-gain them."

"People in leadership positions should engage in serious dialogue around retention of faculty members from under-represented groups."

"Establish a GLBT Center."

"Establish an African American Center."

"Establish a Latino Center."

Key Question for Administration: What Are the Transformational Institutional Practices and Policies That Would Create Spaces for Inclusiveness?

"Upper administration must take on the central apparatuses; which supports barriers in departments and schools. They must develop values that support inclusiveness and provide resources to insure things get done."

"Upper administration must also address the inconsistencies that occur with the tenure and promotion process."

"Review programs, opportunities and events across the campus and support them, as well as communicate them across all channels."

All above quotes from Gause et al. (2010).

Third Year of Initiative

In the 2010/2011 academic year the ICI was renamed the Chancellor's Advisory Committee on Equity, Diversity, & Inclusion with this change making this a permanent standing committee under the Office of the Chancellor. During this latter year the Chancellor was able to secure approval to begin a national search to fill what had been renamed the Chief Diversity Officer/Vice Chancellor of Equity, Diversity, & Inclusion. During this same academic year the Chancellor appointed a search committee with a chair. This search committee received over 200 applications for this administrative position. After a very extensive review and rating system this committee recommended four candidates for campus interviews. The search committee completed all four campus interviews and was about to recommend one of these candidates for this position when the University's Board of Trustees decided that the current economic crisis that the university was facing required that the hiring for this position be closed.

Most of the third year of this initiative, 2010/2011, the co-chairs and their committee members spent trying to figure out ways to sustain all of their accomplishments in view of the decision to close the search for the Chief Diversity Officer. The Committee, after much discussion and brainstorming, recommended to the Chancellor to appoint an Interim Director for the Office of Equity, Diversity, & Inclusion (OEDI) in a part-time position and that it be someone already on staff who could oversee this office and its many related services. In addition, the co-chairs were able to secure a graduate assistantship so that a graduate student would cover the office and related activities when the Interim Director was not available. This coverage of the OEDI, chairing of the Chancellor's Advisory Committee on Equity, Diversity, and Inclusion, and many related services continue to be addressed by this part-time Interim Director and his/her graduate assistant. Obviously, much of the work started by the Committee cannot be continued without hiring a full-time Chief Diversity Officer.

No Changes in Last Three Years

As of the 2013/2014 academic year nothing has changed since the 2010/2011 academic year as the Chief Diversity Officer position is still closed for hiring and the many important functions needed from this individual cannot be carried out by one part-time staff member and a graduate student. As the initial co-chairs of the what seemed to be a very bold and impressive initiative on equity, diversity, and inclusion we are amazed that much of the transformative work that was started has either stopped completed or is being done on a limited basis.

What is even more concerning is in the past two academic years it appears that there are some changes at this university indicating less commitment to diversity and inclusion. For example, in the 2011/2012 academic year the Provost announced that they would be requiring higher SAT scores for incoming freshmen. When a faculty member at a campus wide meeting asked the Provost if he was concerned if this change in admission criteria would negatively impact the university's student diversity he was told that this Southern University is diverse enough so this is no longer a concern. In other words, as long as the university has enough diversity in its student body it does not matter if we put even more importance and weight on an admission criteria, SAT scores, that have been found to often be n unfair way of evaluating minority students.

At the end of the 2012/2013 academic year the Provost announced that the formal faculty mentoring program that was one of the few efforts on the campus that had proven to retain minority faculty was being discontinued. Instead a modified form of this latter mentoring program was put into effect this current year and many of the services that minority faculty reported were most responsive to their needs, for example group mentoring, were eliminated with the new mentoring services being offered. When the Provost was asked at a Faculty Senate meeting why the university decided to make this change he said it too expensive an effort. The cost of this former one year mentoring program was $4,000 per faculty member participant which is not much when one considers that many studies have found that employers spend almost the first year of a person's salary on their initial orientation and training.

Value of Diversity & Inclusion

So how much do we really value diversity and inclusion when they immediately become low priorities once a university's funding is reduced? Think about all the work that had been put into this Initiative on Equity, Diversity, and Inclusion in the first three years and then by the following three years much of its work has not advanced and some of the changes on the campus it had attained have now regressed as shown by the two statements from the University's Provost.

> Which brings us back to the question, how important is diversity? If we truly value it, if closing the achievement gap is a real priority and not just lip service, then funding for diversity should be based budgeted-something we fund no matter the fluctuations in the economy, or the swing of the political pendulum on Capitol Hill, in state legislatures, on higher education boards, or among system or campus leaders. (Clark, 2011)

We as Co-Chairs of this Initiative were able to see some of the beginning transformative changes on the campus even from our committee's initial work. Diversity was beginning to be more than just a number or ratio but rather something to both celebrate and then utilize to enhance all students' learning. Members of minority groups on campus were beginning to feel like they had a voice in changes the administration was making and also in what priorities were being established. Minority faculty members were beginning to provide the administration with more concrete ideas on how they could be made to feel more a part of the campus. Minority staff members were feeling for the first time that their voices were being heard about some very painful challenges they had faced with other members of the campus. GLBTIQQ students and faculty were starting to feel safe to say how they feel on the campus and were making specific suggestions for changes in the campus that could feel more inclusive of them.

These changes are not just extras that higher education can entertain in the good financial times. But rather these are changes that are critical if we are truly to provide students with an educational experience where they learn to embrace diversity, understand the benefits of hearing diverse perspectives, know the importance of questioning what has always been thought or done, and appreciate that the predominant culture in American does not have the only ways of addressing issues or problems. Otherwise, are we truly preparing our young people for the global job market in the years ahead?

Work Cited

Capaldi, E. (2011). Budget cuts and educational quality. *Academe, 97*(6), 10–13.

Clark, C. (2011). Diversity initiative in higher education: Just how important is diversity in higher education? *Multicultural Education, 18*(3), 57–59.

Gause, C. P., Dennison, S., & Perrin, D. (2010). Equity, inclusiveness, and diversifying the faculty: Transforming the university in the 21st century. *Quest, 62*, 61–75.

Oliff, P., Palacios, V., Johnson, I., & Leachman, M. (2013). Recent deep state higher education cuts may harm students and the economy for years to come. Washington, DC: Center on Budget and Policy Priorities.

Umbach, P. (2006). The contribution of faculty of color to undergraduate education. *Research in Higher Education, 47*(3), 317–345.

CHAPTER 5

Re-conceptualizing Higher Education Administration for the 21st Century

Servant Educational Leadership and Knowledge for Public Good in a "Post-racial" Era

Sabrina N. Ross

Knowledge for public good (as opposed to knowledge for profit) is characterized by teaching and leadership decisions that focus on equal access to knowledge and the circulation of knowledge for social betterment (Slaughter & Rhoades, 2004). The continued pursuit of knowledge for public good in higher education is vital because such efforts act as counter-hegemonic forces to resist academic capitalism and destruction to principles of democracy and equity (Rhoades, 2006; Rhoades & Slaughter, 2004; Slaughter & Rhoades, 2004). Although faculty of color who teach for social justice have a long history of supporting knowledge for public good, the emergence of a supposed "post-racial" era threatens to thwart these efforts, requiring faculty of color to focus on eradicating racism and other intersecting oppressions in an era where race/ethnic oppression is presumed by many Americans to no longer exist (Collins, 2009; Smith, 2004). In the 21st century, there is a pressing need for educational administrators, who wield the power and influence to facilitate change in higher education, to engage in moral leadership that promotes knowledge for public good. To overcome the moral passivity inherent in higher education organizations (Samier, 2008), the construct of servant educational leadership, a combination of social justice educational leadership and servant leadership, is offered. Intervention strategies supported by the framework of servant educational leadership are presented to help higher education administrators improve the campus climate for social justice educators of color while simultaneously promoting knowledge for public good.

Two predominant orientations to knowledge (i.e., knowledge for profit and knowledge for public good) currently circulate through institutions of higher education, affecting teaching, learning, and the campus climate in general (Slaughter & Rhoades, 2004). Knowledge for profit, or academic capitalism, is characterized by commoditization of faculty, exploitation of students as a consumer base, and a general adoption of market behaviors by higher education administrators; in contrast, knowledge for public good is characterized by teaching and leadership decisions that focus on equal access to knowledge and the circulation of knowledge for social betterment (Slaughter & Rhoades, 2004). The continued pursuit of knowledge for public good in higher education is vital because such efforts act as counter-hegemonic forces to resist academic capitalism and destruction to principles of democracy and equity (Rhoades, 2006; Rhoades & Slaughter, 2004; Slaughter & Rhoades, 2004).

One group of higher education stakeholders with a long history of pursuing knowledge for public good is faculty of color who teach for social justice. Social justice education involves processes of teaching and learning that are directed at helping students engage in critical reflection on dehumanizing sociopolitical conditions and actions they can take to alter those conditions (Adams, Bell, & Griffin, 2007). Social justice courses transform the public spaces of higher education into sites where empathy, equity, and democratic citizenship skills are cultivated (Gause, 2008; Giroux, 2004; Rhoades, 2006; Ross, 2009); faculty of color who teach for social justice contribute to knowledge for public good by educating students to be informed, compassionate, and active participants in an increasingly diverse U.S. society.

Though vital to the maintenance of principles of democracy and equity in higher education, the social justice work of faculty of color, and particularly faculty of color who teach within predominantly White institutions (PWIs), is exceedingly difficult. A disproportionate number of social justice courses at PWIs are taught by faculty of color (Brayboy, 2003; Perry, Moore, Acosta, Edwards, & Frey, 2006). Despite ubiquitous claims of support for diversity within higher education environments (Brayboy, 2003; Kayes, 2006), faculty of color who work within PWIs experience under-representation, alienation, and marginalization (Aguirre, 2000; Stanley, 2006a). As the designated representatives of diversity at PWIs (Brayboy, 2003), faculty of color who teach for social justice endure challenges to their presence and their curricula (see for example, Dixson & Dingus, 2007; Luthra, 2002; Perry, Moore, Edwards, Acosta, & Frey, 2009; Ross, 2013; Williams & Evans-Winters, 2005).

Now, increasing circulation of the notion of a "post-racial" United States makes the social justice work of faculty of color at PWIs even more difficult and, as a result, jeopardizes the contributions they make to knowledge for public good in higher education. With the 2008 election and subsequent re-election of Barack Obama, the first African-American U.S. president, the rhetoric of a post-racial era in U.S. history (i.e., where issues of race no longer determine life chances and outcomes) has continued to gain prominence. Amidst the circulation of this post-racial rhetoric, however, acts of racism, racial discrimination, and other intersecting forms of oppression have persisted and, in some cases, intensified (Andrews & Tuitt, 2013; Bonilla-Silva, 2013). Within this supposed post-racial era, faculty of color who teach for social justice are charged with the almost impossible task of raising learners' awareness of and desire to alter structures of racism and other intersecting oppressions in an era where race/ethnic oppression is presumed by many Americans to no longer exist (Collins, 2009; Smith, 2004).

Rather than signaling an end to racism, the "post" in post-racial can instead signal the end of traditional approaches to anti-racism and the adoption of new approaches capable of addressing the emerging complexities of racism and other intersecting oppressions (Bonilla-Silva, 2013). Building on the idea of "post" as an invitation to new ideas and approaches, this chapter offers a re-conceptualization of higher education administration in the "post-racial" era that emphasizes moral leadership. Leadership requires both management skills to create stability in organizations and leadership skills to promote change (Kotter, 2001). The argument put forth in this chapter is that for too long, higher education administrators have privileged the use of management skills that perpetuate the status quo, allowing faculty of color who teach for social justice to shoulder the burden of disseminating knowledge for public good on their own. Given the important role that knowledge for public good plays in higher education and the documented difficulties faculty of color who educate for social justice experience within higher education institutions, there is a pressing need for educational administrators, who wield the power and influence to facilitate change in higher education, to engage in moral leadership by partnering with faculty of color in the vital work of promoting knowledge for public good.

Purpose

The organization of educational institutions contributes to an atmosphere of moral passivity within which educational administrators are less likely to act morally when such actions are required (Samier, 2008). One way to overcome the tendency toward moral passivity in educational organizations is through the deliberate infusion of moral and democratic perspectives (Adams & Balfour, 1998). In order to re-conceptualize the role of higher education administration as moral leadership to promote knowledge for public good, this chapter combines literature on social justice educational leadership and servant leadership (Greenleaf, 2002/1977) to develop the concept of servant educational leadership. Servant educational leadership is offered as a framework that higher education administrators can invoke in their work towards knowledge for public good. The chapter also provides specific interventions that higher education administrators, as servant educational leaders, can undertake in the "post-racial" era to improve the campus climate for faculty of color teaching for social justice at PWIs. A review of social justice educational leadership and servant leadership theory follows.

Social Justice Educational Leadership

Like social justice education, social justice educational leadership consists of leadership praxis to address and eliminate marginalizing conditions associated with race, class, disability gender, sexual orientation, and other marginalizing conditions. (Theoharis, 2007). Literature on social justice educational leadership tends to focus on K–12 schools (Diaz, 2011) with only a few empirical studies examining social justice leadership in higher education (i.e., Jean-Marie, 2006; Jean-Marie & Normore, 2008). Literature on social justice educational leadership is difficult to delineate because the act only becomes manifest through the engagement of educational leadership practices; stated differently, each manifestation of social justice educational leadership is specific to the educational practices being undertaken (Bogotch, 2002).

Servant Leadership Theory

Servant leadership is growing in popularity as a leadership model for the 21st century (Parris & Peachey, 2013). Through dedicated focus on service to others, servant leaders help individuals to increase their freedom and autonomy so that they can participate in work for social betterment (Bass, 2000; Parris & Peachey, 2013). While also limited in application to higher education contexts (i.e., Bass, 2000; Hays, 2008; Marina & Fonteneau, 2012), servant leadership theory provides a detailed account of tenets and attributes of servant leaders that facilitate practical application of the theory.

Much of existing literature on servant leadership is derived from the writings of former AT&T executive Robert Greenleaf (Bass, 2000; Sendjaya & Sarros, 2002). Greenleaf (1904–1990) began writing about the concept of servant leadership during the 1960 due to concerns about the process of education and what he perceived as the hopelessness of students on university campuses (Greenleaf, 2002/1977). His work on servant leadership addresses the importance of two primary roles: the servant and the leader, and how individuals embracing both of these seemingly contradictory roles can facilitate social betterment. The primary role of the servant leader is to provide service to others. Service to others suggests that, rather than self-interest or success of the organization, servant leaders are motivated by the primary desire to help others (Greenleaf, 2002/1977). According to Greenleaf, the servant leader exhibits characteristics of sustained and intent listening, facilitation of imagination, empathy, foresight, and persuasion; each of these characteristics help the servant leader in her or his thoughts and actions to serve others (Greenleaf, 2002/1977). The servant leader strives to enable individuals to become freer, more autonomous, and capable of being servant leaders themselves. This emphasis on service to others and the intended effects of this service for social betterment is made clear in the following passage.

> The servant-leader is servant first. It begins with the natural feeling that one wants to serve. Then conscious choice brings one to aspire to lead. The best test is: do those served grow as persons: do they,

> while being served, become healthier, wiser, freer, more autonomous, more likely themselves to become servants? And, what is the effect on the least privileged in society; will they benefit, or, at least, not be further deprived? (Greenleaf, 2002/1977, p. 27)

The importance of building a sense of community is a major theme in servant leadership because the trust established through authentic relationships and community building is a foundation upon which individuals within organizations build their own capacities for servant leadership and social betterment (Greenleaf, 2002/1977). The life and work of the servant leader is holistic in that relationships between individuals, organizations, and society are understood to be inter-related; the servant leader presents an authentic presentation of self in all aspects of life that, according to Greenleaf, ultimately benefits others, society, and self (2002/1977).

Greenleaf's theory of servant leadership gained popularity in the 1970s and continues to grow in popularity more than 40 years after his earliest publication on servant leadership (Marina & Fonteneau, 2012; Parris & Peachey, 2013; Spears, 2010). Currently, scholarship that builds upon Greenleaf's theory of servant leadership is produced through the Robert K. Greenleaf Center for Servant Leadership. Founded in 1964 by Robert Greenleaf, the Greenleaf Center serves as a repository for Greenleaf's work and provides education and training on servant leadership to organizations (Greenleaf Center, 2013). Based on a careful reading of direct quotes and implicit themes in Greenleaf's writings, former president and COE of the Greenleaf Center (1990–2007), Larry Spears identified ten attributes of vital importance to servant leaders including: (1) listening; (2) empathy; (3) healing; (4) awareness; (5) persuasion; (6) conceptualization; (7) foresight; (8) stewardship; (9) commitment to the growth of people; and (10) building community.

Servant leadership theory contains an explicit emphasis on morality through its focus on service to others and its goal of social betterment; as such, the theory is appropriate for use in this chapter's re-conceptualization of higher education administration. The concept of social justice educational leadership (i.e., leadership practices to address and eliminate conditions of marginalization) is also appropriate for use in this chapter; however, the abstract nature of social justice educational leadership and its limited application in higher education settings makes applying the concept difficult. To utilize the strengths of social justice educational leadership and servant leadership, both are used to develop a model of moral educational leadership appropriate for higher education administrators.

For the purposes of this chapter, social justice educational leadership is conceptualized as efforts by higher education administrators to identify and work towards the elimination of factors and conditions within PWIs that impede the social justice work of faculty of color. Servant educational leadership (a combination of servant leadership and social justice educational leadership) is the construct developed to carry out social justice educational leadership within higher education institutions using themes and attributes of servant leadership theory.

The last section of this chapter uses the construct of servant educational leadership to outline specific interventions that higher education administrators can use to facilitate the social justice work of faculty of color. The organization of this final section begins with a literature review of challenges experiences by faculty of color who teach for social justice within PWIs and transitions to a discussion of appropriate higher education interventions supported by specific themes and attributes of servant leadership theory.

Putting it all Together: Servant Educational Leadership, Faculty of Color, and Knowledge for Public Good in Predominantly White Institutions of Higher Education

Vital to reducing challenges experienced by faculty of color at PWIs is a need for higher education administrators to increase their awareness of faculty of color experiences related to social justice education on predominantly White campuses (Dixson & Dingus, 2007; Stanley, 2006b; Williams & Evans-Winters, 2005). Such awareness is a fundamental trait for successful servant leaders; on the importance of awareness in servant leaders, Spears (2010) writes: "Awareness helps one in understanding issues involving ethics, power, and values. It lends itself to being able to view most situations from a more integrated, holistic position" (p. 27). Through awareness, higher education administrators can engage in intervention strategies that improve the campus climate for faculty of color who teach for social justice, and, in doing so, promote knowledge for public good in higher education.

Below, two inter-related themes: resistance from students and other faculty and work overload/ emotional exhaustion derived from literature on challenges experienced by faculty of color who teach for social justice within PWIs are presented, followed by interventions that servant educational leaders can enact to reduce these challenges.

Theme 1: Resistance from Students and Other Faculty

Within PWIs, hegemony is maintained through official curricula that sanctions White, male, middle class ways of knowing (Hoodfar, 1997; Luthra, 2002; Vargas, 1999) and a hidden curriculum that simultaneously posits the views and experiences of individuals placed outside the dominant group as inferior (Collins, 2000). Hegemony encourages faculty of color to be viewed by colleagues and students as outsiders (Stanley, 2006a); this view contributes to the resistance they face from students and other faculty.

Resistance from students. Social justice courses contain knowledge that often challenges long-held common sense notions endorsed by students; the cognitive dissonance produced as students grapple with critical knowledge gained in social justice courses often produces resistance (Ng, 1993; Wang, 2008; Williams & Evans-Winters, 2005). One way that student resistance manifests itself for faculty of color who teach social justice courses is through challenges to professional authority. Male and female faculty of color report challenges to their professional authority and credibility in the social justice courses they teach at PWIs (see for example, Perry et al., 2009), but women faculty of color, in particular, describe student challenges to their authority inside the classroom through verbal and nonverbal acts of disrespect and negative course evaluations (see for example, Brown, 2002; Chaisson, 2004; Muhtaseb, 2007; Ng, 1993; Ross, 2013) and outside of class through grievances reported to senior faculty and administrators (Dixson & Dingus, 2007; Vargas, 1999; Williams & Evans-Winters, 2005).

Resistance from other faculty. Faculty of color note that they are often thought of as special hires or as opportunity hires by their colleagues (Brayboy, 2003; Cleary, 2002; Turner & Myers, 2000). Faculty of color report resistance from their non-minority colleagues that is manifested as subtle and overt acts of racism (Stanley, 2006a) and as disregard for their research activities and scholarship (Turner & Myers, 2000).

Servant educational leadership intervention 1: developing infrastructures that help orient students and faculty to the presence and social justice curricula of faculty of color. In order to adequately address the resistance faculty of color experience from students and colleagues within PWIs, higher education administrators are charged with conceptualizing visions of anti-racist and anti-oppressive higher education environments and convincing students and faculty to join in the work of realizing those visions. Interventions supportive of this goal could include the initiation of campus wide discussions on issues related to diversity and social justice, identifying and altering policies and practices that encourage problematic views of diversity, social justice, and/or faculty of color, and taking steps to ensure that discriminatory actions against faculty of color (e.g., racially-motivated punitive actions by students) are not supported. These interventions are presented below and followed by the servant leadership attributes that support them.

Intervention 1a: Initiating departmental, college, and campus-wide discussions on diversity and social justice. Knowledge of the experiences of faculty of color who teach for social justice at PWIs can be used by higher education administrators as a foundation for discussions about diversity and multiculturalism within the campus community. For students enrolled in social justice courses, discussions initiated by higher education administrators can signal the importance of these courses. Such discussions can be used to challenge student assumptions about who should be teaching them and can also play an important role in orienting students to the dispositions they are expected to adopt relative to faculty of color and issues of diversity and social justice (Williams & Evans-Winters, 2005). For university faculty, discussions about diversity and social justice initiated by higher education administrators within departments, colleges, and campus-wide can go a long way toward communicating university expectations (Dixson & Dingus, 2007) and also convey the importance of having open conversations about issues of race and other intersecting oppressions. Servant leader attributes of listening and conceptualization can be used to support this intervention.

Servant leadership attribute: Listening. For the higher education administrator seeking to improve the campus climate for faculty of color, engaging in thoughtful and reflective listening is imperative. Through purposeful listening to what is spoken and unspoken, servant educational leaders can discern the viewpoints of the university community surrounding issues of diversity and, based on their convictions, make informed decisions about future courses of action. Spears (2010) supports this presentation of the importance of listening for servant leaders. He writes: "The servant leader seeks to identify the will of a group and helps to clarify that will. He or she listens receptively to what is being said and unsaid. Listening also encompasses hearing one's own inner voice" (Spears, 2010, p. 27).

Servant leadership attribute: Conceptualization. Conceptualization involves moving focus beyond short-term goals to broader visions for the institution. In order to understand and work within the intersecting structures of race, class, gender, sexual orientation, and other marginalizing conditions, it is necessary for servant educational leaders to engage in conceptualization by moving beyond superficial solutions associated with day to day realities toward lasting change (Spears, 2010).

Intervention 1b: Altering policies and practices that encourage problematic views about diversity and social justice. Curricular decisions can greatly influence faculty views about the importance of diversity, social justice, and knowledge for public good. At many PWIs, issues of social justice are addressed through a single course that is usually taught by a person of color; this additive, tokenized approach to social justice contributes to the negative experiences of faculty of color (Brayboy, 2003; Dixson & Dingus, 2007; Milner, 2008) because it perpetuates their status as other within the academy. When additive approaches to social justice education are employed, faculty of color are positioned as more concerned with issues of equity and diversity than the rest of their colleagues (Dixson & Dingus, 2007) and this positioning exacerbates their marginalization. This tokenized approach also gives the impression to other faculty that the achievement of diversity goals can be realized without full integration of social justice content throughout the curriculum and without fundamental changes to the conceptualization and day to day operations of the institution (Brayboy, 2003; Dixson & Dingus, 2007). Servant leader attributes of persuasion and building community can be used in support of this intervention.

Servant leadership attribute: Persuasion. Servant leaders privilege persuasion over authority to build consensus and gain support for organizational initiatives (Spears, 2010). From a servant leadership perspective, top-down directives that force compliance are not effective in encouraging support from higher education faculty for socially just policies and practices related to faculty of color. Instead, higher education administrators who view themselves as servant leaders can articulate and communicate the importance of their visions to faculty, and through persuasion, elicit consensus for support of that vision.

Servant leadership attribute: Building community. By repeatedly building strong communities, servant leaders also build strong societies. Greenleaf (2002/1977) captures the significance of community building for social betterment in the following passage:

> All that is needed to rebuild community as a viable life form for large numbers of people is for enough servant-leaders to show the way, not by mass movements, but by each servant-leader demonstrating his or her unlimited ability for a quite specific community-related group. (Greenleaf, 2002/1977, p. 53)

By working to change policies and practices that encourage negative views of faculty of color, servant educational leaders are, at the same time, working to build community within their organizations. Such community building, and the trust that accompanies it, is crucial if social justice goals are to be realized.

Intervention 1c: Exercising awareness of the racialized and gendered dynamics that can influence student complaints about faculty of color. Awareness of the dynamics that come into play when faculty of color teach about issues of inequality within predominantly White settings can help higher education administrators make informed decisions when dealing with punitive actions by students that are motivated by race/ethnicity and/or gender such as student complaints to administrators and negative student course evaluations (Williams & Evans-Winters, 2005). The servant leader attribute of foresight can be used to support this intervention.

Servant leadership attribute: Foresight. "Foresight is a characteristic that enables the servant leader to understand the lessons from the past, the realities of the present, and the likely consequences of a decision for the future" (Spears, 2010, p. 28). Through foresight, servant educational leaders can gain insight from the history of race relations in the U.S. and use those insights to: (1) understand the ways in which hidden curricula that support notions of racial inferiority for faculty of color can influence student decisions to engage in punitive actions against faculty of color; and (2) cultivate appropriate actions to deal with student resistance in ways that support students' continued critical education without penalizing faculty of color.

Theme 2: Work Overload and/or Emotional Exhaustion

Work overload. Social justice educators of color often discuss the excessive workloads they endure due to the rigors of teaching for social justice within PWIs (see for example, Moule, 2005; Roseboro & Ross, 2009) and the cultural taxation they experience when repeatedly asked to engage in service specifically related to their race ethnicity (Aguirre, 2000; Turner & Myers, 2000).

Emotional exhaustion. Levels of psychological and physiological stress associated with teaching about issues of diversity within PWIs can be so great that racial battle fatigue and associated symptoms of nervousness, insomnia, anxiety, and extreme exhaustion occur in faculty of color (Smith, 2004).

Servant educational leadership intervention 2: Developing policies for the implementation of work assignments that are sensitive to the physical and emotional toll of teaching for social justice. Awareness of the excessive time and energy resources that are necessary for social justice education can help higher education administrators to make more informed decisions related to workload, teaching assignments, merit pay, and promotion and tenure (Stanley, 2006). Such awareness can help servant educational leaders to develop and enforce equitable teaching assignments and service expectations for faculty of color who teach for social justice at PWIs.

Intervention 2a: Developing and enforcing teaching assignments that equally distribute the responsibility for teaching social justice courses. Higher education administrators as servant educational leaders can initiate the shifts in academic culture that are needed to improve the campus climate for faculty of color who teach for social justice by developing policies related to course assignments that reflect awareness of the challenges faculty of color face when educating for social justice at PWIs. Many faculty of color report that, as opposed to their White colleagues, they are consistently assigned to teach courses dealing with race, inequity, and/or minority issues (Brayboy, 2003; Cleary, 2002; Perry et al., 2006). Administrators who limit teaching assignments for diversity and/or social justice courses to faculty of color perpetuate institutionalized patterns of marginalization for faculty of color (Perry et al., 2009).

When faculty of color consistently teach diversity and social justice courses they bear the onus for representing, both through their physical embodiment and their teaching, these initiatives (Brayboy, 2003). The marginality and isolated responsibility of faculty of color contributes to their physical and emotional exhaustion at PWIs. Intervening at the program level, higher education administrators could developing and enforce policies and procedures that require the entire program (as opposed to the lone faculty member of color), to infuse social justice themes into the curricula (Dixson & Dingus, 2007). The servant leader attribute of healing can be used to support this intervention.

Servant leadership attribute: Healing. Servant leaders are concerned with the well-being of individuals within their organizations. According to Spears: "… servant leaders recognize that they have an opportunity to help make whole those with whom they come into contact" (2010, p. 27). Higher education administrators who strive to be servant leaders utilize their awareness of the physical and emotional challenges involved in teaching for social justice to develop and enforce equitable teaching assignments that distribute the burden of teaching for social justice among all faculty members and, in so doing, help to make faculty of color whole.

Intervention 2b: Creating service expectations for faculty of color that take issues of cultural taxation into account. Servant educational leaders can use their awareness of the cultural taxation experienced by many faculty of color that disproportionately increases their service obligations to lessen formal service expectations for this group. The servant leader attribute of empathy can be used to support this intervention.

Servant leadership attribute: Empathy. Servant leaders seek empathy and understanding with others. Regarding faculty of color who teach for social justice at PWIs, empathy can encourage higher education administrators to attend to the research and personal stories of faculty of color and the cultural taxation they experience within PWIs and adjust service expectations accordingly.

Servant educational leadership intervention 3: Establishing a critical mass of faculty of color who educate for social justice. Higher education administrators can improve the campus climate for social justice educators of color through the hiring of additional faculty of color to create a more diversified faculty. Increased numbers of faculty of color can alleviate the isolation and alienation reported by so many faculty of color who work within predominantly White institutions (Stanley, 2006b). When faculty of color achieve a critical mass (Collins, 2000) within predominantly White settings, experiences of burnout or work overload can be lessened The servant leader attribute of commitment to the growth of people supports this intervention.

Servant leadership attribute: Commitment to the growth of people. Higher education administrators who are committed to the goals of servant leadership must also be committed to the growth of individuals within their organization. The importance of supporting the growth and development of people is captured in the following passage:

> Servant leaders believe that people have an intrinsic value beyond their tangible contributions as workers. As such, the servant leader is deeply committed to the growth of each and every individual within his or her organization. The servant leader recognizes the tremendous responsibility to do everything in his or her power to nurture the personal and professional growth of employees and colleagues. (Spears, 2010, p. 29)

For faculty of color who teach for social justice within PWIs, higher education administrators can demonstrate commitment to growth by engaging in recruitment and retention strategies targeted towards establishing and maintaining a critical mass of faculty of color within PWIs.

Conclusion

This chapter offers servant educational leadership as a model of moral leadership for higher education administrators in the 21st century. The argument put forth in this chapter is that faculty of color, through their work to educate for social justice, have endured considerable challenges by shouldering the burden of promoting knowledge for public good without adequate support from higher education administrators. The chapter represents a thought project that explores ways in which a re-conceptualized higher education administration based on social justice educational leadership and servant leadership can illuminate higher education interventions capable of supporting knowledge for public good by improving the campus climate for social justice educators of color working within PWIs.

Knowledge for public good serves a vital democratizing function within higher education institutions, but its place in higher education is not guaranteed. Higher education administrators have a choice between moral passivity and moral leadership; they can choose to support knowledge for profit or knowledge for public good. The position supported in this chapter is that 21st century higher educational administrators must be moral leaders who promote knowledge for public good. At a time when racism can exist without racists (Bonilla-Silva, 2013) and the rhetoric of diversity goes unrealized within many predominantly White institutions (Brayboy, 2003), higher education administrators are called upon to qualitatively shift their models of leadership in order to attend to the complexities that arise when faculty of color teach about issues of oppression at predominantly White institutions in the "post-racial" era.

Work Cited

Adams, G., & Balfour, D. (1998). *Unmasking administrator evil.* Thousand Oaks, CA: Sage.

Adams, M., Bell, L. A., & Griffin, P. (2007). *Teaching for diversity and social justice* (2nd ed.). New York, NY: Routledge.

Aguirre, A. (2000). *Women and minority faculty in the academic workplace: Recruitment, retention, and academic culture.* San Francisco, CA: ASHE-ERUC Higher Education Report Volume 27, Number 6.

Andrews, D., & Tuitt, F. (Eds.) (2013). *Contesting the myth of a 'post-racial' era: The continued significance of race in U.S. Education.* New York, NY: Peter Lang.

Bass, B. M. (2000). The future of leadership in the learning organization. *Journal of Leadership Studies, 7*(3), 18–38.

Bogotch, I. (2002). Educational leadership and social justice: Practice into theory. *Journal of School Leadership, 12*, 138–156.

Bonilla-Silva (2013). *Racism without racists: Color-blind racism and the persistence of racial inequality in America* (4th ed.). Lanham, MD: Rowman & Littlefield.

Brayboy, B. M. J. (2003). The implementation of diversity in predominantly White colleges and universities. *Journal of Black Studies, 34*(1), 72–86.

Brown, K. N. (2002). Useful anger: Confrontation and challenge in the teaching of gender, race, and violence. In L. Vargas (Ed.), *Women faculty of color in the White classroom* (pp. 89–108). New York, NY: Peter Lang.

Chaisson, R. L. (2004). A crack in the door: Critical race theory in practice at a predominantly white institution. *Teaching Sociology, 32*(4), 345–357.

Cleary, D. B.-C. (2002). Reflections of an Okanogan-Colville Professor. In L. Vargas (Ed.), *Women faculty of color in the White classroom* (pp. 183–200). New York, NY: Peter Lang.

Collins, P. H. (2000). *Black feminist thought: Knowledge, consciousness, and the politics of empowerment* (2nd ed.). New York, NY: Routledge.

Collins, P. H. (2009). *Another kind of public education: Race, schools, the media, and democratic possibilities.* Boston, MA: Beacon Press.

Diaz, S. M. (2011). Finding our way through the house of mirrors: Higher education, administrative leadership, and social justice. (Doctoral Dissertation). Proquest Dissertations and Theses Database (UMI Number: 3483944).

Dixson, A., & Dingus, J. (2007). Tyranny of the majority: Re-enfranchisement of African-American teacher educators teaching for democracy. *International Journal of Qualitative Studies in Education (QSE), 20*(6), 639(616).

Freire, P. (2001). *Pedagogy of the oppressed.* New York, NY: Continuum International Publishing Group, Inc.

Gause, C. P. (2008). From social justice to collaborative activism: Changing the landscape of academic leadership. *Academic Leadership: The Online Journal, 6*(3). Retrieved from http://www.academicleadership.org/

Giroux, H. A. (2004). Critical pedagogy and the postmodern/modern divide: Towards a pedagogy of democratization. *Teacher Education Quarterly, 31*(1), 31–47.

Greenleaf, R. K. (2002/1977). *Servant leadership: A journey into the nature of legitimate power and greatness.* Mahwah, NJ: Paulist Press.

Hays, J. (2008). Teacher as servant applications of Greenleaf's servant leadership in higher education. *Journal of Global Business Issues, 2*(1), 113–134. Retrieved from http://libez.lib.georgiasouthern.edu/login?url=https://search.ebscohost.com/login.aspx?direct=true&db=bth&AN=31381051&site=ehost-live

Hoodfar, H. (1997). Feminist anthropology and critical pedagogy: The anthropology of classrooms' excluded voices. In S. d. Castell & M. Bryson (Eds.), *Radical interventions: Identity, politics, and differencels in educational praxis* (pp. 211–232). Albany, NY: State University of New York Press.

Jean-Marie, G. (2006). Welcoming the unwelcomed: A social justice imperative of African American female leaders at historically black colleges and universities. *Educational Foundations, 20*(2), 85–104.

Jean-Marie, G., & Normore, A. H. (2008). A repository of hope for social justice: Black women leaders at historically black colleges and universities. In A. H. Normore (Ed.), *Leadership for social justice: Promoting equity and excellence through inquiry and reflective practice* (pp. 1–35). Charlotte, NC: Information Age Publishing.

Kayes, P. (2006). New paradigms for diversifying faculty and staff in higher education: Uncovering cultural biases in the search and hiring process. *Multicultural Education, 14*(2), 65–69.
Kotter, J. P. (2001). What leaders really do. *Harvard Business Review*, December, 3–12.
Luthra, R. (2002). Negotiating the minefield: Practicing transformative pedagogy as a teacher of color in a classroom climate of suspicion. In L. Vargas (Ed.), *Women faculty of color in the white classroom* (pp. 109–124). New York, NY: Peter Lang.
Marina, B., & Fonteneau, D. (2012). Servant leaders who picked up the broken glass. *The Journal of Pan African Studies, 5*(2) 67–83.
McKay, N. (1997). A troubled peace: Black women in the halls of the white academy. In L. Benjamin (Ed.), *Black women in the academy: Promises and perils* (pp. 12–22). Gainesville, FL: University Press of Florida.
Milner, I. V. H. R. (2008). Critical race theory and interest convergence as analytic tools in teacher education policies and practices. *Journal of Teacher Education, 59*(4), 332(315).
Moule, J. (2005). Implementing a social justice perspective in teacher education: Invisible burden for faculty of color. *Teacher Education Quarterly,* (Fall), 23–42.
Muhtaseb, A. (2007). From behind the veil: Students' resistance from different directions. *New Directions for Teaching and Learning,* Vol. 2007 (110), 25–33.
Ng, R. (1993). "A Woman out of control": Deconstructing sexism and racism in the university. *Canadian Journal of Education, 18*(3), 189–205.
Parris, D. L., & Peachey, J. W. (2013). A systematic literature review of servant leadership theory in organizational contexts. *Journal of Business Ethics, 113,* 377–393. DOI 10.1007/s10551-012-1322-6.
Perry, G., Moore, H., Acosta, K., Edwards, C., & Frey, C. (2006). Dialogue on diversity teaching. In N. Peters-Davis & J. Shultz (Eds.), *Challenges of multicultural education: Teaching and taking diversity courses* (pp. 81–111). Boulder, CO: Paradigm Publishers.
Perry, G., Moore, H., Edwards, C., Acosta, K., & Frey, C. (2009). Maintaining credibility and authority as an instructor of color in diversity-education classrooms: A qualitative inquiry. *Journal of Higher Education, 80*(1), 80–105.
Rhoades, G. (2006). The higher education we choose: A question of balance. *The Review of Higher Education, 29,* 381–404.
Rhoades, G., & Slaughter, S. (2004). Academic capitalism in the new economy: Challenges and choices. *American Academic, 1,* 37–60.
Robert, K. (2013). Greenleaf Center for Servant Leadership. Mission, vision, and history. Retrieved from https://greenleaf.org/about-us/
Roseboro, D., & Ross, S. N. (2009). Care-sickness: Black women educators, ethic of care, and a hermeneutic of suspicion. *Educational Foundations,* 23(3–4), 19–40.
Ross, S. N. (2009). Critical race theory, democratization, and the public good: Deploying postmodern understandings of racial identity in the social justice classroom to contest academic capitalism. *Teaching in Higher Education, 14*(5), 517–528. DOI: 10.1080/13562510903186709
Ross, S. N. (2013). The politics of politeness: Theorizing race, gender, and education in White Southern space. In W. M. Reynolds (Ed.), *A curriculum of place: Understandings emerging through the Southern mist* (pp. 143–160). New York, NY: Peter Lang.
Samier, E. (2008). The problem of passive evil in educational administration: Moral implications of doing nothing. *International Studies in Educational Administration, 36*(1), 2–21.
Slaughter, S., & Rhoades, G. (2004). *Academic capitalism and the new economy.* Baltimore, MD: Johns Hopkins University Press.
Smith, W. A. (2004). Black faculty coping with racial battle fatigue: The campus racial climate in a post-civil rights era. In D. Cleveland (Ed.), *A long way to go: Conversations about race by African American faculty and graduate students* (pp. 171–192). New York, NY: Peter Lang.
Spears, L. (2010). Character and servant leadership: Ten characteristics of effective, caring leaders. *The Journal of Virtues & Leadership, 1*(1), 25–30.
Stanley, C. A. (2006a). An overview of the literature. In C. A. Stanley (Ed.), *Faculty of color: Teaching in predominantly White colleges and* universities (pp. 1–29). Bolton, MA: Anker Publishing Company.
Stanley, C. A. (2006b). Summary and key recommendations for the recruitment and retention of faculty of color. In C. A. Stanley (Ed.), *Faculty of color: Teaching in predominantly White colleges and* universities (pp. 361–373). Bolton, MA: Anker Publishing Company.
Theoharis, G. (2007). Social justice educational leaders and resistance: Toward a theory of social justice leadership. *Educational Administration Quarterly, 43*(2), 221–258.
Turner, C., & Myers, S. L. (2000). *Faculty of color in academe: Bittersweet success.* Needlam Heights, MA: Allyn and Bacon.
Vargas, L. (1999). When the "other" is the teacher: Implications of teacher diversity in higher education. *Urban Review, 31*(4), 359–383.
Wang, H. (2008). "Red Eyes": Engaging emotions in multicultural education. *Multicultural Perspectives, 10*(1), 10–16.
Williams, D. G., & Evans-Winters, V. (2005). The burden of teaching teachers: Memoirs of race discourse in teacher education. *The Urban Review, 37*(3), 18.

CHAPTER 6

Good for Whom? The Shifting Role of Higher Education

Jillian Volpe White and Kathy L. Guthrie

This chapter explores the evolving charter between higher education and the public good. Historically, institutions of higher education existed to promote an educated and democratized citizenry that is engaged in the community through socially responsible action. As state support for higher education declines and students contribute more to the cost of higher education, institutions are increasingly focused on the personal and economic gains resulting from participation in higher education at the expense of the public charter. Despite the shifting charter, intuitions can contribute to the public good through student and faculty service in the Twenty-First Century.

Introduction

Since the Colonial period, the mission of American higher education was to foster the public good. The founders of the earliest higher education institutions did not intend for postsecondary education to be a private commodity for individual advancement, but for society to benefit from the development of well-educated citizens in positions of influence (Rudolph, 1990). However, in recent years, Kezar (2004) acknowledged "various social critics and leaders have noted a disturbing trend in higher education: The collective or public good, a historically important component of the charter between higher education and society, is being compromised" (p. 429). With the erosion of state support for higher education, the dynamic of higher education has shifted toward a more individualized view of higher education, which emphasizes the personal benefits of college attendance. Increasingly, market forces are impacting American higher education as institutions seek funding and respond to the pressure to be both more efficient and more prestigious.

Chickering's observation that higher education is seen as a private benefit, operating with a "market mentality" led him to conclude, "the larger issues of interdependence, identity, purpose, meaning, and integrity have been eclipsed by short-term goals oriented toward a well-paying job upon graduation" (2010, pp. 4–5). This shift away from the historic public good mission has resulted in a cultural climate in higher education where the "goals of personal advancement and gratification too often take precedence over social, moral, or spiritual meaning" (Colby, Ehrlich, Beaumont, & Stephens, 2003, p. 7). Kezar (2004) emphasized that in the absence of a charter between higher education and the public good, resources may be diverted away from higher education that will widen existing disparities and diminish civic engagement. Despite this, the public good role of higher education need not be subsumed to economic goals; institutions can be engaged in the community through teaching, community-based research, and service in order to maintain a commitment to the public good. This chapter explores the evolving charter between society and higher education, concluding with opportunities for institutions to engage students and faculty in learning and service that fosters the public good.

Defining Public Good in Higher Education

There are many ideas of what it means to foster the public good. Shapiro (2005) offered the comprehensive view that all institutions, not just public institutions, could contribute to the public good:

> All higher education institutions, both public and private, both nonprofit and for-profit, and from state colleges to research universities to community colleges to a wide variety of technical and professional schools serve a public purpose. Considerable variation in quality, purpose, and aspirations exists in each of these sectors. Nonetheless, they each play a distinctive and important role. (p. 1)

Kezar (2004) provided a list of public good functions, derived from authors in the field, which included: educating citizens for democratic engagement, supporting local communities, preserving knowledge, working with social institutions, developing arts and humanities, and broadening access to ensure a diverse democracy. Whitney (2006) viewed the public good as "educational leaders acting in the public's best interest" (p. 31). She went on to say, "public higher education is viewed as an economic, social, and cultural enterprise that impacts individuals and communities locally, regionally, and globally" (p. 31). Pusser (2006) noted "critical theorists have argued for the centrality of the university as a producer of the public good on two primary dimensions" (p. 17) which were (1) the institution serving as the site of knowledge production and research and (2) the institution serving as a place for critical perspectives and the development of citizens. From an economic standpoint, public good includes the production of human capital and the production of workers (Kezar, 2004). Education for the public good includes educating individuals in order for them to be engaged in society as well as meeting community needs in order to create a more just society.

Moral and civic learning also make up an important component of the public good. Ehrlich (2001) argued that moral and civic learning cannot be separated from one another and institutions should include both. Thornton and Jaeger (2006) summarized five dimensions of civic responsibility in higher education that include "(a) knowledge and support of democratic values, systems, and processes; (b) desire to act beneficially in community and for its members; (c) use of knowledge and skills for societal benefit; (d) appreciation for and interest in those unlike self; and € personal accountability" (p. 52). The National Task Force on Civic Learning and Democratic Engagement (2012), echoed many of these dimensions and called for education for democracy to be "informed by deep engagement" with the values of liberty, equality, individual worth, open mindedness, and the willingness to collaborate with people of differing views and backgrounds toward common solutions for the public good if they continue to reproduce hegemonic structures; it is only when diverse voices are part of the conversation that institutions can foster a public good that create social change.

Jacoby (2009) acknowledged the challenges in defining civic engagement, a term that is somewhat ambiguous in nature and may carry a political connotation. Educating students for civic engagement includes acquisition of content, however, "knowledge and skills are acknowledged to be necessary but not sufficient. Values, motivation, and commitment are also required" (Jacoby, 2009, p. 7). Colby et al. (2003) ventured into "perennially thorny territory" and took the position colleges and universities "ought to educate for substantive values, ideals, and standards, at least in broad terms" (p. 11). There descriptions make it clear civic education includes equipping students with the knowledge, skills, and values to be engaged citizens and also developing relationships with communities in order to produce relevant research and scholarship. It is sufficient for students to know about the community; they must have the conviction to a t on opportunities to create positive change in communities. While there may not be a universally agreed upon definition, it is clear civic education includes developing a sense of personal and social responsibility.

Historical Context of Public Good in Education

Tracing the development of institutions' public good mission provides insight into the current educational climate. In 1803, Joseph McKeen, President of Bowdoin College, said, "It ought always to be remembered that literary institutions are founded and endowed for the common good and not for the private advantage of those who resort to them for education" (Rudolph, 1990, p. 58). Colonial institutions were founded for producing professionals, including doctors and clergy, and for educating certain citizens for participation in democratic society. In the earliest days of higher education, it was not an expectation that youth would attend college; rather institutions were intended to shape political leaders for their contributions to democracy and religious leaders for their contribution to the church (Rudolph, 1990). Most early institutions were closely connected to a religious institution and classical curriculum included both moral and civic learning (Colby et al., 2003, p. 26).

By design, American institutions were more democratic than European institutions, boasting higher enrollments and spreading rapidly because of a "belief in the vital role of colleges in shaping citizens and leaders of the republic" (Colby et al., 2003, p. 27). American colleges were different in that they were "established not by independent groups of faculty and students or by royal initiative, but by private and public communities, and they were meant to serve important civic purposes" (Shapiro, 2005, p. 15). Shapiro (2005) suggested the first truly American contribution to higher education was its commitment to the public good. During the nineteenth century there was a shift towards higher education as an indulgence for the wealthy with a focus on the individual. Over time, the pendulum swung back and in President Roosevelt's 1944 State of the Union Address, he suggested education was a right and not a privilege (Pusser, 2006). The longstanding charter between higher education and society shaped the development of institutions. Higher education institutions were founded to serve the public good and many mission statements continue to emphasize the public good role.

Closely linked to the idea of mission is the emphasis institutions place on effectiveness versus prestige. Effective universities have the ability to deliver on their mission and goals, which typically relate to public policy objectives including expanding access and increasing affordability. Prestigious universities compete for increasingly scarce funding in an effort to replicate a "small number of highly visible institutions" which are "surrogates for quality" (Eckel, 2008, p. 175). Increased competition for status and rankings might cause institutions to shift their focus toward prestige or revenue streams and away from local concerns and contributions to the public good (Rhoads, Li, & Ilano, 2014). Market forces may dominate priorities, hedging out social priorities such as access and affordability (Eckel, 2008).

For the past eight years, the American Association of State Colleges and Universities (AASCU) published an annual policy brief highlighting the Top 10 Higher Education State Policy Issues. This summary of national higher education concerns has consistently drawn attention to tuition policy and state support of higher education (AACSU, 2015). Despite an emphasis on expanding access to education and increasing affordability, American higher education seems to be on the brink of shifting again to a more individualized orientation and away from the public good function. Changing social priorities may either hedge out the public good mission or alter the definition of public good entirely.

Arguments in Favor of the "New" Public Good

The confluence of increasing economic disparity and decreasing state support for higher education creates a challenging environment that may necessitate a shift in the conceptualization of the public good function of institutions. Shapiro (2005) noted "there has been a great deal of discussion in recent years regarding the meaning and consequences of the growing inequality in income and wealth in the United States" (p. 108). If the definition of public good includes broadening access to higher education in order to ensure a diverse democracy, the growing equity in education, this raises questions as to "how we should judge the morally justified distribution of benefits and burdens … should benefits and burdens be distributed equally, by demonstrated need, by merit, by the operation of private markets, or by some utilitarian calculation?" (Shapiro, 2005, p. 109). This is a dense, emotionally charged question with adamant supporters on both sides. While the answer is unclear, it is important to consider who benefits from and who supports higher education when reflecting on the impact of the shifting public good and increasing market orientation of higher education institutions.

Historically, the state has been the largest contributor to higher education. However, "during the past 30 years, state funding for colleges and universities has not kept pace with the rising costs of educating students or the ability of states to fund higher education" (Weerts & Hudson, 2014, p. 134). As state funding diminishes and students pay a greater amount of the cost of their education, is it fair or appropriate for society to expect the public good mission of institutions to continue? Whitney (2006) highlighted two opposing viewpoints: "From a conservative philosophical standpoint, higher education is increasingly seen as benefiting individual students rather than society in general" (p. 45). If students pay a higher percentage of the cost of education, some would argue it seems natural for them to expect a greater personal return at the expense of a public good charter. Conversely, "if we are to be a society that values the comprehensive education of its citizens, then education would be a public good and should be publicly supported" (Whitney, 2006, p. 45). Regardless of which side one supports, "as public institutions of higher learning becomes funded less by the state and more by other sources, redefining the public good appears inevitable" (Whitney, 2006, p. 45). The question of who pays and who benefits also informs conversations about accessibility and affordability in higher education.

Some forces impacting the shifting public good mission of higher education relate to economic goals and the drive to sustain institutional funding. Reasons for this shift include an increase in corporate research partnerships, incentives to privatize, and a tension between efficiency and effectiveness. Public institutions face the question of whether recent declines funding are cyclical or permanent; presumably the funding changes are permanent (Whitney, 2006). Supporters suggest the cost savings from a corporate approach would make higher education more accessible for students; however, they lack evidence to back these claims (Kezar, 2004). Regarding sponsored research, some argue that local industry is promoted through research and development, which can be a form of public good. However, Kezar (2004) notes that the purported cost savings has not been proven. While there are arguments for merging the public good role of institutions with economic aims, this approach lacks evidence and support.

Service and the Public Good

Institutions can contribute to the public good by serving local, national, and global communities. Boyer (1990) emphasized the need for faculty to be more engaged in the community in order to contribute to a wide range of current social challenges. He implored "If the nation's colleges and universities cannot help students see beyond themselves and better understand the interdependent nature of our world, each new generation's capacity to live responsibly will be dangerously diminished" (p. 77). Twenty-five years later, this statement continues to ring true as college graduates face a number of challenging social problems locally and globally. Jacoby (2009) noted consensus among higher education professionals and business leaders around student competence in the areas of personal and social responsibility, in addition to knowledge, practical skills, and applied learning. Kezar (2005) identified the following movements—which engage students, faculty, and staff—as being in line with the historic public good charter of institutions of higher education to serve as a balance to market forces: "service-learning, the K-16 movement, community-college partnerships, and new notions of faculty work life" (p. 43). The public good role of institutions and student benefits from education are not mutually exclusive. Opportunities for civic engagement and service are rooted in learning outcomes and have clear benefits for students. Many institutions are committed to educating engaged citizens; enhancing opportunities for service and reframing research and scholarship can support institutional commitments to the public good.

Although the execution of community service may vary, whether it is a co-curricular service project, structured service-learning at a local not-for-profit agency, or faculty conducting research in service of a public good, institutions can incorporate aspects of service that enhance the public good mission and balance the competing economic demands. Service-learning is one aspect of civic engagement, a broad term that may include learning about social issues, learning about and valuing differences, dealing with controversy in a civil manner, taking a role in community problems, developing empathy, and promoting social justice (Jacoby, 2009). A form of experiential learning, service-learning is course-based and includes application of learning, structured service that meets a defined community need, and reflection (Bringle & Hatcher, 1995). Reflection, a distinguishing feature of service-learning, allows students to develop "further understanding of course content, a broader appreciation of the discipline, and an enhanced sense of personal values, and civic responsibility" (Bringle & Hatcher, 1995, p. 112). Service-learning is closely linked to preparation for citizenship and democratic engagement (Eyler & Giles, 1999). Examples of service-learning partnerships, may include: students in an introductory education course mentoring children in schools, students in a class about the working poor providing tax preparation services for low-income individuals, students in an urban planning transportation class participating in a bicycle and pedestrian count, students in a leadership and sustainability course organizing an energy audit of the campus, or students in a non-profit grant writing class researching and applying from grants on behalf of non-profit agencies. Possible service-learning pairings should focus on both substantive, experiential learning opportunities for students as well as areas of identified community need as vocalized by communities and agencies. The unique mission of the institution and the community context will shape partnership opportunities. Successful service-learning partnerships have clearly defined outcomes and privilege community voices in the planning and execution of reciprocal partnerships. Through service-learning experiences, students can develop skills employers desire, enhance their civic knowledge, and fulfill the institutional public good charter through reciprocal partnerships in the community.

Faculty members play a significant role through teaching, research, and service: "in their role as arbiters of the curriculum, teachers, knowledge producers, and citizens, hold a prominent role in realizing the goal of making higher education more responsive to community and public welfare" (Ward, 2005, p. 217). While some faculty jettison teaching in favor of profitable, market oriented research, students who are taught by these same faculty members are the human capital being educated as part of the workforce that drives the economic engine of the country. In addition to educating students who take knowledge into the community, faculty can contribute to the public good by engaging students directly with the community through service-learning. Faculty can also move toward conducting community-based research, which includes participants in the entire research process, or conduct research with a public goods focus. One study of 70 doctoral students and faculty members in science and engineering found significant intersections and overlap in knowledge production for the public good and academic capitalism (Szelenyi & Bresonis, 2014). Defining public good for these fields as "encompassing a focus on both the serendipitous contributions of university research to society and immediate societal application enacted primarily through an applied research focus," Szelenyi and Bresonis (2014) found expansive intersections "with all participants in our study aware of, and many involved in, both public good-related and academic capitalist values and practices at least to some extent" (pp. 146–147). Finally, faculty can expand the traditional definition of academic service, which often serves the department or discipline, to include service to local not-for-profit agencies, extending their reach into the community and forging partnerships connecting the institution to the community (Ward, 2005).

Public Good in the Twenty-First Century

The charter between institutions for higher education and society is as old as higher education in America. Looking into the twenty-first century, it is critical to assess how the charter will be shaped moving forward. In some ways, the public good charter may overlap with shifting economic priorities; in other ways, institutions and systems require a course correction in order to create energy and resources for the public good. Critics suggested teaching, access, activist leadership, connection to community, and solving social problems are five areas that experience overlap between the economic/private and social/public charter. Through service-learning and public good research, institutions can engage in knowledge production and action that benefits students and society.

In *The Crucible Moment*, the National Task Force on Civic Learning and Democratic Engagement (2012) implored:

> It is time to bring two national priorities—career preparation and increased access and completion rates—together in a more comprehensive vision with a third national priority: fostering informed, engaged, responsible citizens. Higher education is a space where that triad of priorities can cohere and flourish. (p. 13, emphasis in original)

At first glance, it may appear that by asking institutions to prioritize their historic public good charter with society, they must forego other priorities, such as market-oriented research. However, the idea is not to generate competition between these priorities, but to bring them into alignment so the public good role is woven into the fabric of institutions and remains a priority despite changing financial and economic circumstances. In a time of creased economic disparity, it is important to consider how decisions impact the ability of institutions to function within the context of social priorities.

One of the most essential aspects for shaping the future public good role of institutions is galvanizing support from a variety of constituents. In his presidential address to the Association for the Study of Higher Education (ASHE), which focused on the social contract between higher education and society, William Zumeta (2011) concluded negotiating a new social compact would require input from a multitude of stakeholders including all types of higher education institutions, the K-12 system, state governments, non-governmental institutions, underrepresented populations, and the media. The public good role of institutions is not the responsibility of any one sector of society: "creative alliances with public-minded nonprofit agencies, governmental agencies, and businesses can replenish civic capital" (National Task Force on Civic Learning and Democratic Engagement, 2012, p. 69). Enhancing the public good is not limited to non-profit agencies or public entities; all stakeholders have an investment in enhancing the public good mission of institutions. Establishing robust, long-range partnerships requires commitment from faculty and administrators who are willing to make educational partnerships for social good a priority. When generative partnerships are a priority, "interdependency, innovation, multiple perspectives, and a commitment to a long-range investment in the public good define the partnership's core values" (National Task Force on Civic Learning and Democratic Engagement, 2012, p. 64). Institutions must view community partnerships as symbiotic relationships and ensure that all voices, particularly those that have been marginalized in the past, are part of the conversation.

One example of a powerful national program that is engaging institutions in meeting their public good mission, while also focusing on the academic preparation of students, is the American Associate of College and Universities (AAC&U) Liberal Education and America's Promise (LEAP) initiative.

LEAP is a "national advocacy, campus action, and research initiative that champions the importance of a twenty-first century graduates the tools to engage a world with complex challenges" (AAC&U, 2014). One of the essential learning outcomes of LEAP is a focus on personal and social responsibility, which includes civic knowledge and engagement gained through interaction with diverse communities to address social issues (AAC&U, 2014). Through high-impact practices, including service-learning and community-based learning, students develop knowledge, skills, and values to engage in complex problem-solving in a diverse, global context. LEAP is also anchored by Principles of Excellence, one of which is Connect Knowledge with Choices and Actions (AAC&U, 2014). Students, having engaged community issues of concern through high-impact practices, are prepared for citizenship and continued community engagement. Another Principle of Excellence is Foster Civic, Intercultural, and Ethical Learning (AAC&U, 2014). Students understand and apply personal and social responsibility, regardless of their major or intended career goals. The LEAP initiative focus on lifelong learning and engagement makes it a valuable tool for educating students and preparing them for continued investment in the community, amplifying the public good role of institutions.

One of the greatest challenges to expanding the public good role of higher education is institutional support. In order to become a priority of the university, among many competing priorities, the public good mission exemplified through service must become "central rather than marginal, institutionalized rather than fragmented, and strong rather than weak" (Jacoby & Hollander, 2009, p. 227). Service to the community provides value to the institution and the surrounding community, but cannot be undertaken without strong, central support. Regardless of whether the public good priority is reflected in the institutional mission, "without congruence between the values held by faculty and the priorities of tenure and promotion, the integration of service into the curriculum is not likely to occur" (Antonio, Astin, & Cress, 2000, p. 376). In order for community engagement to have scholarly merit, it must be included in research and scholarship in addition to teaching and service (Saltmarsh, Giles, Ward, & Buglione, 2009). Prioritizing community engagement in the tenure and promotion process requires deep change and a shift in academic culture. Support for service-learning and community-based research, in the form of institutional resources and opportunities for publication, may increase faculty incentive to incorporate service and civic learning as a part of their courses. Rhoads, Li, and Ilano (2014) examined current measures of world-class universities, which focus more on research activity and selectivity, and suggested alternative measures that emphasize social justice concerns related to the public good, such as students' engagement in the community and investment in research that promotes the well-being of underserved communities. By making community-engaged scholarship a priority, institutions can better fulfill their public good missions.

Conclusion

Since the founding, the public good role of institutions has been a defining feature of American Higher education. However, proponents of the institutional public good mission are concerned a shift toward market-orientation and Americans growing individualism may overshadow a commitment to the collective good. As state support of higher education declines, institutions must address challenges and priorities; forgoing the public good mission of the twenty-first century. Kezar (2004) identified a primary challenge as "the need to create a good" (p. 432). Together with a diverse and inclusive group of constituents, institutions must evaluate opportunities and challenges for moving forward with the public good mission through teaching, research, and service. There is economic value in both teaching and research; one does not need to subsume the other and forego the public charter in order for an institution to be successful. Additionally, there is opportunity for public good research that engages and benefits community members. Rather than adopting an all or nothing attitude toward market orientation, educational leaders should carefully consider the short and long term consequences of individual choices ant he impact, both positive and negative, or institutional success and congruence with the public good mission. It is incumbent upon institutions to engage students in ways that prepares them for civic engagement and the public good both during college and upon orientation, it is possible for institutional leaders to hold both economic success and the historic public good charter in mind when making significant decisions that impact the orientation of the institution.

Work Cited

AAC&U. American Association of Colleges and Universities. (2014). *An introduction to LEAP.* Washington, DC: AAC&U.

AASCU. American Association for State Colleges and Universities. (2015). *Top 10 higher education state policy issues for 2015.* Washington, DC: AASCU.

Antonio, A. L., Astin, H. S., & Cress, C. M. (2000). Community service in higher education: A look at the nation's faulty. *The Review of Higher Education, 23*(4), 373–397.

Boyer, E. L. (1990). *Scholarship reconsidered: Priorities of the professoriate.* New York, NY: The Carnegie Foundation for the Advancement of Teaching.

Bringle, R. G., & Hatcher, J. A. (1995). A service-learning curriculum for faculty. *Michigan Journal of Community Service Learning, 2,* 112–122.

Brisbin, R. A., & Hunter, S. (2003). Community leaders' perceptions of university and college efforts to encourage civic engagement. *The Review of Higher Education, 26*(4), 467–486.

Chickering, A. W. (2010). A retrospect on higher education's commitment to moral and civic education. *Journal of College and Character, 11*(3), 1–6.

Colby, A., Ehrlich, T., Beaumont, E., & Stephens, J. (2003). *Educating citizens: Preparing America's undergraduates for lives of moral and civic responsibility.* San Francisco, CA: Jossey-Bass.

Eckel, P. D. (2008). Mission diversity and the tension between prestige and effectiveness: An overview of US higher education. *Higher Education Policy, 21,* 175–192.

Ehrlich, T. (2001). Moral and Civic Learning. *Journal of College and Character, 2*(4). https://doi.org/10.2202/1940-1639.1293

Eyler, J., & Giles, D. E. (1999). *Where's the learning in service-learning?* San Francisco, CA: Jossey-Bass.

Jacoby, B. (2009). Securing the future of civic engagement in higher education. In B. Jacoby (Ed.), *Civic engagement in higher education: Concepts and practices* (pp. 5–30). San Francisco, CA: Jossey-Bass.

Jacoby, B., & Hollander, E. (2009). Securing the future of civic engagement in higher education. In B. Jacoby (Ed.), *Civic engagement in higher education: Concepts and practices* (pp. 5–30). San Francisco, CA: Jossey-Bass.

Kezar, A. J. (2004). Obtaining integrity? Reviewing and examining the charter between higher education and society. *The Review of Higher Education, 27*(4), 429–459.

Kezar, A. J. (2005). Creating a metamovement: A vision toward regaining the public social charter. In A. J. Kezar, T. C. Chambers, & J. C. Burkhardt (Eds.), *Higher education for the public good: Emerging voices from a national movement* (pp. 43–53). San Francisco, CA: Jossey-Bass.

Kezar, A. J., & Kinzie, J. L. (2006). Examining the ways institutions create student engagement. The role of mission. *Journal of College Student Development, 47*(2), 149–172.

The National Task Force on Civic Learning and Democratic Engagement. (2012). *A crucible moment: College learning and democracy's future.* Washington, DC: Association of American Colleges and Universities.

Pusser, B. (2006). Reconsidering higher education and the public good: The role of public spheres. In W. Tierney (Ed.), *Governance and the public good* (pp. 11–27). Albany, NY: State University of New York Press.

Rhoads, R. A., Li, S., & Ilano, L. (2014). The global quest to build world-class universities: Toward a social justice agenda. *New Directions for Higher Education, 168,* 27–39.

Rudolph, F. (1990). *The American college and university: A history.* Athens, GA: The University of Georgia Press.

Saltmarsh, J., Giles, D. E., Ward, E., & Buglione, S. E. (2009). Rewarding community-engaged scholarship. *New Directions for Higher Education, 147,* 25–35.

Shapiro, H. T. (2005). *A larger sense of purpose: Higher education and society.* Princeton, NJ: Princeton University Press.

Szelenyi, K., & Bresonis, K. (2014). The public good and academic capitalism: Science and engineering doctoral students and faculty on the boundary of knowledge regimes. *The Journal of Higher Education, 85*(1), 126–153.

Thornton, C. H., & Jaeger, A. J. (2006). Institutional culture and civic responsibility: An ethnographic study. *Journal of College Student Development, 47*(1), 52–68.

Ward, K. (2005). Rethinking faculty roles and rewards for the public good. In A. J. Kezar, T. C. Chambers, & J. C. Burkhardt (Eds.), *Higher education for the public good: Emerging voices from a national movement* (pp. 217–234). San Francisco, CA: Jossey-Bass.

Weerts, D., & Hudson, E. (2014). Engagement and institutional advancement. *New Directions for Higher Education, 147,* 65–74.

Whitney, K. M. (2006). Lost in transition: Governing in a time of privatization. In W. Tierney (Ed.), *Governance and the public good* (pp. 29–49). Albany, NY: State University of New York Press.

Zumeta, W. M. (2011). What does it mean to be accountable?: Dimensions and implications of higher education's public accountability. *The Review of Higher Education, 35*(1), 131–148.

CHAPTER 7

Toward the Global Public Good

A Dialectical Vision for Higher Education

Angelo Letizia

Public institutions of higher education in America are currently chastised as overly bureaucratic, unresponsive to economic needs and for having low graduation rates and academic rigor. Much of the actual knowledge produced by these institutions is also criticized for being pedantic and socially useless (Urban, 2013). Some even view public higher education as dangerous because they see it as bastion of liberal and radical sentiment which seeks to undermine traditional American and free-market values (Giroux, 2011; Newfield, 2008). In light of this, state and federal policymakers, at the behest of their corporate backers, seek to hold higher education accountable to clearly definable economic goals and ensure that higher education produces the information and workforce needed for the global economy.

Perhaps those who fear public higher education for its potential radical elements are correct to fear it. Public higher education can be inclusive, democratic and the producer of radical theories (Newfield, 2008). As a result, public education in America is currently being stripped of its democratic and revolutionary potential (Giroux, 2011; Hill, 2012). Of course higher education has always had market potentialities since the land grant colleges of the 19th century and probably even before. Nonetheless, public higher education today faces unprecedented challenges to its public nature in the form of reduced funding and accountability movements (Zumeta, 2011).

Thomas Jefferson argued that in order for citizens to participate in their government, they must be educated. More than just participate, citizens had to become the "guardians of liberty" and hold their leaders in check (Jefferson, 2010). Education, in Jefferson's view, could only be a public good. And this is precisely what is under attack. What is needed now is a new and revitalized vision of the public good. This is not just a call for more state support of higher education. Those who promote this new public good must no longer simply equate state subsidies with the public good. Rather, a much more expansive view of public goods and the public good must be at the heart of public education.

The main intent of this chapter is to construct a new vision of global public goods and understand how higher education can help produce these goods. Some of the examples of global public goods that are usually cited are world peace and absence of conflict, a clean environment, world financial stability and the creation of knowledge to name a few (Kaul, Grunberg, & Stern, 1999). This chapter incorporates those goods and enumerates new ones: dialectical movement rooted in democratic pedagogy, an understanding of horizontal networks and global civil society, new concepts of just accountability, the creation of new identities not rooted in geography, race and class and an emancipatory conception of science and technology.

Dialectical social movement occurs as a result of the obliteration of unjust and outdated phenomena by the integration of new phenomena to challenge it. The integration of new phenomena occurs as new ideas develop and contradictions grow out of the functioning of old social phenomena (Jay, 1996). In order for dialectical movement to proceed, a clear understanding of its historical context must emerge first.

A Brief History

During the 1930s, after the spectacular collapse of American capitalism, President Franklin Delano Roosevelt enacted a series of sweeping legislation measures which brought the federal government in direct contact with economy (Harvey, 2005). These legislation measures also seriously curtailed the power of American businesses. For their part, many of American businesses relented and accepted the shackling of their power because they really had no other option. Roosevelt made it clear to them that if they did not assent, the United States could be possibly facing a socialist revolution (Harvey, 2005; Wolff, 2012).

Neoliberals, who drew their inspiration from eighteenth century liberals, saw the social welfare legislation of the 1930s and 1940s as detrimental to the market and global business. As their eighteenth century predecessors, neoliberals saw the market as the key to social harmony and functioning. If the market were simply allowed to function, it would guarantee happiness and justice for all (Harvey, 2005; Plant, 2010). However, the rising tide of government intervention in the 1940s and 1950s threatened the functioning of markets worldwide. In 1944, one of the founders of the neoliberal movement, Austrian economist F. A. Haeyk, wrote its seminal text: *The Road to Serfdom*. In it, he argued that modern governments in American and Europe were moving their countries down the roads to serfdom because of increased government intervention and the emasculation of the individual (Plant, 2010). In 1947 a group of likeminded economists, philosophers and thinkers met at the Mt. Perlin hotel in France and penned the Mt. Perlin declaration, which essentially outlined the doctrines of neoliberalism, which were: dedication to the free market, empowerment of the individuals and to wage a fight against government intervention (Harvey, 2005).

In the late 1940s, Hayek came to America and accepted a faculty position at the University of Chicago. His work on neoliberalism influenced many scholars at Chicago, most notably Milton Freidman (Overtveldt, 2007). Freidman was a professor of economics at Chicago from 1946 until 1976. By the late 1950s, while neoliberalism was still a fringe doctrine, it had begun to make a slow entrance into American political circles. The increased power of American industry after the Second World War found them looking for ideological weapons to rebut the political left with (Overtveldt, 2007; Peet, 2009). The 1960s saw further government intervention, in the form of the Lyndon B. Johnson's Great Society programs which entailed heavy taxes on industry, the regulation of workers' rights and the enacting of environmental protections. Business and industry officials and their supporters began to turn increasingly to the ideas of neoliberalism emanating from Chicago (Harvey, 2005; Peet, 2009). Freidman and other scholars at Chicago led an aggressive advocacy campaign aimed at rightwing politicians (Overtveldt, 2007; Reder, 1982). During the 1970s, there was a proliferation of rightwing think tanks and policy organizations which helped to disseminate neoliberal ideas and get them into the political arena (McDonald, 2013; Newfield, 2008).

Higher educational institutions played a pivotal role the social upheaval of the 1960s and 1970s. Students and professors challenged the racist, sexist and authoritarian culture of the United States. The civil rights movement exposed the hypocrisy of a nation which called itself equal. Unprecedented numbers of traditionally under represented students, such as African-Americans, women, minorities and lower income students swelled the ranks of higher education institutions in America (Newfield, 2008). Of course higher education by no means was an equalitarian institution, but radical segments of American higher education challenged the hypocrisy of American society. What's more, students registered black voters and professors challenged the status quo through activism and research (Newfield, 2008). The society of democratic students at Michigan, the protests at Berkeley, the many teach-ins and sit-ins and many others all questioned American values and gave a voice to many marginalized populations (Newfield, 2008). Newfield argued that higher education became a threat to the ruling class and the capitalist system. Scholars read Marx, Fanon and other radical thinkers, they created new race and class based theories, new interpretations of history which questioned the supremacy of Eurocentric views.

In short, the universities became a powerful weapon of social justice. Thus, they also became targets for conservatives (Giroux, 2011; Newfield, 2008). During the mid-1970s, the United States also fell into a severe economic recession. Again, just like the 1930s, many began to seriously question the capitalist system that had wrought such economic hardship (Harvey, 2005; Wolff, 2012). The universities were still a hub of discontent. As a way to rebut what many conservatives saw as a rising tide of communism and radicalism, they turned to neoliberalism and its focus on the market (Newfield, 2008). The close relationship between conservative academics, think tanks and government emerged and helped to push the neoliberal agenda (Harvey, 2005; McDonald, 2013; Newfield, 2008). As the recession worsened, neoliberalism became a sort of demagoguery to a frustrated and beleaguered populace (Peet, 2009). Higher education in particular was in the crosshairs (Newfield, 2008). As Freidman noted in his 1981 classic *Free to Choose*, "public education is a socialist island in a free market sea" (Freidman, 1981 p. 143). He went on to chastise students at public universities, calling them lazy and accusing them of partying on the state's dime, while he lavished praise on private school students. He argued that since they were paying for their education, they took it much more seriously. Freidman went on to argue that education should be a right- but only for those who could afford it (Freidman & Freidman, 1981).

His thoughts epitomized the attitude of many toward public education at all levels. As state coffers lost money, public education, which required massive public expenditure, was scrutinized and questioned. The radical goals of the 1960s were attacked for being too costly, and for requiring a bloated bureaucracy to administer them. Instead, neoliberals argued that colleges had to become more efficient with their resources and must help to spurn economic development (Newfield, 2008). The free market was cast as the pinnacle of social harmony, and the government legislation since the New Deal, while well intentioned, only impeded the functioning of the market (Plant, 2010).

Due to the surge in enrollments, higher education institutions, which were short on resources, began asking states for more money and resources. Up to this time, a relationship of trust had always existed between higher education and their respective states (Zumeta, 2001). But as neoliberalism began to resonate with policymakers and the general public, and as stagflation set in, many questioned why states should fund these increasingly radical institutions. Further, many began to argue that higher education institutions really did not produce anything of value. Instead, overpaid and underworked professors produced useless knowledge and research (Rhoads & Torres, 2006; Vestrich, 2008). While some of their research may be nice to have, it did not contribute to the economic well being of the state. In the largest sense, neoliberal advocates changed the focus of higher education from one of equality of access, which had resonated during the socially contentious 1960s and 1970s to one of accountability, which began to resonate with many policymakers and the general public during the economic recession of the mid 1970s (Prokou, 2013).

Yet this was much more than an economic argument proposed by neoliberals. Higher education became a target of traditional conservatives as well. As Harvey points out, neoconservatism meshes well with neoliberalism. Since neoliberals see an unimpeded free market as the best method to archive social harmony and efficiency, nothing which has the potential to harm the functioning of the market can be tolerated, especially calls for radical utopias and social justice (Harvey, 2005). What is more, many times, and in complete contradiction to most neoliberal theory, government intervention is actually needed to enforce market rules or to create markets where none exist (Harvey, 2005). Neoconservatism and neoliberalism formed a marriage of convenience (Harvey, 2005).

Neoconservatives drew heavily on the work of the conservative philosopher Leo Strauss argued. Strauss argued philosophy was dangerous because it leaves one in a state of perpetual openness. Perpetual openness leaves many unresolved questions and can engender conflict. Thus, Strauss advocated for the need of some type of authority due to the destabilizing nature of unmitigated philosophical introspection (Stanley, 2007). Strauss called this type of philosophical endeavor esoteric knowledge and urged for it to be contained with exoteric knowledge. Exoteric knowledge, such as religious and political ideas could provide much needed order in society. The impact of Strauss's idea on neoconservatives cannot be overstated (Stanley, 2007). In light of Strauss's ideas, many took aim at the "internal barbarians" who were purposely destabilizing society through their reckless philosophical endeavors. Other strands of conservatism also were present, the most visible was democratic realism. Democratic realists assumed that a true democracy could never emerge because citizens are incapable of rational discussion. Instead, democracy consists of politicians who sell themselves and buy their votes in the form of promises (Stanley, 2007). As a result, pedagogy as democracy is ill founded and unrealistic (Stanley, 2007).

Neoliberalism and neoconservatism merged and reinforced each other (Harvey, 2005; Stanley, 2007). They resonated with many policymakers and the general public. Higher education was increasingly seen as liberal, communist, useless and wasteful of crucial state resources. Neoliberalism is the most dominant force in regards to higher education neoconservatism cannot be underestimated (Stanley, 2007; Harvey, 2005). Neoliberals advocated for market based decisions because only the market, free of government influence, no matter how well meaning, can create social harmony (Plant, 2010). Social justice, democracy and philosophical exploration may all be noble goals, but in the eyes of neoliberals, only the market mattered (Harvey, 2005; Newfield, 2008; Zumeta, 2001). Bolstered by neoconservatives staunch defense of Christian values and American militarism, as well as their abhorrence of radical philosophical exploration, neoliberals have drastically shaped higher education policy during the last half of the twentieth century, through journalism, the media, think tanks and lobbying (Giroux, 2011; McDonald, 2013; Newfield, 2008).

This is not to suggest that higher education prior to the rise of neoliberalism was a purely humanistic endeavor. In fact, as Howard Bowen argued in his classic *Investment in Learning*, a central component of higher education has always been its economic and vocational potentials (Bowen, 1996). What makes the neoliberal turn of the late 1970s, which continues into the present, so fundamentally different is the fact that the humanistic potential of higher education is almost completely disregarded, and in many cases, targeted because of their revolutionary potential (Newfield, 2008). By the 1980s, neoconservatives, neoliberals and other opponents of the 1960s protests argued that starving public entities of funds would force them act like market entities or simply cease functioning (Slaughter & Rhoades, 2004). This method continues into the present.

Universities, states and federal government during the 1950s used to rely on trust; universities were trusted to give back to their constituents, and they almost always did (Burke, 2005; Newfield, 2008). The golden age of state university relations came to an abrupt end however. Questions of enrollment declines, economic downturn and growing influence of neoliberalism and neoconservatism spurned the first accountability movements of the 1970s (Burke, 2005). By the 1980s, policymakers questioned the actually quality of a college degree and college teaching (Burke, 2005; Zumeta, 2001). This was spurred on by the Nation at Risk report in 1983 and its accusations of low quality in K-12 education. The 1990s saw efficiency and effectiveness became the guiding principles of accountability. State governments adopted performance based funding policies which focused on outputs and outcomes (Burke, 2005; Zumeta, 2001).

All the while, state funds kept diminishing. So as policymakers called for colleges to be more efficient, they kept cutting off their resources. The early 2000s saw this trend escalate. Policymakers demanded universities produce a trained workforce and drive state economies (Burke, 2005; King, 2000; McClendon, Hearn, Denton, 2006). Higher education was increasingly cast as a private good and students were expected to cover and an ever larger share of the financial burden (Burke, 2005). As Burke notes, by the early 2000s, it was the market, not the commonweal or the public good that drove higher education policy (Burke, 2005).

This strategy of starving public entities of funding in order to force them to become market goods has carried on into the present and is one of the major weapons conservative and neoliberal policymakers use to discipline higher education (Slaughter & Rhoades, 2004; Zumeta, 2011, 2001). While starved of precious state funds, higher education institutions are then held to regimes of accountability by the same policymakers (Alexander, 2000; McClendon, Hearn, & Denton, 2006). When higher education is seen as a market good as it is under neoliberalism it can be scrutinized and made to adhere to numerical goals and targets. At the same time, neoconservatives attack the more abstract and radical ideas emanating from higher education particularly from schools of education (Hill, 2012).

Towards a New Vision of the Global Public Good

The actual configuration and operation of the public sphere in any given society is configured by policies within that society (Marginson, 2007). And the current configuration of higher education policy in the United States is market driven with a splash of neoconservativism. As has been stressed, this policy configuration limits higher education of its true public potential. Thus, we must turn to other conceptions of the notion of public to begin to rehabilitate public education. Marginson notes three realms of what it means to be public; public goods (plural), the public good (singular) and the Habermasian public sphere (Marginson, 2007). Public goods (plural) are perhaps the most readily accessible and easily understandable entities. Public goods plural are more tangible and discreet things, these can include clean air, public safety, and public education (Marginson, 2007). In order for something to be classified as a public good, it is usually declared to be non-rivalrous and non-excludable. If a good is non-rivalrous, all members of a polity can consume it without depleting its stock (Marginson, 2007). Similarly, if a good is non-excludable, no one (at least in theory) can be denied from consuming good (Marginson, 2007). Of course, a truly non-rivalrous and non-excludable good is very rare. Rather, public goods tend to be characterized as almost non-rivalrous and almost non-excludable.

Another facet of public goods is known as externalities (Marginson, 2008). An externality is a by-product that was not necessarily intended or at least not deliberately striven for. These can be positive or negative. For instance, a positive externality of a public education system which produces a highly educated populace is increased rates of civic involvement, lower crime rates, better healthcare and even better selection of marriage partners. There can also be negative externalities.

Externalities occur because within any given polity, there are many different "publics" or groups of people with different and many times competing interests (Calhoun, 1998; Marginson, 2011). These heterogeneous groups can be brought together along lines of occupation, socio-economic status, race, ethnicity, location or any other defining feature. Moreover, individuals almost always belong to multiple groups (Marginson, 2008; Sen, 1999). As a result of these multiple groups, one group's public goods can become another groups' public "bad" or negative externality (Marginson, 2007). For instance, clean air is a public good for everyone, yet economic prosperity for some is also a public good but these two can come into conflict because many times pollution is necessary for companies to produce profit. So public goods can and usually do involve some sort of political bargaining and trade off. Because of the potential for conflict and opposition, Negative externalities and "public bads" necessitate a political mechanism to govern their negative effects. The actions of some groups such as Wall Street bankers, businesses and the financial sector in general as an example will create negative externalities and their effects must be mitigated through the political process. In light of this, even private entities are public in a sense because they have the ability to produce public bads and negative externalities (Kaul, Grunberg, & Stern, 1999). Thus, private entities must be in the purview higher education.

This leads into Marginson's second conception, which he calls the public good singular. The public good of every member of the polity is a much more abstract and murky notion than public goods plural. Public goods in the singular, while multifaceted and opposed, can be seen as the building blocks of the public good singular. Due to this, Calhoun and Mansbridge note that any notion of the public good must always be contested and constantly evolving (Calhoun, 1998; Mansbridge, 1998). The notion of the public good cannot be static because interests and needs of different groups are always changing in relationship to each other. This is because the aforementioned heterogeneous groups are competing with each other, each for their own vision of a public good and specific public goods. In some societies, these differences can render society dysfunctional. In other societies, sometimes an autocratic leader can stifle differences, at least temporarily. Yet in order for society to function healthily, these groups must come together in some kind of harmony (Calhoun, 1998; Mansbridge, 1998).

Giroux has called for a revitalization of the public good in light of the destructiveness of neoliberalism (Giroux, 2011). He asserts that the public good is now associated with the hyper consumption of goods, rampant individualism and little regard for anything save profit (Giroux, 2011). This has created mass disparities in wealth and growing inequities among different groups in society. These inequities and divisions will have ripple effects in a globalized world. This is due to the fact that we now live in a globalized world where there is a continuous global flow of knowledge, ideas, people, goods and money that circulate amongst different regions, different localities, and between various groups and countries (Spring, 2008). It now makes sense to view all societies as globally connected at least in some sense due to the rapid increase in technology of social media and communications. In addition, there is a global economy which is interconnected, the 2008 financial crash is illustrative of this (Held, 2001; Peters, 2010). The connections are dynamic, intricate and complex. In light of this, Marginson and many others have argued for a new conception of public goods and the public good, one that reflects this global nature. In the widest sense, these flows of knowledge can be seen as the arteries of the global public body, sustaining the emerging notion of the global public good. As Marginson notes, building a new world society, rooted in interconnectedness and global understanding is the next great challenge facing humanity (Marginson, 2007).

Yet we cannot just concentrate on the global. Rather the global, regional, national and local all exist simultaneously and they all reinforce each other (Marginson & Rhoads, 2002). Global public goods must be understood as an intricate web of the local, national, regional and ultimately global connections. A robust conception of global public goods, grounded in the glo-na-cal approach, may be the integral building blocks of perhaps the most abstract and most difficult goal to achieve; the global public good (singular). The creation of global public goods, while difficult to achieve, may be necessary to sustain a livable world which is growing increasingly interconnected. Marginson argued for this. Marginson however did not detail or examine what these global public goods may look like or their relation to higher education policy. Higher education policy is only a fragment that configures the public sphere in any given society. Nonetheless, the examination of higher education policy can augment our understanding of the public sphere. These global public goods must be rooted in policymaking but must go beyond it as well.

An exhaustive list of global public goods is impossible to enumerate (and probably unknowable). Instead, scholars should begin to examine possible global public goods and higher education's role in producing them. What follows is a brief list of global public goods, which if produced could go towards enhancing global society as well as the global public good, grounded in a glo-na-cal understanding.

Perhaps the purest public good, the most non-rival and non-excludable good is that of knowledge (Marginson, 2011). And as we are constantly reminded, this is the knowledge economy (Marginson, 2011). The creation of knowledge is also the special purview of higher education institutions yet it is only economic knowledge that is valued (Marginson, 2007; Slaughter & Rhoades, 2004). Accountability measures steer higher education to be economic motors of their states and of the global economy and this is based on producing knowledge and knowledgeable workers who can compete and survive in the global knowledge economy. Yet as Marginson argues, most knowledge generated in higher education is not for profit but rather of free exchange and for the global public good (Marginson, 2007). Knowledge produced and exchanged between actors in higher education can take the form of new political and historical interpretations, cultural diversity, new political understandings as well as scientific advancements (Marginson, 2007). Peer review is the method of choice for policing this knowledge (Truth, 2012). Peer review ensures that knowledge remains unbiased and disinterested. Knowledge, for Marginson, must be put in the service of building the global community (Marginson, 2011).

The spark of emancipatory knowledge is radical creativity (Marginson, 2008). Yet as Marginson notes, radical creativity, the ability for scholars to envision new and more just possibilities and directions for their knowledge production which he calls freedom of power, is constrained by an adherence to neoliberalism. And as discussed earlier, radical creativity frightens neoliberals, and rightfully so (Giroux, 2011). Neoliberalism is market based and embodies a freedom of choice, which is merely the ability to choose between predetermined choices (Marginson, 2006, 2008). Freedom as power, with higher education actors employing it, can be a global public good that can go toward building the global public good. Scholars emboldened with this radical creativity and not restricted by market choices can envision new possibilities for mankind, for alleviating miseries and building a just society. In the widest sense, freedom as power is perhaps the most crucial component of fostering dialectical thinking as a movement of justice because it allows us to envision a just society. Zizek (2009) argued that we must face history; we must make decisions in the face of the dialectic. We can do this with freedom as power and technology is crucial component of this.

Higher education is caught in a cultural and economic dependency on technology and market driven knowledge to power the global economy (Marginson, 2008). Higher education trains the global executives and global businessmen. Applied research is valued over basic research because applied research has the potential to yield immediate profits (Slaughter & Rhoades, 2004; Rhoads & Torres, 2006). College administrators are hoping their faculty research will lead to lucrative patents and long term revenue for the university in the form or royalties. Technology has an exclusionary effect on society under capitalism.

Yet, as Suoranta and Vaden note, there is a "second economy" in regards to technology. This alternate vision to capitalist technology is not a market at all. Rather the second market is a socialist conception of technology; all information is free and open to all (Marginson, Murphy, & Peters, 2010; Suoranta & Vaden, 2007). In academia, there has been a movement by many faculty to digitize their publications and thus render them open access in an effort to bypass the exploitive actions of publishers (Marginson, Murphy, & Peters, 2010; Suoranta & Vaden, 2007). There is nothing for sale, no profit to be made. Back in the 1960s, Marcuse argued that technology has the potential to liberate humanity from nature, from hunger, disease and oppression (Marcuse, 1990). Similarly, the essence of technology in the second economy is the fact that it should lead to creation of socially useful knowledge and ultimately an enhancement of human life (Hall, 2013; Suoranta & Vaden, 2007). Technology, as part of the second economy and in use of social justice is a global public good which can lead to this global public good.

Perhaps the most effective way to make freedom as power and the second economy of technology global public goods (plural) and use them to create the global public good (singular) is to cast them as *movement*. Peters argues that knowledge in society most move vertically among legal and hierarchical structures, horizontally among social institutions and organizations and even three dimensionally as a cross between the two (Peters, 2010). This idea of knowledge movement elides with Marginson's third conception of the public sphere, that of the Habermasian sphere of social criticism (Marginson, 2007). Marginson, following Habermas argues that there should exist a sphere outside the orbit of government which can critique society and government. This sphere is made up of informal groups, volunteer organizations, civic organizations and other non-hierarchical associations (Marginson, 2007). Habermas did not believe that higher education could participate in this sphere, but Marginson said it could. Higher education, drawing on the notion of movement, can take its place in the public sphere as a vehicle of social criticism. The Habermasian sphere and the use of social criticism can help define and establish the elusive notion of the global public good (singular). More than this they can engender vertical and horizontal social movement.

The public sphere as social criticism can be framed as *dialectical* movement. Dialectical movement can be thought of as a forward movement of history, society and reality toward justice and human happiness. In this case, this movement is directed toward the creation of the global public good (singular). If higher education research and scholarship is held strictly accountable to the market as it is presently, higher education institutions cannot take their place in the horizontal networks of the public sphere. This vision of the global public good (singular) underpinned by a concept of dialectical movement is one that higher education policymakers should try to capture in policymaking, or be made to see by horizontal pressure. Of course, as many of the critical theorists argued, there is no goal to reach, utopia is not possible, but this does not mean we should ever stop trying to achieve it (Jay, 1996).

Global public goods are the building blocks of the global public good (singular). Yet, the global public good is also a precondition for the flow of global public goods (plural) which circulate through regional, national and local networks (Marginson & Rhoads, 2002). Thus they have a reciprocal and interconnected nature. Global public goods and the global public good however will be extremely difficult to foster under higher education accountability regimes. Accountability systems for higher education spawn from neoliberalism, and communal notions are the antithesis of neoliberalism (Giroux, 2011; Hill, 2012). Yet communal notions, undergirded by concepts of altruism are key to establishing the global public good.

Altruism is a complex concept, yet what it boils down to is concern for another (Wolfe, 1998). What makes one person care for another, what makes one person put another's welfare above their own? The answer is a combination of evolutionary, biological, cognitive and moral factors (1998). And while the answer is complex, it should be the cornerstone of any conception of the global public good. As Wolfe bluntly notes, in the increasingly connected world we have to learn to live with each other. Altruism, care for another and ultimately world peace and the absence of conflict is in everyone's interest and it can be promoted through an understanding of altruism (Kaul, Grunberg, & Stern, 1999). It also elides with Marginson's call for producing a global community.

One of the preconditions for world peace however stems from another global public good which is of the utmost importance in modern society; that of financial stability (Kaul, Grunberg, & Stern, 1999). Financial security for the world economy, not the financial gain of the few at the expense of the many is perhaps the most crucial global public good (plural). Financial security, which stems from a system to insulate the poor and low income individuals and families from the vicissitudes of the volatile global market is the foundation of peace because it ensures the safety of all.

As has been stressed throughout this paper, the public good is always a contested good, forged by heterogeneous groups. These groups can be aligned according to community, ethnicity, geography and many other characteristics. In addition, an individual many times belongs to more than one group (Calhoun, 1998). Yet, as Amartya Sen argues, there are many different identities that people may align with, such as occupation or social activity (Sen, 1999). These other identities are not rooted in geography or physical characteristics; rather they are usually of higher and more abstract cohesiveness. This is an excellent starting point for higher education and higher education policy. Drawing on Sen's idea of identity, higher education policymakers, or those who seek to influence higher education policymakers, can push for higher education to create new and more beneficial identities. These new abstract and more complex identities can help to dialectically drive higher education; scholars, educationalists and dialecticians can be the locus for these new identities. They can replace the more primal identifications in use today, which are rooted in base characteristics such as geography and race.

For a true notion of the global public good (singular), it must only be beneficial for this generation, but for posterity (Sandler, 1999). A public good in this generation cannot be a public bad for the next generation, such as debt, pollution or political tension (Sandler, 1999). A concern for posterity is at the heart of the social contract and education in general (Giroux, 2011). The point of education is to create a livable world for children as they become adults (Giroux, 2011). Thus, policymakers must not only legislate from their current constituents, but for the future.

Lastly, and perhaps most importantly, Giroux further argues that pedagogy should be synonymous with democracy (Giroux, 2011). As mentioned earlier, the public good is an endlessly contested political concept (Calhoun, 1998; Mansbridge, 1998). Under neoliberalism however, education is synonymous with the market. In the most dramatic sense, Tuck argues that neoliberalism is imperialistic because it dispenses with any notions of citizenship, communality or the public good. (Tuck, 2013). In light of this degradation of the public good, education and educators must teach people citizenship, create spaces for democratic discussion and show citizens how they can create positive social change and ultimately influence the dialectical movement of history (Giroux, 2011). This is how global public goods can be integrated into higher education pedagogy.

In sum, the global public good can be built with a new class of global public goods including; a sense of freedom as power, a liberating vision of technology, a sense of altruism, world peace, financial security and intergenerational conceptions. Further, the global public good as underpinned by all of these concepts must be understood as a *dialectical* sense of movement toward a more just state of being. Dialectic movement can be the glue which holds all the various concepts together. Instead of seeing this new vision of the public as an aggregate of various components, these components must become integrated and fluid and they must dialectically move toward a more just and democratic state. Each of the components must inform each other. For instance, democratic pedagogy can help students' realize new identities for themselves. New forms of knowledge, such as cultural, artistic and philosophical knowledge can also be used to create new and higher identifies. Intergenerational concepts can be used to inform decisions on technology as justice, and technology as justice can help scholars create externality profiles as well as map out new schemes for worldwide financial security. Most importantly, the notion of dialectical progression would underpin all of these endeavors. Technology as justice, new identities, financial security and all the concepts listed above would all be part of a larger dialectical movement toward a just state. As mentioned earlier, the dialectic is process and goal. As a goal, it is never static, but always able to incorporate new concepts and always able to progress further.

The global public good is a radical new vision of public goods and the public sphere which can dialectically transcend the current attack. Yet this dialectical movement will not happen without deliberate human action. The role and mission of public institutions in any given polity is configured by policy (Marginson, 2007). Consequently, the current policy system of accountability largely structures higher education in the United States like the market, which in the long run diminishes notions of the commonweal and the social fabric (Giroux, 2011; Hill, 2012). Thus, if policymakers and supporters work from an expanded view of the notion of the public to create policy, the mission and scope of public institutions will augment. Yet it is unlikely that policymakers and their neoliberal supporters will magically adopt these policies predicated on the global public good. Rather, as Zumeta argues, sometimes policymakers have to be shown what accountability truly means, what they *should* want and do (Zumeta, 2011).

Policy is a vertical structure; there is a clear hierarchy and clear positions of authority in that hierarchy (Peters, 2010). If one is at the bottom of that hierarchy, they have very little power to influence the upper positions. Thus, in order to educate policymakers and circumvent the hierarchy of policy, it is necessary to act upon the horizontal structures of society. Horizontal networks are flat; they are building blocks of global civil society. Organizations such as Amnesty International, environmental groups and the communist party to name a few constitute some of the organizations in global civil society. Another example could be individual schools and departments in universities. While they also occupy vertical positions (at the bottom of a state led hierarchy) they may be better able to effect change through their existing horizontal connections as well as by forging new ones with different social groups and organizations. This action can take the form of lobbying, social activism, scholarly pursuits and media action.

In a wider sense, this horizontal movement can be dialectical. Horizontal movement is another dimension of social change, one that many radical scholars and journalists have begun promote (Hedges, 2013; Peters, 2010). Horizontal movement however cannot simply be directed toward amelioration or temporary change, it cannot be a band aid. Rather, to be truly effective, horizontal movement must inspire dialectical transformation toward justice. Further, higher education institutions can drive this change. Scholars can push for a new vision of the global public good, rooted in ideas such as the creation of knowledge, the promoting of radical creativity, technology as justice, viewing public education as an organ of criticism, promoting altruism, world financial stability, new identity creation, intergenerational goods and democratic pedagogy, as well as whatever other goods that scholars can conceptualize. These global public goods can transcend the paltry amount of state subsidization higher education institutions are given to create a new vision of the global public good (singular). Scholars can work to weave these goods together in a dialectical movement. This can be done in their scholarship, through activism and engagement with the public, and perhaps most importantly, through their pedagogy. This would be a true movement toward a more just state, which would be grounded in human need and human justice. This is also true accountability and what higher education faculty need to impress on state policymakers and the general public (Zumeta, 2011). Situated historically, globalized society of the 21st century is on a historical precipice and faculty can take control of it instead of being led down a suicidal path of neoliberalism.

Work Cited

Alexander, K. (2000). The changing face of accountability: Monitoring and assessing institutional performance in higher education. *The Journal of Higher Education, 71*(4), 411–431.

Bowen, H. (1996). *Investment in learning: The individual and social value of American higher education* (2nd ed.). Introduction by Cameron Fincher. Englewood Cliffs, NJ: Transaction publishers.

Burke, J. (2005). The many faces of accountability. In Joseph Burke (Eds.). *Achieving accountability in higher education*. San Francisco, CA: Jossey-Bass.

Calhoun, C. (1998). The public good as a social and cultural project. In W. Powell & E. Clemens (Eds.), *Private action and the public good.* New Haven, CT: Yale University Press.

Freidman, M., & Freidman R. (1981). *Free to choose: A personal statement.* New York, NY: Harcourt Brace.

Giroux, H. (2011). *On critical pedagogy.* New York, NY: Continuum.

Hall, R. (2013). Educational technology and the enclosure of academic labor inside higher education. *Journal of Critical Education Policy Studies, 11,* 52–82.

Harvey, D. (2005). *A brief history of neoliberalism.* Oxford: Oxford University Press.

Hedges, C. (2013). *Our invisible revolution.* Retrieved from http://truth-out.org/opinion/item/19658-our-invisible-revolution

Held, D. (2001). Law of states, law of peoples. In D. Held & A. McGrew (Eds.), *The global transformations reader: An introduction to the globalization debate* (2nd ed.). Malden, MA: Blackwell Publishing.

Hill, D. (2012). Immiseration capitalism, activism and education: Resistance, revolt and revenge. *Journal for Critical Education Policy Studies, 10,* 1–34.

Jay, M. (1996). *The dialectical imagination: A history of the Frankfurt School and the Institute of Social Research, 1923–1950.* Los Angeles, CA: University of California Press.

Jefferson, T. (2010). *Notes on the state of Virginia.* Introduction by Peter S. Onuf. New York, NY: Barnes and Noble Press.

Kaul, I., Grunberg, I., & Stern, M. (1999). *Global public goods: International cooperation in the 21st century.* New York, NY: United Nations Development Programme.

Labree, D. (1998). Educational researchers: Living with a lesser form of knowledge. *Educational Researcher, 26*, 2–9.
McDonald, L. (2013). In their own words: U.S. think tank "experts" and the framing of educational policy debates. *Journal of Critical Education Policy Studies, 11*(3), 1–28.
Marcuse, H. (1990). Philosophy and critical theory. In D. Ingram & J. Simon-Ingram (Eds.), *Critical theory: The essential readings*. New York, NY: Paragon House.
Mansbridge, J. (1998). On the contested nature of the public good. In W. Powell & E. Clemens (Eds.), *Private action and the public good*. New Haven, CT: Yale University Press.
Marginson, S. (2007). The public/private divide in higher education: A global revision. *Higher Education, 53*, 307–333.
Marginson, S. (2011). Higher education and public good. *Higher Education Quarterly, 65*, 411–433.
Marginson, S., Murphy, P., & Peters, M. (2010). *Global creation: Space, mobility and synchrony in the age of the knowledge economy*. New York, NY: Peter Lang.
Marginson, S., & Rhoads, G. (2002). Beyond nation states, markets, and systems of higher education: A glonacal agency heuristic. *Higher Education, 43*, 281–309.
McClendon, M., Hearn, J., & Denton, R. (2006). Called to account: Analyzing the origins and spread of state performance-accountability policies for higher education. *Educational Evaluation and Policy Analysis, 28*(1), 1–24.
Newfield, C. (2008). *Unmaking the public university: The forty year assault on the middle class*. Quincy, MA: Harvard University Press.
Overtveldt, J. (2007). *The Chicago school: How the University of Chicago assembled the thinkers who revolutionized economics and business*. Canada: Agate Publishing.
Peet, R. (2009). *Unholy trinity: The IMF, World Bank and WTO* (2nd ed.). New York, NY: Zed Books.
Plant, R. (2010). *The Neoliberal state*. Oxford: Oxford University Press.
Prokou, E. (2013). Equity and efficiency in Greek higher education policies in the past three decades: A shift of emphasis to the issue of efficiency/"quality assurance" in the 2000s. *Journal of Critical Education Policy Studies, 11*(3), 29–51.
Reder, M. (1982). Chicago economics: Permanence and change. *Journal of Economic Literature, 22*, 1–38.
Rhoads, R., & Torres, C. (2006). *University, state and market: The political economy of globalization in the Americas*. Palo Alto, CA: Stanford Press.
Sandler, T. (1999). Intergenerational public goods: Strategies, efficiency and institutions. In. I. Kaul, I. Grunberg, & Marc A. Stern (Eds.), *Global Public Goods: International cooperation in the 21st century*. New York, NY: United Nations Development Programme: Oxford University Press.
Sen, A. (1999). Global justice: Beyond international equality. In. I. Kaul, I. Grunberg, & Marc A. Stern (Eds.), *Global Public Goods: International cooperation in the 21st century*. New York, NY: United Nations Development Programme: Oxford University Press.
Slaughter, S., & Rhoades, G. (2004). *Academic capitalism and the new economy: Markets, state and higher education*. Baltimore, MD: The Johns Hopkins University Press.
Spring, J. (2008). Research on globalization and education. *Review of Educational Research, 78*, 330–353.
Stanley, W. (2007). Critical pedagogy: Democratic realism, neoliberalism, conservatism and a tragic sense of education. In P. McLaren & J. Kincheloe (Eds.), *Critical pedagogy: Where are we now*? New York, NY: Peter Lang.
Suoranta, J., & Vaden, T. (2007). From social to socialist media: The critical potential of the wikiworld. In P. McLaren & J. Kincheloe (Eds.), *Critical pedagogy: Where are we now?* New York, NY: Peter Lang.
Truth, F. (2012). Pay big to publish fast: Academic journal rackets. *Journal of Critical Educational Policy Studies, 10*, 54–105.
Tuck. E. (2013). Neoliberalism as nihilism? A commentary on educational accountability, teacher education and school reform. *Journal of Critical Education Policy Studies, 11*(2), 324–347.
Urban, W. (2013). Anti-progressivism in education: Past and present. *International Journal of Progressive Education, 9*(1), 14–24.
Vestrich, R. (2008). The academy under siege: Threats to teaching and learning in American higher education. *American Academic, 2*, 55–71.
Wolfe, A. (1998). What is altruism? In W. Powell & E. Clemens (Eds.), *Private action and the public good*. Pp. 36–46. New Haven, CT: Yale University Press.
Wolff, R. (2012). *Democracy at work: A cure for capitalism*. Chicago, IL: Haymarket Books.
Zizek, S. (2009). *First as tragedy, then as farce*. New York, NY: Verso Press.
Zumeta, W. (2001). Public policy and accountability in higher education: Lessons from the past and present for the new millennium. In Donald Heller (Eds.) *The states and public higher education policy*. Baltimore, MD: The Johns Hopkins University Press.
Zumeta, W. (2011). What does it mean to be accountable? Dimensions and implications of higher education's public accountability. *The Review of Higher Education, 35*(1), 131–148.

CHAPTER 8

Private For-Profit Universities

Inflating Academic Degrees and Hurting the Economy?

Andrea S. Dauber and Kim Hunt

Introduction

Higher education in the United States is at risk of devaluation owing to the dramatic increase of for-profit universities. Without entrance requirements such as minimal SAT or ACT scores, these institutions primarily employ faculty with M.A.s, allow students with poor levels of college preparedness into their programs, have lower academic standards, and eventually release graduates into the workforce who compete with graduates from traditional universities with corresponding higher standards in a globalizing market. Meanwhile, the structures of the education system and the American labor market mandate that young people aim for a college degree to be able to compete with their peers for entry-level positions that will steer their occupational careers into well-paying, middle or upper class jobs. From an international perspective, the U.S. has one of the most privatized higher education systems among developed nations. Other developed countries rely more heavily on public universities or colleges that make it easier to maintain certain academic standards while for-profit universities, despite accreditation, do not aspire to the same level of academic quality. Whether or not the American college-educated workforce of the 21st century will remain competitive on a global market will also be a question of entrepreneur commitment to quality and quality management of profit-oriented quantity.

Transnational Markets and Higher Education

Transnational markets, the flow of capital, goods and people, the rise of developing countries and the world's future economic, social, political and ecological challenges will have to be met by every nation-state to varying degrees. Leading developed nations, in the process of transitioning to a post-industrial state, must rely heavily on one major asset: the education of the prospective and the existing workforce. The demand of higher education is met differently by each country, depending on the degree of capitalization of the education system. Higher education in the U.S. has an outstanding reputation world-wide, with some universities ranking amongst the top positions in the world. According to the

Academic Ranking of World Universities, eight American universities were in the top 10 in 2015, among them prestigious non-profit and public universities such as Harvard, Stanford, UC Berkeley, or Princeton (Shanghai Jiao Tong University, 2015).

However, private and public non-profit universities in the U.S. are under attack; not from the outside, but from within the higher education system; and it has gone unnoticed by many. While traditional state universities and public colleges will undoubtedly continue to exist, other providers of higher education services have been pushing rigorously onto the educational market. Context factors such as rising tuition costs, increasing numbers of applicants who intensify competition, decreasing need-based financial aid, the pressure on young people to obtain degrees, the necessity for older generations to 'update' their education to stay competitive, and a poorly structured labor market contribute to the current development.

The national and global landscape of higher education is undergoing constant change, particularly in the context of globalization. Systems must respond to increasing or decreasing numbers of potential students, the need for specific skills and knowledge by the economy, immigration and to a lesser extent, emigration. In the past two decades, one spin-off in these processes has been the substantial increase in for-profit universities and colleges that extend their services to students of younger and older cohorts.[1] Morey (2004) reported that there were approximately 4000 private colleges which enrolled an estimated 1.8 million students by the late 1980s. At present, their number has grown to over 2.4 million, an increase of almost 50 percent (NCSL, 2015).

The proliferation of for-profit universities and colleges is increasingly drawing scholarly attention. Researchers have examined a variety of variables, such as the growth in numbers of for-profit schools (Deeming, Goldin, & Katz, 2012; Morey, 2004; Wilson, 2010), funding sources of universities and colleges and financial aid for students (Belfield, 2013; Cellini, 2010; Laband & Lentz, 2004), characteristics of faculty and students (Deeming, Goldin, & Katz, 2013; Kinser, 2002) and governmental regulation efforts (Bennet, Lucchesi, & Vedder, 2010). Alongside these scholarly investigations of for-profit companies providing higher education service, a number of federal or state institutions produce a large number of statistics that provide a basis for the comparison of public and private non-profit universities and private for-profit universities. Because for-profit universities have recently been subject to regulations and accreditation processes, it is vital to evaluate their role in the context of higher education in the U.S. This demands a more thorough examination of student populations and faculty on the micro level and opportunity structures, labor market demands, and changing demographics from a macro perspective. A more precise picture must, for example, be developed about the factors that drive a person's decision to study at a for-profit university, why they choose online programs over on-site classes as well as aspects such as gender, ethnicity, race and socio-economic background. By the same token, scholarly examination of for-profit universities' performance must move into the center of attention. If these companies have the right to issue degrees, but lack decades or even centuries of history, tradition and expertise, it must still be ensured that the quality of education does not differ from that of traditional universities.

In this contribution, we will draw connections between the micro and the macro level by critically evaluating how aspects such as aggressive advertising, funding, quality of instruction, qualification of instructors and student performance shape the development of U.S. higher education and the workforce of the 21st century. From an international perspective, we will also discuss how the increasingly visible problem of university segregation is embedded in the structure of the American labor market and the lack of alternatives to higher education in the transition from adolescence to young adulthood.

For the purpose of comparing indicators of private and public non-profit universities versus private for-profit universities, we will review secondary data from the College Board Advocacy and Policy Center, the Education Commission of the States, and the U.S. Department of Labor. On the supply side, the indicators we will consider reflect the stages course that students go through in the course of their educational career. As a student enters a university, GPA, SAT, and other types of scores will matter in terms of admission. In this regard, acceptance rates will be of importance as well. As students transition through their programs, retention rates and dropout rates matter in terms of successful completion of a program.

On the demand side, it will be essential to examine different profiles of lecturers and professors at for-profit and non-profit universities. Moreover, the length students spend in courses throughout a semester is important to consider as well for the overall academic qualification of those students upon graduation. The sources that fund both types of organizations, the degree to which this is the case and how students are affected by funding policies differently will be given consideration against the background that not every student has the financial means to pay for college tuition. How universities receive funding and provide their students with scholarships will therefore be a crucial aspect in the evaluation of for-profit universities as well.

To complement this perspective we will include reflections about the American labor market structure. It might well be that the market demands college graduates; however, supplying this demand with graduates who did not receive the same quality of education that is acknowledged as a general standard could lead to negative effects in the long-run, inflation of degree holders' salaries being just one of them. Moreover, the dramatic increase of for-profit universities places traditional university degrees at risk of devaluation if quality differs, but both educational paths lead to a tertiary degree. For-profits do not use entrance exams, primarily employ faculty without terminal degrees, and have lower academic standards. Yet, enrollment in these institutions has grown more than 225% over the past two decades (NCSL, 2015).

Aside from the political debate over the use of federal monies, the issue of social stratification within America's higher education system is revived. For-profit universities emphasize they counter social inequality by accepting students who otherwise would not have a chance to receive a degree. Students with a low high school GPA, or just a GED and poor, or no, SAT or ACT scores can ultimately obtain degrees and compete for better paying jobs, fueling the idea of the American Dream. However, tuition at non-profit universities is generally just a fraction of tuition at for-profit universities. This begs the question of long-term affordability for students from lower or lowest socioeconomic strata. Moreover, as the international perspective will demonstrate, instead of pushing ill-prepared students through university programs which cause them high debt, it might be better to provide them with alternative routes to higher skill levels and mastery of a field.

How students at for-profit universities are educated relates directly to questions about their human capital. As enrollment numbers show, the labor market is increasingly becoming saturated with graduates many or most of whom most likely cannot compete with their peers from traditional universities in terms of basic college skills such as professional communication, literacy, or critical thinking. Perhaps this is insignificant if for-profit and non-profit graduates compete for different types of jobs. However, recent and presumably future contractions of the labor market may intensify graduates' competition, resulting in less diverse choices about where to apply. To increase their graduates' chances of securing employment upon completion of a program, many for-profit universities provide career services to students. While 'placement' is officially prohibited, for-profits invest significant resources into establishing networks with corporations which could benefit their graduates. Moreover, the quality of education is outweighed by quantity; the sheer numbers of graduates, not their qualifications, is the emphasis in for-profit universities to appeal to the boards of directors which must focus on stockholders' profits.

The effect of for-profit higher education on the labor market and the status quo of public colleges and universities can be expected to vary because for-profit companies offering higher education degrees do not all follow the same business model. However, we generally hold that graduate performance in the labor market can be predicted through certain indicators. For example, studies have indicated that college performance and completion vary contingent on students' and graduates' SES status (Lundberg, 2013; Sirin, 2005; Titus, 2006). We would expect the same for labor market preparedness.

For-Profit versus Non-Profit: Quantitative and Qualitative Aspects in Comparison

In general terms, a non-profit organization is defined as an organization whose primary purpose is for public benefit and does not distribute profits but instead re-invests profits into the organization. These organizations come in many forms and cross many different segments of the marketplace. For-profit universities cover a wide range of educational services, from beauty schools to technical colleges with a general education add-on to resemble non-profit universities in their structure.

Most non-profit institutions are classified as 501(c)(3) or 501(c)(4) organizations under the IRS tax codes. In U.S. higher education, there are two types of non-profit universities, public and private. Public universities are traditionally funded primarily through state funds, although this is slowly changing in recent years, while private, non-profit universities are funded primarily through donations, foundations, and government funding in the form of financial aid for students. In theory, for-profit universities are funded primarily through student fees. However, the majority of these fees come from government-backed federal aid for students and veterans' benefits (U. S. Senate Committee, 2012).

Controversies about Funding of Higher Education Institutions and Resource Allocation

According to a US Senate report from 2012, for-profit higher education corporations such as Apollo Group, which runs University of Phoenix, and Bridgepoint Education which runs Ashford University, obtained over 85% of funding for the year 2010 from federal student aid in one form or another (U.S. Senate Committee, 2012). This same report stated, $32 billion per year of taxpayer money is used by for-profit university students to attend school although more than 50% of these students leave before completing their degree program. Due to this high percentage of reliance on federal monies, the federal government enacted the 90-10 rule which stated institutions of higher education could not receive more than 90% of their funding from federal student aid, however, this rule exempted money aimed at veterans and their families (Riegel, 2013). In his 2016 budget plan, President Obama has proposed closing this loophole and requiring money aimed at veterans and their families to count on the 90% side (Wong, 2015). What makes this issue so controversial are the relative costs of programs at for-profit and non-profit schools. Moreover, the importance of budgets and profit for for-profit universities can be gauged when comparing compensation rates for administrators in the for-profit and the non-profit sector. For example, according to the UC annual report on executive compensation, the outgoing head of the University of California system reported an annual salary of $591,000 (University of California, 2013). The non-profit UC system includes eight campuses throughout the state and "has an annual budget of $24 billion, 230,000 students, 191,000 faculty and staff, five medical centers and three national laboratories" (University of California, 2013, para. 11–12). Comparatively, it has been reported that Bridgepoint Education's CEO Andrew Clark oversees two campuses hosting 81,810 students with an annual budget of $209.4 million. His total yearly compensation in 2012 was $2,247,766. Ashford University, which is one of two universities under the Bridgepoint Education umbrella, employed "56 full-time faculty members in 2011, with 2,458 part-time faculty members and 875 instructional staff" (Fain, 2010, para. 8). These numbers give rise to the assumption that profits are given priority over student resources at for-profit universities. What exactly do you mean by student resources?

The salaries of top administrators at for-profit schools lead to a discussion of disparity of wealth among those running the for-profit institutions and those who are attending. According to Baum and Payea (2005), tuition at a two-year public university was merely 19% of two-year private for-profit university tuition in the academic year 2010–2011. While this is undoubtedly a problem for students from low and lowest socio-economic strata, for-profit universities employ aggressive advertising to conceal this inconvenience. With a dropout rate of over 50% in for-profit schools, individuals already in the lower socioeconomic strata will have an even more arduous task to fulfil their debt obligations. According to Baum and Payea (2012), who report for the College Board:

> For-profit institutions accounted for 12 percent of all students enrolled in 2008–09, 28 percent of those who entered repayment in FY 2009, 48 percent of those who defaulted by the end of September 2010, and 47 percent of those who defaulted by the end of September 201.1. (p. 20)

It must be added, though, that dropout rates do not reveal how many of those students went on to a different for-profit university, a public university or how many stay out of higher education.

The Center for Studies in Higher Education at UC Berkeley sums up the issue of cost, financial aid, and loan default:

> FP [for-profits] have been highly effective in helping students secure taxpayer subsidized financial aid; but not very effective in graduating those students and helping them gain employment to then pay off their high debt levels. This has led to relatively high default rates among their former students. (Douglass, 2012, p. 8)

Some politicians such as Senator Tom Harkin from Iowa are aware of this imbalance and have pointed out that a substantial percentage of the profits for these institutions derive from federal education grants and loans (Blumenstyk, 2012). However, President Obama's efforts to regulate for-profit universities more strictly have largely deflagrated. The National Center for Education Statistics reported that in the academic year 2010–2011, 73% of students at four-year, for-profit universities received federal financial aid compared to 35% of students at private, non-profit universities (Baum & Payea, 2012). In sum, the data show that for-profit higher education institutions receive a disproportionate amount of public money which by and large does not have the desired effect of successfully serving students in lower socioeconomic status to enhance their chances for social mobility. Unlike many European nations that have a long history of government-funded education (cf. Glaeser & Shleifer, 2001), higher education in the U.S. is funded from a mix of sources, including government funding, private donations and private capital.

Quality of Education

The quality of post-secondary education is one of the most crucial factors in terms of future workforce competitiveness. Obviously, for-profit universities must handle a conflict of interests. They, like any for-profit business, must answer to their stockholders. Although their primary purpose is to provide an educational product, they have a legal obligation to answer to their stockholders first. Understandably, the interests of stockholders do not have to correspond with the interests of students who purchase a product based on the information they receive through advertising. In order to be competitive on the market, for-profit universities must provide a product that is satisfactory to customers if they do not want to forgo profit or even run out of business. Interestingly, though, for-profit universities are not always living up to the claims they make in terms of providing an equal education compared to non-profit universities at a more affordable and efficient manner. As stated earlier, one of for-profit universities' strategic arguments is they reach students who are ignored or turned away by traditional universities which is why they fill a gap in higher education services (Lederman, 2009). While it is accurate that for-profit universities seek to attract a different student population, for example active military members or veterans, a problem emerges regardless of this approach. Theoretically, for-profit universities would have to provide more than an equivalent level of educational quality to level the relative educational, socio-economic and cognitive disadvantages many of the students struggle with when they enter their programs.

According to US News College Ranking (2015), which is an often referred to source in higher education to retrieve information about rankings used by most college admissions departments, the acceptance rates for these for-profit institutions are generally very high. Most of these schools, such as Ashford University, have acceptance rates of around 90%. In comparison, the public and private non-profit institutions, such as UC Berkeley in 2015, had an acceptance rate of just 16% and the University of Southern California had an acceptance rate of just 18% (US News, 2015). There are two possible explanations for this drastic difference in acceptance rates. According to for-profit executives, the higher acceptance rates are reflective of the ability to offer a college education to those who are traditionally ignored by non-profit institutions. These for-profit universities emphasize they counter social inequality by accepting students who otherwise would not have a chance to receive a degree (Lederman, 2009). The argument is these students not only deserve the chance to earn a college degree but that with this college degree, they can move beyond the confines of their current socioeconomic status and origin. One of the strongest arguments made against pushing students into higher education without vetting, is they simply do not have the educational background from K-12 to succeed.

Acceptance at a traditional non-profit school is a rigorous process. Students must submit an application, high school GPAs, SAT and/or ACT scores, written essays, and sometimes, interviews just to begin the application process. Applications then undergo an intense scrutiny by the university to determine the right mix of students for their next incoming class. Average SAT scores for non-profit schools such as UC Berkeley and USC average around 2000. Average GPAs of entering freshmen at these same schools are 3.7. For-profit universities tend to not use these types of acceptance standards. For example, according to Ashford University (2013), the only criterion for enrollment is a high school diploma or GED, an application form for school, and a deposit. As soon as a student is accepted they are rushed off to a financial aid counselor to secure student loans, a few grants for those who qualify, and a handful of scholarships. Experts in the field have pointed to the aggressiveness with which for-profit universities recruit and enrol students, aiming at enrolling as many students as fast as possible, irrespective of academic fitness (Wilson, 2010). The lower acceptance standards and 90% acceptance rates of these for-profit schools could be justified if it were not for the statistics on retention rates.

When comparing the same universities, the retention rates are nearly an exact mirror image of acceptance rates according to statistics provided by the College Board (Baum & Payea, 2012). This seems to contradict the argument that for-profit institutions provide an education for students because the non-profit universities will not. Burdened with staggering amounts of debt, students who drop out of for-profit programs do not have their degree in hand to secure a better job and hence, repay the formerly acquired student loans.

The structure of programs and learning models of most for-profit universities are important components in assessing the quality of education students receive. The quality issue is further exacerbated through the amount of required classroom hours for receiving credentials. Traditional non-profit universities run on a semester or quarter system. Many for-profit universities run their entire courses in a mere 5–8 weeks, depending on the school. Kinser (2002) described the semester system of the University of Phoenix which consists of five weeks with four classroom hours a week. Other private for-profit institutions of higher education have similar models. For example, at DeVry University, which has more than 90 locations throughout the U.S. and enrolls the largest share of America's undergraduate population (Smith-Barrow, 2013), one semester, which is referred to as "session", usually has three on-site classroom hours for a three-credit class. The classes run over seven weeks with finals being taken in the last week. Students usually take these finals online through their online modules, which run parallel to on-site instruction. During a session, students must log into their modules and partake in online discussion threads usually a specified number of times (DeVry, 2014). In comparison, at a traditional university a semester has approximately 4.5 months with one hour of classroom time for every credit unit per class each week. This ratio raises the question how justified it is to assume that both curricula convey the same in-depth knowledge and quality. At for-profit universities, students rush through comparably short "semesters" to receive their degrees faster to enter the primary labor market faster. The universities advocate this system because it is an integral element of their advertising strategy. The faster a degree can be completed, the faster the student will supposedly generate higher income. Whether or not these students are better educated and trained in such short periods of time than students at traditional universities remains in question.

The quality of education is not just influenced through the structure of programs and amount of classroom hours; the qualification of instructors must be considered as well. The U.S. Bureau of Labor Statistics' Occupational Handbook (2013) describes that, "most commonly, post-secondary teachers must have a Ph.D." (para. 3). However, the majority of faculty members at for-profit institutions do not hold terminal degrees or have never taught at a traditional university. Instead, they tend to have a Master's Degree and have worked in their jobs for many years. This issue has recently been encountered by the requirement of accreditation agencies that a certain percentage of faculty members hold a terminal degree in the field they teach. The majority of instructors working in for-profit universities are hired as adjuncts, are paid substantially less than they would be in non-profit institutions and receive no benefits unlike their tenure-track or adjunct counterparts in non-profit universities. They are also expendable and can be cut back or replaced with lower cost faculty whenever budgeting issues arise. Further, Morey (2004) stated, "… for-profit institutions have separated instructional delivery from the design of their course … it removes faculty from their important role of control over the curriculum and diminishes the need for subject matter expertise" (p. 145). Finally, tenured and non-tenured faculty at non-profit institutions usually conduct research in their field of study. This enables lecturers and professors to stay current within their field, bring new and relevant information into the classroom and often affords the students the opportunity to collaborate with faculty who are renowned within their field and expand their own knowledge and expertise. For this purpose, non-profit universities and colleges often have undergraduate research programs which pair students with tenure- track faculty or full professors for one or two semesters, advancing students' academic, social and analytical skills.

Higher Education and Structural Aspects of the U.S. Labor Market

Higher education and the U.S. labor market have developed a highly dependent relationship over the past decades. In comparison with other developed nations, the situation is rather unique in the U.S. owing to the largely missing country-wide acknowledged alternatives to college or university education for young people. Just how dependent the labor market is on the supply of university graduates becomes apparent when comparing the structure of the American labor market with those of other countries. A good example is provided by Germany whose apprenticeship system has a century-long tradition. German high school graduates choose between entering a university or a college and starting an apprenticeship with an employer. Hairdressers, bank tellers, administrators, car mechanics and industrial sales representative are examples of occupations that graduates can aspire to take. While under formal contract with an employer who will function as their instructor as well, graduates pass through a two or three year apprenticeship during which they spend 50% of their time in school and 50% at their job. They receive a salary that varies contingent on the type of occupation they learn. After they complete their apprenticeship, they may be offered to stay with their employer or they may apply to other employers throughout the country.

France follows a similar, yet less labor market-oriented system. High school graduates can choose to enter a university, start an apprenticeship, or add some years to their high school education to receive certificates that enable them to seize a variety of occupations. Italy offers a range of alternatives to a university education as well. There certainly is variation in the Anglo-American countries; in Canada, students can obtain certificates or diplomas in non-degree-granting educational institutions, enter a regular university or take part in apprenticeship programs. Canada's "red seal" program facilitates geographical mobility of professionals because of standardized qualifications. This is one of the major differences between Canada's and the United States' validity and applicability of such alternatives to degree programs at universities.

Over the past decades, the match between educational systems and required qualifications for labor markets has been subject to an "elevator effect" in many countries. Draut (2005) described this phenomenon for the United States: "In many ways, a bachelor's degree has become equivalent to what a high school degree used to be: the bare minimum for competing in the economy. As a result, a master's degree is becoming the new bachelor's degree" (p. 99). In the context of this development, the structure of the American labor market is exacerbating the situation for high school graduates. If they do not obtain a degree, their chances of having a white-collar career are drastically diminished. Programs that issue certificates are not universally accepted throughout the country. A certified realtor can work in the state where they took the test and obtained the license, but they probably cannot pursue this occupation in a different state unless they re-take tests and become certified again.

U.S. employers tend to have loose and comparatively short-term commitments with their employees, a relationship mediated through various institutions such as the law, the job market and the economy. After all, it is much more profitable for companies to reap the benefits of a young, preferably college-educated and mobile workforce that enters the labor market in search of full-time jobs. After these young employees have gathered some experience on the job, they usually look to ascend to better paying and more responsible positions, often in a different company. In other words, the bond between employees and employers is often not strong enough to retain highly qualified employees.

It follows that the demand- and supply-side of the American labor market mandate at least two requirements: young people must preferably obtain a college degree if they want to develop a rewarding occupational career, at least in certain industries, and employers must have access to qualified people. Kerckhoff (2003) compared Great Britain's, America's and Germany's school systems and examined the different pathways that young people can take upon leaving school at age 16, 18 or even older. American society structures the transition from school to work, or from adolescence to young adulthood, in a way that young people do not have much of a choice but to enroll in community colleges, colleges or universities to obtain a B.A. or M.A. to be considered for entry-level jobs that can develop into careers. In fact, the vast majority of high school graduates aspires to obtain a postsecondary degree. In October 2012, 66.6% of 2012 high school graduates were enrolled in colleges or universities (Bureau of Labor Statistics, 2013). The unaddressed question is how many of these 66.6% have an academic level that qualifies them for higher education. For-profit universities nullify the validity of this question by allowing virtually anybody into their programs.

International Perspective

UNESCO's 2011 report on the globalization of for-profit universities suggests a necessity for a different model than that which is currently used in the U.S. According to Giesecke (2006), one of the key issues of the US model is its focus on investors seeking substantial financial return. At the same time, other countries, particularly in the Middle East, India, and Europe, are increasingly looking into the options for-profit universities can provide, but they are nervous about the negative reports that have been leveled at for-profit universities in the United States. After conducting interviews with students and faculty members in central and eastern European countries, it was found that for-profit universities are met with mistrust and negativism. Interviewees felt students at private universities were inferior in preparation and performance, the instructional programs were weak, and programs are tailored to gain entry into the job market for graduates rather than for long-term societal issues and concerns (Giesecke, 2006).

Weinberg and Graham-Smith (2012) argued that corporatization of higher education potentially destroys collegiality and any type of corporate higher education must be tailored to each country's needs and regulations rather than as a one-size-fits-all model. If there is evidence that other developed and even developing countries express skepticism towards profit-oriented higher education, then why has it been successfully expanding in the United States? Presumably, the culture of an economy is a key factor in this process. Moreover, the availability of public resources plays a key role. The CHEA and UNESCO (2011) pointed out that developing countries have given more importance to the market because public resources did not suffice to reach the United Nations 2000 Millennium Development Goal in areas other than higher education. In other words, the for-profit schools have stepped in to fill a gap created by the inability of the non-profit and public schools to serve the increasing needs of higher education for the non-traditional student.

Discussion and Conclusion

Has the U.S. created an education utopia where everyone can reap the benefits of a university degree or is it headed towards an education dystopia that diminishes, intentionally or unintentionally, the worth of higher education by state institutions? What is the outlook for America's workforce who must compete with ascending countries such as India or China in a globalizing world economy? While a definitive answer cannot be given yet, current trends and signs must be researched more intensely. Researchers have stressed the positive spin off that for-profit universities have had on non-profit universities (Wilson, 2010). Increasingly more non-profit universities look to the for-profit sector for innovative ideas and start implementing some of the elements first put forward by proprietary schools, for example online programs. For-profit schools are not large-scale competitors yet; however, they are picking up speed fast. Simultaneously, they do not seem to be serious competitors from an insider perspective. The indicators evaluated in this chapter all point to a substantial gap in quality aspects between non-profit and for-profit universities. Both demand- and supply side agents in the for-profit sector differ substantially from agents in the non-profit educational sector. The problem is that supply-side agents might never develop that same insider perspective. Not all students might know the difference between a traditional and a profit-oriented education, and if for-profit universities manage to appeal to them because of aggressive advertising, seemingly stronger financial support, and tools that facilitate employment, this aspect might never really matter. However, for-profit institutions invest considerable resources into establishing networks with businesses. While placement of students is officially prohibited, it is almost impossible to reveal intricate relationships between for-profit institutions and businesses. In the long run this could result in a shift away from the traditional focus and values of non-profit universities to the seemingly stronger labor market readiness promise of for-profit universities if future generations of students encounter quickly contracting and expanding labor markets.

Additionally, private for-profit universities and colleges are cultivating the fast-track degree. Many specifically advertise this concept, implying that students can obtain a degree much faster at a for-profit school. To argue they receive the same amount and quality of higher education in these programs would require substantial longitudinal empirical evidence. It is clear that the U.S., just like any developed country, will need a large number of professionals and well-educated individuals in the future to successfully compete with developing economies. If for-profit students finish their programs faster than non-profit students, this might have a negative effect on the employability of the latter on the aggregate level. At present, the University of Phoenix has more than 455,600 students enrolled. The impact on the U.S. economy's competitiveness when these students enter the labor market cannot be estimated, but it should raise concerns that these students were not educated according to the same quality standards that employers would generally expect of B.A. and M.A. graduates. In this context, further concern must be raised regarding future immigration trends. While immigration reform is pending, it is clear that the U.S. will have to open its gates to highly skilled immigrants to maintain its innovative potential and stabilize and expand the U.S. economy. With more highly educated immigrants entering the U.S. labor market, the issue of competitiveness of the native workforce will be even more pressing, particularly if these high skilled immigrants come on temporary visas.

Connected with this trend is the question of how an increase in for-profit B.A.s, M.A.s and even Ph.Ds will affect the non-profit degrees' ROI. A number of factors must be taken into consideration in this equation, ranging from academic integrity, to employability of graduates, to quality of programs, to financing. The inflation of traditional academic degrees is a long-term risk if the market is flooded with mediocre for-profit graduates who did not develop the same kind of academic foundation that is traditionally cultivated at non-profit universities. This might exacerbate the "elevator effect" that Draut (2005) has pointed to; what is a Bachelor's degree today might be a Master's degree in the future.

A simple way to mediate this effect would be to revoke the right to use the labels "university" or "college" and replace them with another label which distinguishes them from non-profit universities, particularly because not all for-profit university students are aware of the difference between both institutions. Additionally, adding a short abbreviation to B.A., M.A. and Ph.D. degrees to demonstrate that these degrees differ in terms of quality and speak differently to a job applicant's overall qualification could be another way to set both types of institutions apart. While this might not matter too much to employers who will likely know how to evaluate degrees from both types of universities, an institutionalized distinction could prevent the devaluation of non-profit university degrees regardless. Because students who enter for-profit universities generally have a lower level of preparedness, they cannot potentially reach the level of knowledge and skills of student who enter a public, especially 4-year university the same amount of time. This is particularly true when for-profit universities design their curricula in a way that a semester is substantially shorter than a regular semester at a public institution.

Other countries have designed different ways of separating public university degrees from private for-profit universities or colleges. For example, a degree obtained at a private or public technical college in Germany carries the addition "FH" (Fachhochschule, *engl.* University of Applied Sciences). The official distinction of these two notations can immunize public university degrees against devaluation, simply because entering public universities requires better GPAs and higher levels of academic preparedness. Moreover, students would probably be better aware of the differences between private for-profit and public non-profit and for-profit universities and could make more informed choices about the marketability of their degrees, depending on what they want to do after their undergraduate program. Universities build good or bad reputations, and parallel to these, employers, often through informal processes, form opinions about the quality of human capital to be expected from a graduate depending on the university they attended. It can be said that the market needs more transparency in these matters, particularly because for-profit students accumulate on average higher debts in for-profit universities. And students who would like to move on to a traditional university might not be able to do so if their private for-profit degree is not accepted, potentially for good reasons. At present, different student populations seem to be rather unaware of these intricacies.

In future research, consideration should be given to the relative quality of online programs as non-profit universities are increasingly adopting them as well. Moreover, in evaluating a potentially negative impact that for-profit higher education has on the value of university degrees and the overall qualification of the workforce, research should differentiate between primarily technical institutes and universities and colleges that confer traditional four-year degrees.

Note

1 For the sake of text flow we will refer to private non-profit universities and colleges as for-profit universities and to public and private non-profit universities and colleges as non-profit universities. It would certainly make sense to further differentiate the different types of schools in analyses; however, in this contribution we will take a rather general look at differences between for-profit education and non-profit education and their providers.

Work Cited

Baum, S., & Payea, K. (2005). Education pays: 2004. *College board connect to college success*. Retrieved from http://www.collegeboard.com/prod_downloads/press/cost04/Educati onPays2004.pdf

Baum, S., & Payea, K. (2012). Trends in student aid. *Trends in higher education*. Retrieved from http://trends.collegeboard.org/sites/default/files/student-aid-2012-full-report-13020 1.pdf

Belfield, C. R. (2013). Student loans and repayment rates: The role of for-profit colleges. *Research in Higher Education, 54*, 1–29. DOI:10.1007/s11162-012-9268-1

Bennet, D. L., Lucchesi, A. R., & Vedder, R. K. (2010). *For-profit higher education. Growth, innovation, regulation*. Retrieved from http://www.centerforcollegeaffordability.org/uplo ads/ForProfit_HigherEd.pdf

Blumenstyk, G. (2012, November 7). Obama's victory spells continued scrutiny for for-profit colleges. *The Chronicle of Higher Education*. Retrieved from http://chronicle.com/article/Obamas-Victory-Spells/135590/

Bridgepoint Education, Inc. (2013, October 25). *Bloomberg Businessweek*. Retrieved from http://investing.businessweek.com/research/stocks/people/person.asp?personId=30396776&ticker=BPI

Bureau of Labor Statistics. (2013). *College enrollment and work activity of 2012 high school graduates*. Retrieved from http://www.bls.gov/news.release/pdf/hsgec.pdf

Cellini, S. R. (2010). Financial aid and for-profit colleges: Does aid encourage entry? *Journal of Policy Analysis and Management, 29*(3), 526–552.

Council for Higher Education and Accreditation, & United Nations Educational, Scientific and Cultural Organization. (2011). *Exploring the future of international for-profit higher education and quality assurance: Where are we now and where do we go from here?* Retrieved from http://www.chea.org/pdf/UNESCO_document.pdf

Deeming, D., Goldin, C., & Katz, L. (2012). The for-profit post-secondary school sector: Nimble critters or agile predators? *The Journal of Economic Perspectives, 26*(1), 139–164.

Deeming, D., Goldin, C., & Katz, L. (2013). For-profit colleges. *The Future of Children, 23*(1), 137–163.

DeVry University, Inc. (2014). Academic calendar. Retrieved from http://www.devry.edu/degre e-programs/academic-calendar.html

Douglass, J. A. (2012). *Money, politics, and the rise of for-profit higher education in the US: A story of supply, demand and the Brazilian effect*. Informally published manuscript, Center for Studies in Higher Education, UC Berkeley. Retrieved from http://cshe.berkeley.edu/p ublications/docs/ROPS.JAD.ForProfitsUS.2.15.2012.pdf

Draut, T. (2005). The growing college gap. In J. Lardner & D. A. Smith (Eds.), *Inequality matters* (pp. 89–101). New York, NY: The New Press.

Fain, P. (2010, July 10). Rise of the accreditor. *Inside Higher Ed*. Retrieved from http://www.insidehighered.com/news/2012/07/10/profit-ashford-university-loses-accreditation-bid

Giesecke, H. (2006). Legitimacy seeking among new private institutions of higher education in Central and Eastern Europe. *Higher Education in Europe, 31*(1), 11–24. doi:10.1080/03797720600859072

Glaeser, E. L., & Shleifer, A. (2001). Not-for-profit entrepreneurs. *Journal of Public Economics, 81*(1), 99–115. Retrieved from http://scholar.harvard.edu/glaeser/files/1-s2.0-s004727270 0001304-main.pdf

Kerckhoff, A. C. (2003). From student to worker. In Mortimer, J. T. & Shanahan, M. J. (Eds.), *Handbook of the life course* (pp. 251–267). New York, NY: Kluwer Academic/Plenum Publishers.

Kinser, K. (2002). Faculty at private for-profit universities: The University of Phoenix as a new model? *International Higher Education, 28*, 13–14.

Laband, D. N., & Lentz, B. F. (2004). Do costs differ between for-profit and not-for-profit producers of higher education? *Research in Higher Education, 45*(4), 429–441.

Lederman, D. (2009, October 8). Served, yes, but well-served? *Inside Higher Ed*. Retrieved from http://www.insidehighered.com/news/2009/10/08/pell

Lundberg, S. (2013). The college type: Personality and educational inequality. *Journal of Labor Economics, 31*(3), 421–441.

Morey, A. I. (2004). Globalization and the emergence of for-profit higher education. *Higher Education, 48*(1), 131–150.

National Conference of State Legislatures (NCSL). (2015). *For-profit colleges and universities*. Retrieved from http://www.ncsl.org/issues-research/educ/for-profit-colleges-and-universi ties.aspx

Riegel, D. J. (2013). Closing the 90/10 loophole in the Higher Education Act: How to stop exploitation of veterans, protect American taxpayers, and restore market incentives to the for-profit college industry. *The George Washington Law Review, 81*(1), 259. Retrieved from http://www.gwlr.org/riegel/

Shanghai Jiao Tong University: Center for World-Class Universities. (2015). Retrieved from http://www.shanghairanking.com/

Sirin, S. R. (2005). Socioeconomic status and academic achievement: A meta-analytic review of research. *Review of Educational Research, 75*(3), 417–453.

Smith-Barrow, D. (2013). 10 universities with the largest undergraduate populations. *US News*. Retrieved from http://www.usnews.com/education/best-colleges/the-short-list-college/ar ticles/2013/12/03/10-universities-with-the-largest-undergraduate-populations

Titus, M. A. (2006). Understanding college degree completion of students with low socioeconomic status: The influence of the institutional financial context. *Research in Higher Education, 47*(4), 371–398.

University of California. (2013). *Compensation at the University of California.* Retrieved from http://compensation.universityofcalifornia.edu

U.S. Department of Labor, Bureau of Labor Statistics. (2013). *Occupational outlook handbook.* Retrieved from http://www.bls.gov/ooh/education-training-and-library/postsecondary-tea chers.htm

US News. (2015). *U.S. News College Rankings.* Retrieved from http://colleges.usnews.rankingsandreviews.com/best-colleges

US Senate Committee on Health, Education, Labor and Pensions. (2012). *For profit higher education: The failure to safeguard the federal investment and ensure student success.* Retrieved from http://www.help.senate.gov/hearings/hearing/?id=cdd6e130-5056-9502-5dd 2-e4d005721cb2

Weinberg, A. M., & Graham-Smith, G. (2012). Collegiality: Can it survive the corporate university? *Social Dynamics, 38*(1), 68–86. doi:10.1080/02533952.2012.700181

Wilson, R. (2010). For-profit colleges change higher education's landscape. *The Chronicle of Higher Education.* Retrieved from http://chronicle.com/article/For-Profit-Colleges-Chang e-/64012/

Wong, A. (2015, February 23). The downfall of for-profit colleges. *The Atlantic.* Retrieved from http://www.theatlantic.com/education/archive/2015/02/the-downfall-of-for-profit-colleges/385810/

CHAPTER 9

Post-Racial Higher Ed.: Implications of Mergers Between HBCUs and PWIs

Nia I. Cantey, Cara Robinson, and Michael Harris

Introduction

Debates continue to mount to clarify current social-structural problems, with racism as the backdrop. Racism, once discussed as an overt endemic in American society is now discussed as a problem of the past, in light of racial progress and the election of Barack Obama as president. However, racial advancement in America did not create a society devoid of racial tension, discrimination and prejudice. Arguably, the Obama era brings with it a new racism (Bonilla-Silva, 2014) which is a hidden phenomenon demonstrated "through laws, policies, and formal and informal practices" as a web of institutional racism (Miller & Garran, 2008, p. 63) which places marginalized groups (people of color, women, and low income populations) at a disadvantage on multiple levels (i.e., macro, mezzo, and micro). Miller and Garran (2008) identify nine types of institutional racism: residential, educational, employment, accumulation of wealth and upward mobility, environmental and health, mental health, and criminal justice, political, and media (p. 63). These forces are impacting higher education and are in fact creating a climate that makes conditions more conducive to bring a change. In this chapter we will discuss the forces that are currently impacting higher education, making the argument that these forces are in fact creating a climate that makes conditions more conducive to change. We will focus on examining institutional racism in higher education through an amalgam of critical race in higher education (Delgado, 1999; Ladson-Billings & Tate, 1995) and neoliberalism (Brentnall, 2013).

Specifically, this chapter explores the language and discourse surrounding proposed mergers between historically black colleges and universities (HBCUs) and predominately white institutions (PWIs) in contrast with their historical counterparts (see Harris-Stowe and UT/TSU mergers). We will examines the implications of these proposed mergers for HBCU students, faculty, and the Black community in their continued struggle for social, political, social control, and economic (Bonilla-Silva, 2014) equity. The analysis presented in this chapter will highlight the embedded mission to ostracize marginalized communities through macro (i.e., unequal funding); mezzo (i.e., inconsistent leadership); and micro (i.e., racial micro-aggressions, stereotyping) level forms.

Scrutiny of the educational system and policies is not exclusive to higher education as both public and private schools are equally securitized when addressing socio-political injustices. For instance in K-12, the premise of the No Child Left Behind Act of 2001 (NCLB) was to improve student achievement with the "goal of closing the academic achievement gap that exists between students living in poverty, student of color, and other students" (Cameron, 2011, p. 24). While well intended, NCLB shortcomings as a landmark in education reform failed to provide adequate funding and maintained inconsistency in standards at the federal, state, and local levels, particularly when ensuring all marginalized groups were achieving annual benchmarks (Howard & Reynolds, 2008, pp. 79–80).

This reality leads to similar inequities in higher education. For example, in California, two state schools (UC Berkeley and UCLA), non-Asian minority freshman enrollment dropped by almost half in the year following the ban on race as a factor in admissions (Miller & Garran, 2008; Bronner, 1998). This also includes discriminatory practices in screening measures for admissions on both undergraduate and graduate level programs which are structured by and for upper-middle-class whites (Feagin, 2010, p. 178). Additionally, decreased state funding and financial aid to colleges and universities have disproportionately impacted Blacks and Latinos (Brown et al., 2003) at alarming rates. These trends debunk the notion of a post-racial, color blind society when separate and unequal begets a new racism in the web of educational institutionalized racism, especially, higher education.

Like the new racism and the web of institutional racism, critical race theory (CRT) (Delgado, 1999) equally challenges a colorblind premise. In particular, scholars highlight critical race theory inequity within higher education (Ladson-Billings & Tate, 1995) to include racial micro-aggressions on college campuses and the multiple dimensions of institutional poverty (Taylor, 2006). Arguably proposed mergers in the 21st century are designed to eradicate HBCUs although the need for them remains relevant for educating black youth, supporting the black community, and providing opportunities for advancement in the workforce (Cantey, Bland, Mack, & Joy-Davis, 2011). While the mergers during the post-Brown era were in response to overt inequality the proposed mergers in the Obama era are in response to covert forms of inequality.

"The duality was clear, we really had two different education systems, and this was the plantation school."—Rita Geier

Historical Mergers

Landmark U.S. Supreme Court case Brown v. Board of Education in 1954 is the genesis of federal law ruling, separate educational facilities are inherently unequal, however, many other federal rulings shaped and continue to effect higher education to include, Morrill Act of 1862, the Hatch Act of 1887, the Second Morrill Act of 1890, Plessy v Ferguson, the Civil Rights Act of 1964, and the United States v. Fordice (1992). Along with federal rulings, state lawsuits equally attempted to dismantle racial discrimination in education prior to the 1954 Brown v. Board of Education ruling (see Murray v Maryland, 1936; Missouri ex rel Gaines v. Canada, 1938; Sweat v Painter, 1950; McLaurin v Oklahoma Board of Regents of Higher Education, 1950). Although these notable cases were instrumental in addressing inequality and racism within higher education, Brown v. Board of Education in 1954 was the catalyst for desegregation in public schools K-12, colleges, and universities.

In the post-Brown v. Board of Education era, one strategy employed to promote integration and diversity specific to colleges and universities was to force mergers between HBCUs and PWIs. These mergers took place in response to desegregation court cases and their associated policies. One notable merger occurred in St. Louis, Missouri between Harris Teachers College, a White teachers college and Stowe Teachers College, a college for Black teachers, to form Harris-Stowe State University.

Established in 1857 as a normal school by the St. Louis Public Schools, Harris Teachers College (PWI) was the first public teacher education institution. In 1906, the College offered in-service education for St. Louis white teachers. Thirty-three years after Harris Teachers College, the St. Louis Public Schools founded Stowe Teachers College (HBCU) in 1890, as a normal school for future black teachers of elementary schools in the city of St. Louis (www.hssu.edu). For the next sixty-four years these two colleges worked separately in segregated communities to educate and prepare future educators in St. Louis, until Missouri implemented a desegregation plan in response to Brown v. Board of Education and merged the two colleges in 1955 (Morris, 1999). This merger resulted in Harris Teachers College as the remaining institution. With this merger the identity and history of Stowe Teachers College as a contributing institution was omitted. This omission garnered several complaints from Stowe Teachers College alumni along with the St. Louis community. Consequently, the name was changed in 1979 to Harris-Stowe College to acknowledge the legacy of the black college; later the college became a university (www.hssu.edu).

Another noted merger involved Tennessee State University (TSU) and the University of Tennessee-Nashville (UTN). Tennessee State University was founded in 1912 as a historically black college and university. In 1968, the University of Tennessee-Nashville sought to expand and offer evening and weekend classes for UTN students in downtown Nashville two miles from an underfunded and neglected HBCU. The emergence of a newly constructed building for predominately white students illuminated a glaring de facto segregation in middle Tennessee. Subsequently, the Geier lawsuit was filed to halt completion of the new building contending that Tennessee was in violation of Title VI "obligation to provide equal access to education" (Vanderbilt Lawyer, 2012). The lawsuit was filed in 1968 and almost forty years later in 2001 a desegregation agreement; Consent Decree was reached. However during this thirty year emotionally and racially charged dispute the two universities in 1977 (TSU and UTN) merged resulting in Tennessee State University as the surviving institution (Bell, 1992) in response to the Geier lawsuit.

Both mergers occurred during an era when disparity and racial discrimination in academia were widespread and reflected the realities of the separate but equal legacy; a legacy which left Black institutions on an unequal foundation with inadequate funding, facilities, and access to opportunity. While both mergers sought to improve the separate educational systems the route to each one varied. Harris-Stowe College merger was initiated by St. Louis Board of Education and TSU-UTN's merger was prompted by a faculty from TSU. Faculty, Rita Geier posited, "we really had two different education systems, and this was the plantation school" (Vanderbilt Lawyer). Her concerns of separate and unequal facilities and funding between the two universities resulted in a long contentious and racially charged lawsuit. Although the era dictated the racial tension between the universities the outcomes of the both mergers also highlight a sharp distinction of how the racial tension is interpreted during a post-racial society. For instance, in St. Louis the university, albeit after protest, included the merging university's name to reflect a joint university merger whereas in Nashville the surviving university is TSU without any account of UTN. The failure to account for UTN as a part of the TSU-UTN merger suggests to some faculty the outcome was a takeover as opposed to a merger which omitted the legacy of UTN. This notion of a takeover in lieu of a merger is suggestive of proposed mergers in the 21st century between PWIs and HBCUs.

Mergers & the 21st Century

Over the past 30 years mergers between institutions of higher learning have become a progressively common strategy to reduce financial burdens and create broadened academic opportunities while increasing efficiencies (Harman & Harman, 2003). These mergers have been voluntary and involuntary and they have taken the form of consolidations (two similarly-sized institutions) and takeovers (merger between a small and large institution) (Koontz, 2009). Due to reduced financial capacities within state funding streams, many policymakers propose mergers as a means to decrease fiscal burdens and the duplication of services. Subsequently, mergers have proven to have significant impact on institutional culture, public dialogue and employee well-being. Most mergers face backlash from college/university employees, students and, often, the greater community (McBain, 2012; Wallace, 1998). While mergers and proposed mergers between all types of institutions of higher education have proven challenging, the historical legacy of mergers between PWIs and HBCUs as well as the ongoing role of race as a central factor in American social, political and economic life puts these mergers at the forefront of discussions surrounding public policy, political dialogue and the social-economic realities of higher education and American society.

Over the last decade several mergers between HBCUs and PWIs have been proposed. The most notable of these proposals included those to merge the University of New Orleans with Southern University (New Orleans) in Louisiana, reduce the role of HBCUs (e.g. Elizabeth City State University) within the larger North Carolina higher education system while merging UNC-Greensboro with North Carolina A&T, and, in Georgia, the proposal to merge Savannah State University with Armstrong Atlantic University as well as Albany State University with Darton College. Each of these proposed mergers failed to progress. The following section discusses the reasons behind the development of each of these proposed mergers, the reaction to the proposals and the subsequent decision not to merge institutions. First, a discussion of the current landscape for and debate surrounding HBCUs, their competitiveness and purpose is offered.

Debating the Modern HBCU

Over the past two decades HBCUs have come under increasing public scrutiny for financial, academic and social concerns. This public scrutiny is a key component of the debate surrounding HBCU and PWI mergers as it provides a context for the influencing role of these issues in shaping public dialogue and political discourse in the merger proposals.

Some in the public sphere question the social necessity of HBCUs. In their opinion, HBCUs were created during a time of segregation; therefore, they call into question the continued need for their presence. This sentiment can be seen in the dialogue surrounding proposed mergers as, often; proponents of mergers bring forward concerns related to their perception of HBCUs as exclusionary institutions primarily focused on serving one segment of society. These concerns are reflective of a larger stream of public discourse in which products, institutions and other services geared toward the black community are accused of being examples of reverse racism. While this argument has little factual legitimacy, the power of this argument is strong among many voting groups (e.g. Republicans). As a result, it cannot be dismissed as an influential contextual factor in the merger debates.

Another key contextual factor is the role limited finances play at HBCUs. Due to the overall financial strain on the nation's economy and higher education in particular, the fiscal efficiency and accountability of HBCUs is central to the discussion over mergers. The high profile fiscal problems and mismanagement of a few HBCUs (e.g. Delaware State University, Fisk University) has brought into question the overall fiscal status of HBCUs and is, therefore, a key component of the dialogue around merger proposals. HBCUs face a legacy of historical underfunding from state government, student bodies facing enhanced financial strain in the current American economy (which results in reduced revenue for institutions) and decreases in alumni and corporate giving. These counteracting realities have left many HBCUs in a state of economic crisis (Jennings, 2013). "[A]lmost every HBCU that has lost its accreditation has done so due to finances and double-digit default rates" (Jennings, 2013, para. 14). Moreover, there are, "vast inequities between [state] funding for flagship universities and HBCUs, based on funding per student." (Gasman, 2010; Minor, 2008) For example, in North Carolina,

> University of North Carolina-Chapel Hill and North Carolina State University are appropriated roughly $15,700 in state funding per student. In contrast, students at historically black North Carolina A & T

> and Fayetteville State University receive roughly $7,800 each in state appropriations. (Gasman, 2010, p. 2)

In addition, there is currently a pending court case filed against the State of Maryland arguing for equity in funding. Federal funding also poses a problem for HBCUs as, in 2005, federal research dollars were unevenly distributed amongst HBCUS. Close to 53% of federal dollars went to the just ten institutions (Gasman, 2010). Due to these funding inequities as well as historical racial inequities between the minority and majority communities in the United States, HBCUs find themselves serving student bodies who are in greater overall need of enhanced access to financing versus their counterparts at PWIs.

In addition to the financial strains faced by HBCUs and their student bodies, academic accountability and success is a common discussion point at the heart of proposed mergers. "On average, HBCU six-year graduation rates were 33.7% in 2011 compared with a national average of 58%" (Malveaux, 2013, para. 8). In recent years, many states (and the new proposal put forward by the Obama Administration to rank higher education institutions on a set of metrics) have passed higher education policies focused on a set of performance measures related to graduation, retention and academic achievement. These policies, however, do little to take into account the aforementioned differences between the student bodies served at HBCUs and, with many of the policies tied to funding, may serve to actually further marginalize HBCUs and their students. Discussions surrounding academic success without concurrent discussions about inequitable funding, societal inequality and the importance of HBCUs as historical facets of American society do little to actually improve student success. These discussions do serve, however, to promote the idea that HBCUs require some assistance from PWIS through new policies and restructuring, including institutional mergers. These three factors—the "need" for HBCUs in modern society, the financial condition and capacity of HBCUs, and the academic success of HBCU students—are all integral parts of the debates surrounding the proposed mergers discussed below.

University of New Orleans and Southern University (New Orleans)

On January 18, 2011, Louisiana Governor Bobby Jindal (R) asked the Louisiana Board of Regents to review the potential of a proposed merger between the PWI University of New Orleans (UNO) and the New Orleans branch of the HBCU Southern University (Southern). The idea was to have both institutions leave their affiliated systems (UNO in the Louisiana State University system and Southern in the Southern University system) to join the, predominantly white, University of Louisiana system. Despite a 2006 study opposing the merger of the two institutions, Governor Jindal cited low enrollments, low graduation rates and financial strains as the key reasons behind the proposed merger.

> The governor said that UNO's six-year graduation rate is 21 percent, while SUNO's rate is 5 percent, although some records indicate that the latter figure has gone up a bit recently. Since 2005, when many people left New Orleans and never came back, UNO has seen its enrollment drop by 32 percent, to 11,700. SUNO's enrollment has fallen by 14 percent, to 3,100. (Jaschik, 2011, para. 6)

It is important to note that the lasting effects of Hurricane Katrina had significantly impacted the student body and structural integrity of both institutions, "Both neighboring universities were flooded in 2005 when levees were breached in the aftermath of Hurricane Katrina. They have struggled for years to regain their pre-Katrina enrollments and to boost dismal graduation rates" (Mangan, 2011, para. 4). The proposal was met immediately with skepticism and anger as stakeholders from both institutions saw the merger as an affront to the history and status of their respective universities.

As of 2011, the University of New Orleans (a member of the Louisiana State University system) had an enrollment that was 57% white and 17% black while Southern University's (New Orleans) enrollment was 96% black. This disparity in enrollment is a contributing factor to the stakeholder challenges that followed the proposal. From the beginning, the merger debate was racially charged. Governor Jindal did little to head off this type of reaction as he failed to seek adequate minority representation on the TBR governing board nor did he make outreach to key leaders from Southern prior to the proposal (Grace, 2011). Governor Jindal actually did little to address the issue of race as a factor in the merger. As a result of the former, in February 2011, seven students from Southern filed a lawsuit to halt the study of the merger based on grounds that the racial diversity of the governing body did not reflect Louisiana's diversity.[1] Between January and May 2011, numerous public meetings were held to address the merger proposal. Opponents cited the lack of awareness surrounding the role of HBCUs in supporting black students in achieving academic success, the unfairness of graduate assessments which do not take into account transfer graduates and the legacy of historical and post-Katrina underfunding of Southern. Proponents continued to focus on the improved efficiencies and academic opportunities that the merged institution would provide for both student bodies. Ultimately the merger proposal was pulled from consideration in the Louisiana legislature due to a variety of public pressure and strong resistance from the legislature's Black Caucus. The Republican House Speaker stated that it was a "sad day for education" when he had to pull the bill while Governor Jindal stated, "We continue to believe the status quo for students in New Orleans is unacceptable and we're not going to give up on our fight to improve educational opportunities" (The Louisiana Weekly, 2011, para. 7).

North Carolina

In 2013, Governor Pat McCrory proposed $135 million in cuts to North Carolina's public higher education system. Supporters of the Governor's plan have publicly stated that there needs to be a reduction in the number of institutions currently in the state system (sixteen). Senator Pete Brunstetter, co-chairman of the Senate Appropriations Committee, said, "I think our members definitely envision that there could be some consolidation between campuses, and we might need to go from 16 down to 15, 14, something like that." (Browder, 2013, para. 5) This proposal has definitely raised concerns regarding the status of North Carolina's five public HBCUS—Elizabeth City State University, North Carolina Central University, Fayetteville State University, North Carolina A&T, and Winston-Salem State University. In a preemptive move, these five institutions (in partnership with the six private North Carolina HBCUs) have called upon the Governor to provide more resources to HBCUs statewide.

Georgia

In 2008, Chair of the State's Higher Education Committee, Georgia Representative Seth Harp, proposed merging two HBCUs with geographically local PWIs: Savannah State University with Armstrong Atlantic University and Albany State University with Darton College. In a December 4, 2008 interview with National Public Radio, Harp cited the national economic slowdown (Georgia's higher education system, at the time of the interview, already faced a six percent cut), the need to emphasize desegregation and the fiscal inefficiencies of two geographically co-located institutions as reasons for his proposal. Harp also stressed that the proposal was to maintain the HBCU as the surviving institution in the mergers not the PWIs.

While Harp's proposal ultimately failed to gain support with the Georgia Board of Regents, the debate surrounding it had common elements with the debates in other states—financial efficiencies, academic success and the historical legacy of HBCUs. For example, Senator Bill Cowsert, co-Chair of the Higher Education Committee did not support the proposal and stated, "I think the HBCUs offer a unique educational opportunity and they are greatly valued by their community" (Sabry, 2009, section 3). The Georgia debate, and Seth Harp, did emphasize another aspect of the debate, however, the role of segregation in the founding and continued operation of HBCUs. Harp argued that Savannah State and Albany State were formed as black institutions and it was, therefore, against desegregation orders to maintain their status as such.

Conclusion

Proposed mergers in the 21st century between HBCUs and PWIs have been unsuccessful. They have, however, touched upon many aspects of American society in the supposed post-racial era. As the cases in Louisiana, North Carolina and Georgia demonstrate there is still a significant disconnect between research showing the importance of HBCUs to black students and their unique needs and policymakers. In addition, public debates have shown that discussions surrounding the performance and funding of HBCUs has not addressed historical or modern (e.g. Hurricane Katrina) legacies contributing to cited factors in proposed mergers. Finally, as in Georgia, there is clearly uneasiness about the status of HBCUs as an institution started for African-Americans. While a variety of factors throughout the merger debates were given, race played a central role in the reaction and discussion in the public sphere. This can be captured by the famous lines of the English poet Matthew Arnold in describing the birth of the modern era: "Wandering between two worlds, one dead the other powerless to be born." The use the birth and death metaphor, a metaphor that is not only appropriate but helps to explain the emotional intensity of our situation. Institutions of higher education are organic artifacts. They live and grow and evolve as a result of the human interactions that take place within them. We use human metaphors to talk about institutions when we consider elements like growth or health of the institution. For this reason we cannot discount the human element in this enterprise for at the end of the day, education and leadership are all about people and relationships.

Implications

Critical Race Theory (CRT) seeks to study the role of race in all elements of society (e.g. social relations, economics, history) and to change the factors which contribute to racism as a key foundational driver within society (Delgado & Stefancic, 2001). CRT scholars established a framework for its use in higher education in the late 1990s. This framework is used to analyze the role of mergers in higher education historically in the "post-racial" context.

The centrality of race and racism in society: The experiences of those who were part of the historical institutional mergers and the reactions of stakeholders to the proposed mergers all clearly demonstrate the central role of race in policymaking, public discussion and final decision-making. Two approaches were utilized by key policy figures in the proposed mergers. Governor Jindal attempted to ignore race as a factor and Representative Seth Harp in Georgia made race one of the key factors. Both, however, failed to note the important role HBCUs play in the black community or how financial realities and race are inextricably tied in American society despite financial concerns playing the major role in merger proposal dialogue.

While policymakers largely avoided race in modern merger discussions, those with direct merger experiences from historical mergers note the role race played post-merger. Racial factors played a substantial role in post-merger administrative and faculty relations. One black faculty member noted that the merger actually contributed to a significant decline in campus pride and a reshaping of identity among black faculty and students. Despite the integration of two campuses, many black faculty members felt the PWI had direct control over finances and faculty decision-making. At the same time, a white faculty member felt that, over time, white faculty members were kept out of important administrative positions. Modern political discussion surrounding mergers have neglected to discuss the short and long-term role race plays in institutional culture and politics. Subsequently, the political sphere's focus on finances does not even acknowledge the role race plays in finances.

The challenge to dominant ideology: The focus on finances as the main factor in proposed mergers does little to nothing to challenge the existing structure of American society. This structure is one that benefits majority groups at the expense of minority groups and is a direct cause of many conditions afflicting HBCUs in the modern context. The historical benefit of the HBCU for black students has been to create a safe educational experience without the traditional constraints of mainstream society with the concurrent promotion of the black community and self-pride.

In public discussions surrounding mergers it has been found that many whites find this historical benefit offensive. According to this strain of thought, the very need for HBCUs was thrown out with desegregation. Despite the continuing segregation found in America's housing, educational and financial markets the dialogue of the offensive HBCU holds strong. The HBCU itself poses a challenge to the dominant ideology.

The centrality of experiential knowledge: The experience of African-Americans is a central component in the examination of HBCU-PWI mergers. Often, in the public domain, the experiences of minorities are subjugated to that of the majority population. In the public discussion surrounding the proposed mergers the African-American reaction to the proposals are presented as race-based and inflammatory. For example, in reviewing stories regarding the Louisiana merger, the public meetings held by members of the black community were presented as ignoring financial and academic concerns at the expense of race. CRT asserts that race as a central component of society and the experiences of minorities is an essential part of such discussions and should not be dismissed simply because the majority population deems it as an unnecessary factor.

Note

1 On February 24, 2011, a judge ruled against the student lawsuit, allowing the study to proceed.

Work Cited

Bell. D. (1992). *Faces at the bottom of the well: The permanence of racism.* New York, NY: Basic Books.

Bonilla-Silva, E. (2014). *Racism without racists: Color-blind racism and the persistence of racial inequality in America* (4th ed.). Lanham, MD: Rowman and Littlefield Publishers.

Brentnall, H. (2013, July 28). Neoliberalism and the commercialization of higher education. *The International.* Retrieved from http://www.theinternational.org/articles/448-neoliberalism-and-the-commercialization-o

Bronner, E. (1998, April 1). Black and Hispanic admissions off sharply at University of California. *New York Times*, A1.

Browder, C. (2013, March 21). UNC system could lose campuses. *WRAL.com.* Retrieved from http://www.wral.com/unc-system-could-lose-campuses/12252716/

Brown, J. K., Carnoy, M., Currie, E., Duster, T., Oppenheimer, D. B., Shultz, M. M., & Wellman, D. (2003). *White-washing race: The myth of a color-blind society.* Berkeley, CA: University of California Press.

Cameron, M. L. (2011). *No child left behind: A review from a critical race theory lens.* University of Minnesota. Published Dissertation. Retrieved from http://conservancy.umn.edu/bitstream/110069/1/Cameron_umn_0130E_11951.pdf

Cantey, N., Bland, R., Mack, L., & Joy-Davis, D. (2011). Historically black colleges and universities: Sustaining a culture of excellence in the twenty-first century. *Journal of African American Studies.* DOI: 10.1007/s12111-011-9191-0

Delgado, R. (1999). *Critical race theory: The cutting edge* (2nd ed.). Philadelphia, PA: Temple University Press.

Delgado, R., & Stefancic, J. (2001). *Critical race theory: An introduction.* New York, NY: New York University Press.

Feagin, J. R. (2010). *Racist America: Roots, current realities, and future reparations.* New York, NY: Routledge.

Gasman, M. (2010). Comprehensive funding approaches for historically black colleges and universities. *University of Pennsylvania Graduate School of Education.* Policy Brief, Retrieved from http://www.gse.upenn.edu/pdf/gasman/FundingApproachesHBCUs.pdf

Grace, S. (2011, January 30). Jindal takes strategic aim at UNO and SUNO. *The Times-Picayune.* Retrieved from http://www.nola.com/opinions/index.ssf/2011/01/jindal_takes_strategic_aim_at.html

Harman, G., & Harman, K. (2003). Institutional mergers in higher education: Lessons from international experience. *Tertiary Education and Management, 9*(1), 29–44.

Howard, T., & Reynolds, R. (2008). Examining parent involvement in reversing the underachievement of African American students in middle-class schools. *Educational Foundations, (22)*1–2 Winter-Spring, 79–98.

Jaschik, S. (2011, January 19). Another black college merger is proposed. *Inside Higher Ed.* Retrieved from http://www.insidehighered.com/news/2011/01/19/louisiana_governor_wants_to_merge_black_and_white_colleges_in_new_orleans

Jennings, R. (2013, January 6). Sustaining the future of HBCUs. *Diverse Issues in Higher Education.* Retrieved from http://diverseeducation.com/article/50503/#

Koontz, K. (2009, May). The impact of mergers in higher education on employees and organizational culture. Master's Thesis. Retrieved from http://www2.uwstout.edu/content/lib/thesis/2009/2009koontzk.pdf

Ladson-Billings, G., & Tate, W. (1995). Toward a critical race theory of education. *Teachers College Record, 97*(1), 47–68.

The Louisiana Weekly. (2011, May 23). SUNO/UNO merger bills die, pulled before vote. *The Louisiana Weekly.* Retrieved from http://www.louisianaweekly.com/sunouno-merger-bills-die-pulled-before-vote/

Malveaux, J. (2013, September 2013). Obama metrics would hurt historically black colleges. *USA Today.* Retrieved from http://www.usatoday.com/story/opinion/2013/09/10/obama-college-plan-hbcus-column/2795871/

Mangan, K. (2011, May 18). Proposed merger of 2 New Orleans universities is called off. *The Chronicle of Higher Education.* Retrieved from http://chronicle.com/article/Proposed-Merger-of-2New/127583/

McBain, L. (2012, May). College and university mergers: An update on recent trends. *American Association of State Colleges and Universities.* Retrieved from http://www.aascu.org/policy/publications/policymatters/2012/collegemergersupdate.pdf

Miller, J., & Garran, A. M. (2008). *Racism in the United States: Implications for the helping professions.* Portland, OR: Brooks/Cole Cengage Learning.

Minor, J. T. (2008). *Contemporary HBCUs: Considering institutional capacity and state priorities. A research report.* Michigan State University, College of Education, Department of Educational Administration. East Lansing, MI. Retrieved from http://steinhardt.nyu.edu/scmsAdmin/uploads/002/151/MINOR_Contemporary_HBCU_Report_2008.pdf

National Public Radio. (2008, December 4). Lawmaker suggests HBCU, majority school merger. *National Public Radio podcast.* Podcast retrieved from http://www.npr.org/templates/story/story.php?storyId=97802436

Sabry, M. (2009, January 30). HBCUs drawing scrutiny. *Inside Higher Ed.* Retrieved from http://www.insidehighered.com/news/2009/01/30/hbcu

Taylor, K. A. (2006). Poverty's multiple dimensions. *Journal of Educational Controversy.* Retrieved from http://www.wce.wwu.edu/resources/cep/ejournal/v004n001/a002.shtml

Wallace, S. (1998). In search of vision and values: The Minnesota higher education merger. *New Directions for Community Colleges,* Vol. 1998 (102), 5–17.

CHAPTER 10

Managing Anger and Mistrust in the Academy

Five Steps for Engagement

Paul Watkins

As a school administrator making a career shift to higher education, I was struck with how parents continued to hover over their children. Parents found letting go difficult. Not recognizing the young adult their child had become produced blind spots not easily overcome.

University executives are no less immune than school administrators from the protective wrath of parents stung by the missteps of their young. Confronted with the pressures of anger, anxiety, and emotion how can university registrars, deans, directors or student affairs deal effectively with anger? How can they make informed, ethical decisions and effectively resolve conflict under trying conditions? How can they balance privileged power with multi-racial and multi-cultural mistrust? Most importantly, how can they strengthen university-home relations to minimize the destructive influence that anger and mistrust bring to the university?

These are difficult questions to answer, but I believe that these five strategies, associated with the negotiating process, offer some insight. Projecting confidence, grounding expectations, focusing response with inquiry, and creating space for solutions all contribute to the de-escalation of mistrust and anger.

Step One: Demonstrate Confidence

Recent studies demonstrating the complex workings of our brain suggest that under unusual pressure emotions take over the reasonable pre frontal lobes just behind our forehead and activate the more primal inner cortex. Once confronted with anger, calm and precise thinking must overcome the chaos of emotions in voice and posture. Daniel Goleman in his book, *Working With Emotional Intelligence,* describes this as "emotional competence." As a result, emotional competence manages the disruptive emotions and impulses, maintaining the confidence found in reason and good judgment.

Confidence does not mean the administrator digs in for a fight. Instead, give angry parents credibility by hearing them out. Saying such things as "I'm not sitting here and listening to you shout," "Anger will get us no where," or "Its in both out interests to calm down" may seem reasonable, but it may be more

helpful allowing a full voice to grievance. Consider a full-throated injustice like landing a big fish. You allow the frustration to play out and exhaustion to set in before landing a suitable agreement.
The burden of proof can now turn to the parent: "you may have a point, and I might be wrong. Let's examine the facts together." Compare this position with: "No, I'm sorry your facts are all wrong and I can prove it." Even if you have the proof at hand, you won't win respect and from the parent's point of view you haven't won the argument.

Step Two: Establish Ground Rules

A second strategy for dealing with difficult parents is to establish ground rules that provide a nonthreatening environment conducive to reasonable discussion.

Home Court Advantage. University administrators have an advantage because most meetings are held on their turf. This gives them the authority to set rules of conduct that parents will usually accept. In some instances barriers of color, gender, and power must be crossed. White, male, administrators must be sensitive to the fact they could be looking at a situation through a lens of privilege. While these barriers require a wider conversation White male administrators must understand the positionality of color and/or gender in the conversation. It is critical to understand that you are endowed with privilege and power. As a result people of another color or gender may respond to you differently. It is critical to respect race, gender, and heritage regardless the level of emotion. Talking down to or a cynical challenge to another's point of view only exacerbates mistrust regardless of turf.

Setting Time Limits. When both parties know they have a limited time to resolve their differences, they work harder to get directly at the issues. But be careful about imposing arbitrary time constraints. They can keep important information and feelings from being heard.

Rules of Conduct. Raised voices and profanity must be restricted if a conference is to be constructive. The administrator has the right to set limits to threats of harm or repeated profanity. "I have no intention of using profanity toward you and I would ask that courtesy of you" is a reasonable expectation of any meaningful dialogue.

Arranging Furniture. The seating for confronting anger and mistrust can represent symbols of interest and empathy. A desk between the administrator and the aggrieved presents an unspoken divide, which is unnecessary. Sitting at a round table puts everyone at a common place. Siting with a parent or parents without any barriers presents an equal footing and openness to issues.

Step Three: Keep Focused

During difficult conversations, particularly when race or cultural issues are at stake, the administrator must stay engaged and remain emotionally, intellectually, and socially involved with the conversation. Singleton and Linton (2006) warn that you cannot allow the "heart and mind to 'check out' of the conversation." Administrators, particularly white administrators, are conditioned to avoid talking about race. People of color, according to Singleton and Curtis are very aware of and talk often about race. University leaders must be aware of the natural inclination to lean back from issues of color. Instead, lean into the conversation and create space for the conversation around equity, privilege, and power to unfold.

Identifying and assessing the source of anger aids in understanding the parent's expectations, and develop a clear picture of possible outcomes. If both heart and mind are in the conversation maintaining a consistent focus is almost guaranteed regardless of demands and pressures.

Step Four: Ask Questions

"When two partners agree, one of them is not necessary." Dealing with difficult parents brings truth to this often used conundrum above. While conversations of disagreement are uncomfortable, such conversations provide a chance to learn and improve if the right questions are asked. Asking questions unearth and clarify issues and feelings. Because parents are often threatened by hard facts, whenever possible put facts into the form of questions. For example, instead of making a statement like, "Here are the facts I have gathered. First ..." you might turn it into a less intimidating question, "Could I ask a couple of questions and see if the facts I have been given are correct?" Such an approach gives parents an opportunity to clarify, refute, or accept the facts presented.

Questions promote engagement and help parent and administrator learn from one another about what can be accomplished. Engaging questions help move the conversation forward, clarify issues, and collect information that may spotlight solutions. Here are a few examples of questions, which can help maintain momentum.

Questions Probing for More Evidence. These questions help to clarify statements of fact the seem unrelated to the issues of disagreement. The facts they question may be erroneous or unsupported. Probing questions should be phrase as a simple request and not stated as a challenge to anyone's intelligence. Some examples might include: How do you know that? How did come by that information? If some one doubted that information, what would be your interpretation?

Questions Clarifying Assertions or Assumptions. Often emotion prompts one to confuse their thinking and confuse the issues. We saw earlier how the primal cortex may take over from the more reasoned frontal lobe when someone feels threatened. Clarifying question are an invitation for one to convey meaning. Here are some examples: Could that be put another way? Do you have an example of what you are saying? I'm still unclear. Can you give me another example?

Questions That Summarize and Draw Synthesis. Finally a valuable type of question is the one that invites the person to summarize or synthesize the issues as they have been discussed. These questions call on participants to identify important ideas, and think about them in ways that may lead to a solution both parties can live with. Summarizing and synthesizing questions may sound like these: What do you see remains unresolved about ...? Based on our discussion, what do we (not you) need to understand better? Or, "What would you like to see happen now?"

Skill in mixing the different question alters the pace and direction of the conversation, keeping both parties alert and engaged. Mixing questions offers only half of the equation. Listening with empathy demonstrates value in what the other person is saying. Listening intently boosts an understanding for the other person's point of view and the degree of commitment to his or her argument.

Step Five: Buy a Little Time

When anger builds, it becomes difficult to understand a problem well enough to make any substantive decisions that serve either side. Emotion can often boil over into personal attacks, ignoring the legitimate focus of concern. At these moments, creating timely pauses in the discussion can help.

Silence is a powerful tool in negotiating a difficult conference, particularly when responding to an angry attack or an unreasonable proposal. Silence provides the precious time needed to avoid making quick response without thinking it through. By simply not responding to an angry outburst, you can force parents to be more reasonable in stating their case.

People often feel uncomfortable with silence, particularly if they have doubts about the strength of their position. If questions are posed for which there are insufficient answers, a few moments of silence may compel parents to break the stillness either by answering their own question or rephrasing it. Another method for slowing down the pace of a difficult conference is to take notes. By looking up from your legal pad and asking softly, "I'm sorry, could you repeat that form me? I want to be sure I have down correctly" you not only buy time, but demonstrate that the parents' concerns are important enough to be accurately recorded. Another time-buying technique is to invite a third party unrelated to the issue, perhaps a secretary, to sit in on the conference. Having another person present gives the occasional break from talking, allowing time for reflection with a fresh perspective.

Perhaps the most important aspect of buying time is perspective. In the midst of a losing streak Aaron Rodgers, Green Bay's quarterback, told fans in a press conference to R-E-L-A-X. Later that 2014 season Green Bay made the National League final playoff game. His comments slowed things down and allowed perspective for critics, fans, and the team. The same applies here. This chapter identifies the softer skills of managing conflict and provides tools to navigate a difficult conversation (Confidence, focus, inquiry). These tools are important in leveraging a reasonable outcome to anger and emotion. Creating space from emotion allows time to assess the tools and how they are applied.

The challenge for university administrators in managing anger from others is not to suppress conflict, but to minimize its destructive nature. Transform it into a positive creative force for change. By managing conflict, the discussion can move forward toward a collaborative understanding of issues and develop creative solutions to difficult problems.

Work Cited

Goleman, D. (1999). *Working with emotional intelligence.* New York, NY: Bantam Books.

Singleton, G. E., & Linton, C. (2006). *A field guide for achieving equity in schools: Courageous conversations about race.* Thousand Oaks, CA: Corwin Press.

CHAPTER 11

Creating Emotionally Intelligent Global Leaders

Kathy L. Guthrie and Tessly A. Dieguez

Emotional intelligence is a critical concept in leadership (Goleman, 1999); however, is it applicable to different cultural contexts beyond Western societies? This chapter argues that when examining specific emotional intelligence competencies, most notably empathy, adaptability, and organizational awareness, it can lead to international leadership effectiveness. This chapter explores using emotional intelligence competencies to teach global leader efficacy, which is critical in the 21st century.

The need and urgency of leadership development in higher education has continued to grow over recent years. Sometimes missing from this discussion is the idea of how leadership constructs, programs, and curricula can be transferred to an international context. According to Jokinen (2005), "The dynamics, complexity, and diversity now characteristic of the global environment are diffusing into the domestic environment, making increasing demands on management and leadership competencies at all organizational levels" (p. 199). Much of the literature frequently interchanges the terms "leadership" and "management" (Jokinen, 2005). For the purpose of this chapter we refer to leadership as a process separate from management. Kellerman (2012) states there are over 1,500 definitions and 40 models of leadership. Leadership, as a social construct, holds different meanings to different people. Rost (1993) specifically defined leadership as, "an influence relationship among leaders and followers who intend real changes that reflect their mutual purposes" (p. 102). This definition will serve as the foundation for this chapter.

Emotional intelligence is one of the many conceptualizations used to teach practices of leading and leadership. Goleman, Boyatzis, and McKee (2002) compiled an overview of specific competencies that can be honed in the development of emotional intelligence; however, it is sometimes unclear how emotional intelligence can be viewed in an international context. Some critics of leadership research, most notably Earley and Ang (2003) and Hofstede (1980) argue much of the research on emotional intelligence does not account for cultural differences. According to Den Hartog, House, Hanges, and Ruiz-Quintanilla (1999), leadership research is influenced by the culture in which it is conducted.

Earley and Ang (2003) propose the concept of cultural intelligence, a separate construct from emotional intelligence.

When developing global leaders, is emotional intelligence enough for effective leadership in an international context, or is the separate construct of cultural intelligence also necessary? This question needs to be asked when creating leadership development programs for students to be able to lead globally. While it is true that cultural contexts are often overlooked in common leadership pedagogies, the development of certain emotional intelligence competencies advocated by Goleman et al. (2002), most notably empathy, adaptability, and organizational awareness, will lead to the same results cultural intelligence tries to achieve. We will work to explain how the specific emotional intelligence competencies provide similar leadership lessons as those of cultural intelligence.

Emotional and Cultural Intelligence

Intelligence refers to the mind's ability and capacity to understand and learn (Gardner, 2006). Intelligence is essentially a computational capacity, the ability to process information. Gardner (1999) discusses how one has multiple intelligences including linguistic, mathematical, musical, kinesthetic, spatial, naturalist, intrapersonal, interpersonal, and existential. Goleman (1999) furthers Gardner's multiple intelligences theory to include emotional intelligence. Boyatzis, Goleman, and Rhee (1999) and Goleman et al. (2002) placed the behaviors of Emotional Intelligence into four overall clusters: (a) emotional self-awareness (recognizing one's emotions); (b) emotional self-management (regulating one's emotions); (c) social awareness (recognizing emotions of others); and (d) relationship management (maintaining emotional ties to others). Researchers have explored emotional intelligence and how it relates to student success and development in higher education (Jaeger & Eagan, 2007; Pritchard & Wilson, 2003); however, a better understanding of the relationship of cultural competencies and emotional intelligence is needed.

Earley and Ang (2003) developed the idea of cultural intelligence as "a person's ability to adapt effectively to new cultural contexts" (p. 59). They divide cultural intelligence into four different components—meta-cognitive, cognitive, motivational, and behavioral (Ang & Van Dyne, 2008; Earley & Ang, 2003). Like Goleman's emotional intelligence competencies, these components are hierarchical (Lee & Templer, 2003). The meta-cognitive component refers to one's level of awareness during intercultural interactions (Ang & Van Dyne). The cognitive component refers to culture-specific skills and knowledge (Earley & Ang), motivational component refers to one's level of desire to engage in other cultures, and behavioral component refers to the "capability to actually engage in behaviors that are adaptive" (Earley & Ang, p. 10).

Earley and Ang (2003) adamantly point out that cultural intelligence is a construct separate from emotional intelligence, and was developed because emotional intelligence was unable to stand on its own when examined with regards to cultural differences. They write, "Unlike social and emotional intelligence researchers, we are concerned with these capabilities with regard to a new cultural environment that is unfamiliar to a person" (p. 68). Cultural intelligence is an important addition to the conversation, especially when cultural context is taken into consideration.

Criticisms of Emotional Intelligence

Leadership research has been criticized for being ethnocentric (Blunt & Jones, 1996; Earley & Ang, 2003). Some (Elenkov & Pimentel, 2008; Jordan, Ashton-James, & Ashkanasy, 2013) have specifically criticized the construct of emotional intelligence. As mentioned before, one of the most common criticisms is that emotional intelligence does not account for cultural differences. Hofstede's (1980) model of Cultural Dimensions provides one of the most well-known conceptualizations of cultural differences. Hofstede (1980) argues that cultural differences are based on the dimensions of power distance, uncertainty avoidance, individualism-collectivism, and masculinity-femininity. Alon and Higgins

(2005) retool these dimensions into the more palatable "equality/hierarchy, direct/indirect, individual/group, task/relationship, and risk/certainty" (p. 508). Differences in cultural dimensions can lead to misunderstandings in the practice of leadership (Hofstede, 1980).

Goleman's (1999) research in particular has been the target of some heated criticism. Jordan et al. (2013) argue that Goleman supports emotional intelligence as a "magic bullet" (p. 201) for effective leadership, and that his claims are "extravagant" (p. 204). Murphy and Sideman (2013) believe the characteristics of Goleman's conceptualization of emotional intelligence are in line with what they consider a fad, which emerges suddenly, attracts fanatical believers who do not use critical thinking, presents itself as a solution to a myriad of problems, leads to controversy, and collapses easily (p. 283).

Leadership versus Management

The criticisms surrounding emotional intelligence are not without merit. However, upon further investigation, many of the arguments used against emotional intelligence can be challenged. Many of the criticisms surrounding emotional intelligence and leadership research in general use the terms "leadership" and "management" interchangeably (Blunt & Jones, 1996; Hofstede, 1980). Blunt and Jones argue against many Western managerial competencies, such as "survival of the fittest", and describe "the thrusting, demanding, driven creature of the Western model" (pp. 15–17). However, it seems safe to say that this hypothetical creature has not honed its emotional intelligence competencies. House (1995, cited in Den Hartog et al., 1999) writes:

> Almost all prevailing theories of leadership and most empirical evidence is North American in character, that is, "individualistic rather than collectivistic … stated in terms of individual rather than group incentives; stressing follower responsibilities rather than rights; assuming hedonistic rather than altruistic motivation, and assuming centrality of work and democratic value orientation." (pp. 227–228)

However, these concepts are not in line with progressive leadership research or Goleman's (1999) conceptualization of emotional intelligence.

Emotional Intelligence Competencies

Criticisms of emotional intelligence often lack a thorough review of emotional intelligence competencies outlined by Goleman (1999) and Goleman et al. (2002), namely empathy, adaptability, and organizational awareness. Countless examples of emotional intelligence's "shortcomings" are, upon further examination, simply a result of a lack of cultivation of these three specific competencies. Jordan et al.'s (2013) argument that Goleman (1999) uses emotional intelligence as a "magic bullet" (p. 201) is an oversimplification. While the concept of emotional intelligence may seem simple in theory, actually cultivating its competencies are significantly more difficult. Developing emotional intelligence is challenging because it requires the very thing you are trying to develop. A high level of self-awareness and management is needed to develop these competencies. Finally, much research that focuses on skills, abilities, and behaviors related to international leadership effectiveness mirror these three competencies of empathy, adaptability, and organizational awareness.

Empathy

Goleman et al. (2002) writes, "Empathy makes a leader able to get along well with people of diverse backgrounds or from other cultures" (p. 255). Two different measures of global leadership competencies Jokinen (2005) discusses cite "empathy" (pp. 202, 204) and "cultural sensitivity" (p. 203). The Global Leadership and Organizational Behavior Effectiveness (GLOBE) research program is a long-term research program designed to conceptualize, operationalize, test, and validate a cross-level integrated theory of the relationship between culture and societal, organizational, and leadership effectiveness (House, Hanges, Javidan, Dorfman, & Gupta,, 2004). A team of 160 scholars worked together since 1994 to study societal culture, organizational culture, and attributes of effective leadership in 62 cultures. In the GLOBE study, skilled communication and encouragement were found to be universally endorsed (Den Hartog et al., 1999). The ability to empathize is necessary for both of these attributes. Earley and Ang (2003) write, "There are anecdotal cases (many of them) of individuals who show great empathy within their own culture—seemingly high on 'emotional intelligence' and other forms of social intelligence—yet they fail to adjust to new cultures adequately" (Earley & Ang, p. 4). This argument demonstrates a misunderstanding of the concept of empathy, which, by Goleman's definition, includes understanding of other cultures. Focusing on being a skilled communicator, both verbally and non-verbally, and encouraging others, is critical for empathy across cultures.

Adaptability

Criticisms of emotional intelligence often have to do with adaptability as well. According to Goleman et al. (2002), people with well-developed adaptability are flexible and able to adjust to change well. Some of the characteristics of varying measures of global leadership competencies that Jokinen (2005) discusses include "role flexibility" (p. 202), "managing adaptability" (p. 202), "openness to experience" (p. 203), and "ability to change leadership style based on the situation" (p. 203). Earley and Ang (2003) describe the behavioral component of cultural intelligence as the "capability to actually engage in behaviors that are adaptive" (p. 10). This is without a doubt in line with Goleman, Boyatzis, and McKee's idea of adaptability. Earley and Ang (2003) also argue that self-awareness isn't enough for cultural intelligence, that "a certain level of cognitive flexibility is critical … since cultural situations require a constant reshaping and adaptation of self-concept to understand a new setting" (p. 71). To counter their point, Goleman et al. does not argue that self-awareness is the only competency necessary for emotional intelligence—adaptability is key as well.

Organizational Awareness

Just as with empathy and adaptability, criticisms of emotional intelligence often cry out for the very things offered by the organizational awareness competency. Organizational awareness understanding both the organization and its leaders regarding current abilities, capacity, and results. Earley and Ang (2003) describe "knowledge of social environment" (p. 68) as a key part of the cognitive element of cultural intelligence. Universally desired characteristics in the GLOBE study included "informed" and "motive arouser" (Den Hartog et al., 1999, p. 239). These are related to organization awareness. Characteristics of varying measures of global leadership competencies Jokinen (2005) discusses that are in line with organizational awareness include "curiosity and concern about context" (p. 202), "seeing the big picture" (p. 207), and "knowledge of the company's worldwide business structure" (p. 203). Again, these concepts are directly related to organizational awareness.

Emotional Intelligence Competencies and Functioning in Other Cultures

The cultivation and development of empathy, adaptability, and organizational awareness would have a positive effect on functioning in other cultures because of a greater understanding of context. Empathy, or the attempt to understand the backgrounds and contexts of where people of other cultures are coming from, would positively enhance intercultural interactions. For example, if an American expatriate living in Japan empathized with the high power distance culture there (Hofstede, 1980), he or she would feel more comfortable with a rigidly hierarchical work environment structure. Another example would be understanding Spain's traditional working hours of 10–12 am and then 4–7 pm and why culturally that is important.

Adaptability, or the ability to adjust to whatever situation someone is thrown into, would also positively affect cultural interactions. For example, if a university career counselor made an effort to understand the collectivistic nature of Hispanic cultures, he or she may adjust his or her advising style so as to not pass judgment on a student with a strong cultural background for not wanting to detach from his or her family unit.

Organizational awareness, or knowledge about another culture, also increases leadership efficacy in other cultures. For example, if someone working in the Netherlands is aware of the direct nature of Dutch culture, he or she may be less offended by what may seem like harsh feedback from his or her perspective. Likewise, understanding British culture of being more passive is worth noting. While further research is needed on this topic, it is plausible that well-developed empathy, adaptability, and organizational awareness would have a positive impact on leadership effectiveness in different cultures.

Discussion

Earley and Ang (2003) write, "Emotional intelligence presumes a degree of familiarity with culture and content that may not exist" (p. 8). Perhaps this is true for some aspects and applications of emotional intelligence, however, the competencies of empathy, adaptability, and organizational awareness do not presume these things. In Earley and Ang's review of emotional intelligence, empathy is the only competency mentioned. Various researchers have determined that empathy, respect for others, role flexibility, concern with context, knowledge of the bigger picture, and knowledge of other countries are critical for global leadership success (Jokinen, 2005).

Jokinen (2005) writes that the items which appear most frequently in a review of the research on global leadership competencies "[indicate] that emotional intelligence represents a major component of global leadership competency" (p. 203). She discusses two arguments about those who are successful in global leadership—either they have developed their own set of unique skills, or "global leaders have just developed their (general) competencies into a higher (global) level" (p. 200). We agree with this argument. It is essential for global leaders to have extremely well-developed emotional intelligence competencies, and while for some there is no need for an entire separate construct, others may find the concept of cultural intelligence helpful.

We recognize that the international context *is* often overlooked in leadership research and education, and that is something leadership researchers and educators, should work to change by including the specific emotional intelligence competencies of adaptability, empathy, and organizational awareness. There are many possibilities for developing these emotional intelligence competencies that are directly related to international leadership success. Leadership training programs and curricula can continue to be developed to include honing of these specific competencies while focusing on international contexts.

Conclusion

In conclusion, developing the specific emotional intelligence competencies of empathy, adaptability, and organizational awareness may have similar results that cultural intelligence seeks. Thus, the separate construct of cultural intelligence is not always necessary if the international context is taken into consideration. Intentionally teaching and learning emotional intelligence with international contexts in mind is critical to the future of creating global leaders with higher education. Cultural intelligence has been proposed as a construct, which helps people function in other cultures. However, emotional intelligence competencies of empathy, adaptability, and organizational awareness can lead to greater leadership effectiveness in different cultures. In the future, training and curricular models should work to include focus on developing these specific competencies in the discussion of leadership and emotional intelligence in an international context. Both the emotional intelligence competencies of empathy, adaptability, and organizational awareness, and cultural intelligence are critical in creating emotionally intelligent global leaders for the 21st century.

Work Cited

Alon, I., & Higgins, J. M. (2005). Global leadership success through cultural and emotional intelligences. *Business Horizons, 48*(6), 501–512.

Ang, S., & Van Dyne, L. (2008). *Handbook of Cultural Intelligence: Theory, Measurement, and Applications.* Aramonk, NY: M.E. Sharpe.

Blunt, P., & Jones, M. L. (1996). Exploring the limits of Western leadership theory in East Asia and Africa. *Personnel Review, 26*(1/2), 6–23.

Boyatzis, R. E., Goleman, D., & Rhee, K. (1999). Clustering competence in emotional intelligence: Insights from the emotional competence inventory (ECI). In R. Bar-On & J. D. A. Parker (Eds.), *Handbook of emotional intelligence* (pp. 342–362). San Francisco, CA: Jossey-Bass.

Den Hartog, D. N., House, R. J., Hanges, P. J., & Ruiz-Quintanilla, S. A. (1999). Culture specific and cross-culturally generalizable implicit leadership theories: Are attributes of charismatic/transformational leadership universally endorsed? *Leadership Quarterly, 10*(2), 219–256.

Earley, P. C., & Ang, S. (2003). *Cultural intelligence: Individual interactions across cultures.* Stanford, CA: Stanford University Press.

Elenkov, D. S., & Pimentel, J. R. C. (2008). Social intelligence, emotional intelligence, and cultural intelligence: An integrative perspective. In S. Ang & L. Van Dyne (Eds.), *Handbook of cultural intelligence: Theory, measurement, and applications* (pp. 289–303). Aramonk, NY: M. E. Sharpe.

Gardner, H. (1999). *Intelligence reframed: Multiple intelligence for the 21st century.* New York, NY: Basic Books.

Gardner, H. (2006). *Multiple intelligences: New horizons* (2nd ed.). New York, NY: Basic Books.

Goleman, D. (1999). What makes a leader? *Harvard Business Review, 82*(1), 82–91.

Goleman, D., Boyatzis, R., & McKee, A. (2002). *Primal leadership: Learning to lead with emotional intelligence.* Boston, MA: Harvard Business School Press.

Hofstede, G. (1980). Motivation, leadership, and organization: Do American theories apply abroad? *Organizational Dynamics, 9*(1), 43–63.

House, R. J., Hanges, P. J., Javidan, M., Dorfman, P. W., & Gupta, V. (Eds.). (2004). *Culture, leadership, and organizations: The GLOBE study of 62 societies.* Thousand Oaks, CA: Sage.

Jaeger, A. J., & Eagan, M. K. J. (2007). Exploring the value of emotional Intelligence: A means to improve academic performance. *NASPA Journal, 44*(3), 512–537.

Jokinen, T. (2005). Global leadership competencies: A review and discussion. *Journal of European Industrial Training, 29*(3), 199–216.

Jordan, P. J., Ashton-James, C. E., & Ashkanasy, N. M. (2013). Evaluating the claims: Emotional intelligence in the workplace. In K. R. Murphy (Ed.), *A critique of emotional intelligence: What are the problems and how can they be fixed?* (pp. 189–210). New York, NY: Routledge.

Kellerman, B. (2012). *The end of leadership.* New York, NY: HarperCollins Publishers.

Lee, C. H., & Templer, K. J. (2003). Cultural intelligence assessment and measurement. In P. C. Earley & S. Ang (Eds.), *Cultural intelligence: Individual interactions across cultures* (pp. 185–208). Stanford, CA: Stanford University Press.

Murphy, K. R., & Sideman, S. (2013). The facilitation of emotional intelligence. In K. R. Murphy (Ed.), *A critique of emotional intelligence: What are the problems and how can they be fixed?* (pp. 283–299). New York, NY: Routledge.

Pritchard, M. E., & Wilson, G. S. (2003). Using emotional and social factors to predict student success. *Journal of College Student Development, 44*(1), 18–26.

Rost, J. C. (1993). *Leadership for the twenty-first century.* Westport, CT: Praeger.

CHAPTER 12

Adjunct Faculty as Commodities

Christopher Cumo

The word "adjunct," also known as a part time faculty member, was once benign. A university hired one when enrollment was too high or to cover a specialty course that no full time faculty member could teach. This use was casual and infrequent (Fuller, 2011). Presently, 75% of all college and university faculty teach part time. In the process the adjunct has ceased to be a person with hopes, aspirations and yearnings. He or she is simply a commodity and/or a unit of production. He or she is a piece of dust lying moribund on the tombs of the forgotten.

How did this drastic change happen? One might cite a number of factors, including the overproduction of Ph.D.s, but the most significant feature may be the rise of the corporate university. In a nation that worships capitalism, this alteration may have been inevitable. Take journalism as a parallel. Many magazines and newspapers rely on freelance writers for virtually all, and in some case all, of their content. Freelance journalists are paid per piece, so that the 18th century concept of piecework still flourishes. These writers receive a token payment, no benefits of any kind, and have virtually no hope of upward mobility.

The corporate university has simply applied these lessons to academe, whereby part time faculties are as powerless as independent contract journalists. This essay explores the many perils of this system. For now it suffices to say that part time faculty and the abuses that imperil them appear to be here to stay.

An Adjunct Dies

Margaret Mary Vojtko was once an adjunct at Duquesne University in Pittsburgh. She is no longer, first because the university refused to rehire her in 2013 after 25 years' service (Anderson, 2013). The administration at Duquesne severed ties despite the fact that the 83-year-old French instructor was battling cancer. In fact doctors had given her only six months to live, but the university rid itself of her anyway. She received no severance pay. The university did nothing to ameliorate her poverty and poor health. Second, Vojtko is no longer an adjunct because a heart attack rather than cancer claimed her.

Vojtko, despite 40 years of research, never completed her doctorate, making it easy for the university to marginalize her, in fact to marginalize all part time faculty whatever their accomplishments. Despite strong teaching evaluations, the university let Vojtko go because it deemed her teaching substandard. Vojtko claimed, however, that the university fired her because she did not have a Ph.D.

That Vojtko had worked well into her 80s is not mysterious when one reflects on the fact that she had no health insurance and no pension. Expensive cancer treatments had made her penniless and virtually homeless. She could not afford to heat her home in the winter, leaving her to inhabit a restaurant at night. Perhaps, as Hemingway (1984) ventured, it was a "clean well lighted place." She had tried sleeping in her office at Duquesne, but security removed her as though she were simply a vagrant.

For most of her career, Vojtko earned just $2500 for a three-credit course, though in her last years pay had risen to $3000 or $3500 per course. Still she made no more than $25,000 teaching eight courses per year, an overload. In her later years, though, the university had taken away most of Vojtko's courses so that she earned less than $10,000 per year. According to one study this amount is less than one fifth the pay of a female porn star for about 100 days' work per year (Weisman, 2012).

This is not the place to critique the sex industry. In fact I believe no critique is in order. Sex workers deserve respect, dignity and a living wage. It seems strange in this context that the corporate university does not think these values apply to part time faculty.

The adjuncts at Duquesne have allied with steelworkers in unionizing in hope of bettering their lot, but Duquesne, using its status as a Catholic institution, replies that it need not recognize the union. This seems strange given former pope Benedict XVI's statement that the Catholic Church has always supported workers' rights to bargain collectively. Indeed, where part time faculties are unionized, wages are 25% hirer than among non-unionized adjuncts (Anderson, 2013). If Duquesne is out of step with the church, it understands its place in corporate America. Duquesne does not concede that it has done anything wrong. If all other colleges and universities hire adjuncts, why shouldn't it? The university won't even admit that the hiring, and firing, of adjuncts is a form of exploitation.

In the end Duquesne abandoned Vojtko, old, feeble, and riddled with cancer, when she most needed help. "Hiring adjuncts instead of tenure track faculty is unquestionably great for a university's bottom line (Anderson, 2013). From every other perspective, though, it's a scourge." Curiously Duquesne has an endowment of more than $230 million, yet it will not share even a fraction with part time faculty.

Confessions of a Former Adjunct

Margaret Vojtko's story is more than an abstraction. It is a reminder of my own experiences. I was once a young Ph.D. with presumably bright prospects. The faculties at my mid-tier public university encouraged me to teach part time to hone my skills in the classroom, garner good evaluations, and publish frenetically. I followed this advice. During the next six years I published two books and a number of articles, essays, reviews, and short stories, all in print. True, only the peer-reviewed work really counted, but my books and articles qualified in this regard.

I also taught more than my share of classes at two public universities and one Catholic university. I had received my undergraduate degree from the last and hoped to parlay my part time teaching into a tenure track job there. Although, I am narrowly trained as a historian of science, I never taught a course in my specialty. Fortunately, I was publishing on a variety of topics and so matured quickly into a jack-of-all-trades, which every adjunct must be. I taught military history, the U.S. surveys, economic history, and philosophy. The courses in military history and economic history were new. The tenured faculty, not wishing to prepare new lectures, gave me the courses.

At first, eager and optimistic, I secured high evaluations. Students so liked me that they enrolled above the threshold to take my classes. But as the years passed, my optimism turned to bitterness. I chaffed at the tenured faculty, many of who did not have a terminal degree or publications, who insisted that students call them "doctor." Meanwhile they took pains to refer to me as "mister." To be sure this sounds petty, but it reminded me that the tenured disdained me. When the history department finally posted a full time position, its members crafted the job description to exclude me. Maybe this was unintentional, but I found it curious that the department suddenly needed an expert on Russia when no such specialty had been taught before.

As my desperation and bitterness worsened, my temperament poisoned the classroom atmosphere. I knew the time had come to leave academe, but this decision was certainly not on my terms. I had applied to hundreds of positions over those six years, yet received only one interview, at a small Catholic college similar to the one at which I had taught. This interview came early in my career, and when I did not receive an offer, I knew that the odds were very much against me.

I am not alone in having left academe. A friend tells me that former adjuncts at Cornell University settle for jobs as janitors to earn something akin to a living wage. One way or another, we must all make peace with the academy, but this is difficult to do because it embraces capitalism rather than people. It has learned how to devalue as it has forgotten that people have value.

The Numbers

Indeed, only about half of all Ph.D.s in history and English find a tenure track job (Seligman, 2012). Some search committees discard all applicants who are adjuncts and others will not hire their own adjuncts, preferring someone out of state. One university to which I applied hired an ABD rather than one of the innumerable Ph.D. applicants. What happens to the other half? The Woodrow Wilson National Fellowship Foundation believes that Ph.D. need not settle for penury as adjuncts. They can join the managerial elite in business. Others retrain. I know one former adjunct who earned an MLS and is now ensconced at a sizeable metropolitan library. Another graduated from a well-respected law school and is now a lawyer in private practice in California.

For a while I thought of going to law school or earning a Ph.D. in psychology so that I could establish my own practice. Instead I settled for the job I had held on and off again since adolescence. I resumed my work as a landscaper: cutting grass, running a weed eater until my hands shook from fatigue, and spreading mulch (Cumo, 2003a, 2012). Because of the heat and humidity where I live, I worked in shorts, sandals, and virtually nothing else. I was vulnerable to the sun, flies and mosquitoes. Fortunately biology equipped me for this work. I tan quickly and become dark after only a week or so of constant sun exposure. My vitamin D levels are high enough to impress my primary care physician. I sweat profusely, shedding excess heat, replenishing my fluids by drinking more than one gallon of water each day I am in the field. This is not what I envisioned doing with my Ph.D. but, honestly, it's better than being an adjunct.

I don't know how many other Ph.D.s cut grass, though the number must be vanishingly small. I suspect that large numbers get trapped in the adjunct system. They believe, as I once had, in the concept of upward mobility. The idea is as old as America itself. Who hasn't read Horatio Alger or at least have heard of him? Hard work guarantees success in this world of fantasy, so adjunct take as many classes as they can, deliver dynamic lectures, grade scores of papers and expect a tenure track job to reward their diligence and dynamism. Some end up in this trap for years and even decades, as Vojtko did. In some ways the biological world makes more sense than the part time system. An insect with the misfortune to stray too near a Venus's Fly Trap does not suffer years or decades. Digestive juices truncate its life in a week or so. Yet the adjunct endures the "slings and arrows of outrageous fortune" for much longer (Shakespeare, 1984).

Perhaps MacBeth had the adjunct in mind when he dismissed life as "a tale told by an idiot full of sound and fury, signifying nothing" (Shakespeare, 1955). These are the moments when I ponder my former existence as an adjunct and the current existence of those who are still ghosts in the classroom. These moments are my nadir, my descent into nihilism.

The Dimensions of the Problem

For part time faculty who are new to the enterprise, it must seem as though such exploitation cannot persist long. Certainly this was what Marx and Engels though about the oppression of the working class (Marx & Engels, 1848). In fact the misuse of adjuncts has blighted academe at least since the 1970s (Fuller, 2011). It was at this juncture, university by university, that academe made its pact with the devil. The use of adjuncts gave universities what they most needed: flexibility. In flush times, hire all the adjuncts who will take the work. When enrollment dips, simply refuse to renew adjuncts' contracts. Does the cost of medical coverage for an aging core of full professors increase the blood pressure of nervous administrators? Simply hire disposable faculty who receive no medical coverage and earn obscene wages.

This is an unequal system in which pay, benefits and prestige flow to the top of academe and all the work devolves on part time labor. The adjunct is not a professional but rather a unit of labor. This is the reduction of adjunct to commodities that we witnessed earlier. This system of abuse is ripe for Marxian analysis, but that has not happened, I suspect because Americans are so enamored with capitalism. The adjunct system is capitalism at its most ruthless. It is the personification of the widening income chasm that President Obama notes. Yet curiously no politician that I know has targeted casual labor. Society will always have poor people, according to the Jesus of the Gospel of Matthew.

Now, of course, the working poor have advanced degrees. Many, as we have seen, have the terminal degree in their field and publications. The situation is dire in the humanities (Seligman, 2012). Sylvia DeSantis *Academic Apartheid* (2011) is full of anguished stories of adjuncts in the humanities, particularly English. In fact English is the perfect discipline of exploitation. Tenured and tenure track faculty take the literature courses, loading up on their specialties, selecting only upper level courses when they can, leaving the grading intensive composition courses to adjuncts. Though they make only a fraction of what the tenured earn, adjuncts in English are stuck with all the time intensive grading. Because pay is so poor for adjuncts, they must teach an overload of course, worsening the time constraints. Grading consumes weekends and holidays. The routine of marking papers never ends so that the inevitable must happen: the overburdened, overworked adjunct may not be able to give every paper due consideration (Cox, 2011). As an adjunct I too felt this pressure.

What is most perplexing about this system is that tenure track and tenured faculty do not appear to care. These are the professors, often with liberal leanings, who lament the injustices done to women and minorities but who cannot seem to widen their vision to the present and to their institution. Injustice is injustice, whether the temptation is to pay women less than men or adjuncts less than full time faculty. Yet this insight seems not to have ascended the academic ladder. Assistant professors dare not question the system for fear of jeopardizing their chances at tenure. Yet those with tenure, the associate and full professors, do not advocate on behalf of part time faculty though their job security and the long tradition of academic freedom should predispose them to critiquing the adjunct system. They do not critique the system because they benefit from it. They must find someone to do the arduous work of grading. Because they do not wish to do it, adjuncts must. Because they do not wish to teach introductory courses with massive numbers of students, adjuncts must fill the void.

The situation is dire for those in the humanities because, despite what the Woodrow Wilson National Fellowship Foundation says, few options exist for humanists (Cumo, 2003). Outside the ivory tower, there are not many jobs that beg for an M.A. or a Ph.D. in English or history. When I first contemplated what I should do after leaving the adjunct sweatshop, I thought that my publication record, and in general my writing skills, such as they are or are not, might help me transition to journalism. I was wrong. As I had done in academe, I blanketed the country with resumes and cover letters, responding to virtually anything that journalismjobs.com posted. No one was interested, though my hometown paper let me write features and cover meetings for $1 per inch of text. I agreed only after I made clear to the editor that I wanted a job if one arose. In due course the paper posted a job description. I applied but did not receive an interview. The editor pulled me aside afterwards, telling me that I was overqualified.

If the humanities are in the doldrums, the situation is much different in the sciences, where only about one third of Ph.D.s want to teach (Seligman, 2012). This number also holds for engineering and education Ph.D.s (or Ed.D.s). Because the number of scientists, engineers, and educators seeking entre into the academy is much smaller than the phalanx of folks in the humanities, competition is less keen and the desperation less palpable. *Academic Apartheid* (2011) does not contain a single account of scientists, engineers, or educators who taught part time, leading me to suspect that the numbers are small (Cumo). I know one woman with a Ph.D. in plant pathology who will never teach part time because the job of a scientist is to research not squander her talent in the classroom.

Scientists and their ilk need not surrender to life as an adjunct because, unlike the humanities, jobs abound for science graduates outside academe (Cumo, 2002). One year, out of curiosity, I searched the job listings of the American Society of Agronomy, finding some twenty jobs for agronomists at the U.S. Department of Agriculture alone. That year universities worldwide did not post twenty openings for a historian of science. These opportunities enable scientists never to enter the adjunct trap.

In some ways the greatest injustice that adjuncts suffer is the mismatch between their aspirations and reality. Many if not most of them entered graduate school and wanted to teach because they valued the life of the mind. They knew how to think critically, how to read texts, and how to ask all the right questions. But in the adjunct trap these skills do not count for much. One is too busy trying to cobble together an existence to indulge the life of the mind. Grading and preparing for courses far outside one's specialty at a moment's notice consume the adjunct. Do not misconstrue my meaning. Adjuncts love to teach. They thrive in the classroom and most earn high marks for their teaching. What they neither want nor need is the imperative that they forever prepare new courses for a variety of colleges and universities within commuting distance, all because they cannot afford to turn down a course. The failure to do exactly as one is told is a sure way not to be renewed next term. In many ways, the lack of job security makes cowards of us all. We cannot surmount our injustices. We cannot complain about the system because no one will want to hire us to teach introduction to philosophy or the myriad other courses that adjuncts teach.

Ironically given their treatment, adjuncts make the modern university possible (Fuller, 2011). Their penury allows universities to erect opulent buildings, to make the university a type of country club that will attract students and even tenure track faculty. More than a century ago the slave served the plantation economy in much the way that the adjunct now serves the corporate university (Fuller, 2011). The analogy with slavery is overdrawn. After all adjuncts can quit as I did, an action forbidden to slaves. But the mistreatment of part time faculty is startling. The corporate university has descended into apartheid (Fuller, 2011). This injustice betrays American values of upward mobility and accountability and truncates the nobility that universities once claimed. The corporate university, in this sense, has degenerated into a class system, one in which one class of faculty merit tenure while the lower class merits nothing more than penury. Perhaps this is really a caste system given its imperviousness to reform.

Among other things, pay separates these classes. By one account McDonald's and Burger King pay more per hour than does the corporate university (DeSantis, 2011). One adjunct calculated her pay at \$3.50 per hour (Blackwell, 2011). Part of the problem, of course, is that adjuncts are in gross oversupply. With so many people competing for so few jobs, wages must fall. Any job market will conform to the law of supply and demand. This is just how capitalism works. In some cases high school dropouts earn more per hour than highly educated part time faculty (DeSantis, 2011).

Capitalism, at least in Republican terms, in the terms of the corporate university, also works by trickle down economics. That is, the wealth that adjuncts create through their labor will, having been appropriated by the university, disperses throughout the university, benefiting everyone including part time faculty. But what if trickle down economics does not work? The trickle down approach of the 1920s led to the Great Depression of the 1930s. In this case one must acknowledge that the corporate university has stolen the wealth that adjuncts had created in the first place. Money does not trickle down. The elites appropriate it.

One senses that women comprise a disproportionate share of adjuncts. This would not surprise one given the tendency to devalue women's accomplishments and the work they do. Whenever women have entered an occupation, pay has tended to decline. The argument was once that women only worked for "pin money." What excuse can the corporate university devise today? Are female academics less gifted than men and so more likely to teach part time? This is absurd, but the fact remains that women are underrepresented as tenured faculty and over represented as part time faculty.

Adjuncts suffer from the old and putatively discredited "Great Chain of Being." Naturalists once thought that all life could be arranged from the most primitive to the most complex. At the bottom were bacteria, and atop the ladder, of course, were humans. Some naturalists went even farther to use the Great Chain of Being to support racism. At the bottom of the ladder was the orangutan, just above which stood Africans. These naturalists, all of them white, believed that black women interbred with male orangutans. The offspring were worthy only of slavery. Above Africans stood Native Americans with Asian above them. Atop the ladder, of course, were whites. I do not know where these naturalists placed Arabs, Polynesians and others. These people apparently did not interest white naturalists. Now the Great Chain of Being has shifted to the corporate university, where adjuncts occupy the bottom rung. Above them are assistant professors, then associate professors, and then full professors. I do not know where to place administrators. They have nice titles and offices, but they do not seem to work as hard as adjuncts. In fact no one else in the corporate university appears to work as hard as part time faculty.

Because adjuncts occupy the bottom of the Great Chain of Being, they receive only disdain from those above them. The professors regard adjuncts as second-class citizens and as an inferior grade of human. By any measure adjuncts are inferior. Worse many adjuncts internalize this sense of inferiority (DeSantis, 2011). They come to believe that if they had worth, they would be on the tenure track. Adjuncts come to expect overwork and a lack of respect. They become accustomed to holding office hours at a local McDonald's or even outdoors near a soybean field.

In fact, it is difficult to argue with the premise that in the twisted world of the corporate university, soybeans have become more important than adjuncts. The land grant universities, the agricultural experiment stations, and the USDA spend millions of dollars every year studying soybeans. Where is the investment in part time faculty? Why is a legume more important than a human?

The lack of autonomy is another cross adjuncts must bear. At one university where I taught part time, the administration deemed me sufficiently unqualified to choose my own textbook or prepare a syllabus. For a fee, a tenure track member of the department selected the textbooks and wrote the syllabi for all courses that adjunct would teach. Apparently a Ph.D. and publications did not qualify me to complete these elementary tasks. From experience I know that it is difficult to fit content into someone else's textbook and syllabus.

Universities often do not offer adjuncts the simplest tokens. Part time faculty must even pay to park at many universities (DeSantis, 2011). I circumvented this problem by bicycling to the universities where I taught. In some cases this meant a commute of more than twenty miles per day, but I refused to pay to park. The dean called me "weird" for cycling to work. I was skilful, able to cycle on snow and ice. One day I reached campus to learn that snow had canceled classes. No one had bothered to telephone me. I had pedaled more than ten miles for nothing other than exercise. My primary care physician still encourages me to cycle, even though it now serves no utilitarian purpose.

The inescapable truth is that universities marginalize adjuncts and coerce them to work in abysmal conditions (Reagan, 2011). How many part time faculty willingly submit to such injustice? Ironically, students are not always aware of an adjunct's plight. They assume that an adjunct must be a professor; otherwise he or she would not be standing before them. One adjunct worked in retail and had the embarrassment of selling clothes to her students, who quickly connected the dots. In other cases students know who has tenure and who does not. In many of these cases, students view adjuncts as "easy" (Lusiak, 2011). Adjuncts cannot award low grades for fear of retaliation on student evaluations.

Are There Any Solutions?

In one sense there may not be a solution to the adjunct problem. One website counsels historians that they cannot find a real job in academe. These jobs have disappeared as the corporate university has gutted the profession by substituting low wage labor for the once mighty professorial elite. If this is true, if it is becoming impossible to find a tenure track job, then the adjunct problem is bound to worsen. It may be too late to do anything constructive. Already, the Catholic university where I taught has created a division that hires *only* part time faculty. The dean is the sole full time employee. The University of Phoenix, a for profit institution, hires part time faculty (Cumo, 2003). Brown Mackie College hires adjuncts. The list is much longer but the trend is frighteningly clear.

If prospects for real employment are worsening, what options does one have? Adjuncts already enmeshed in the trap have, it seems to me, two options. One is to remain on the periphery and unionize. As the death of Margaret Vojtko makes clear, unions are in a difficult position. The corporate university stiff-arms unions, refusing to negotiate with them. In some places, however, unions have won concessions and can boast of better pay, some benefits, and incremental improvements in job security. Those adjuncts not prepared to fight their institution for the right to bargain collectively should not sacrifice their lives to an institution that does not care about them. These adjuncts should take the second option, leaving academe. There is life outside the ivory tower, though one may need to retrain, as some have.

Another solution, again very difficult to achieve, would be to put collective pressure on universities to stop awarding so many graduate degrees (Seligman, 2012). How many more English or history Ph.D.s does the United States realistically need? The current surplus only exacerbates the adjunct problem. Universities will resist this reform because graduate students, like adjuncts, are a source of cheap and easily exploited labor. But the adjunct problem will go away only when universities mirror medical schools in keeping close track of the number of entrants to match the number of jobs, real jobs, not part time positions. No physician, outside of special circumstances, would submit to part time work. Why should the holders of graduate degrees endure such abject labor conditions?

Yet another solution would be to restore the meaning of "professional." Conceptual changes are the most difficult to achieve, but in this endeavor change of some kind is long overdue. To put the matter bluntly, either an adjunct is a commodity or a person. If adjuncts are just commodities, then the language of exploitation takes precedence. The need for a Marxist revolution, even in America, becomes stark and unavoidable if conditions reach their nadir. If an adjunct is a person, then one must ask of what kind? It is easy to define adjunct as laborer, as the woman at Walmart or the man cutting grass is a laborer. But this is still not precise enough because we must situate the context of labor. The labor is without question intellectual, calling for the transmission of complex ideas in terms that undergraduates can understand. By its nature intellectual labor is the work of a professional. Once adjuncts can define themselves as professionals, it will be more difficult to marginalize them, to pay them so poorly, and to deny them the fruits of their labor in every sense of the word.

Robert Fuller (2011) suggests that adjuncts must launch a new civil rights movement. The attempt to right the wrongs of sexism and discrimination must grapple anew with the adjunct trap. Once more a disenfranchised and oppressed class of people must agitate for their rights. But how, one might ask? By any means necessary. Unionization is part of the answer, but the moment may not be ripe for widespread union agitation. For one thing adjuncts earn so little that union dues might impose hardship. If unions are to succeed they must win concessions first and ask for dues later. If unions are only part of the answer, adjuncts must confront squarely the issue of rebellion. The United States was founded on the notion of rebellion. Adjuncts must do the same.

As a first step toward rebellion, adjuncts must educate the larger world about what is wrong with the corporate university. The corporate university should be an easy target for adjuncts because of the way it treats students and parents, not just part time faculty. As the corporate university raises tuition, making higher education a hardship for parents and their children, it slashes pay and perks to its part time faculty. Adjuncts must make clear to everyone that this behavior benefits the corporate university alone. Students do not benefit from the overuse of adjuncts. Who wants an overburdened, underpaid person as a teacher? Students and parents, once they are educated about the adjunct trap, should demand that universities convert from contingent to permanent employees. Ultimately the withholding of tuition may be the only gesture that the corporate university will acknowledge.

Even with these efforts, the problem may worsen before it improves. In state after state, Republican governors and legislatures (Ohio is a good example) have slashed funding to public education. Public universities under duress have an even greater incentive to hire more and more adjuncts. The universities are bereft of money that under Republican authority now goes to subsidize business. Private corporations, it turns out, benefit from the use of adjunct faculty in this circuitous fashion.

This state of affairs means that adjuncts must retaliate against capitalism itself. As an economic system it has impoverished part time faculty and a lot of other people. The rebellion, if it is to succeed, must target American capitalism. The adjunct who wants to be more than a commodity must rebel. Perhaps adjuncts should reread *The Communist Manifesto*. "The proletarians have nothing to lose but their chains. They have a world to win" (Marx & Engels, 1848).

Work Cited

Anderson, L. V. (2013). *Death of a professor*. Retrieved from Salon.com

Blackwell, J. (2011). Guest Parking in the Ph.D.-only zone. In S. M. DeSantis (Ed.), *Academic apartheid: Waging the adjunct war* (pp. 37–44). Newcastle: Cambridge Scholars.

Cox, T. (2011). Tenuous, not tenured: A long time being part-time. In S. M. DeSantis (Ed.), *Academic apartheid: Waging the Adjunct War* (pp. 45–52). Newcastle: Cambridge Scholars.

Cumo, C. (2002, Jan–Feb). Scientists don't have to visit. *The Adjunct Advocate Magazine*, 36–37.

Cumo, C. (2003a, May–June). Phoenix rising. *The Adjunct Advocate Magazine*, 16–18.

Cumo, C. (2003b, 15 August). *The Chronicle of Higher Education,* C5.

Cumo, C. (2012). The grass isn't always greener. *Akronlife Magazine*, 12.

DeSantis, S. M. (2011). Introduction. In S. M. DeSantis (Ed.), *Academic apartheid: Waging the adjunct war* (pp. 1–3). Newcastle: Cambridge Scholars.

DeSantis, S. M. (2011). Profound treachery. In S. M. DeSantis (Ed.), *Academic apartheid: Waging the adjunct war* (pp. 87–90). Newcastle: Cambridge Scholars.

Fuller, R. W. (2011). Foreword. In S. M. DeSantis (Ed.), *Academic apartheid: Waging the adjunct war.* (pp. ix–xi). Newcastle: Cambridge Scholars.

Hemingway, E. (1984). *A clean, well-lighted place. The heath guide to literature*. Lexington, MA: D.C. Heath.

Lusiak, C. (2011). The ladder and the adjunct. In S. M. DeSantis (Ed.), *Academic apartheid: Waging the adjunct war* (pp. 21–26). Newcastle: Cambridge Scholars.

Marx, K., & Engels, F. (1848). *The communist manifesto*. Chicago: The Great Books Foundation.

The Sad Death of an Adjunct Professor Sparks a Labor Debate. (2013). Retrieved from www.npr.org.

Seligman, A. I. (2012). *Is graduate school really for you?: The whos, whats, hows, and whys of pursuing a Master's or Ph.D.* Baltimore, MD: Johns Hopkins University Press.

Shakespeare, W. (1955). *MacBeth*. Chicago: The Great Books Foundation.

Shakespeare, W. (1984). *Hamlet. The heath guide to literature*. Lexington, MA: D.C. Heath.

Teeuwen, R., & Hantke, S. (Eds.). (2007). *Gypsy scholars, migrant teachers and the global academic proletariat: Adjunct labour in higher education*. Amsterdam & New York, NY: Rodopi.

Weisman, A. (2012). *Here's what female porn stars get paid for different types of scenes*. Retrieved from www.businessinsider.com/heres-what-female-porn-stars-get-paid-for-different-types-of-scenes

CHAPTER 13

The Unintended Consequences of New Residence Hall Construction

Issues of Access and Student Success

Elizabeth C. Jodoin and Christopher Gregory

Introduction

Suite and apartment-style living is quickly becoming the preferred option on campuses nationwide. However, the increasing cost to the student in order to live in suite and apartment-style residence halls with upgraded amenities may be burdensome. The purpose of this chapter is to highlight the complexities within the intersection of residence hall design and student facility preference with issues of student success and access. Exploring the complexities of residence hall design with student access and success may encourage institutional administrators and housing and residence life personnel to think more holistically regarding residence hall design.

Living on-campus has been empirically shown to positively impact student academic success, student satisfaction, enrich interpersonal skills, and improve rates of retention (Pascarella & Terenzini, 2005; Reynolds, 2007; Wallace, 1980). On-campus housing offers close proximity to courses and campus resources for students (Agron, 2007). Physical features of on-campus housing are important to students, not only helping to determine which school they attend, but also in regards to their overall satisfaction with their chosen institution (Amole, 2009; Reynolds, 2007). With the many benefits of on-campus living, institutions have a duty to ensure that no student is limited in their ability to reside on campus should they choose. Unfortunately, this is not the current reality of higher education. Costs for on-campus housing continue to rise, even outpacing the rate of tuition increases in many cases. Coupled with the current trend of larger and more private residence halls, students from lower socio-economic classes are being priced out.

Institutions are renovating traditional residence halls, i.e. double-occupancy rooms, to offer larger rooms and more amenities to students (Balogh, Price, & Moser, 2009). Furthermore, suite and apartment-style living is quickly becoming the preferred option on campuses nationwide (Balogh et al., 2009). The average square foot per resident in 1997 was 250 square feet, compared to 357 square feet in 2006. This increase in square footage, along with in-residence amenities such as on-site fitness centers, classrooms, and technology may be desired by students, but comes with a larger price tag (Agron, 2007). Compounding this issue is the pressure universities feel to compete with spacious, amenity-filled, off-campus housing facilities (Balogh, Grimm, & Hardy, 2005; Mulvaney, 2013). As such, the increasing cost to the student in order to live in larger, new and/or renovated housing with upgraded amenities and technology may be burdensome. Along with the increased cost, there is evidence to suggest the overall student experience is diminished for students living in more private accommodations. The long touted benefits of living on-campus may also be affected by moving students from traditional style halls to more private suite and apartment-style accommodations.

The purpose of this chapter is to highlight the complexities within the intersection of residence hall design and student facility preference with issues of student success and access. Based on current literature, there are a myriad of negative outcomes to current housing trends that have not been thoroughly discussed or evaluated. The authors' goal is to encourage institutions to examine possible inequalities and/or financial barriers to access of contemporary on-campus housing design as well as the overall impact to the student experience. First the impact on living on campus will be reviewed. Second, student facility preferences will be explored. Third, contemporary housing design and costs will be examined. Finally, the impact of housing costs and construction trends at one large Southeastern public institution will be discussed. This institution, which we will name Southeastern University, has an approximate total enrollment upwards of 15,000 students and is comprised of 33% ethnic minority enrollment. Currently, approximately 5,000 on-campus beds are available, and there is no requirement for first-year students to reside on-campus.

Exploring the complexities of residence hall design with student access and success will offer a necessary first step in creating a body of work that may help institutional administrators and housing and residence life personnel to think more holistically regarding residence hall design. Utilizing a more comprehensive viewpoint, institutional administrators may be encouraged to examine possible financial barriers to on-campus living and how this may impact specific student populations.

The Impact of Residing On-Campus

Research showing the benefits of living on-campus is vast and has been the subject of thousands of studies and is nearly unequivocal. Synthesizing many of these studies through an exhaustive search of available literature, Pascarella, Terenzini, and Blimling (1994) concluded that residential students are more active with campus organizations, interact more often with faculty, are significantly more satisfied with their college experience, and have higher rates of retention and graduation. Looking closer at the reasons living on campus may have such positive results is important as the explanations are multifaceted. Tinto (1987) found that social integration and interaction with other students is a chief contributor to persistence and graduation. Higher levels of social and extracurricular involvement also lead to on-campus students having significantly higher satisfaction levels with their college experience than peers who commute (Pascarella, 1985). These peer interactions also help students understand and make sense of what they are learning (Whitt, Edison, Pascarella, Nora, & Terenzini, 1999).

Palmer, Broido, and Campbell, in a 2008 commentary on the educational role in college student housing, found that these earlier findings were reinforced. Citing the 2005 study by Pascarella and Terenzini, the authors underscore current research by noting the following: (1) place of residence has little if any impact on cognitive growth, but on-campus students are more satisfied and are retained at a greater rate, (2) residence effects are primarily indirect, and (3) residential effects on student learning and development are greatest in residential environments that are intentionally designed to achieve those effects.

Sickler and Roskos (2013) note that new residence halls may have a positive impact upon student recruitment. The benefits of living on-campus are frequently used as a recruitment tool by university administrators, both in recruitment of students to university and the retention of students to live on-campus. A quick review of the housing websites of Southeastern University and three other large public universities in the same state reveals similar themes. Better grades, a more satisfying college experience, and more interactions with peers are listed as benefits of living on-campus. In addition, a shorter commute to class, more access to other university services, and more support from staff are listed as supplementary advantages of on-campus living.

What does this mean for the current trend of suite and apartment-style housing? As is highlighted elsewhere in this chapter, suites and apartments are a newer phenomenon; therefore most research related to students living on campus was conducted in the traditional, double-loaded corridor, residence hall setting. More recent research has looked at the differences in experiences students living in suites and apartments may have from those living in traditional style halls. One such study found that students living in suite-style housing reported less interaction with hall-mates and other students overall than did peers living in traditional style housing (Brandon, Hirt, & Cameron, 2008). Students in suite-style housing also report experiencing a diminished sense of community when compared with students in traditional housing (Devlin, Donovan, Nicolov, Nold, & Zandan, 2007). While current research has not fully assessed this topic, what has been evaluated has shown a gap in the experience for on-campus students based on housing accommodations.

Student Facility Preferences

A survey of American college students found that "students were quite discriminating about their living and learning spaces" (Reynolds, 2007, p. 68). In an examination of 1,902 students at one large public institution, first-year students indicated that type and size of room, related amenities, cost of room, and age of the buildings were the most important housing considerations when choosing their academic institution. In addition, first-year students reported that they were more likely to live on-campus the following year if they currently resided in new halls, had their own bedroom, and lived in a suite-style residences as compared to students who were at present living in traditional style halls, shared a room, and lived in an older building (Sickler & Roskos, 2013).

Furthermore, the top reasons for wanting to move residence halls for first-year students were a desire for a different type or size of room, the location of the hall and age of the building, proximity to friends, associated amenities, and cost of the room (Sickler & Roskos, 2013). Similarly, living in newly refurbished housing has been shown to increase student satisfaction (Thomsen & Eikemo, 2010). In a study of Nigerian residential students, it was found that privacy, characteristics of the bedroom, and social density were factors that determined satisfaction with on-campus housing (Amole, 2009).

Institutions are keenly aware of student desires and are retrofitting their on-campus residential facilities accordingly. Extant research indicates that today's college student is seeking more private residential units on campus (Alkandari, 2007; Balogh et al., 2005). For example, the percentage of campus construction projects that created individual bathrooms in rooms grew from 43.1% in 2001 (Agron, 2002) to 67.0% in 2004 (Agron, 2005). In addition, information gathered from chief housing officers regarding residential construction projects completed during 2001–2003 indicated that new construction focused upon building apartments with a semi-private or private bath (31.9%), single apartments (23.0%), and suite-style residences (20.4%) (Balogh et al., 2005). Balogh et al. (2005) noted that "in line with student preferences for privacy, slightly more than half (52.2%) of all new construction projects consisted of 81% to 100% single-occupancy bedrooms, compared with only 23.3% of new construction projects containing 81% to 100% double-occupancy bedrooms" (p. 52).

Similar findings are reported in a more recent survey of chief housing officers regarding campus construction projects completed during 2006–2007 (Balogh et al., 2009). New construction projects primarily focused upon building suite-style apartments, building apartments with private or semi-private baths, as well as single apartments. Double occupancy rooms were noted as being constructed more frequently than in previous years. However, privacy was a priority, as these double rooms were designed to include private or semi-private bathrooms, which is a shift from traditional style residence halls with a group bathroom. Suite-style residence halls and single apartments were primarily geared towards housing upperclassmen. In addition, participants reported that fewer double occupancy rooms and more suites existed after renovations were completed. Common amenities reported were wireless Internet access, laundry facilities, security systems, air conditioning, and furniture (Balogh et al., 2009).

Issues of Student Access

Students from low-income families may be at a disadvantage from the start regarding having access to on-campus housing. As Southeastern University is a public institution, we will explore the current costs for public institutions of higher education in the United States. The College Board (2012) notes for an in-state student at a public institution, "room and board charges account for more than half of the total charges for these students" (p. 3). This results in an average annual cost of $9,498, manifesting a 3.6% increase for room and board from 2012 (The College Board, 2013). Furthermore, household incomes for families in the bottom 20% of the population have decreased the most in the past decade (The College Board, 2012). These increases in room and board, in addition to familial financial struggles, may result in students from low socioeconomic backgrounds residing at home versus on-campus. In sum, "the cost of living poses a significant hurdle for many students" (The College Board, 2013, p. 8).

Extant research shows that living at home in an effort to reduce the cost of higher education negatively impacts student retention (Bozick, 2007). In a national sample of 10,614 first-year college students, students in the lowest quintile of household income (<$21,032) were more likely to live at home with their parents or in an off-campus apartment during their first year, as compared to students in the highest quintile of household income (>$80,001), who were more likely to live on-campus their first year. These statistics may be due to lower-income students not being able to afford living on-campus and thus they opt to remain at home. In addition, 77.4% of students with the highest household income persisted into their second year of college, as compared to only 55.9% of students with the lowest household income. Factors such as working greater than 20 hours per week while enrolled in college and living at home have been shown to impede retention and academic success (Bozick, 2007).

While scholarships, grants, and various forms of public and private financial assistance are available to qualified students, expenses for American higher education are increasing at a rate greater than the average family income (Vedder, 2012). Even if a student receives financial aid or acquires loans, the cost of on-campus housing may consume a large percentage of their annual aid allotment. Vedder (2012) notes that "tuition fees have risen at well over double the rate of inflation, and adjusting for inflation, tuition charges are over double what they were a generation ago" (2012, p. 1). The current average cost of tuition for an in-state public institution in 2013 is $8,893.00, a 2.9% increase from 2012 (The College Board, 2013). Specifically, at Southeastern University, tuition alone increased by 50.2% during the years 2000–2005. Furthermore, tuition in Southeastern University's specific state higher education system increased by 169% in the time span from 1985 to 2005, while per capita income only increased by 34% during this same time span within this state (Gillen & Vedder, 2008). Finally, the estimated debt per borrowing student at Southeastern University is $19,677, the greatest of all institutions within this public state system (Gillen & Vedder, 2008), indicating that students at this particular institution may have little help in the form of family contributions to their college expenses.

Stoner and Cavins (2003) note that "to fund residential renovation and new construction, college and university officials traditionally have opted to increase room rent, reduce the cost of the housing and residence life program, or both" (p. 17). However, housing rates charged to students will not generate enough income to fund future housing projects (Stoner & Cavins, 2003). The fact that on-campus housing offers a steady revenue stream to the institution is a well-known concept (Grube, 2010). Grube (2010) states that "certainly, the only way that constructing new residential facilities makes sense for an institution is to deliver housing that is desired by students and then charge an ample fee to ensure fiscal responsibility for the institution instead of creating a financial strain" (p. 48). These increases in tuition and housing costs, in addition to the lack of increase in per capita income, all present a challenge for students and their families to continue to absorb the increasing costs of higher education, and may negatively impact the student's ability to academically succeed.

Implications for Practice

Smith (2014) notes that,

> Many students face a stark choice: go to college and acquire a mountain of debt that will come due right after graduation, or forgo college altogether. Sadly, this choice is the primary one confronting those who stand to gain the most from higher education: the economically disadvantaged and people of color. (p. 42)

Students from minority backgrounds may also be the most loan-averse and may be fearful to take out educational loans (Burdman, 2005). In addition, factors such as the family's income level, the educational level of one's parents, and one's immigrant status have been found to impact attitudes towards taking on educational debt. While fully exploring the impact of race and socioeconomic status upon educational borrowing behavior is beyond the scope of this chapter, the rising cost of higher education may deter minority students from applying for financial aid and grants in the first place due to fears about loan repayment.

The increased financial burden upon students and their families is not solely due to increased tuition or housing rates, but is also related to increased interest rates on loans, reductions in state aid, as well as the failure of grant programs to match increases in tuition (Burdman, 2005; Smith, 2014). Nationally, 37 million students across the United States have student debt (Kamenetz, 2014). During the 2012–2013 academic year, students borrowed a total of $8.8 billion in funds from private, state, or institutional funding sources; $238.5 billion was borrowed from Federal sources; and another $44 billion of institutional grant aid was offered (The College Board, 2013). Repayment of loans may be no easy feat for recent graduates, with statistics noting that 10% of student borrowers during the 2010–2011 year defaulted on their loans. While loan forgiveness programs such as those included within the Higher Education Opportunity Act of 2008 exist (American Library Association, 2014), these programs may not be applicable to all student-borrowers.

The movement to create more on-campus housing opportunities is related to generating "student experiences, revenue streams, and recruitment tools" (Grube, 2010, p. 47). Reynolds (2007) notes that "the built environment is fundamentally related to recruitment and retention; a positive relationship does exist that is profound and interrelated" (p. 78). It's clear students are preferring suite and apartment-style housing options which offer more amenities and privacy (Li, Sheely II, & Whalen, 2005). Universities may be responding to these desires by creating assignment processes that place freshmen in traditional-style housing, and upperclass students into suites and apartments. This compels students to either pay more to stay on-campus after their freshmen year, or to search for lower-cost options off-campus. Even those students who can afford to stay on-campus may be negatively impacted.

Although current research suggests that students who move into suite and apartment-style housing options are more satisfied with their accommodations than peers living in traditional-style housing (Palmer et al., 2008), they experience less of a sense of belonging and connection to their hall mates (Brandon et al., 2008; Devlin et al., 2007). The professed benefits of living on-campus may prove to be diminished if students are not in the traditional environment that leads to interactions with peers. Worse yet, students from minority ethnic groups and lower socio-economic backgrounds who most need the peer support and access to institutional programs may be forced off-campus after their freshmen year due to the rising cost of on-campus housing.

If more students move off-campus due to financial concerns or in a desire to acquire more luxurious off-campus facilities, the sense of community and the overall sense of belonging on campus may dwindle (Gose, 1998). While Southeastern University has certainly worked to build residence halls that students, particularly upperclass students, will desire to live in for the duration of their college experience, these more luxurious options come with a larger price tag. In this manner, upperclass students are funneled towards the more expensive suite-style and apartment-style housing options, while freshman are channeled towards the less expensive traditional-style double room designs.

Housing officers and university administrators must fully understand the ramifications of the types of residential space being constructed and the options available to students as they matriculate. In addition, institutional administrators may wish to consider the overall institutional mission and student demographics when campus housing projects are being implemented. There is no question that institutions of higher education certainly need to charge tuition and fees; however it is imperative that current residential building plans not further disenfranchise low-income or minority students in the long-term by way of furthering increasing college debts. Housing options of varying costs and types need to be available to all students, and in particular upperclass students. Although varied campus housing options and luxury amenities are vitally important in today's institutional climate, the best housing options for students may not align with what students ultimately want, but may align with what is affordable for students in order to improve student access, enhance interpersonal experiences, and to promote institutional retention efforts.

Work Cited

Agron, J. (2002). Room to grow: 13th annual residence hall construction report. *American School and University.* Retrieved from http://asumag.com/mag/university_room_grow

Agron, J. (2005). Betting the house: 16th annual residence hall construction report. *American School and University.* Retrieved from http://asumag.com/mag/university_betting_house

Agron, J. (2007). 18th annual residence hall construction report. *American School and University.* Retrieved from http://asumag.com/Construction/res_halls/university_th_annual_residence

Alkandari, N. (2007). Students' perceptions of the residence hall living environment at Kuwait university. *College Student Journal, 41*(2), 327–335.

American Library Association. (2014). Federal student loan forgiveness. *American Library Association.* Retrieved from: http://www.ala.org/educationcareers/education/financialassistance/loanforgiveness#higher%20ed

Amole, D. (2009). Residential satisfaction in students' housing. *Journal of Environmental Psychology, 29*(1), 76–85.

Balogh, C. P., Grimm, J., & Hardy, K. (2005). ACUHO-I construction and renovation data: The latest trends in housing construction and renovation. *Journal of College and University Student Housing, 33*(2), 51–56.

Balogh, C. P., Price, K., & Moser, R. (2009). ACUHO-I construction and renovation data: The latest trends in housing construction and renovation. *Journal of College and University Student Housing, 36*(2), 82–91.

Bozick, R. (2007). Making it through the first year of college: The role of students' economic resources, employment, and living arrangements. *Sociology of Education, 80*(July), 261–285.

Brandon, A., Hirt, J. B., & Cameron, T. (2008). Where you live influences who you know: Student interaction based on residence hall design. *The Journal of College and University Housing, 35*(2), 62–79.

Burdman, P. (2005). *The student debt dilemma: Debt aversion as a barrier to college access.* Berkeley, CA: Center for Studies in Higher Education. Retrieved from https://escholarship.org/uc/item/6sp9787j

The College Board. (2012). *Trends in college pricing.* New York, NY: Author. Retrieved from http://trends.collegeboard.org/sites/default/files/college-pricing-2012-full-report-121203.pdf

The College Board. (2013). *Trends in college pricing.* New York, NY: Author. Retrieved from http://trends.collegeboard.org/sites/default/files/college-pricing-2013-full-report.pdf

Devlin, A. S., Donovan, S., Nicolov, A., Nold, O., & Zandan, G. (2007). Residence hall architecture and sense of community: Everything old is new again. *Environment and Behavior, 2008*(47), 478–521. doi: http://10.1177/0013916507301128

Gillen, A., & Vedder, R. (2008). *North Carolina's higher education system: Success or failure?* Washington, DC: Center for College Affordability and Productivity. Retrieved from http://files.eric.ed.gov/fulltext/ED536274.pdf

Gose, B. (1998, February 13). Colleges invest millions on improvements to keep upper class men in campus housing. *The Chronicle of Higher Education,* A52–A53.

Grube, S. A. (2010). Student housing growth: Expanding past institutional borders in an urban environment—A campus and community perspective. *The Journal of College and University Student Housing, 37*(1), 44–59.

Kamenetz, A. (2014, June 9). The one thing Obama didn't say about student loan repayment. *National Public Radio.* Retrieved from http://www.npr.org/blogs/ed/2014/06/09/320351501/the-one-thing-obama-didn-t-say-about-student-loan-repayment

Li, Y., Sheely II, M. C., & Whalen, D. F. (2005). Contributors to residence hall student retention: Why do students choose to leave or stay? *Journal of College & University Student Housing, 33*(2), 28–36.
Mulvaney, E. (2013, July 8). College Station follows trend with growth in upscale, off-campus student housing. *Houston Chronicle.* Retrieved from http://www.houstonchronicle.com/business/real-estate/article/College-Station-follows-trend-with-growth-in-4651514.php#/0
Palmer, C., Broido, E., & Campbell, J. (2008). A commentary on "the educational role in college student housing". *The Journal of College and University Housing, 35*(2), 87–99.
Pascarella, E. T. (1985). The influence of on-campus living versus commuting to college on the intellectual and interpersonal self-concept. *Journal of College Student Personnel. 26,* 292–299.
Pascarella, E. T., & Terenzini, P. T. (2005). *How college affects students: A third decade research.* San Francisco: CA: Jossey-Bass.
Pascarella, E. T., Terenzini, P. T., & Blimling, G. S. (1994). The impact of residential life on students. In C. C. Schroeder & P. Mable (Eds.), *Realizing the educational potential of residence halls* (pp. 22–52). San Francisco, CA: Jossey-Bass.
Reynolds, G. L. (2007). The impact of facilities on recruitment and retention of students. *New Directions for Institutional Research, 135,* 63–80.
Sickler, S., & Roskos, B. (2013). Factors that play a role in first-year students' on-campus housing decisions. *The Journal of College and University Student Housing, 39*(2), 10–31.
Smith, C. (2014). Student debt: State policies leave families with few good options. *Education Digest, 79*(7), 42–46.
Stoner, K. L., & Cavins, K. M. (2003). New options for financing residence hall renovation and construction. *New Directions for Student Services, 101,* 17–27.
Thomsen, J., & Eikemo, T. A. (2010). Aspects of student housing satisfaction: A quantitative study. *Journal of Housing and the Built Environment, 25,* 273–293.
Tinto, V. (1987). *Leaving College; Rethinking the causes and cures of student attrition.* Chicago: University of Chicago Press.
Vedder, R. (2012). *Twelve inconvenient truths about American higher education.* Washington, DC: Center for College Affordability and Productivity. Retrieved from http://files.eric.ed.gov/fulltext/ED541358.pdf
Wallace, J. A. (1980). The philosophy of university housing. *The Journal of College and University Student Housing, 10*(2), 23–25.
Whitt, E., Edison, M., Pascarella, E., Nora, A., & Terenzini, P. (1999). Interactions with peers and objective and self-reported cognitive outcomes across 3 years of college. *Journal of College Student Development, 40*(1), 61–78.

PART TWO

Equity and Access

Social and equitable justice should no longer delineate our humanity based on markers of difference, but should call to the oneness of our condition—the ability to access to equitable learning environments and to experience success without barriers to opportunity. As citizens of this constitutional republic, we must realize that to improve our economic and social conditions, we have to be vigilant in the pursuit and advancement of knowledge. We understand ethnicity, ideology, value, race, gender, and class politics are frameworks and constructs for defining our social culture because they interact with one another in shaping human behavior.

In the first chapter, Talha Siddiqi and C. P. Gause highlight American Higher Education Institutions continue to seek opportunities to grow their enrollments and budgets. Many institutions provide educational opportunities for foreign nationals as a means of achieving this objective. The International Student is very visible on today's campuses; however, with this visibility comes issues regarding equity, cross-cultural engagement, misunderstandings regarding customs, and the pressure to assimilate into American culture. They present the perspectives and challenges of International students who attend a predominantly white institution (PWI) in the Midwestern part of the United States.

In the second chapter, Donna Marie Peters, Sonja Peterson-Lewis, Rickie Sanders, Elizabeth L. Sweet, Karen M. Turner and Kimmika Williams-Witherspoon explore the experiences of women faculty of color who teach University-required Race and Diversity courses and/or other courses that contain significant race or race-related content. Because of the subject matter/content (race and diversity) and their goal of encouraging ways of thinking that further social justice, they relied almost exclusively on pedagogies akin to Friere's critical consciousness building and the Socratic Method.

In the following chapter, Jay Poole explore queer and queerness situated in education and schooling by employing a personal lens, an approach which may be viewed by some as queer in and of itself. Despite the fact that queer approaches have been part of academic literature and discussions for twenty years or more (some would argue much longer), he finds that most of his academic colleagues remain either confounded or offended when I bring up the topic.

In this chapter, Gust A. Yep, Sage E. Russo, and Rebecca N. Gigi present a description of the social and cultural context of U.S. Trans visibility with a focus on Caitlyn Jenner. They identify their theoretical and pedagogical orientation to the project. Next, they unpack U.S. mainstream representations of Jenner and explore how such representations might be producing what they call "the new trans normativity" at this historical moment and discuss its potential symbolic and material consequences. They conclude with a summary and exploration of the theoretical and pedagogical implications of their analysis.

Tara Jabbaar-Gyambrah and Seneca Vaught assert despite increasing numbers of Black students enrolling in higher education, fewer Black professionals are being promoted to senior level administrative positions in higher education. Does the dual burden of racial consciousness and gender expectations play any role in this disparity? Balancing career and family life is a challenge for most academics but can be particularly challenging for Black faculty and administrators in higher education. They examine the challenges that Black middle level administrators and tenure-track faculty face in higher education as they attempt to move above the "glass ceilings" and break through the "tinted windows" of higher education.

Brenda L. H. Marina presents and critically examines the findings and the silent voices of women in academia and their respective experiences of the "glass ceiling". These findings are synthesized with literature related to concepts and "syndromes" that identify conceptual patterns of significance and assign meaning for women on a career path in academia.

P. Brandon Johnson presents findings from a qualitative study purposed with understanding their experiences of African American males participating in a living learning community (LLC) at a Historically Black College and University (HBCU). Specifically this chapter investigates the experiences of first-year African American males who participated in an LLC on an HBCU campus to see how, if at all, LLC participation impacted their retention.

Dalia Rodriguez, Mary Cannito-Coville and Tremayne S. Robertson they highlight perspectives from young black males in schools and university contexts, and addresses the construction and performance of black masculinity. They ask the following questions: How do Black male boys and college students construct, perform, and express black masculinity in a society that perceives them as threatening and dangerous? How are they perceived by whites, especially in an era where surveillance has become normalized? Their lives often sensationalized and rarely understood for their complexities, it becomes critical to address the nuances of how Black males construct and perform black masculinity in educational and overall social contexts.

Brent E. Johnson and James H. Campbell discuss the usage of Black male athletes as property to be controlled by the hegemony of their sport specifically and modern society in general. It is their attempt to examine Black masculinity through lens of Critical Race Theory (CRT) in sport. They believe this analysis provides a tool to examine the tensions that the black male athlete must endure while participating in sport at collegiate and professional levels. The title "You Can't Piss Down My Back And Tell Me It's Raining" was chosen to bring to bear the notion that the African American male participating in Division I basketball and football at Predominantly White Institutions (PWIs) and in professional football and basketball are held captive by the system that profits monetarily from their labor and told that it is in their best interest.

Jewell E. Cooper and Joseph N. Cooper presents the personal narratives of a single African American mother and her son to highlight how educational success was cultivated through the transmission of cultural and social capital. Using an auto ethnographic approach, a mother and son present critical reflections on their lived experiences within a culture in the southeastern United States. Their stories reflect how parental leadership can serve as a vital form of social justice in equipping African American children with the skills necessary to succeed in a society where the odds are against them.

Steven Randolph Cureton highlights lethal vigilante violence has an active pulse in America. More specifically, in those instances where young white males are confronted by social, cultural, and academic situations that challenge their sense of value, some may define these as severe injustices, and obstacles to their rite of passage to manhood. He asserts, we are witnessing adolescent, high school, and college aged white males' inability to effectively cope with feeling vulnerable, unaccepted, bullied and criticized. The rational for rampage killings is that it represents justice for males who feel tormented by their peers. Moreover, the school yards, and campuses where rampage shootings are carried out appear to make sense because masculine affirmations must take place in the arena where the male felt emasculated.

CHAPTER 14

The Perspectives of International Students at Southern River University

A Predominantly White Institution (PWI) in the Midwest

Talha Siddiqi and C. P. Gause

American Higher Education Institutions continue to seek opportunities to grow their enrollments and budgets. Many institutions provide educational opportunities for foreign nationals as a means of achieving this objective. The International Student is very visible on today's campuses; however, with this visibility comes issues regarding equity, cross-cultural engagement, misunderstandings regarding customs, and the pressure to assimilate into American culture.

Public universities in the United States have a long tradition of participation in international activities. Many prestigious and selective colleges have utilized international programs to provide cross-cultural and study-abroad experiences for their students (Paulson, 2014). Colleges and universities have utilized curriculum enrichment via international studies majors or area studies to enhance their curriculum. Many campuses provide sponsorships for foreign students to come to campus to study. Because of these various internationalization initiatives, international students are becoming more prevalent on the campuses of American universities.

The foci of this chapter are the stories and perspectives of International students attending a predominantly white institution (PWI) in the southern Midwestern region of the United States. The stories of international students are limited in the academic literature; particularly, as it relates to how global politics and cultural barriers impact their integration into campus and local communities. We are interested in the perceptions of this population and ways to utilize their narratives to impact services and enhance the socio-cultural experiences for campuses with a significant International student population.

International Students in the United States

The United States of America (USA) accommodates the largest international students' population in the world. According to the Organization for Economic Co-operation and Development (OECD), foreign students' population in the USA was recorded at 741,000 with an increase of approximately 30% that used to be just 570,000 a decade ago (OECD,2015). The overall population of international students in the U.S. has grown to 900,000 with a record increment of 72% within past 15 years. Although increased number of foreign enrollments provide enormous financial contributions to the U.S. economy it comes with many challenges. These challenges range from managing the diverse populations on campus, in classrooms, and in the local communities.

According to *Open Doors 2015*, the number of international students enrolled in U.S. higher education increased by ten percent to 974,926 students in 2014/15, with 88,874 more students than last year enrolled in colleges and universities across the United States (IIE, 2015). There are 73% more international students studying at universities and colleges in the United States now than were reported 10 years ago. International students comprise five percent of the more than 20 million students enrolled in U. S higher education. There is currently a decrease in the number of American students enrolled in American colleges and universities. China remains the top sending country, with almost twice the number of students in the U.S. as India, but India's rate of growth and absolute increases outpaced China's (IIE, 2015). The number of students from Saudi Arabia in the United States to nearly 60,000; which represents a 11% increase. This is due impart to the largely funded Saudi government scholarship program, which is currently in its 12th year. The top three countries of origin—China, India, and South Korea now represents approximately 51% of the total enrollment of international students on campuses in the United States (IIE, 2015). According to the National Association of Foreign Student Advisors (NAFSA) the 974,926 international students studying at U.S. colleges and universities contributed $30.5 billion and supported more than 373,000 jobs to the U.S. economy during the 2014–2015 academic year (www.nafsa.org). In addition to the economic impact on the U. S. economy and university budgets, international students offer important insights and perspectives to campus and community leadership, viewpoints regarding equity and diversity, and opportunities to create progressive collaborative learning environments. However, all of this may come at a price. The increasing number of international students enrolled in American colleges and universities has pointed attention to the lack of special services to help international students adjust to the host culture, which has created various problems on university campuses.

The Setting

Southern River University or SRU as it is affectionately called by both students and alumni is located near the Mississippi in the southeastern part of a Midwestern state. Southern River University enrolls approximately 11,200 undergraduate and graduate students. It is located in a small regional center that has a population of 38,000, so the city is considered a "town and gown" community. Ninety percent of the city residents are White, 8% are African Americans, and 2% are considered "other."

The student headcount based on race and ethnicity consists of the following: 8,551 White students; 1,030 African American students; 1,139 Nonresident Alien students; 120 Asian students; 200 Hispanic students; and 988 not reporting any race and/or identity. Approximately 68% of the student body identity as female. There are several civic, religious, and community organizations in the town in which SRU is located. The majority of the churches are United Methodist, Lutheran, Baptist, Catholic and Presbyterian. There is an Islamic Center or Mosque located in the city with a very active Islamic community. SRU does not keep an actual count of students who identify based on particular religious beliefs; however, it is noted that many of the international students who attend SRU identify as Muslim, Hindu, and Buddhist. The Islamic Center is located approximately five blocks from the administrative building of the university. It serves as a gathering place for all Muslims in the community and region.

Method

This study utilized Qualitative case study design. Data were collected via questionnaires and individual interviews with 11 international students studying at a regional university in the southern region of a state located in the Midwestern part of the United States. For the purpose of this study, we will use the name Southern River University (SRU) as a pseudonym for the university in this study. Case study was the most appropriate qualitative research method for this study because it provided opportunities to gather artifacts within the institution and the experiences of the participants are influenced by cultural, social, and political contexts of that institution (Stake, 2005).

The following eight questions were developed to guide the interviews:

1. What is your gender?
2. Where are you from?
3. What things have you experience while being here?
4. Are there any positive and/or negative things you experienced?
5. What are your favorite things you like to do on campus?
6. What are your experiences on campus inside of class and outside of class?
7. Do you have friends who are from other countries?
8. What are other things you can tell us about your time here in the United States that we did not ask?

The questions were disseminated anonymously via a student email list developed by the Office of International programs. Students were given a link to access the survey and could not begin the survey until they gave electronic consent. Students were also given the link to the survey via several social media platforms. Through peer conversations, many students noted they received the link to the survey; however, had difficulty completing it due to their limited English language ability. Those who indicated this also informed the researchers they wanted to receive assistance in completing the surveys questions. The researchers met with those students who wanted assistance in completing the surveys. The researchers assisted those participants by reading the surveys questions to them and recording their answers. Some participants had problems writing their answers legibly in English. The researchers wrote the answers as dictated by the participants. Eleven students contacted the researchers. Seven were males and four were females.

The students represented the following countries: India, Nepal, France, Ecuador, Jordan, Costa Rica, and Saudi Arabia. Participants were undergraduates and graduate students with majors in the College of Business, College of Health and Human Services, College of Education, College of Liberal Arts, and the College of Science, Technology, and Agriculture. They were interviewed for approximately 30 minutes and were asked the same set of questions. Interviews were conducted in classrooms, offices, or in non-formal settings on and off campus. The interviews were conducted during the 2015 and 2016 calendar year.

The researchers noted, once the questions were completed, students begin to engage in informal levels of conversations. Students shared information regarding their experiences both on and off campus. They also discussed their perspectives regarding attending this university and also some of the problems they were experiencing with their instructors. We provide the questions and responses in the next session so you are able to surmise the brevity of our interviews. We follow this section with a data analysis of the conversations that were held after we stopped writing their answers to the surveys interviews. We discovered the "data" presented in the informal conversations provided more of a context for their experiences and perspectives. We asked the students why they did not present the informal information during the completion of the survey and most of them expressed that the survey felt more like and academic exercise. "One in which, Westerners would engage, instead of really trying to get to know me."

Questions and Responses:

Malik

Please select your gender:
Male

Where are you from?
Jordan

Why did you choose to come to this college and/or university?
I applied for couple of universities and it was the best choice of all of them.

What things have you experienced while being here? Are there any positive and/or negative things you experienced?
Positive: people are very helpful and friendly
Negative: different cultures

What are your favorite things you like to do on campus?
Studying

Tell us about your experiences on campus inside of class and outside of class.
Yes, I do have friends from all around the world.

Bashir

Please select your gender:
Female

Where are you from?
Saudi Arabia

Why did you choose to come to this college and/or university?
Because I got admission.

What things have you experienced while being here? Are there any positive and/or negative things you experienced?
People are very friendly and nice.

What are your favorite things you like to do on campus?
Going to the gym.

Tell us about your experiences on campus inside of class and outside of class.
Yes, I have friends from many countries and this is really nice to meet different people and have a background of different culture.

Suresh

Please select your gender:
Male

Where are you from?
India

Why did you choose to come to this college and/or university?
It had a great business program referred to me by some of my friends who had graduated from this university. It is a good university and has a good value for money.

What things have you experienced while being here? Are there any positive and/or negative things you experienced?
I have experienced a mix of positive as well as negative things. There have been times where I was appreciated for my work and effort; on the other hand, there have been times that I felt that I am being discriminated by the domestic students. I won't point at someone but there have been instances where I have been denied opportunities (unofficially) only because I am an International student.

What are your favorite things you like to do on campus?
Get involved in on-campus organizations
Serve the campus community
Volunteer
Work out
Play different sports and try different kinds of food.

Tell us about your experiences on campus inside of class and outside of class.
The in-class experience is not that much appraising as the out of class experience is. In the class, I don't have friends who would talk to me or share their class work or knowledge with me. Out of the class, I find people who became friends and are absolutely willing to me with all the stuff that I need help in. Yes, I love friends from different countries and around the world.

What are other things you can tell us about your time here in the United States that we did not ask?
There have been instances where people who are typically from the countryside have a very narrow approach towards the international students. Especially, being from a so-called third world country, they think that we are another group of more guys trying to harm them in any way, shape, or form. It is a common ideology that they have. Even when you try to be nice and being a change in their thinking, their stereotypes never let you grow and being a change.

Zyad

Please select your gender:
Male

Where are you from?
Saudi Arabia

Why did you choose to come to this college and/or university?
Because I got my admission.

What things have you experienced while being here? Are there any positive and/or negative things you experienced?
Yes, learning time and money management.

What are your favorite things you like to do on campus?
Drinking coffee.

Tell us about your experiences on campus inside of class and outside of class.
Learning new things such as research. Yes, I have.

What are other things you can tell us about your time here in the United States that we did not ask?
Chilling with friends and traveling with my wife.

Lala

Please select your gender:
Female

Where are you from?
India

Why did you choose to come to this college and/or university?
Because it's affordable and it was closer to my sister's university.

What things have you experienced while being here? Are there any positive and/or negative things you experienced?
Yes, I have experienced both positives and negatives. I have learned a lot by staying in the U.S. and have realized the meaning of independent life which according to me has helped me become a better individual. I have had negative experiences too as I have been judged by my skin color.

What are your favorite things you like to do on campus?
I like to get involved on campus by giving interviews/applying for different organizations to keep myself busy. Also, I love to hang out with my friends during my free time or make new friends.

Tell us about your experiences on campus inside of class and outside of class.
Yes, I have many friends who are from other countries. My experience on campus inside of class and outside class is great as I got to know so many people because of in-class group activities and by staying on campus dorms.

What are other things you can tell us about your time here in the United States that we did not ask?
My time in the United States is amazing till now. The only problem is I don't get to celebrate my country's festivals the same way as I did back home. Also the food is really different and we have to go to St. Louis to eat Indian food. One drawback of staying on campus is that you have to pay to stay in your room during vacations which gets really expensive when you add up with food expense.

Ricky

Please select your gender:
Male

Where are you from?
Costa Rica

Why did you choose to come to this college and/or university?
I came before through cultural exchanges and I liked the school.

What things have you experienced while being here? Are there any positive and/or negative things you experienced?
Most of them positive. I have learned to interact with different cultures, work collaboratively, and respect different kinds of thinking. I have experienced many different treatments from different cultures and religious groups, but all good. (Most of what you find in here is foreign due to the diversity on campus)

What are your favorite things you like to do on campus?
Observe the different behaviors according to the culture.

Tell us about your experiences on campus inside of class and outside of class.
All of them are! I am the only Costar Rican on campus. That means that I can't interact with people from my country as most internationals do. In class I am almost always alone because there are several cultural groups (such as Chinese, Arabic, Indians, etc.).

What are other things you can tell us about your time here in the United States that we did not ask?
The behavior of Americans toward international. However, I don't think in this place are like all over the country. This is a small town and people tend to be more gentle in rural areas.

Tham

Please select your gender:
Male

Where are you from?
Hyd, India

Why did you choose to come to this college and/or university?
This college provides the courses in which I wanted to pursue my master's and this is a state university.

What things have you experienced while being here? Are there any positive and/or negative things you experienced?
Keep up with the plan of study to maintain and achieve good grades in the academics.

What are your favorite things you like to do on campus?
I like to move around and use the campus recreation center most of the time.

Tell us about your experiences on campus inside of class and outside of class.
The classes are pretty good and well equipped with updated technology. The outside environment is good and makes us feel calm. We can say a perfect education environment.

Results—"Off the Record"

Data obtained from the surveys and informal interviews were analyzed using content analysis and the following results below:

International students who participated in this research project indicated, although SRU is located in a "lovely" small town in the Midwest, they still had some difficulties with adjustment. There were cultural differences, challenges with making new friends (social integration), differences in the educational system with regard to cooperative learning and sharing versus individual responsibility for completing assignments. International students indicated they enjoyed the amenities offered by the university, to include the recreation center, having a Subway and Starbucks on campus; but they also felt socially isolated because of the small number of students who may be from their home region and/or country.

Students indicated they utilized services sponsored by the Office of International programs; however, those who were graduate students did not utilize the resources provided by the center. International students at the graduate level relied upon services that were provided off campus i.e. those provided by the Islamic Center, community organizations, and local churches. Graduate students indicated having family members who lived in the region. This provided them opportunities to still connect to their home country and culture.

Many students reported issues with their communication skills to include both speaking and writing. They expected the challenge before they came to the United States; however, they did not realize the level of writing intensive courses and group projects that they would encounter in their courses that required them to better understand the professor's dialogue and classroom interactions. They biggest conflict; particularly in the classroom setting with American students and themselves was the tension in the duality between being an "individual student" versus operating out of a "collective identity" which was learned behavior established in the fabric of their upbringing from their home country. Negotiating the rules and policies of the U. S. educational system and the assertiveness of most American students was a stressor for those International students who participated in this project.

International students who participated in this project indicated they enjoyed making new friends, the social activities provided by the university, and also the ability to engage in "dating" rituals. Two of the participants in this project met their future spouses while attending the university and one student "came out" as a gay man while attending SRU. The student who "came out" stated he would be killed in his home country for being gay and was excited that he could live out his "true identity" in the United States. One of the participants who met his future spouse did get married to an American white female and she converted to Islam. Both families were exciting regarding this union and have been quite supportive.

Conclusions and Recommendations

International students who participated in this project were apprehensive during the survey process. Students became very open with regard to their perspectives regarding attending Southern River University at the end of completing the survey. The change in behavior took place after the participants completed "the academic" exercise (the surveys). The results of this project revealed International students still experience many difficulties negotiating the American Higher Education system. Even with the "safe" environment of a regional predominantly white institutions (PWI) in the Midwest, they find themselves having to adjust to various cultural norms, language proficiency, and social isolation. The students who participated in this project enjoyed several of the amenities, services, and location of Southern River University; they did note that adjusting to the "way things are done" can be difficulty. Many students in this project reported having many friends; but also discussed the financial difficulties they experienced as well. They did report relying on family in the region for support and that Southern River University was definitely a place to get a "good" education.

International students who participated in this project, especially at the graduate level, recommended more co-curricular activities and that the colleges, departments, and university should have orientation programs for international students that address academic responsibilities and expectations, as well as the cultural values, beliefs, and norms that exist on the campus. They believe these orientation programs should also have members of the student university community and not be done in isolation. International students have arrived on this campus during the holiday season or when campus is closed and this has to do with when they receive their visa and the permission to travel from their host country. International students recommend that someone is available to meet them and provide as much information as possible when they arrive because of the level of stress and anxiety they are experiencing when arriving to the United States (a new country). International students are making life transitions when they arrive in the United States to attend an institution of higher education. Students who participated in this project recommend that early connections to support staff, university counseling services, the Office of International programs, and empathetic faculty early in the arrival is essential to their success.

International students who attend institutions of higher education in the United States have gone through rigorous educational programs. They want faculty to know they have the academic aptitude to be successful. They recommend that faculty get to know them and really want faculty to understand that just because they appear to be silent in class or have limited capacity for speaking English fluently, does not mean they are not capable of doing the work and rising to the academic expectation. International students in this project desire to be challenged and want to fully participate in the academic process. They recommend faculty continue to encourage them to seek out student support services and other programs so that they can become peer mentors for their fellow international students.

Work Cited

Institute of International Education. (2015). *Open doors 2015: Report on international educational exchange*. New York, NY: Institute of International Education.

OECD. (2015). Education Database: Foreign/international students enrolled. *OECD Education Statistics* (database). Retrieved October 20, 2015 from doi: http://dx.doi.org/10.1787/data-00205-en

Paulson, A. (2014, November 17). *Record 900,000 international students in US: The top countries they hail from*. Retrieved October 26, 2015 from CS Monitor Website: http://www.csmonitor.com/USA/Education/2014/1117/Record-900-000-international-students-in-US-the-top-countries-they-hail-from

Stake, R. E. (2005). Qualitative case study. In N. Denzin & Y. Lincoln (Eds.), *Handbook of qualitative research* (pp. 443–466). New York, NY: Sage.

CHAPTER 15

Treading Treacherous Waters

A Conversation with Women Faculty of Color on Teaching Race

Donna Marie Peters, Sonja Peterson-Lewis, Rickie Sanders, Elizabeth L. Sweet, Karen M. Turner and Kimmika Williams-Witherspoon

Introduction

The ideas for this chapter came together with considerable struggle—not unlike most collaborative efforts, but also not unlike those experiences we have difficulty putting into words. The most difficult ideas to put into words are those things we know to be true but fear no one else would understand—or, more troubling, fear no one else would want to hear.

In *Teaching to Transgress* (1994), bell hooks draws on her experience as a Black woman in the university classroom to make the argument that the standard educational experience—which relies largely on a power dynamic between the teacher and the student—is problematic. *Teaching to Transgress* is actually hooks' musings on what an alternative education might look like. She puts forth two observations that are foundational. First, the insistence that learning should be enjoyable and connected to the personal lives of the student; and second, the practice of revering the mind and ignoring the body (embodiment) is a practice that confers power to a bankrupt and impotent pedagogy. This practice of erasing the body and denying its place in the classroom is the focus of our work here which highlights the impact of microagressions on the minds and bodies of women of color who teach Race and Diversity courses. While hooks perceptively notes the importance of acknowledging the relatedness between mind and body, she does not discuss the political and practical fallout faced by faculty who must teach content that introduces difficult socio-political historical content to audiences that either oppose or are offended by that body of information. Given the perfect storm created by the current political economy of higher education, the historical antecedents of the "Race" requirement in many Universities' curricula, and the often-uncritical deployment of student evaluations as a means of assessing faculty suitability for teaching such courses, this is a problem that needs to be discussed. Added to these factors are others such as the state of the US economy, which has seen wages fall and tuition rates increase and the emergence of a consumerist/customer satisfaction mentality in post-secondary education. Together, they point to the increased vulnerability and delicate position of women faculty of color in the academy. Ironically, these dynamics emerge at a time when the election of the first African American president has signaled to some that U. S. society is now a postracial society—one in which race no longer matters.

Much of the recent work on post-racial societies and its implications has focused on the symbolic importance of the election of Barack Obama, the experience of international students, and the greater visibility of people of color in the public sphere (see Apollon, 2011; Brown, 2003; Bush, 2011; Dawson & Bobo 2009; Lopez, 2010; Wise, 2013). At the same time however, this literature suggests that the term "post-racial" is a misnomer. More than anything, this literature signals a "shape shifting" of racism that allows for both racial stereotypes and racial exceptionalism to exist side by side. The more things change, the more they stay the same.

In this chapter, we extend the conversation about teaching race beyond this literature, pick up where hooks left off in her acknowledgement of the importance of mind/body synthesis; and explore the experiences of women faculty of color who teach University-required Race and Diversity courses and/or other courses that contain significant race or race-related content. Because of the subject matter/content (race and diversity) and our goal of encouraging ways of thinking that will further social justice, we relied almost exclusively on pedagogies akin to Friere's critical consciousness building and the Socratic Method. We are not aware of research, which specifically examines the impact of various pedagogies on teaching race and/or diversity.

After some background about the history of designated/required Race and Diversity courses at Temple University, we provide a description of the Academic Center on Research in Diversity (ACCORD) Research Group, and a brief discussion of our methods. Following that, we share what emerged from the discussions and conversations among the members of the research group and conclude with "Lessons Learned" and "Proposals for Future Work".

Background and Context

The requirement that students take a Race and Diversity course has been in the Temple University curriculum for over two decades. To date, much of what we know about these courses is information gleaned from teaching evaluations and pertains primarily to the student experience. This information suggests student attitudes vary from *strong enthusiasm* to *strong resentment*. What makes race focused courses different from other courses is that students *come* into the class with preconceived attitudes, experiences and prior knowledge. These preconceived notions affect (1) classroom interactions; (2) student attitudes (3) student performance on assignments; (4) student learning; and (4) course/faculty evaluations. However, the student resistance generated by incongruity between their worldview and the introduction of new ideas that most courses bring, begs the question of whether the goals of Race and Diversity courses are being accomplished and what can be done to make the courses maximally effective for students and less stress-inducing for the faculty teaching them.

These concerns make it especially important to examine the experiences of faculty based on their relative positionality in the academy. Research shows that faculty variables such as gender and race are related to the perception of faculty legitimacy in the academy, with faculty of color and women often being more vulnerable to negative stereotyping than others (Aguirre, 2000). The experiences of women of color,—whose vulnerability to race and gender biases in the academy have been explored elsewhere (see Bordo, 2003 & Crenshaw, 1991; Davis, 2004; Moraga & Anzaldúa, 1981, Thomas & Hollenshead, 2001) become particularly informative and important to examine.

Course evaluations reveal student attitudes. The attitudes and classroom experiences of faculty, however, are usually neglected in traditional course evaluations. The experiences of faculty members who teach Race and Diversity courses specifically have been explored in the work of Littleford, Ong, Tseng, Milliken, and Humy (2010); Peters-Davis and Shultz (2005); Laubscher and Powell (2003). Much of this research focuses on "microaggressions"—subtle racist acts that are manifested in myriad ways, often without the perpetrator or even the victim being aware. They are "subtle, stunning, often automatic, and nonverbal exchanges, which are 'put downs'" (Pierce, 1978, p. 66). Derald Sue expanded the term to include

> … brief and commonplace daily verbal, behavioral, and environmental indignities, whether intentional or unintentional, that communicate hostile, derogatory, or negative racial slights and insults to the target person or group. … These exchanges are so pervasive and automatic in daily conversations and interactions that they are often dismissed and glossed over as being innocent and innocuous. (Sue et al., 2007, p. 273)

Microaggressions are complicated by the fact that the *perpetrator* is not only oblivious to the effect on the receiver, but is also likely to be offended by the insinuation that she/he has engaged in an act of racism. Because people have different racial realities that make it difficult to interpret interracial events independently of their personal experiences, dialog about microaggressions can be thorny (Sue et al., 2007). Again, as noted, this is exacerbated by the belief among many that we live in a post-racial and colorblind society where racism no longer exists.

For the people who experience them, however, the microaggresions elicit a visceral reaction. They land on a body that is raced and gendered. Typically, a person who has been at the receiving end of such behaviors is left wondering if what happened is indeed real, and looks to other people who can relate to similar experiences for validation. Perpetrators reject the incident as non-racial, thus cancelling the experience of the recipient (Joshi, McCutcheon & Sweet, forthcoming).

Literature on racial microaggression has grown. Some scholars have developed ways of categorizing microaggression (Sue et al., 2007), others have documented its impact (Solorzano, D., Ceja, M., & Yosso, T. 2000). Sue et al. (2007) proposed a classification system including: the more aggressive ***microassaults*** (distinguished from overt racism where the perpetuator is anonymous), the subtle yet racially demeaning ***microinsults***, and ***microinvalidation*** the questioning or delegitimization of the ideas, existence and/or experience of the non-white body.

Microaggression theory has been used to identify and locate the experience of students of different races (Solorzano et al., 2000) and ethnicities—Latino/a undergraduates (see Clark et al., 2011; Gomez et al., 2011; Yosso et al., 2009). Solorzano et al. (2000) attempted to study the linkages between racial stereotypes, cumulative racial microaggressions, campus racial climate, and academic performance of African American undergraduates, using critical race theory as a theoretical underpinning. The range of microaggressions included *invisibility* experienced by the students, a perception of lower expectations, insinuations about affirmative action and tokenism, which over time led to self-doubt, feelings of exhaustion, frustration, isolation, and resentment.

The impact of racial microaggressions registered in the form of severe bodily stress (anxiety, vulnerability, loss of energy and enthusiasm, feelings of alienation and *outsiderness*), particularly when students confronted the perpetuator. Coping mechanisms consisted of creating counter spaces by building communities in academic and social contexts. As was the case in the early days of "date rape", those studying racial microaggressions emphasize the importance of naming the injuries, both for purposes of validation, as well as learning how to appropriately address these behaviors.

These studies indicate that being well-intentioned with goals to promote social justice is not enough. Our work will contribute to this growing body of literature and at the same time, *unpack* the current sociocultural context, which many (misrepresent) as "postracial" society in the U.S. Our purpose, then, is to explore the experiences and observations of women of color who teach University-required Race and Diversity courses and other courses that place strong emphasis on race. We examine these experiences through intensive, openended conversational interviews. We are particularly interested in unearthing how the intersectionality of race and gender is associated with particular classroom experiences.

We plan to expand our study and invite a larger group of colleagues who are willing to discuss their teaching experiences and observations. Our broader research project aims to explore issues that affect teaching and ultimately improve teaching effectiveness and learning outcomes in the contested domain of race. By extension, our work should be useful to the growing knowledge base about teaching and learning in other contested subdivisions of the social sciences such as religion, class, sexuality and gender studies. This chapter should also make a contribution to students, faculty and progressive institutions that recognize and seek to seize the opportunities that exist when the legacy of race, ethnicity and other arenas of difference are discussed in a climate of openness and collegial sharing. For departments in the planning stages of implementing related courses in their curricula, this work should prove valuable.

We see this paper as an initial contribution to a larger conversation—a pilot investigation or precursor to a more in-depth examination of the topic. We neither replicate the literature that exists, nor pretend to offer a comprehensive treatment—even if that were possible. We are aware this work is based only on one University and thus might be perceived as narrow and parochial. We argue, however, that the ideology of post-racialism—the larger sociocultural context of our work—is ubiquitous and unbounded; thus, we expect our work to have unlimited applicability.

The Accord Research Group

Our group of six women of color met several times over a period of three months in 2014. While the meetings were prompted by the immediate goal of contributing to this edited volume, all but one of the six women are members of Temple University's Academic Center on Research in Diversity (ACCORD) and the Faculty Senate Committee on the Status of Faculty of Color (FOC). The FOC, meets twice a month and is formally charged with advising the faculty and administration on issues of concern to faculty of color. In that regard, issues pertaining to the classroom experiences of faculty of color frequently come up for discussion. The six group members are of all ranks—from non—tenure track to full professor. Length of service ranges from five years to 27 years at Temple; altogether, there is a combined total of 135 years teaching experience at various universities. A mix of Colleges (Liberal Arts), Schools (Media and Communication; Center for the Arts) and with disciplines (Geography and Urban Studies/ Planning, Sociology, African American Studies, Theater and Journalism) are represented. Most of the collaboration took place electronically and via conference calls. Face to face meetings occurred several times on Temple University's campus. The then Associate Vice Provost and Director of the Teaching and Learning Center and a former non-tenure track faculty person, whose research specialty is critical race theory and microaggressions, co-facilitated the conversation described here. We chose these two colleagues because of their knowledge of teaching strategies, classroom dynamics, student learning, race theory and their interest in the issues we were raising. Their role was (1) to encourage us to think deeply about our teaching experiences and (2) to push for greater depth in our responses.

The facilitators asked us to respond to the following six questions:

What has been your experience teaching Race classes?

How have your students reacted (in class, on evaluations, etc.) to your teaching race or incorporating race in your course(s)?

1. Have you changed your teaching strategies as a result of student reactions? If so, how?
2. How has teaching race impacted your career?
3. How has teaching race impacted your scholarship?
4. Aside from General Education curriculum goals for Race and Diversity studies classes do you have additional goals when you teach/discuss race in your class(es)?

The questions proceed from the premise that because everyone comes to Race and Diversity courses with experiences and preconceived notions about race, teaching race poses unique challenges to students and faculty. Given that data has shown dual effects of race and gender on teacher's classroom experiences (Griffin, Pifer, Humphrey, & Hazelwood, 2011; Modica & Mamiseishvili, 2010; Smith, 2007, 2009; Stewart, 2012; Sule, 2011), the questions posed to the group in this study are rooted in the assumption that the teaching experiences of faculty of color—and *especially* women of color—may be particularly instructive.

History of "R" Designated Courses at Temple University

> *Few students are aware of it, but the race course required by the core curriculum with the intention of promoting racial understanding has its origins in a violent incident of racial conflict …*
>
> ~The Temple News, April 26, 2005

In the late 1980s, many universities around the country introduced courses aimed at sensitizing students to issues of race and diversity. Although this concern was prompted at Temple by a number of location-specific events, in general universities perceived students to be lacking skills seen as essential for success in a racially diverse and globalizing world. Temple University was an institutional leader in establishing Race Studies courses. Accounts differ, however, as to why.

According to the April 27, 1990 *Philadelphia Inquirer:*

> A dispute over a broken window at a Temple University fraternity house escalated into a street brawl between students that attracted a crowd of several hundred spectators. Several injuries were reported. Police and witnesses said that after a window was broken in the Phi Kappa Psi fraternity on Broad Street near Susquehanna Avenue around 11:20 p.m., a group of fraternity brothers charged out with sticks and bats and encountered a group of other students gathered in the plaza outside Johnson Hall, a dormitory. Temple police, attempting to break up the fight, quickly radioed for city police assistance. Four police vans were dispatched and the disturbance was brought under control in a matter of minutes, police said. Four students were taken into custody by Temple security police. City police said they made no arrests.

In contrast, the student newspaper The Temple News, on April 26, 2005, wrote about the origins of the university's race requirement in the following story that we have paraphrased:

> [I]t all began on the night of April 26, 1990 during the annual Temple University Spring Fling event, when a group of white fraternity brothers approached an African American male student [Sean Patrick Anderson] wielding bats, sticks and two-byfours. They thought it was Anderson who had broken the window in their fraternity house on Broad and Susquehanna Avenue. The African American student was incredulous but the damage had been done and things happened fast as the student was hit with a bat and struck across the back with a twoby-four. Several black football players came to the aid of the student. After someone pulled a fire alarm and students began to pour out of dorms, the police arrived. Temple police beat eight black students. All those handcuffed were black (Philadelphia Daily News and Philadelphia Inquirer). At 2 a.m., President Peter Liacouras met with students in the residence halls and announced the suspension of the fraternity.

The following Monday, 400 black students sat down and blocked traffic on North Broad Street … for an hour in protest. The number of daily protesters exceeded 1000 by Thursday … Black students united in a group called Concerned Black Students and presented a series of demands to the University. (Editor, *Temple News*, 2005)

Students' demands included firing the head of campus security, permanently suspending the fraternity, establishing an allblack dormitory and student union, and adding a requirement that every student enrolled at Temple take a course on race. It was the latter demand that gained traction. After several meetings between students, administrators and faculty, a proposal was submitted by the Faculty

Senate Educational Programs and Policies Committee to add a requirement that every undergraduate would take at least one course on race. In December 1991, the Faculty Senate recommended adding the Race Studies requirement to the curriculum. In the two decades since the Race Studies requirement was established, the course offerings have been broadened to include all aspects of diversity, though race continues to be prominently featured. As of this writing, there are 27 Race and Diversity courses with multiple sections offered each semester by various schools and colleges.

Discussion

Pamela Barnett, former Associate Vice Provost and Director of the Teaching and Learning Center/ cofacilitator: ***What has been your experience teaching Race classes?*** Several common elements surfaced among the participants regarding their experience teaching race classes, primarily the challenge relating to students who see themselves as members of a post-racial and post-colonial society. Are these students devoid of racial preference, discrimination, and prejudice?

Many scholars and social commentators regard this post-racialized notion as an ideological fictive expressing a desire for 21st century multiracial acceptance.

ELS: It's hard to teach race because we're in a *postracial* society—you know, we have a black president, so therefore race is something historical and people—especially younger people seem to really think that it's passé—that it's ancient history. And they have a very hard time even getting to the point where it's something worth even discussing.

KMT: I've had students who say it's basically my generation's problem. And this goes to your point about being post-racial—and there's no problem because they have white friends. I'm talking about particularly African American students. There's a lot of interracial dating. And it goes back to "it's you all, and once you [the older generation] die off, there won't be any problems."

KWW: It's more than European Americans who don't want to confront the history of racism in this country. In general studies and theater basics courses, I have African American students who don't want to be anything other than *a theater student*, or a communications student or whatever ... They feel as if they'll be *othered* or somehow stigmatized by identifying with anything else.

ELS: One of the things that Kimmika said that really struck a chord with me is this idea of not wanting to confront the history of racism in this country. And for me, as a Native woman, this has a broader context as well. Not only the racism, but also the imperial colonial past that this country represents. Slavery was so long ago; we can't talk about that now. And according to some of my students everything has been fine since slavery, and they think we haven't done anything else since then. When we talk about US colonialism and imperialism and their disastrous impacts on other countries and their people, I get pushback. There's this idea of not wanting to confront historical or contemporary colonialism or imperialism—of not recognizing the benefits people in the U.S. have because of these structures. This is privilege that they carry and it is very, very hard to get some students to recognize their privilege.

As a group we were very concerned with the various pedagogies and strategies we used to convey information. For example, we are intent not simply to lecture but rather to find ways to engage the students in dialogue, conversation, projects and discussion. This can become especially difficult in classes with more than 25 students, which most Race and Diversity courses have. Since much of the course material resulted in cognitive dissonance and "pushback," in some instances some of us felt it was more effective to let "authorities" impart the message.

KMT: One video I found for this semester's radio reporting class, which I think is interesting, is *1964* produced by PBS. It doesn't go back to 1619 or anything if we're talking about slavery and African Americans ... It's not so far back in the day that students think it's outdated and they talk about the foundation being laid for what we're dealing with today, like the Tea Party and Civil Rights.

DMP: You know, the students are challenged to see the world through a variety of lenses and experiences. And I feel that putting them through this discomfort is sort of like what we call *disequilibrium*. And so I think I have grown to expect the basic pushback.

Most of the group thought that even with innovative and novel pedagogies, there were aspects of the teaching experience that were sometimes troubling.

SPL: And it's particularly disturbing—when you think of all the efforts that went into changing the civil rights lay of the land—that there are African American students who don't want to confront information that suggests that the playing field might be a little bit different for them. Some are threatened by the idea. And anything that produces dissonance is going to get some pushback. And that's what we're speaking of: the pushback.

RS: I find it interesting that my white colleagues can say things that I cannot say. I mean, not that I cannot say, but when I say them, I either feel or *am made* to feel "that's not true …" But my white colleagues can say exactly the same thing, and it *is* true. Before this semester, talking about race was impossible because my black students would shut down; my white students would look at me and it felt like I was getting daggers, and then they wouldn't say anything …

We were also keenly aware of the very fragile position we occupied in the classroom. All of us could recount stories of students who would attempt to "remind us of our place" by being openly disrespectful.

RS: I had a student come up after class one day and tell me—because I asked her to revise a paper; this was a white student—to *stop riding her ass*. Really!? I have no doubt she would *not* have said that to a white male. And I have little doubt that she would have said it to a white female.

KWW: There is a level of disrespect that happens in the academy to women, and then particularly to women of color. And that's whether you teach in the race curriculum or not. I always felt bad about forcing people to call me Dr. WilliamsWitherspoon. First of all, the name is too long; okay, it just really is. But I've begun to do that now. Either Dr. Kimmika or Dr. WilliamsWitherspoon, because I know that there is a tendency to disrespect women and women of color in particular in the academy, so when we're having those difficult questions and conversations, and it's getting a bit, you know, agitating for them to sort of answer my query, then because they've had to call me Dr., Dr., Dr., all through the semester, it keeps some of that (disrespect) at bay. But then there's always that one student that crosses the line.

SPL: A student with poor attendance and less than a 40% final average in a course—not an R course—came to see me months after the course ended. I reviewed all her assignments with her and gave strategies for improving her future performance. About an hour into our meeting, she said, "You mean you are not going to change my grade? I have to take the course again?" I told her I couldn't just give her passing grade without cause, but that I would help her develop a plan for improving her future work. I was in the middle of talking through and writing out a study plan when she just walked out of the room.

Each of the ACCORD research members talked about similar disrespectful narratives where disgruntled students are constantly undermining their credibility as academicians.

SPL: I found her standing at the elevator and asked if she was leaving. She said an expletive and something like, "You'll see." Shortly thereafter, she filed a grievance, but it was found baseless. Months later, I received a message that contained a note she had sent to an office. Her note claimed that I made the course assignments challenging specifically to make her life miserable! She demanded that I not be allowed to teach the course … Why? Because *she* found the course hard.

Many of the ACCORD research members talked about the student perceptions that women and faculty of color should not have the authority to exact such rigorous standards.

SPL: Such was the case with an older student who claimed I discriminated against her age-wise because after I sat with her for two hours to guide her through a very simple formula, I left it to *her* to push the calculator button to get the final answer so she could take some credit for having done the assignment as homework! Both these students [the other mentioned above] happened to be African American females and I have seen this behavior cut across several demographics. Often, these experiences stem from the assumption that certain professors do not have the right to hold standards.

ELS: Its mental energy, and physical too … when I have an incident where a student is very aggressive, I feel stressed. I go home and try to deal with the stress. Then, I can't sleep because I'm thinking about it. So, I lose sleep over it. I feel like students often connect the disrespect to my presumed incompetence, as a Native American woman. The linkage to my being makes it hard for me to separate or disconnect from it. It consumes me. My husband always says, "Don't worry about it" or "don't let it stress you out." But it does.

For all of us, such experiences produced fatigue and exhaustion.

KMT: When I teach my online race media studies class, which is usually once a year, I am so focused on race—I'm exhausted. I need sometimes to step back and process student comments and try to figure out how I'm going to respond to them in a way that addresses whatever they're talking about. Also, in a way that encourages them to think critically, honestly and be curious about issues of race and class in a media context. I don't want them to feel so overwhelmed, they shut themselves down … But I'm drained at the end of that semester because of all of these strategies that we've all been sharing, and constantly trying to think through. And it just takes a toll on me emotionally.

SPL: It sounds like teaching under siege. [Affirmations from group]. And there's only so much psychological space that you can devote to that kind of problem solving and still accomplish other things. I often calm myself by thinking about my ancestors and what their lives were like. In comparison, mine is relatively easy. But anytime you have to devote extreme time to thinking about how to stay out of the sights of somebody who's gunning for you … there is a tiredness you feel because there is only so much brain space that you can devote to staying safe and at the same time get other important things done.

KWW: Every day is a matter of staying alive in the academy because once you get the label of being the troublemaker, or the angry black woman—especially for those who are not tenured; and if you're a nontenure-track or adjunct—oh my God!

DMP: I ask myself why do I put myself through this? Why teach? And even teach the race classes. But you know what? I don't mind the pain, the ulcers, the gray hair, because I have this feeling that this is about progress, and moving this generation forward. I have great faith in the millennials. They have positive traits as a group: they're optimistic, they're engaged, they're team players, they have liberal political attitudes, and many are socially committed because they say that they want to work towards making the world a better place to live.

RS: I'm the oldest one in the room. And I've been in the academy for longer than anybody. Until fairly recently, I was the only African American woman geographer Full Professor *in the world.* For the longest time, I thought that the things I was feeling were not legitimate feelings. But everything that happens lands on a body that's raced and gendered and holds the stockpiled impact of all time and all space. So it's the embodiment of the microaggressions, the accumulated effect of what happens over the course of a day that I feel makes my experience different.

SPL: I think the idea is that the microaggressions that you experience while you're teaching about race are replications of the microaggressions that you experience just living your life.

KWW: There's a part of me, thinking back to the ancestors that makes me feel that I have to be willing to go into the trenches to teach this second generation of students because I can help change their minds. And if indeed the millennials are more liberal, more open—minded, more politically active, if they really are *that*, then here's an opportunity to touch these individuals in ways that will have ramifications years—countless years—down the road.

ELS: I feel like I have skills based on my experience in everyday life. I feel and understand racism. It is not my cross to bear, but I feel like it's my mission. It's social justice, and I need to do it, but I need some protection or backup.

Shangrila Joshi, Visiting assistant professor/Co-facilitator: **How have your students reacted to your teaching race or incorporating race in your course, in class, or on your evaluations, etcetera?**

The common element that surfaced in this discussion is a unanimous concern with the Student Feedback Forms (SFFs), Temple University's mandatory teaching evaluation instrument. These are administered once during the semester during the last two weeks of class. Last year a decision was made by a joint faculty and staff committee to administer the instruments in an online format. Several of us were troubled by this and thought that revisiting the process of evaluating teaching would be a critical first step in demonstrating the institution's commitment to supporting faculty, especially faculty of color, as well as faculty from other marginalized groups.

KMT: What I find is that looking at student evaluations generally for all my classes, I think students don't realize race and gender play a part in how they're relating to me.

SPL: There should be a date stamped on evaluations because sometimes what students say is a matter of their reacting to something that happened that day—to your having said "no" to their taking an exam three weeks late, or to your having returned a paper that they have to rewrite. Keeping the form open for so long allows evaluations to change depending upon what a student has just experienced in a class on a particular day—or what grade students expect to get.

ELS: Well, they have research that shows evaluations are directly tied to the grade that students think they will get.

KWW: And if you talk a lot about race, and make some people feel uncomfortable about the history of racism in this country, then that comes out in the evaluations.

ELS: At another institution, I was teaching a book called The *Devil in the White City*, which is about the Chicago World's Fair. The devil is the guy who was murdering women in Chicago throughout the duration of the fair. I had a group of students *en masse* go to the Dean and complain that they were sick of learning about race. This book is called the White City because the *walls* of the buildings constructed for the fair were white—there is nothing about race in that book! So their going to the dean shows that the students didn't even open the book. After my supervisor reviewed the syllabus at the request of the dean, he suggested that I tone down the emphasis on race.

KWW: I found that I got a better response from the students if every day I reminded them that this was a race course and not a theater course. But when they thought that it was a theater course that I was just dealing with race, then they were very agitated.

How have you changed your teaching strategies as a result of student reactions? Or have you; if so, how?

SPL: Letting the textbook or documentarybased experts say it is something I do to minimize conflict and stress because I don't see fighting over established historical truths as my cross to bear. I like to choose my crosses.

RS: What I want to share is *not* how my teaching has changed but how *I* have changed as a result of student reactions. Students will come to me, and tell me how they really enjoy my class. And that should make me feel very good, and it does. At the same time, however, I know that those same students will put something on a teaching evaluation, intentionally or not, that will do me harm. I don't know whether to believe them or not. And so there's a distrust that has entered some of my interactions with my students, and that's unfortunate.

ELS: Sounds like a cycle of violence.

RS: The problem is that nobody has our back. Will the administration even entertain the possibility that the teaching evaluations are not an accurate gauge of teaching? And if not, that is a problem.

KMT: There is research that shows gender and race negatively impacts student feedback forms. We should have an opportunity to respond to the forms so we can at least give them a context. There should to be a groundswell of faculty saying *we need* to have a way to respond.

ELS: I get feedback that the course is too hard. If you only believe what the students say, and the students only want an easier class, then it puts faculty in a bind.

KMT: I'm thinking about how I've changed, and I know I've changed because when I grade, I'm constantly thinking if this student challenges the final grade, I need to have a paper trail, I need to be very specific on the feedback that I give to the students because this may show up in another place or form. It's frustrating because I'm taking the extra time—I guess to show that the person who's teaching this class knows her stuff. And it's time consuming. And it's exhausting.

KWW: It does make you second-guess yourself, and you're hyperconscious of everything that you do.

Looking to the future of Race and Diversity courses at Temple, all of the faculty members agreed to the importance of the race curricula and its impact on their own creative and scholarly output.

With the extra commitment of time you put into your race content courses, how have they impacted your teaching and career?

KWW: It means that you're spending less time doing your research or writing or whatever it is, doing *this* work. Here at a place called the *Diversity University,* the assumption is that if those of us who teach in the race curriculum don't do it, then who will? And so that's what continues to drive me.

DMP: As universities change Temple has remained true to its mission. At least we can teach these courses here.

KWW: Even as they streamline the education—the process to allow students to get through the University in four years—you're still trying to come out with a product—a global citizen that can do critical thinking on all of these areas, regardless of whatever the ultimate job at the end of the rainbow might be. I'm hoping that students will continue to recognize the importance and reassert their commitment to the Conwellian tradition. That's what Temple used to be, and I would hope that's what Temple continues to be.

KMT: Even though we have a different population or a changing demographic of students who are coming in with higher SAT scores and more middle and upper—middle class backgrounds staying on campus, it's important that we readily articulate the Conwellian mission, as in years past.

DMP: But if students haven't learned to interact with different populations while in college, how will they interact with others in the workforce? Because it isn't one color, one creed, one race, one sex. We are living in a global, multiracial society. And we need faculty members committed to teaching young people how to live in our rapidly changing society.

KMT: And we should not be the only ones responsible for, or thought to have the capacity and the competency to teach these courses. These should be courses that everyone should be teaching.

How has teaching race impacted your scholarship?

Responses to this question varied based on whether or not "race" per se was part of the participants' research and writing interests. Those who teach about race and who also have research interests that entail writing about race or its effects, spoke of differential responses from publishers depending upon whether or not their perspective or research findings were considered in vogue or politically correct.

ELS: I started publishing on race because of my experiences teaching race.

RS: Me as well.

DMP: Ditto.

[Other faculty nod their heads.]

KMT: The types of journals the administration respects and expect you to publish in are not the publications that necessarily would be interested in issues of diversity I want to talk about. However, that's always—at least for me—the struggle, finding that balance of what I want to write about versus what I should write about to get published in the mainstream high impact journals.

SPL: I had an experience in which an editor returned an article to me with all kinds of accolades—how well researched, how strong it was, how objective. … Yet, he rejected it, claiming that the topic was off the path of what the journal published. However, a number of the most relevant articles in my literature review had come from that very journal. It seems that the real issue was that they had a problem with the highly racialized and politically incorrect positions some of my participants voiced. So even if you do not teach race per se, if your research has findings deemed politically incorrect at the moment, it can affect publication opportunities.

KMT: And then beyond the journals, if you're talking about a discipline such as journalism where perhaps you're also trying to get op-eds published, you know the emphasis is getting into publications such as the *New York Times* or the *Wall Street Journal.* Well, given what I or someone else dealing with issues of diversity might have to say, such publications may not be interested. So you publish in *minority* media. But for those individuals usually judging your work, this is not as respected; it doesn't count, or at least not for much.

KWW: So, it's a double-edged sword. We're committed to doing the work and writing, but we also know that we're writing to what is perceived as a second-tier audience, only because we're being forced to write that way.

As for tools and "best practices," most of the research group suggested that their syllabi, as contracts, set the tone in engaging their students.

"Do you have specific goals for when you teach or discuss race in your classes?"

KWW: Absolutely. We all have learning goals embedded in our syllabi.

RS: I don't teach the Race and Diversity courses, but I have specific goals on my syllabi. They may be there to foster critical thinking or to learn how to write a well—argued essay … but I also have other goals, and I guess they're personal. I want my students, to appreciate how they are *raced, classed,* and *gendered.*

ELS: I want my students to know that racism still exists—and how it manifests in our everyday lives.

DMP: And I want to help students critically understand how race matters. In the words of one of my favorite writers, James Baldwin, *"Color is not a human or personal reality; it is a political reality."*

SPL: I think the prospect of appreciation some years down the line keeps you trying in any class. I read an article that said that teachers who say that they are willing to wait for their students to appreciate them many years down the line are just giving an excuse for getting poor evaluations. But I have noticed that by the time students graduate and spend a little time working or they've gone into graduate school, they begin getting jobs or hearing conversations that engage some of the skills or concepts you've taught them. They then realize that it wasn't just you—that you were actually teaching from an academically sound base; that you weren't teaching your personal opinion or ideology—that you were actually teaching ideas they will have to deal with in the world and things that, if they learn, are going to put them a few steps ahead of the competition.

KWW: And they are better able to articulate the language now because of you.

SPL: I'd rather be appreciated now rather than later. [laughter] There was a time when I liked the now—later decision. I have more now in my life than I have later. But the question is, are our experiences different from our colleagues?

Conclusion-Lessons Learned and Proposals for Future Work

You cannot tell what are the lives of these [women] who surge about you.

Upon your own people sympathy and knowledge you hold; you can enter into their lives ... But these [women] are strange to you ... their likeness to you does not help you; it serves rather to emphasize their difference ... you might as well look at a brick wall ... You do not know the first thing about them ...

~W. Somerset Maugham, On a Chinese Screen

We set out to explore the experiences and observations of women of color who teach Universityrequired Race and Diversity courses and other courses that place strong emphasis on race. Realizing that we all occupied the intersectionality of race and gender and seemed to have familiar sounding stories to share, we seized the opportunity to come together and examine our experiences through conversation and dialogue.

So, after our many hours together, what do we know? Do we now see our classroom experiences in a different light? Do we understand our experiences better? Do we now know why we tread the treacherous and emotionally challenging waters to do what we do? Do we know what resources we draw on to stay afloat? Answering these questions presupposes we have answers to more fundamental philosophical and moral questions; e.g. what is desirable?; what is possible?

Despite intragroup differences—age, training, professional status, disciplinary background, teaching philosophy and epistemology—there were several things we agreed on. First, our shared experience of occupying a raced and gendered body has consequences for what goes on in the classroom. Second, we all agreed that our primary reason for being in the academy is to teach our students to engage different perspectives and imagine a better world. This is *the* important work we do; we do it for them, but we also do it for ourselves. Third, we agreed all classrooms are racialized. Even when we are not teaching Race and Diversity courses, we confront the prevailing ideology that racial equality is a zero sum gain *versus the our gain is their loss* paradigm. Guiding students to the point where they can clearly see how race privilege and how race privileges have structured the world in a way that is detrimental and challenges deeply held beliefs. In these instances, privilege is fraught with difficulty. It is not unlike the very contentious debates that ensued among faculty during the initial discussions in the Faculty Senate around implementation of the Race proposal. The mere suggestion that this is not the case produces the fight or flight response. The goal is not to induce guilt, as many students think, but to stimulate the imagination. Unless we can facilitate more open discussions about how individuals are raced, classed and gendered etc.—no one wins.

We present this very personal conversation among ourselves not simply so other women of color will recognize they are not alone. We would be remiss if the message ends here. Rather, what we hoped for was to reveal the continued marginalization of women of color in the academy *despite* the rhetoric of a post-racial society. Our objectives are goals that university administrators *should* be deeply invested in. Over the next year, we plan to expand our study and invite a larger group of colleagues who are willing to discuss their teaching experiences and observations. We hope to target women faculty of color and others who teach race and diversity courses. Our overall research goal is to explore issues that affect teaching and learning outcomes and, ultimately improve teaching effectiveness in the contested domain of race. Our hope is that we will be taken seriously.

Work Cited

Aguirre, A. Jr. (2000). Women and minority faculty in the academic workplace: recruitment, retention, and academic culture. *ASHE-ERIC Higher Education Report, 27*(6), Jossey-Bass Higher and Adult Education Series.

Apollon, D. (2011). *Don't call them "postracial": Millennials' attitudes on race, racism and key systems in our society*. New York, NY: Applied Research Center.

Bordo, S. (2003). *Unbearable weight*. University of California Press.

Brown, M. K. (2003). *Whitewashing race: the myth of a colorblind society*. Oakland, CA: University of California Press.

Bush, M. E. (2011). *Everyday forms of whiteness: Understanding race in a 'postracial' world*. Rowman & Littlefield.

Crenshaw, K. (1991). Mapping the margins: Intersectionality, identity politics, and violence against women of color. *Stanford Law Review, 43*(6),1241–1299.

Davies, B., & Bansel, P. (2005). The time of their lives? Academic workers in neoliberal time (s). *Health Sociology Review, 14*(1), 47–58.

Davies, B., & Petersen, E. B. (2005). Neoliberal discourse in the academy: The forestalling of (collective) resistance. *LATISS: Learning and Teaching in the Social Sciences, 2*(2), 77–98.

Davis, B. A. (2004). The slippery slope of student evaluations for black women faculty. In *Building bridges for women of color in higher education: A practical guide for success*. University Press of America.

Dawson, M. C., & Bobo, L. D. (2009). One year later and the myth of a post-racial society. *Du Bois Review: Social Science Research on Race, 6*, 247–249.

Editor (2005, April 26). Race requirement began with a brawl. *The Temple News*. Retrieved from http://temple-news.com/race-requirement-began-with-brawl/

Griffin, K. A., Pifer, M. J., Humphrey, J. R., & Hazelwood, A. M. (2011). (Re)Defining departure: Exploring black professors' experiences with and responses to racism and racial climate. *American Journal of Education, 117*(4), 495–526.

Gutiérrez y Muhs, G., Niemann, Y. F., González, C. G., & Harris, A. P. (2012). *Presumed incompetent: The intersections of race and class for women in academia*. Utah State University.

Harley, D. A. (2007). Maids of academe: African American women faculty at predominantly white institutions. *Journal of African American Studies, 12*(1), 19–36.

Hart, J., Grogan, M., Litt, J., & Worthington, R. (2008). Institutional diversity work as intellectual work at the University of MissouriColumbia. In *Doing diversity in higher education: Faculty leaders share challenges and strategies*. Rutgers University Press.

Heilman, M. E., & Welle, B. (2006). Disadvantaged by diversity? The effects of diversity goals on competence perceptions. *Journal of Applied Social Psychology, 36*, 1291–1319.

hooks, b. (1994). *Teaching to transgress*. New York, NY: Routledge.

Howard, T. C., & Flennaugh, T. (2011). Research concerns, cautions and considerations on Black males in a 'postracial' society. *Race Ethnicity and Education, 14*(1), 105–120.

Hull, G. T., BellScott, P., & Smith, B. (1982). *All the women are white, all the blacks are men, but some of us are brave: Black women's studies*. Feminist Press at CUNY.

Joseph, T. D., & Hirshfield, L. E. (2011). "Why don't you get somebody new to do it?" Race and cultural taxation in the academy. *Ethnic and Racial Studies, 34*(1), 121.

Joshi, S., McCutcheon, P., & Sweet, E. L. (2015). Visceral geographies of whiteness and invisible microagressions. *ACME: An International E-Journal for Critical Geographies, 14*(1), 299–322.

Landry, P. (1990, April 27). Students in brawl at temple. *Philadelphia inquirer*. Retrieved from http://articles.philly.com/1990-04-27/news/25918839_1_fraternity-brawl-students

Laubscher, L., & Powell, S. (2003). Voices inside schools: Skinning the drum: Teaching about diversity as "Other". *Harvard Educational Review, 73*(2), 203–224.

Lewis, A. E., Chesler, M., & Forman, T. A. (2000). The impact of "colorblind" ideologies on students of color: Intergroup relations at a predominantly White university. *Journal of Negro Education, 69*(1/2), 74–91.

Littleford, L. N., Ong, K. S., Tseng, A., Milliken, J. C., & Humy, S. L. (2010). Perceptions of European American and African American instructors teaching racefocused courses. *Journal of Diversity in Higher Education, 3*(4), 230.

Lopez, I. F. H. (2010). Is the "post" in postracial the "blind" in colorblind? *Cardozo L. Rev., 32*, 807.

McBride, D. A. (1999). *James Baldwin now*. New York University Press.

Modica, J. L., & Mamiseishvili, K. (2010). Black faculty at research universities: Has significant progress occurred? *Negro Educational Review, 61*(14), 107–122.

Moore, S. E., Alexander, R., & Lemelle, A. J. (2010). *Dilemmas of black faculty at predominantly white institutions in the United States: Issues of the postmulticultural era*. Edwin Mellen Press.

Moraga, C., & Anzaldúa, G. (1981). *This bridge called my back: Writings by radical women of color.* Watertown, MA: Persephone Press.

Perry, G., Moore, H. A., Edwards, C., Acosta, K., & Frey, C. (2009). Maintaining credibility and authority as an instructor of color in diversityeducation classrooms: A qualitative inquiry. *Journal of Higher, 80*(1), 80–105.

PetersDavis, N., & Shultz, J. (2005). *Challenges of multicultural education: Teaching and taking diversity courses.* Paradigm Publishers.

Pierce, C., Carew, J., Pierce-Gonzalez, D. & Willis, D. (1978). An experiment in racism: TV

commercials. In C. Pierce (Ed.), Television and education (pp. 62–88) Beverly Hills, CA: Sage.

Smith, B. P. (2007). Student ratings of teaching effectiveness: An analysis of endofcourse faculty evaluations. *College Student Journal, 41*(4), 788–800.

Smith, B. P. (2009). Student ratings of teaching effectiveness for faculty groups based on race and gender. *Education, 129*(4), 615–624.

Smith, B. P., & Hawkins, B. (2011). Examining student evaluations of black college faculty: Does race matter? *Journal of Negro Education, 80*(2), 149–162.

Solorzano, D., Ceja, M., & Yosso, T. (2000). Critical race theory, racial microaggressions, and campus racial climate: The experiences of African American college students. *The Journal of Negro Education, 69*(1/2), 60–73.

Stewart, P. (2012). The uphill climb. *Diverse: Issues in Higher Education, 29*(11), 16–17.

Sue, D. W., Capodilupo, C. M., Torino, G. C., Bucceri, J. M., Holder, A., Nadal, K. L., & Esquilin, M. (2007). Racial microaggressions in everyday life: implications for clinical practice. American psychologist, 62(4), 271.

Sule, V. (2011). Restructuring the master's tools: Black female and Latina faculty navigating and contributing in classrooms through oppositional positions. *Equity & Excellence in Education, 44*(2), 169–187.

Thomas, G. D., & Hollenshead, C. (2001). Resisting from the margins: The coping strategies of black women and other women of color faculty members at a research university. *The Journal of Negro Education, 70*(3), 166–175.

Vargas, L. (2002). *Women faculty of color in the white classroom.* P. Lang.

Wise, T. (2013). *Colorblind: The rise of postracial politics and the retreat from racial equity.* City Lights Books.

CHAPTER 16

Being Queer in the Classroom

Understanding and Applying Queer Theories

Jay Poole

It has been over a decade and a half since William Pinar's edited volume *Queer Theory in Education* was published (Pinar, 1998). At that time, I was in the midst of earning a master's degree in social work and the world was poised to mark the turn of the century and the millennium. The United States was still reeling from the AIDS crisis and the gay rights movement was struggling to redefine its direction and identity as a political force. The television show *Will and Grace* (1998) brought into peoples' homes a nice, clean-cut gay lawyer, his zany effeminate gay-male friend, and an all American straight girl, laughingly pushing the boundaries of what the American public could tolerate relative to main stream media's depiction of gay people and life and, perhaps, one of the first prime time looks at a queer family. In the so-called gay community, the word queer was being heard and used not as a demeaning term; rather, to be "queer" could mean that one was living and acting beyond and between what was expected relative to sexuality and gender roles—even heretofore established deviant gender and sexuality roles. In the 1940s and 1950s and beyond, dominant groups used "queer" as a slur toward anyone perceived to be other than heterosexual, including those who did not seem to follow traditional gender roles. Queer in the 1990s was taken up in the vocabularies of those who railed against dominance. Indeed, queerness became a location for opposition to dominant paradigms. Pinar and the authors that are represented in his book grapple with the concept of queer and queerness, particularly as it may or may not be situated in the field of education. In his introduction, Pinar eloquently speaks to important historical markers relative to queer theories in education and I will not repeat that effort here; rather, the focus of this essay will be to explore queer and queerness situated in education and schooling by employing a personal lens, an approach which may be viewed by some as queer in and of itself. Despite the fact that queer approaches have been part of academic literature and discussions for twenty years or more (some would argue much longer), I find that most of my academic colleagues remain either confounded or offended when I bring up the topic. In many cases people jump to the conclusion that I am attempting to address sexuality in some way and, thankfully, they are mostly supportive in their efforts to accommodate my ramblings. When I begin to explain what I mean when I refer to queer, they often remain fixed on the sexual aspect of the concept despite my best efforts to explain how queer may operate in many settings, including the classroom. Some self-disclosure here: I do consider my self to be queer and I often use queer approaches in my teaching and writing among other activities; thus, I consider myself to be queer in the classroom. What I hope to do here is provoke the reader to consider what queer may mean, how queer approaches may be considered and used as pedagogical tools, and how queerness may be taken up as a lens that serves to destabilize, critique, and question.

I would be remiss to avoid situating this discussion of queerness in contexts of sexuality and gender identities. Indeed, some would say that queer theories in education, at least in recent times, grew out of the struggles of those whose sexual and gender identities did not conform to dominant, heterosexual paradigms. As the modern gay rights movement and its offshoots began to destabilize essential identities that had emerged early on in its history, the cooption of "queer" began to emerge in the vernacular of some parts of the so-called gay community and as part of identity politics that resulted from the struggles to gain political power. *Queer Nation* most notably took up the word in the 1990s within their slogan that proclaimed a queer presence to the world, "We're here, we're queer, get used to it!" (Queer Nation, 2014). Queerness, derived from the use of the term queer as a descriptor of that which does not quite fit particular spaces, began to open opportunities for those who drifted between, among, and outside known sexual and gender spaces and "queer" seemed to call into question the sexual and gender codes that shape(d) identity and, interestingly, began to emerge in the academy as a space for calling into question all practices that reflected hegemony and dominant structures, which served as supports for oppression. Writers such as Foucault, Teresa deLauretis, Dianna Fuss, and Judith Butler, to name a few, began to academically "trouble" what had become reified as "normal" within gender and sexual definitions and practices as well as politics. Coupled with feminist approaches, so-called queer theories began to offer opportunities to (re)imagine possibilities. Butler (1990) asserted that gender was rooted in the performance of particular characteristics and that such performances were reinforced through social structures. Her work pointed out that heterosexuality was central in the construction of gender around the binarial view of male/female (based in biological definitions) and that we are driven to reify the notion of particular gender roles by performing heteronormatively constructed gender. Butler also pointed out that agency was an integral part of how genders and sexualities are performed with one being able to engage in fluid performances of gender and sexuality (Alsop et al., 2002). It is with the fluidity and plurality of gender [and sexual] performance that one may begin to disrupt what has been deemed normal and/or natural; thus, queering how gender and sexuality is/becomes defined/identified. Indeed, queer as an identity space has emerged in popular culture as young people (and old) begin to explore gender and sexual practices and politics that work the margins of what has been defined as normal, not only within dominant cultural spaces but, also, in so-called normal spaces within marginalized groups. For example, the Internet is filled with voices and practices that rail against what has become normalized (Ross, 2005). Certainly, the work of those who call dominant practices and politics into question has opened possibilities for deconstructing what we have come to know as "male," "female," "man," "woman," "gay," "lesbian," "bisexual," and "transgendered," yet our social order remains rather steadfast in its insistence on particular identities and practices associated with gender and sexual roles. Often it is in our schools that this discourse is played out, with students being the actors on a stage that can become perilous.

Many of the models aimed at addressing heterosexism and homophobia in schools call for the use of multiplicity with regard to using reading materials, visual images, films, guest speakers, panels, experiential techniques and personal narratives to expose students to positive messages about sexual and gender identities (Cullen & Sandy, 2009; Goldfarb, 2006; Little & Marx, 2002). Additionally, the involvement of stakeholders and the community becomes important in work to address heterosexism and homophobia (Garber, 2002; Wehbi, 2004). In the communities formed in schools one of the challenges in confronting homophobia or other prejudices is addressing the values, attitudes, beliefs, and behavior not only of students but also of teachers, staff, and administrators. Historically, teacher education has focused on pedagogical methods in an effort to produce teachers who can follow and implement curriculum plans. It seems that notions of moral and spiritual dimensions of the classroom are not routinely a part of teacher education courses and Purpel and McLaurin (2004), and Shapiro (2006), among others, call for schooling and education to take up moral and spiritual dimensions and aspects when engaging with students not only in the classroom but in all spaces where education can and does occur. The so-called progressive educators have long been associated with the disruption of bigotry, prejudice, and discrimination by exploring and promoting tolerance, empathy, acceptance, and celebration of so-called difference. Recognizing that tolerance simply asks us to deal with difference, the progressives moved toward an emphasis on empathy or identification with the "other." Taylor (2002) describes this effort:

> Having long recognized that information alone is not enough to produce empathy (Steward & Borgers, 1986), attitudinal changes from bigotry to compassion are sought through such devices as exposing students to positive representations of marginalized groups, providing access to the voices of silenced populations, facilitating role-playing experiences that let students of dominant culture simulate marginalized people's oppressive experiences, and providing students with corrective information about the oppressive experiences of the members of such groups. The goal of such lessons is for students to project themselves into the difficult social situations of others unlike themselves, recognize their common humanity, and move in the process from disrespect to solidarity. (p. 223)

Of course, it would be utopian to assume that simply awakening empathy is the answer to dispelling homophobia and heterosexism or other forms of oppression; indeed, deep foundational beliefs and values whose roots are often embedded in religious doctrine and practice are many times in conflict with embracing empathy for those who are considered immoral, particularly when foundational beliefs are conservative or fundamental. Taylor (2002) proposes that in the case of resisting an empathic lens based on personal foundational beliefs that reinforce "otherizing" those who are sexually and gender nonconformists the educator may employ a deconstructive model that addresses aspects of sociocultural phenomena that serve to marginalize particular groups. Using the prophetic voice, the educator calls into question systems and elements of systems, including those grounded in religion, in an attempt to promote a critical reading; however it is clear that deconstructive experiences are not always transformational. As Taylor (2002) points out:

> … even deconstructive classrooms often maintain the bifurcated tradition of Western scholarship which shoos matters of religious faith offstage into the personal arena, leaving them unscrutinized. In practical terms, the academic avoidance of discussing personal religious beliefs lets homophobic Christians complete Education degrees and arrive in classrooms with their prejudices intact, never having experienced the conflict between their faith and a commitment to just teaching practices. It also lets passive anti-homophobes grossly underestimate the continuing prevalence of homophobia in their future teaching colleagues, confirming our likeliest allies in a complacent attitude that homophobia is extinct when, for the sake of lesbian and gay students and the children of lesbian and gay parents, we need teachers to be alarmed at the damage homophobes continue to do. (p. 228)

The academic, critical exercise of tearing apart ideas and structures, while certainly a step in the direction of being progressive as an educator seems to fall short if one does not interrogate personal values, attitudes, and beliefs. As one of my professors often said, "go deeper" as if to suggest that there was more to explore (or tear apart) between and beyond where I was and often it was within my own self that became a fruitful, albeit frightening, place of discovery. Further, if one engages in deconstruction as a practice and, perhaps, a pedagogical model, what is one left with? A pile of rubble that was once structured identity or theory? Pinar (1998) addresses this in the Introduction of *Queer Theory in Education* and, following a discussion of identity politics and essentialism, points out that, "A queer pedagogy would, presumably, call forth and speak to a resturcured self." (p. 8). Thus a question is raised about what it means to deconstruct. What are we hoping to gain from deconstruction? Of course the answer to such a question has been the subject of many books and articles, penned by scholars far more learned that I; thus, I will not make any attempt to "answer" the question. Rather, I will take inspiration from it as an educator and I will consider what an answer might be like if one approached an answer using a queer lens.

I suppose a good place to begin would be to (re)consider the notion of queer approaches to pedagogy (or anything really). At its core, queer in this context is about being or doing differently—beyond what is normal or expected. Most certainly the roots of considering how queer pedagogy may apply are in efforts relative to sexual and gender identity concerns and those efforts are still needed and important; however, I believe that we can consider queer approaches beyond sexual and gender identities while still taking up oppression and what operates to support it. For instance, could an algebra class be queer? I propose that queerness may indeed be considered in any learning context and that any teacher could take up queer pedagogies. For instance, the algebra teacher may initiate a discussion about why Algebra came into existence as a form of math and may also discuss how it plays a role in supporting significant social structures, e.g., the banking industry. This discussion may go further into how algebra may or may not be used to improve peoples' quality of life. Many students may find it strange that they are talking about such things in math class and I would guess that many math teachers would find it strange to engage in such discussions. Looking at this from another direction, seeing someone teach queerly would probably raise many eyebrows among those in the status quo. I am thinking here of the scene in *Dead Poet's Society* (1989) when the teacher takes his students outside and marches them around the courtyard to demonstrate how to recognize and rise up against compliance. In the scene the teacher takes a queer approach, acts queerly, and creates opportunities for the students to take queer actions—eyebrows are definitely raised. Lesson learned—don't simply do what others do. But, did this exercise result in new identities, consideration of new possibilities, or a re-structured way of being? As a result of this deconstructive pedagogical endeavor have the students now restructured themselves as "radicals" or "rebels," which may be construed as simply other identities that support particular structures and ways of being or taking action? While this scene seems to represent a queer approach we can take the notion of queerness further than we see it taken. I believe that queer can and should take us beyond simply deconstructing what we know; rather, queerness takes us into what we do not know or into realms of what we believe cannot be known. Queer becomes a process of unknowing. Revisiting the *Dead Poets Society* scene for a moment these questions may be raised in the spirit of queer pedagogy—Where is the interrogation of the structures that got them to march in time to start with? What paradigms were/are at work that support a privileged, private education where being compliant is most certainly part of the curriculum? Is "carpe diem" simply representative of a newfound identity that serves to rail against the mainstream while serving the needs, wants, and desires of the self? What is problematic with leaving queer pedagogy simply linked to deconstruction is that reconstruction of identity, which inevitably follows deconstruction, rebuilds identities that begin to limit other imaginings and possibilities. Indeed, de Lauretis (1994), who is credited with coining the "queer theory" term criticized it almost as soon as it was used because it became exactly what it was supposed to critique—a sort of codified identity. Thus, as we consider how to be queer in the classroom, we must consider how to push beyond simply constructing something new out of what we deconstructed.

Luhman (1998), writing in Pinar's book, pushes us to consider how a post-identity pedagogy may be imagined pointing out that subversion is central to the consideration of pedagogies that may be queer. Luhman (1998) states, "Subversiveness, rather that being an easily identifiable counter-knowledge, lies in the very moment of unintelligibility, or in the absence of knowing." (p. 147). It is the state of unknowing that promotes discovery and imagining new possibilities. Becoming a queer pedagogue implies that one engages in a process of disrupting "normal" and embracing the effort to relish (un) knowing what is known in order to know what lies between and beyond what is known. Being queer in the classroom means that one has to disrupt the notion that teaching is a transferential process; rather, teaching is an engagement with what is known, how it may be unknown, and how new possibilities emerge as unknowing occurs.

Of course, this notion of unknowing is not simple and moreover, the process of unknowing is one that is often tedious and complex. In order to further ponder the notion of unknowing it may be helpful to consider complacency within the context of the educational process that occupies many educators' pedagogical tool bags. I suspect that a good number of us who identify as teachers would say that if our students would just "act right" and do their work as they have been told, all would be okay. Indeed, in many school settings the students who are most complacent are those who are deemed academically "successful." Their homework is turned in on time, they have the "right" answers, they don't disrupt the classroom, and they are "nice" kids. Engaging a queer approach would disrupt complacency and encourage both teachers and students to call ideas, structures, and processes into question. In the queer classroom, both teachers and students alike engage in the disruption of what is known and take up a critical examination of how and why what is known came to be. Learning becomes messy and unpredictable and power is examined and disrupted as the teacher/student binary is diffused and (re) imagined as reciprocal and fluid. A personal example of this would be my own struggle with the notion of mental illness and what we know about it. As a teacher of clinical social work I ask students to learn about diagnosing mental disorders using the current edition of the *Diagnostic and Statistical Manual of Mental Disorders* published by the American Psychiatric Association. Before I queered my pedagogical approach to this task I had students carefully consider the details and nuances of each diagnostic category, discuss them, address questions, and then take a test to see if they had "learned" what they needed to know. Now that I have become queer in my teaching, some of the questions I ask of the class (and myself) include: Why do we have this manual of mental disorders to begin with? Where did it come from and why do we hold it in such high esteem? What does mental disorder mean? What structures support the idea that people have mental illnesses? How do I (we) play a role in perpetuating the practice of diagnosing mental disorders? And, the list could go on. What is important to recognize here is that there are no finite answers to these questions; rather, they are intended to provoke and disrupt what we think we know about mental illnesses. It is this process of provocation, questioning, and unpacking that becomes, in my opinion, queer pedagogy. Further, how I am in the classroom is influenced by queerness; thus, I become queer in the classroom through my own reflective and introspective work relative to how I work with and among my students. Shlasko (2005) in her excellent article entitled *Queer (v.) Pedagogy* states,

> Where a mainstream educator might begin the planning or design process by asking hirself [Shlasko's word], "What information shall I convey to my students?" a queer educator (that is, an educator engaging in a queer pedagogy) could ask instead, "What questions shall we ask of each other? After we explore those questions, what will have been left out? And then, what other questions shall we ask of each other?" (p. 128)

It is in this space of willingness to move beyond the boundaries constructed within traditional approaches to teaching that queerness may emerge and be taken up as an intentional tool to promote learning (and unlearning). While noble and, perhaps, effective, efforts to simply teach people about queers or queer theories is not what I am suggesting here. Rather, I am encouraging readers to consider how queerness and queer approaches may be engaged in any classroom as an intentional pedagogical tool. Abes (2008) referring to Brueggemann and Moddelmog (2002) hints at this same encouragement and states,

> Whether offering queer theory courses to explicitly introduce students to this complex approach to identity or disrupting the norm and decentering privileged identities in courses across disciplines, queer pedagogy can challenge students' to think more complexly about their sense of self. (p. 73)

Indeed, if we as teachers can foster an environment where our students and we can engage in a thoughtful, provocative, reflective, and imaginative process of inquiry our selves are bound to be affected and, potentially, transformed. There is a refreshing and energizing aspect to imagining how teaching may be experienced much differently than simply transferring knowledge from one person's head to another. Davis and Sumara (2000) take up the notion of *complicity* in their article *Another Queer Theory* and play with it's queered meaning as a space for further expansion of the complex as well as being compliant with some wrongdoing, e.g., engaging in routine, conforming teaching practices. Shlasko takes up this notion of complicity in education and states,

> If education is "complicitous," then the goal of queer pedagogy must be to constantly multiply the possibilities of knowledge. We cannot simply search for the answer, because the answer is never quite reachable. "Events are inextricable … experiences are irreducible … [and] we are not converging on a unified and complete understanding of the universe" (Davis and Sumara, 2000, p. 108). (p. 128)

Freire (1998) and Greene (1988), both hailed as scholars in critical pedagogy, note that a state of being "unfinished" is a desirable state of being—we are all works in progress with learning being an ongoing endeavor. It is in this notion of being unfinished that we can connect to queer theories and queer approaches to teaching. This blows apart the idea that we simply convey "facts" to our students who then regurgitate those facts in some form or fashion. Indeed Freire (1998) warns against what he calls the banking system of education as limiting and oppressive. Further, queer approaches push against what is known into territories of what we do not know or, as Britzman (1998) states, "queer theory offers education techniques to make sense of and remark upon what it dismisses or cannot bear to know" (p. 214). Further, Britzman (1998) suggests that, in order to engage in queer pedagogies, we evaluate how we read information in order to locate our selves, power and oppressive structures in our reading practices. Obviously, extending this reflexive and reflective work with students is part of the queer learning environment, engaging students in deeply evaluating why they read (perceive and think) the way they do. It is within these processes that we can begin to locate heteronormativity, patriarchy, racism, sexism, and other systems that support oppression and oppressive actions. I believe that the consideration of power and systems and practices that inform and support it may be gleaned from queer practices in education so that teachers and students are not simply left on an unending loop of questioning. In fact, some would say that queer or critical approaches might result in being stuck in a repetitive cycle of questioning such that no position is ever taken and I think that this warning is something to heed. If we take up queer as a critique of normalcy, then it follows that queer pedagogies provoke normal and encourage taking a stand against simply complying with what has been deemed normal—ordinary—expected. Perhaps then as projects, queer approaches to teaching trouble normal and encourage action to de-normalize in order to stand against oppressive structures. Indeed this spills into the political realm and as feminists have pointed out, the personal is political, which may create opportunities for activist pedagogies (Poole & Church, 2011). As a result of critical inquiry and destabilization of what we know, possibilities emerge that may result in new directions, new knowledge, and imagined ways of doing and being that have not heretofore been considered. That, in my view, is one of the most exciting aspects of what queer approaches to education have to offer. I have been rejuvenated as I witness the academy's embrace of community-engaged scholarship, participatory action research, and interdisciplinary self-directed studies as possibilities for engaging between and beyond the boundaries set by traditional practices in higher education. Further, scholar/teachers such as Ileana Jimenez (2011) are queering classrooms in middle and high schools with great fervor. As Halberstam (2003) points out, "Queer studies can work on many fronts simultaneously: we can exploit this wave of new technologies to bring new methods and topics to the classroom; at the same time, queer public intellectuals can try to bring activism to the university and theory to the "community" (p. 364). If nothing else I hope this work will provoke readers to explore the notion of queer theory more in depth, and moreover, I hope that readers will take up queer theories as they consider how they engage in teaching and learning. For it is within the exploration of the known that we encounter the unknown, giving us possibilities for imagining what we could know. Embracing those possibilities, for me, is what is means to be queer in the classroom.

Work Cited

Abes, E. (2008). Applying queer theory in practice with college students. *Journal of LGBT Youth, 5*(1), 57–77.

Alsop, R., Fitzsimons, A., & Lennon, K. (2002). *Theorizing gender.* Cambridge: Polity Press.

Britzman, D. (1998). Is there a queer pedagogy? Or stop reading straight. In W. Pinar (Ed.), *Curriculum: Toward new identities.* Pp. 211–231. New York, NY: Garland Publishing.

Brueggemann, B., & Moddelmog, D. (2002). Coming-out pedagogy: Risking identity in language and literature classrooms. *Pedagogy, 2*(3), 311–335.

Butler, J. (1990). *Gender trouble: Feminism and the subversion of identity.* New York, NY: Routledge.

Cullen, F., & Sandy, L. (2009). Lesbian Cinderella and other stories: Telling tales and researching sexualities equalities in primary school. *Sex Education, 9*(2), 141–154.

Davis, B., & Sumara, D. (2000). Another queer theory: Reading complexity theory as a moral and ethical imperative. In S. Talburt, & S. Steinberg (Eds.), *Thinking queer: Sexuality, culture, and education* (pp. 105–130). New York, NY: Peter Lang.

de Lauretis, T. (1994). Habit changes. *Differences, 6*(2/3), 296–313.

Freire, P. (1998). *Pedagogy of freedom: Ethics, democracy and civic courage.* New York, NY: Rowman & Littlefield Publishers.

Garber, L. (2002). Weaving a wide net: The benefits of integrating campus projects to combat homophobia. *Journal of Lesbian Studies, 6*(3/4), 21–28.

Goldfarb, E. (2006). A lesson on homophobia and teasing. *American Journal of Sexuality Education, 1*(2), 55–66.

Greene, M. (1988). *The dialectic of freedom.* New York, NY: Teachers College Press.

Halberstam, J. (2003). Reflections on queer studies and queer pedagogy. *Journal of Homosexuality, 45*(2–4), 361–364.

Jimenez, I. (2011). *Teaching feminism in high school: Moving from theory to practice.* Retrieved September 18, 2013 from http://www.ontheissuesmagazine.com/2011fall/2011fall_jimenez.php

Little, P., & Marx, M. (2002). Teaching about heterosexism and creating an empathic experience of homophobia. *Journal of Lesbian Studies, 6*(3/4), 205–218.

Luhman, S. (1998). Queering/querying pedagogy? Or, pedagogy is a pretty queer thing. In Pinar, W. (Ed.), *Queer Theory in Education* (pp. 141–156). Mahwah, NJ: Erlbaum.

Pinar, W. (1998). *Queer theory in education.* Mahwah, N 1: Lawrence Erlbaum Associates.

Poole, J., & Church, M. (2011). Making the personal political in the classroom: Possibilities for activist education. *The South Atlantic Philosophy in Education Society's Annual Yearbook Volume 2011,* 125–134.

Purpel, D., & McLaurin, W. (2004). *Reflections on the moral and spiritual crisis in education.* Washington, DC: Peter Lang.

Queer Nation. (2014). *History.* Retrieved March 3, 2014 from http://queernationny.org/history

Ross, M. (2005). Typing, doing, and being: Sexuality and the Internet. *Journal of Sex Research, 42*(4), 342–352.

Shapiro, H. S. (2006). *Losing heart: The moral and spiritual miseducation of America's children.* Mahwah, NJ: Lawrence Erlbaum Associates.

Shlasko, G. (2005). Queer (v.) pedagogy. *Equity and Excellence in Education, 38*(2), 123–134.

Taylor, C. (2002). Beyond empathy: Confronting homophobia in critical education courses. *Journal of Lesbian Studies, 6*(3/4/), 219–234.

Wehbi, S. (Ed.). (2004). *Community organizing against homophobia and heterosexism: The world through rainbow-colored glasses.* New York, NY: Routledge.

CHAPTER 17

The New Transnormativity? Reading Mainstream Representations of Caitlyn Jenner in the University Classroom

Gust A. Yep, Sage E. Russo, and Rebecca N. Gigi

The emergence of trans visibility in U.S. mainstream media—for example, Caitlyn Jenner, Carmen Carrera, Chaz Bono, Chelsea Manning, and Laverne Cox, among others—has been aptly called the "transgender turn" in cultural affairs and academic scholarship (Stryker & Currah, 2014, p. 3). Mainstream culture makers, such as print media and television writers, interviewers, photographers and producers, have not only created a trans visibility but have in effect produced a particular type of trans subject for public consumption. Indeed, they have constructed, assembled, framed, and formulated "what trans looks like" for the general public. Such media representations have generated important exchanges and contestations over the meanings of trans, representations of trans lives, and the politics of trans images and subjectivities in the cultural domain. In the university classroom, these representations offer new opportunities to critically discuss, examine, and unpack the social construction of gender and its potentially violent symbolic and material consequences in society. Subscribing to bell hooks' (2010) vision of teaching as "a prophetic vocation" (p. 181) and committed to social justice and education as "the practice of freedom" (hooks, 1994, p. 13), we examine critical ways of reading trans representations in U.S. mainstream media in the university classroom. More specifically, using tenets of critical pedagogy (e.g., Freire, 1970, 1973; McLaren & Leonard, 1993) and transing (e.g., Stryker, Currah, & Moore, 2008; Yep, Russo, & Allen, 2015), we examine, in this essay, representations of Caitlyn Jenner[1] in popular culture to unpack, highlight, and demystify their deep and profound connections to larger structural and cultural processes, such as cisgenderism and heteropatriarchy, in U.S. culture. To do so, our essay is divided into five sections. We start with a description of the social and cultural context of U.S. trans visibility with a focus on Caitlyn Jenner before we identify our theoretical and pedagogical orientation to the project. Next, we unpack U.S. mainstream representations of Jenner and explore how such representations might be producing what we call "the new transnormativity" at this historical moment and discuss its potential symbolic and material consequences. Finally, we conclude with a summary and exploration of the theoretical and pedagogical implications of our analysis.

Caitlyn Jenner and the Social and Cultural Context of Trans Visibility

Over the last few years, trans identities and communities have steadily made their way into U.S. mainstream media and popular culture. The recognition of trans celebrities, activists, and public figures like Caitlyn Jenner, Carmen Carrera, Chaz Bono, Chelsea Manning, and Laverne Cox, among others, have increased trans visibility to the general public. Yet trans visibility in media representations has consciously portrayed trans communities as completely separate from mainstream cultural narratives, "othering" them in the process (Yep et al., 2015). In doing so, hyperanxiety about the preservation of heteronormative and heteropatriarchal structures of power feel threatened, reinforcing the cultural gender hierarchy currently valued by Western ideals. For example, in a recent interview with *Time* Magazine on the growing visibility of the "transgender movement," Laverne Cox (star of the popular Netflix series *Orange is the New Black*) addresses how increased trans visibility has the possibility to change attitudes since "more of us are living visibly and pursuing our dreams visibly, so people can say, 'Oh yeah, I know someone who is trans.' When people have points of reference that are humanizing, that demystifies difference" (Steinmetz, 2014, para. 2). These points of reference come at a price since transparency is highly valued by the audiences who consume this media and is directly tied to maintaining visibility. Steinmetz strongly believes "this new transparency is improving the lives of a long misunderstood minority and beginning to yield new policies, as trans activists and their supporters push for changes in schools, hospitals, workplaces, prisons and the military" (2014, para. 2). If a transperson does not display a certain level of transparency—whether it be a willingness to educate cisgender people about trans issues at any given time or explicitly discuss their bodies and sexual orientation, for example—then their existence and legitimacy within society becomes questionable, further detaching trans lives from humanistic qualities and maintaining marginalization. To put it more simply, the current trans visibility is based on a voyeuristic transparency of trans lives designed mostly for cisgender audiences with the potential corollary effects of simultaneously increasing understanding of this group and further otherizing and exoticizing trans realities.

In 2015, Caitlyn Jenner's very open transition has captured the attention of many mainstream media outlets. Months prior to Jenner's two-hour exclusive interview with Diane Sawyer confirming her transition, rumors flooded Internet and print media about secret surgeries, life in seclusion, and uncertainty as to why Jenner's physical appearance was seemingly changing. Buzz Bissinger's (2015) twenty-two page *Vanity Fair* article told Caitlyn's life story from previous marriages, relationships with her children, and the gritty details of her recent surgeries. This level of extreme transparency arguably makes Caitlyn the most "acceptable" or "good" trans citizen in mainstream media to date as it directly challenges the old trans narrative of hiding, lying and deceiving, and conforms to notions of heteronormative behavior that is strongly valued by U.S. society (Yep et al., 2015). Because of this, Jenner has been the recipient of increased popularity, media attention and praise; with the addition of a reality television show titled *I Am Cait*, documenting her life post-transition. Although increased trans visibility is much needed in mass media in order to validate marginalized identities, the oversaturated visibility of Caitlyn's transition in mainstream media provides a false assumption that the instantaneous, hyper-visible, hyper-transparent nature of her transition is or should be considered the new norm, invalidating the experiences and lifestyles of those in trans communities where this is simply not a desired or viable option. Caitlyn Jenner's transition further complicates trans visibility and how the media chooses to present it, providing an imperative and pressing opportunity to analyze the ways her transition has been represented in U.S. mainstream media.

Theoretical and Pedagogical Orientation

Paulo Freire (1970), in his classic volume *Pedagogy of the oppressed*, accurately observes that education, including the university classroom, can be domesticating or liberating. Domesticating education reaffirms social inequalities through a one-way relationship whereby the teacher is considered an active "depositor" of knowledge and the students are the passive recipients or "depositories" of knowledge (Freire, 1970, p. 53). In this model, the teacher is the active subject, the students are passive objects, and knowledge is lifeless, static, and apolitical. In contrast, liberating education attempts to subvert and change social inequalities through an interactive, co-created relationship between teacher and students by using a problem-solving approach, such as questioning the current social construction of gender in mainstream media representations. This approach creates spaces to understand how power relations function in society and to find creative ways to intervene in socially unjust situations. In this sense, education becomes "the practice of freedom" rather than the "practice of domination" (Freire, 1970, p. 62).

Adhering to the vision of a liberatory classroom, teaching is, in hooks' (2010) words, "a prophetic vocation" (p. 181). More specifically, this orientation to teaching is characterized by five critical features (hooks, 2010). First, it is active in "telling the truth" (p. 181)—that is, it highlights dynamics of oppression, suffering, and subordination (e.g., the symbolic and material violences of cisgenderism on trans bodies and identities). Second, it engages students as active learners—that is, they become co-creators of knowledge rather than ignorant and passive recipients of information (e.g., inviting students to understand their own gender fluidity). Third, it invites both teacher and students to engage in self-reflection—that is, to pay attention to affective, cognitive, behavioral, and bodily responses to power relations and knowledge production (e.g., discussing personal and collective reactions to patriarchy in U.S. culture). Fourth, it fosters critical thinking—that is, it encourages critical interrogation of the "who, what, when, where, why, and how" (p. 183) of a particular situation (e.g., unpacking the relationship between cisgenderism, patriarchy, and transphobia). Finally, it creates spaces to imagine new horizons—that is, to envision different social and cultural possibilities and realities (e.g., a social world with multiple gender expressions). Taken together, this orientation to teaching is transgressive, liberating, and creative.

Guided by critical pedagogy and trans theory, our examination of critical ways of reading trans representations focuses on the development and cultivation of "critical consciousness" in the university classroom (Freire, 1973, p. 44). As a central goal of critical pedagogy, critical consciousness refers to ways of seeing, relating, and interacting with the dynamics of power and domination in society (Shor, 1993). Critical pedagogy, according to Giroux and Shannon (1997), raises "questions about how culture is related to power—why and how it operates in both institutional and textual terms—within and through a politics of representation" (p. 5). Cultural texts, such as mainstream representations of transpeople,

> become not merely serious objects of struggle over how meaning is constituted, but also practical sites that register how power operates so as to make some representations, images, and symbols under certain political conditions more valuable as representations of reality than others. [Cultural] texts in this instance become pedagogical sites through which educators and others might analyze the mechanisms that inform how a politics of representation operates within dominant regimes of meaning [such as cisgenderism and heteropatriarchy] to produce and legitimate knowledge about gender, youth, race, sexuality. … (Giroux & Shannon, 1997, p. 7)

In short, mainstream representations of Caitlyn Jenner are important pedagogical sites for the development and cultivation of critical consciousness.

With a focus on examining and deconstructing "how gender is contingently assembled and reassembled with other structures and attributes of bodily being," transing complements the critical pedagogy project by providing an important tool for unpacking constructions and representations of gender in society (Yep et al., 2015, p. 70). More specifically, transing analyzes gender (a) in relation to other vectors of social and bodily difference (e.g., gender intersects with race, class, sexuality, age, etc.); (b) as simultaneously a performative act and administrative structure (e.g., gender is both microscopic and macroscopic); (c) in terms of multiplicity rather than duality (e.g., gender as a galaxy rather than a binary); and (d) in terms of the subjectivity and narrative viewpoint of people inhabiting a gender (or genders) (e.g., understanding how trans experiences are presented from a cisgender perspective in mainstream media) (Yep et al., 2015, In press).

Taken together, critical pedagogy points to the importance of analyzing mediated representations as a potential site for the development and cultivation of critical consciousness in the university classroom. Further, transing offers ways to unpack and analyze the social construction of gender and its potential symbolic and material consequences. In the next section, we use these tools to unpack mainstream representations of Caitlyn Jenner in U.S. popular culture.

Unpacking U.S. Mainstream Representations of Caitlyn Jenner

With the increased visibility of mainstream representations of transpeople, mostly fueled by a capitalist desire to cater to the current hottest "controversial" topic, some representational patterns—regurgitated through the multitude of news and gossip websites, magazines, and television programs—are beginning to emerge. Similar to the ways other marginalized and oppressed groups have historically been represented, "trans visibility" has largely been portrayed through reductionist, heteropatriarchal, cisgenderist lenses leading to the reiteration of "classic trans narratives." These narratives encompass hegemonic discourses surrounding transpeople and trans identities that are often employed in media to assure that trans identities are palatable for a mainstream cisgender audience (Irving, 2008; Mock, 2012; Siebler, 2010, 2012; Skidmore, 2011). Undoubtedly, this lack of representational diversity of trans communities in mainstream media only perpetuates the marginalization of their stories, identities, and lives.

To unpack the most common classic trans narratives and their key features, we turn to Caitlyn Jenner's *Vanity Fair* article (Bissinger, 2015)—the twenty-two-page story and accompanying photographs—as our central site of analysis. Three main themes emerged from our close reading of Caitlyn Jenner in the *Vanity Fair* article as well as in other mainstream media representations of Jenner and other transpeople. They are: (a) Pathologization of trans experiences, (b) obsession with the body, and (c) reification of the gender binary.

While the three themes are the most apparent, it is important to note that they are not the only classic trans narratives that perpetuate reductionist portrayals of transpeople in mainstream media. In addition, while we are separating these themes for clarity, they are in reality operating simultaneously, always constituting each other, and are never mutually exclusive. For example, in a particularly poignant example that encompasses a range of classic trans narratives and themes, almost immediately after the opening of the article, Jenner states, "I wish I were kind of normal. It would be so much more simple" (Bissinger, 2015, para. 5). Although this statement was made by Jenner, Bissinger's decision to include it within the first five paragraphs of the article positions the reader to think about it through a lens that views Jenner as anything but "normal." In this sense, it utilizes Caitlyn's internalized pathologization, to position transpeople as abnormal and their bodies as a site of complication, putting the responsibility to "fix" such abnormality on the trans individuals themselves, instead of focusing on deeper sociocultural issues, namely, the ways we understand, maintain, and enforce stringent Western sex and gender systems. By doing so, Bissinger reinforces cisgender identities as the default and desired gender identity, affirming the gender binary. The focus on the individual instead of the larger social system prevents society from addressing the deep structural and systemic changes that must be made for trans lives to be legitimized and validated (Spade, 2011). Keeping in mind their interconnectedness, we discuss, in the following sections, each theme in greater detail.

"It's Always About What's 'Wrong'": Pathologization of Trans Experiences

This theme refers to the ways that trans experience is regarded as medically or scientifically "abnormal" and presents transness as something that needs to be urgently "fixed." It often takes the form of mainstream media creating a mental and physical hierarchy of a person's relationship to biological sex, gender identity, and gender expression. Pathologization of trans experiences takes two primary forms: (1) psychological and (2) social.

Psychological pathologization positions transpeople as mentally unstable (or ill), confused, and/or misguided, among other dysfunctional features. It is often deployed through the use of the "wrong body" narrative and/or depicting transpeople as experiencing a constant state of pain, turmoil, panic, and self-victimization. A prototypical example includes Bissinger's (2015) reference to Caitlyn's journey as "a tragic one, a painful one, and a harmful one, for so many years, not just to himself but to others he should have been closest to, and a lonely one …" (para. 26). Though Bissinger finishes the list with brave, funny, and "maybe, just maybe, because it is far too early to tell, a triumphant one," the underlying message here is that transpeople are first tragic, and (maybe) secondly brave and triumphant, qualifying her experience as anything but ordinary. In the same vein, when Jenner posits that she was not comfortable in her "own skin" before hormones, surgery, and coming out as Caitlyn, she is harkening back to the "wrong body" narrative that seemingly helps cisgender people understand the trans experience by reinscribing the binary onto the body (e.g., a boy trapped in a girl's body or vice versa) and severely limits the ways that people can express and inhabit gender (McQueen, 2014; Mock, 2012). This state of discomfort adds to the narrative that transpeople need to experience dysphoria or discomfort as a central component of the trans experience (binaohan, 2014). The wrong body narrative is harmful as it ultimately reinforces the gender binary and the pressure for transpeople to "pass" as the hegemonic ideal of their "true" gender.

Similarly, Bissinger's (2015) choice to include Caitlyn's fifteen-second panic attack after waking up from multiple surgeries reinforces the idea that the choice to transition in order to "fix" the discomfort caused by living in the "wrong body" might have been too hasty or too drastic, cementing the assumption that transpeople are always in a constant state of pain or turmoil until they are able to identity and realize their "authentic" identity. It employs the idea that transpeople are not capable of mentally or emotionally handling their transition and disregards the fact that anyone might have a similar feeling waking up from a major surgery. This is an example of the way that transpeople's experiences are often reduced to their trans identity instead of acknowledging that their transness is only component of their humanity.

Social pathologization pertains to the ways that transpeople are portrayed as social outcasts or pariahs. It is often fostered through discourses of transpeople as liars, deceivers and cheaters, which affirm the unquestionable existence of an authentic or true self (Yep et al., 2015). Films like *Boys Don't Cry* further the narrative that transpeople are always attempting to trick people of the "opposite" sex into "homosexual" interactions and generally ends with the transperson being found out and beaten or murdered (Rigney, 2004). Thus, in order for transpeople, or other marginalized identities, to be "good" citizens, they must share their story and have a ceremonial "coming out" so that everyone is aware of their trans status (Klein, Holtby, Cook, & Travers, 2014; Skidmore, 2011). Caitlyn Jenner's story might be the most documented coming out story in trans history. The mass circulation of Caitlyn's very personal information contributes to the demystification of her identity. She answers the questions about her surgeries and transition (unlike trans activists like Laverne Cox and Janet Mock), she provides intimate details about her personal life with spouses and children to be analyzed (insinuating her trans identity was the primary or sole reason for her imperfect relationships), and uses palatable metaphors and arguments to defend her trans identity (e.g., the wrong body narrative). This extreme transparency arguably makes Caitlyn the most palatable or "good" trans citizen in U.S. mainstream media to date as it directly challenges the narrative of hiding, lying, and deceiving.

"It's All About the Body": Obsession with the Body

Media attention on transpeople re-centers the common trope of the body, that is, an unrelenting focus on their physical body instead of their character, achievements, or interests. An infamous example of this obsession includes Katie Couric's invasive questioning about the state of Carmen Carrera's genitals in an interview on her show. This narrative helps maintain focus on the trans body, rather than the transperson, and simultaneously creates and maintains a social distance from the cisgender body. Additionally, focusing on transitioning or the body reduces trans identities to their transness, leaving limited space for the exploration of their human qualities. This obsession with the trans body tends to revolve around two main themes: (1) The body as a site of truth and (2) the body as a site of social value.

The body as a site of truth implies that gender is explicitly and directly tied to the physical body. This narrative relies heavily on essentialist arguments used to invalidate trans identities assuming that it would be impossible for someone to not identity with the sex and gender they were assigned at birth, similar to the consequences of social pathologization (McQueen, 2014). Common features include the focus on a person's transition, specifically surgeries or hormone treatments and the state of their genitalia. The combination of invalidating a transperson's body, while only focusing on their body creates the normalization of mainstream disavowal of a transperson's identity and lived experience (binaohan, 2014; Mock, 2012; Rigney, 2004; Siebler, 2012). In the *Vanity Fair* article, Bissinger (2015) begins by explicitly divulging the details of Caitlyn's surgeries and history with hormone therapy. This is often the first question that talk show hosts ask their trans interviewees as a way to require transparency from the transperson, while also maintaining the focus on the body. Only asking transpeople deeply personal questions about genitalia and the body maintains cisgender people as the invisible center, perpetuating the marginalization of trans bodies and identities (Willox, 2003). Further, as Laverne Cox explained to Katie Couric in a subsequent interview, focusing on a person's transition takes time away from being able to speak about humanizing transpeople by focusing on the other aspects of their lives and the numerous struggles that trans communities are facing in the United States and abroad.

The body as a site of social value refers to the ways bodies are regarded and respected within a neoliberal social system of late capitalism. In this sense, the human body must be seen as productive within society to be deemed valuable and legitimate (Irving, 2008; Spade, 2011). In Jenner's case, along with other famous transwomen, the body as a site of social value also refers to the ways that bodies—especially hyperfeminine ones—are objectified and hypersexualized for the heteropatriarchal gaze (Vaes, Paladino, & Puvia, 2011). For example, in his segment about Caitlyn Jenner's *Vanity Fair* expose, comedian John Stewart satirically welcomed Caitlyn into womanhood by highlighting the misogynistic comments about her appearance, in the same way other celebrity women are constantly objectified and hypersexualized.

Caitlyn's body as social value can most easily be ascertained through the photographs that accompany the *Vanity Fair* article. There are five photographs, including the cover image, featured in the article. Except for the cover photo where Caitlyn is featured looking directly into the camera, the other images present her as avoiding the gaze of the viewer. This is a nonverbal technique commonly used to portray women as submissive, primarily present for their sexual value (Bratu, 2013; Vaes et al., 2011). Indeed, in the photographs, Caitlyn's body appears to be the prominent visual feature. In addition, in most of the pictures, Caitlyn is constructing her identity through getting ready (e.g., standing in front of well lit mirrors, reclining blissfully in a hair and makeup chair). This plays into the common narrative that womanhood is tied to the body—constructed through a preoccupation with hair, makeup, clothing, and overall appearance—ready for consumption by the heterosexual male gaze. Similarly, though Caitlyn is positioned with a computer in one photo, she appears disinterested, which seems to suggest that her new appearance outweighs any other aspect of her personhood, including character traits or personal achievements.

"It Always Comes Back to Two Genders": Reification of the Gender Binary

Perhaps unsurprisingly, the most common theme within the classic trans narratives is the reification of the gender binary. While the argument has been made that trans individuals who identify within the binary are inherently reifying it, our aim is to discuss the ways that the representation of trans identities reifies the binary—not the people themselves. Our analysis suggests that the reification of the binary within trans narratives comes in two main forms: (1) Affirmation of the binary and (2) defense of the binary. While seemingly quite similar, the subtle difference between affirmation and defense lies in the way the theme is presented.

Affirmation upholds the binary by regarding it as a fact or just a part of the "natural order" of things. Heavily relying on essentialist ideologies of sex and gender, affirmation of the binary acknowledges cisgender identities as the default, natural, or normal—thus, unquestionable—gender identity. In doing so, cisgender identities remain the invisible center, consequently pathologizing and otherizing trans identities.

In the tagline of the article which reads, "From Olympic athlete to transwoman ..." Bissinger (2015) uses the notion of two separate entities as if Caitlyn cannot be both simultaneously. This rigid upholding of the binary seals off any space for non-binary representation and gender fluidity. The insinuation that a transperson's identity is segmented and mutually exclusive before and/or after transition works to invalidate the individual's trans identity by negating that the person has had an identity all along. Additionally, not all people are aware of their trans identity from a young age, as might be suggested by other popular trans narratives, so to disregard gender fluidity ultimately invalidates a range of trans identities. On a similar note, throughout the article Bissinger (2015) only refers to Jenner as Caitlyn (using she/her pronouns) once he is finished telling the story of her transition, still using he/him pronouns to describe the beginning stages of transition surgeries and hormones. This implies that womanhood, she/her pronouns, and femininity are distinctly tied to the body, disregarding the idea that they are socially constructed and exist in the social imagination, and are only to be used once Caitlyn's transition is "complete." Bissinger (2015) never addresses his use of pronouns and names, normalizing the seemingly subtle affirmation of the binary and otherizing trans and fluid identities.

Defense of the binary, on the other hand, actively perpetuates heteropatriarchal cisgenderism by reacting when the hegemonic sex and gender systems are directly confronted or attacked. Due to the fragile nature of social constructs, the gender binary must be defended, guarded, and upheld at all times to prevent it from crumbling.

Bissinger (2015) takes a few paragraphs to speak about his experience being around Caitlyn pre- and post-transition. He recollects that it was "weird" and "anyone who says it isn't weird is giving themselves far too much credit" (para. 24) since "it is a strange story regardless of the important inroads made by transgender men and women into the cultural mainstream" (para. 26). In this sense, Bissinger (2015) is already pathologizing Caitlyn's experience, in turn defending the binary, by delineating it as weird and strange, but goes one step further by implying that regardless of how many transpeople tell their stories in the media, it will always be strange. He goes on to comment that he misgendered Caitlyn multiple times, but Caitlyn kindly let him off the hook. In fact, Bissinger (2015) reveals that he has cross-dressed before (perhaps with the hope of establishing credibility and alleviating transphobic guilt), so his "miscues have nothing to do with intolerance" (para. 26). In the defense of his own actions and letting himself off the hook for misgendering Caitlyn multiple times, Bissinger (2015) metaphorically lets the reader off the hook, giving in to the already popular societal notion that trans identities are less important than cis preferences for grammar and convenience. This seemingly subtle message works to normalize the disavowal and invalidation of Caitlyn's identity, as well as trans identities in general by privileging the binary and use of assumed pronouns, ultimately upholding the binary by defending the forceful oppression onto a trans body.

The New Transnormativity?

Caitlyn Jenner's hyper-visibility and hyper-transparency in U.S. mainstream representations, which have made her into a "good," "palatable," and "acceptable" trans subject in the popular imagination, suggest, in our view, the emergence of a "new transnormativity"[2] at this historical juncture. Indeed, this new transnormativity has produced new standards through which trans identities, experiences, expressions, and aesthetics—in short, trans lives—are to be measured and judged in the cultural domain. To put it differently, the new transnormativity has created a social hierarchy through which to view, interpret, judge, and assess trans lives in U.S. society. These standards and their accompanying social hierarchy emerge in the context of neoliberal ideologies, policies, and practices characterized by a blinding focus on individualism and individual responsibility, erosion of community and the "public good," massive government deregulation and the expansion of the "free" market designed to magnify global corporate profit at the expense of collective wellbeing and sustainability, which Elia and Yep (2012, p. 881) call "neoterrorism," a concept they introduced to highlight the insidious personal and cultural effects of neoliberalism. In terms of transpeople, Elia and Yep (2012) note, "neoterrorism has produced a docile, domesticated, and normative gender and sexual minority citizen who fully participates in consumption and the process of economic production of the neoliberal world order" (p. 885). It is in this context that the new transnormativity registers as a new mode of cultural intelligibility.

What does this new transnormativity look like? Based on our analysis and the themes presented in the previous section, we argue that the new transnormativity consists of three interrelated and defining foci: (a) Fixing trans "pathology" through consumption, (b) concern about physical appearance and transparency, and (c) centering the individual at the expense of the cultural and the political.

Accepting the mainstream cultural view that trans phenomena are psychological and social pathologies, one of the central features of the new transnormativity is to find ways for trans individuals to fit into the mainstream sex and gender system. In this sense, it does not contest the hegemony and tyranny of the system. Indeed, by promoting ways to fix the "pathology," it further reifies and solidifies the sex and gender system as normal, natural, and unquestionable. The process of fixing requires consumption of services from various industries in the neoliberal economy, such as psychological, medical, and cosmetic, among many others, which also increases and naturalizes surveillance of the trans body (Beauchamp, 2014). This may include services from psychologists for a diagnosis of Gender Identity Disorder or Gender Dysphoria to authorize the process for gender transitioning; medical doctors to begin hormone therapy and other treatments; multiple surgeons to construct or remove gendered body parts; voice therapists to change the quality, pitch, and resonance of the individual's voice; cosmetologists to enhance the person's gendered appearance, and so on (Erickson-Schroth, 2014). As demonstrated by representations of Caitlyn Jenner, to fix the "pathology" is indeed a long and costly endeavor. With the erosion of social services, including medical care, under neoliberal policies, such costs become, in most cases, the sole responsibility of the transperson. As such, a "good" transperson, under the new transnormativity, is one who can afford these costly and ongoing services.

Related to the need to fix one's gender to conform to the strict binary system of mainstream culture is the focus on gender appearance and transparency, which representations of Caitlyn Jenner clearly demonstrates. This feature of the new transnormativity is manifested in two ways. First, the trans body must be corrected and presented in ways that can "pass" in mainstream culture, that is, it must symbolically and materially present itself in gender unambiguous terms (e.g., to look and act like a man or a woman). Failure to do so exposes the person to a range of violences ranging from social disapproval and punishment to physical aggression and death. Second, the trans body must be ready for voyeuristic public consumption, that is, it must be transparent to others without regard for intrusion and invasion of personal privacy of the transperson (e.g., expectation of transpeople to reveal their trans identity to others). Failure to do so produces accusations of the transperson as deceitful, fraudulent and deceptive, which carry a range of potential harms, including murder. Upholding the normality of cisgender bodies through cisgenderism, transparency "otherizes" the trans body and presents it as abnormal, out of the ordinary, and pathological for public scrutiny. Reifying the gender binary system, the focus on passing makes the trans body palatable and sanitized for public consumption. As stated previously, to pass requires ongoing consumption of a range of services and products in the neoliberal economy. In addition, passing allows trans bodies to participate in the economy as productive citizens and consumers (Irving, 2008).

Finally, consistent with the neoliberal landscape from which it emerges, the third feature of the new transnormativity is its almost exclusive focus on the individual. Trans phenomena are presented as individual "choices" and "events," divorced from their social, cultural, and political contexts. Mainstream media representations tell the reader and the viewer that Caitlyn Jenner finally "chose" to be herself after many years of personal agony and torture without engaging with and examining the tyranny of the cultural system that produced and maintained the agony and torture in the first place. Gender, in this instance, becomes an individual choice rather than a cultural matrix of invention, production, enforcement, and discipline. By doing so, gender is detached from the cultural domain and becomes depoliticized and gender justice movements, including trans movements, are undermined and subverted. Further, by depoliticizing gender, it evades analysis and scrutiny and its connection to patriarchy and other systems of subordination, marginalization, and oppression are concealed and obscured, thus, preventing deep cultural change (Spade, 2011).

In sum, the new transnormativity not only leaves the gender binary intact; it further solidifies it. By upholding the gender binary, it seals off the leakiness, slippages and instability of the categories of "woman" and "man" through which heteropatriarchy is founded (Butler, 1990). As an overarching system of male dominance through the institution of heterosexuality, heteropatriarchy is utterly dependent on the notion of two intelligible, coherent, separate, and "opposite" genders (Yep, 2003). Through the "heterosexual matrix," such genders are presumed to be oppositionally defined, "naturally" complementary in desire and attraction, and hierarchically organized through the compulsory institution of heterosexuality to secure patriarchal domination of women and other genders (Butler, 1990, p. 151). As such, the new transnormativity is complicit with heteropatriarchy. In addition, the new transnormativity creates a hierarchy, through which trans lives are judged, making those who will not or cannot adhere to its demands marginalized in their communities as well as in mainstream society.

Summary and Implications

Mass media representations of transpeople offer new opportunities to critically discuss and examine gender as constructed by society in the university classroom. Alexander McKay noted that "promoting gender equality in a democratic sexuality education involves expanding students' critical awareness of the wide range of ideological perspectives on the meaning of gender equality and the best means to reach it for both individuals and society" (1999, p. 171). Through the development and cultivation of critical consciousness in the classroom, we can better understand how transing communication uncovers the intersections of identity that encompass gender, the perception of gender as a galaxy, and addressing how our current understandings of gender originate from the privileged cisgender perspective. Using Caitlyn Jenner's representation of trans communities and saturation of "what trans looks like" in recent popular media, we hope to engage readers to think about the ways transpeople are pathologized, connected to bodily obsessions, and forced to continually fit in the rigidness of the gender binary by way of increased trans visibility, as well as being confronted with oppression and violence that is associated with violating heteronormative social structures of power.

To develop and enhance critical consciousness in the classroom based on both critical pedagogy and transing, four qualities are particularly important in critical reading practices (Shor, 1993; Yep et al., In press). First, it attempts to increase awareness of power (i.e., ways power operates and functions, visibly and invisibly, in society at both microscopic and macroscopic levels). Through critical reading of representations of Caitlyn Jenner, the relationship between gender and power can be made more visible (e.g., how Jenner was described and visually represented as a transwoman, such as focus on her appearance and clothes, that presented her as an sexual object rather than a human subject). Second, it seeks to enhance critical literacy (i.e., ways of reading, thinking, writing, speaking and discussing multiple layers of meanings of a cultural text, event, or social situation). For example, while seemingly celebrating Jenner's new public gender identity, U.S. mainstream representations also pathologized her as anything but "normal" and objectified her for public scrutiny and consumption. Third, it attempts to develop modes of desocialization (i.e., ways to unlearn regressive values, such as sexism, racism, classism, and homophobia, operating in society). By understanding how the gender binary pathologizes trans lives and upholds heteropatriarchal power, for example, a process of internal psychic decolonization can begin to take place. Finally, it seeks to potentially initiate social change (i.e., ways of transforming and altering unequal distribution of power in a social system). To conceive of gender as a galaxy—that is, a social universe with multiple gender performances, expressions, and identities—could lead to the depathologization of trans lives and potentially deep cultural change.

By examining mainstream representations of "what trans looks like" through Caitlyn Jenner in U.S. popular culture, the social construction of gender and its potentially violent symbolic and material consequences can be critically discussed, examined, and unpacked through critical pedagogy and transing. More specifically, they offer analytical tools, such as critical reading practices, that can be applied to a wide range of social phenomena and events, including representations of gender normativity and non-normativity. Extending such critical reading practices in the classroom into the student's own lived experiences and realities has the potential to create new social worlds, such as "the opening and creation of spaces without a map, the invention and proliferation of ideas without an unchanging and predetermined goal, and the expansion of individual freedom and collective possibilities without the constraints of suffocating identities and restrictive membership" (Yep, 2003, p. 35). This critical, transgressive, and creative endeavor is, to invoke Berlant and Warner's (1998) terms, "queer world-making," in which "queer" does not automatically signify sexuality but anything (including gender) at odds with regimes of the normal (such as cisgenderism, the gender binary, and heteropatriarchy). Through the development and cultivation of critical consciousness and the expansion of new horizons for social constructs and relational arrangements, liberatory education can truly become, in hooks' (1994) words, "the practice of freedom" (p. 207).

Notes

1 To respect and honor Jenner's subjectivity as a self-identified transwoman, we use feminine pronouns (e.g., "she," "her"), whenever possible, to refer to Caitlyn in this essay.

2 Our use of the term "new transnormativity" was inspired by Duggan's (2003) work on the "new homonormativity." Although these normativities are conceptually distinct, they also share some commonalities, such as reification of heteropatriarchy, focus on the individual, depoliticized citizenship, and emphasis on consumerism, that are characteristic of neoliberalism in the twenty-first century.

Gust thanks John Elia, my friend and colleague, for our ongoing dialogue about research and pedagogy; Dr. Jessica Holliday, Huy, Nikki, and the entire staff at Park Animal Hospital in San Francisco, for their excellent work and for taking care of Pierre with love; and Yogi Enzo and Pierre Lucas, my furry bodhisattvas, for their constant love, playfulness, and companionship. Gust dedicates his portions of the essay to Tony, Tyler, Dino, Copper, Pinto, and Grekko—may you continue your adventures and walks beyond "The Rainbow Bridge."

Work Cited

Beauchamp, T. (2014). Surveillance. *TSQ: Transgender Studies Quarterly, 1*(1–2), 208–210.

Berlant, L., & Warner, M. (1998). Sex in public. *Critical Inquiry, 24*(2), 547–566.

binaohan, b. (2014). *decolonizing trans/gender 101*. Toronto, Ontario, Canada: biyuti publishing.

Bissinger, B. (2015, July). *Caitlyn Jenner: The full story*. Retrieved from http://www.vanityfair.com/hollywood/2015/06/caitlyn-jenner-bruce-cover-annie-leibovitz

Bratu, S. (2013). The communication function of advertising. *Journalism Studies, 14*(2), 11–16.

Butler, J. (1990). *Gender trouble: Feminism and the subversion of identity*. New York, NY: Routledge.

Duggan, L. (2003). *The twilight of equality?: Neoliberalism, cultural politics, and the attack on democracy*. Boston, MA: Beacon Press.

Elia, J. P., & Yep, G. A. (2012). Introduction: Sexualities and genders in an age of neoterrorism. *Journal of Homosexuality, 59*, 879–889.

Erickson-Schroth, L. (Ed.). (2014). *Trans bodies, trans selves: A resource for the transgender community.* New York, NY: Oxford University Press.

Freire, P. (1970). *Pedagogy of the oppressed.* New York, NY: Continuum.

Freire, P. (1973). *Education for critical consciousness.* New York, NY: Continuum.

Giroux, H., & Shannon, P. (1997). Cultural studies and pedagogy as performative practice: Toward an introduction. In H. A. Giroux & P. Shannon (Eds.), *Education and cultural studies: Toward a performative practice* (pp. 1–9). New York, NY: Routledge.

hooks, b. (1994). *Teaching to transgress: Education as the practice of freedom.* New York, NY: Routledge.

hooks, b. (2010). *Teaching critical thinking: Practical wisdom.* New York, NY: Routledge.

Irving, D. (2008). Normalized transgressions: Legitimizing the transsexual body as productive. *Radical History Review, 100,* 38–59.

Klein, K., Holtby, A., Cook, K., & Travers, R. (2014). Complicating the coming out narrative: Becoming oneself in a heterosexist and cissexist world. *Journal of Homosexuality, 62*(3), 297–326.

McKay, A. (1999). *Sexual ideology and schooling: Towards democratic sexuality education.* Albany, NY: State University of New York Press.

McLaren, P., & Leonard, P. (Eds.). (1993). *Paulo Freire: A critical encounter.* London: Routledge.

McQueen, P. (2014). Enslaved by one's body? Gender, citizenship, and the "wrong body" narrative. *Citizenship Studies, 18*(5), 533–548.

Mock, J. (2012, July 9). Trans in the media: Unlearning the "trapped" narrative & taking ownership of our bodies. Retrieved from http://janetmock.com/2012/07/09/josie-romero-dateline-transgender-trapped-body/

Rigney, M. (2004). Brandon goes to Hollywood: *Boys Don't Cry* and the transgender body in film. *Film Criticism, 28*(2), 4–23.

Shor, I. (1993). Education is politics: Paulo Freire's critical pedagogy. In P. McLaren & P. Leonard (Eds.), *Paulo Freire: A critical encounter* (pp. 25–35). London: Routledge.

Siebler, K. (2010). Transqueer representations and how we educate. *Journal of LBGT Youth, 7*(4), 320–345.

Siebler, K. (2012). Transgender transitions: Sex/gender binaries in the digital age. *Journal of Gay & Lesbian Mental Health, 16*(1), 74–99.

Skidmore, E. (2011). Constructing the "good transsexual": Christine Jorgensen, whiteness, and heteronormativity in the mid-twentieth-century press. *Feminist Studies, 37*(2), 270–300.

Spade, D. (2011). *Normal life: Administrative violence, critical trans politics, and the limits of law.* Brooklyn, NY: South End Press.

Steinmetz, K. (2014, May 29). The transgender tipping point. Retrieved from http://time.com/135480/transgender-tipping-point/

Stryker, S., & Currah, P. (2014). Introduction. *TSQ: Transgender Studies Quarterly, 1*(1–2), 1–18.

Stryker, S., Currah, P., & Moore, L. J. (2008). Introduction: Trans-, trans, or transgender? *WSQ: Women's Studies Quarterly, 36*(3–4), 11–22.

Vaes, J., Paladino, P., & Puvia, E. (2011). Are sexualized women complete human beings? Why men and women dehumanize sexually objectified women. *European Journal of Social Psychology, 41,* 774–785.

Willox, A. (2003). Branding teena: (Mis)representations in the media. *Sexualities, 6*(3–4), 407–425.

Yep, G. A. (2003). The violence of heteronormativity in communication studies: Notes on injury, healing, and queer world-making. In G. A. Yep, K. E. Lovaas, & J. P. Elia (Eds.), *Queer theory and communication: From disciplining queers to queering the discipline(s)* (pp. 11–59). New York, NY: Harrington Park Press.

Yep, G. A., Russo, S. E., & Allen, J. K. (2015). Pushing boundaries: Toward the development of a model for transing communication in (inter)cultural contexts. In L. G. Spencer & J. C. Capuzza (Eds.), *Transgender communication studies: Histories, trends, and trajectories* (pp. 69–89). Lanham, MD: Lexington.

CHAPTER 18

The Double-Edged Sword

Fighting for Equity and Professional Advancement in Higher Education

Tara Jabbaar-Gyambrah and Seneca Vaught

Introduction

Despite increasing numbers of Black students enrolling in higher education, fewer Black professionals are being promoted to senior level administrative positions in higher education. Does the dual burden of racial consciousness and gender expectations play any role in this disparity? Balancing career and family life is a challenge for most academics but can be particularly challenging for Black faculty and administrators in higher education. This chapter examines the challenges that Black middle level administrators and tenure-track faculty face in higher education as they attempt to move above the "glass ceilings" and break through the "tinted windows" of higher education. Is it possible for Black professionals to have a healthy and balanced home life while advancing in academia? What are some of the institutional conflicts and interpersonal barriers that have contributed to the lack of upward mobility for Black professionals? We discuss practical solutions to address these challenges and contribute to a greater level of personal satisfaction and professional advancement for black faculty.

There are significant forces that impede the professional advancement of Blacks in higher education. Discrimination, tokenism, lack of support from supervisors, differential treatment, and lack of quality mentorship, are just a few of the reasons why there are not many Blacks in top-ranking roles. Equity and fair practices as it relates to employment and promotion for Black professionals has always been a challenge in American society. Dating back to slavery until now, underlying the issue of "equity" has been embedded in stereotypical and discriminatory practices that have decreased access and growth in the work force. These practices have affected Black men and women in different ways but with interrelated consequences—one being the lack of advancement in high profile positions in higher education, such as becoming a president, provost, or vice president of finance. Chun and Evans (2011) provide some startling data on this pattern:

> Nearly 85 percent of the top-ranked positions in doctorate-granting institutions are held by whites and 66 percent are held by males. The only exception to this pattern is the chief diversity officer position—70.8 percent of these positions are held by African-Americans, with white incumbents holding 12.3 percent.

What this mean is that there Whites hold the majority of senior level administrative positions and the majority of them are men, and although, Blacks are concentrated in senior level position, such as the Chief Diversity Officer, it is path that does weld much power. Maybe there is not enough guidance, preparation, or seeking out mentors to assist with navigating the cultural and political process of promotion. Consequently, there are fewer Blacks who actual have the opportunity to serve in senior level positions.

There is not much research focused on Blacks in administrative roles that lead to the college presidency. Interestingly, there has been an increase of literature on Blacks in Chief Diversity Officer positions that may, or may not serve as a pipeline to the presidency or provost line. Jackson (2004) found that the number of Blacks in executive level positions from 1993 to 1999 decreased by 6.02% however there was an increase of Black departmental chairs. As of 2011, the number of Black faculty employed as a full-time Assistant, Associate or Full Professor in colleges and universities are substantially lower than White faculty. Of that faculty whose race/ethnicity was known, only 6% were full-time Black faculty. If we examine the data for full-professors, 84% are White (60% White male and 25% White female) while there are 4% Black. There are many factors may impact the lack of growth of Black faculty in institutions of higher education, including but not limited to: decrease in the number of Blacks enrolled in doctoral programs, the absence of mentors that provide guidance throughout the tenure track process, deficient hiring practices and policies to diversify the pool of faculty applicants, and institutional discrimination.

The Civil Rights Act of 1964 serves as the nation's benchmark legislation which forbid the discrimination on the basis of race, color, religion, national origin, and sex in hiring, firing, and promotion. This act continues to serve as the benchmark of Civil Rights Movement and on one hand, it has helped to provide equal access to all people in the work place, but on the other hand, it has impacted the intersection of race and gender in a contradictory and complex ways. This is particularly true in how Black academics interpret their role and their relationship to social justice issues within the academy. Seldom are Black academics afforded the luxury of their individual actions being only representative of them or their individual goals representing only their personal ambitions. Rather, Blacks are vicariously representative of their race. Even when Blacks are attending to address personal wrongs, their complaints are racially translated to be representative of the broader Black American community. This places a particularly heavy burden on Black academics in general but mainly on Black women.

For example, in 1991 Anita Hill, an Oklahoma law professor, accused Clarence Thomas of sexual harassment during her time working for him. What made this case complex was the fact that Clarence Thomas had been nominated by President George H. W. Bush replace Thurgood Marshall as the court's first Black justice—Thomas' and Hill's political ideology was not representative of the broader policy consensus among black intellectuals in the Black public at large. The case went before the Judiciary Committee and in her testimony, she shared graphic incidents of degrading comments that Clarence Thomas made to her while she was employed at two government agencies. In his testimony, Thomas called the entire process "[a] high tech lynching for uppity blacks."

Although the Senate voted 52–48 to confirm Clarence Thomas for the Supreme Court Justice seat, the unstated dilemma here was that blacks were forced to prioritize in a rather public forum whether the prospects of racial advancement outranked gender equality. Since the case, American women have become more actively involved in political roles and public life in a variety of fields. While this progress is significant, there remains a significant gap when it comes to Black women in tenured faculty or higher level administrative positions in higher education. What role does the complex intersection of race and gender continue to play?

In this chapter, we seek to shed light on some of the institutional conflicts and interpersonal barriers that have contributed to the lack of upward mobility for Black academics using three metaphors that engage concepts of race and gender. We use the familiar term "glass ceiling" to define the "unseen" barriers that prevent minorities, particularly women, from advancing to more powerful positions. In the case of academia, this would encompass attaining tenured and/or senior level administrative positions. When we refer to the "tinted window" we are invoking a metaphor to express the complex racial lens that Black academics experience the academic setting through. Particularly, Black men who find themselves torn between responsibilities within the academy to uplift the race, but also to set examples of exemplary manhood in their homes and the community. Of course this term harks back to W.E.B. Du Bois notion of double consciousness, grappling with what it means to see oneself through the eyes of others. Here, we seek to emphasize the role of racial perception in the academy as it relates to the responsibilities Blacks take upon themselves on behalf of advancing the race. Black academics bear these burdens vicariously with serious consequences for how their work and its' impact is perceived by other non-black academics.

We invoke the imagery of a double-edged sword to emphasize the desire Black academics have to cultivate family life while combating discrimination in the workplace. "Moving on up" or achieving the American dream for Black academicians is seldom a test of one's personal desires but rather one's determination to succeed and to pave the way for the success of others. "Making it" is perceived not just in the sense of making it to the top, but being able to balance life and bring others along as well. Personal successes are never equated with individual efforts alone but are indicative of a reciprocal relationship with the broader Black community that extends to include houses of worship, immediate and extended family, past acquaintances, and underrepresented communities. We weave these three metaphors to argue that the dual burden of racial consciousness and gender expectations plays a major role in professional advancement and negatively impact the home life and personal satisfaction.

Black women are isolated culturally, emotionally, and intellectually from allies facing significant challenges. As Stephanie Jones (2013) has written, race and gender play a defining role for career advancement of women in academic but in different and quite nuanced ways. For example, in an article, "Black Women in the Economy: Facing the Glass Ceilings in Academia" the authors document the experiences of Black women in academia as it relates to teaching and research. Interestingly, it was indicated that before the 1960s Black women were not employed at higher education institutions. However, after the Civil Rights Act of 1964, there was a tremendous growth of Black women that pursued doctoral degrees. Those that obtained their doctoral degree were generally locked into three companies: higher education, industry, and government. There are two key findings, first, Black women who eventually were employed in higher education focused on teaching, administrative and service work. This was to their disadvantage because it did not give them the opportunity to research which is crucial to being promoted. Second, there is a lack of mentorships or networking opportunities to assist Black women with moving up the ladder towards tenure and promotion.

Furthermore Black women face a glass ceiling reinforced with the burden of racial responsibility that negatively impacts home life and personal satisfaction. Historically, institutional conflict with the dominant gender discourse, until rather recently, was framed from White feminist perspectives. The inability for Black women to advocate for their unique perspectives on race, family, and social welfare were overshadowed by one-dimensional discussion of equal pay and affirmative action that negated many Black feminist academics equally important concerns for social justice. Ultimately, American society was much more attuned to the sentiments of Western European feminisms than many of the demands of the women's liberation movement.

In 2003 the *Grutter vs. Bolinger* case set a precedent for the enrollment of underrepresented students and the "not-so-new" gender politics. The Supreme Court ruled that race, among other factors, could be considered as a form of affirmative action in the school admissions process to achieve an ethnically diverse class at colleges and universities race could be used as one of those. However, this was a case that was part of a broader strategy by the Center for Individual Rights (CIR) to challenge affirmative action using white female plaintiffs. The strategy presented a disturbing message for many Black feminists who saw how cultural warriors were using gender politics in an attempt to dismantle rather benign and limited social justice policies.

Although *Grutter* was a narrow victory for supporters of affirmative action it signaled the shifting political climate of things to come and battles that would shape the future and how differently many Black and White women viewed the most effective way of shattering the glass ceiling. Most recently, in the *Schutte v. Coalition to Defend Affirmative Action*, the U.S. Supreme Court "reversed the 6th Circuit Court of Appeal's determination that Michigan's Proposal 2 that prohibits the consideration of race as one of many factors in admissions decisions was unconstitutional." Both of these cases profiled the way that gender priorities of White women in the public square conflicted with widespread beliefs among Black academics.

Interpersonal factors have also greatly diminished Black women's satisfaction with higher education and their prospects for advancement. Hosts of what Chambers (2011) calls "microassaults, microinsults, and microinvalidations" have been documented reasons for the lack of retention among minority and faculty. The interpersonal annoyances, often laden with gender and racial meaning, have undermined efficiency and cooperation necessary for advancement in higher education. Unequal expectations, repeated efforts of justify the relevance and significance of scholarship and academic projects, and disproportionate service loads make the road to tenure a troubling path. Additionally Black women have cited unfairness and a lack of clarity as additional barriers.

Chun and Evans (2011) explored how Black administrators handled subtle, covert, and/or overt discrimination in their work environments. In their study, they found that Black administrators had to deal with enormous amounts of stress and were often subject to "double-standards" when related to their job responsibilities. In one of their interviews, a Black female administrator shared her story of how she was constantly singled out by a discriminatory supervisor. It caused an enormous amount of stress, which led to high blood pressure that was "uncontrollable." Ironically, once she was terminated from her position, her blood pressure returned to normal with medications.

Despite the numerous interpersonal factors Black women face, critical pedagogues must engage structural factors to understand the impact of these experiences. In an article, "Understanding the Employment Disparities Using Glass Ceiling Effects Criteria" Jackson and O'Callaghan found that exclusionary practices in higher education unfairly limit the promotion and progression of people of color. These factors collectively predetermine outcomes and help maintain an unfair advantage against Black women.

More specifically, Jackson and O'Callaghan laid out four possible paths that people of color take when in higher education: (1) they chose to leave the academy (2) they are denied tenure and promotion (3) they develop a low morale and their job performance begins to diminish (4) the small few that make it to senior-level positions report a high level of job satisfaction.

In addition to the "glass ceiling" and the host of complementary challenges that Black women face in academia, there is also a notable "tinted window" that inhibits the advancement of Black men in higher education. As a metaphor, the tinted window suggests that in a so-called post-racial era, unprecedented opportunities for advancement, institutional transparency, and cultural serious challenges affecting the prospects and opportunities for Black professional advancement persists.

Black men face a tinted window that obscures opportunities for an authentic Black masculinity and personal fulfillment. The tinted window involves black men coming to terms with the complex and conflicting ideas about the role of race and manhood in negotiating their way through American society. Most of the traits of masculinity that are necessary for self-preservation in Black urban America are not acceptable forms of self-expression in the culture of academia. Paradoxically, Black men are victimized by non-black colleagues using characteristics of "typical" masculine aggression that they are denied to invoke.

Micro-aggressions and passive aggressive characteristics that are not tolerated in the Black community are the predominant form of academic politicking. These forms of incivility can be demoralizing and often accompanied by racial slurs and cultural insensitivity. A passive aggressive Black man becomes a walking paradox, embodying the very characteristics that are contradictory to his validation, history, and momentary triumph over anti-black forces in broader American society. Thus, the tinted window presents a Du Boisian barrier for Black men.

Black men identifying as feminists face uphill battle against institutional norms. Racial stereotypes, gender bias, and popular misconceptions about Black men permeate administrative and academic expectations. In the past some Black men have used these stereotypes to advance themselves but in other situations these strategies have backfired. Collectively, as a tinted window, these stereotypes obscure the complex role and contributions that Black men make to higher education but also the lost opportunities for personal and professional growth.

Black men attempting to balance family life and professional expectations face barriers to professional advancement that are seldom acknowledged or considered because of self-reinforcing stereotypes about gender and race. For example, Black fathers face challenging circumstances that pit their family interests against institutional norms. Black fathers seeking to take a more proactive role in the care and development of his children and or extended family may face stigmas regarding his ability as a competent worker that complicate relationships outside of work and on the job.

The tinted window is duplicitous because it prevents both the academy and Black men from the seeing the inherent violence of the system. One would be quick to point out the violent machismo of Black men but scholars have been loath to discuss the psychological and emotional violence that is implicit a part of the academic system. One can easily and rightly point to the emotional distress caused by a Black man yelling at woman as a form of violence but one would be less inclined that the numerous micro-aggressions and unrealistic work expectations of Black male faculty cause higher forms of stress and increase likelihood of premature death. We accept the latter form of violence because of the victim and the method but both examples stem from the same source: power.

Because Black men and women wield a double-edged sword in their battle for academic justice, they face greater burdens that their colleagues and lower prospects for institutional advancement. Black men and women share challenges of seeing the important work they perform in the service of diversity support to young Black women and men as mere "service" unrelated to the "real" work of academics. In addition to this insult, they are forced to persistently battle to persuade colleagues on the merits of their advocacy for Black students. This creates a dual burden, one that all faculty face in arguing for more resources but in addition to the equally important but elusive goal of respect for the important work of advocacy for Black students.

Black men and women often wield a double-edged sword, using their academic influence and/or expertise to help others like them. They work not only for self but for eradication of racial inequality and gender equity. They work with and for Black students, their families, and the broader communities in ways in which their personal advancement is intricately tied in the well-being of others. This sense of double duty—what Kerry Ann Rockquemore refers to as keeping ones' soul—exacerbates the demands of an already unwieldy workload causing emotional distress and numerous professional challenges.

For many academics, the divisions between the workplace and home life may overlap but the idea of duty to a broader community is less common. Some have urged for Black faculty to abandon these "pet projects" in the interest of a more robust research agenda—meaning a certain type of research that is devoid of broader commitments to racial advancement and commensality with Black students. Attempts to do so may be fraught with a loss of identity, community, and connection to a greater cause that often were the driving decisions for many Blacks to pursue careers in higher education.

Tenure and promotion policies continue to favor methods of assessment that augment rather than challenge the racial and gendered bias in the status quo. For example, in "The Status of Equity for Black Faculty and Administrators in Public Higher Education in the South" Perna, Gerald, Baum and Milem examine the status of full-time Black administrators, tenured and tenure track faculty from 1993 to 2001 in 19 states in the South, limited to 4-year public and flagship institutions. They found Blacks experienced substantial inequity in tenured and tenure track positions at 4-year public institutions in most of the 19 states in 2001, while administrators experienced greater equity. Understanding the context of experiences of Black faculty their research also found that there was a significant degree of inequity for Black full than assistant professors.

One of the ways that they assessed the inequity was through disaggregating by looking at the number of underrepresented faculty and administrators as compared to students enrolled at the institution. This provided them the baseline evidence for percentage of ethnic diversity needed minimally to support the campuses progress towards equity. Thus, as the demographics of the American population transforms, colleges/universities should reflect the same for their faculty, administrators and students. Research has shown that academic support from underrepresented faculty and administrators has increased retention rates for minority students. Often constituents that would typically be allies (i.e., White women, liberals, other ethnic minorities) are pitted against Blacks in the preservation of their own self-interest and zero-sum games.

Conclusion

Because Black men and women wield a double-edged sword in their battle for academic justice, they face unique challenges and particularly heavy burdens that lower prospects for institutional advancement. The personal, familial, and cultural aspects of racial consciousness and gender expectations deeply influences the professional prospects of black academics in a variety of ways. Far too frequently, Black women are isolated culturally, emotionally, and intellectually from allies facing significant challenges. Black men and women both face a tinted window that obscures opportunities for an authenticity and personal fulfillment. What does all this mean for higher education as our society continues to grow in terms of diversity? How do we prepare and encourage black professionals to stay in higher education while assisting them moving up the career ladder?

In 2011, I can recall a conversation that bloomed while I sat in Senior Leadership Program that helped prepare faculty and administrators for advance roles in higher education (i.e., Vice President, Provost, etc.), "there are not many people of color that are staying in higher education," one of my colleagues explained and they turned to me to ask why. I too, was puzzled, but access to growth and promotion was the first response that spurred out of my mouth. Black faculty face a variety of unique demands that make their bids for tenure and promotion, a challenging prospect in itself, much more frustrating than their non-black colleagues.

"Faculty of Color in Academe: What 20 Years of Literature Tells Us" reviewed literature focused on faculty of color from 252 publications by more than 30 scholars. The authors found that there continues to be an underrepresentation of Black faculty nationwide, with only 17% being full-time faculty. This disparity continues to pervade higher education because of the lack of support for diversity across all contexts including national, institutional and departments. Although there has been an increase in the number of Chief Diversity Officer positions developed at public and private institutions, there still is a lack of departmental and institutional effort to recruit and retain talented faculty of color. Some barriers to tenure and promotion of faculty of color include: (1) negative student evaluations (2) undervaluation of research (3) unwritten rules and policies regarding the tenure process.

As we move further along into the 21st century, trends are showing that our cities are growing more diverse and the need for high quality professionals to lead the helm of institutions in the area of student and academic affairs is in dire straits. The Hispanic population is expected to double, "from 53.3 million in 2012 to 128.8 million in 2060 and the Black population is expected to increase from 41.2 million to 61.8 million." As our population continues to grow more diverse, it is essential that the demographics of the people in American society line up with the diversity of faculty, staff, and students in colleges and universities. If this does not happen, there will be a slow decrease in the retention of these groups on university and college campuses.

Future Implications and Solutions

Although the number of Black faculty and administrators has increased since the Civil Rights Era, there is still a disparity in the percentage of those individuals in senior level positions in higher education. Future researchers should dedicate time to understanding how the lack of underrepresented faculty and administrators will impact the retention of students. Especially, if there are fewer and fewer individuals left to advocate for their access to higher education institutions. More than this, in what ways can strong mentorship help Black professionals move up the hierarchal ladder to promotion?

There are practical solutions to address these challenges and contribute to a greater level of personal satisfaction and professional advancement for Black faculty and administrators.

1. There is a vast need for mentorship. One who can guide and advise you through your career path and help you to avoid the pitfalls of life. This is an area of dire straits as for Black faculty and administrators. There are too little mentors who are able to commit to guiding others through the process of getting tenure and being promoted. Many mentors also are unable or unwilling to advise effectively to unique status of Black faculty. In her dissertation, *In their own words: African women narrate their experiences to leadership*, Choates found that African American women who were in senior-leadership roles acquired their positions as a result of some kind of mentorship, or sponsorship. Although several of the relationships may not have been formal, each provided some kind of sponsorship to help them move up their career ladder.
2. Disclose all opportunities for advancement, course downloads, administrative assistance, etc. to Black faculty, develop a policy and make them mandatory. Many institutions make the assumption that Black faculty will take advantage of institutional mechanisms to ease the pressures of academic life. However, many Black faculty are concerned that inquiring about such opportunities or requesting them will bring unwanted attention and stigma from colleagues. Administrators have a key role to play in this process by making sure opportunities that help all faculty deal with the pressures of academic life are available but also that faculty can take advantage of them without being negatively impacted in the short term. There have been studies conducted on paternity leave programs but the stigma of men taking them without them being mandatory.
3. Start the development process early, by developing mentoring programs that reward leadership, cultural competency, and administrative excellence necessary for senior administrative positions. Black administration and faculty are often involved in a variety of important formal and informal processes across campus that are essential to making the university run smoothly and efficiently. However, much of that work is not properly acknowledged or home for professional advancement. Academic institutions could more effectively gauge their commitment to Black faculty by integrating many of the activities that there faculty as examples of professional development.

4. Develop national hiring and promotion practices that stress equity and fairness. Importantly, this means developing instruments that effectively assess the impact of cultural workers. A part of this process is reviewing current affirmative action standards and diversity policies. Admittedly this is not an easy task which is why many of the current techniques have persisted for so long. However, with the rise of literature on the engaged university there are new mechanisms that are promising.

5. Reward Black faculty and administration comparatively for the challenging mentoring work that they do with younger faculty and black students. All attempts to address racial and gender disparities need to be somewhat comprehensive in scope. However, universities tend to perceive cultural work among minorities as less significant than other major committee work and research. Institutions that are serious about addressing racial inequality and gender disparities should embrace pipeline programs that integrate mentoring opportunities for Black faculty and administrates on-campus, regionally, and internationally.

6. Acknowledge faculty commitment to diversity issues, advisement, leadership, and mentoring with same level of support as other academic and student support programs. Many institutions have developed mentoring and advisement strategies to address racial disparities but fail to give an adequate acknowledgment of the invested time and resources of faculty and administrators. It is incumbent on universities to view the time invested in the development of Black administrators, students, and faculty on equal terms.

7. Public and private institutions should develop creative ways to increase diversity within the executive leadership level. Provide economic opportunities to serve in various senior-level positions on a temporary basis to build expertise to move into Provost and President role. Despite the fact that some institutions may send some Black faculty and administrators on specific leadership development programs, in some cases, some are not promoted or still lack key experiences, such as: managing million dollar portfolios and supervising a large staff, which keep Black professionals stagnant. It is crucial that effective mentoring programs be developed to assist with this process. By offering Black professionals an opportunity to serve in senior level positions on a 3–6 month basis with a comprehensive economic package, it will help to fill this gap in their experiences.

Work Cited

Chun, E., & Evans, A. (2011). Creating an inclusive leadership environment in higher education. *The Higher Education Workplace,* Fall 2011, Retrieved May 7, 2014, from http://www.cupahr.org/hew/files/HEWorkplace-Vol3No2-Inclusive-Leadership.pdf

Brown, W. (2007, July 12). Increasing power, not just numbers—senior level African American Administrators. *Diverse Education*, Retrieved February 19, 2014, from http://diverseeducation.com/article/8344/

U.S. Department of Education, National Center for Education Statistics. (2013). The condition of education 2013 (NCES 2013-037). *Characteristics of Postsecondary Faculty*. Retrieved March 12, 2014, from https://nces.ed.gov/fastfacts/display.asp?id=61

U.S. Department of Education, National Center for Education Statistics. (2013). The condition of education 2013 (NCES 2013-037). *Characteristics of Postsecondary Faculty*. Retrieved March 12, 2014, from https://nces.ed.gov/fastfacts/display.asp?id=61

Siegel, J. (2011). Clarence Thomas-Anita Hill supreme court confirmation hearing 'empowering women' and panel member Arlen Specter still amazed by reactions. *World News*, October 24, 2011. Retrieved May 5, 2014, from http://abcnews.go.com/US/clarence-thomas-anita-hill-supreme-court-confirmation-hearing/story?id=14802217

James, J. (1991, December 1) Anita Hill: Martyr heroism & gender abstractions. *The Black Scholar, 22*(1/2), 17–20.

Cotter, D. A., et al. (2001, December 1). The glass ceiling effect. *Social Forces, 80*(2), 655–681; Stith, A. (1998). *Breaking the glass ceiling: Sexism & racism in corporate America: The myths, realities & solutions* (1st ed.). Warwick Publishing.

Du Bois, W. E. B. (2008). *The souls of black folk* (p. 12). Arc Manor LLC.

Jones, S. J., Taylor, C. M., & Coward, F. (2013, July 22). Through the looking glass: An autoethnographic view of the perceptions of race and institutional support in the tenure process. *Qualitative Report, 18*(29), 2.

Woody, B., Brown, D., & Green, T. (2000, January 1). Black women in the economy: Facing glass ceilings in academia. *Trotter Review, 12*(1), http://scholarworks.umb.edu/trotter_review/vol12/iss1/8.

Nolan, D. S. (2014, April 24) *The national association of diversity officers in higher education on Schutte v. Coalition to defend affirmative action.* Retrieved May 7, 2014, from http://www.nadohe.org/news

Jones, Taylor, and Coward, "Through the Looking Glass"; Lawrence, J. H., Celis, S., & Ott, M. (2014, April 3) Is the tenure process fair? What faculty think. *Journal of Higher Education, 85*(2), 174, 179; Chambers, C. R. (2011). Candid reflections on the departure of black women faculty from academe in the United States. *Negro Educational Review, 62/63*(1–4), 233–260.

Jackson, J. F.L., & O'Callaghan, E. M. (2011). Understanding employment disparities using glass ceiling effects criteria: An examination of race/ethnicity and senior-level position attainment across the academic workforce. *The Journal of the Professoriate,* 92.

Twale, D. J., & De Luca, B. M. (2008). *Faculty incivility: The rise of the academic bully culture and what to do about It* (p. 9). Jossey-Bass.

B. N. Williams, & S. M. Williams (2006, February), Perceptions of African American male junior faculty on promotion and tenure: Implications for community building and social capital. *Teachers College Record, 108*(2), 287–315. doi:10.1111/j.1467-9620.2006.00649.x. For perspectives on black male feminists see Ikard, D. (2007). *Breaking the silence: Toward a black male feminist criticism.* LSU Press; Lemons, G. L. (2013). *Black male outsider: Teaching as a pro-feminist man.* SUNY Press; Digby, T. (2013). *Men doing feminism.* Routledge.

Brown-Glaude, W. (2008). *Doing diversity in higher education: Faculty leaders share challenges and strategies* (pp. xi–xii). Rutgers University Press.

Rockquemore, K. A., & Laszloffy, T. A. (2008). *The black academic's guide to winning tenure without losing your soul* (pp. 4–5). Lynne Rienner Publishers.

Perna, L. W., Gerald, D., Baum, E., & Milem, J. (2007, March). The status of equity for black faculty and administrators in public higher education in the south. *Research in Higher Education, 48*(2), 193–227.

"U.S. Census Bureau Projections Show a Slower Growing, Older, More Diverse Nation a Half Century from Now," December 12, 2014, Retrieved March 12, 2014, from http://www.census.gov/newsroom/releases/archives/population/cb12-243.html

Van Ummersen, C. A. (2005, January). No talent left behind: Attracting and retaining a diverse faculty. *Change: The Magazine of Higher Learning, 37*(6), 26.

CHAPTER 19

Identifying and Coping with Academe's Glass Ceiling

A Critical Analysis

Brenda L. H. Marina

This chapter presents and critically examines the findings and the silent voices of women in academia and their respective experiences of the "glass ceiling". These findings are synthesized with literature related to concepts and "syndromes" that identify conceptual patterns of significance and assign meaning for women on a career path in academia. There are some salient variables that contribute to this intangible construct (Bain & Cummings, 2000, 2010; Jackson & O'Callaghan, 2007, 2009; Stanley, 2006a). Tangible *manifestations* of gender-based obstacles, i.e., lower salary, appointment at lower rank, slower rate of promotion, lower recognition through awards, and not being retained, is evidence of a widespread problem. While these *manifestations* of gender-based obstacles have been consistently observed at many universities, businesses, and governmental organizations; there simply are not enough critical analyses that probe and report on the *root causes* (Dominici et al., 2008) of under-representation of women in full-time professorate and leadership positions in academia. This chapter signals recognition of the still sub-optimal situation of the glass ceiling in academia and of the need for continued efforts to address this problem. In the final pages of this chapter, strategies utilized to cope with obstacles and contemporary ideologies are offered to promote greater personal and professional success while breaking the glass ceiling in American higher education.

The Glass Ceiling

The "glass ceiling" is a metaphor for the levels of leadership beyond which women have not been admitted. Meyerson (2004) contends that it is not just the ceiling that's holding women back; it's the whole structure of the organizations: the foundation, the beams, the walls, and even the air. This "glass ceiling" also refers to barriers faced by women who attempt, or aspire, to attain senior levels in corporations, government, nonprofit organizations, and education. This vertical challenge has also been consistently discussed with respect to ethnic and racial minorities when they experience barriers to advancement.

Although invisible an intangible, the "glass ceiling" does have a visible and tangible commission and legislation. The Glass Ceiling Act of the Civil Rights Act of 1991 was designed to combat gender based discrimination in the workplace. The passing of a 1991 Civil Rights Act, lead to the formulation of the Federal Glass Ceiling Commission for the purpose of conducting studies and preparing recommendations concerning barriers and opportunities for women (Federal Glass Ceiling Commission, 1995). The Lilly Ledbetter Fair Pay Act of 2009 was a welcomed sign of progress. This law was an answer to the *Ledbetter v. Goodyear Tire & Rubber Company* United States (U.S.) Supreme Court decision holding that the statute of limitations for presenting an equal-pay lawsuit begins at the date the pay was agreed upon, not at the date of the most recent paycheck, as a lower court had previously ruled (Grossman, 2009).

Considering the influences and manifestations on several levels, I have sought to ascertain the change in the prevailing glass ceiling over the past 25–30 years. In particular, I wanted to better understand the saga of the perpetual "glass ceiling" above my head—in the academy. I further this analysis and drill down to the *root* causes of the glass ceiling effect by noting the layered social, cultural and political behaviors that play out at the national, and state level, as well as considering what has occurred in the business world and the K-12 arena. These entities have served as a "role model" for the higher education arena.

The National Glass Ceiling

Nationally, glass walls and ceilings have been systematically constructed as a consequence of cultural attitudes, behaviors, and practices in the United States. The U.S. population is still approximately 51% female, the same as it was three decades ago. Women have made great strides in the workforce on a national level, yet they still are not proportionally represented in the chief leadership positions. As such, I highlight a few statistics germane to the conversation about women in the United States workforce (Institute of Women's Policy Research, 2014):

- Women's participation in the labor force accounted for 57.7% of the working age women population in 2012, compared to 70.2% participation rate for men.
- In 2012, the unemployment rate of White women was 7%, of Black or African American women 12.8%, of Asian women 6.1%, and 10.9% of women of Hispanic or Latino ethnicity.
- Women who worked full time in wage and salary jobs had median usual weekly earnings of $706 in 2013. This represented 82% of men's median weekly earnings.
- In 2013, forty percent of Hispanic women work in service and other occupations with poverty wages, as well as 32% of black women and 14% of white women.

Calculating gender differences may seem complicated, but the politics are simple (Clift, 2014). While writing this chapter on "Equal Pay Day", President Obama unveiled executive orders aimed at narrowing the wage gap. Equal Pay Day took place on April 8th; marking how much extra time women would have to work into 2014 to earn as much as men. The very next day, this legislation was voted down. While legal and cultural barriers have decreased over time and women have become more prominent in the workforce, over all, state by state, the numbers vary, with 64 cents for women in Wyoming to one dollar for men and 85–90 cents to the dollar for women in the Beltway around Washington, D.C.

The State Level Glass Ceiling

The glass ceiling remains intact for women appointed policy leaders in the executive branch of most state governments. Study after study has shown that when women run for office, they perform just as well as their male counterparts. While there have been no differences emerge in women and men's fundraising receipts, vote totals, or electoral success, women remain severely under-represented in U.S. political institutions. Large gender disparities are also evident at the state and local levels, where more than three-quarters of statewide elected officials and state legislators are men. Men occupy the governor's mansion in 44 of the 50 states, and men run City Hall in 92 of the 100 largest cities across the country. The lack of recruitment is an explanation for why women are less likely than men to consider a candidacy. When women have been encouraged to run by a party leader, elected official, or political activist, they have considered running. Women are just as likely as men to respond favorably to the suggestion of a candidacy. They are just less likely than men to receive it (Lawless & Fox, 2012).

The Business Sector Glass Ceiling

The glass ceiling remains intact for women in business and management. For example, in New York's top 100 companies, women hold 40 of 341 executive positions (11.7%). These women are in 31 different companies; as such a majority of these companies have no women executives. The glass ceiling has been virtually impervious to many qualified women, especially women of color, attempting to assume leadership roles. Women of color held 3.2% of board seats in the Fortune 500 in 2013, down from 3.3% in 2012 but up from 3.0% in 2011. With the business sector being hit hard by the financial crisis, it's imperative that companies tap into the expertise, talents, and perspective that women offer (Nauman & Wolverton 2008).

The Education Administration (K-12) Glass Ceiling

The glass ceiling remains intact for women leaders in education Administration (K-12). Throughout American history, the education profession has been a predominately female occupation. The American school superintendency has been a leadership position dominated by white males since the inception of the position (Konnert & Augenstein, 1995). This pattern of male-dominated leadership is a "glass ceiling effect" for women which prevent them from obtaining higher administrative positions (Baker, Graham, & Williams, 2003; Mainiero, 1994).

A recent national study indicated that the percentage of female superintendents has increased nearly four times since 1992. The study, released by the American Association of School Administrators, noted that from a survey of about 2,000 superintendents nationwide, only 24% were women; this is a 13% increase since the last survey taken a decade ago.

The Higher Education Administration Glass Ceiling

The glass ceiling remains intact for women leaders in higher education administration. Historically, educating women was met with strong resistance by White men, specifically early on in America's colleges and university systems. In proportion to men, women are likely to be hired less frequently, promoted at a slower pace, disproportionate in lower ranked positions in higher education and are more likely to be the lowest paid. The underrepresentation of full-time women faculty of color (WFOC) in the academy has been well documented in the literature. WFOC—(i.e., defined as Black, Hispanic, Asian/Pacific Islander, and American Indian/Alaska Native in the United States)—comprised 11.5% of all assistant, 8% of all associate, and 4% of all full professors (U.S. Department of Education, 2012). While there have been interventions by leaders in higher education, women are still under-represented in faculty and leadership positions. Despite the barriers to inclusion, White women have made significant gains in academia, coming only second to their White male counterparts holding specific academic ranks (Holmes et al., 2007). Women of color and African American women in particular continue to face racial inequities beyond the barrier of gender (Nichols & Tanksley, 2004). African American women, as a separate group, face both racial and gender disparity which posits a different dynamic in their quest to succeed in higher education. Despite the steady gains that African American women have made, their voices are still not heard within the sometimes-cold nature of the academy (Holmes et al., 2007; Thomas & Hollenshead, 2001; Valverde, 2003).

African American women administrators have been (are) constantly challenged because they are viewed as inferior; have been (are) over scrutinized by peers, superiors, and students; have been (are) assumed to be affirmative action hires and thus are less qualified; have been (are) considered tokens; have (had) to work harder than others in order to gain respect; and have been (are) denied access to sources typically given to someone in that position (Valverde, 2003). In looking at the current state of affairs for African American women in academe, they continue to face isolation, demoralization, and opposition in attaining equity in university administration, (Holmes et al., 2007). The lack of representation in top level management poses a problem for higher education institutions who try to justify their representation of being social change agents. And, what is more unfortunate is the lack of representation of African American women on governance boards (Valverde, 2003). Governance boards within institutions form policies and the lack of representation of African American women means little or no voice in the formulation of policies that reflect issues faced by other African Americans.

As a woman of color, pause to note my positionality and confirm my exposure to gendered and raced socialization in the academy, and more specifically at predominantly White institutions (PWIs). I can identify with the challenges mentioned, as such; my ongoing reflexivity (Creswell, 2013) enhances the trustworthiness of the literature and the statistics. My ways of understanding my lived experiences as an African American woman in U.S. higher education are intimately connected to my knowledge of other historical and contemporary African American women's experiences of racial, gender, and class discrimination, their strategies of survival, and their wisdom cultivated to resist and transcend these intersecting forms of oppression (Collins, 2000).

Deeper Roots: The Syndromes

The Professional Victim Syndrome

I reiterate that glass walls and ceilings have been systematically constructed as a consequence of cultural attitudes, behaviors, and practices in the United States. Ridgeway (2001) asserts that "status beliefs embedded in gender stereotypes create a formidable maze of obstacles that hold women back from positions of high authority and leadership" (p. 650). Reviewing accounts from government, business and education (K-12 and Higher Education Administration) illuminates the contemporary realities of gender equity in the labor market in general and in higher education in particular in our male dominated society. The obscure obstacle of the glass ceiling has infringed on the lives of women in public leadership, resulting in a phenomenon called the "professional victim syndrome". In general, contemporary women in academia and leadership positions frequently experience the "professional victim syndrome," defined as,

> the condition confronted by many public leaders, especially executive branch policy leaders, university faculty, administrators, presidents, and superintendents of schools, who faced a career crisis in which his/her professional and personal reputation was being tarnished, and he/she had the challenge of navigating the political waves in order to survive, literally and figuratively, as a leader and a person. (adapted from Polka & Litchka, 2006)

I further describe this syndrome to return to critically examining *root* causes for the glass ceiling.

Davis (2007) conducted a study on women in educational leadership related to women superintendents' perceptions of career advancement barriers and strategies to overcome those barriers. The three barriers for women superintendent advancement receiving the highest mean score in the Davis study were: conflicting demands of career and family, existence of the "buddy system" in which men refer other men to jobs, lack of political know-how. The next two highest scores for barriers were: exclusion from the informal socialization process of "good ole boy network" and gender bias in screening and selection process (Davis, pp. 61–62).

The women interviewed exhibited great strength and *self-confidence*, were *confident* in their ability to lead and expressed a strong sense of satisfaction in the job they held. All the women superintendents agreed that women need to mentor other women and develop better networking to promote and sustain their increased presence in contemporary educational leadership (Davis, 2007). It should be noted that even with a mentor available, many women still had an apprehensive relationship with power and the traits necessary to be a leader (Kantrolwitz, 2007).

The chances of surviving a "professional victim syndrome" are dependent on whether or not the person has core beliefs and values as a foundation, and whether or not, he/she is persistent in using them. Additionally, the contemporary women pursuing public or academic leadership roles need to ensure that a network exists of family, friends and trusted colleagues including a key mentor. Those who have such a network will be better equipped to survive the Professional Victim Syndrome (Polka & Litchka, 2006) and continue the quest to shatter glass ceilings.

The Marilyn Munster Syndrome

The Professional Victim Syndrome extends its tentacles deeper in women of color. With that being said, I wanted to articulate this phenomenon in another way. During a conference in 2007, a colleague introduced and described "the Marilyn Munster" syndrome. With no other literature that even hinted to this condition, I gathered narratives over the past seven years to authenticate this hypothetical syndrome. Based on the narratives gathered I define the "Marilyn Munster" syndrome for women of color in general and African American women in particular aspiring to leadership positions as: *an accomplished women who is constantly shifting between her professional and personal self at work, home, and with friends. This woman feels isolated and undervalued and this feeling is particularly acute in her professional life. This woman also feels that her role or title is minimized because of her race or gender. These feelings lead to a sense of isolation that may be described as workplace marginalization.*

Marilyn Munster is a fictional character who may be viewed as an example of a marginalized woman. Marilyn Munster was not a woman of color; she was blond and blue-eyed. She spoke well and dressed nicely—and from all appearances she came from a good family. Although she was not Latin, African American, Asian, or Native American, I suggest that some of the challenges she faced parallel challenges faced by professional minority women: Marilyn did not look or act like members of her family; she was different in appearance and demeanor; she was well-mannered, considerate, intelligent and compassionate and because of these attributes she did not fit in with her family (Marina & Ortega, 2008).

The premise of the television series, *The Munsters* (1964–1966) is that the viewing public would find it interesting to watch weekly episodes in which the predicaments of this normal looking young woman unfolded. Week-after-week viewers saw Marilyn overcoming one challenge after another. She learned how to survive in a family that could not offer her the naturally protective and nurturing environment other typical American families presumably enjoy and in which she should have been allowed to develop to her full potential.

Marilyn's remarkable innate abilities somehow allowed her to manage to survive in spite of the weird circumstances in which she found herself. Marilyn's strength became apparent and viewers saw how resourceful she became. At an early age, she found ways to cope, grow-up, survive and prosper. It may be argued that because she was different she was marginalized by her own natural family group. Marilyn Munster's experience is not unlike many women of color. In spite of having little support from naturally occurring family and social groups, some women of color manage to find ways to thrive and prosper. They break through the glass to become scholars, surgeons, philosophers, lawyers, professors, and engineers and they manage to make their way in any number of other arts, sciences and disciplines.

Concluding Thoughts

Women aspiring to be leaders, especially women of color, must focus on their personal coping skills in order to overcome the barriers to achieving their career leadership objectives. It has become apparent that women cannot wait on policies and legislation to mitigate the contemporary realities of gender equity in the labor market in general and in higher education in particular. Identifying and coping are foundational first steps to taping on the glass doors, walls and ceilings in the workforce.

Women of color are relatively new to the workforce. Because they are relative newcomers, they experience professional challenges similar to, but deeper that the experiences regarded as professional victimization. When confronted with professional and personal attacks that have the possibility of damaging their careers, women of color typically have fewer resources to depend upon and must somehow navigate the system alone. They must become resourceful or they will not survive.

Women in general have the potential to become professional victims. All women of color in higher education, whether as faculty or professional positions of leadership, have the potential to become professional victims and/or experience the Marilyn Munster syndrome. It is imperative that women aspiring to work in leadership positions recognize the omnipresence of these syndromes and similar identity crises that are at the *root* of glass ceiling. It is crucial for women to understand the value of knowing one's self and the need for remaining proactive to be prepared to deal with obscure obstacles in the work environment.

Differences in *confidence* and career ambition between men and women have been cited as factors in preventing women from moving into senior and executive positions. An Institute of Leadership and Management study revealed that women managers are hampered in their careers by lower ambitions and expectations. Women often lack *self-confidence* and *self-belief*, which leads to less risk taking and more cautious career choices.

Strategies that should be considered by women in all aspects of the workforce: develop political know-how, develop a strong self-concept, learn the characteristics of the work environment and position you wish to obtain, obtaining the support of family, friends, and a mentor, attend workshops to improve professional skills, learn coping skills, gain access to community power, and increase visibility in professional circles.

In a study of 322 male and female executives, Goodson (2000) found that women are less comfortable promoting themselves than men. Many women believe that self-promotion is unacceptable and have been taught that hard work alone will put them on par with men at some point. It appears that women who do make it to the top often fail to reach out to others coming up the ranks behind them. Goodson (2000) noted that the "essence" of the glass ceiling today may just be that when women get to the top of the corporate ladder, they pull up the ladder behind them. This critical analysis of findings and manifestations, my literature searches and narrative inquiries on the successes, failures, and experiences of women in leadership positions in higher education still merits further analysis. I have considered the "essence" of the prevailing glass ceiling and end with the critical question: Are women responsible for the glass ceiling?

Work Cited

Bain, O., & Cummings, W. (2010, November). *Academic glass ceiling; A comparative analysis.* Paper Presented at the 35th annual conference of the Association of the Study of Higher Education (ASHE), Indianapolis, IN.

Bain, O., & Cummings, W. (2000). Academe's glass ceiling: societal, professional-organisational, and institutional barriers to the career advancement of academic women. *Comparative Education Review, 44*(4), 493–514.

Baker, B., Graham, S., & Williams, S. (2003, Spring). *Teaching under a glass ceiling: A study of gender equity in federal education career fields.* Retrieved June 12, 2008 from Advancing Women: ttp://www.advancingwomen.com/awl/spring2003/BAKER~1.HTML

Clift, E. (2014). What equal pay day? McConnell slams paycheck fairness act. *The Daily Beast.* Retrieved from http://www.thedailybeast.com/articles/2014/04/09/what-equal-pay-day-mcconnell-slams-paycheck-fairness-act.html

Collins, P. H. (2000). It's all in the family: Intersections of gender, race, and nation. In U. Narayan & S. Harding (Eds.), *Decentering the center: Philosophy for a multicultural, postcolonial, and feminist world* (pp. 156–176). Bloomington, IN: Indiana University Press.

Creswell, J. (2013). *Qualitative inquiry and research design: Choosing among five approaches* (3rd ed.). Thousand Oaks, CA: Sage.

Davis, Sheryl, (2007). *Career paths of female superintendents in Georgia.* Unpublished Dissertation. College of Education, Georgia Southern University.

Dominici, F., Busch-Vishniac, I., Landau, B., Jarosz, J., Stokes, E., Gillian, R., … Fried, L. (2008). *Women in Academic Leadership: Analysis of root causes for under-representation.* Retrieved December 12, 2008 from www.biostat.jhsph.edu/~fdominic/NIHwomen/extra1/

Federal Glass Ceiling Commission. (1995, November). *A solid investment—making full use of the nation's human capital. A report.* Washington, DC: U.S. Department of Labor.

Goodson, S. (2000). Are women responsible for the glass ceiling? *USA Today,* Society for the Advancement of Education. Retrieved November 5, 2010 from http://findarticles.com/p/articles/mi_m1272/is_2659_128/ai_61586738/

Grossman, J. (2009). *The Lilly Ledbetter fair pay act of 2009: President Obama's first signed bill restores essential protection against pay discrimination.* Retrieved March 15, 2010 from http://writ.news.findlaw.com/grossman/20090213.html

Institute of Women's Policy Research. (2014). Retrieved April 6, 2014 from http://www.iwpr.org/

Jackson, J. F. L., & O'Callaghan, E. M. (2007). *The glass ceiling effect: A misunderstood form of discrimination [Annotated bibliography].* Milwaukee, WI: Institute on Race and Ethnicity, University of Wisconsin System.

Jackson, J. F. L., & O'Callaghan, E. M. (2009). What do we know about glass ceiling effects: A taxonomy and critical review to inform higher education. *Research in Higher Education, 50*(5), 460–482.

Kantrolwitz, B. (2007). Women and leadership. *Newsweek, 16,* 49–65.

Konnert, W., & Augenstein, J. (1995). *The school superintendency: Leading education into the 21st Century.* Lancaster, PA: Technomic Publishing.

Lawless, J., & Fox, R. (2012). *Men rule: The continued under-representation of women in U.S. politics.* Washington DC: Women & Politics Institute, School of Public Affairs.

Mainiero, L. (1994). On breaking the glass ceiling: The political seasoning of powerful women executives. *Organizational Dynamics, 22*(4), 5–20.

Marina, B., & Ortega, R. (2008). Unpublished Paper. Presented at the COMPA Conference. Bermuda.

Meyerson, D. (2004). A modest manifesto for the shattering the glass ceiling. *Harvard Business Review, 78*(1), 125–136.

Nauman, M., & Wolverton, T. (2008). Women as business leaders? Study shows little progress. *Mercury News.* Retrieved December 16, 2008 from www.mercurynews.com/ci_11006472

Nichols, J. C., & Tanksley, C. B. (2004). Revelations of African-American women with terminal degrees: Overcoming obstacles to success. *The Negro Educational Review, 55*(4), 175–185. Retrieved August 30, 2008 from ERIC database.

Polka, W., & Litchka, P. (2006). *Illegitimi non carborundum: The contemporary school superintendency and experiences related to the professional victim syndrome.* Unpublished Research Project. College of Education, Georgia Southern University

Polka, W., Litchka, P., & Davis, S. (2008). *Female superintendents and the professional* victim syndrome: Preparing current and aspiring superintendents to cope and succeed. *Journal of Women in Educational Leadership, 6*(4), 293–311.

Ridgeway, C. L. (2001). Gender, status, and leadership. *Journal of Social Issues, 57*(4), 637–655.

Stanley, C. A. (2006a). An overview of the literature. In C. A. Stanley (Ed.), *Faculty of color: Teaching in predominantly White colleges and universities* (pp. 1–29). Bolton, MA: Anker Publishing Company.

Thomas, G. D., & Hollenshead, C. (2001). Resisting from the margins: The coping strategies of black women and other women of color faculty members at a research university. *Journal of Negro Education, 70*(3), 166–175. Retrieved from http://www.jstor.org/stable/3211208

U.S. Department of Education. (2012). Full-time instructional faculty in degree-granting institutions, by race/ethnicity, sex, and academic rank: Fall 2007, fall 2009, and fall 2011. *National Center for Education Statistics.* Retrieved from http://nces.ed.gov/programs/digest/d10/tables/dt10_260.asp

Valverde, L. A. (2003). *Leaders of color in higher education: Unrecognized triumphs in harsh institutions.* Walnut Creek, CA: AltaMira Press.

CHAPTER 20

African American Males in A Living Learning Community

Their Experiences at an HBCU

P. Brandon Johnson

Introduction

In recent years, the retention of African American male students has been an increasing concern for institutions of higher education (Palmer & Young, 2008). However, previous studies on African American males typically has centered on their experiences at Predominantly White Institutions (PWIs) (Harper, 2005, 2008; Harper et al., 2011; Harper & Quaye, 2007), to which Kimbrough and Harper (2006) suggested, "much of the national attention [is] being placed on issues facing Black students at Predominantly White Institutions … the quality of life at HBCUs for [Black American] students—especially [Black] men—has gone virtually unnoticed" (p. 190). This despite evidence African American males experience campus disengagement, attrition, and decreased involvement at HBCUs (Palmer, Maramba, & Dancy, 2013).

This research emphasis on African American males at PWIs has highlighted the efficacy of a multitude of programs such as: African American Male Initiatives (AAMI) (Bledsoe & Rome, 2006; Bailey, 2006; Catching, 2006; Johnson & Moore, 2011; Laster, 2006; Palmer et al., 2013), participation in Black Greek Letter Organizations (BGLO) (Harper, 2005; Harper & Quaye, 2007; Taylor & Howard-Hamilton, 1995), and religion (Watson, 2006) on their ability to affect their experiences and student success outcomes. LLCs are an alternative program shown to affect several student outcomes (Inkelas & Weisman, 2003; Inkelas & Associates, 2007; Inkelas, Daver, Vogt, & Leonard, 2007), yet has not been investigated regarding its impact on African American males or its application on an HBCU campus.

Similar to studies on African American males, the majority of current LLC research has taken place at PWIs (Inkelas & Associates, 2007; Inkelas et al., 2007; Jessup-Anger, Johnson, & Wawrzynski, 2012; Soldner, Rowan-Kenyon, Inkelas, Garvey, & Robbins, 2012; Yao & Wawrzynski, 2013), and those studies focusing on males have been limited to small samples of predominantly White male students (Jessup-Anger et al., 2012; Yao & Wawrzynski, 2013). The lack of research on the experiences of African American males at HBCUs and in LLCs adds to the dearth of contemporary literature that can provide insight into the academic and social experiences of these students (Palmer, Davis, & Maramba,

2010; Strayhorn, 2010). Such information can benefit practitioners and researchers alike by investigating another possible variable in the African American male success equation.

In an effort to provide further insight into the social and academic experiences of African American males at HBCUs, this chapter presents findings from a qualitative study purposed with understanding their experiences of African American males participating in an LLC. Specifically this study investigated the experiences of first-year African American males who participated in an LLC on an HBCU campus to see how, if at all, LLC participation impacted their retention.

African American Male LLC

The LLC used for this study was created in 2010 in response to a university system report that emphasized the need to increase the educational attainment of African American males. LLC students participated in an orientation that grants early campus move-in, and involved them in team-building activities such as skits, problem-solving games, academic workshops, and participation in a community service activity. They received training to navigate the institutions website and utilize additional university technological resources as well as increase their familiarity with campus through individual and group tours, were involved in out-of-class activities such as service learning, trips to museums associated with the Civil Rights movement, and at other programmatic activities to encourage social development, to provide a balance with the academic components of the program.

These students also were enrolled in two cohort first-year experience courses: FYE 100 in the fall and FYE 101 in the spring; each course being taught by one of the two program coordinators who also served as academic advisors for the LLC student. Because of the number of students wanting to participate in the program, each of the cohort sections contained students who did not live in the residence halls as part of the LLC. Additionally, LLC students have the ability to register early if they participated in at least five hours of tutoring assistance each semester. During the academic year, regularly scheduled evening workshops conducted and students were assigned peer mentors, some of whom were previous LLC participants.

Method

This chapter is based on findings from a qualitative case study investigating the experiences of first-year African American males participating in an LLC on an HBCU campus. Stake (2005) noted that case studies are a choice of what to study, or a bounded system, enclosed by time and place. They also provide a clear methodology when investigating a particular topic, prioritizing until a depth of understanding is achieved (Merriam, 2009; Yin, 2014).

This case study sought to not only understand the overall experiences of these first-year students but also asked questions concerning the effect of their pre-entry characteristics on their first-year experiences, how their participation affected their academic and social integration, and finally how LLC participation impacted their retention.

Research Locations

Three locations were utilized to conduct research for this case study. The first is the six-story, co-educational, double occupancy, suite-style residence hall that housed the 37 LLC participants. Each suite contained four rooms (two students per room), a common area, and a bathroom. The second and third location were the two classrooms where each section of the FYE 101 course was held.

Data Sources and Collection

Data were collected over a four-week period during the spring 2015 semester and began after students returned from spring break. Within this bounded system, data were obtained through 12 semi-structured interviews (Shank, 2006), 12 passive participant observations (Spradley, 1980) in the LLC residence hall, and 4 observations in the FYE 101 classroom. Research conducted by Guest, Bunce, and Johnson (2006) on reaching qualitative data saturation informed the frequency of interviews and residence hall observations used for this study. Four was the maximum number of classroom observations available during the defined research period, as the FYE 101 course met only once per week. Additionally, institutional reports were obtained to provide information on the students' high school GPA, SAT and ACT scores, and their fall-to-fall retention rate.

Data Analysis

Coding

A combination of open coding (Corbin & Strauss, 2007) and In Vivo coding (Creswell, 2013; Saldana, 2013) were used to analyze the data from the interview transcription and observation field notes. A cross-categorical analysis of data from the interviews, residence hall observations, and classroom observations generated 13 overarching categories and 3x sub-categories that addressed each of the research questions associated with this study.

Institutional Reports

In addition to the interviews and observations, four institutional reports or documents were used and consisted of: an end-of-year report, a program academic progress tracking report, a student pre-entry information list, and a retention report. Information from the various reports were reviewed to create a comprehensive picture of the pre-entry characteristics, academic preparedness, and academic progress of the LLC students.

Findings

Data collected from the interviews, observations, and information obtained from institutional reports were analyzed and distilled into 13 primary categories and 3x sub-categories. Findings are presented in the following sections that represent each of the 5 research questions. Each subsequent section includes one or more of the coded categories associated with each question.

Experiences of First-Year African American Males

The first research question sought to understand the experiences of first-year African American males who participated in an LLC on the campus of an HBCU. Based on the data, four categories were created to address this question, and consisted of behavior change experiences, interpersonal connectivity experiences, LLC privilege experiences, and family affiliation experiences.

Behavior Change Experiences

Several of the interview participants expressed having experienced a change in some aspect of their behavior since joining the LLC. Most participants commented on how they perceived a change in behavior from life before college compared to how they act now in college. This transition seemed to move from an antisocial or isolated behavior to behavior indicating more social openness. Hogan commented:

> Before I was in college and I saw someone like my roommate, I would probably not like them, I'd rob them. (laughs) That was the type of environment I had at home. I wasn't attracted to those type of people, but those type of people were attracted to me. They had an influence on me. But now I'm in college … me and my roommate are best friends. My roommate is up there (raises hand to indicate a higher socioeconomic level) and I'm like here (lowers hand to indicate a lower socioeconomic level). We got a lot of things in common. [*sic*]

The data revealed another behavior change attribute regarding the participants' approach to their college academics. Participant comments revolved around how they changed or adapted their study habits to survive in the college environment. Orlando commented about not studying in high school but also spoke about a tip he learned to improve his studying and memory retention:

> I never studied. I would just cram. Like even if it was exams I'd cram. I never needed to really. I was always good at retaining information in high school. Now it's more like … one of the best tips I got from the program, was when he [LLC coordinator] was teaching in class. Like the day of, when they teach you something when you go to your room just read or go over it. And it's what I've been doing lately because I've been struggling in chemistry, like when we go over a topic I'll go to YouTube and I'll search the topic and watch a video and help me keep it in my memory that way.

Kerry noted that participation in "the FYE class where we go over topics like that [study skills]" affected his study habits. However, in his comments, Christopher said, "The program, it affects your study habits but it's all up to the person … it offered me a lot of help but I did not take it at first."

Interpersonal Connectivity Experiences

All of the participants who perceived a social behavior change attributed that change to the interaction with their program peers. Furthermore, some type of peer interaction was mentioned by every one of the research participants in varying degrees and situations.

Ricky emphasized the importance of the skit during the early arrival orientation when he said, "Yea, we probably would have never clicked like we did if we did not do the skit." This skit, which involved all of the LLC students, served as the first interpersonal connectivity experience. Ricky's comments also alluded to the formation of a bond between the LLC students as a product of their skit participation which was evident in the residence hall.

During residence hall observations, many of the students in the observed suites left their doors open and would freely walk in and out of each other's rooms. Christopher described this as typical for his suite when he said:

> In our suite you would just about find all of our doors open. Cus that's just how we do, you know. We're real close in there you know we just walk in the next room and have a conversation go back to our room and then go to somebody else room … like one big happy family. [*sic*]

The closeness that was exhibited in the residence hall manifested as social grouping in the classroom. In both sections of the FYE 101 course, the LLC participants sat together. They would sit with either their roommate or other students from their suite. If the student's roommate or suitemates were not in that particular FYE 101 section, the students would sit with other LLC students. Konrad said that for his suite, "Yea, we always, [sit at] the same table. You can catch us in the cafeteria together or in the gym working out together too. We do a lot of things together." The same LLC student grouping was also evident in Classroom B.

LLC Privilege Experiences

Students' were asked to compare their lives within the LLC with their perception of those not in the LLC. The participants expressed a variety of perceived benefits associated with LLC participation and that other students were missing out on a great opportunity.

The LLC program offered several components that could be viewed as perks, such as the early arrival orientation, workshops, peer mentors, program coordinators (who serve as academic advisors and teach sections of the FYE courses), and early spring registration. Christopher talked about how he used his early registration privileges to create a schedule he knew he could follow. He also spoke about how non-LLC students were amazed at his schedule:

> So, some people don't benefit from early registration so they end up having those early classes that the majority of nobody wants to go to. I have like one class one day and people are like "how did you get

> that" and I tell them it's the program that I'm in. The early registration helped me get the classes at the times I knew I could wake up and go to them. [*sic*]

Hogan gave his opinion on the difference between LLC and non-LLC participants:

> I feel bad for them [non-LLC students]. Cus they don't have the same opportunities that I've got (laughs). Like they don't have early registration unless they are athletes. Like they don't got, you know, they do nothing, they don't do nothing really. They just go to class and chill like that. [*sic*]

Although the participants acknowledged their differences because of their LLC participation, a few expressed desires to share what benefits they could with other non-LLC members. Additionally, participants commented on their use of the peer mentors and other academic support resources integrated into the program, as well as their participation in special campus events.

Family Affiliation Experiences

The final category was derived from student comments about how they perceived their relationship with the other members of the LLC as a type of family. Participants used terms such as "family," "brother," "brothers," "brotherhood," or "big brother" when describing their experiences with other LLC members and coordinators. Mathew described it as, "like a brotherhood really, since everyone stays in the LLC residence hall. The majority of the LLC is basically in the same major." Christopher commented on how one of the LLC program components has given him a similar brotherhood experience when he said:

> So all the [program] workshops, all the males that are involved with [the LLC program], I've gotten kind of close with them. It's like another brotherhood, a family-type thing. Um they, all of us, we get along so it helps build you back up if you're down.

Konrad likened his experiences to that of having an older brother when he said:

> I'm getting advice from mentors that are also in the program that are sophomores, juniors, and seniors that are remembering their freshman year. They can tell me things they messed up or things they could have done or should have done. It's like having an older brother who has experienced it all and can lead you through it and can tell you what to do and what not to do.

Other participants shared similar feelings about their experiences but attributed them to their perceived experiences within individual suites, rather than the program as a whole.

Pre-entry Characteristics and Perceived First-Year Experiences

The second research question sought to investigate the impact of a student's pre-entry characteristics on their perceived first-year experiences. These characteristics represented the academic and family background components each student brought with them to college.

Concerning academic pre-entry characteristics, this study placed an emphasis on the student's high school GPA because it was the primary measure used to select and recruit students for the LLC. Participants' first-generation college student status, socioeconomic status, and household type were used to establish the family background characteristics.

Perceived academic performance and perceived benefits of LLC participation were the two categories created to address this research question. The category of perceived academic performance is split into three sub-categories of average performing student, mid-range performing student, and high performing student, which was drawn from institutional data revealing the students' high school GPAs.

Perceived Academic Performance

Family background was categorized by the students' perceived high, middle, or low economic status, whether they came from a single- or two-parent household, and if they were a first-generation college student. Findings are presented in the three sub-categories of high performing students, mid-range performing students, and average performing students. Four students were included in each of the three performance categories.

Average Performing Students

The first sub-category discussed is the average performance category, which includes high school GPA's between 2.5 and 2.9. Herbert, who identified himself as coming from a middle-class, single-parent household, described his fall semester academic performance:

> Like the first semester I missed like a month or so because of medical issues, I had a liver transplant two years ago and I was having another episode so I was out. And plus before that classes, like I don't think I was in the right classes. Like my SAT or ACT scores, that's what put me in calculus and I was going straight from discrete math to calculus and that wasn't … so first semester I did not do too good. And when I got back [the LLC coordinator] helped me register for classes for this semester and classes that I needed to be in and not like last semester.

When asked why he joined the LLC, Orlando said: "I knew that coming out of high school I was kinda lazy like with school work and stuff and I figured this would help motive me." Orlando identified himself as coming from a middle-class, single parent household. Konrad, identifying himself as coming from a middle-class two-parent household, reported that his high school studying was limited to finding quick ways to remember items prior to exams. He added: "I was aware of some studying techniques like I knew how to study but not to my maximum potential. And that's like what the LLC has helped me kind of reach that maximum."

Mid-Range Performing Students

This category consisted of earned GPA's between 3.0 and 3.49. Mathew came from a single-parent home and was not a first-generation student. But Mathew thought of his family's socioeconomic status as low, "nearly poverty stricken" in his words. Mathew spoke about some of his difficulty and recovery within the first semester:

> First semester was a little rough getting here. I did not think it was going to be true, but got caught up with the females. First semester was kind of tragic. Ended up with a 2 [GPA] flat but now things are better cus I know what I have to do and right now I've got all A's.

John was not a first-generation student but did come from a single-parent home. He perceived his family as having a high socioeconomic status. When asked about his academic experiences during the first year, John responded:

> Taxing, like extremely taxing. Like I was not prepared, especially not first semester. It was not even the difficulty of the work but just the workload itself. And like the perfectionism of the professors like it really really got me down. This semester I was kinda better at it, kinda ready for it sort of. But yeah, it was sort of a rough ride.

High Performing Students

The final sub-category of high performing students included GPAs between 3.5 and 4.0. Jamel was a first-generation student from a two-parent household and perceived his family's socioeconomic status as middle class. Concerning additional pre-entry characteristics, Jamel said, "I don't think my high school prepared me for college at all. The only problem I've had with classes is math and that's my biggest weakness." However, Jamel stated that he did know how to study prior to attending college, "I knew how to study I just did not need to … But now I have to study a lot more, I think I could study more and I would do better."

Hogan came from a single-parent household but did not identify as a first-generation student. Although Hogan did not make any mention of knowing how to study prior to college he did express that he was dyslexic and was taking medication for Attention Deficit Disorder.

Perceived Benefits of LLC Participation.

Previously, several of the interview participants commented that they came to college with certain pre-entry characteristics that might have posed a risk to their academic success. Others possessed the necessary skills to succeed but had not been required to exercise those skills in high school. Students also mentioned not wanting to be like other family members who did not succeed in college. These students felt that this program was going to assist them in overcoming known and unknown obstacles. Other students viewed the program as offering positive assistance for their first year of college. Herbert joined the LLC after hearing a presentation from the coordinators during new student orientation. He said, "So I decided to join because of what [the coordinators] said. That it's a good mentoring program and helps you get on track." When asked what made him joining the program, Marcus said, "It seemed like a good idea to be around a supportive group to make the first year of college easier." Kerry thought that the LLC would help facilitate an easier transition to college. Whereas Jamel thought that the LLC "seemed like something good and positive and I wanted to do something else besides sitting in my room all the time."

LLC Participation and Academic Integration

The third research question sought to understand the effects of LLC participation on a student's perceived academic integration. Based on the data, three categories were created to address this research question, which included informing the student, using academic support services, and coordinator access.

Informing the Student

The LLC offered several channels through which the students could obtain information about campus academic support services, as well as program-specific support services. Students were first introduced to campus and program academic support services through presentations during the early arrival orientation. After orientation, the LLC students were reminded about academic support services through their FYE 100 and 101 courses. Instructors/LLC coordinators also served as the academic advisors for the LLC students, making advisement sessions an additional venue for sharing information about support services. Finally, the coordinators conducted "foot campaigns" where they visited the LLC residence hall to remind them about support services and perform an additional check-up on the students. According to the LLC end-of-year report, the coordinators conducted 3 foot campaigns, making 59 student contacts.

Using Academic Support Services

Often reacting to poor test scores or grades, students experiencing academic difficulty made the most use of support services. Some comments did imply proactive use as well, however these instances were in the minority.

"I don't think, if I was not in the LLC I would be going to the tutorial lab … I probably would not even know about it or where it was." This was a comment from Herbert after being asked how the LLC has impacted his study habits. Konrad commented about using tutorial services when he said:

> We are require to go to tutorial lab which is basically free tutoring for any subject. Originally I was like I don't really need it, it's a waste of time. I can just study by myself. But the more and more I went I kind of realized that oh, I did not really think of it this way. And I'm kind of getting new perspective on certain classes or certain topics we're studying in the class. So, the program … even thought it was like required it's still like benefited me.

Others attended the tutorial lab as a means of improving from some academic difficulty. For instance, Jamel used the tutorial services to overcome some math difficulty. Christopher however was more reluctant to use tutoring when he shared:

> The program like I said it offered me a lot of help but I did not take it at first. When I really started focusing on my grades and realizing that I wanted to make better grades. I started going to the tutorial lab and meeting my mentor more and studying on my own and going to the library.

He also spoke about an additional component of the LLC, being assigned a peer mentor:

> Yeah, the program, they blessed me with a mentor. My mentor he called me one day and asked if we could meet in the library and I was like sure. I meet with him once a week and we go over all the work I have and he helps me out. So the program has helped me … it's making me stay on the right path so it's not letting me fall back at all. It's keeping me where I need to be.

In addition to the peer mentors mentioned, the LLC coordinators were mentioned as additional mentors and sources of motivation.

Coordinator Access\

An LLC coordinator is a multi-faceted position, requiring the individual to serve as the FYE instructor as well as the academic advisor for the LLC students. These different duties created multiple opportunities for the LLC students to gain access to address any problems that arose during the academic year.

When asked about how the LLC affected his academic experience, Kerry spoke about his advising sessions:

> If anything it's been the advising periods that we have. They really there to make sure you're on track. It's not really to have someone overbearing you, but to have someone looking over your shoulder to make sure you're still on track. [*sic*]

The LLC students were not limited to the scheduled advising sessions. They were free to seek out their advisor when they needed them. Such was the case during classroom observation debriefing sessions with the coordinators. Each of the debriefing sessions was interrupted by at least two LLC students who did not have appointments and were in need of assistance or advice.

The second touchpoint between student and coordinator was the FYE 100 and 101 courses in which the coordinators served as instructors. Course enrollment was determined by which coordinator served as the student's advisor. If the students attended every session of class, they had contact with their advisor/coordinator 15 times per semester where the instructors used class time to remind students of advising-related material such as registration and financial aid deadlines as well as academic support services. Kerry also shared his thoughts on having his advisor as an instructor when he said:

> I think it helps because if you go to class you're going to have to see them. It helps, the way he teaches he puts his personal info into so we feel more comfortable with each other. So it's easier going to him for help because you really know them rather than just going to meet someone to just talk about your grades and stuff.

The third and final touchpoint was through the "foot campaigns" the coordinators conducted in the residence hall. These door-to-door check-ins were used to meet the students in their environment and reinforce previously disseminated information.

LLC Participation and Social Integration

The fourth research question sought to understand the impact of LLC participation on first-year African American male students' perceived social integration. Based on the data, two categories were created to address this research question. One category is creating a social network, and the second category is event attendance.

Creating a Social Network

Interview participants expressed that the LLC was instrumental in making friends and facilitating peer connections outside of the LLC. Several of the interview participants directly credited their involvement in the LLC with making friends and other peer connections on campus, especially when they did not know many people. Konrad spoke specifically about the program's impact on him making friends when he said:

> I'd say it's impacted it pretty … it's been a large impact. Without the LLC, I would not have had the core groups of friends I have today. It's kind of weird how we all got paired up, but everything happens for a reason and we are a pretty close-knit group.

In the process of remarking on their perceptions of how the program impacted making friends, Hogan and Ricky elaborated on what they perceived to be the improved quality of friends they were making. Hogan spoke about how his friends are positive and push him to do better when he said, "It's like I'm making good friends, like they make me and drive me to do better and become better myself. I'm making friends that are driving me to do better." Ricky shared a similar sentiment when he said:

> It actually helped me look for smart friends you know. Not looking for smart friends but like putting myself around ppl that are good for me. Cus like none of my friends partake in alcohol or marijuana. That's just because my family do stuff like that and I already see where we at because of stuff like that. So I don't want to be around that no more that's why I'm here. I did not come here to do what I was doing or around at home so I mean.

Contrarily, two students shared that they did not think the LLC had any impact on making friends or their social interactions. Jamel commented:

> I don't think it has because I just hang out with people that I meet anywhere. When I'm in my room I hang out with my suitemates, when I'm in class I hang out with my class friends and so on.

He continued saying, "I probably would have had a more diverse group of friends." Marcus shared a similar comment stating, "I don't think it's impacted me making friends. I think I would have made the same friends no matter."

Event Attendance

According to the interview responses, the members of the LLC were very active in attending campus events, even when the attendance for mandatory programs was excluded.

When asked if they attended any campus or social events during their first year, the respondents produced an extensive list of programs and events. Athletic events were the most referenced, followed by campus parties and homecoming activities (including step shows, concerts, fashion shows, and talent shows). Christopher commented on how the LLC contributed to his event attendance when he said,

"A lot of the times I find out about different events from the people that actually live in the residence hall with me." When the students heard about an event, they often chose to attend it together. Konrad added:

> We'll see a flier for a poetry slam but it will also talk about HIV awareness and things like that and it's on a Tuesday night. So we'll get our work done as a group, and as a group we'll also go to that program. Or just lectures, things like that, people speaking about Ferguson, Missouri, or race relation(s). And well go to that too. So it's [the LLC] kinda by requiring us to go it started us down that path were we have to go to this that and this, but then now it's like we don't have to go but its sounds pretty interesting so why not go. So it's opened up some doors.

Jamel and Mathew did not share the same views as the rest of the participants. Jamel felt that he still would have sought out and attended similar programming without the LLC. Mathew expressed a similar sentiment when he said, "It hasn't affected me going to any, or exposing myself to high quality programs they offer around campus."

LLC Participation and Retention

The final research question asked how, if at all, first-year African American male retention was impacted by the students' perceived LLC participation. Two categories were created to address this research question and consisted of life without the LLC and LLC student retention.

Life without the LLC

When the students were asked how they felt their experiences would be if they were not in the LLC, many of them commented about the impact it would have on their academic and social lives. Hogan simply said, "I would probably just, to be honest I'd be out this school by now." Herbert expressed concern about his grades but also spoke about how not having as much access to his advisors would affect him differently:

> [I] Probably be on academic probation and some other stuff. Because, I guess I know I haven't met other advisors from different majors but I know that they … I don't think they would be as helpful as [the LLC advisors] with advisement or classes. Cus I hear from other people who have declared majors that it's hard to get in touch with their advisors.

Participants also felt that not being in the LLC would have stifled the amount of information they would have received and limited their social development. Timothy said:

> If I was not a part of [the LLC] I wouldn't know important stuff like how to make a better resume and how to get around and scholarships, registration, and basic stuff like that. I probably be in my dorm all day not really doing anything. Like I met my first friends through the program so it would probably be harder finding friends.

Konrad reflected on his first-year social experiences when he said:

> They would be extremely different. I would be one of those lost freshmen who does not really fit in with a particular group and I'm kinda feeling my way around. I don't know exactly what to get involved with. Unless you're on a sports team or in a LLC, you really don't have that guidance or that sense of where to go. I don't know if I would be struggling academically but definitely socially. [*sic*]

LLC Student Retention

First-year student retention was measured by the number of students enrolled in fall semester who returned for the successive fall semester. When each of the 12 students were asked how they felt about returning the following fall semester, all 12 participants responded with confidence and surety they would return. Eleven of the twelve students returned for their second academic year of college. Of the 11 retained, 7 of the students earned cumulative GPAs above a 3.0, the highest of which was a 3.58. Three earned GPAs in the 2.0 to 2.9 range. Two students earned GPAs below a 2.0 placing them on academic suspension. One was granted a waiver of suspension by the department allowing him to return for the subsequent fall. The other student earned a GPA below 1.0. He did not seek a suspension waiver and did not return for the following fall semester.

Discussion

Data suggests that from their participation in a LLC, first-year African American males perceived themselves as having four distinct experiences: a change in behavior, peer-to-peer connections, privilege from the perceived benefits of the program, and a perceived sense of family. Some of their pre-entry characteristics, such as a lack of study knowledge seemed to have an initial negative effect on some of the students. But through LLC participation they expressed finding solutions to address these incoming inadequacies. Further findings also suggested that the structure and activities of the LLC program facilitated the students' perceived academic and social integration, and the students attributed their confidence in retention to their participation in the LLC.

Implications

Previous LLC research has only documented the ability of these programs to increase social connectivity, engagement, persistence, and retention of students at PWIs, but this is no longer the case. Data from this study suggest that the benefits of LLC participation can now be extended to first-year African American males and HBCU campuses. Based on the findings from this study, higher education practitioners could benefit from the implementation of LLCs on HBCU campuses with low African American male engagement and retention as targeted programs intended to improve student outcomes. This study also creates a foundation for future research concerning first-year African American males, LLCs and HBCUs. It offers a unique perspective on the experiences of students participating in a residential college program which has previously been the subject of single, multi-institutional, and national studies (Inkelas & Associates, 2007; Inkelas et al., 2007; Jessup-Anger et al., 2012; Soldner et al., 2012; Yao & Wawrzynski, 2013). This study opens the door for further investigation and possible testing of this program's effect on the first-year African American male population.

Conclusion

This study was purposed with addressing certain unexplored areas in higher education research. Addressing these areas has the potential to expand known information concerning the LLC experience for African American male college students. It also has the supplemental benefit of adding much needed research concerning the academic and social experiences of African American men at HBCUs (Palmer et al., 2010; Strayhorn, 2010). LLCs are not a panacea to ensure the success of African American male college students. They do, however, share many components with several other programs linked with the success of this student population such as student government associations and Greek letter organizations.

From this, LLCs have the capacity to serve as an alternative to participation in campus organizations such as BGLO's which have prohibitive membership requirements that exclude mass participation, or student government associations which require being elected. Not every African American male will have an interest in such organizational participation and should have access to alternative avenues to achieve the success outcomes of involvement, engagement, persistence, and retention.

The findings from this study do not allow for the statement to be made that the retention of first-year African American males at an HBCU is directly connected with their LLC participation. What can be said is that these students believed fully that participation in the LLC would enhance their first-year experience and ensure their retention. There was a perception of value placed on LLC involvement by each of the students, and for 11 of them, that commitment to involvement resulted in their retention.

Work Cited

Bailey, (2006). The Black man on campus (BMOC) project. In M. J. Cuyjet (Eds.), *African American men in college* (pp. 274–280). San Francisco, CA: Jossey-Bass.

Bledsoe, T., & Rome, K. D. (2006). Student African American brotherhood. In M. J. Cuyjet (Eds.), *African American men in college* (pp. 257–264). San Francisco, CA: Jossey-Bass.

Catching, C. C. (2006). Black men's collective: Rutgers, the state university of New Jersey. In M. J. Cuyjet (Eds.), *African American men in college* (pp. 281–287). San Francisco, CA: Jossey-Bass.

Corbin, J., & Strauss, A. (2007). *Basics of qualitative research: Techniques and procedures for developing grounded theory.* Thousand Oaks, CA: Sage.

Creswell, J. W. (2013). *Qualitative inquiry and research design: Choosing among the five approaches* (3rd ed.). Los Angeles, CA: Sage.

Guest, G., Bunce, A., & Johnson, L. (2006). How many interviews are enough? An experiment with data saturation and variability. *Field Methods, 18*(1), 59–82. doi: 10.1177/1525822X05279903

Harper, S. R. (2005). Leading the way: Inside the experiences of high-achieving African American male students. *About Campus, 10*(1), 8–15. doi: 10.1002/abc.118

Harper, S. R. (2008). Realizing the intended outcomes of Brown: High-achieving African American male undergraduates and social capital. *American Behavioral Scientist, 51*(7), 1029–1052. doi: 10.1177/0002764207312004

Harper, S. R., Davis, R. J., Jones, D. E., McGowan, B. L., Ingram, T. N., & Platt, C. S. (2011). Race and racism in the experiences of Black male resident assistants at predominantly White universities. *Journal of College Student Development, 52*(2), 180–200. doi: 10.1353/csd.2011.0025

Harper, S. R., & Quaye, S. J. (2007). Student organizations as venues for Black identity expression and development among African American male students. *Journal of College Student Development, 48*(2), 127–144. doi: 10.1353/csd.2007.0012

Inkelas, K. K., & Associates. (2007). *National study of living-learning programs: 2007 report findings.* Retrieved from http://drum.lib.umd.edu/bitstream/1903/8392/1/2007%20NSLLP%20Final%20Report.pdf

Inkelas, K. K., Daver, Z. E., Vogt, K. E., & Leonard, J. B. (2007). Living-learning programs and first-generation college students' academic and social transition to college. *Research in Higher Education, 48*(4), 403–434. doi: 10.1007/s11162-006-9031-6

Inkelas, K. K., & Weisman, J. (2003). Different by design: An examination of outcomes associated with three types of living-learning programs. *Journal of College Student Development, 44*(3), 335–368. Retrieved from http://search.proquest.com/docview/195174228?accountid=14604

Jessup-Anger, J., Johnson, B. N., & Wawrzynski, M. R. (2012). Exploring living learning communities as a venue for men's identity construction. *Journal of College and University Student Housing, 39*(1), 162–175. Retrieved from http://web.a.ebscohost.com/ehost/pdfviewer/pdfviewer?sid=3457aa7f-7002-4511-9f74-90b5055a2ec2%40sessionmgr4005&vid=6&hid=4109

Johnson, P. B., & Moore, J. A. (2011). Living learning communities: An intrusive model for the retention of African American males. Charleston, SC: *Proceedings of the Consortium for Student Retention and Data Exchange (CSRDE).* 7th Annual National Symposium on Student Retention.

Kimbrough & Harper (2006). African American men at Historically Black Colleges and Universities: Different environments, similar challenges. In M. J. Cuyjet (Eds.), *African American men in college* (pp. 189–209). San Francisco, CA: Jossey-Bass.

Laster, E. (2006). Black male rap session: University of Louisville. In M. J. Cuyjet (Eds.), *African American men in college* (pp. 285–287). San Francisco, CA: Jossey-Bass.

Merriam, S. B. (2009). *Qualitative research: A guide to design and implementation.* San Francisco, CA: Jossey-Bass.

Palmer, R. T., Davis, R. J., & Maramba, D. C. (2010). Role of an HBCU in supporting academic success of underprepared Black males. *Negro Educational Review, 61*(1–4), 85–106. Retrieved from http://search.proquest.com/docview/818559849?accountid=14604

Palmer, R. T., Maramba, D. C., & Dancy, T. E. (2013). The male initiative on leadership and excellence (mile) and its impact on retention and persistence of Black men at Historically Black Colleges and Universities (HBCUs). *Journal of College Student Retention, 15*(1), 65–72. doi: http://dx.doi.org/10.2190/CS.15.1.e

Palmer, R. T., & Young, E. M. (2008). Determined to succeed: Salient factors that foster academic success for academically underprepared Black males at a Black college. *Journal of College Student Retention, 10*(4), 465–482. doi: 10.2190/CS.10.4.d

Saldana, J. (2013). *The coding manual for qualitative researchers* (2nd ed.). Thousand Oaks, CA: Sage.

Shank, G. D. (2006). *Qualitative research: A personal skills approach* (2nd ed.). Upper Saddle River, NJ: Pearson.

Soldner, M., Rowan-Kenyon, H., Inkelas, K. K., Garvey, J., & Robbins, C. (2012). Supporting students' intentions to persist in STEM disciplines: The role of living-learning programs among other social-cognitive factors. *Journal of Higher Education, 83*(3), 311–336. doi: 10.1353/jhe.2012.0017

Spradley, J. P. (1980). *Participant Observation.* New York, NY: Holt Rinehart and Winston.

Stake, R. E. (2005). Qualitative case studies. In N. K. Denzin & Y. S. Lincoln (Eds.), *The Sage Handbook of Qualitative Research* (3rd ed., pp. 443–466). Thousand Oaks, CA: Sage.

Strayhorn, T. L. (2010). When race and gender collide: Social and cultural capital's influence on the academic achievement of African American and Latino males. *The Review of Higher Education, 33*(3), 307–332. doi: 10.1353/rhe.0.0147

Taylor, C. M., & Howard-Hamilton, M. F. (1995). Student involvement and racial identity attitudes among African American males. *Journal of College Student Development, 36*(4), 330–336.

Watson, L. W. (2006). The role of spirituality and religion in the experiences of African American male college students. In M. J. Cuyjet (Eds.), *African American Men in College* (pp. 112–127). San Francisco, CA: Jossey-Bass.

Yao, C. W., & Wawrzynski, M. R., (2013). Influence of academically based living-learning communities on Men's awareness of and appreciation for diversity. *Journal of College and University Student Housing, 39*(2). Retrieved from http://web.b.ebscohost.com.libproxy.uncg.edu/ehost/pdfviewer/pdfviewer?vid=2&sid=f6065523-8c90-4fbe-851e-171d838d2b04%40sessionmgr115&hid=102

Yin, R. K. (2014). *Case study research: Design and method* (5th ed.). Thousand Oaks, CA: Sage.

CHAPTER 21

Black Masculinity & Surveillance

Gender and Racial Performances in K-12 and University Contexts

Dalia Rodriguez, Mary Cannito-Coville, and Tremayne S. Robertson

Introduction

Representations of black males often depicted as criminals render violence synonymous with blackness. Black males have been constructed as being disrespectful, unintelligent, hypersexualized, violent, and threatening, held suspect, marginalized, rendered invisible, and increasingly are under social and institutional surveillance (Collins, 2005; Feagin, Vera, & Imani, 1996; Ferguson, 2001a hooks, 2004). Tied to the historical legacy of racism, these culturally violent messages contribute to the misrepresentation, policing, and surveillance of Black males.

The U.S. populace has been so thoroughly conditioned to experience Black boys and men as the embodiment of social transgression, that accepting accounts of alleged criminal behavior, even in situations where no evidence is presented is natural, eradicating Black male bodies in various ways. Society's readiness to judge Black men as guilty, without evidence has been a common occurrence (Harper, 1996). Black boys in general are socially constructed to be "naughty by *nature*" and are seen as "mischievous" troublemakers that "can stand up for themselves" (Ferguson, 2001b, p. 85). These messages can be delivered blatantly in racist discourses; however, the same sentiment is often delivered in less overt ways such as the social and formal policing of black bodies, in various educational settings, as well as communities.

Masculinity can be policed socially and formally. We primarily focus on the social policing of masculinity to discuss practices that occur in places of social contact such as schools and colleges and refer to the process of maintaining social hierarchies within a hegemonic societal system. Formal policing, on the other hand, focuses on policing as it refers to a formal institution of maintaining law and order (i.e. the police force). These practices of policing work individually and collectively to preserve the status quo that ultimately protects a system in which whites benefit disproportionately. These practices of policing construct black bodies as moving targets of oppression. They are viewed as a threat that are therefore in need of policing. Their social construction as a threatening force operates in a way that causes whites to believe that without formal policing, black bodies would cause a violent societal upheaval. Their very presence results in surveillance and increased regulation of black bodies (Calmore, 2006) through means of formal policing such as law enforcement agencies and state sanctioned policies.

This chapter highlights perspectives from young black males in schools and university contexts, and addresses the construction and performance of black masculinity. We ask the following questions: How do Black male boys and college students construct, perform, and express black masculinity in a society that perceives them as threatening and dangerous? How are they perceived by whites, especially in an era where surveillance has become normalized? Their lives often sensationalized and rarely understood for their complexities, it becomes critical to address the nuances of how Black males construct and perform black masculinity in educational and overall social contexts.

Literature Review

The way in which Black male students have been written about, at all levels of education has been through a deficit approach (Harper, 2012). Educational scholars often portray Black males negatively, highlighting the various "problems" associated with Black males (Bonner & Bailey, 2006), relegating Black males beyond love (Duncan, 2002). Most of what we read about young Black males focus on the problems of crime, violence, drugs and poor academic achievement (Hrabowowski, Maton, & Greif, 1998; Noguera, 2003). The challenges that Black male students encounter are often understood as not only natural but also a product of their own design (Davis, 2003). Studies about black men in particular, too often focus on "ghetto culture" which reduces Black masculinity to classed and sexualized depictions of violent hustler, drug dealers, and pimps.

Moreover, much of our academic understanding of the construction of masculinity for students of color in K-12 settings comes from urban settings where the majority of students are students of color. A portion of this article asks, what happens to the social construction of masculinity for students of color in predominantly white school spaces? Urban schools with high percentages of students of color often lack resources as a result of school funding systems tied to formulas that promote white privilege and maintain racial inequalities (Caton, 2012, p. 1069), while wealthier, often suburban and predominantly white schools offer not only more resources but also more positive learning environments (Brown, 2011, p. 130). The economic disparities in urban schools lead to problems hiring experienced teachers, buying textbooks, adequately heating and cooling buildings, providing enough chairs, desks and learning space, providing academic and emotional support, and offering extracurricular activities. Student-teacher relationships become strained and racial gaps widen as students of color feel alienated from their schools.

Black males are consistently placed at risk for failure (Davis, 2003). Rates of Black male school attrition, relatively poor academic performance, and college enrollment and persistence are seen, in part, as a function of Black males' inability or disinterest in fulfilling their roles as conventional learners in school settings (Davis, 2003; Harper, 2009, 2012). While much has been said about the failure of the public educational system to adequately prepare young Black men to enter college or the workforce, there tends to be less discussion about the educational experiences of those who actually succeed in college (Cuyjet, 2006; Harper, 2009; Wilson, 2007).

Moreover, while there have been several studies that primarily focus on college access, retention, academic engagement, and black male students' experiences at historically white universities (Cuyjet, 1997; Harper, 2006, 2009; Harper & Nichols, 2008; Harper et al. 2011; Smith, Yosso, & Solorzano, 2007; Smith, Allen, & Dantley, 2008), these studies focus on understanding gendered racism, *not* an understanding of how Black males are gendered (McGuire, Berhanu, Davis, & Harper, 2014). Despite the large contributions of previous studies, few studies have critically examined the gendered performance and expressions of Black male undergraduate students (Davis, 2003; McGuire et al., 2014). Moreover, while there has been research about college men as "gendered" (Dancy II, 2010; 2011; Davis, 2001 Harper, 1996, 2008; Harper & Harris, 2010; Harris, Palmer, & Struve, 2011) in higher education contexts, not much research has been conducted at all on their masculinities. During the last several decades (McGuire et. al.2014), these studies have rarely included men of color in general, and Black male students in particular (Kimmel, 2008).

Critical Race Theory, Black Feminist Thought & Black Masculinity Studies

In an effort to address the absence of research on performances of Black masculinities in predominantly white educational spaces, as well as to inform educational research as to how black masculinity is (re)constructed, we work from Critical Race Theory (Bell, 1987, 1992; Crenshaw, Gotanda, Peller, & Thomas, 1995; Delgado, 1988/1989, 1995; Matsuda, 1996; Solorzano, 1998; Solorzano & Yosso, 2002; Williams, 1991; Wing, 1997), Black Feminist Thought (Collins, 2015; hooks, 1996; Lorde, 1984; Williams, 1991), and Black Masculinity Studies (Alexander, 2004; Cooper, 2006; Jackson & Hopson, 2011; Johnson, 2006, Mutua, 2006; Neal, 2006). In no way is the following description of these theories meant to be exhaustive, but rather concise, highlighting the interconnections between them.

Critical race theory begins with the premise that racism is a normal part of society and is a permanent part of American life (Bell, 1987, 1992). Critical race theorists (Bell, 1987; Crenshaw et al., 1995; Delgado, 1988/1989, 1995; Matsuda, 1996; Solorzano, 1998; Williams, 1991; Wing, 1997) expose different forms of racism and critique legal, educational, and other social institutions that perpetuate inequality. Critical Race Theory scholars also employ alternative methodologies such as storytelling, parables, chronicles, counter-stories, poetry, fiction and revisionist histories.

For the marginalized, counter-storytelling can serve as a powerful means of survival and liberation (Delgado, 1988/1989). Writing counter-stories can also serve as a tool for unmasking and challenging majoritarian stories (Bell, 1987, 1992; Solorzano & Yosso, 2002) that uphold racial privilege. Stories can also serve as a means to destroy complacency and challenge the status quo. These counter-stories can build a sense of community among those at the margins of society by providing a space to share their sense of reality and experiences (Delgado, 1989). Stories build consensus, a common culture of shared understandings. Second, stories can challenge the dominant's perspective. And lastly, storytelling teaches people about how one can construct both story and reality. Narratives that focus on the marginalized can therefore empower the storyteller as well those that listen.

Black feminist thought enables us to do anti-racist and anti-sexist work through a lens of the "new racism" (Collins, 2005). Black feminist thought is a standpoint epistemology that challenges domination of all women of color and marginalized peoples. Black feminist thought has recently served as a means of unmasking and gaining a deep understanding of the experiences of Black women (Hill Collins, 1998). Beginning with the assumption that African-American women create oppositional knowledge that aims to resist oppression and search for justice, critiquing institutional practices the U.S. Black women face collectively. Black feminist thought also involves discovering, re-interpreting and analyzing the ideas of subgroups within the larger collectivity of black women who have continuously been silenced (Lorde, 1984; Smith, 2000). As a collective group, one of the main goals is to name one's own reality (Collins, 1998). African American women's voices are specialized bodies of knowledge that have been excluded from the social science literature (Bell-Scott, 1998). The foundation of Black feminist thought and its adaption by black masculinity scholars (Cooper, 2006; hooks, 2004; Mutua, 2006; Neal, 2006) allow us to identify how black masculinity is constructed, performed, expressed, and experienced in educational contexts.

As a field, Black Masculinity Studies centers on race, gender and sexuality in a way to empower Black men and boys to confront controlling images and consider how Black masculinity is constructed, re-imagined, and dominated through surveillance, criminalization, commodification, hypersexualization and deficit models that dehumanize Black bodies (Cooper, 2006; Harper, 2006; hooks, 2004; Mutua, 2006; Neal, 2006; Staples, 1982). Jackson and Hopson (2011) posit masculinity as "largely implicit social meanings that come to be accepted as truths about how males are supposed to think, behave, or function" (p. 1). Rejecting the commercial adaptation of masculinity by Black men and boys, black masculinity scholars advocate for a "new black man" in the "new racism" that performs a race and gender which affirms their spirit despite narrowing tropes (Alexander, 2006; Awkward, 1995; Carbado, 2008; Collins, 2005; hooks, 2003; Johns, 2007; McCall, 2011; Neal, 2006).

We define masculinity as the socially constructed and influenced behavior, demonstrations, or performances of men (Berger & Luckman, 1967; Butler, 2006; Kimmel, 2002; Alexander, 2006). Gender is socially constructed in the everyday, through social interactions, conversations, and relationships (Connell, 1995; Kimmel & Messner, 2007), influencing our understanding about our social contexts. We found Mutua's work on progressive black masculinities useful in making sense of some of the student data. Mutua (2006) defines progressive black masculinities as "… unique and innovative practices of the masculine self actively engaged in struggles to transform social structures of domination." Progressive black masculinities actively stand against social structures of domination, and simultaneously value, validate, and empower black humanity in all its variety. They also require rejecting not only the images currently associated with black masculinity but also the structural power relations that cause them. New definitions of black masculinity grounded in strength of commitment to families, communities or social justice principles might create space for Black men to redefine black male strength in affirming ways. Progressive masculinity has implications for Black young male's partners, children, and communities.

This article seeks to share stories that unveil the truths about how both black males in schools and colleges construct, and perform, and express their racialized and gendered identities. More specifically we address what their masculinities mean, particularly in a social and political climate that fosters and structurally supports surveillance and control of black male bodies. This article focuses on how young black males work to make sense of their own identities, while simultaneously rejecting stereotypical images of black males, as well as challenging educational social structures, redefining black masculinity in their own terms.

Method & Data Analysis

Interviews with 10 high school students who identify as Black males in grades 9–12 were conducted. In order to recruit participants, student names were pulled at random from a list of students who identified in the school database as Black male. Students were asked mainly open-ended questions in a private setting with interviews lasting one class period, or about 45 minutes. Questions were designed to gain more insight into their experiences as Black males in a predominately white school and community. Questions included topics on race, gender, age, teacher-student interactions, administration-student interactions, and policing in schools and communities. We also conducted 10 in-depth interviews with Black male students on a predominantly white college campus. Interviews ranged from 1 to 2 hours, and included topics such as experiences with racism and discrimination with professors, types of support services including mentoring and outreach programs, as well as relations with white students, professors, administrators, and campus/community police.

We began every interview with small talk, in an effort to make the participants feel comfortable and establish rapport, eventually discussing the consent forms and emphasizing the confidentiality of the data. We approached all interviews as a flexible process in which "interviewees have substantial experience and insight" (Charmaz, pp. 312). Following Gubrium and Holstein (2001), we believe interviews are not merely neutral conduits, but instead a site where knowledge is constructed and co-constructed between researcher and participant. We conducted all interviews more as conversations between two equals, rather than as distinctly hierarchical, question-and answer exchange. To contextualize words and meanings constructed by both researcher and participants, the interviewer tries to tune into the interactively produced meanings and emotional dynamics within the interview itself (Denzin & Lincoln, 2000; Ellis & Berger, 2002). Douglass' (1984) writes about "creative interviewing" where the interviewer expresses common ground with their respondents, so that both interviewer and interviewee share a narrative space. Respondents and researchers share information, the interview context is more comfortable, and the hierarchal gap between researchers and respondents is diminished (Cook & Fonow, 1986; Ellis & Berger, 2002; Ellis, Kiesinger, & Tillman-Healy, 1997).

Individual interviews were transcribed no more than 24 hours after being conducted. An initial follow-up reading produced initial insights and working codes of themes and patterns. Data analysis was an ongoing process. In addition to the transcribed interviews, observations were documented as to interactions, dialogue, and reactions of both interviewee and interviewer. Grounded theory (Charmaz, 2006) guides our methodological approach, with the idea that data is generated from the ground up. Despite the time-consuming and tedious process of transcribing, we transcribed all interviews because we felt that this would allow us to more intimately listen and understand what our participants voiced. After conducting open coding, there were several iterations of re-coding. In an effort to further complicate the findings theoretically, we consistently have written detailed memos to further complicate our analysis. Analysis of data and generation of theories from data were constantly compared over the course of the research process.

High School Context

In order to gain a better understanding of how Black male high school students experience their schools and communities, part of this study was conducted at Riverport Central Schools, a suburban school district in the Northeast that serves a predominately white student body. White students comprise 90% of the student body, while black students account for 3.5%. Riverport claims nearly a 100% graduation rate with a college attendance rate almost as high, as well as many state and federal accolades for excellence in academics and extracurricular activities. Riverport's academic and extracurricular success should be commended, however, while the school works to produce college-ready young scholars of all of its students, this educational process is experienced in particular ways for students of color. The high school students interviewed from Riverport reveal feeling that their behavior is under constant scrutiny and that they are socially policed to behave in a way that is read as "white" (reword), including speaking in a low tone, using particular vernacular and not showing outward signs of emotions(gender performance), as a way to counter the stereotypes of black boys as threatening. Overall, society and schools construct Black bodies as criminals rather than products of structural oppression and thereby reinforce their need for policing (Ferguson, 2001).

DeAndre is one of several students that reveal how constructions of black males as dangerous contributes to a particular framing of black males as gang members within the school. DeAndre is an 18 year old Senior who said he was excited to have the opportunity to share his experiences because he felt like he had to keep a lot of his emotions bottled in while in school. DeAndre showed this enthusiasm by smiling and speaking fast as he bounced in his seat as if the words were tripping on themselves to get out. He stood about 5¢8² tall with a solid yet skinny frame, a buzzed haircut and medium black skin tone. DeAndre wore blue jeans, a black sweater and a flat gold chain as he talked about his transfer to Riverport just before high school in 8th grade from the nearby city school district.When asked what it means to be a black male in Riverport DeAndre responded:

> *It carries sort of expectation, and also stereotypes. Expectations meaning some people, automatically assume that, especially if you're physically fit, that you're some type of athlete, you're good at some type of sport, and then the stereotypes on the same note that you're going to be better than them, and by them I mean other Caucasian students. And you're gonna, you know, be scary … And most of the time, the blacks, the African American students at this school, came from a different school, so then they think you're part of some type of gang … Well not a gang but like you were in some type of mischievous activities that you're gonna steal and basically stereotypes like that.*

The construction of black males as dangerous gang members generates fear of black male students that perpetuates stereotypes and sets an expectation that black male students will perform their masculinity in a hypercriminalized way. When asked how he feels when he hears those stereotypes DeAndre provides an example of how stereotypes play out within his school peers by giving an example of his white friend Alex. DeAndre says:

> *At first I was infuriated, like 9th and 10th grade I would be mad and upset like "yo that's not me, I want you guys to like me for me, not for these stereotypes". But through the years, you become numb to certain things and I just became passist. And, like, ok, I'm about to go meet one of my friends, like let's say Alex. And Alex is like "yo you should come to this baseball game" and I'm like ok sure. "we go". I've got to go to this baseball game with Alex, now I gotta meet Alex's friends who believe the stereotypes that Alex believed before he met me so now I gotta through that whole process again. So now I've become pretty lenient, I've become pretty expectant of it, and that's really not, that's not, that's not good.*

DeAndre experiences a type of violence towards his identity that forces him to choose between performing his masculinity in a way that purposefully counters or plays into the stereotypes. DeAndre does not have the luxury of "being himself" because his is constantly aware of how others are perceiving him as a black male.

Terrance, a 17 year old Black male senior who moved to Riverport from another rural district several hours away when he was 10 years old, speaks about how he feels that he has been targeted for social segregation by students and staff at the school until he is complimented for his behavior that is viewed as being "white". These interactions demonstrate how students of color are racialized and constructed a threat to whites. Terrance's short black curly hair and light brown eyes sparkled as he clutched a backpack against a fitted maroon long sleeve shirt. He held the backpack during the entire interview and swiveled nervously back and forth in his chair as he gazed out the window while he talked:

> *I don't know if it's Riverport itself or the school but I think people here are just generally—I don't wanna say closed minded but—people have these facades up. There's this intense pressure to adhere to some norm, something xenophobic, nobody wants to be that outsider. I see it a lot in my interactions with people that I'm not really familiar with. The things they praise about me or notice about me, they'll be like "oh you know, you talk pretty well, oh you sound pretty white, oh you know, you're really easy to talk to. You're not all loud and up in my face" or the best thing is they like to talk about things that don't mean anything.*

The actions of the students and staff who meet the majority white paradigm is driven by a fear of students that are viewed as different. Black males are under constant watch and scrutiny by students and staff that racialize their behaviors and construct students of color as an "other". The students of color are being surveilled for their actions. The students have to learn how to navigate white spaces as a black male and, in order to do so, they must demonstrate behavior deemed appropriate to the predominantly white culture. This form of cultural violence requires the students to be strategic in deciding what parts of his personality and culture the student wishes to demonstrate. The black male student must decide what portion of himself he is willing to reveal to the white school staff in order to be accepted and, more in all reality, to be deemed worthy of receiving an education. Terrance has to speak in a particular way that requires him to speak softly and with a standardized American English. Terrance shows how the social construction of stereotypes of black males creates an expectation that they perform their masculinity in a particular way in order to work to break the stereotype to defy expectations and be socially accepted.

Micka helps us to see how being constructed in this way alienates Black students and makes them targets for discrimination. Ironically, Micka is the only participant who was born and raised in Riverport; yet he still has internalized that he is perceived as a threat. Micka is a light skinned Black man who claims Black and Puerto Rican descent. He speaks slow and with drawn out words, and his eyes remained half opened and fixed on the floor for most of the interview. Micka wore a blue hooded sweatshirt with white writing of the clothing brand Aeropostale, wooden rosary beads, blue jeans, white sneakers and fake diamond earrings about the size of a nickel. As he spoke in slow, careful sentences,

Micka seemed to sink deeper and deeper into his blue hooded sweatshirt while keeping his eyes locked on the floor as if the gravity of his words increased with each sentence and weighed him down. Micka says:

> *It's hard sometimes because we know, it feels at times like they don't like seeing [us], cause … the way it's been lately is a lot of Black people have been comin' out here and a lot of Black people have been doing really good things so I feel like it kinda, it gets them mad sometimes, "cause I feel like, I don't know, I'm on a radar. That people are just waiting for me to mess up, waitin" for me to do something.*

Micka's description of his experiences in the school demonstrate the way in which Black males are surveilled in the school context. The surveillance is not always technical in terms of electronic monitoring through cameras. Micka feels unwelcome and as though he is being watched for signs of failure rather than success. Furthermore, the monitoring of his actions causes him to behave in a guarded, but also a strategic manner which could potentially have ramifications for his academic performance if he is focused on performing in a particular way as to avoid disturbing the watchful radar. Black males are held to a cycle of expected performance of their masculinity in both schools and communities. Black students in predominantly white institutions that go between a majority and minority culture in school and at home "must negotiate the racism and discrimination" and are expected to "conform to dominant gender role expectations (e.g., to be successful, competitive, aggressive), as well as meeting culturally specific requirements (e.g., cooperation, promotion of group, and survival of group) of the Black community, which often conflict" (Davis, 2001, p. 24).

University Context

The second part of this study focuses on gaining insight into black male undergraduate students' experiences in a predominantly white university. In particular, we wanted to understand how both their racialized and gendered experiences, and the multiple ways in which black male undergraduate students constructed, expressed, and navigated a predominantly white institution, while under surveillance.

Most college student participants did not consider themselves campus leaders (one was committed to leadership positions on campus organizations and/or fraternities). While some students (one) in the study held campus leadership positions, indicating a responsibility to community (McGuire, 2014), others were not as involved on campus, but still demonstrated a commitment to their own communities by being highly involved in community organizations such as local church groups. Despite Black male students continuously being held under surveillance in every facet of their lives on college campus, students were committed to their families, their communities, as well as worked hard to achieve academically. There were also contradictory ideals that conveyed black male college students—at times their performances reflected hegemonic cultural notions (particularly in relation to gender) and students expressed and enacted their masculinities in ways that "simultaneously reflected and rejected hegemonic cultural notions," which varied depending on social context.

Commitment to Family

Marsharn stood at about 6 ft. 4 inches, muscular, with long dreads, slightly above his shoulders and towered over most students. He asked to meet about a class assignment and we decided to meet at a cafe on campus. We order our coffee and shortly thereafter, Marsharn excuses himself as he realizes that he forgot to put money in the meter. I quickly walk over to the bookshelf filled with board games, magazines and newspapers. I flip through several piles, in search of something interesting to read. About five minutes later, I hear Marsharn apologizing profusely, "No … it's o.k … it's not a problem." I look up to see a White male, in typical college attire, t-shirt with khaki shorts, slowly reaching to get his coffee, shrugging his shoulders, cringing—shoulders up to his ears. "No, it's o.k." Marsharn backs up slowly, raising both hands, palms facing the White male student, as if to indicate he can have the table. The White student continues cringing. "It's ok … It's ok …" Marsharn repeatedly says.

Marsharn continues apologizing as the white male's look of fear is an indication of how Black males are perceived as threatening, dangerous and feared. His reaction to the white student also raises questions as to how Black male students use their black masculine performances to navigate the academy. What other possible reasons could be attributed to Marsharn's decision to place his hands up? Most evident is that placing his hands up is an indication that Marsharn does not want to be perceived as a threat. However, what other meanings may his actions have? Aware of how whites perceive him, and expect him to act, Marsharn's performance consciously works to dispel the stereotype of the threatening black male. All Black male students interviewed agreed with the sentiment "That's how whites expect me to act, so I'm not gonna act that way." Frustrated by racist stereotype of the dangerous black male, students intentionally performed their race and gender in a way that contradicted prevailing narratives about Black men. When asked how he deals with a racist act committed against him, Marsharn says the following:

> I feel like, naturally my first feeling is just to … fight, but it's like, that's, basically that's what they [whites] want to happen. They just want to see that come out of you. I just got to, like I said, stay focused and think about why I'm down here and make the wisest decision.

Marsharn's quote is reflective of John's argument, who disputes Anne Ferguson's argument that Black boys in schools are often forced to fit into the binary of "Bad Black boys" and "school boys." Instead, Johns (2007) argues that many Black male boys are aware of how teachers perceive them as "trouble" and simultaneously feel that they want to be in school—contributing to the interactions between students and teachers and contradictory feelings, affecting self-perception. Not fitting into this binary complicates notions of Black masculinity. For some students, fitting into the Bad Black boys binary was not an option. For example, many Black boys considered it an opportunity as well as a responsibility to dispel the myth of bad Black boys. This conscious decision to dispute the stereotype of the dangerous Black male indicates that the issue is more complex than the simple desire to accommodate whites. Instead, Marsharn strategically makes choices about his racialized and gendered performances, working consciously to disrupt hegemonic ideas of the dangerous Black male stereotype (Steele, 1997; Steele & Aronson, 1995; Smith, Allen, et al., 2007). By playing a submissive role, he hopes not to trigger fear in the white male student—and not be read as dangerous. Playing a submissive role also helps Marsharn move along spaces as seamlessly as possible. A conscious decision to perform his black masculinity in a particular way, can simultaneously serve as a form of agency. Consciously performing his Black masculinity in a particular way becomes a form of knowledge as to how to act, navigating the white academy.

Marsharn, a single father, who's daughter was 10 months old, was raising his daughter after his partner abandoned them. For Marsharn, being successful in college was the only option. Marsharn's investment in finishing college signifies more than simply receiving a degree for the sake of having one. His daughter daughter served as one of his biggest motivators in completing his degree. There are many reasons in which Black males behave, interact, and react to whites in particular ways—and in this case as non-threatening. Knowing that he serves as the primary caregiver to his daughter, and his overall familial responsibilities, confronting racist perpetrators may not be an option as the risks may be too big. While he was tired of dealing with racism, he felt that remaining in college would help him provide so much more financially to his daughter. In this way his racialized and gendered performance was at least somewhat linked to his decision to remain in college—finishing his degree was also a matter of economic survival for him, ensuring the well-being of his family.

While Marsharn was tired of dealing with racism, he also felt that remaining in college would help him provide so much more financially to his daughter. In this way his decision to perform his black masculinity was at least somewhat linked to his decision of ensuring the well-being of his daughter.

Finishing his degree was not only a matter of economic survival, but it was also him prioritizing his family. This not only counters the common representation(s) of Black males as absentee and irresponsible fathers (Hutchinson, 1994), but it also tells us how prioritizing the role of family is critical in the decision-making process about their racialized and gendered performances. We see a new definition of black masculinity, grounded in strength of commitment to families (Mutua, 2006) communities or social justice principles, creating space for Black college students to redefine black male strength in affirming ways.

Commitment to Community

Jamaal, an 18 year old African American who sat in one of my courses. He used to sit in class, in his usual student casual attire—jogging pants and a blue football jersey. Having grown up in a predominantly Black neighborhood, he attended a racially diverse school, and struggled after attending a historically white university when it came as a bit of a shock when experiencing racist residence hall advisors, university staff, and classmates. Black male bodies are also under surveillance in various spaces across the campus including in their own respective living spaces, dining halls, classrooms, as well as the local community. Jamaal continued with another story in which he challenged racism and explained that on the way to a party with six other friends (who were all Black and male):

> We got out the car, we wuz just walkin' to one of my cars and then a van came up and it was honking at me, like get the hell off the street. So I just turned to look to see who it is, so they pulled up like, like basically like this close to me, like if you don't move, I'm going to hit you. This wuz a white girl and a white guy in a van. Then they pull up, like they pull up a little further and they just stopped the van. So then all the guys I wuz with … my roommate, he got really mad, because they almost hit me. So then the van pulls off. We about to leave, we goin' home and we see the van again. The guy that wuz driving, he pulled over too, and he looked in the (our) car. Then they sped off real fast. I guess they got scared. But by the time we wuz about to pull off, it was like a whole bunch of police cars out there. And then I'm like we didn't do nut'n, so just be cool, ya know. We ain't gotta say nut'n'. So then the police basically tell us to get out the way. They said they lookin' for somebody. So they tell us to move. So we drive off … we think everything OK.

Shortly thereafter, Jamaal and his friends see the police cars turn around, and the police follow them. The police pull them over and yell, "Get out of the car!" Jamaal said, "One by one, carrying guns, they tell us to back up." So I back up into my car, and they put handcuffs on us. They (the police) say, "We have reason to believe that somebody in your car has a gun." Feeling like he deserved an answer, Jamaal responds, "Well you have to tell me something. Don't I have a right to know why you handcuffin' me? You all can check the car … we ain't got no gun."

Despite the threat to his life, Jamaal demands an answer as to why they are pulled over. Through a masculine performance, Jamaal demands an answer. Similar to Chandler's (2011) findings, black males demonstrated a masculine performance. His masculine performance allows him to challenge the racist police officer's assumptions of being dangerous, and more specifically of carrying a weapon. Moreover, Jamaal uses this experience to resist larger social structures. In addition to challenging the police officer, he files a formal complaint against the police officer. One can argue that Jamaal uses his masculine performance to "stand against social structures of domination" (Mutua, 2006).While Jamaal's gendered performance simultaneously feeds into normalized masculinity, it also serves as a way to directly address racism in his life. Jamaal's performance is empowering to himself, allowing him to feel a sense of control over racist acts he consistently experiences, particularly when under surveillance by law enforcement and/or university security, and dominant society overall.

Aware of how whites perceive him as threatening, Jamaal's instinct is to fight, but he also realizes that this is how whites expect him to act. During his interview, as a response to the question, "How do you think whites perceive you?" his response, "I already got two strikes against me, so I can't get into any trouble" is telling. It indicates his own awareness as to how being black and male work against him. While Chandler argues that black males have an organized schizophrenia (She argues that black men feel they have to perform their racialized and gendered masculinities in order to assimilate into dominant society), we argue instead for more of a strategic performance of black masculinity. The performance of black masculinity does not have to entail assimilation, but rather, as a navigational skill (Solorzano & Yosso, 2001), which becomes critical in maneuvering through the college setting. Organized schizophrenia suggests that black males have to "hide" their true selves.

In this instance, Jamaal questions the police about being racially profiled and he begins questioning the police officers. Despite being upset, Jamaal says, "I try to take things in stride." Jamaal's expression of "taking things in stride" demonstrates his own need to demonstrate a masculine performance. Showing anger may indicate a loss of power and control—a departure from Black manhood (Chandler, 2011). While he demonstrates how upset he is by requesting the police officer's badge number, he also makes certain to express that he takes things in stride, he makes a conscious decision not to express his own vulnerabilities. In other words, "manning up" becomes a kind of barometer by which some Black males determine acceptable performances of masculinity (Chandler, 2011). Becoming too visually upset would indicate a loss of power and control over his own life.

Paradoxically, Jamaal's defensiveness becomes a way to assert his agency. Again, Jamaal utilizes his masculine performance, in order to confront and challenge the police officer's racist acts. Jamaal challenges the officer by stating he did not break any laws, demanding an answer as to why he was pulled over. While performing his own masculinity, he also confronts the racist police officer, by demanding his badge. In other words, Jamaal uses a masculine performance to productively confront racism.

While Jamaal's masculine performance feeds into normalized masculinity (masculine performance), this masculine performance paradoxically serves as a way to directly address racism at the institutional level. Jamaal's performance is empowering to himself, allowing him to feel a sense of control over racist acts he consistently experiences, particularly when under surveillance by law enforcement and/or university security, and dominant society overall. With the guidance of two deans at his university, he actively challenges racism by filing a formal complaint against the police officer. This appears to be different than Chandler's notion of survivor's mode because Jamaal doesn't "disassociate" from the event, yet he takes it on directly from the beginning of the harassment by confronting the officers and follows up with a formal report with university administration and police. He does not "get over it" and "move on" in an attempt to project a mastery, dominance or control of the event (i.e. I'm past that … been there done that); he asserts himself in a way that sustains a relationship with the painful incident—reporting. In other words, Jamaal moves from victim to survivor, assuming he has experienced racism previously similar to this police stop or otherwise, essentially working against racism and for the betterment of other African American male college students.

Succeeding Academically: Self Reliance and Self Assurance

All of our participants also worked hard to succeed academically and demonstrated concerted efforts to do well while in college. Some of this commitment derived from external pressure (family, as previously discussed). However, often the commitment to succeed came from a strong sense of self-reliance and self-assurance of all participants. Some students spoke of having to work extra hard to demonstrate, in particular to white faculty that they were capable of doing strong work. Matthew said:

> With teachers, many times, they don't expect you to carry out your work, and if you are then they're sorta surprised that you're concerned about your work and your grade, and concerned about your overall quality. And many times I'll go in the classes and talk to the professors and let them know I'm very concerned about my grade and the overall learning environment in the class, and so that, many times that catches them by surprise that I'm so concerned about my grades and willing to know more things about the class. I think many times they expect you to come in and if you're falling [behind] not to come see

> them and just to fall off, because many times the campus can be overwhelming with lots of students and you can get lost in the mix. And so, they don't expect you to keep up, they expect you to fall out and if you're failing to not even talk to them or you know work things out. Many times what I do is go in, and work things out and talk to them, ya know that I'm on top of my things.

Moreover, Matthew continued explaining how white classmates also questioned his academic abilities, and he was often questioned as to whether or not he would perform (when doing group projects) and classmates questioning whether or not he would even show up for group meetings. Again, Matthew expressed a strong sense of self-assurance of his academic abilities:

> many times you see that, them (whites) questioning whether or not I was gonna make the meeting. One time I had this girl, this white girl, she emailed me like four times, and I kept telling her, ya know, I'm gonna be at the meeting, I'm gonna be at the meeting and I asked my partner ya know, this girl keeps emailing me. And he was like … "well, she probably just wants to make sure that you're coming." And she kept asking me, did I do my work, did I do my work. I said, yeah, I have my work, I'm capable of doing things. With students, many times they're thinking you're inadequate for the job or you're not capable of carrying out your end of it … I feel like, naturally my first feeling is just to, want to fight, but it's like, I don't know—it's like, that's basically that's what they (whites) want to happen. It's like they want to, they just want to see that come out of you, not, I mean, basically I just got to, like I said stay focused and think about why I'm down here and make the wisest decision. I got to stay focused …

Conclusion

What emerged from these young black males is not how power limits their lives, nor how they demonstrate hyper-masculine behavior, but rather, how they navigate white spaces, in very particular circumstances. Hall (2006) states: "Specifically for males of color, adolescence is burdened by such factors as hypermasculinity, racial awareness in a predominantly white society, negative imagery tied to minority status, and social labeling and mistreatment" (p. 17). It is important to explore how young black male students experience schools and how school dynamics can affect student performance of masculinity in both K-12 and higher education settings. Their voices offer insight into possible areas of amelioration; and improving student experiences in and with educational institutions serves not only to benefit the student and their families but their communities as well. More specifically, these stories point to Mutua's (2006) notion of progressive masculinities.

Black males are being "undereducated" and pushed out of educational institutions and into prisons at a strikingly racially disproportionate rate (Laura, 2014). Laura (2014) cautions of the consequences of this criminalization of black students:

> Black boys who have been sorted, contained, and then pushed out of schools become Black men—men whose patterns of hardship are pronounced and deeply entrenched; men who constitute nearly 50% of the adult males in prison; men who have been well primed for neither college, career, nor full participation in our democracy, but instead for punitive institutionalization. (Laura, 2014, pp. 21–22)

The use of educational institutions to surveil black students occurs as what Brown (2011) refers to as a "culture of militarism" in schools and society that attempt to socialize poor youth of color that have been socially constructed and policed as uncivilized. Surveilling black students to conform to dominant white values and norms causes them to perform their masculinity in a particular way or face rejection and punishment (Hope, 2010).

Despite their masculine performances, students also demonstrated a sense of responsibility to other African American college students as well as the Black community, broadly. Black male students also performed an empowered Black masculinity by drawing on their own agency and directly addressing racism (Harper, 2009). Not all Black male college students adhered to the limiting conceptions of black masculinity. None of the college students chose to perform the role of a threatening black male. Both Black boys and Black male college students were aware of how whites perceived them, and how their own hypervisibility often lead to social policing and surveillance in educational spaces. While white teachers, professors, students and administrators often perceived these young men as threatening, these students worked to disrupt theses cultural images. Students challenged these notions of Black masculinity, disrupting hegemonic ideas of the threatening Black male image. Defying the stereotypical image of a threatening and dangerous black male, these students search for and demonstrate different modes of human expression within a very narrowly defined black masculinity.

Work Cited

Alexander, B. K. (2004). Racializing identity: Performance, pedagogy, and regret. *Cultural Studies/Critical Methodologies, 4*(12), 12–27.

Alexander, B. K. (2006). *Performing black masculinity: Race, culture, and queer identity.* Lanham, MD: AltaMira Press.

Awkward, M. (1995). *Negotiating difference: Race, gender, and the politics of positionality.* Chicago, IL: University of Chicago Press.

Bell, D. (1987). *And we are not saved.* New York, NY: Basic Books.

Bell, D. (1992). *Faces at the bottom of the well.* New York, NY: Basic Books.

Berger, P., & Luckman, T. (1967). *The social construction of reality.* New York, NY: Knopf Doubleday Publishing Group.

Bonner, F., & Bailey, K. (2006). Enhancing the academic climate for African American college men. In M. Cuyjet's (Ed.), *African American men in college.* San Francisco, CA: Jossey-Bass.

Brown, W. (2010). *Walled states, waning sovereignty.* New York, NY: Zone Books.

Brown, A. (2011). Racialised subjectivities: A critical examination of ethnography on Black males in the USA, 1960s to early 2000s. *Ethnography and Education, 6*(1), 45–60.

Butler, J. (2006). *Gender trouble.* New York, NY: Taylor & Francis.

Calmore, J. O. (2006). Reasonable and unreasonable suspects: The cultural construction of the anonymous Black man in public space (here be dragon). *Progressive Black Masculinities,* 137–154.

Caton, M. T. (2012). Black male perspectives on their educational experiences in high school. *Urban Education, 47*(6), 1055–1085.

Charmaz, K. (2006). *Constructing grounded theory: A practical guide through qualitative analysis.* Introducing Qualitative Methods Series. Thousand Oaks, CA: Sage.

Chandler, K. (2011). How to become a 'Black Man': Exploring African American Masculinities and the performance of gender. In R. L. Jackson & M. C. Hopson (Eds.), *Masculinity in the black imagination: Politics of communicating race and manhood.* New York, NY: Peter Lang.

Collins, P. (1998). *Fighting words: Black women & the search for justice.* Minneapolis, MN: University of Minneapolis.

Collins, P. (2005). *Black sexual politics: African Americans, gender, and the new racism.* New York, NY: Routledge.

Cook, J. A., & Fonow, M. M. (1986). Knowledge and women's interests: Issues of epistemology and methodology in feminist sociological research. *Sociological Inquiry, 56,* 2–27.

Cooper, F. R. (2006). Against bipolar black masculinity: Intersectionality, assimilation, identity performance and hierarchy. *U.C. Davis Law Review, 39*(3), 853–905.

Crenshaw, K., Gotanda, N., Peller, G., & Thomas, K. (Eds.). (1995). *Critical race theory: The key writings that formed the movement.* New York, NY: New Press.

Cuyjet, M. (2006). *African American men in college.* San Francisco, CA: John Wiley & Sons.

Davis, J. E. (2003). Early schooling and academic achievement of African American males. *Urban Education, 38*(5), 515–537.

Delgado, R. (Ed.). (1995). *Critical race theory: The cutting edge.* Philadelphia, PA: Temple University Press.

Denzin, N. K., & Lincoln, Y. S. (2000). *Handbook of qualitative research* (2nd ed.). Thousand Oaks, CA: Sage.

Douglass, J. D. (1984). *Creative interviewing.* Thousand Oaks, CA: Sage.

Duncan, G. A. (2002). Beyond love: A critical race ethnography of the schooling of Black males. *Equity & Excellence in Education, 35*(2), 131–143.

Ellis, C., & Berger, L. (2002). Their story/my story/our story: Including the researcher's experience in interview research. In J. F. Gubrium & J. A. Holstein (Eds.), *Handbook of interview research: Context and method* (pp. 849–875). Thousand Oaks, CA: Sage.

Feagin, J., Vera, H., & Imani, N. (1996). *The agony of education: Black students at white colleges and universities.* New York, NY: Routledge.

Ferguson, A. (2001a). *Bad boys: Public schools in the making of Black masculinity.* Ann Arbor, MI: University of Michigan Press.

Ferguson, A. (2001b). *Bad boys: Public schools in the making of black masculinity (Law, meaning, and violence).* Ann Arbor, MI: University of Michigan Press.

Gubrium, J. F., & Holstein, J. A. (2001). *Handbook of interview research.* Thousand Oaks, CA: Sage Publications.

Hall, H. (2006). *Mentoring young men of color: Meeting the needs of African American and Latino students.* Lanham, MD: Rowman & Littlefield Education.

Harper, P. B. (1996). *Are we not men?: Masculine anxiety and the problem of African-American identity*. New York, NY: Oxford University Press.

Harper, S. R. (2004). The measure of a man: Conceptualizations of masculinity among high-achieving African American male college students. *Berkeley Journal of Sociology, 48*(1), 89–107.

Harper, S. R. (2006). Enhancing African American male student outcomes through leadership and active involvement. In M. Cuyjet's (Ed.), *African American college men* (pp. 68–94). San Francisco, CA: Jossey-Bass.

Harper, S. R. (2012). *Black male students success in higher education: A report from the National Black Male Achievement Study*. Graduate School of Education, Center for the Study of Race and Equity in Education. University of Pennsylvania.

Heitzeg, N. A. (2009). Race, class and legal risk in the United States: Youth of color and colluding systems of social control. *Forum on Public Policy. Vol. 2009* (2) Winter.

hooks, b. (1989). *Talking back*. Boston, MA: South End Press.

Hope, A. (2010). Seductions of risk, social control, and resistance to school surveillance. In T. Monahan and R. D. Torres (Eds), *Schools under surveillance: Cultures of control in public education* (pp. 230–246). New Brunswick, NJ: Rutgers University Press.

Hrabowowski, F., Maton, K., & Greif, G. (Eds.). (1998). *Beating the odds: Raising academically successful African American males*. New York, NY: Oxford.

Hutchinson, E. O. (1994). *The assassination of the Black male image*. New York, NY: Simon & Schuster.

Jackson, R. L., & Hopson, M. C. (2011). *Masculinity in the black imagination: Politics of communicating race and manhood*. New York, NY: Peter Lang.

Johns, D. J. (2007). Re-imagining Black masculine identity: An investigation of the "problem" surrounding the construction of Black masculinity in America. In *The state of Black America: Portrait of the black male*. National Urban League. New York, NY: New York.

Kimmel, M. (2008). *Guyland: The perilous world where boys become men*. New York, NY. Harper Collins Publishers.

Kimmel, M. S., & Messner, M. A. (2007). *Men as gendered beings. Men's lives*. New York, NY: Pearson.

Laura, C. T. (2014). *Being bad: My baby brother and the school-to-prison pipeline*. New York, NY: Teachers College Press.

Matsuda, M. (1996). *Where is your body? And other essays on race and gender in the law*. Boston, MA: Beacon Press.

McCall, N. (2011). *Makes me wanna holler: A young black man in America*. Vintage.

McGuire, K. M., Berhanu, J., Davis, C. H., & Harper, S. R. (2014). In search of progressive black masculinities critical self-reflections on gender identity development among black undergraduate men. *Men and Masculinities, 17*(3), 253–277.

Mutua, A. D. (Ed.). (2006). *Progressive masculinities?* New York, NY: Routledge.

Neal, M. (2006). New black man. New York, NY: Routledge.

Noguera, P. (2003). The trouble with Black boys: The role and influence of environmental and cultural factors on the academic performance of African American males. *Urban Education, 38*, 431–459.

Smith, W., Allen, W. R., & Danley, L. (2007). "Assume the position ... You fit the description": Psychosocial experiences and racial battle fatigue among African American male college students. *American Behaviorial Scientist, 51*(4), 551–578.

Smith, W., Yosso, T., & Solorzano, D. (2007). Racial primes and Black misandry on historically White campuses: Toward critical race accountability in educational administration. *Educational Administration Quarterly, 43*(5), 559–585.

Solorzano, D. (1998). Critical race theory, race and gender micro-aggressions, and the experience of Chicana and Chicano scholars. *Qualitative Studies in Education, 11*(1), 121–136.

Solorzano, D., & Yosso, T. (2001). Critical race and LatCrit theory and method: Counterstorytelling. *International Journal of Qualitative Studies in Education, 14*(4), 471–495.

Solorzano, D., & Yosso, T. (2002). Critical race methodology: Counter-storytelling as an analytical framework for education research. *Qualitative Inquiry, 8*(1), 23–44.

Steele, C. M. (1997). A threat in the air: How stereotype shape intellectual identity and performance. *American Psychologist, 52*(6), 613–629.

Steele, C. M. & Aronson, J. (1995). Stereotype threat and the intellectual test performance of African Americans. *Journal of Personality and Social Psychology, 69*(5), 797–811.

Williams, P. (1991). *The alchemy of race and rights*. Cambridge, MA: Harvard University Press.

Wilson, V. R. (2007). On equal ground: Causes and solutions for lower college completion rates among Black males. In *The state of Black America: Portrait of the Black male*. New York, NY: The Bekham Publication Group. National Urban League.

Wing, A. (1997). *Critical race feminism: A reader*. New York, NY: New York University Press.

CHAPTER 22

You Can't Piss Down My Back and Tell Me It's Raining

James H. Campbell and Brent E. Johnson

Introduction

This chapter discusses the usage of Black male athletes as property to be controlled by the hegemony of their sport specifically and modern society in general. It is our attempt to examine Black masculinity through lens of Critical Race Theory (CRT) in sport. This analysis provides a tool to examine the tensions that the black male athlete must endure while participating in sport at collegiate and professional levels.

The Maryland colonies' original edict was expanded into a public policy on Blacks, stipulating that "Black people shall constitute an available, uncompensated, noncompetitive, well-disciplined, permanently subordinated work force, which shall be separated from the white society." (Anderson, 1994).

Preface

The title "You Can't Piss Down My Back And Tell Me It's Raining" was chosen to bring to bear the notion that the African American male participating in Division I basketball and football at Predominantly White Institutions (PWIs) and in professional football and basketball are held captive by the system that profits monetarily from their labor and told that it is in their best interest. They have not been emancipated by this oppressor. In fact this system has convinced these young men that they are receiving benefits that outweigh the vast amounts of cash that this revenue generating sport produces. The sweat equity that these young men contribute to the university provides for the supplementation of budgets for other sports programs, 6 and 7 figure salaries for coaches, substantiating video game, apparel, shoe and television contracts and merchandising sales. Last year, the National Collegiate Athletic Association (NCAA) men's basketball tournament generated $1.15 billion in television ads. All television revenue, ticket, and jersey sales, likeness promotions and other sources of income go to the NCAA, the schools, the coaches, the event staff, and everyone else involved in the business-except the players creating the value. Ninety percent of the NCAA revenue is produced by 1% of the athletes. Go to the skill positions-the stars, states Sonny Vaccaro (who signed his shoe contract with Michael Jordan in 1984), ninety percent (of the one percent), are Black.

The NCAA is the institution that is at the forefront of collegiate athletics in the United States. This institution according to the NCAA manual operates with the purpose of the organization is designed to be a vital part of the educational system. A basic purpose of this Association is to maintain intercollegiate athletics as an integral part of the educational program and the athlete as an integral part of the student body. By so doing, a clear line of demarcation exists between intercollegiate athletics and professional sports. The NCAA was designed to be the governing body of amateur athletics. Its sole purpose is to maintain the integrity of amateur athletics and promote academic excellence in higher education. In maintaining the integrity of amateur athletics the NCAA strictly prohibits the student athlete from earning any monetary reward or prize from their athletic abilities. According to the NCAA manual in the section Use of Overall Athletics Skill—Effect on Eligibility: Participation for pay in competition that involves the use of overall athletics skill (e.g., 'superstars' competition) constitutes a violation of the Association's amateur-status regulations; therefore, an individual participating for pay in such competition is ineligible for intercollegiate competition in all sports. Student athletes are also permitted to have their own business only if some specific criteria is met. According to the NCAA manual a student-athlete may establish his or her own business, provided the student-athlete's name, photograph, appearance or athletics reputation are not used to promote the business.

These types of sanctions prevent the athlete from pursuing his ability to earn a fair wage with the use of his intellectual and physical property. With the denial of the student athlete to receive any monetary gains as a stakeholder in the revenue generation of the sports program in which he participates he is systematically excluded from the process of wealth distribution. In this way the NCAA and colleges and universities collude to prevent student athletes from directly benefiting from his sweat (personal) equity.

The Black collegiate student population is less than 5%. However, Black student athletes make up 43% of the football roster at USC (80% of the starters) and nearly 90% of the USC men's basketball team, 100% of the starters in 2013. At UCLA, Black athletes make up approximately 51% of the football roster and approximately 72% are starters. In basketball, Black student athletes make up 80% of the team and starters. The combined athletic department revenue for USC and UCLA was more than $139 million. Basketball and football represent the only revenue-generating sports (Sacramento Observer, 2013). Yet, college athletes receive only scholarships as compensation.

In popular society the athlete is put on a pedestal for a variety of reasons. They are admired for their athletic ability, fame, fortune, success and often times for their personalities. These personalities are what initially attracted me to the realm of sport. The charismatic Ervin "Magic" Johnson seemed so personable that I felt as though I was connected to this man an in reality I had not met the man. Kareem Abdul Jabbar's stoic persona on the court being juxtaposed by his comedy feature in the movie Airplane and fight scene with Bruce Lee in Game of Death pulled me into sports culture in a way that only can be described as obsessive. In becoming a fan of Jabbar I also became aware of his personal platform of social justice, equality and civil rights. I was introduced to the human dimension of the man. This introduction ignited my passion for pursing the liberties of Black athletes as they have been subjugated on multiple fashions. As a very visible example of blackness, the masculinity of these athletes is constantly scrutinized by the dominant society.

Black masculinity in regards to the black athlete takes on a performative appearance as it is consistently under the gaze of the Dominate culture. As Black men and former athletes ourselves, we bring our own unique experiences combining athletics, post-secondary educational training, research, and lived experience as negotiates of otherness in sport and society. As DuBois was successfully able to combine his lived experience with conceptual frameworks, we to are attempting to integrate Critical Race Theory for the purposes of providing a theoretical foundation for the disparity in understanding the tensions of "being a Black male" and the common misconceptions and beliefs about the capabilities of Black males.

The black male form has been commodified in the United States for many years prior to the formation of the country. Back masculinity--once defined mainly by an urban aesthetic, a nihilistic attitude, and an aggressive posturing--has made its way into the cultural mainstream in the last two decades. Though there are numerous contributing factors, this image of Black masculinity has developed largely as a result of the commodification of hip-hop culture, and the ubiquity of rap music and the "videomercials" that sell it. More specifically, it is the result of the popularity of the urban "gangsta.

In contemporary times the Black male is viewed as a dominant physical specimen both athletically and socially. As discussed in earlier sections the Black male has not been given the benefit of being thought of as an intellectual being. Harry Edwards (1984) states:

They must contend, of course, with the connotations and social reverberations of the traditional "dumb jock" caricature. But Black student athletes are burdened also with the insidious racist implications of the myth of "innate black athletic superiority", and the more blatantly racist stereotype of the "dumb Negro" condemned by racial heritage to intellectual inferiority. Under circumstances where there exists a pervasive belief in the mutual exclusivity of physical and intellectual capability (p. 8).

In keeping with the notions of CRT, Black masculinity in sport is a microcosm of the broader culture. Mary Jo Kane (1996) writes, "Sport consists of a set of ideological beliefs and practices that are closely tied to traditional power structures" (p. 95). These power structures often are attached to the notion of black males possessing according to

Ferber (2007) "their animal-like nature, emphasizing their sexuality, aggressiveness, and physical power" (p. 19). The paradigm of Black man as athlete or entertainer further perpetuates the dynamics of white supremacy in that the Black man is viewed according to Ferber (2007) as a safe individual if the white man can control him. This is indicative of the "coach is similar to the white male father figure" (Ferber, 2007, p. 20). Gause (2008) asserts the image of Black men is viewed as naturally violent, bestial, and hypersexualized.

This combination of violence and sexuality made Black men inherently unsuitable for work until they were trained by white men and placed under their discipline and control. To explain these relations, white elites created the controlling image of the buck. Unlike images of African natives who roam their wild homelands like beast untamed by civilization (colonialism), the representations of the buck described a human animal that had achieved partial domestication through slavery (p. 56).

However when there is a Black man that does not conform to the narrative of being a child under the control of his white father figure he is viewed as a troublemaker. The troublemaker is ostracized and made an example of by the media especially when they are involved in an altercation that stems from what is assumed to be the primitive nature of the black man. Violators of the safe Black man role have very public interactions with the law. Some of these violators have been O.J Simpson, Aaron Hernandez, Ray Lewis, Plaxico Burress, Ron Artest, Stephen Jackson, Michael Vick, Rae Carruth, Allen Iverson, Kobe Bryant, Tiger Woods and Latrell Sprewell. Collins (2005) states that Latrell Sprewell who was suspended by the National Basketball Association for an altercation in which he attacked and choked his head coach P.J. Carlesimo, received an undue amount of scrutiny from the media that may be indicative of the ways in which Black masculinity is depicted as over sexed, aggressive, violent, confrontational and reckless.

Black masculinity in the United States has been directly associated with criminal activity. Black men are arrested and convicted at a disproportioned rate compared to other racial groups. Weathersbee shows that one third of black men from the age of maturity to age 40 that they will have an encounter with the legal system including probation, incarceration or parole (Weathersbee, 2006). A majority of whites still stereotype Black people as violence-prone, inclined to live on welfare, and disinclined to hard work. Many continue to stereotype Black Americans as unintelligent.

Black masculinity is a subjective notion that has very little validity in the depiction of the lived existences of Black men. It might be considered a cloak spread over the Black man to subjugate him to conform to the notions that the dominant society perpetuates as their narrative of what constitutes blackness. In other words, despite the countless Black males in sport and society that have progressed sport and society forward in athleticism and courage (Arthur Ashe and Jesse Owens just to name to such men), the framework that surrounds the idea black maleness has been defined by norms heavily influenced by white maleness.

Critical Race Theory

Critical Race Theory (CRT) is a movement inspired by a collection of activists and scholars interested in studying and transforming the relationship among race, racism, and power (Delgado & Stefancic, 2006, p. 1). Originating in the field of law, critical legal studies, CRT, like the civil rights initiatives, is working toward a more egalitarian society. However, unlike the civil rights movement, CRT opposes the incremental process used in more traditional movements (Delgado & Stefancic, 2006). Guided by four basic tenets (racism as ordinary or color blindness, interest convergence, racism as a social construct, and different experiences between whites and people of color) CRT, unlike critical legal studies, also broadens its scope beyond the legal disciplines to include micro and macro issues of race and power in all aspects of society. As athletics is often regarded as society operating in a micro-context and used by researchers to examine phenomena, we to agree with this premise and engage in interrogating Black masculinity as it pertains to sport.

Critical Race Theory and Sport

Using CRT as the lens of this study implicitly implies that there are injustices and inequalities in the field of sport that revolve around race. The uses of the term revolve implies that race is the central loci from which the problem stems. According to Hylton (2004) "the political "race" focus, the emancipatory edge for black people, is not the starting point, yet this is a crucial element of CRT" (p. 92). CRT has as a part of its tenet of racial realism the notion of colorblindness. Colorblindness was discussed in a previous section of this review. "Colorblindness offers a largely normative claim for a retreat from race that is aspirational in nature" (Cho, 2009, p. 1598). The notion is especially applicable to the issue of sport. It has been determined that the majority will concede superiority to the minority in sport. In doing so the minority that performs a particular sport at its highest level may be viewed by the majority as more than his race. In fact the participator may be viewed as race less. This notion is seen explicitly in the country of Argentina according to Bass (2005), through exceptionalism Argentina has effectivelydesignated itself as white by being contrary to other Latin American countries. An imperialist European country is Argentina's self image. As the footballers (soccer players) of Argentina compete in international matches the racial realism has been introverted as the Argentinians view themselves with a colorblind notion. Hylton (2004) makes the argument that "players 'deprioritize' their identifiable 'Asian culture' have serious ramifications for the identities of Asians in football, sport and the wider society" (2009, p.14). The ability to be other than what is observable is something that individuals identified as black do not have the option of adhering to in forming their identity. Delgado, R., & Stefancic, J. (2005) asserts the positioning of Black and white has been static in society. These classifications create the binary necessary for the "other" to exist. In popular culture the most notable attempt of an individual in sport to exempt themselves from being positioned in the black category is golfer Tiger Woods. He classified himself as "Cablinasian" a mixture of the racial classifications of Caucasian, Black, Indian and Asian. What is notable is that the Caucasian is listed as the primary classification.

In this chapter CRT will be used to give voice to the Black male athlete. CRT provides the opportunity for Blacks in sport to speak about their experiences from their point of view instead of the story being told from the perspectives of the broader community. Counter storytelling according to Hylton (2009) gives the observer the opportunity to hear testimonies that may be viewed as disturbing. It is disturbing because as an academician there is a notion of knowledge that is adhered to in a way that it constitutes truth, however this truth is formed from an on-lookers perspective. With meaning manufactured through ethnographic studies observation is subjective and voice is minimalized. "For those lost in the epistemological strictures, provided new ways of seeing and understanding" (Hylton, 2009, p. 52). For academics the use of counter storytelling will offer an opportunity to examine the ontological question of being a Black athlete. According to Birrell (1989) "it will yield the epistemological grounding for a new analysis that would celebrate the distinctiveness of Black culture" (p. 215).

CRT in sport will provide a lens to examine the lived existence of the Black male student-athletes that participate in Division I intercollegiate basketball at a PWI. Thus, creating a platform to share their stories as they see fit without the overbearing gaze of the institution upon them. Overbearing in the sense that the institution takes on the responsibility of parenting these young adults. "CRT has a tradition of interrogating or questioning ideologies, narratives, institutions and structures of society through a critical lens" (Zamudio, Russell, Rios, & Bridgeman, 2010, p. 11). CRT in sport has limitations as any, however the upside is very promising as a lens to assist in extrapolating epistemological truisms.

Racial realism, an idea incorporated within the CRT tenet of racism as normal, postulates that racism is endemic and a permanent part of our current society and our social history.

According to Bell (1992a):

> Black people will never gain full equality in this country. Even those herculean efforts we hail as successful will produce no more than temporary "peaks of progress", short-lived victories that slide into irrelevance as racial patterns adapt in ways that maintain white dominance … We must acknowledge it and move on to adopt policies based on what I call: "Racial Realism." (p. 373)

Are we concluding that this modern-day colonialist system we know as division I athletics will most likely always exist within our society? The answer is "yes". However, as Bell (1992a)states later in this passage, this mindset is not to foster hopelessness but reality. Do not expect that the NCAA will all of a sudden become inoculated with a dose of critical consciousness. Nonetheless, the continued struggle for improved conditions and more equitable treatment can still be obtained. The Northwestern University football team just might be attempting the type of imaginative strategy necessary to create a more humane relationship between college athletes and the NCAA. In March 2014, the National Labor Relations Board ruled that Northwestern football players are university employees who have a right to unionize. College athletes, defined as amateurs by the NCAA, often devote 50–60 hours a week to their sport. Kain Colter, former quarterback and face of this movement, reported spending 50–60 hours a week on football.

In April 2014, members of the Northwestern football team had the opportunity to vote in order to decide to unionize USA Today, 2014). Although the outcome of the vote has yet to be determined and Northwestern University may appeal based on the outcome, this incident may become the catalyst toward a more just system for college athletes.

Summary

In conclusion I would like to reiterate that the black male athlete has a bevy of obstacles to overcome to participate in collegiate and professional athletics. The ridicule and demining treatments given to an athlete such as Mr. Jackie Robinson as depicted in the film "42" have subtlety changed however the tensions of being a black male athlete in America are still present. This mind-set or philosophy requires us to acknowledge the permanence of our subordinate status. That acknowledgement enables us to avoid despair, and frees us to imagine and implement racial strategies than can bring fulfillment and even triumph (Bell, 1992, p. 374). Can the Black athlete ever produce the amount of counter-hegemonic agency to create an economically equitable space? Can the ongoing collusion between the NCAA and the university system be toppled by a critical mass of collegiate athletes who also view themselves as political agents of change? Unfortunately, imbedded in the American fiber is the legally sanctioned extraction of labor disproportionately taken from people of color and the poor. The collusion of the university system and the NCAA is a glaring example of this process. Although the dismantling of this system anytime soon is doubtful, teams like the Northwestern Wildcats and athletes such as Brandon Jennings (who chose to play basketball oversees rather than provide a year of his work and talent as a collegiate amateur) might be providing the "young and talented" with alternatives in which to choose or strategies in which to employ. If more young athletes exercise these options, the NCAA-university partnership will have to yield to the notion of compensating its work force and silent partner, the collegiate athlete.

Work Cited

Anderson, C. (1994). *Black Labor White Wealth: The search for power and economic justice.* Bethesda, MD: PowerNomics Corporation of America.

Bass, A. (2005). *In the game: Race identity, and sports in the twentieth century.* New York, NY: Palgrave Macmillan.

Bell, D. A. (1992a). *Faces at the bottom of the well: The permanence of racism.* New York, NY: Basic Books

Bell, D. A. (2004). *Silent covenants: Brown v. Board of education and the unfulfilled hopes for racial reform.* Oxford and New York, NY: Oxford University Press

Delgado, R., & Stefancic, J. (2005). *The derrick bell reader.* New York, NY: New York University Press.

Birrell, S., (1989). Racial relations theories and sport: Suggestions for a more critical analysis. *Sociology of Sport Journal, 6,* 212–227.

Cho, S. (2009). Post racialism. *Iowa Law Review, 94,* 1589–1649.

Crenshaw, K. W. (1988). Race, reform, retrenchment: Transformation and legitimation in anti discrimination law. *Harvard L aw Review, 101,* 1331–1387.

Crenshaw, K. W. (1993). Beyond racism and misogyny: Black feminism and 2 Live Crew. In M. J. Matsuda, C. R. Lawrence, R. Delgado, & K. W. Crenshaw (Eds.), *Words that wound: Critical race theory, assaultive speech, and the First Amendment* (pp. 111–132). Boulder, CO: Westview Press.

Delgado, R. (1988). Critical legal studies and the realities of race-Does the fundamental contradiction have a corollary? *Harvard Civil Rights-Civil Liberties Law Review, 23,* 407–413.

Delgado, R., & Stefancic, J. (1989). Why do we tell the same stories? Law reform, critical librarianship, and the ripple helix dilemma. *Stanford Law Review, 42,* 207–225.

Delgado, R. (1990). When a story is just a story: Does voice really matter? *Virginia Law Review, 76,* 95–111.

Delgado, R., & Stefancic, J. (1992). Images of the outsider in American law and culture: Can free expression remedy systemic ills? *Cornell Law Review, 77,* 1258–1297.

Delgado, R. (1995). *Critical race theory: The cutting edge.* Philadelphia, PA: Temple University Press.

Delgado, R., & Stefancic, J. (2001). *Critical race theory: An introduction.* New York, NY: New York University Press.

Delgado, R., & Stefancic, J. (2012). *Critical race theory: An introduction* (2nd ed.). New York, NY: New York University Press.

Delpit, L. (1988). The silenced dialogue: Power and pedagogy in educating other people's children. *Harvard Educational Review, 58,* 280–298.

Dixson, A. D., & Rousseau, C. K. (2006). *Critical race theory in education: All god's children got a song.* New York, NY: Routledge.

Edwards, H. S. (1984). The dumb jock. Sociology of sport: Homewood, Illinois., Dorsey Press.

Gutierrez-Jones, C. (2001). *Critical race narratives: A study of race, rhetoric and injury.* New York, NY: New York University Press.

Ferber, A. L. (2007). The construction of black masculinity: White supremacy now and then. *Journal of Sport and Social Issues, 31*(1), 11–24.

Gause, C. P. (2008). Integration matters: navigating identity, culture and resistance. New York: Peter Lang.

Hylton, K. (2004). 'Race', sport and leisure: lessons from critical race theory. *Leisure Studies, 24*(1), 81–98.

Hylton, K. (2009). *"Race" and sport: Critical race theory.* Abingdon: Routledge.

Ladson-Billings, G., & Tate, W. F. (1995). Toward a critical race theory for education. *Teachers College Record, 97,* 47–68

Nelson, H. L. (2001). *Damaged identities, narrative repair.* Ithaca, NY: Cornell University Press.

Parker, L., Deyhle, D., & Villenas, S. (1999). *Race is, race isn't: Critical race theory and qualitative studies in education.* Boulder, CO: Westview Press.

Taylor, E., Gilborn, D., & Ladson-Billings, G. (Eds.). (2009). *Foundations of critical race theory in education.*NY: Routledge.

Williams, P. J. (1991). *The alchemy of race and rights.* Cambridge, MA: Harvard University Press. (first chapter)

Zamudio, M., Russell, C., Rios, F., & Bridgeman, J. L. (2010). *Critical race theory matters: Education and ideology.* New York, NY: Routledge.

CHAPTER 23

Mother to Son

The Role of Cultural and Social Capital in African American Intergenerational Success

Jewell E. Cooper and Joseph N. Cooper

Introduction

This chapter presents the personal narratives of a single African American mother and her son to highlight how educational success was cultivated through the transmission of cultural and social capital. As a lifelong educator, Dr. Jewell E. Cooper instilled in her children core values that emphasized educational attainment, personal networking, cultural awareness, and social consciousness. She transmitted these values through various strategies such as being actively engaged in their early educational experiences, establishing key social relationships for them beyond their biological family within the community, and providing them with educationally enriching opportunities outside of school. Specifically, she used her involvement with the Black church, African American social organizations, and historically Black colleges and universities (HBCUs) to expose her children to individuals and environments that promoted positive self-identities and high academic expectations. Using an autoethnographic approach (Patton, 2002), a mother and son present critical reflections on their lived experiences within a culture in the southeastern United States (U.S.). Their stories reflect how parental leadership can serve as a vital form of social justice in equipping African American children with the skills necessary to succeed in a society where the odds are against them.

Story of an African American Mother

The famous poem by Langston Hughes titled "Mother to Son" describes the story of an African American mother who overcame trials and tribulations to provide a better life for her children. The main protagonist in the poem explains to her son how she persevered even though she was often discouraged and exhausted by her life circumstances. More importantly though, she encourages her son to never give up no matter what challenges he may face because she is a living testimony that success is possible through faith and persistence. This poignant poem serves as a narrative for many African American mothers who raise their sons in a society where they face significant obstacles in nearly every facet of life (e.g., increased likelihood of growing up in poverty, receiving inequitable educational opportunities, facing higher levels of unemployment, being incarcerated and/or criminalized, and experiencing poor health outcomes) (Bell, 1992; ETS, 2011; West, 1993). These unique challenges are a byproduct of the systemic racism within the United States (U.S.), which privileges Whiteness and the values, norms, and beliefs of people from European descent while devaluing the lived experiences, culture, and perspectives of people from African descent (Ladson-Billings, 1994).

In the face of these perilous challenges, African American families have relied on their spirituality, collective identity, cultural values, intellect, and social networking to overcome and sustain as a people. A cornerstone of African American subsistence in the U.S. has been the strength of the family. Specifically, the parental leadership exhibited by countless African American mothers and fathers (and grandparents, extended family members, and surrogate family members) has served as a vital tool in the promotion of social justice and equity as well as the creation of intergenerational success. Education (both traditional and non-traditional) and communalism are two core values within African American culture that have contributed to intergenerational success sand mobility (Hale, 1994; Woodson, 1990). Throughout history, African Americans have used education to undermine the system of White supremacy in the U.S. In other words, education was the gateway for African American upward mobility (e.g., economic, political, and social). Connected to education is the African American cultural value of communalism. Specifically, the Black church and historically Black educational institutions (e.g., historically Black colleges/universities (HBCUs)) were and continue to be safe havens and beacons of hope for African Americans in the U.S. (Boykin, 1986; Fleming, 1984). These social institutions were established with the unique mission of providing African Americans a place for spiritual and cultural expression, empowerment, and uplift. In concert with the persevering spirit of the protagonist in Langston Hughes' poem and the history of African Americans who have excelled against all odds, this chapter describes how a single African American mother successfully transmitted intergenerational success to her son by providing him with vital cultural and social capital.

Autoethnographic Research

An autoethnography is a study of "one's own culture and oneself as part of that culture" (Patton, 2002, p. 85). This unique type of qualitative inquiry involves the use of personal narratives to describe one's lived experiences within a culture. Autoethnographies are inherently reflexive because the method requires the author to engage in "multiple layers of consciousness, connecting the personal to the cultural" (Patton, 2002, p. 85). The autoethnographic approach in this chapter was incorporated to elucidate the lived experiences of a single African American mother and her son. Hence, the researchers use their personal experiences as the primary data source to present creative analytic insight into their lives and culture (Patton, 2002; Richardson, 2000). Using first-person narratives, each author offers individual perspectives on their life experiences. The first author describes her life experiences from childhood to adulthood specifically highlighting the various challenges she faced raising two African American boys on her own. The second author describes his experiences as a young African American male being raised by a single mother and how the transmission of cultural and social capital from his mother contributed to his educational attainment and personal development.

Cultural and Social Reproduction Theory

In his theory of cultural and social reproduction, Bourdieu (1973) posited the transmission of capital (economic, cultural, and social) is a byproduct of the structure (e.g., classes) and nature (e.g., extent or strength) of relationships within a given context (e.g., society, community, family, etc.). Bourdieu (1973) primarily focused on the reproduction of power, privilege, and inequalities within different social structures. However, his theory also serves as a useful framework to examine how families leverage their capital to cultivate intergenerational success and mobility for their children to counter systemic inequalities in a society (e.g., African American families in the U.S. society dominated by European

American values, norms, and structures) (Coleman, 1988). Within this theory, there are three primary forms of capital: (1) economic, (2) cultural, and (3) social (Bourdieu, 1986). The current chapter will focus on the transmission of cultural and social capital within the context of an African American family. Cultural capital refers to the acquisition of knowledge, values, or norms associated with a dominant culture in a given context (e.g., educational background, language, behavioral expectations, etc.). Bourdieu (1986) suggested children who have access to certain cultural resources (e.g., ways of thinking congruent with dominant cultural values, books, education, etc.) are more likely to excel academically than those who are not privy to these resources. Hence, a child's academic achievement can be attributed to factors aside from economic resources.

Moreover, social capital refers to the presence of or access to key relationships with individuals that result in a privileged or advantageous position (Bourdieu, 1986). Often times, social capital is institutionally transmitted through group membership (e.g., family, organization, etc.). Similar to other forms of capital, social capital is not inevitably transferred, but rather consciously and subconsciously reproduced by a set of practices and strategies. Regarding family structures, Coleman (1988) explained the primary difference between social capital and other forms of capital (economic and cultural) is the time and effort expended by family members (e.g., parents) towards their children's intellectual development. More specifically, the transmission of social capital and access to a parent's human capital is predicated on the physical presence of the family member and the amount of attention provided to the child by a parent. Bourdieu's (1973) theory of cultural and social reproduction serves a useful lens to examine how the transmission of cultural and social capital from a single African American mother to her son contributed to successful academic outcomes and positive overall development.

An African American Mother's Perspectives on Intergenerational Success

Throughout my childhood, my parents instilled in me a set of values that helped me to overcome significant challenges in my life. Although, my father passed away when I was just 14 years of age, the lessons he taught me while he was here have been pivotal in my personal and professional growth. Similarly, my mother has also contributed to my spiritual foundation, which continues to serve as my source of strength. My life has been a journey filled with several major obstacles. Nonetheless, my possession of immeasurable forms of cultural and social capital sustained me while I fought off what seem to be insurmountable challenges. The following sections describe my story and highlight how cultural and social capital played a pivotal role throughout my life.

Setting the Stage—Preparation for Teaching and Mothering

I am a middle aged, city-born, college-educated, African-American Southern female, Christian (Baptist), middle child in a family of three raised by two rural-born African American parents, and a single/divorced mother of two adult sons. I use this descriptive exercise with my students to call their attention to something I call "the factual me." My factual self-descriptions cause me to think of myself from a critical, yet holistic perspective. For example, my middle age status leaves me with vivid memories growing up during a time where there was no central air conditioning in homes and black and white televisions were the primary form of home entertainment. Unfortunately, I am also left with memories of the height of the Civil Rights Movement in the South. Those memories include sitting at the back of the bus, Ku Klux Klan (KKK) billboards and burning crosses, drinking from Colored-only water fountains, sitting in the balcony at movie theatres, back-of-the-building restrooms as well as outhouse facilities, and segregated schools and churches. Even though the memories of segregation imprinted feelings of fear, doubt, and confusion in me at times, my recollections of segregated schools and churches also instilled in me a sense of enormous possibilities.

I grew up with parents who were high school graduates and college attendees. Limited financial resources and the death of a parent (on my mother's side) stifled their educational pursuits. Nonetheless, both my father and mother valued education and were determined that my siblings and I would earn college degrees. I grew up loving school and in loving it, I learned how "to do school" as I say. I worked hard and was rewarded through excellent and above average grades. I believe my love for school was also borne out of the demonstrations of good teaching I witnessed from predominantly African American teachers. These teachers not only embodied the tenets of culturally relevant teaching (Ladson-Billings, 1994) before it was coined as such, but they were also byproducts of the Civil Rights movement and knew that we represented the next generation of African Americans who could benefit from the future of integration. Therefore, they taught and disciplined us with love and hope as if we were their own children. This priceless cultural capital bestowed upon me by my teachers provided me with numerous benefits. It not only enhanced my desire to excel academically and my sense of racial pride, but it also inspired me to pursue a career as a teacher. I wanted to continue the legacy of good teaching they provided for me.

Similar to how my teachers affected my educational interest, my encounters in the Black church influenced my future parenting style. Having been reared in rural Black Baptist church settings, I was used to experiencing live portraits of spirit-filled praise and worship celebrations about the goodness and promise of God. Whether my father was the preaching or not, each time I entered these churches, I was reminded that if I continued "leaning on the everlasting arms" of Jesus Christ, "trust and obey" His word, and "acknowledge Him in all my ways" that even in bad times, everything would be alright. However, when I turned 14 years of age, everything was not alright. After being diagnosed with a hematology-related cancer that could only be treated with massive experimental dosages of chemotherapy, I was left wondering why me.

In spite of this devastating news, I was determined not to let this disease disrupt my two joys in life, which were attending school and church. Being around the church folk became the psychological, emotional, and social anchor I needed to persevere through the Hell-on-Earth experience (also known as chemotherapy) to which I was exposed. In my darkest hours of the before and after treatment, I would remember the sounds of church members' prayers of supplication and intercession, soulful singing, testimonies of praise and thanksgiving, and pleas for salvation. A year later, I remembered the same faith-filled demonstrations of these church folk as I entered remission and my father entered the final months of his life. He succumbed to a different form of cancer. "Leaning on the everlasting arms" helped me to not question God in the death of my father. Trusting and obeying God aided me in understanding that my illness was only a chapter in my life that would ultimately lead to a greater purpose. Acknowledging Him in all my ways caused me to have an unshakeable belief in God that I wanted to share with my children that I would hopefully one day parent. This same acknowledgement led me to not only love my children dearly, but to also parent them as if I could physically depart from their lives through death at a moment's notice, knowing that no matter what, everything would be alright. Essentially, the cultural and social capital I acquired through my upbringing, particularly my spiritual foundation through church involvement, equipped me with the knowledge and strength I needed to face the life's harshest challenges. As a result, I was committed to passing along these same values and beliefs to my children as my parents did for me.

Conscious Preparation for Teaching—Unconscious Preparation for Mentoring

During my junior year of high school, I knew I wanted to earn a doctorate so I could teach in college. Initially, I wanted to teach students how to teach, in part, by being a student teacher supervisor. I also knew there was only one college at which I wanted to teach—Bennett College, presently known as Bennett College for Women, one of two historically Black colleges for women in the U.S. In preparing to meet my goals, I planned to go to college with the intent on majoring in teacher education. I decided I wanted to apply to a HBCU for my undergraduate degree. During this same time, the federal government via the Supreme Court mandated that White schools, including institutions of higher education, begin enrolling more ethnic minorities or they could lose federal funding. Since my father recently passed away, my mother would not allow me to attend an out-of-state institution. Therefore, along with three in-state HBCUs, I also applied to one in-state predominantly White institution (PWI), which consequently offered me "the best deal" financial package for enrollment. Fortunately, the school was renowned for its teacher education program. I graduated in three and half years with a degree in Intermediate Education (Grades, pp. 4–9) with a concentration in English.

After graduating, I taught middle school Language Arts and Social Studies in a nearby county school system in North Carolina for three years. This experience helped me develop my pedagogical skills. I continued to hone those skills later when I taught the same content at a middle school in a Tennessee school system. Marriage was the primary reason I moved to Tennessee. While teaching in Tennessee, I earned my Master of Science degree in Education at Memphis State University, now known as The University of Memphis. Between teaching jobs, I also worked as a secretary in the English Department at Vanderbilt University and in the Department of Biochemistry at the University of Tennessee Center for the Health Sciences. The latter two jobs whetted my professional appetite even more to become a college professor.

With a toddler and an infant son in tow, I spent five years as a stay-at-home mom; however, restlessness overtook me about not using my college degree. At this point, we had moved back to North Carolina. I also did not want to completely depend on another person's funds—not even my husband's—to live. Therefore, I began teaching at a Saturday enrichment program, funded by a U.S. Department of Education grant awarded to Bennett College. I also worked part-time as a grants assistant at Bennett. While I worked, one of my sons attended the child development laboratory (CDL) school at Bennett College. Later, both my sons continued their preschool attendance at a CDL at North Carolina A&T State University (NCA&TSU). In other words, my sons began their college socialization process at the tender age of three. After preschool ended and their attendance in public school began, both sons would accompany me anywhere I had to go on campus that was permitted. They virtually became my "back pockets."

Being those "back pockets" I introduced them to the campus life and community of students, faculty, and staff at Bennett. Throughout elementary school, they navigated the campus like professionals. Known to everyone on campus, my sons would accompany me to class at times, to meetings, and to after school hours events. They knew "their places" in that they were quite aware of times they needed to be quiet and still, and they knew when it was appropriate to be active and rambunctious boys. All I was concerned about was that they would not embarrass me while we were on campus. Therefore, they received pre-arrival lectures on how to behave and the consequences of not being obedient to my wishes.

Somehow, I did not worry about my older son, Adam, and his behavior. I did, however, worry about my younger son, Joseph or "Joey" as we call him. His demeanor was challenging at times. Though old folks would call him independent, defiant, and determined to have his way, he clung to me in a way my older son did not. His attachment to me became most amplified during my marital separation and ultimate divorce. At eight years of age, Joey would not allow me to go many places alone if he knew it. I surmised it was his childlike fear of abandonment based on his understanding of what it meant for his parents to be divorced. It would only be later that I learned he was not only making sure that I would return home, but he was also paying attention to more of my actions than I thought.

Becoming a single parent dictated my actions where my sons were concerned. They still accompanied me to Bennett College when necessary. For 12 Saturdays in the Fall and 12 Saturdays in the Spring, they sat in the back of the classroom as I taught Language Arts to third through eighth graders in the Saturday Academy at NCA&TSU. On some days during the summer, they sat in the back of the classroom as I taught English to 10–12th graders in the Intensive Summer Science Program (ISSP), a four-week residential enrichment program housed at Bennett College that served 100 African

American teenagers from across the U.S. Joey and Adam would sit and listen to me teach grammar, mechanics, and writing skills. In fact, Joey, in particular, would question me on what was taught as we rode home on some Saturdays. He would also comment on my instructional delivery not only during Saturday Academy or ISSP, but also when I taught during the regular school day. Since I taught curriculum and instruction courses, I was preparing pre-service teachers to teach. Therefore, I modeled for them what I considered through study and practice sound culturally relevant/responsive pedagogy. To my surprise, Joey was internalizing everything he saw and heard and would later apply these lessons in his educational pursuits.

The cultivation of cultural and social capital was an important goal of parenting for me. I intentionally exposed them to as many educational experiences outside the academic environment of traditional schooling that I could afford whether it was summer academic or sports camps. In addition, we went to the library each week where they were required to read for specified times as assigned by their teachers. I would often peruse the newspaper weekly to discover when the circus, the Ice Capades, special children's events, or other educational activities would be in town. They took swimming lessons, horseback riding, skating lessons, gymnastics, and karate lessons. When I was invited to join Jack and Jill of America (an African American mothers' and children's organization that was born during the 1930's during the Jim Crow era as an avenue to expose African American children to educational, social, and leadership opportunities that were denied to them), I agreed to provide them with yet another opportunity to develop their cultural and social capital. Considered a middle class organization, I wanted my sons to take advantage of whatever exposure this group could offer them. I also desired for them to associate with African American children who had similar goals, who lived outside their neighborhood, and who did not attend their schools or our church. In other words, I wanted them to cast a wider net of friendships and associations for early networking purposes.

Along the same lines, I encouraged their participation in youth activities at church; however, because of Joey's competitive sports activities—soccer and basketball, practices and actual competitions would occur during the week and on weekends—Joey's church youth activities were minimal especially during his sports seasons. Nevertheless, when sports season ended, I intentionally required their church activities to be made a priority in their lives. In fact, they were dedicated members of the Youth Group I led for a period of time. Joey became so involved in the Youth Group activities that he served as president for an annual term.

We Are All In School Now—Co-Educational Journeys

Retaining my job at Bennett required me to earn a doctoral degree, one of my earlier goals of my life. On one hand, I eagerly accepted the challenge in an academic sense. After all, I loved "to do school." On the other hand, accomplishing this goal while I was parenting two young sons and working full-time appeared to be Herculean task. The Young Women's Christian Association (YWCA) became a blessing in disguise. At the time, my greatest, immediate challenge was transporting my children from afterschool care to evening care on days when I would be attending graduate classes. The YWCA was their afterschool provider. This program provided transportation from their respective schools to the YWCA each afternoon. Miraculously, when I began attending graduate school, the YWCA began an evening program where the boys could transition from afterschool to evening care until 8:00 pm. My evening classes ended at 7:00 pm. The YWCA was only three miles from my graduate school campus. My first problem was solved. Additionally, I felt comfortable with this arrangement because my sons were safe, loved, and cared for at the YWCA. The women who worked in the afterschool program also volunteered to care for my sons outside the YWCA program. They became another support system for the boys and me.

My students and colleagues at Bennett College also came to my aid where care for my sons was concerned. My students who already knew my sons readily volunteered to "sit" with them while I was taking evening classes or writing papers. Those young women would assist them with homework, take them to the school's dining hall for meals, take them to sports practices if need be, pick them up from afterschool care at the YWCA on various days, and generally care for them as if they were their younger brothers. No doubt, my sons felt special in that they remained within the collegiate environment and thought they were "big boys" who were cared for by their "big sisters." My colleagues replaced the students when needed. By this time, "word got around" about my divorce and my attempt to attend graduate school. Different colleagues demonstrated their support of my efforts by assisting me with childcare when they could or when they felt I was in the greatest need.

I did not want to abuse the assistance I was being given by my students, colleagues, and the YWCA staff. Therefore, at times my sons would accompany me to the university library where I would read journal articles and book chapters and write papers while the boys would do homework. They learned how to chart their course on the floors of the library and helped me find books through their knowledge of the Dewey Decimal System. They also checked out books from the Teaching Learning Center, a youth/young adult library that was a part of the larger library. It was not unusual to see us all reading a book or doing homework at the same time. They knew I valued the importance of reading so they had to as well.

Weekday sports nights and weekends became juggling acts. Joey was participating in the Amateur Athletic Union (AAU) basketball tournaments and competitive soccer leagues. Select school nights were reserved for basketball games and weekends were dedicated to soccer. For me, weekends were prime time to do statistics homework and write papers. In gymnasiums and on soccer fields, I found myself completing statistics assignments and writing papers about ethnic identity development in African American adolescents while Joey led his respective basketball and soccer teams. My older son, Adam watched the game and signaled me when Joey had the ball so I could see him pass, shoot, or kick it. There was a big part of me that felt guilty by not giving my full attention to Joey's performances. I did not know how he perceived my double duty—watching him play sports while doing my school work. For me, however, managing to do both was necessary in being a good mother and a good graduate student.

Even at home, my duties were divided. I was a Mom and a student. When we were not attending to our daily maintenance needs or doing what needed to be done as household chores, we were reading, writing, or watching television in the basement. That is where my home office was situated. Books and papers were strewn around the room everywhere. For as long as I can remember, my sons were surrounded by books and papers. They grew up knowing that I loved reading the newspaper and books. When riding in the car from place to place, we engaged in conversations about school, work, social relationships, plans for the future, and whatever was happening in the world at the time. Our engagement also included precautionary advice and reprimands if they were not behaving in a manner that was appropriate to the task or situation. In other words, no matter was off limits for dialogue. If I did not know the answer, I found someone who did.

Preparing to Let My Gifts Go—The Manifestation of Intergenerational Success

My experiences in church taught me early on that children are given to us on loan as gifts. They are given to us to love, nurture, and guide with our life's roadmap until it is time to let them go to chart their own courses of living. By the time my older son entered high school, I had completed graduate school. While my sons were no longer my "back pockets," this time was replaced with sports practices and tutoring sessions. On one hand, with driver's licenses in tow, I breathed a sigh of immense relief because they could transport themselves where they needed to go. On the other hand, I realized that their daily presences with me were numbered. Sooner rather than later, they would be graduating from high school and entering college. Therefore, I became more conscious of the quality of time I spent with them.

During this same time, I was led to change jobs. I moved from Bennett College to The University of North Carolina at Greensboro (UNCG). With this move, the demands of my job changed. For example, at Bennett I taught classes during the day. At UNCG, I taught in the late afternoon/early evening. This change caused me to leave class at 7:00 pm and drive sometimes 40 miles to a basketball game in a nearby county in time to see half the game. It was imperative for Joey to see me at the game, even if I did arrive after half-time ended. After all, other parents and family members were present for their player-sons. I needed to be there for mine and he needed to know that I made the effort to get there.

After Adam left for college, Joey would come to my office UNCG in the afternoons to do his homework. I would be preparing for class or writing manuscripts for publication while he was doing his work. Even while I taught class, he would work in my office. When he was there, we would have rich conversations. Problem solving became a regular activity. Talking about girlfriends was a constant. Our mother-son relationship was also developing into a best friend duo, something that he and I valued and cherished. Once both sons were off to in-state colleges, they rarely came home, but our lines of communication via cell phone were always open.

For Joey, enrollment in graduate school introduced him to a more focused meaning of his major—kinesiology. In fact, I attended his thesis defense. The format of the defense was similar to a dissertation defense. Joey's delivery was masterful! He answered questions from his thesis committee with confidence and rigor. I actually left the defense awe-struck and with a vision of what Joey could be become if he continued his line of research. We walked away from the defense with me commenting that he should seek a doctoral program in kinesiology to continue his study of Black athletes in college. Further, I was fully convinced that Joey should seek a Ph.D. program after he was awarded the kinesiology's research award as a Master's student. My confidence was buoyed even more because his Master's degree program was from a highly regarded Research I institution.

During the year Joey took off between the Master's degree and entry into a Ph.D. program, I sent him peer-reviewed articles and recommended books and book chapters to read. I hoped he would keep his research skills up as well as his "academic writing rhythm." We continued having conversations about critical race theory, social reproduction theory, other epistemologies, and methodologies related to his and my area of research. As he read, he also applied to the three top programs in kinesiology in the country. Additionally, he investigated and read the studies of researchers at these institutions with whom he wanted to work. When he entered the University of Georgia (UGA) Kinesiology Ph.D. program, he was well prepared for its academic demands by my estimation. I let him go physically, but I continued to share with him the experience I learned through my years in the academe. I mentored not only as a professor to a first-year Ph.D. student, but also I mentored as a "mother to son."

An African American Son's Perspectives on Intergenerational Success

One of the primary values my mother instilled in me was the importance of education. In fact, a significant part of my childhood and adolescence was spent on the campuses of institutions of higher education. As a lifelong educator, my mother intentionally provided me with various forms of cultural and social capital to increase my chances at excelling academically. It was not until I became an adult and earned my Ph.D. that I realized how vital these experiences were to my holistic development. In my family, the consistent presence of my mother made up for the "structural deficiency" in the family associated with the absence of my father (Coleman, 1988, p. 210). In order to understand the impact of her parenting on my development, I will highlight key experiences throughout my life that made me the person I am today.

Plant the Seeds and They Will Grow—Early Childhood Educational Experiences

As a toddler, my mother enrolled me in the CDL preschool program at NCA&TSU. Being on the campus of NCA&TSU (a HBCU), my initial introduction to an educational setting involved being surrounded by a critical mass of African-Americans. I would later learn that the social capital I acquired as a preschooler at the CDL would manifest in the fact that many of my preschool friends would later be my classmates in elementary, middle, and high school. I also developed several other meaningful friendships with my CDL classmates throughout my childhood albeit in lesser capacities than with my closer friends. I also acquired a significant amount of cultural capital (e.g., interpersonal skills, language acquisition, etc.) as a preschooler at CDL, which enhanced my readiness to excel as a kindergartner the following year. The small class size combined with the knowledgeable and caring instructors provided me with the attention I needed to develop cognitively and non-cognitively. My mother recognized the importance of this early childhood educational experience for my educational and personal development.

After CDL, my mother enrolled me in a local magnet school called Jones Elementary School for my kindergarten year. As a magnet school, Jones enrolled a large number of students from diverse backgrounds (e.g., racial, ethnic, socioeconomic, etc.). In addition to the core curriculum (e.g., reading, math, social studies, and science), Jones offered kindergarteners the opportunity to begin to learn a foreign language. In my class, we were introduced to Spanish as a second language. We learned how to read and write basic words in Spanish. The combination of a being in a diverse classroom environment and being presented multicultural curricula instilled in me at an early age a deep appreciation for people who were different from me. I also benefitted from having an outstanding kindergarten teacher, Mrs. Light, who took a particular liking to me. In fact, as one of the top performers in her class, I was invited along with another classmate to a special dinner at her house as reward for my academic performance. My positive experiences at Jones established a foundation for my future academic success. More specifically, both my acquisition of capital (cultural and social) and positive educational experiences at CDL and Jones increased my interest in school. These initial experiences would be beneficial reference points for me because in my subsequent schooling experiences I would encounter unique challenges as an African American male (e.g., negative stereotypes based on my race and gender, underrepresentation of people like me in advanced courses, etc.), which challenged my initial positive feelings about school.

After my kindergarten year, my mother enrolled me in a school closer to our house called Morehead Elementary. Similar to Jones, Morehead was a multicultural school with a range of educational resources. It was during my years at Morehead that I began to realize how the cultural and social capital I had acquired in my previous educational experiences benefitted me. For example, at Morehead, nearly half of the students were African American and the other half were White. A majority of the African American students who attended Morehead grew up in different neighborhoods than the one I grew up. In contrast, many of the White students grew up in a similar neighborhood as mine. At the time, I was being raised in a two-parent upper middle class household in a predominantly White neighborhood. At school, the cliques were divided along racial lines, which were also based along the neighborhood you grew up in. This presented a challenge to me because I had similarities and differences with both groups. Thus, I had to rely on my cultural and social capital to connect with each group. With my fellow African American classmates, I used my relationships and cultural knowledge I acquired from CDL and Jones to connect with them. With my fellow White classmates, I used the social relationships I made with friends who lived in my neighborhood as a way to connect with them. I realize now my mother's intentional efforts to provide me with diversified educational experiences taught me how to network and understand people from different backgrounds. This vital life skill would prove to be pivotal in my future success both personally (e.g., having a wide social network) and educationally (e.g., knowing how to communicate with people from different cultural backgrounds).

In addition to the racial differences at Morehead, I was also introduced to a wide range of negative stereotypes associated with my race. For example, I began to observe that doing well academically was viewed as "acting White" and any African American students who did well academically were subject to ridicule (Fordham & Ogbu, 1986, p. 176). These racial microaggressions were particularly harsh for

African American males since racially society deemed me to be less intelligent and as a male I was supposed to be behaviorally deviant (Sue et al., 2007). Little did I know, the pervasiveness of these negative stereotypes had a powerful influence on me and began to affect my attitude toward school. In an effort to combat this stereotype, my mother spent a significant amount of time, energy, and resources to ensure that I performed at my optimal level academically and did not succumb to these pressures. For example, my mother would regularly attend my teacher-parent meetings to discuss my progress with my teachers and identify areas of improvement. It was always clear to me that my mother deeply cared about my education and academic success. During these years, my mother would also purchase a wide range of children books and read them aloud to me to help me develop my reading comprehension skills. I remember whenever we had a book fair at school she would accompany me and purchase books for us to read together. Her presence and support reinforced to me that doing well academically was a family expectation regardless of what stereotypes I encountered at school.

Another example of when she leveraged cultural capital to help with my development was with my annual science fair projects. Each year starting in third grade, I had to complete a science project for the school-wide science fair. My mother would always put forth extra effort to assist me and ensure my science project was among the most comprehensive and decorated. She knew many of the White students' parents would help them with their projects and she wanted to make sure I had the same resources and produced the highest quality project possible. I remember our countless trips to Office Depot to purchase materials and going to the public library to research different topics. I would later realize that my mother was transmitting to me vital cultural capital that instilled in me the importance of education and putting forth my best effort in everything I do.

It Takes a Village to Raise a Child—Community Support in Child-Rearing

A major turning point in my life took place mid-way through my third grade year when my parents got divorced. I was eight years old and although I was too young to fully understand what was taking place I knew that my life was about to change drastically. Around this time, my mother enrolled my brother and me in an after school program at the YWCA. At the YWCA, I experienced an environment filled with caring administrators and counselors. Essentially, the YWCA staff served as extended family members to my brother and me while we were in their care. Each of the staff members were aware of our family situation and made a concerted effort to comfort us. I remember one day my brother and I got into a heated fight after a basketball game and we were sent to the after school superintendent's office. Instead of scolding us for our bad behavior, she told us how much she loved us and wanted us to know that we could talk to her about any difficulties we were facing due to our home situation. Beyond our time at the YWCA, many of the staff members would also babysit us when my mother had to work or was out of town. During these times, they would reinforce to us the values our mother taught us about respect, caring for others, hard work, and doing our best academically. These acts of kindness were typical among the YWCA staff and created a sense of belonging among my brother and me during a critical time in our lives.

At the YWCA, my brother and I were also exposed to a wide range of culturally enriching activities such as swimming, karate, gymnastics, arts and crafts, and dance. We would also take field trips to different places such as the Natural Science Center, the zoo, museums, historical battleground sites, theme parks, and other recreational facilities. This exposure to different cultural activities enriched my childhood and facilitated my holistic development. Furthermore, these cultural experiences enhanced my educational performance as well because I was being exposed to different concepts that I would learn in my classes (e.g., lessons about human and animal development I saw at the Natural Science Center and the zoo would be discussed in my science classes). Also at the YWCA, my brother and I had the opportunity to interact with a diverse group of young people who attended different schools throughout Guilford County. The tremendous amount of social capital we acquired through this experience facilitated our positive educational experiences throughout our primary and secondary schooling. Our expansive social connections at both the schools we attended and other schools in the county enhanced our sense of belonging in the community. Similar to my early educational experiences, I was developing my interpersonal skills and cultural knowledge, which would later contribute to my academic success and positive social relationships.

Around the same time my parents got divorced, my mother was also teaching at Bennett College as an instructor. I remember her routinely taking my brother and me to campus. We would often sit in the corner of her office and play while she met with her students, graded papers, and worked on various tasks. One particularly fond memory of mine of this time was when I used to watch her type on her typewriter and later her computer. I would be mesmerized by the fact that she could type so fast without looking at the keys. This memory would come back to me when I took a keyboarding class during my ninth grade year in high school. I was committed to learning how to type because I wanted to be like my mother. Her role modeling socialized me to appreciate the ability to use a computer and develop strong writing skills.

During her time at Bennett, we were with her so regularly that we knew all of her colleagues and students by name and they knew us. She would affectionately refer to us as her "back pockets." Several days she would take us to her classes and we would to sit in the back corner quietly. I remember being captivated by mother's teaching style as she communicated to her students. In addition to being intrigued by the classroom setting, I was fascinated with the entire college environment. I used to love sitting in the auditoriums, library, and computer rooms while she taught. It was something about being in that environment that made me feel "smart."

I also remember several times when my mother's students would babysit my brother and me. During these babysitting sessions, they would take us to the school cafeteria, their dorms, and the gymnasium. We were able to get an up close and personal look into the lives of college students. We learned so much from being around them and more importantly we felt their love for us. These enriching experiences not only influenced my interest in attending college, but also instilled a sense of security and empowerment being around so many African-Americans on a college campus.

During my high school years, after my mother earned her Ph.D., she took a position as an Assistant Professor at the UNCG. I spent a significant amount of my time at school either in her office, at the main library, or one of the classrooms in her building. When we were hungry, she would take time out to walk us over to local hot dog and milkshake restaurant, which was located on the main part of campus. I remember enjoying those walks from her building, the School of Education building, to the restaurant because it made me feel like I was a college student. I remember sitting in her office while she met with students and worked on her research. I particularly remember looking at her extensive bookshelf with books on topics ranging from race to education to history to a host of other topics. I remember having a sense of pride knowing that my mother had read those books and it made me feel like I must be smart too since I was her son. The cultural capital I acquired by being on a college campus with my mother particularly her office had an immeasurable impact on my academic self-efficacy and motivation.

Quite honestly, her office was and continues to be one of the most inspiring aspects of my childhood. Seeing the books and papers in her office revealed to me how hard she worked to make our lives better. It was also an illustration of the power of education because I remember the days when I was younger before my parents got divorced and my mother was at home with us. Through her hard work, dedication, perseverance, and intellect she had earned her Ph.D. while raising two African American boys on her own. Today, she is an Associate Professor at one of the top institutions of higher education in the state of North Carolina with a collection of teaching excellence and service awards and widely recognized in the community and state as an exceptional educator.

When we were not in her office, we would sit in on her classes in the back and she would often tell stories about us to her students, which made us feel really special. It was as if she was acknowledging our presence in the room and validating our sense of belonging there along with her students. Similar to our experiences as younger children watching her at Bennett, our experiences at UNCG provided us with another opportunity to enhance our cultural capital. Even though, as an adolescent, a majority of the content was beyond my understanding, the mere fact that I was in an academic environment at an institution of higher education and watching my mother engage in teaching left an indelible impression on me. Seeing my mother teach these college students from diverse backgrounds about education, theory, policy, and best pedagogical practices signaled to me that I was capable of achieving high levels of success as well.

Moreover, my mother's role modeling allowed me to feel comfortable in academic spaces where I otherwise would not feel comfortable particularly as an African American male. More often than not, in my academic classes, I would be one of the few if not the only African American in the class and I would seldom have a teacher who shared the same racial and cultural background as me. As an ethnic minority, coupled with the lack of emphasis on cultural diversity in the curriculum, I began to think academic spaces and achievement for were reserved for Whites (similar to my initial thoughts back at Morehead). The primary reason I was able to overcome these challenges was due to the opportunities and resources (cultural and social capital) my mother instilled in me outside of the classroom throughout my childhood.

Another major factor of my childhood was our involvement in a local Black church. Ever since I can remember, my mother, brother, and me attended church together. When I was 12 years old, I was baptized at a Black church on the southeast side of Greensboro, North Carolina. We regularly attended Sunday School and were active in the Youth Group. In fact, during my high school years, my mother served as co-leader of our Sunday School class. As a result, our attendance and engagement in Sunday School was not an option. Although, I complained about getting up early and having to go to Sunday School, I would later learn to appreciate the foundational knowledge about the Bible and the Christian experience I acquired in these classes. Similarly, in Youth Group we participated in several culturally enriching activities such as community service and fields trips (e.g., museums, parks, theatres, etc.). These activities were beneficial in expanding my appreciation for different cultures as well as enhanced my knowledge about history, the arts, geography, politics, and a wide range of other topics. Essentially, this cultural capital made me a more well-rounded person and a better student.

Our involvement in this Black church also increased my social capital as I was able to interact with a group of African Americans from diverse backgrounds (e.g., socioeconomic, etc.). My socialization experiences at church involved learning about African American cultural values such as collective identity, perseverance, and educational attainment. Collective identity was evident every Sunday as well as other days of the week when members would come together to worship and/or perform various acts of stewardship. There was a feeling that we all had an obligation to one another to uplift our race and engage in acts of kindness towards one another. Perseverance was embodied in the fact that many of the adults in the congregation had lived through the Civil Rights era in the U.S. and frequently described how far we have come as a people. In addition, several members had testimonies of overcoming various hardships (e.g., cancer survivors, loss of loved ones, growing up in violent households, living with low financial resources, etc.), which served as an example of the strength of our spirit as Christians and as African Americans. Along the same lines, the pastor would also highlight in his sermons the important role of having a persevering spirit and thus this theme became synonymous with church membership.

Socially, I was able to establish meaningful friendships with other African Americans who shared similar ambitions and interests. Among my church friends we shared set of expectations. These expectations included excelling academically, being active in leadership and social organizations, performing community service, and planning to attend college. Since we all were involved in the same organizations it was easy to stay on track because we all held each other accountable. Overall, this social network fostered positive academic and personal habits for me and enabled me to maximize my potential.

A Product of My Environment—Involvement in Academic Enrichment Activities

On the weekends when I was in elementary school, my mother was a teacher in a college preparatory program for African American high school students called Saturday Academy. Every Saturday morning, from 9:00 am to 12:00 pm at NCA&TSU my mother would teach English and writing skills to a group of high school students. Her lessons would help prepare the students to take the Scholastic Aptitude Test (SAT) as well as to improve their performance in their high school English courses. Although, my brother and I were too young to participate in the classes my mother would occasionally have us sit in the classrooms while she taught. Other times, she would allow us to sit outside and play until the class was over. Nonetheless, our attendance to these Saturday Academy sessions exposed us to critical mass of African American teachers and students who served as positive role models.

During my middle school years, my mother provided us with opportunities to attend academic enrichment camps. For example, the summer after my sixth grade year, my brother and I attended a National Aeronautics and Space Administration (NASA) summer camp at Bennett College. This six-week summer camp program focused on enhancing knowledge and skills in the areas of science, math, and technology. An integral part of this camp involved staying on campus in the dormitories. This was a major benefit of this camp because it allowed us to experience the life of a college student, which increased our desire to attend college. In addition, all the instructors were African American and either taught at the post-secondary or secondary level. In the program, I was able to take advanced classes in areas such as physics, algebra, biology, and computer applications. Moreover, a majority of the participants at this camp were African Americans from different parts of the country. The preponderance of academically focused African American students and caring teachers created an optimistic academic environment for learning and excelling. The academic skills and networking relationships I developed at the NASA camp were immeasurable and helped prepare me for my future educational pursuits.

Another summer academic enrichment camp my mother enrolled me in was an Exercise and Sport Science Camp at the UNCG. Participants in this program included a diverse group of students from schools across Guilford County. Similar to my schooling experiences, this camp strengthened my interpersonal skills through collaborative projects. For example, in small groups were assigned different laboratory assignments where we would conduct experimental tests measuring participants' abilities to perform various physical tasks. We had to work together to set up the experiment, collect the data, analyze the findings, and write up a final report. These collaborative assignments were not only exceptional learning experiences, but also positive social interactions that helped me understand the various similarities I shared with students from different backgrounds. Even though, we were different racially and socioeconomically, we all possessed a shared level of intellectual curiosity and desire to have fun. Aside from my peers, professors from the Exercise and Sport Science department at UNCG taught all classes at the camp. The experience of working with nationally recognized scientists heightened the academic rigor of the camp and challenged all students to maximize their potential.

In addition to academic enrichment camps, my mother also transmitted cultural and social capital to me by having us participate in different social organizations. One such organization was the Greensboro Chapter of Jack & Jill of America, Inc. Jack & Jill is a national organization of mothers focused on providing quality social, cultural, and educational opportunities for children from infancy through high school. Jack & Jill is also a predominantly African American organization. As a member, I participated in regular community service activities and culturally enriching activities (e.g., attending theatre plays, museums, pre-professional business workshops, colleges and universities, etc.). During high school, I also attended annual teen conferences for the Mid-Atlantic Region, which involved a weekend conference of chapters from North Carolina, South Carolina, and Virginia. At this conference, we learned about parliamentary procedures, organizational management, and leadership. My junior and senior years I served as President of the Greensboro Chapter. This vital experience prepared me for future leadership opportunities and instilled in me a level of professionalism and social etiquette.

Along with Jack & Jill, my mother encouraged my brother and me to participate in other extra-curricular activities such as the Greensboro Youth Council (GYC) and ANYTOWN. GYC is a youth volunteer organization designed to develop leadership, governing skills, responsibility, and community activism among high school students in Guilford County. ANYTOWN is a weeklong residential summer camp sponsored by the National Conference for Community Justice (NCCJ) designed to bring a diverse group of students together to engage in meaningful conversations and activities on issues such as diversity, inclusivity, and social justice. Both GYC and ANYTOWN enhanced my cultural and social capital through collaborative activities (e.g., community service, critical conversations, team building tasks, problem solving, conflict resolution, etc.) with a diverse group of peers.

Throughout my childhood, my mother also provided me with academic support to ensure I excelled at the highest level possible in my classes. During the end of my elementary school years, it was apparent that I was experiencing difficulty with my reading and comprehension. As a result, my mother arranged for me to meet with a reading tutor after school twice a week. Although, I would cry and fuss about going to these sessions, I would later appreciate them because both my reading and comprehension increased significantly from these one-on-one sessions. Similarly, in high school my mother arranged for me to attend a tutoring center operated by a family of one of her former students. At these sessions, I would complete my homework assignments and receive extra practice and assistance with my reading comprehension and math skills.

During my junior and senior years in high school, when I was taking advanced math courses, my mother arranged for me to meet with a popular tutor that was highly recommended by several parents of students who were enrolled in similar courses. Working with this tutor not only helped me improve my performance in my classes, but also enhanced my preparation for the math portion of the SAT. Regarding the SAT preparation, my mother also enrolled me into a Kaplan SAT prep course offered at UNCG. Her social capital allowed her to find out about this program and register me before the enrollment was full. Although, I had taken the SAT several times before, she knew I needed to increase my verbal score in order to be considered for admission to my top college preferences, which were Wake Forest University and the University of North Carolina at Chapel Hill (UNC-CH). Another example of how she used her social capital to help me academically was when she arranged for me to meet with one of her colleagues who is a renowned mathematician who served as a consultant for the Educational Testing Services (ETS), which produces the questions for the SAT. My mother's social capital provided her with access to information about the aforementioned academic support services, which in turn greatly influenced my academic achievement in high school.

Throughout my childhood, my mother also enrolled my brother and me in various programs offered by the local Young Men's Christian Association (YMCA). Our participation in these programs afforded us a wide range of experiences that helped us develop holistically. For example, my brother and I participated in several YMCA sports from kindergarten through sixth grade (in seventh grade we started playing on our school-sponsored teams). We participated in baseball, basketball, and soccer. We also had the opportunity to attend outdoor summer camps where we received lessons on horseback riding, camping, and archery. The cultural and social capital we acquired through these camps facilitated the development of our interpersonal, physical, critical thinking, and leadership skills.

Conclusion

In conclusion, all of my personal and professional success is a reproduction of the cultural and social capital transmitted to me by my mother. This capital was transmitted to me through my early educational experiences, involvement in community organizations, and participation in academic enrichment programs. My exposure to different educational contexts such as college campuses as a child increased my interest in education and comfort level in academic spaces. My involvement in African American organizations such as our church and Jack & Jill, Inc. created a sense of cultural empowerment.

Moreover, my participation in educationally and socially enriching activities with peers from diverse backgrounds enhanced my social network, interpersonal communication, and leadership skills (e.g., YWCA, YMCA, NASA summer camp, etc.). Collectively, these experiences helped me become the man I am today. Educationally, I earned two bachelor's degrees from UNC-CH, a master's degree from UNC-CH, and a doctoral degree from the University of Georgia (UGA). Currently, I am an Assistant Professor at the University of Connecticut (UConn) in the Department of Educational Leadership. My mother's transmission of cultural and social capital serves as a blueprint for how to facilitate positive developmental outcomes for African American children growing in the 21st century. For her love, support, and guidance I am eternally grateful.

As a mother, I can honestly say that I do not know of any other mother in her "right mind" who does not want more for her children than she has for herself. I follow suit. While I fully attest that "life for me has been no crystal stair" given my biology in time as well as circumstances that have, in part, defined my lived experiences, my responses to those experiences, chiefly supported through family, schooling, church, and community, guided me in parenting my sons. My transmission of cultural and social capital to both my sons and especially to Joey was quite intentional. It is a gift I hope to keep on giving, not only to him and Adam, but also to others whom I "mother" through various roles of teaching, scholarship, and service. For helping others succeed is an extension of my love for my sons and my desire to uplift the race (Woodson, 1990). What better capital to socially reproduce? What better capital to transmit than from "Mother to Son!"

Work Cited

Bell, D. A. (1992). *Faces at the bottom of the well.* New York, NY: Basic Books.

Bourdieu, P. (1973). Cultural reproduction and social reproduction. In R. Brown (Ed.), *Knowledge, education, and cultural change* (pp. 71–112). London: Tavistock.

Bourdieu, P. (1986). The forms of capital. In J. G. Richardson (Ed.), *Handbook of theory and research for the sociology of education* (pp. 241–258). New York, NY: Greenwood Press.

Boykin, A. W. (1986). The triple quandary and the schooling of Afro-American children. In U. Neisser (Ed.), *The school achievement of minority children: New perspectives* (pp. 57–92). Hillsdale, NJ: Erlbaum.

Coleman, J. S. (1988). Social capital and the creation of human capital. *The American Journal of Sociology, 94*, 95–120.

ETS. (2011). A strong start: Positioning young Black boys for educa-tional success a statistical profile. In E. T. Service (Ed.), *ETS's addressing achievement gaps symposium* (pp. 1–5). Washington, DC: Educational Testing Service.

Fleming, J. (1984). *Blacks in college.* San Francisco, CA: Jossey-Bass Publishers.

Fordham, S., & Ogbu, J. U. (1986). Black students' school success: Coping with the "burden of 'acting white'." *The Urban Review, 18*, 176–206.

Hale, J. E. (1994). *Unbank the fire: Visions for the education of African-American children.* Baltimore, MD: John Hopkins University Press.

Ladson-Billings, G. (1994). *The dreamkeepers.* San Francisco, CA: Jossey-Bass.

Patton, M. Q. (2002). *Qualitative research and evaluation methods* (3rd ed.). Thousand Oaks, CA: Sage Publications.

Richardson, L. (2000). Writing: A method of inquiry. In N. Denzin & Y. Lincoln (Eds.), *Handbook of Qualitative Research* (2nd ed., pp. 923–929). Thousand Oaks, CA: Sage.

Sue, D. W., Capodilupo, C. M., Torino, G. C., Bucceri, J. M., Holder, A., Nadal, K. L., & Esquilin, M. (2007). Racial microaggressions in everyday life: implications for clinical practice. American psychologist, 62(4), 271.

West, C. (1993). *Race matters.* Boston, MA: Beacon Press.

Woodson, C. G. (1990). *The mis-education of the Negro.* Trenton, NJ: Africa World Press. (Original work published in 1933)

CHAPTER 24

Hulking Out

White Males' Response to Bullying, Humiliation, Rejection, Isolation and Perceived Injustice in an Academic Setting

Steven Randolph Cureton

Introduction

Lethal vigilante violence has an active pulse in America. More specifically, in those instances where young white males are confronted by social, cultural, and academic situations that challenge their sense of value, some may define these as severe injustices, and obstacles to their rite of passage to manhood. Unfortunately, we are witnessing adolescent, high school, and college aged white males' inability to effectively cope with feeling vulnerable, unaccepted, bullied and criticized. The rational for rampage killings is that it represents justice for males who feel tormented by their peers. Moreover, the school yards, and campuses where rampage shootings are carried out appear to make sense because masculine affirmations must take place in the arena where the male felt emasculated. Offering mental illness as significantly related to rampage shooters is a comfort impulse because it seems that such lethal violence was cold blooded. However, the evidence should force academic administrators, health professionals, and law enforcement agents to consider that rampage killings represent justifiable targeted bloodletting splurges carried out by trouble-minded males operating in a kill-self mode.

The Beast: Lethal Violence

Somewhere lurking is a beast, with a pulse quickened by anger over perceived instances of humiliation and injustice. This beast seeks retribution, and is attentive to the moment when people shall hear his roar, feel his might, and absorb his violence. It's a hulking rage that is triggered by an overwhelming sense of shame, and torment that must be acted upon. People who deserve to live will die, and the wounded will be scarred for life. The aftermath is shaken faith, deep sorrow and the search for answers to understand a lethal rampage that came from an unlikely person.

The narrative is becoming all too familiar. The most unusual offenders used lethal violence against unsuspecting victims in unlikely spaces and places. Unfortunately, terrible but justified fears have forced a hasty gravitation towards proclaiming mental illness, which is now the scapegoat for atypical murder. From 1979 to 2014, three hundred and twelve students and faculty members were killed and at least another four hundred and seventy two were wounded.

Elementary, high schools, and college campuses have unfortunately become stages for rampage shootings. The horror of Columbine High school produced fifteen deaths in 1999, which was eclipsed by the tragedy of thirty two deaths on Virginia Tech's campus in 2007, and then there was the unspeakable nefarious event where twenty children were killed in cold blood at Sandy Hook elementary in 2012. Parents, loved ones, and friends were left with a depth of sorrow that even gospel seemingly is reduced to cliché statements. In our pursuit of explanations, too many legal agents, social science researchers, and mental health professionals have blamed mental illness as the most significant contributor to these mass murders. However, the social fact is that mental illness does not stand alone as the reason for targeted violence or rampage shootings (Cornish & Clarke, 1986; Fantz et al., 2014; Fessenden, 2000; Hempel, Meloy, & Richards, 1999; Klein, 2012).

Given males pursue acceptance and respectable status amongst peers, murder becomes an attractive alternative when functional interaction and communication to gain acceptance and recognition has failed. Murderous outcomes could be related to extreme emotional deficits associated with being confronted with circumstances that humiliate, and challenge masculinity, devalue human dignity, negate social status, assassinate character, and/or create uncomfortable stress (Fox, Levin, & Quinet, 2005; Gilligan, 1997; Katz, 1988). In other words, when males find themselves marginalized by social institutions, peer groups and/or intimate personal groups with no seemingly acceptable way to become meaningful participants, a few males anoint themselves as superior beings, and then gravitate to murder as a cold blooded method of imposing crystal clear messages of "I matter and you don't."

The crux of the matter is that shooting sprees on school grounds are disconcerting because white males are more likely (than their black male peers) to employ their version of vigilante justice to counter various forms of peer level social dismissal (Kimmel, 2008; Kimmel & Mahler, 2003; McGee & Debernardo, 1999; Schwyzer, 2012; Rocque, 2012).Vigilante justice has gained relative applause in instances where there is a collective understanding that there is a deserving population but has alternatively created moral panic in instances where such behavior has been labeled as killing in cold blood (Estes, 2005; Gilligan, 1997; Muschert, 2007). The actions of rampage shooters, fundamentally implies underlying psychological conflicts that manifest as rage; therefore, it's an easy next step to offer mental illness as significantly related to mass murder. However, what if it turns out that rampage shooters rationally deliberate murder, evaluate strategies to sacrifice symbols of their humiliation, and are ultimately satisfied with the finality of life that results from lethal predation? This chapter discusses rampage shootings on school grounds as a product of reasoning criminals who have defaulted to a transformative kill self-mode of operation.

Core Principles of Social Acceptance, Compensatory Reaction and Murder

Family dynamics and family processes are critically important in socializing individuals. The nuances of culture, normative expectations, social development, perceptions, self-esteem and self-efficacy, impact the interpersonal value systems we use to relate to others. As individuals mature, they emerge from the bosom of the family with social, economic, cultural, spiritual, and physical appearance characteristics that will be confronted by diverse institutions, and social networks that present discretionary social value assessments and treatment outcomes relative to confirmation, acceptance, validation, marginalization, isolation and victimization (i.e. deviant, criminal and violent).

When males experience adverse social value assessments and humiliation, they may perceive these experiences as unfair, and be compelled to act on what has now become a social imbalance impeding their happiness and/or comfort levels. Depending on the relentless nature of value assessments and treatment, boys can respond by investing in conventional socially approved methods to achieve relative integration and assimilation, be satisfied with the nuances of their status in the institutional and social network hierarchies, or they can wage a troublesome masculine campaign (actions focused on toughness, self-reliance and taking control of situations using aggressive tactics) to force validation, acceptance and even rejection out of fear (Chatterton, 2010; Cohen, 1955; Harro, 2000; McCall, 1994; Oliver, 1989; Rothenberg, 2002; Wallace, 2007).

As soon as boys are presented with opportunities to independently socialize with peers and as soon as boys become enrolled in school, they have to consistently compete for acceptance from peer groups, and academically perform at a sustainable level worthy of grade promotion. For the most part, boys campaign for respect amongst peer groups, and feel a sense of entitled acceptance and academic praise from educational authority figures and teachers by virtue of just being present at school. Make no mistake about it boys mature well into adulthood with a competitive energy and a sense of deservedness. In some cases where campaigns for respect are suppressed and school acceptance is tempered by warranted criticisms and discipline, males (regardless of age) may be inclined to respond with troublesome behaviors. Agnew's General Strain Theory, Gilligan's Saving Face Perspective and the Diathesis Stress Model provide generic assumptions that seem logical enough to explain the use of violence to counter being disrespected by peers, and/or challenged by school authority figures and teachers (Agnew, 2006; Gilligan, 1997; Hooley & Gotlib, 2000).

According to Agnew (2006), the teenage lifestyle carries with it apprehension, angst, uncertainty, frustration, insecurity, and even concern with respect to navigating through social circumstances related to family dynamics, family processes, parent-child relationships, peer group associations, opposite sex relationships, and academic progress. Males (i.e. young boys, adolescent, teenage, young adult, and adult) enthusiastically pursue satisfactory relationships, and acceptable academic performance; however, to the degree that these males experience negative relationships with parents and/or encounter awkward moments with peers, attractive girls, school authority figures, and teachers because of personal attributes and characteristics, they become stressed. The behavioral manifestation will depend on psychodynamic conflicts, personality, definitions of the situation (as humiliating), and problem solving. The generic assumption here is that family, peer group, heterosexual relationships, and academic circumstances can become traumatic events for males who become angry, frustrated, depressed, and ultimately motivated to engage in deviant, criminal and violent behaviors, particularly when there is no evidence of positive counteracting forces to prevent such behavioral outcomes (Agnew, 2006). If behaviors go un-checked, fail to alleviate grief; and/or does not provide some level of functional balance, then actions can elevate to a mass killing in a public arena that is easily accessible, and provides the largest number of defenseless, unsuspecting, symbolic targets.

Gilligan (1997) contends that routine interactions amongst similarly circumstanced individuals and competing peer groups, contribute to the construction of meaningful social networks, sub-culturally specific normative expectations, and social hierarchies where public persona is a form of social currency that can increase and decrease in value.

Instances where males have experienced functional inclusion, it's likely that they will be conformists or act in accordance to group expectations. Alternatively, when males have encountered circumstances that cause his peers to socially ridicule, scorn, criticize, become socially distant, and devalue his social capital to the point where he is rebuffed and/or has become an outcast, then there is a distinct possibility that he will entertain the idea of becoming violent to offset any perceived loss of peer group approval.

Let me begin with the common empirical observation that people feel incomparably more alarmed by a threat to the psyche or the soul or the self than they are by a threat to the body. The death of the self is of far greater concern than the death of the body … People will sacrifice their bodies if they perceive it as the only way to avoid losing their souls, losing their minds, or losing face … In addition, a person only develops a stable, integrated, and differentiated sense of selfhood or identity through the process of interacting with other humans in the community, or culture (Gilligan, 1997:96). … *I have yet to see a serious act of violence that was not provoked by the experience of feeling shamed and humiliated, disrespected and ridiculed and that did not represent the attempt to prevent or undo this loss of face, no matter how severe the punishment …*

The purpose of violence is to diminish the intensity of shame and replace it as far as possible with its opposite, pride, thus preventing the individual from being overwhelmed by the feeling of shame. Violence toward others, such as homicide, is an attempt to replace shame with pride (Gilligan, 1997, pp. 110–111).

These quotes seem to suggest that fatal violence is a defense mechanism against feeling ashamed and/or paranoia about perceptions that peers no longer respect the social legitimacy of a person. Murder seems to be an extreme and unnecessary action; however it is the strongest protest against any agent attempting to bring public shame to the offender. The generic assumption here is that the human spirit thrives under conditions that promote positive social capital (a positive self-image). Hence, when males perceive that their peers have lost respect for them by consistently engaging in behaviors that render shame, and/or whenever males perceive that school officials, and teachers are creating undue hardships then some may turn to murder to regain a sense of superiority (Gilligan, 1997). The targeted areas for murder are most likely public places, and spaces where the murderous desire will garner the most attention.

It logically follows that shooting rampages are ritualistic sacrifices of people that are reduced to offensive objects that have encroached upon the dignified humanity of an offender.

Hooley and Gotlib (2000) offer a succinct examination of the Diathesis Stress Model. The Diathesis Stress Model fundamentally suggests that behavioral outcomes reflect vulnerabilities to specific disorders, and sensitivities to life course events and situational circumstances. In other words, people can be predisposed to mental disorders by virtue of biological factors that are present or developed soon after birth. Mental health can be negatively impacted by stressful events and/or social circumstances that become traumatic enough to effect diminished capacity because people are differently susceptible to environmental conditions, and act based on whether their experiences negatively affect functional thinking, ability to suppress subconscious conflicts and self-regulation. The generic assumption relative to rampage shooters is that males have certain impulses (i.e. selfish pursuits with no regard for reality) that are normally held in check by internal constraints; however, when confronted by traumatic events (e.g. home life, peer group or school experiences that weaken psychological equilibrium), behaviors may no longer yield to morality because subconscious conflicts erupt. Murdering those perceived to be the source of stress seems like a functional alternative because at least the intensity of the trauma is reduced (Hooley & Gotlib, 2000).

Agnew's General Strain Theory, Gilligan's Saving Face Perspective and the Diathesis Stress Model have in common the assumptions that males are confronted, challenged, and exist in social settings that validate, accept, allow for positive identification or can negate respect, suppress identities, challenge entitlements, and cause people to feel insignificant, tormented, and ashamed.

If males experience approval they move throughout life in a mostly conventional way; however if they experience distressing, and traumatic circumstances in the absence of counteracting forces then their behavior may drift towards depravity. Even though, the focus of this chapter has been on males, it should be noted that these very same principles can apply to females who when faced with similar conditions engage in victimless crimes or targeted deviant, criminal, and violent acts, including fatal violence (Agnew, 2006; Gilligan, 1997; Hooley & Gotlib, 2000).

Nature and Extent of Targeted Violence, Mass Murder and Rampage Shootings

Lethal events that encroach upon the serenity of educational institutions underscore the reality that academic settings are not immune to violence. Ultimately, gun violence resulting in death and casualties depends on individuals' motivations, rationalizations, coping strategies, access to firearms, and calculated opportunities (factoring in the degree to which people, and places are prepared to defend against an attack).The circumstances surrounding school shootings appear to be related to the culture of honor, which emphasizes positive social capital related to masculinity (i.e. perceived rights and entitlements to personhood, dignity, respect, praise, acceptance, and social status), pressure moments related to the pursuit of a meaningful existence with family, friends and peer groups in social settings and mental health challenges (i.e. conditions that interfere with one's ability to effectively rationalize and engage in socially acceptable behaviors) (Agnew, 2006; Gilligan, 1997; Hooley & Gotlib, 2000; Meloy, Hempel, Mohandie, Shiva, & Gray, 2001).

The data from 1979 to 2014 reveal 201 targeted (e.g. specific person defined as the target), rampage (e.g. lethal violence resulting in at least 1 killing and several casualties), and mass murder (e.g. student used firearm resulting in 3 or more murders with several casualties) shooting events with student assailants where 312 were killed and over 472 were wounded (Fantz et al., 2014; Klein, 2012; McGee & Debernardo, 1999; Muschert, 2007; Rocque, 2012). There were an additional 16 campus shootings resulting in several more murders and casualties perpetrated by individuals who were not students. The context for these shooting events was problematic relationships (domestic abuse and jealousy), relationship termination, stalking, and post relationship violence. In these instances shooters were faced with circumstances that proved demeaning to their sense of entitlement to a partner they were currently involved with or the relationship had ended.

Out of the 217 school shootings, 28 happened on college campuses, involving 21 undergraduate and 6 graduate students, and 1 college professor (between 1979 and 2014). In every case, it appears that students and a professor were disgruntled about negative evaluations concerning their academic performance and progress. Undergrad students facing the pressure from parents to perform well in school combined with less than ideal grades, relationship problems, pressures related to sexual orientation, and roommate issues more than likely experienced enough frustration, and stress over their inability to be successful, which led to overwhelming strain. Graduate students responded with lethal violence in retaliation for perceived injustices related to professors negatively evaluating their classroom performance, writing and research ability. Additionally, graduate students generally believed that they were far more capable than their grades reflected, and responded with violence in those instances where they were dismissed from the program.

In the single case involving a female professor at the University of Alabama, 3 professors were murdered, and 3 others were wounded during a faculty meeting. It was determined that her motive was denial of promotion and tenure. Obviously the professor felt academically disrespected, entitled to tenure, and perceived that those who did not support her promotion to tenure created an unjust hardship (Fantz et al., 2014; Klein, 2012).

When compared to homicides involving firearms in neighborhoods, public places and work settings, school yard and campus shootings are a rare occurrence. Nevertheless, the dramatic nature, media coverage, and public concern manufactures a moral panic. Targeted school violence weakens collective faith in social regulation and control (Katz, 1988; Muschert, 2007). There were 8 targeted school shootings with at least 1 dead, several wounded and a suicide (7 of which were self-inflicted and 1 was suicide by cop). Additionally, there were 9 instances where a student went on a shooting rampage resulting in mass murder (3 or more killed), with casualties and a suicide (all self-inflicted) (Klein, 2012). In these cases students experienced problematic socializing happenstances where they were deemed outcasts and thus became desperately isolated, and perhaps convinced that their reputation was beyond repair in a manner that would be acceptable to those peer groups they felt were critical to their happiness (Andriolo, 1998; Kalish & Kimmel, 2010; Preti, 2006).

High school shootings (100 cases) were more common than elementary (17 cases), middle school (24 cases) and college campus (16 cases) between 1979 and 2011 (Klein, 2012). Males more than females, overwhelmingly (95%) participated in school shootings.

The data indicate that perceived challenges to masculinity and relationship troubles (i.e. arguments, abuse, break-ups, and jealousy) were identified as possible antecedents to school shootings 70% of the time and grievances with school authority figures were identified as possible causes to school shootings 30% of the time. Challenges to masculinity came in the form of verbal and physical bullying, fighting, stealing, destroying personal property, attempts at character assassination by gossiping and taunting about clique affiliations, sexual orientation, and the over-all perception that an enemy has been created because of some level of perceived cruelty. Relationship troubles included arguments, abuse, break-ups, jealousy, stalking, and the overall perception that girls are not supposed to reject boys. Grievances with teachers included disagreement over graded assignments, and the perception that a teacher had embarrassed a student in front of his peers. Additionally, school shooters seemed to have adverse reactions to instances where they felt judgments at their school hearings were biased, and had problems with accepting or adjusting to disciplinary actions related to in-school suspension or suspension from school grounds altogether (Kimmel, 2008; Kimmel & Mahler, 2003; Larkin, 2007; Leary, Kowalski, Smith, & Phillips, 2003; Newman, Fox, Roth, Mehta, & Harding, 2004; Vossekuil, Fein, Reddy, Borum, & Modzeski, 2002).

Agnew's General Strain Theory and Gilligan's Saving Face Perspective similarly suggest that social network dynamics, processes and circumstances operate to impact individuals in ways that affect behavioral outcomes. Agnew's General Strain Theory implies that individuals may be inclined to sever ties from conventionalism and engage in drastic behaviors when they experience events that threaten their dignity (Agnew, 2006). Gilligan's Saving Face Perspective implies that seeking masculine identities involve investing in a culture of honor that emphasizes being in control of structural, and situational circumstances in a manner befitting of respect (Gilligan, 1997).

A logical assumption derived from General Strain Theory and the Saving Face Perspective would be that males are likely to act out when confronted by events that cause his peers to devalue his social capital to the point where he is disrespected, rejected, or made fun of in public. The data shows that school shooters were males who experienced direct assaults to their manhood (i.e. masculinity, relationship troubles, and problems with school authority figures); hence, it's logical to conclude that rampage shootings have been used as a mechanism to reclaim some measure of respect, overcome embarrassment, and to get back at specific persons or people who represent a symbol of his humiliation (Agnew, 2005, 2006; Felson, Allen, South, & McNulty, 1994; Gilligan, 1997).

Race and Killing Moods

Living in a violent society with access to lethal weapons provides ideas and resources to carry out fatal revenge on designated targets. This country has been witnessing males turn to violence as a means to problem solve in cases where they have not been accepted, are experiencing challenges to their dignity, and/or are finding themselves having to exist outside of important peer groups. In other words, as males seek to negotiate their manhood within their respective social arenas, they are relatively prepared to handle social challenges, competition, and obstacles preventing a comfortable transition to achieving respectable social status. The seemingly incomprehensible acts of targeted violence, and rampage shootings resulting in casualties and mass murder (on primary and secondary school grounds, and on college campuses across the country) has generated public concern, and unsettling fear as these terrorists-like events are being largely committed by suburban white males.

The most notable of rampage killings resulting in mass murder and suicide were Columbine in 1999 (two White male shooters), Virginia Tech in 2007 (an Asian male shooter), Sandy Hook in 2012 (White male shooter), and Isla Vista in 2014 (assailant self-identified as Euro-Asian). In 2008, a young African-American woman (not a student) went on a rampage killing 3 in Baton Rouge Louisiana. A roll call of rampage shootings on school grounds from 1996 through 2008 suggest that white males (17) were triggermen in school shootings in Moses Lake Washington, Bethel Alaska, Pearl Mississippi, West Paducah Kentucky, Stamps Arkansas, Jonesboro Arkansas, Edinboro Pennsylvania, Springfield Oregon, Littleton Colorado, Conyers Georgia, Fort Gibson Oklahoma, Santee California, New York New York, Red Lion Pennsylvania, Cold Spring Minnesota, Jacksboro Tennessee, and Cleveland Ohio. A school shooting in Dover Delaware was committed by a black male (Rocque, 2012). Other studies examining rampage shootings have concluded that there is a tendency for white males more than black males or white and black females to engage in school shootings (Kimmel, 2008; Kimmel & Mahler, 2003; McGee & DeBernardo, 1999). It's safe to suggest that rampage shootings are more likely to occur in low crime suburban and rural areas, which may speak to why shootings are more likely to be carried out by white males. However, when dealing with targeted acts of violence on school grounds, such school shootings where there is a specific grievance between minority combatants are more likely to be carried out on inner city school yards (Casella, 2001; McGee & DeBernardo, 1999; Newman et al., 2004). In spite of having a good deal of data for why school shootings occur, there is a hesitancy to offer a one size fits all profile for rampage shooters. Social science theories can only offer educated guesses regarding the potential for a person to engage in a school shooting.

Biological, psychological, and sociological theories have cast a wide net by offering pre-dispositional risk factors (e.g. mental health issues, psychodynamic conflicts and personality traits) and social context variables (e.g. private home troubles, peer group interaction, conflict issues, and contempt and condemnation for school officials) (Fast, 2008; Langam, 2009; Larkin, 2007; Leary et al., 2003; Vossekuil et al., 2002). Similarly biological, psychological, and sociological explanations have been used to indirectly explain racial differences in school shootings (Rocque, 2012). Upon closer inspection, answers to racial variation in shooting perpetrators, perhaps can be gleaned from differential socialization between white and black males. Generally speaking, in a white patriarchal society, white males may benefit from white privilege (an ascribed social credit that reinforces positive self-esteem, acceptance, and access to life chances that promote life course success). White privilege promotes intra-racial confidence because socially approved institutions, and social structures appear to be geared towards advancement. More specifically, white privilege is favored racial inclusion, and assumes that white males have an inherent ability to carve out an acceptable, and reasonably respectable identity as well as achieve social, academic, financial, and employment success. Essentially, white privilege is a cultural context that bolsters notions of entitlement because of racial supremacy, integrity, intellectualism and deservedness (Rothenberg, 2002). Institutional challenges to assumed intellectualism, and/or peer group rebuffing creates a disjunction between the benefits of white privilege and reality of circumstance. Hence, when white privilege is negated this could lead to troublesome behavioral outcomes particularly in instances where white males are rejected, criticized, marginalized, and/or made to feel insecure, uncertain, ashamed and indignant.

White males attempting to remedy their marginalized status turn their personal problems of adjustment to a community problem in those instances where they chose to target symbols (schools, school officials, and peer groups) of their social down fall. Parents can become targets too, particularly when white males feel their parents have been inept in preparing them for the realities of life. In other words, it logically follows that when white males experience negative experiences that counter the advantages of white privilege, they may perceive these experiences as an unjust campaign that undermines their humanity. Essentially, stressed, strained, traumatized, and feeling awkward with no directives on how to remedy their situation, may lead some white males to identify with rampage shooters because they view them as warriors, avengers or heroes (Fox et al., 2005; Langam, 2009; McGee and DeBernardo, 1999; Sullivan & Guerett, 2003).

African-Americans' legacy in this country includes, systematic denial of citizenship rights, inequitable justice as well as psychological warfare on the humanity of blackness (Cleaver, 1996; Cureton, 2011; Dyson, 1996; Haley, 1964; Magida, 1996). Moreover, in a white patriarchal dominant society black males have encountered black caste codes (an ascribed condition focused on blacks' criminality), which fosters suspicion, moral panic, threat, fear, and the type of opportunity channeling that negatively impacts self-esteem, and restricts life chances leading to less than ideal social, academic, employment, cultural, economic and legal sanction outcomes (Alexander, 2010; West, 2001; Wilson, 1987, 2009).

Given there are varying degrees of racial acceptance, tolerance, challenge, rebuffing, suppression, oppression, discrimination and alienation, expressions of black masculinity will differ from expressions of white masculinity (Anderson, 1999; Cureton, 2011; Cureton & Wilson, 2012; Estes, 2005; Williams, 2004; Wilson, 1987, 1996). African-American families (middle, working and lower class) have to socialize their children in a manner that equips them with the necessary tools to successfully navigate the demands of conventional society and mainstream institutions as well as the normative expectations attached to intra-racial subcultures operating in their neighborhoods and social networks (Anderson, 1990, 1999; Chatterton, 2010; McCall, 1994). Dysfunctional family dynamics and family process circumstances create family pressure, and failure to address the stresses related to negotiating black personhood. Whenever the family falls short on providing acceptable ways to adjust to institutional and social network challenges, black males will seek out alternative ways to defend themselves. Specifically, black males contend with estimations of their criminality from educational institutions, which take the form of negative labeling, unwarranted attention, value assessments, and strict disciplinary actions in the classroom, in school suspensions or out of school suspensions. In an effort to counter their displeasure with these circumstances, black males respond by adopting a nonchalant attitude, uncaring disposition, and perhaps a gravitation away from the perceived benefits of academic success. Consequently, black males rebel against schools and invest in subcultures that provide avenues for success that devalue the merits of education (Cohen, 1955; Katz, 1988; Majors, 1993; Nirvi & Maxwell, 2012; Wilson, 2009).

Another immediate concern for black males is having to confront immediate challenges to their respectability (earned social status within peer groups), and having to vigorously proclaim and defend masculine status. Associating, affiliating, and identifying with deviant, criminal and/or violent subcultures that emphasize aggressive manhood provides normative expectations that are consistent with street codes, street elitism and gangsterism. Blacks males are expected to adopt a set of rules that promote violence as a way to problem solve or settle grievances with perceived combatants (Anderson, 1990, 1999; Cureton, 2002, 2008, 2010, 2011; Cureton & Wilson, 2012; Katz, 1988; Oliver, 1989; Wallace, 2007). To the degree that black males invest in subcultures that focus on earning social status away from the confines of school, and negotiating a cool pose to combat school rejection, they are less likely to engage in rampage shootings on school grounds compared to white males who identify with classroom avengers. Additionally, black males who subscribe to street codes or gangsterism may engage in targeted violence against clearly defined persons more so than revenge violence against anonymous people, who represent a symbol of personal dissatisfaction. (Canetto, 1997; Majors, 1993; McGee & DeBernardo, 1999).

The take away from this racial examination of responses to school experiences and peer interaction is that both white and black males condemn school officials for actions taken against them, and both white and black males respond to peer group challenges. However, the differences in racial responses appear to be related to contextual socialization, white privilege for white males, and black caste codes for black males. White privilege indirectly creates a chasm of undefined ways to counter rejection, and black caste codes indirectly creates a defined set of subcultural meanings to counter rejection.

It could be argued that differences in socialization lead to differences in lethal violence on school grounds. It would prove beneficial for school officials to become culturally aware of differences in socialization because the psychological definitions that take root in white and black boys' lives could very well represent the difference between rampage shootings, and targeted violence. It is not safe to assume that by the time white males reach college they have successfully dealt with the pitfalls of white privilege, and that black males have overcome the adverse effects of black caste codes. It's also not the case that institutions of higher learning are exempt from labeling, judging, rejecting, challenging, marginalizing, and disciplining in objectionable ways. Therefore, institutions of higher learning have to answer the call to create a thoroughly comprehensive inter-racial environment with tangible evidence of diversity as well as gender sensitive (male and female) instruction, guidance, and counseling. Colleges and universities can either embrace an improved effort to address the nuanced needs of its male population or brace for the impact of mass lethal violence on their campuses.

Note on Mental Illness

The cold blooded senseless nature of lethal violence aimed arbitrarily at symbols resulting in rampage shootings, mass murder, and suicide shocks the collective conscience, creates moral panic, and fear that there is little control over motivated offenders who intend to inflict wholesale devastation. A-typical killings in public places often force public figures to pursue immediate answers, without the full set of social facts concerning the event. A significant amount of energy is dedicated towards aligning rampage shootings resulting in mass murder, and suicide with mental illness.

An examination of research reveals that 50–67% of targeted lethal violence, and rampage shootings resulting in mass murder and suicide have been attributed to a mental health component inclusive of probable psychosis, adjustment disorders, mood disorders, delusional disorders, depression, schizophrenia, mental health trauma (resulting from disruptive events) and diagnosed diminished capacity conditions requiring professional counseling, prescription medication and/or mental health facility treatment. However, when identifying a history of diagnosed mental health pathologies and/or disease that requires professional attention as a precursor to rampage shootings, the number of instances decrease from as high as 67% to somewhere between 11% and 15% (Dikel, 2012; Hooley & Gotlib, 2000; Rocque, 2012).

In most cases, there is much speculation about a rampage event, after the fact whereby a host of professional and legal agents, along with politicians, and peer group associates chime in offering ad hoc explanations as to why the perpetrator used lethal violence as a means to an end. It's far too easy to review rampage shootings as the result of psychosis, diminished capacity, loss of contact with reality, impaired insight, and/or hallucinations of a better existence because these thoughts in and of themselves are not necessarily deviant but become elevated as illogical musings when they are acted upon in non-conventional ways. The moral panic becomes somewhat calmed when the public can be convinced that mental illness is the stand alone culprit in rampage shootings (Fessenden, 2000; Hempel et al., 1999; Langman, 2009). Explaining rampage shootings as the result of individuals breaking from reality, severing emotional connections, and suffering from an emotional breakdown, certainly restores some degree of comfort as the public may be inclined to think that controlling, regulating, and treating mental disorders prevents cold blooded senseless murder.

The social scientific method of evaluation should include an examination of the relationship between prior mental health issues and rampage shootings. Additionally, there is much to be gained from examining the impact of adverse social factors, events, and circumstances on lethal predation in public places and spaces. In order to effectively address the problems that males are experiencing, it is necessary to examine the probability that rampage shooters rationally explored the realities of their actions, and became comfortably resigned to the fact that imposing the death penalty on people, and causing others to suffer is justly warranted (Gilligan, 1997; Katz, 1988). How scary would it be if it turns out that rampage shooters are less likely to be suffering from mental health issues, and are more likely to be reasoning criminals? It's a probable fact that rampage shooter sacrifice life in order to gain re-entry into peer conversations that had been exclusionary, or to cure an imbalance brought on by perceived injustices, unfair criticisms, rejection and denial. Rampage shooters in similar fashion to conventional citizens may not be suffering from anything other than wanting to matter; however, the major difference is using murder (after some degree of processing social facts, strategic analysis, and opportunity assessment) as some form of social currency. If the goal is to increase academic setting safety, then there are implications that should be acted upon when rampage shooters are understood as suffering from mental health issues or determined to be deliberate thinkers who rationally process information, and decide to intentionally kill in mass (Cornish & Clarke, 1986; Gilligan, 1997; Katz, 1988; Tuck & David, 1986).

Jack Katz's Theory of Righteous Slaughter

Jack Katz's theory of Righteous Slaughter, offers a reasonable analysis of a typical homicide because the theory embodies core questions (e.g. what are the killer's motivations, relative to the victim, how will his actions solve the problem, and what significant social facts make the scene an appropriate place to carry out the crime?) that speak to rampage shootings carried out on school property. Just as Gilligan (1997) posits that violence results from an individual attempting to regain respectful consideration in the eyes of his intimate social circle after suffering some measure of disgrace; Katz (1988) argues that individuals will use murder to sacrifice individuals perceived to have infringed upon their rights to exist free from ridicule, slander, and/or challenge to personhood. Essentially, Gilligan (1997) and Katz (1988), seem in agreement that murder is a reasonable outcome to seize respect from people perceived as deeply offensive in a humiliating manner.

Jack Katz (1988) argues that a righteous slaughter (murder) serves the purpose of protecting socially acceptable statuses. Katz contends that social groups believe that every person is entitled to socially approved goods (e.g. manhood, womanhood, respect, love, and family). In the event that any one of these are threatened, ridiculed, or harmed by another person, the response would be an emotional reaction that runs the risk of being lethal, especially if humiliation is involved. According to Katz, when a person is humiliated (feels the burden of a character assassination), he/she may free fall into rage (an overwhelming emotional imbalance where one is propelled by blinding anger), which then leads to engaging in chaotic behavior (conduct that falls outside the boundaries of conventionalism) resulting in sacrificial violence (the source of humiliation is eliminated) (Katz, 1988).

Recall that the ingredients for high school, and college campus shootings involve the contextual realities of differential socialization relative to white privilege and black caste codes, problematic socializing happenstances resulting in desperate isolation, and some level of awareness that reputations have suffered excessive damage. Precursors to lethal predation involved perceived challenges to masculinity and relationship troubles (i.e. verbal and physical bullying, arguments, abuse, break-ups, and jealousy), attempts at character assassination through gossiping, and taunting over clique affiliations, sexual orientation, and the over-all perception that an enemy has been created because of some level of perceived torment. Additionally, school shooters seemed to have adverse reactions to grievances with grade assessments, educational progress in challenging programs, instances where they felt judgments at their school hearings were biased, and had problems with accepting or adjusting to disciplinary actions related to school suspensions (in school or suspended from school grounds altogether) or dismissal from undergraduate and graduate level programs (Andriolo, 1998; Kalish & Kimmel, 2010; Kimmel, 2008; Kimmel & Mahler, 2003; Larkin, 2007; Leary et al., 2003; Newman et al., 2004; Preti, 2006; Vossekuil et al., 2002).

All of the above circumstances can lead to humiliation setting off a chain reaction resulting in rampage shootings, mass murder and suicide. It is very possible that any combination of the above mentioned circumstances can become so devastating and reach a tipping point whereby an individual loses sense of self value and/or becomes overwhelmingly bitter enough to be propelled in to a kill self-mode.

Once humiliation has reached the depths of despair as to ignite the kill self-mode, some males may become intent on killing tormentors as well as themselves in an effort to reclaim some measure of dignity, while simultaneously sacrificing a part of the self that allowed the humiliation to happen in the first place. Essentially, in life and death, he becomes resigned to the fact that the narrative of his life will become far more meaningful after the murder and suicide than it is now or that his social currency will be elevated from victim to superior predator. Even though he will not be around to experience the changing narrative, the thought of it sustains him enough to carry out the act (Canetto, 1997; Gilligan, 1997; Katz, 1988; Preti, 2006; Range & Leach, 1998; Stack & Wasserman, 2009).

Educational Institutions Become the Stage for the Grand Finale

Education is significantly related to improved life chances, and academic settings are in many ways social arenas where individuals have to demonstrate an ability to negotiate socially acceptable status, and strive to achieve academic success. In cases where students experience functional peer group inclusion, and achieve academic success, school is perceived as the best of times. Alternatively, when students are rejected by their peer groups, marginalized, made to feel insignificant, and are unable to successfully overcome academic challenges, then school perhaps becomes the worst of times. Perceived social exclusion, humiliating social experiences, negative evaluations from teachers, unwarranted attention from school officials, the threat, and/or pending dismissal from school grounds or academic programs generates stress, anxiety and strain leading students to defer to vigilante actions aimed at settling social disputes and perceived injustice.

As students proceed into advanced stages of their education, failure to successfully integrate with socially approved groups and/or inability to handle the demands of college courses elevates tension as graduate and undergraduate students may perceive failure as detrimental to their goals to secure the American dream. The majority of students take advantage of the numerous resources to improve their college experience; however, a few drift into despair, and use violence as a method to transcend failure (Gilligan, 1997; Katz, 1988; Langam, 2009; Levin & Fox, 2001; McGee & DeBernardo, 1999; Sullivan & Guerett, 2003).

Institutions of higher learning (similar to high schools) while designed to prepare students for entry into a phase comprised of establishing a lifestyle of significant friendship networks, romantic relationships, job security, resources, and material acquisitions necessary for supporting a family can become a source of contempt. Institutions are microcosms of society utilizing curriculum instruction, governing bodies, culture, honor codes, and diverse social networks to provide opportunities for students to become well rounded citizens. However, these very same components can be perceived as creating academic courses that unfairly rank students' intellectual ability, and social atmospheres that devalue inter-personal skills. Institutions of higher learning perhaps take for granted that their diverse majors, campus life activities, campus groups, counseling services, student out-reach programs, and professor-to-student rapport provides a fundamentally sound college experience while at the same time serving as enough of a safety net for troubled students. The flipside is that the college environment while providing numerous opportunities for inclusion inherently has just as many opportunities for students to be confronted by exclusion leading to alienation.

The narrative for rampage shootings on school grounds reveals issues with personal accountability, jaded perceptions of reality, image construction flaws, and a need to elevate to superior status by lethal means (Fast, 2008; Langam, 2009; Larkin, 2007; Leary et al., 2003; Newman, 2004; Vossekuil et al., 2002). High schools, colleges, and universities have undergone significant changes relative to prevention of and preparedness for rampage shootings, since the mass murder events at Columbine in 1999 and Virginia Tech in 2007. Additionally, given, the increased attention to high school and campus shootings, the Secret Service along with the Department of Education has worked diligently to develop a Safe Schools' Initiative. The blueprint seems to be proactive, and reactive to the reality that no academic setting is immune to rampage shootings. The prevailing theme aimed at prevention seems to be anchored in information gathering and campus security (Vossekuil et al., 2002). Information gathering is extremely critical in prevention because it involves collaborative efforts from mental health professionals, local law enforcement, campus security, school administrators, staff and professors. Mental health professionals, counselors and perhaps professors have to tune into potential shooter's motivations, which is difficult to ascertain without having consistent contact with potential shooters. In spite of the difficulty, the Secret Service has developed a framework for threat assessment or a method by which facts about a potential threat are gathered (by mental health professionals, and counselors) and used to prevent a potential attack (Reddy et al., 2001; Vossekuil et al., 2002). Anytime there are attempts to assess criminality, and predict the actions of would be criminals there is the potential for discretionary actions (i.e. labeling, profiling, channeling opportunities, engaging in unwarranted surveillance and information sharing) (Reddy et al., 2001). However, there has to be some element of trust that threat assessments will proceed with the ultimate goal of risk assessment and prevention.

Moreover, with the understanding that crimes occur with the convergence of motivated offender and opportunity, schools and campuses have been making efforts to increase environmental surveillance, secure otherwise unguarded areas, increase law enforcement presence, have law enforcement and school personnel engage in active shooter exercises, and ensure that emergency alert systems are efficiently disseminated to students, and faculty (particularly for college campuses). Unfortunately, schools and campuses have so many free spaces or unprotected locations, that it will always be difficult to completely eliminate the risk of a shooting event (Reddy et al., 2001; Rocque, 2012; Vossekuil et al., 2002).

Conclusion: Safety Checks and Balances

What more can educational leadership do to deter individuals from carrying out rampage shootings given it's almost impossible to know with certainty the intentions of motivated offenders? This may seem very basic but a potential solution rests with educational seminars that train ground zero persons (i.e. professors, advisors, residence hall counselors, and other individuals who have consistent contact with students) to become more aware of student motivations. Seminars could certainly emphasize Agnew's General Strain theory, Gilligan's Saving Face Perspective, differential race socialization (e.g. white privilege, black caste codes, cool pose, and code of the street) and Katz's Righteous Slaughter Perspective (Agnew, 2006; Alexander, 2010; Anderson, 1999; Gilligan, 1997; Katz, 1988; Rothenberg, 2002; Wilson, 2009). Additionally, perhaps the presence of full-time social network specialists (who would examine all things social media related to the institution, monitor social networking patterns of students, and research grapevine posted material), college experience coaches, (similar to life coaches whose job it is to monitor the academic and social dynamics of college students), student anonymous reporting call in centers (similar to crime stoppers), troublesome relationship and/or grievance hotlines (similar to call centers concentrating on domestic abuse, alcoholism and suicide), faculty, peer sponsors, peer level mentors (who are perhaps affiliated with diverse socially accepted groups), and campus safe/inclusivity zones could prove significant in preventing school massacres. In terms of community outreach, perhaps a small community/school center where parents or legal guardians of students are welcome to routinely visit campus, accompany their sons/daughters to classes, and even a reversal of rules prohibiting disclosure of students' grades to parents could be a step towards deterring school shootings on college campuses. Also, it could make a difference if there were public places known for professor/student gatherings where professors and students could mingle naturally over breakfast and lunch. Furthermore, high schools and universities should invest more time in exchange programs where professors guest lecture in high school classrooms and/or college bound students are allowed to visit select classes in order to be exposed to the college experience.

More and more colleges and universities are becoming saddled with budget issues, and administrative functions that seem to be turning schools into business operations. It may be time to return to embracing the reality that as educational agents, duties will have to include, teaching students, assisting with a student's well-being, and risk management (this holds true for high school teachers as well). If our schools and colleges are already being proactive in the areas mentioned above then they are on the right path to reducing the potential for a rampage shooting. Unfortunately, even with all the safe guards in place (i.e. the blueprint for threat assessment, target hardening, campus preparedness, and educational leadership awareness) there simply is no such thing as a full proof plan to prevent rampage shootings because human nature is unpredictable.

However, it remains a daily duty to provide a healthy and safe environment for learning, and after all the consistent hard work, the reality remains that every time violence bypasses schools, so many people are blessed to continue their life's journey. Finally, even though prayer is relatively objected to in schools, prayer just might be a necessary ingredient for prevention.

Research Note: Without Sanctuary or Leisure, Moving in on Soft Targets

Emanuel African Methodist Episcopal Church in Charleston, South Carolina has a storied legacy of survival, spirituality, and strength that makes it a pillar in the black community. On June 17, 2015, a 21 year old white male motivated to start a race war, entered the church and engaged in a nefarious deed ending the lives of 9 African-Americans who were in attendance for Bible study. This mass murderer made sure that 9 African-Americans would have no sanctuary for worship and prayer. The nation was encapsulated in disbelief, and mourned in a manner that erased racial lines of division. Politicians and leaders offered familiar narratives of condolences and embraced routine rhetoric focusing more on the forgiving nature of black people. Unfortunately, it was all a routine ending in turning the page in similar fashion to what was done in 2012 when 20 beautiful children were murdered at Sandy Hook Elementary School in Newtown, Connecticut. Currently, movie theatres and/or places of leisure have become soft targets where mass murderers can get maximum results before facing an equitable defense that could effectively thwart their attack. Additionally, social media has become part of the equation where violence has found a way to stream into our everyday lives. On August 26, 2015, a disgruntled gunman, two years removed from his job as a news reporter murdered two former co-workers while they were broadcasting a story live at Smith Mountain Lake in Moneta, Virginia. This gunman then went on to reach out to the public declaring a sadistic victory over some perceived injustice before committing suicide.

Again, America finds itself in a state of shock relative to the cold-blooded nature of a killing from a person who was on nobody's radar when it came to lethal targeting. It seems we are living in a time where it's logical to suggest that home grown terrorism has invaded American's routine activities. Therefore, there is a desperate need to address variables related to socialization, personal motivations, mental health, and the psychological processes operating in the minds of individuals that prove related to mass murder in sanctuaries, movie theatres, and other public places and spaces. It could very well be that the steps needed to protect America's student population are also necessary to protect people in the work force and the general public.

Work Cited

Alexander, M. (2010). *The New Jim Crow: Mass incarceration in the age of colorblindness.* New York, NY: New Press.
Andriolo, K. (1998). Gender and the cultural construction of good and bad suicides. *Suicide and Life-Threatening Behavior, 28*(1), 37–49.
Agnew, R. (2006). *Pressured into crime: An overview of general strain theory.* Oxford: Oxford University Press.
Agnew, R. (2005). *Why do criminals offend?: A general theory of crime and delinquency.* Los Angeles, CA: Roxbury Publishing Company.
Anderson, E. (1999). *Code of the street.* New York, NY: W.W. Norton and Company.
Anderson, E. (1990). *Street wise.* Chicago: The University Press of Chicago.
Canetto, S. (1997). Meanings of gender and suicidal behavior in adolescence. *Suicide and Life Threatening Behavior, 27*(4), 339–351.
Casella, R. (2001). *Being down: Challenging violence in urban schools.* New York, NY: Teachers College Press.
Chatterton, W. (2010). *Losing my cool: Love literature and a Black Man's escape from the crowd.* New York, NY: Penguin Press.
Cleaver, E. (1996). *Soul on ice.* New York, NY: Random House.
Cohen, A. (1955). *Delinquent boys: The culture of the gang.* New York, NY: Free Press.
Cornish, D., & Clarke, R. (1986). *The reasoning criminal: Rational choice perspectives on offending.* New York, NY: Springer-Verlag.
Cureton, S. (2002). Introducing Hoover: I'll ride for you gangsta. In C. R. Huffs (Ed.), *Gangs in America III.* Ps. 83–100. Thousand Oaks, CA: Sage.
Cureton, S. (2008). *Hoover crips: When Cripin' becomes a way of life.* Lanham, MD: University Press of America.

Cureton, S. (2010). Lost souls of society become hypnotized by Gangsterism. *Journal of Gang Research, 18*(1), 39–52.

Cureton, S. (2011). *Black vanguards and black gangsters: From seeds of discontent to a declaration of war*. Baltimore, MD: University Press of America.

Cureton, S., & Wilson C. (2012). The deceptive black knight campaign: Clique loyalty and sexual conquest. *Journal of Black Masculinity, 2*(3), 1–24.

Dikel, W. (2012). *School shootings and student mental health-what lies beneath the tip of the iceberg*. NSBA Council of School Attorneys. Reprinted with permission.

Dyson, M. (1996). *Race rules: Navigating the color line*. New York, NY: Vintage Books.

Estes, S. (2005). *I am a man: Race manhood and the civil rights movement*. Chapel Hill, NC: University of North Carolina Press.

Fantz, A., Knight, L., & Wang, K. (2014). How many school shootings since Newton? *CNN Latest News*.

Fast, J. (2008). *Ceremonial violence: A psychological explanations of school shootings*. New York, NY: The Overlook Press.

Felson, R., Allen, L., South, S., & McNulty, T. (1994). The subculture of violence: Individual vs. school context effects. *Social Forces, 73*(1), 155–173.

Fessenden, F. (2000). They threaten seethe and UnHinge then kill in quantity. *New York Times*.

Fox, J., Levin, J., & Quinet, K. (2005). The will to kill: Making sense of senseless murder (2nd ed.). New York, NY: Pearson.

Gilligan, J. (1997). *Violence*. New York, NY: Vintage Books.

Haley, A. (1964). *The autobiography of Malcolm X*. New York, NY: Ballantine Books.

Harro, B. (2000). The cycle of socialization. In M. Adams, W. J. Blumenfeld, R. Castaneda, H. W. Hackman, M. L. Peters, and X. Zuniga (Eds.), *Readings in diversity and social justice*. New York, NY: Routledge.

Hempel, A., Meloy, J., & Richards, C. (1999). Offenders and offense characteristics of a non-random sample of mass murderers. *Journal of the American Academy of Psychiatry and Law, 27*, 213–225.

Hooley, J., & Gotlib, I. (2000). A diathesis-stress conceptualization of expressed emotion and clinical outcome. *Applied and Preventive Psychology, 9*, 135–151.

Kalish, R., & Kimmel, M. (2010). Suicide by mass murder: Masculinity, aggrieved entitlement, and rampage school shootings. *Health Sociology Review, 19*(4), 451–464.

Katz, J. (1988). *Seductions of crime: Moral and sensual attractions to doing evil*. New York, NY: Basic Books.

Kimmel, M. (2008). Profiling school shooters and shooters' schools: The cultural contexts of aggrieved entitlement and restorative masculinity. In B. Agger & T. W. Luke (Eds.), *There is a gunman on campus: Terror at Virginia tech*. Lanham, MD: Rowman and Littlefield.

Kimmel, M., & Mahler, M. (2003). Adolescent masculinity, homophobia and violence: Random school shootings, 1982–2001. *American Behavioral Scientist, 46*(10), 1439–1458.

Klein, J. (2012). *The bully society: School shootings and the crisis of bullying in America's schools*. New York, NY: NYU Press.

Langman, P. (2009). *Why kids kill: Inside the minds of school shooters*. New York, NY: Palgrave Macmillan.

Larkin, R. (2007). *Comprehending columbine*. Philadelphia, PA: Temple University Press.

Leary, M., Kowalski, R., Smith, L., & Phillips, S. (2003). Teasing rejection and violence: Case studies of the school shootings. *Aggressive Behavior, 29*(3), 202–214.

Levin, J., & Fox, J. (2001). *Deadlines: Essays in murder and mayhem*. Boston, MA: Allyn and Bacon.

Magida, A. (1996). *The prophet of rage: A life of Louis Farrakhan and His Nation*. New York, NY: Basic Books.

Majors, R. (1993). *Cool pose: The dilemmas of black manhood in America*. New York, NY: Simon & Schuster.

McCall, N. (1994). *Makes me Wanna Holler: A young black man in America*. New York, NY: Vintage Books.

Meloy, J., Hempel, A., Mohandie, K., Shiva, A., & Gray, T. (2001). Offender and offense characteristics of a nonrandom sample of adolescent mass murderers. *Journal of the American Academy of Child and Adolescent Psychiatry, 40*, 719–728.

McGee, J., & DeBernardo, C. (1999). The classroom avenger. *The Forensic Examiner, 8*(5–6), 16–18.

Muschert, G. (2007). Research in school shootings. *Sociology Compass, 1*(1), 60–80.

Newman, K., Fox, C., Roth, W., Mehta, J., & Harding, D. (2004). Rampage: The social roots of school shootings. New York, NY: Basic Books.

Nirvi, S., & Maxwell, L. (2012). *Researchers sound alarm over black student suspensions*. Retrieved from EdWeek.org

Oliver, W. (1989). Black males and social problems: Prevention through Afrocentric socialization. *Journal of Black Studies, 20*(1), 15–39.

Preti, A. (2006). Suicide to harass others: Clues from mythology to understanding suicide bombing attacks. *The Journal of Crisis Intervention and Suicide Prevention, 27*(1), 22–30.

Range, L., & Leach, M. (1998). Gender culture and suicidal behavior: A feminist critique of theories and research. *Suicide and Life-Threatening Behavior, 28*(1), 24–36.

Reddy, M., Borum, R., Berglund, J., Vossekuil, B., Fein, R., & Modzeleski, W. (2001). Evaluating risk for targeted violence in schools: Comparing risk assessment, threat assessment, and other approaches. *Psychology in the Schools, 38*(2), 157–172.

Rocque, M. (2012). Exploring school rampage shootings: research, theory and policy. *The Social Science Journal, 49*, 304–313.

Rothenberg, P. (2002). *White privilege: Essential readings on the other side of racism*. New York, NY: Worth Publishing.

Stack, S., & Wasserman, I. (2009). Gender and suicide risk: The role of wound site. *Suicide and Life-Threatening Behavior, 39*(1), 13–20.

Sullivan, M., & Guerett, R. (2003). The copycat factor: Mental illness, guns and the shooting incident at heritage high school, Rockdale county Georgia. In M. H. Moore, C. V. Petrie, A. A. Braga, & B. L. McLaughlin (Eds.), *Deadly lesson: Understanding lethal school violence*. Washington, DC: NAP. Pp. 25–69.

Tuck, M., & David, R. (1986). The theory of reasoned action: A decision theory of crime. In D. B. Cornish & R. V. Clarke (Eds.), *The reasoning criminal: Rational choice perspectives on offending*. New York, NY: Springer-Verlag.

Vossekuil, B., Fein, R., Reddy, M., Borum, R., & Modzeski, W. (2002). *The final report and findings of the safe school initiative: Implications for the prevention of school attacks in the United States*. Washington DC: U.S. Department of Education, Office of Elementary and Secondary, Safe and Drug-Free Schools Program and U.S. Secret Service, National Threat Assessment Center.

Wallace, D. (2007). It's a M-A-N Thang: Black male gender role socialization and the performance of masculinity in love relationships. *Journal of Pan African Studies, 1*(7), 11–22.

West, C. (2001). *Race matters*. New York, NY: Vintage Books.

Williams, S. (2004). *Blue rage black redemption*. Pleasant Hill, CA: Damamli Publishing Company.

Wilson, W. (2009). *More than just race: being black and poor in the inner city*. New York, NY: W.W. Norton Company.

Wilson, W. (1996). *When work disappears: The world of the new urban poor*. New York, NY: Knopf.

Wilson, W. (1987). *The truly disadvantaged: The inner city, the underclass, and public policy*. Chicago: University of Chicago Press.

PART THREE

Critical Pedagogy and Social Justice

Critical pedagogy is a liberating theoretical framework which provides scholars and essayists with tools to critique and deconstruction institutions of power. It causes educators to question how constructions of reality are legitimized by the dominant culture. It enables scholars to critical our past, reflect upon our present, and transform our future. Critical pedagogy is a vehicle for decolonizing our curriculum and "lived" experiences. It awakes in us a social and political actors the desire to transform our environments. It is the framework for questioning the "isms" in our society. Through this framework it helps us to "make-sense" of the ways in which human rights are manifested in the everyday lives of our society. It becomes our foundation for engaging in and practicing the habits of social justice.

In this first chapter, Kelly Concannon and Laura Finley provide definitions of social justice and social justice education. They use these definitions to make claims regarding the most effective social justice practices in academe. They follow with the challenges of social justice education, including the overall commodification of higher education and limitations of service learning initiatives, but also propose effective pedagogical-based approaches to social justice education as well as efforts to engage students in social justice activism off-campus.

In the second chapter, Ty-Ron M. O. Douglas examines the theme of *hope* within the context of his own spiritual positionality and his philosophical journey from Plato to Richard Rorty during a Philosophy of Education course experience as a graduate student. He frames his argument around the controversial notions of Big Truths (Ts) and little truths (t's) as tangible, yet sometimes misguided, manifestations of man's nihilistic pursuit of meaning in a confusing world. He believes this topic is important for all educators—particularly educators in American Higher Education, because they possess and promote varying notions of truth that collide with, create, clarify, and even confuse the beliefs of their students—many of whom no longer learn about God in schools and invariably wrestle with their own notions of truth.

In the following chapter, Lalenja Harrington shares her experiences writing poetry for a class that turned into a "dialogic encounter." Through the activity she found herself focusing on that discovery element of social justice—the moment when each individual is empowered not only to find their voice, but to speak it aloud-ideally in an environment where their perspective is respected and of value. She takes us through the creative process. She shares her moments of "becoming" and the freedom/expectation to examine one's own position, whether it be for an individual or for an entire community, are at the core of a critically-thinking, socially-just society.

Toby S. Jenkins utilizes tropes from the "Wizard of Oz" to highlight the field of education continues to face serious challenges with issues of satisfaction, retention, and completion of students of color. She argues many wounded learners are in need of alternative places of inclusion and creative educators that can "work their magic" so that these learners are truly engaged and included. She also argues, part of the problem is that in our attempts to "transform" education, we stand still. We continue to examine the same spaces to better understand their faults and problems rather than taking a creative and inspiring journey (the yellow brick road) towards fresh perspectives. We focus on pathology rather than possibility.

Robert E. Randolph explores the importance of literacy to the project of social justice. Through critical analysis and personal insights, he contextualizes literacy and poetry—as critical discourses of power and resistance, conditions of positionality, and essential curriculum for those engaged in higher education. He further contends that writing is a queer act, precisely because it requires the writer to deviate from normalcy, incorporate differences, and employ a praxis and pedagogy of affect(ion).

Melissa A. Odegard-Koester reflects on the politics of leading, by sharing an epigraph from bell hooks. She shares the impact of bell hooks' teaching and reflections on race, class, gender in education, and sexuality on her own growth. She discusses her own writing on reflective pedagogy and uses a critical pedagogical lens to contextualize her personal and professional history as it relates to the leadership and the politics of leading. She concludes with student perspectives and their definitions of leadership.

Laura Finley, Victor Romano, Glenn A. Bowen, and Celeste Fraser Delgado begin with a discussion of the benefits and potential limitations of service-learning, particularly in relation to marketing a university or college. They address how service-learning fails when it does not fully engage the three key stakeholders: students, faculty, and community partners. They respond to concerns by documenting best practices and exemplary service-learning programs, from both scholarly literature and extensive experiences utilizing the pedagogy.

Pearlie Strother-Adams presents some of the problems that often plague African American and minority tenured and tenure track faculty within their classrooms and academic departments at predominately white institutions. She also discusses how individual faculty student conferences and faculty-peer mentoring can make the difference in both retention and overall success of faculty. She introduces educators to the concept of innovative faculty-student conferences and the "power" and possibility it has to help improve relations between minority professors and their students.

Lalenja Harrington & Remington Brown present the collaborative process involving the development of strategies for exploring desired post-graduation outcomes of students with intellectual disabilities (ID) attending college. The authors discuss how they collaborated together to structure and conceptualize a pilot study designed to highlight student perspectives on the impact of college on post-graduation outcomes. In the same vein as Participatory Action Research studies, this chapter serves as a much-needed platform for the voices of students who have historically been relegated to the margin.

Sarah J. Dhilla discusses "online" education and the debate it has sparked between faculty and administrators regarding the ownership of online courses. Longstanding academic presidents has granted faculty ownership of their scholarly work; however, the emergence of online learning has called that tradition into question. Administrators claim that online courses are distinctly different than their face-to-face counterparts in terms of investment and development and the institution is entitled to course ownership. Faculty argue that they should retain the copyright as the course authors and that institutional ownership is a violation of their academic freedom.

John J. Lee asserts, in educational institutions, there are many ways students become marginalized or feel "Othered." Some of these categories of marginalization include race, gender, skin color, and sexuality, but one category not often discussed, particularly in higher education, is by language. Each student comes to school with unique background experiences, cultural practices, and even attitudes toward learning. For ELLs (English language learners), one of their academic needs may be specialized language instruction, yet there exists several complications in the way they are placed into their English courses as well as the labeling of these students as they enter postsecondary institutions. He investigates these issues.

Brian Collier highlights day after day, channel after channel, cable networks and satellite companies provide hours upon hours of "classic" television shows that are now in syndication. Depending on the network, one has the privilege to ingest hours of classic "black" sitcoms. Although these stations are rare, they do provide a very clear insight into African American culture. These sitcoms are places where multiple worldviews, stereotypes, and identities have been developed. He questions the intent and the impact of Black television. He argues the content and the context inextricably go hand in hand. The same can be said for the educative process and Historically Black Colleges and Universities. He utilizes the syndicated television shows *The Fresh Prince of Bel-Air* and *A Different World* as texts and curriculum to interrogate.

CHAPTER 25

Social Justice Education in Higher Education

Laura Finley and Kelly Concannon

Introduction

According to many scholars, one of the functions of academe is to help create a more peaceful and just world (Bok, 1988; Boyer, 1996; Marullo & Edwards, 2000). The Association of American Colleges and Universities (AACU) has implored institutions of higher education to take seriously the call of educating and not just preparing students to be active contributors in their communities.

Liberal Arts colleges have for a long time integrated curricula that emphasize social justice. In recent years there has been a surge in more specific, formal programs that are tied to the college or university mission. This is perhaps in response to research showing that, while students are likely to say they received multicultural coursework, they are much less likely to report having received specific coursework on social justice (Singh et al., 2010). Many private schools have social justice programs, often housed in social work, sociology, or education. Even some public universities like Arizona State have added graduate programs in social justice (Smith, 2012). Colleges of Business, too, have begun to integrate social issues in their curricula, although such efforts focus largely on corporate social responsibility rather than social justice (Toubiana, 2014). As is clear from these examples, colleges and universities are increasingly emphasizing social justice.

Yet, as many have noted, higher education's rhetoric far exceeds its actual performance regarding its commitment to civic engagement, social justice, and preparing students to better their communities. It is not enough to merely say you are promoting social justice or to offer specific courses or programs. Rather, campuses must also consider the pedagogical methods being used (Harkavy, 2006). Bok (1988), Boyer (1996), Marullo and Edwards (2000) and others have criticized higher education for focusing far too much on the "scholarship of discovery" and too little on methodologies that engage (Marullo & Edwards, 2000, p. 895).

For many faculty and staff in higher education, it remains unclear precisely how to define social justice, how to teach these concepts in classroom setting, and what are the most effective strategies to get students invested in larger questions of social justice education *outside* of the classroom. We begin this chapter by providing definitions of social justice and social justice education. We then use those definitions to make claims about the most effective social justice practices in academe. We will not only outline the challenges of social justice education, including the overall commodification of higher education and limitations of service learning initiatives, but also propose effective pedagogical-based approaches to social justice education as well as efforts to engage students in social justice activism off-campus. We assert that reflexivity and collaboration are essential, and we maintain that educators and student affairs professionals must resist the traditional framing of heroic teacher and inspired student, instead drawing attention to the more messy and complex ways in which teaching and learning occurs within multiple institutional contexts.

Definitions of Social Justice and Progressive Pedagogy

Social justice can be defined in many ways. Calderwood (2003) says "social justice works to undo socially created and maintained differences in material conditions of living so as to reduce and eventually eliminate the perpetuation of the privilege of some at the expense of others" (p. 302). Bell (1997) defines social justice as being both a goal and a process, while Marullo and Edwards (2000) refer to it as an

> attempt to alter the structural or institutional practices that produce excessive or unjustified inequalities or that treat people unfairly—for example, discriminating against people on the basis of race, sex, social class, religion, nationality, ethnicity, sexual orientation, or disability status. (p. 899)

Building on these definitions of social justice, "The goal of social justice education is full and equal participation of all groups in a society that is mutually shaped to meet their needs" (Bell, 1997, p. 3) while, "the process for attaining the goal of social justice … should be democratic and participatory, inclusive and affirming of human agency and human capacities for working collaboratively to create change" (p. 4). Thus, the focus is on both the end result—addressing structural inequalities—as well as *how* one achieves these end results. We believe that both elements should be visible as we work towards progressive ends.

Social justice education draws from a variety of pedagogical traditions, such as peace education, critical pedagogy, multicultural education, civic education, anti-oppressive education, and partnership education (Bajaj & Brantmeier, 2011; Eisler, 2000; hooks, 1994; Kushamiro, 2009). It also draws from multiple disciplines, including composition and rhetoric, women's studies, educational studies, and sociology. Oftentimes these focal points are inextricably linked to progressive outcomes that can be accomplished through both engagement with course materials as well as through research and activism, where students and teachers are asked to move outside of the confines of the classroom to engage in advocacy and activism. Most definitions of social justice education integrate the notion of praxis, as offered by famed Brazilian educator Paulo Freire (1970). To Freire and his followers, praxis is the combination of reflection and action, all with the intent of challenging the status quo, reducing inequalities, offering voice to those who are marginalized and improving communities (Cipolle, 2010). Hackman (2005) explains

> Social justice education does not merely examine difference or diversity but pays careful attention to the systems of power and privilege that give rise to social inequality, and encourages students to critically examine oppression on institutional, cultural, and individual levels in search of opportunities for social action in the service of social change. (p. 104)

Further, Hackman (2005) has identified five essential components of social justice education:

1) Content mastery;

2) Tools for critical analysis;

3) Tools for social change;
4) Tools for personal reflection; and
5) An awareness of multicultural group dynamics. (p. 104)

We add that social justice education should address multiple relationships to power and privilege in an equitable way. That is, social justice education must acknowledge and address the historical and current power differentials between students, between teachers and students, and between academe and the community. Oftentimes, students are rendered powerless when they learn about social inequalities, as they are taught in ways that fail to highlight the social structural roots of the problem. Students are often led to believe that there is little, if anything, that they can do to address these larger issues. Likewise, communities often feel as though academics live in the so-called "ivory tower" and don't understand the real issues they face (Finley, 2004). The examination of power differential and active attempts to reduce them, we argue, is essential if higher education is to have any role in eradicating social inequalities.

Social Justice Education in the College Classroom

In this section, we provide a review of literature related to enacting social justice education inside the college classroom. We highlight the most essential components involved in creating a classroom in which students learn both the content and the motivation to engage in social justice activism and advocacy.

Resisting "Power Over" Pedagogies

Despite good intentions, the traditional relationships to power and privilege oftentimes prevail even as teachers and students engage in classroom-based social justice education. Faculty often want to appear as all-knowing and thus use largely or even exclusively pedagogical methods that demonstrate their power over students (Sperber, 2000). Students, too, are generally accustomed to this dominator-style teaching (Eisler, 2000), and thus resist methods that are more engaging and in which power is shared. These "student" and "teacher" roles are deeply engrained and reinforced in popular culture that depicts the heroic teacher inspiring and saving his or her passive and apathetic students (Sperber, 2000). It is challenging for both groups to overcome these roles (Finley, 2004), and thus, careful and critical reflections of both our theories and our practices is necessary in order to ensure that social justice education involves both the content and methods that will reach and inspire students. Research is clear that in order to inspire and prepare students to become advocates for social justice, professors and instructors must step out of the traditional role of lecturer and utilize more egalitarian and participatory instructional methods. That is, social justice educators should move away from "banking" styles of presentation to more egalitarian methods that are more likely to be memorable to students and to excite them to take action (Astin & Astin, 2000; Freire, 1970).

The Importance of Dialogue

Classrooms must be safe spaces where students feel comfortable to engage with knowledges in ways that might be disruptive, uncomfortable, and sometimes unsettling. This shift calls for an awareness that students bring with them different experiences, insights, and opinions. In her research about how college students become social justice allies, Boido (2000) found that students were most impacted by serious and sustained dialogue about social justice issues. While it sounds quite simple to facilitate a classroom discussion, in reality, careful attention must be paid beforehand to ensure that all students feel safe and encouraged to participate. And, as Boido (2000) found, it is essential that students feel comfortable expressing different viewpoints, as often students note that their peers are hesitate to offer divergent views in class in case they appear to be racist, sexist or otherwise unpopular. It is through dialogue in these safe environments that students can work through and challenge some of these ideas, oftentimes allowing students a more firm place to stand when it comes to their beliefs and attitudes about social issues.

Students should be given the opportunity to outline their overarching perceptions about what they have learned in a classroom and the kind of work that they expect to do within a particular location. Further, students should be provided time and space to candidly discuss how their perceptions about who experiences social injustices and significantly *who does not experience* such injustices, allowing for a more critical conversation about their work. Further, these opportunities can allow students to begin to discuss how their individual perceptions are not only related back to *their* histories and identities, but more significantly, how these attitudes are reflected through different elements of popular culture (Sperber, 2000). These moves allow conversations to begin with the individual, but end with a more systematic discussion of cultural attitudes and beliefs about multiple relationships to power and privilege. In the process, students and teachers collaboratively create understandings of social justice that are relevant and accessible.

Attention to Sociological Roots of Inequalities

Additionally, students better understand social justice issues and become more committed to working as allies when they were asked to participate in perspective-taking exercises coupled with structured opportunities for personal reflection (Boido, 2000; Mayhew & Deluca-Fernandez, 2007; Nagda, Gurin, & Lopez, 2003). In their study of five social-justice oriented classes, Mayhew and Deluca-Fernandez (2007) found that students were most likely to report greater understanding and commitment to social justice when they are taught from a sociological approach that emphasizes societal structures and inequalities. That is, students must understand how the inequalities that we seek to reduce or eradication are *socially created* in order to take action to undo them.

However, scholars are clear that social justice education can be integrated into any class, not just sociology courses. Several social justice initiatives emphasize the relationships between careful dialogue and engagement with course materials. For example, in "Writing with the Community: Social Cognitive Rhetoric, Intercultural Discourses, and the Community Literacy Center," Thomas Deans (2000) acknowledges the power of reflective work that integrates course materials, dialogue, and action. He explores the significance of the Community Literacy Center, where participants work directly with urban residences on issues related to language and literacy. The project calls for consistent dialogue and reflection on individual's interactions with others in an attempt to engage in social activism.

Sharing Our Activism and Inviting Participation

Social justice initiatives and experiences need to be presented to students in order to allow course materials to resonate in meaningful ways. In other words, educators must share with students their work and can invite them to join. In Boido's (2000) study, students also noted that the social justice activism or advocacy to which they became involved was rarely self-initiated. Rather, they were "recruited" by professors or by peers (Boido, 2000). In addition to discussing their own social justice activism, guest speakers to inform students of local opportunities, especially if these opportunities are not part of the overarching structure of the course.

It is clear that the classroom can be an important place to introduce social justice education. Yet classroom-based activities are not the only, or perhaps even the most important, ways to do social justice education.

Social Justice Education Outside the Classroom

One popular method of social justice education that involves off-campus activity is service-learning. Service-learning is a form of experiential education in which students engage in community service that benefits groups or organizations in need while simultaneously enhancing their knowledge of course content. Research has documented the tremendous benefits of service-learning for students, universities, and community organizations. In particular, students may learn more about social inequalities and can become part of solving them, thereby promoting social justice (Alberle-Grasse, 2000; Astin & Astin, 2000; Dale & Kalob, 2006; Harkavy, 2006; Koliba, 2000; Mayhew & Deluca-Fernandez, 2007; Osanloo, 2009; Roschelle, Turpin & Elias, 2000).

Community-based research (CBR) is also ideally suited as method of social justice education. "CBR is collaborative, change-oriented research that engaged faculty members, students, and community members in projects that address a community-identified need" (Strand et al., 2003, p. 5). CBR helps students understand social issues and the research process and allows them to see themselves as change agents. It helps communities address critical social issues, and it helps universities build strong connections with community agencies (Strand et al., 2003). CBR offers a challenge to the power dynamics noted earlier in the chapter, as it involves equally students, faculty, and community partners (Cox, 2009 & Strand et al., 2003).

In addition to service-learning and CBR, which are more structured efforts, professors and student affairs staff can simply encourage interested students to take part in local activities in which they are involved. For instance, these authors have introduced students to a scholarship and mentoring program for girls, involving students who have a passion for mentoring young women in monthly meetings with mentees. At first these students simply shadowed the faculty mentors, but after attending monthly meetings and engaging in thoughtful reflection about what they experienced, the college students were able to come up with lessons they were comfortable leading. Thus what began as an additional way to learn about some of the issues experienced by at-risk girls turned into an opportunity for college students to become mentors and to take on powerful leadership roles. Both authors are involved with a non-profit organization that helps victims of domestic violence. As that social issue comes up in courses taught by each of the authors, we have attempted to inspire interested students to get involved as well. Several have done so, and now routinely attend events sponsored by the non-profit, assist with its annual holiday party, and coordinate activities for the survivors' children. One of the authors has also engaged students in anti-death penalty work, building on classroom-based knowledge to help students facilitate vigils on dates of executions, prepare petitions and collect signatures, and coordinate community presentations that help teach others about the problems with capital punishment.

Campus-based programming can and should introduce students to local social justice agencies and efforts. Offering speakers, panel discussions, film screenings and group trips can provide students with important opportunities to interact with social justice advocates, to learn about their work, and to identify areas in which they can assist. Student Affairs staff can encourage students to participate by promoting local efforts on campus, by facilitating transportation to off-campus activities, and by hosting reflection or "debriefing" sessions after students have engaged in social justice activities.

Challenges in Enacting Social Justice Education in Higher Education

Higher education has been drastically influenced by a globalized marketplace; thus, one challenge in enacting social justice education is the commercialization of higher education. Peter Katopes (2009) argues that the business model of education creates a problematic definition of the purpose of education. Because of the focus on the "product," students and teachers are situated in a tenuous relationship. In other words, this consumer model of education oftentimes produces conflicting outcomes and purposes, especially for faculty and administrators who are interested in creating conditions through which students can begin to imagine their roles as global citizens who are not only responsible for their own welfare but for the welfare of others as well. He argues that

> the business model, which prizes "customer satisfaction" or "efficiency" above all else, has led in higher education to an imbalance in the relation between student and institution, has led to a culture of entitlement and instant gratification, and has causal ties to the current fiscal crisis. (Katopes, 2009)

The business model of education can sometimes be in conflict with social justice education. It takes work to position students as not only customers and/or consumers of education to global citizens who should be invested in issues that matter. Thus, the question of student satisfaction—particularly when instructors and programs are intended to destabilize students to think critically about their own relationships to power and privilege and to do so in classrooms that resist more traditional methods of instruction—can be tricky:

> In this highly competitive education market, customer (student) satisfaction has become paramount. The more satisfied the student, the argument goes, the more he or she is willing to persist at the institution, the greater the graduation statistics, and the more enhanced the reputation of t College ought not to be merely a place where someone learns "skills" and racks up credentials, but rather an environment and an experience in which students learn, in addition to history and literature and mathematics, also how to begin to navigate the adult civilized world in an adult. (Katopes, 2009)

As Harkavy (2006) notes, "when universities openly and increasingly pursue commercialization, it powerfully legitimizes and reinforces the pursuit of economic self-interest by students and contributes to the widespread sense among them that they are in college solely to gain career skills and credentials" (p. 14). It is difficult to teach "others-before-self" in a culture in which individual gain is the presented as the primary goal.

Excessive bureaucracy can also stymy social justice education, both on and off campus. Policies, procedures, rules and regulations can be difficult to navigate in any institution, but the siloed nature of most colleges and universities is particularly challenging for faculty, staff, and students who want to initiate certain types of programs. Even starting a new club or organization on many campuses requires extensive paperwork that is off-putting to some social justice-oriented students.

Lukanioff (2012) documents the growth in bureaucracy since 1992, highlighting how the "most conspicuous component" in the rise in cost of higher education is the increased salaries of top administrators and the growth in the number of people employed as campus administrators. Thus "students are not paying for an exponential increase in the quality of their education, but rather for a massive increase in campus bureaucracy" (Lukanioff, 2012, p. 73). The expansion of campus judicial boards, for instance, has resulted in "the criminalization of everything" (Lukanioff, 2012, p. 116). Students, faculty, and staff may be hesitant to engage in social justice initiatives if they fear repurcussions.

Another challenge for social justice educators is the increasingly narrow space for free speech on many campuses. In his book *Unlearning liberty: Campus censorship and the end of American debate,* Lukianoff (2014) details the many restrictions campuses have on student and faculty free speech. "Free speech zones" have become more common on campuses. These are designated areas in which the campus community is allowed to speak publicly. While the classroom itself can be more open, given that faculty generally have more academic freedom than others on campuses, the stifling of freedoms does inevitably impact every part of the higher education experience. Lukianoff (2014) explains the problem with censorship on campus, stating that, "an environment that squelches debate and punishes the expression of opinions, in the very institution that is supposed to make us better thinkers, can lead quickly to the formation of polarized groups in which people harbor a comfortable, uncritical certainty that they are right" (p. 9). Further, even if one does not personally experience censorship, fear that any kind of public dissent might result in punishment is likely to have a chilling effect on public speech (Lukianoff, 2014). In particular, this silencing of debate results in "a shallow and incomplete understanding of important issues and other ways of thinking" (Lukanioff, 2014, p. 11), thereby reducing the likelihood that students will become social justice change agents. In fact, as Lukanioff (2014) notes, designating specific locations and enacting hyper-restrictive free speech policies teach college students exactly the opposite of what they should be learning. "Empowering students to question everything, even the administration, may make administrators' lives harder, but it's what you need to do if you want to educate a free people as opposed to an obedient one" (Lukanioff, 2014, p. 156). These constraints make it more difficult for instructors to create spaces through which students will feel comfortable to engage in their ideas, namely if these ideas run counter to the overall climate of the campus.

Yet another issue, according to Harkavy (2006), is that "disciplinary ethnocentrism, tribalism, [and] guildism strongly dominate American universities today and strongly work against their actually doing what they rhetorically promise to do" (p. 14). Described as the "disciplinary fallacy," the problem is the notion that academics are "duty-bound only to serve the scholastic interests and preoccupations of their disciplines and have neither the responsibility nor the capacity to help their universities keep their long-standing promises to prepare America's undergraduates for lives of moral and civic responsibility" (p. 15). A lack of incentives to teach about and for social justice may also prohibit faculty from doing so (Marullo & Edwards, 2000). If faculty and staff are not encouraged, recognized, or awarded for integrating social justice education into their classrooms and campus programs, many will shy away from doing so.

There are some other challenges that are unique to faith-based colleges and universities. Students, faculty and staff who wish to advocate for social justice initiatives that might be in contrast to the spiritual leadership of the institution may also be discouraged if not prohibited from doing so. For instance, a group of students seeking to represent their university in an off-campus gay rights march might not be prohibited from taking part, but might be told they cannot use university transportation, wear gear with university logos or insignia, or hold university signage.

Pitfalls of Service Learning Projects

Although service-learning has great potential as a means of furthering social justice goals, it is not always conducted in a way that does so. One concern is that service-learning opportunities are designed by those in academe, rather than by the community groups to be served. Thus the needs of the course and the students may come well before the needs of the community, making it less likely that any real transformation will occur (Cushman, 1999; Eby, 1998; Marullo & Edwards, 2000). The short-term focus of most academic service-learning programs, what has been called the "drive-by model," may actually be more harmful and disruptive to communities than it is advantageous (Hollander, 2010). Disadvantaged people being served by these organizations may be viewed as little more than lab rats, objects to be studied (Eby, 1998; Himley, 2004). This type of program can reinforce misconceptions about social problems, their causes, and about groups of people (Eby, 1998; Herzberg, 1994). Rather than dramatic social change, service-learning that involves students as individual saviors can reinforce the idea that what is needed is yet another hero to swoop in and save others (Illich, 1990).

Colleges and universities may use service-learning as a "public relations tool," encouraging it to enhance their reputation and recruit students rather than as a legitimate pedagogical method and as a means of ensuring the campus' commitment to social justice in the community. These programs can easily be watered down, becoming little more than volunteering, or what many have called "McService" (Eby, 1998). This type of service-learning often focuses on direct service rather than on more activist activity, favoring work like preparing and serving food over helping to coordinate a town hall meeting on a pressing issue. These are what Marullo and Edwards (2000) have called the "charity model" of service, and they are not capable of solving social problems.

Additionally, professors and instructors must be careful to ensure that students play significant roles in creating and assessing service-learning projects. Efforts must be made to ensure that students and educators share power and that students' voices are heard (Epstein, 2011; Marullo & Edwards, 2000). As Epstein (2011) points out, "teachers who use pedagogical practices that enable students to be active and empowered can teach them to use their voices in socially productive ways" (p. 177).

Some scholars dispute the usefulness of service-learning initiatives for bringing about social justice and argue for a shift from a focus on "service" and into a conversation about community engagement (Deans, 2000). In *Service- Learning in Theory and Practice,* Dan W. Butin (2010) argues that the future of service learning in higher education involves a combination of sustained engagement and intellectual exploration.

Summary of Best Practices for Social Justice Education in Higher Education

In a project supported by the NCTE Commission on Social Justice entitled *Narratives of Social Justice Teaching*, Miller, Beliveau, DeStigter, Kirkland, and Rice (2008) argue for the role of narrative in the exploration of social justice teaching. The authors place value on a "fourthspace"—where teachers can reflect on pedagogies and practices (p. 1). Just as students need opportunities to reflect on what they are learning, faculty and staff need these opportunities as well. Campuses should provide faculty and staff with ongoing professional development so they are prepared to teach and reinforce social justice content (Rodriguez, Chambers, Gonzalez, & Scheurich, 2010). We echo Calderwood's (2003) call for the development of a "professional community for social justice," in which those engaging in social justice education can provide support and encouragement for one another and can celebrate achievements and small victories.

As noted earlier, dialogue is essential in enacting social justice education. Intergroup dialogue (IGD) has been proven to be a useful technique in furthering students' understanding of others and of social issues, both when utilized in classroom settings and outside of them (Nagda & Zúñiga, 2003; Nagda et al., 2003). IGD

> brings together students from two or more social identity groups to build relationships across cultural and power differences, to raise consciousness of inequalities, to explore the similarities and differences in experiences across identity groups, and to strengthen individual and collective capacities to promote social justice. (Nagda & Gurin, 2007, p. 35)

Best practices in service-learning for social justice include the development and sustenance of true partnerships between academe, students, and community groups to be served (Jacoby, 1996). Thus, we place value on the cultivations of real relationships. Making sense of these relationships and what complicates our outcomes in real situations *matters* insofar as "taking it to the streets" may produce more conflict than an alleviation of multiple relationships to power and privilege. Further, these partnerships need intensive reflection opportunities for students to consider the impact of their service, how it connects to course material, and how it relates to structural, not just individual change (Cushman, 1999; Eby, 1998; Herzberg, 1994). Campus-community collaborations for service-learning and CBR help students, community members and, in a challenging economy, they can help the public see the relevance of higher education (Strand et al., 2003). Deans (2000) argues that we need to be clear of the types of relationships that we are formulating with the community, as these definitions will help create or constrain the types of work we can accomplish.

Research clearly shows that undergraduate students are most likely to get involved when they are taught about social inequalities and local efforts to address them, when they receive the encouragement from their professors, and when the bureaucratic roadblocks to engaging in social justice activism are minimal. Institutions must pay close attention to the ways that their policies and practices either encourage or discourage social justice advocacy and activism. Students can and should have a role in shaping some of the rules and procedures that impact their ability to take action on and off campus.

Conclusion

Throughout this chapter we have argued for the creation of a working definition of social justice education that is complex, open, and accounts for different relationships to power and privilege. We have highlighted the importance of challenging the simple and stereotypical narratives of heroic teacher and passive student in order to identify the often ambiguous and complex teaching and learning moments that accompany the pursuit of peace and social justice. We resist more traditional methods through which to discuss social justice education and argue that social justice education is messy, complex, and oftentimes is difficult to codify in terms of intended outcomes and results, particularly when we are placing value on both the epistemological *and* ontological aspects of what we do in out classrooms in general, and in higher education in particular. Further, we have highlighted the importance of seeing social justice education as not just a classroom-based set of knowledge but instead an affinity toward understanding the social roots of inequalities, to reflecting deeply on our own role in sustaining or reducing those inequalities, and in taking action in and *with* communities to promote a peaceful and more just world. In sum, as Kevin Kumashiro (2009) argues,

> The question for educational reforms is not *whether* schools should be addressing issues of oppression … The question needs to be *how* schools should be differently addressing issues of oppression. And therein lies the reason for recentering education on issues of social justice, that is, on a movement against oppression. The problem of common sense calls on us to engage in *anti-oppressive* forms of education, i.e., in forms of education that explicitly work against multiple oppressions (pp. xxxvii).

Work Cited

Alberle-Grasse, M. (2000). The Washington study-service year of Eastern Mennonite University: Reflections on 23 years of service-learning. *American Behavioral Scientist, 43,* 848–857.

Astin, A., & Astin, H. (2000). *Leadership reconsidered: Engaging higher education in social change.* Battle Creek, MI: W. K. Kellogg Foundation. Available at www.wkkf.org

Bajaj, M., & Brantmeier, E. (2011). The politics, praxis, and possibilities of critical peace education. *Journal of Peace Education, 8*(3), 221–224.

Bell, L. A. (1997). Theoretical foundations for social justice education. In M. Adams, L. Bell, & P. Griffin (Eds.), Teaching for diversity and social justice: A sourcebook (pp. 3–15). New York, NY: Routledge.

Boido, E. (2000). The development of social justice allies during college: A phenomenological investigation. *Journal of College Student Development, 41*(1), 3–18.

Bok, D. (1988). *Higher learning.* Ambridge, MA: Harvard University Press.

Boyer, E. (1996). *The basic school: A community for learning.* New York, NY: John Wiley & Sons.

Butin, D. (2010). *Service-learning in theory and practice: The future of community engagement in higher education.* New York, NY: Palgrave.

Calderwood, P. (2003). Toward a professional community for social justice. *Journal of Transformative Education, 1*(4), 301–320.

Cipolle, S. (2010). *Service-learning and social justice.* Lanham, MD: Rowman & Littlefield.

Cox, P. (2009). Brief report of community ownership of local coalitions: Community members' perspectives. *Journal of Community Psychology, 37*(6), 789–794.

Cushman, E. (1999, January). The public intellectual, service-learning, and activist research. *College English, 61*(3), 328–336.

Dale, C., & Kalob, D. (2006, May). Embracing social activism: Sociology in the service of social justice and peace. *Humanity & Society, 30*(2), 121–152.

Deans, T. (2000). *Writing partnerships.* Urbana, IL: National Council of Teachers of English.

Eby, J. (1998). *Why service-learning is bad.* Retrieved February 17, 2014 from http://www.messiah.edu/external_programs/agape/servicelearning/articles/wrongsvc.pdf

Eisler, R. (2000). *Tomorrow's children.* Boulder, CO: Westview.

Epstein, S. (2011). Who's in charge?: Examining the complex nature of student voice in service-learning projects. In T. Stewart & N. Webster (Eds.), *Problematizing service-learning: Critical reflections for development and action* (pp. 175–200). Charlotte, NC: Information Age.

Finley, L. (2004). Teaching peace in higher education: Overcoming the challenges to addressing structure and methods. *Online Journal of Peace and Conflict Resolution, 5*(2).272–281

Freire, P. (1970). *Pedagogy of the oppressed.* New York, NY: Continuum.

Hackman, H. (2005). Five essential components for social justice education. *Equity & Excellence in Education, 38,* 103–109.

Harkavy, I. (2006). The role of universities in advancing citizenship and social justice in the 21st century. *Education, Citizenship and Social Justice, 1*(1), 5–37.

Herzberg, B. (1994, October). Community service and critical teaching. *College Composition and Communication, 45*(3), 307–319.

Himley, M. (2004, February). Facing (up to) "the stranger" in community service. *College Composition and Communication, 55*(3), 416–438.

Hollander, E. (2010). Foreword. In D. W. Butin (Ed.), *Service-learning in theory and practice* (pp. vii–xii). New York, NY: Palgrave Macmillan.
hooks, b. (1994). *Teaching to transgress: Education as the practice of freedom.* New York, NY: Routledge.
Illich, I. (1990). To hell with good intentions. In J. Kendall (Ed.), *Combining service and learning: A resource book for community and public service* (Vol. I, pp. 314–320). Raleigh, NC: National Society for Internships and Experiential Education.
Jacoby, B. (1996). *Service-learning in higher education.* San Francisco, CA: Jossey-Bass.
Katopes, P. (2009, February 16). The "business model" is the wrong model. *Inside higher education.* Retrieved February 17, 2014 from http://www.insidehighered.com/views/2009/02/16/katopes
Koliba, C. (2000). Moral language and networks of engagement: Service-learning and civic education. *American Behavioral Scientist, 43,* 825–838.
Kumashiro, K. (2009). *Against common sense: Teaching and learning towards social justice* (2nd ed.). New York, NY: Routledge.
Lukanioff, G. (2014). *Unlearning liberty: Campus censorship and the end of American debate.* New York, NY: Encounter Books.
Marullo, S., & Edwards, B. (2000). From charity to justice: The potential for university-community collaboration for social change. *American Behavioral Scientist, 43,* 895–912.
Mayhew, M., & Deluca-Fernandez, S. (2007). Pedagogical practices that contribute to social justice outcomes. *The Review of Higher Education, 31*(1), 55–80.
Miller, SJ., Beliveau, L., Destigter, T., & Kirkland, D. (2008). *Narratives of social justice teaching.* New York, NY: Peter Lang.
Lukianoff, G. (2014). *Unlearning liberty: Campus censorship and the end of American debate.* New York, NY: Encounter Books.
Nagda, B., & Gurin, P. (2007). Intergroup dialogue: A critical dialogic approach to learning about difference, inequality, and social justice. *New Directions for Teaching and Learning, 111,* 35–45.
Nagda, B., Gurin, P., & Lopez, G. (2003). Transformative pedagogy for democracy and social justice. *Race, Ethnicity and Education, 6*(2), 165–191.
Nagda, B., & Zúñiga, X. (2003). Fostering meaningful racial engagement through intergroup dialogues. *Group Processes and Intergroup Relations, 6*(1), 111–128.
Osanloo, A. (2009). Civic responsibility and human rights education: A pan-educational alliance for social justice. *Intercultural Education, 20*(2), 151–159.
Rodriguez, M., Chambers, T., Gonzalez, M., & Scheurich, J. (2010). A cross-case analysis of three social justice-oriented education programs. *Journal of Research on Leadership Education, 5*(3.5), 138–153.
Roschelle, A., Turpin, A., & Elias, R. (2000). Who learns from service-learning? *American Behavioral Scientist, 43,* 839–847.
Singh, A., Hofsess, C., Boyer, E., Kwong, A., Lau, S., McLain, A., & Haggins, K. (2010). Social justice and counseling psychology: Listening to the voices of doctoral trainees. *The Counseling Psychologist, 38,* 766–795.
Smith, M. (2012, January 31). Social justice revival. *Inside higher education.* Retrieved February 3, 2014 from http://www.insidehighered.com/news/2012/01/31/colleges-embrace-social-justice-curriculum
Sperber, M. (2000). *Beer and circus: How big-time college sports is crippling undergraduate education.* New York, NY: Holt.
Strand, K., et al. (2003). Principles of best practice for community-based research. *Michigan Journal of Community Service-Learning,* 1–15.
Toubiana, M. (2014). Business pedagogy for social justice? An exploratory investigation of business faculty perspectives of social justice in business education. *Management Learning, 45*(1), 81–102.
Zimmerman, T., Krafnick, J., & Aberle, J. (2009). A university service-learning assignment: Delivering the FAIR curriculum to K-12 students to promote social justice. *Education, Citizenship and Social Justice, 4*(3), 195–210.

CHAPTER 26

The Audacity of Humanity

Searching for Hope, Longing for Peace

Ty-Ron M. O. Douglas

Introduction

The angry outcries from many *Christian* sects to Barak Obama's audacious and successful presidential campaigns (in which *hope* was a central theme) exemplify the polarization that has resulted from the abuse of religion and Christianity. Suspicion of spirituality, religion, and faith abounds inside and outside of the academy. Scholars who see their spirituality as inseparable from their work as advocates of social justice are often challenged with naming their "prophetic pragmatism" (West, 1999) without being labeled *anti-intellectual* or libeled as close-minded. Naming and embracing one's positionality as a Christian academician can be a highly nuanced and difficult process (Cozart, 2010). Drawing from my positionality as a self-identified *non-traditional Christian intellectual*, this chapter reveals personal elements of my philosophical encounters with Plato's (1992) "philosopher-king," Rorty's (1999) notion of "consensus," and discourses of hope.

In this chapter, I examine the theme of *hope* within the context of my own spiritual positionality and my philosophical journey from Plato to Richard Rorty during a Philosophy of Education course experience as a graduate student. I frame my argument around the controversial notions of Big Truths (Ts) and little truths (t's) as tangible, yet sometimes misguided, manifestations of man's nihilistic pursuit of meaning in a confusing world. I believe this topic is important for all educators—particularly educators in American Higher Education, because we possess and promote varying notions of truth that collide with, create, clarify, and even confuse the beliefs of our students—many of whom no longer learn about God in our schools and invariably wrestle with their own notions of truth.

Barak Obama's audacious and successful presidential campaigns (during which *hope* was a central tenant) and the recent outcry from many *Christian* sects—typified by a *Christian* minister in Kansas in 2008 who posted the disturbing billboard message: "America, we have a Muslim president. This is a sin against the Lord"—reveals the polarization that has resulted from the abuse of Christianity. By drawing on what some may describe as *primitive* Biblical principles, in one sense my argument reflects traditional Christianity; yet, in another sense, it is far from traditional in that it espouses teachings that are no longer common in traditional, mainstream, or nominal Christianity. For example, unlike Rorty (1999), who reduces Christianity to New Testament teachings, my perspective encompasses the whole Bible as my standard for truth, hope, and wisdom in ways that many Christians no longer acknowledge or accept. As such, this chapter is as much an analysis of man's philosophical pursuit of hope as it is an articulation and acknowledgement of my positionality as a *non-traditional Christian intellectual* within the context of my course experience. Certainly, suspicion of spirituality, religion, and faith abounds inside and outside of the academy. Scholars who see their spirituality as inseparable from their work as advocates of social justice are often challenged with naming their "prophetic pragmatism" (West, 1999) without being labeled *anti-intellectual* or libeled as close-minded. Naming and embracing one's positionality as a Christian academician can be a highly nuanced and difficult process (Cozart, 2010). Drawing from my positionality as a self-identified *non-traditional Christian intellectual*, this chapter reveals personal elements of my philosophical encounters with Plato's (1992) "philosopher-king," Rorty's (1999) notion of "consensus," and discourses of hope.

Because I understand that the language, label, and legacy of Christianity as a "tool" (Rorty, 1999, p. 65) for bludgeoning and beguiling the masses is as real as the God of Christianity, I cautiously begin navigating through the treacherous web of opinions at the origin of humanity's philosophical dilemma: The Garden of Eden. White (1911) explains the following:

> It is a masterpiece of Satan's deceptions to keep the minds of men searching and conjecturing in regard to that which God has not made known and which He does not intend that we shall understand. It was thus that Lucifer lost his place in heaven. … Now he seeks to imbue the minds of men with the same spirit and to lead them also to disregard the direct commands of God. Those who are unwilling to accept the plain, cutting truths of the Bible are continually seeking pleasing fables that will quiet the conscience. (p. 523)

Philosophy—which can be defined as the love or pursuit of wisdom—has always been a part of the human experience, although it transcends the existence of humanity (White, 1911). The biblical account of the creation and fall of Adam and Eve (see Genesis 1–3) suggests that this couple was not only given the responsibility of tending the Garden, but they also had the privilege of learning about the intricacies of the universe directly from God. Arguably, then, philosophy—in its purest form—was valuable to humanity and validated by God, as long as we did not abuse our freedom by disobeying the parameters of the Creator, the source of wisdom. In this light, Kant's (1960) belief that laws are meant to make people free and individuals must be free to follow the law is not new. In the Bible, Genesis 3: 4, 5 outline the deceptive introduction of the counterfeit to the human race: "Then the serpent said to the woman 'You will not surely die. For God knows that in the day you eat of it *your eyes will be opened, and you will be like God, knowing good and evil*'" (New King James Version—emphasis mine). As such, it can be contended that philosophy as we know it began with Adam and Eve's disobedience. And since then humanity has *vainly* sought to explain the world and our existence, while simultaneously and systematically denigrating God to meaningless conjecture.

Plato (1992) posits many intriguing and insightful ideas. His beliefs in education as the journey of the soul towards "the good" and his focus on "justice" are rooted in what appears to be a sincere desire to improve the human condition. Like Plato, I believe that each person has a nature, but I disagree with him on its quality. Plato believes we find happiness when we find that nature (p. 49); I believe we find happiness when we allow God to change our nature: "The heart is deceitful above all things, And desperately wicked" (Jeremiah 17: 9). Nevertheless, Plato's value to Western philosophy is exemplified by his claims that disharmony, internal conflict, and war occur when people are working outside of their specialized function, and that violence is the result of violating boundaries. I concur. But I also believe that philosophy, like nominal Christianity, often violates those boundaries. Although Plato acknowledges that there is a Truth to be found and—upon its discovery—we must align ourselves with it, he, like Adam and Eve, was deceived; to misappropriate the magnitude of man's fallen condition through the misguided hope in education as the magic cure-all is merely a mutation of the swindling, self-indulged subtleties espoused by the serpent (Satan) in the Garden; on this charge, Kant is also guilty. While some may suggest that Plato, who penned his thoughts 2400 years ago, predates the Bible and Christianity, it is my contention that—as a descendent of Adam—Plato merely predates Christianity as a religion and not Christianity as the experience. Biblical record suggests that Christ is the Creator in the Old Testament and the crucified Savior of the New Testament:

> In the beginning was the Word, and the Word was with God, and the Word was God. He was in the beginning with God. All things were made through Him, and without Him nothing was made that was made. … And the Word became flesh and dwelt among us, and we beheld His glory, the glory as of the only begotten of the Father, full of grace truth. (John 1: 1–3, 14)

The writings of E. G. White (1911, 1958) and T. E. White (2000) suggest that a Christian whose interpretation is based on the acceptance and legitimacy of the whole Bible, must consider that Christ is not only the Redeemer in the New Testament, but also the Creator in the Old Testament. This acknowledgement is significant because many scholars and contemporary philosophers attempt to position Plato and his writings as predating Christianity. This argument must be questioned in light of the Biblical record that suggest that Christianity is a relational experience that began (for humanity) when we were created in the Garden of Eden.

In this postmodern society where the prevailing sentiment is the belief in varying and independent little truths, there is a growing unwillingness by many to even consider the possibility that Truth exists. We have run the full gamut: the experiment—started by Adam and Eve's disobedience and continued by philosophers like Plato and Kant, who fail to recognize God as the Truth—has left humanity with many holes to plug in our collective conscience. The post-modern proliferation of little t's, albeit "rational" (Rorty, 1999), is only rivaled by the proliferation of anti-depressants and Tylenol in our post-modern society: the holes and the corresponding headache of our arrogance just won't go away! Rorty's (1999) pragmatism and ancillary *hope* in man's "ability to communicate" (p. 204), adjust, and find "eventual agreement" (p. 72) is a far less likely prospect than the Second Coming that he mockingly questions. Many would have placed the likelihood of seeing a black President in the United States in the same realm of near impossibility as the return of Christ. Still, the rapid deterioration of the environment and morality seem to suggest that Rorty may have put his hope in the wrong occurrence; beyond the frightening prospect that the pursuit of social justice is "the only basis for a worthwhile human life" (p. 204), we are forced to grapple with the reality that humans are killing ourselves and each other. Hope, in this regard, seems insufficient.

During the sixteen weeks of a *Philosophy of Education* graduate course, I sought to heed Lisa Delpit's warning—as cited by Hudak (2001)—that "we see what we want to see and hear what we want to hear" (p. 256). During those sixteen weeks, I saw a young, black senator from Chicago rise from relative obscurity to the personification of *The Audacity of Hope*. I got behind the eyes of Plato, Kant, and Rorty, and I saw and learned many things. One thing I did not see through their philosophical and political lenses, however, was hope. All of these philosophers appear to put their faith in something or someone other than Jesus Christ and that, for me, is a hopeless and depressing prospect. I recognize that my position is dependent on the acceptance and interpretation of the Scriptures, and I understand that there are many, like Rorty (1999), who would view my perspective with "suspicion." I respect our power of choice and our capacity to disagree amicably. But unlike the Christians Rorty (1999) describes, I do not believe one can "become a member of a particular sect or denomination *in order to* prepare for [the second coming]" (p. 201). Instead, one prepares by accepting and obeying the Truth (God), through the growth of a daily love relationship: "I am the way, the truth, and the life. No one comes to the Father except through Me" (John 14: 6). And like Plato, I believe we experience and know the Truth as we get closer to it.

Similar to Plato's philosopher-king who must share with others still in the cave, I, too, must share, while carefully dodging the sermonic overtures that often set off the two-headed trip-alarm of skepticism and cynicism. The abuse of God and religion has made this tough though, for there are many who, with Mahatma Ghandi, would declare: "I like your Christ, I do not like your Christians. Your Christians are so unlike your Christ." To that, I am reminded that "faith is the substance (realization) of things *hoped* for, the evidence (confidence) of things not seen" (Hebrews 11:1). Ironically, Rorty (1999) quotes a portion of this biblical passage when describing his "willingness to refer all questions of ultimate justification to the future" (p. 27). Each of us, then, must decide where we will place our faith and hope.

In the penultimate class of my graduate Philosophy of Education class, I will never forget the stifling silence and eventual grunts that greeted the professor's request to my classmates and me to articulate our thoughts on *hope*. The silence was a pretty accurate barometer of people's real sense of *hope*. Before the medicating thoughts of an Obama presidency or the optimism about the power and potential of our "interconnectivity" could kick in, there was an obvious sense of ineptitude. In a world searching for answers, there seems to be few alternatives that help us sleep better at night, and the booming sales of the pharmaceutical industry suggest that our days are no easier to get through.

The search for hope and peace mirrors the daunting task of sharing the world with individuals whose little t's (and big T's for that matter) can only be described as terrorism. I cringe at the thought of religious organizations whose central edicts promote the destruction of others. I cringe at the abuse of true Godliness by religious organizations and religious people who very well may, as Rorty (1999) suggests, "cause much more suffering in the United States than Abiel Guzman managed to cause in Peru" (p. 205). I cringe at the thought of the maturation of "malleable" children (Plato, 1992) who are being encouraged to see *The Communist Manifesto* and *The Bible* as having equal value (Rorty, 1999). If education, as Kant (1960) suggests and I concur, shapes the nature of society in the future, then I am not looking forward to lying in the hard bed that we have made for ourselves and our posterity (p. 11). Plato (1992) would assert that our children lack more "self-control" than ever; Kant (1960) would bemoan the lack of "discipline" in this generation of youth; and many would agree that the growing propensity towards ethical *normalization* promises to leave our society morally bankrupt. Plato (1992) would declare that our "appetites" are running amuck.

Taken together, the perpetuation of Godless schooling and irresponsible parenting, along with the desire for moral inclusivity and "consensus," is a formula for "compromise" and chaos (Rorty, 1999); Plato would certainly be appalled. Worse still, if, as Rorty suggests, exposure creates the propensity for "sympathy," then we are raising an immoral generation of young people who will not only have little respect for God but little sympathy for those who do. In addition, the willingness to do anything in the name of "consensus," "growth" (Rorty, 1999), and the greater good creates a dangerous concoction. Even Delpit (2006) is "more concerned now with the development of the character of our youth than [she] was when [she] originally wrote *Other People's Children*" (p. xvi), and I believe the "causal pressures" of a desperate world community and the volatile times in which we live will create a deceptively "useful" solution: Apostate Protestantism. Through the merging of church and state and in the name of the *greater good*, many will soon declare that Kant's belief that *one must be free to follow the laws* was historically *reason*able, but contextually replaceable. The events of the Dark Ages stand as a chilling warning of what could lie ahead. Even Rorty would be amazed at "what [people's] peers [may] let them get away with." Moreover, I believe that the same wound that mars the fabric of Plato's Big T without *the Big G* (God) encroaches onto Rorty's ideas, through the inevitable diminution of *the Truth* to little truths. Man's futile attempt to be God, coupled with the worship of vast and varied pseudo-gods (i.e. the worship of man and possessions) (Douglas, 2012), facilitates the use of philosophy as an anesthesia—or "tool" (Rorty, 1999)—to numb the pain created by the abyss between humanity and hope. As educators and leaders in American Higher Education, we must have the audacity to create institutions and spaces of hope and healing. While large-scale reforms and political inertia may discourage many educators from envisioning and engaging in critical practices that can heal, I am reminded that the first and most important system that one has agency over is *the institution of self.* We cannot lead students any further than we are prepared to go (hooks, 1994). We must seek to know our authentic selves and be willing to utilize the pedagogical power that exists in our stories, our belief systems, our journeys, and our survival—inside and outside the academy. That was my approach as a graduate student; this continues to be my approach as a professor.

Like hooks (1994), I now teach with the understanding that teaching is a sacred art which requires that I care for the "whole" student. My leadership and teaching is grounded in the belief that "true education is the harmonious development of the physical, the mental, and the spiritual powers" (White, 19011 p. 13). I am a respecter of difference who is willing to consider perspectives that are different from my own. I believe that a profound love for humanity, coupled with a love for my subject matter and the power of ideas, must be present in order to teach and lead effectively (Darder, 2002). I concur with Freire that "teaching is an act of love" (Darder, 2002). I also see credence to McLaren's description of love as "the oxygen of revolution, nourishing the blood … [and] spirit of struggle" (McLaren (2000) as cited in Darder, 2002, p. 148). As a non-traditional Christian intellectual and professor in this age of great religious intolerance and legitimate discontent with the status quo, I seek to teach with hope and love for all people (Douglas, 2013; Douglas & Nganga, 2015). I refuse to run away from the critical conversations that invariably emerge in classrooms that embrace and consider the Big T's and little T's that students bring with them to class. This is an audacious yet necessary undertaking—both for my students, and for me, as a walking institution of healing who seeks to live out my faith and pedagogy in authentic, relevant, and liberating ways.

Work Cited

Cozart, S. C. (2010). When the Spirit shows up: An autoethnography of spiritual reconciliation with the academy. *Educational Studies, 46*(2), 250–269.

Darder, A. (2002). *Reinventing Paulo Freire: A pedagogy of love.* Boulder, CO: Westview.

Delpit, L. (2006). *Other people's children.* New York, NY: The New Press.

Douglas, T. M. O. (2012). Resisting idol worship at HBCUs: The malignity of materialism, Western masculinity, and spiritual malefaction. *The Urban Review, 44*(3), 378–400.

Douglas, T. M. O. (2013). Confessions of a border crossing *brotha*-scholar: Teaching race with all of me. In D. J. Davis & P. Boyer (Eds.), *Social justice and racism in the college classroom: Perspectives from different voices* (pp. 55–67). Bingley: Emerald Publishing Group.

Douglas, T. M. O., & Nganga, C. (2015). What's radical love got to do with it? Navigating identity, pedagogy, and positionality in pre-service education. *International Journal of Critical Pedagogy, 5*(3), 58–82.

hooks, b. (1994). *Teaching to transgress: Education as the practice of freedom.* New York, NY: Routledge.

Hudak, G. M. (2001). "Addicting epistemologies? Neo-conservative, Thich Nhat Hanh, Lisa Delpit." In G. M. Hudak & P. Kihn (Eds.), *Labeling: Politics and pedagogy* (pp. 251–260). London: Routledge/Falmer Press.

Kant, I. (1960). *Education.* Ann Arbor, MI: The University of Michigan Press.

Plato. (1992). *Republic.* G. M. A. Grube & C. D. C. Reeves (Trans.). Indianapolis, IN: Hackett Publishing Company (Original work written c. 380 B.C.)

Rorty, R. (1999). *Philosophy and social hope.* New York, NY: Penguin Books.

West, Cornel. (1999). The Cornel West Reader. New York, NY: Civitas Books.

White, E. G. (1911). *The great controversy between Christ and Satan.* Nampa, ID: Pacific Press Publishing Association.

White, E. G. (1958). *The story of patriarchs and prophets.* Nampa, ID: Pacific Press Publishing Association.

White, T. E. (2000). *Scandal of the universe.* Belleville, ON: Essence Publishing.

CHAPTER 27

On Becoming

Exploring self, Equity in Education and the Poetry of Critical Thinking

Lalenja Harrington

mmm girl
listen to the inspiration
of power all around you
and position yourself
legs wide
at the door to that nothing place
where all those insidious voices
whisper and hiss
alone at this crossroad
you are insensitive
to the sharp-toothed tearing
of double standards
that inch slowly down your back
I will speak when I feel like speaking
you say
over and over
until you are heard
until the night stops its breathing
quieting sound with a blanket of heavy wool
so that it can take in the beauty
of your razor focused
intent
and knowledge
of becoming
–Lalenja Harrington

Poetry has long been an incredibly important part of my life. I believe that there is potential for poetry in each one of us, regardless of age, experience, ability or facility with words. In my mind, it is a great equalizer. The freedom that lies within the craft of writing a poem, can help people tap into thoughts and ideas that are sometimes too hard to articulate in formal writing and discussion. I have watched children and grow n folk alike surprise themselves with the depth of imagery and metaphor that they find within their own voices. I believe that there is great power in that discovery.

So when I was given the opportunity to write the above piece for my Social Justice in Higher Education class, I found myself focusing on that discovery element of social justice—the moment when each individual is empowered not only to find their voice, but to speak it aloud-ideally in an environment where their perspective is respected and of value. Those moments of "becoming" and the freedom/expectation to examine one's own position, whether it be for an individual or for an entire community, are at the core of a critically-thinking, socially-just society. As Patricia Hill Collins has said, "both the changed consciousness of individuals and the social transformation of political and economic institutions constitute essential ingredients for social change" (Collins, 1990, p. 221). With Collins' words in mind, in this narrative I will explore my poetic response in light of the following:

1. my own position, relationship with poetry as a catalyst for transformation/social justice

2. the power of "becoming" and resistance through the framework of the "poetry of critical thinking," as expressed through the writings of women of color

3. the role of poetry and collaborative writing in higher education

THE POWER OF THE WORD

Growing up, my mother's bookshelves were filled with the words of women. Ntozake Shange, Alice Walker, Audre Lorde, Nikki Giovanni, Sonia Sanchez, Adrienne Rich … the wall to wall bookshelf was like a tapestry of poetic images in warm reds and browns, quilted wisdom that I could wrap around my gangly young frame, from which I drew power that allowed me to grow into the woman that I would be. At the feet of these incredible women, my consciousness began to change—eyes closed with newborn softness, forced open by unapologetic attacks on race, power and privilege.

Discovering Self, My Position

As a young girl of mixed heritage, identity was a constant source of tension and discomfort for me. Was I black enough? Should I feel guilty about liking the same things that my white friends liked? What did it mean to have good hair and fair skin? If I claimed my blackness, was I strong enough? Was I "down" enough"? Could I reject commonly held beliefs about black women and still claim that identity for myself? Encountering poems like *When I was growing up* by Nellie Wong helped me to begin to come to terms with the vulnerability that comes with true self-reflection,

> When I was growing up,
> read magazines
> and saw movies, blonde movie stars, white skin
> sensuous lips and to be elevated, to become
> A woman, a desirable woman, I began to wear
> imaginary pale skin (Moraga & Anzaldua, 1983, p. 7)

as well as the rawness and pain touched on by Charlene McRary in her poem *I used to think,*

> If I could be a cream-colored lovely
> with gypsy curls,
> Someone's pecan dream and sweet sensation
> I'd be poetry in motion …

If I were beautiful, I could be angry and cute
instead of an evil, pouting mammy bitch
a nigger woman, passed over
conquested and passed over,
a nigger woman
to do it to in the bushes (Smith, 1983, pp. 57–58)

Nina Simone's song *Four Women*, stopped me in my tracks, caused a paradigm shift in my thinking: I was all of these women and I claimed them all.

My skin is black/My arms are long, My hair is woolly/my back is strong
Strong enough to take the pain/inflicted again and again
What do they call me/my name is aunt sarah, my name is aunt sarah

My skin is yellow/my hair is long/between two worlds/I do belong
My father was rich and white/he forced my mother late one night
What do they call me/my name is saffronia/my name is saffronia

My skin is tan/my hair is fine/my hips invite you/my mouth like wine
Whose little girl am I/anyone who has money to buy
What do they call me/my name is sweet thing/my name is sweet thing

My skin is brown/my manner is tough/I'll kill the first mother I see/my life has been too rough
I'm awfully bitter these days/because my parents were slaves
What do they call me/my name is peaches

Ntozake inspired as she told a story of the colored girl that was also me:

she's been dead so long
closed in silence so long
she doesn't know the sound
of her own voice
her infinite beauty
she's half notes scattered
without rhythm/no tune
sing her sighs
sing the song of her possibilities
sing a righteous gospel
let her be born
let her be born
& handled warmly. (Shange, 1977, pp. 4–5)

With time, I came to understand that the responsibility to "handle her warmly" was mine, as well as all members of any socially just community—to welcome and celebrate the perspective and position of those who have traditionally been marginalized and discounted. I struggled to drop my own "Cry-Smile mask" spoken of here by Jid Lee in *This Bridge we call home*,

> As a doctoral student at a mid-western university, I first realized that most students expected me to reinforce their stereotypes: as an Asian woman, I was to tell them how grateful Asian immigrants were for the opportunity to live in a free country far superior to our own oppressive native lands. Because I didn't accommodate this expectation, I became unpopular until I adopted my Cry-Smile mask. But when I moved to a southern regional university as a tenure-track assistant professor, I needed a much thicker mask, capable of withstanding the omnipresent, violent statements of racism and prejudice. (Anzaldua Keating, 2002, p. 398)

and reject those stereotypes that sparked work like Simone's *Four Women*—I began to celebrate the fullness of my own colored girl. In *Homegirls: A Black Feminist Anthology*, Renita Weems expressed this in the following passage,

> Over the years, the Black woman novelist has not been taken seriously. "Shallow," emotional," "unstructured," "reactionary," "just too painful," are just some of the criticisms made of her work. That she is a woman makes her work marginal. That she is Black makes it minor. That she is both makes it? But these criticisms have not stopped the flow of her ink. The Black woman writer has insisted on portraying the tragic and the fortunate of her lot. And in so doing, she answers the question posed by actress/ activist Abbey Lincoln some twelve years ago in her essay titled "Who will revere the Black woman?" The Black woman artist will revere the Black woman. For it is her duty to record and capture with song, clay, strings, dance and in this case ink. The joys and powers of Black womanhood. And the person who is sane, secure and sensitive enough to revere her art is the same person who will revere her life. (Smith, 1983, p. 94)

I myself began to revere the Black Woman, starting the work that Collins mentions, and setting the stage for my own personal transformation of consciousness.

Understanding impact of racism. privilege, and oppression

I believe that the diasporic connection that I experienced in studying the writings of women of color has been an essential part of my continued development as a critical thinker and proponent of social justice. It was almost impossible *not* to transform my thinking as I was steeped in poems, essays and other writings that challenged racism, privilege, power and oppression—described here through Sensoy and DiAngelo's lens of social justice:

> Racism: "the historical accumulation and ongoing use of institutional power and authority that supports discriminatory behaviors in systemic and far-reaching ways." (Sensoy & DiAngelo, 2012, p. 116)
>
> Privilege: rights and advantages conferred by socially constructed practices that value one group of people at the expense of others. (p. 58)
>
> Oppression: when power is combined with prejudice and discrimination, oppression occurs; involving "institutional control, ideological domination, and the imposition of the dominant group's culture on the minoritized group (p. 39)"

The emphasis on community and the collective displayed by women of color writers/artists, as well as their dedication to shining light on systematic abuses of power and authority, were essential parts of what I tapped into as a young woman. Nikki Giovanni called out for urgency and action in the face of dehumanizing practices,

> The Black Revolution is passing you bye,
> negroe
> Anne Frank didn't put cheese and bread away for you
> because she knew it would be different this time …
> tomorrow was too late to properly arm yourself
> see you can do an improper job now
> see you can do now something, anything, but move now
> negro. … (Giovanni, 1979, pp. 24–25)

Audre Lorde spoke about the invisibility of being a black woman artist in a white, patriarchal world in *To the Poet Who Happens to Black and the Black Poet who Happens to be A Woman*:

> No cold spirit ever strolled through my bones
> on the corner of Amsterdam Avenue

No dog mistook me for a bench
nor a tree   nor a bone
No lover envisioned my plump brown arms
as wings   no misnamed me condor
But I can recall without counting
eyes
canceling me out
like an unpleasant appointment
Postage due
stamped in yellow red purple
any color
except Black and choice
and woman
alive
(Lorde, 1994, p. 6)

I, along with the women that I was reading, rejected the hegemonic ideal of "Individualism" where race is made irrelevant because there are "no intrinsic barriers to individual success", and where "failure is not a consequence of social structures but of individual character." (Sensoy & DiAngelo, 2012). I read and re-read bell hooks "essays on the commodification and appropriation of race."

> Words like other and difference are taking the place of commonly known words deemed uncool or too simplistic, words like oppression, exploitation and domination. Black and white in some circles are becoming definite no-nos, perpetuating what some folks see as stale and meaningless binary oppositions. Separated from a political and historical context, ethnicity is being reconstituted as the new frontier, accessible to all, no passes or permits necessary, where attention can now be focused on the production of a privileged, commodifiable discourse in which race becomes synonymous with culture. There would be no need however, for any unruly radical black folks to raise critical objections to the phenomenon if all this passionate focus on race were not so neatly divorced from a recognition of racism, of the continuing domination of blacks by whites, and (to use some of those out-of-date uncool terms) of the continued suffering and pain in black life. (hooks, 1990, pp. 51–52)

resonating with the idea that color blind practices were indeed dangerous in their tendency to reinforce "white supremacy through the normalization and silence that surrounds and supports their (white folks) institutionalized white privilege" (Weiner, 2007). I also think that there is great value in Weiner's assertion that white people who are serious about eradicating racism, will use their privilege "toward the goal of destroying their privilege" (Weiner, 2007, p. 61).

It is this self-reflection and awareness that encouraged writers like Diana Courvant to explore the privilege that allowed her "to pretend that being a white woman confronting racism is hard." In her essay, *Speaking of Privilege*, Courvant acknowledged that she has "dangerous moments" where she imagined that it might have "been nice" to have been born of color, so that she could have absorbed "the reality of racism" instead of having to force it into visibility. She also evoked the idea of intersectionality as she admitted that she also has "dangerous moments" where she allows herself to let her disability become an "excuse for not doing the work of confronting oppressions that privilege" her (Courvant, 2002). Angela Davis highlights issues that have arisen within the women's right's movement around privilege, power and intersectionality,

> The inestimable importance of the Seneca Falls Declaration was its role as the articulated consciousness of women's rights at midcentury. It was the theoretical culmination of years of unsure, often silent, challenges aimed at a political, social, domestic and religious condition which was contradictory, frustrating and downright oppressive for women of the bourgeoisie and the rising middle classes. However, as a rigorous consummation of the consciousness of white middle-class women's dilemma, the Declaration all but ignored the predicament of white working class women, as it ignored the condition of Black women in the South and North alike. (Davis, 1983, p. 53)

This is a struggle that I believe faces most students of color in higher education—acknowledging the privilege that accompanies our position as "academics" even within an oppressive educational, political and cultural system, particularly for those of us who consider ourselves to be "social justice" scholars. We have a responsibility to examine our own motives and advantages gained by our position so that we are not recreating Seneca Falls, and we must examine our own complicity and willingness to "collaborate in our own victimization" (Collins, 1990). Slam poet Patricia Smith explores this complicity in *Nothing Pulling Him Down,*

> He kept those black hands flat on the table,
> away from the throats of the men
> who nodded tolerance when they passed him
> in the halls, then struggled to keep
> his hands away from his own throat.'
> Kept his eyes level,
> his mouth shut,
> and every month his bank account fattened.
> corporate magic. Used to be
> that was all he asked, just to be there. (Smith, 1993, p. 62)

Sonia Sanchez challenges us to think about lethal consequences of internalizing oppression,

> I see you blackboy
> bent toward destruction watching
> for death with tight eyes. (Sanchez, 1984, p. 42)

Audre Lorde's asks us to fight the pull of internalized oppression by re-framing our identities; for example, we as women should view our desire to nurture not as "pathological but redemptive." When we can claim the knowledge that our power is real, "our real power is rediscovered" (Lorde, 1994). In her poem *Koko*, Angela Jackson echoes this with,

> There are different kinds
> Of naked., if you can understand
> What makes it funny is I get
> Up in the morning in real life and cook and
> Clean house like any woman but
> Then before morning I let the
> Growl out the pocket of my mouth
> And she come out in a
> Holler be naked and long-legged
> Split the smoke room swoop
> And fly up in somebody eye.
> Used to be a time when a woman
> Didn't go around making such suits
> For anybody to wear
> She just stay home and sew. But
> I take the spool and go upside a man's
> Head he know he been struck by lightning. (Jackson, 1993, p. 91)

And so, with all of these words and many others at my fingertips, my introduction into the power and poetry of critical thinking began.

"Poetry" of critical thinking

A stripped down definition of critical theory might describe it as a "scholarly approach that explores the historical, cultural, and ideological lines of authority that underlie social conditions

(Sensoy & DiAngelo, 2012, p. 1)." Some central points further identified by Joseph Kincheloe (2007) include critical engagement, rejection of economic determinism, focus on relationships among power, culture and domination, impact of desire, reconceptualization of hegemony and ideology, and the centrality of interpretation. Critical theory is grounded in a concern with power and the oppression of human beings, and the state of human suffering as a result of the social order. (Kincheloe, 2007) Nikki Giovanni challenges scholars of color to dig deep in critically examining their own consciousness,

> Just because our hair is natural doesn't mean we don't have a wig. We are niggers-in-residence at white universities and talk about voting as a means to take over a city, and then we put James Brown down for supporting Hubert Humphrey. Its all a wig. (Giovanni, 2003, p. 46)

As Kincheloe states, critical thinkers, educators and scholars should find excitement in "attaining new levels of consciousness and ways of being." It is imperative to understand how dominant ideology "constructs subjectivity/consciousness via education, the media and other cultural sites. (Kincheloe, 2007, p. 33)." As I move deeper into my own scholarly life, continued transformation is non-negotiable for me—I cannot claim criticality without a commitment to continue challenging myself and my relationship with hegemonic ideology. I am drawn to bell hooks description of her "revolutionary" relationship with critical pedagogy,

> For me, critical pedagogy (expressed in writing, teaching and habits of being) is fundamentally linked to a concern with creating strategies that will enable colonized folks to decolonize their minds and actions, thereby promoting the insurrection of subjugated knowledge. (hooks, 1990, p. 8)

and embrace her concept of insurrection and resistance; it does indeed feel like a battle is being waged on critical thinking in our academic, cultural and political communities these days.

Reflections of Resistance

Resistance is an important concept for me for two reasons: (1) the discover y of one's motivation to resist requires a critical examination of one's position and beliefs about self-worth, and (2) the empowerment that comes along with such an evaluation can then act as a launching pad for further transformation, as alluded to by hooks in the above quote. In *Affirmative Acts*, June Jordan highlights the following elements of resistance:

· absence of fear;

· affirmation of self-worth;

· resolute holding to one's entitlement to the power one was exercising;

· manifest support;

· the stunning energy of rage. (Jordan, 1998, p. 145)

If we look at each element of Jordan's framework, we can find echoes of resistance.

Within the books on my mother's shelves, I found resistance, discovery, and most importantly, a commitment to ask the hard questions and seek the uncomfortable truth. These writings helped set the stage for me to speak my own truths, and although I did not realize the profound impact that this foundation would play in my life, that is often the power of words.

SHARING THE WORD

In college I began playing around with my own writing and exploration of self, but it was not until I walked into the Can Tab Lounge in Cambridge MA after I graduated, that I found a community that was as welcoming and powerful as the books with which I had spent so much time at home. Each night, in that basement of a room, I watched poet after poet get up on the stage, touching on a bevy of universal and personal truths—griots in action. Booing was not allowed—all voices were supported and all perspectives heard and respected. The stage became a place that I was able to question injustice and advocate for my own sense of personal "rightness," a place that I could continue to work through some of my own demons around sexism, racism and oppression along with the other word warriors all around me. As Ntozake Shange (1977) said so beautifully, "I found god in myself, & I loved her/loved her fiercely" (p. 63).

I found great joy in the slam scene, and continued to write and perform for some years, but as my interests changed, moving beyond the restrictions of a three-minute poem format, I found myself losing focus. How was I to continue transforming my writing to stay true to the sense of empowerment and self-fulfillment that I had found through speaking my own truth on stage? How else could I encourage others to open their minds to the power of poetry and wordsmithing? It was a chance activity in my role as an advocate for people with disabilities that helped me find a vehicle for the continued fruits of my love affair with metaphor.

I had been working within the field of disability advocacy for many years, when I was given the opportunity to facilitate a writing group for people of all levels of ability. Naysayers were initially skeptical about how this was going to work with folks with intellectual disabilities, but in the end, people are people—and everyone has a unique voice—so we went at it. The experience made a lasting impression on all of us. We found poetry in the everyday, with everyone bringing their own words or images as inspiration. About a painting of a woman in red we wrote:

Alone
in the crying room

depression
is an uncomfortable chair

where you must sit
head down

Trapped within
the angles of yourself

nothing to hold onto
in the storm
of your
raw burning red

shame

(The Arc of High Point, 2007, p. 48)

People who had never considered poetry as a possibility, began walking around with composition books and looking for inspiration in every corner. People whose voices were not generally heard or even respected, began finding places to insert their point of view in a poetic way. People with disabilities in the group began to challenge the stereotypes of incompetency and inability, and in the resulting spaces, created themselves anew as writers with valuable viewpoints. It was fabulous.

The purpose of the group was never to deny or ignore the fact the it contained people with varied abilities—the point was to create an inclusive unit that celebrated the unique characteristics of each of its members. That was the beauty of it, experiencing the synergy of all the individual working parts in the creation of a cohesive whole. June Jordan speaks to this idea of "cultural pluralism" here,

I am a cultural pluralist because I am in my right mind … And, therefore, I do not propose that those many peoples should be homogenized into one prime-time sitcom. I reject E Pluribus Unum as a guideline or goal. I have to! Yes, I understand the hierarchical urge of individuals and groups wanting to imitate or, better yet, merge with Dominant Culture because, otherwise, they fear disastrous dependency, invisibility, or extinction. And I even understand the pathological urge to act like the Number Ones; I understand the urge to copycat the hateful, violent, and disgusting, dominant history of dominant response to those who differ from those who would dominate. But the hierarchical urge is undemocratic, at least, and I believe, immoral, besides. (Jordan, 1998, p. 136)

As with many minoritized groups, people with disabilities have historically been discounted, discriminated against, condescended to, oppressed and dominated by the "Dominant Culture" that Jordan discusses. Segregation is still in full force for this community, and it often requires great efforts of advocacy and resistance for people with disabilities to receive basic human rights, to simply have choice in their lives. I think that we have to be cautious in our advocacy for those rights, however, to ensure that we don't confuse equality and equity. People with disabilities often utilize different tools/strategies to have full access to their communities (equity) and desire the same respect as a human being given to any other member of their community (equality).

Current philosophical trends in advocacy call for self-determination, self-direction, empowerment and personal responsibility. People with disabilities are willing to fight the fight to have control over their lives, with the understanding that, "if you don't have control you cannot take responsibility … How can anyone be responsible without power? Power implies choice." (Giovanni, 2003, p. 6) As critical educator, Shirley Steinberg (2012) has pointed out, "domination limits self-direction and democratic community building while emancipation enables it." These ideas of power, choice and self-direction are at the very center of advocacy for any people who have been subjugated, oppressed or disenfranchised, and it is here that I have been able to bridge my personal and creative interests in social justice, with my professional interests in inclusive higher education.

In *Is everyone really equal?* Sensoy and DiAngelo (2012) discuss the concept of Transformative Academic Knowledge as a method for ensuring that education and knowledge reinforces a society that is just,

> Transformative academic knowledge refers to the concepts and explanations that challenge mainstream academic knowledge and that expand the canon. TAK questions the idea that knowledge can ever be outside of human interests, perspectives, and values. Proponents of transformative academic knowledge. Assume that knowledge is not neutral and that it reflects the social hierarchies of a given society. They believe that a key purpose of conceptualizing knowledge in this way is to make society more just. TAK is knowledge that challenges the traditional canon. (Sensoy & DiAngelo, 2012, p. 10)

I believe that the post-secondary education movement for students with intellectual disabilities can be considered TAK. The inclusion of students with ID in college courses challenges traditional teaching methods and course frameworks, requiring faculty and instructors to implement more universally designed strategies. These changes will ultimately make college courses more accessible to a broader expanse of students, opening doors that have rarely been accessible to oppressed people, and this ultimately has the potential to upset the current status of collegiate education, where the primary audiences for critical pedagogy are the privileged, rather than the oppressed (Weiner, 2007).

> It is so vitally important that those who work in spheres that deal with issues of knowledge and education listen carefully to the insights of colonized people. (Kincheloe, 2008, p. 6)

I consider collaborative writing (CW) to be a "transformative" method that makes room for multiple voices and "insights of colonized people." As an educational exercise, it is a way to avoid "pedantic teaching" where the instructor/faciliatator "might sometimes have to sacrifice what s/he thinks or knows to be right in an effort to create the conditions for students to investigate the conditions, relations, and contradictions that make things appear right or wrong (Weiner, 2007, p. 67)." Through the "performance" of writing, CW acts a conduit of critical pedagogy that "disrupts those hegemonic cultural and educational practices that reproduce the logics of neoliberal conservatism (Denzin, 2007, p. 128)."

> Drawing on the complex traditions embedded in participatory action research, as well as the critical turn in feminist discourse, and the growing literature for and by indig. peoples, crit. Performance pedagogy implements a commitment to participation and performance with, not for, community members. (Denzin, 2007, p. 138)

It is also my belief that CW can be used as a method of exploratory qualitative research where "knowable communities" are "engaged in cultural and political reflection and struggle (Leistyna, 2012, p. 217)." As with Participatory Action Research (PAR) or Action based research, with this model, there is a focus on doing research with others, "rather than on them," as described below,

> Action based research has always had a qualitative political and transformative agenda explicitly woven in its theoretical and empirical fabric … AR is thus substantively different from applied research in that praxis is not seen as a distinct separation between theory and practice, given that knowledge is constructed and evaluated in the midst of action as the two dialectically feed off of each other in the process. (Leistyna, 2012, p. 204)

I have tried CW in a number of settings, with a variety of audiences, and I am inspired by the experience each and every time. I am always amazed by the synergy that develops as a group of people begin to tune into a common vision/direction, and by the joy that people experience when presented with the finished product. I want to see every classroom as well as the community at large work this way, with communal decision making for the good of all, in an environment where ALL voices are important. How do we begin to structure our classrooms in this way? How do we open the door for these types of experiences in education?

The opportunity to co-lead a class on prejudice and discrimination for my Social Justice in Higher Education seemed like the perfect place to bring collaborative writing to the table. My co-leaders and I saw this as another level of access and opportunity for the creation of an authentic "community" voice, a voice that is truly the sum of its parts; that would not exist without the unique points of view of each of its members. When done correctly, collaborative writing is a perfect example of how a community of diverse members can come together, honor the individual contributions, ideas, and strengths of its members towards a unified goal. It was my hope that the transformative power of the written and spoken word would be as impactful for my classmates as it has been for me in my life.

A Community of Unsuspecting Poets

The Process

On the day of the exercise, I walked into the classroom with a feeling of anticipation and possibility. Having been in this class for several weeks, I knew that our small community was ripe for creativity and expression, particularly with a topic like prejudice and discrimination. The goal of the exercise was twofold: to highlight a justice-oriented "process", as well as the creation of a creative "product," expression of thoughts about the impact of discrimination and prejudice.

After starting the learning activity with a poem to "prime the pump" we shared resources and facts from the course materials to highlight our responses and thoughts about the topic. The class was instructed to write down one word that was most salient to them from our presentation. Seven of those words were then chosen randomly for a Seven Word Spill. The only rule of the exercise was that all seven words had to be used in the poem. The seven words chosen for the poem were *power, insidious, inspiration, double-standards, insensitive, listen* and *becoming.*

Once the words were identified, students were asked to begin coming up with descriptive phrases using the seven words, which were then written on a whiteboard for everyone to see. The class was so energized by the topic that we could not write the phrases fast enough, ideas were coming at us like fastballs. We included as many voices as possible in the exercise, and made decisions based on group feedback whenever possible. As one of the co-leaders all of my hopes were realized—the creative process brought out excitement and meaningful contributions, phrases began to build on and inform one another, and the root of our community poem began to take its shape. The volume of responses and time constraints created an opportunity to adjust the activity, and we were all given the chance for an extension—everyone was asked to use the work that had been done up until that point, to write their own poems individually. I am used to having a final product at the end of this exercise, and I have to admit, I was skeptical about whether students were going to follow through—but they did with great thought and intention.

After reviewing the work that we did in class, my own poem snuck up on me and tackled me in the restaurant where I was eating dinner, refusing to let go until I was finished bringing it forward. The writing was stream of consciousness, determining its own direction as I wrote. In looking at it afterward I can sense the weight of all of the revolutionary women that I have read over the years, pushing it forward and out—rooted in that moment of resistance, refusal to accept society's standards, assumptions and misconceptions about one's self, and concluding with the moment of becoming. After listening to poems from the class, I recognized the ways in which other students critically examined their own positions, and brought their own responses and experiences with discrimination/prejudice to the fore. We were a community of unsuspecting poets/writers, and performers, reflecting a "comprehension of the simultaneity of oppressions that has helped to create a political atmosphere particularly conducive to coalition building (Smith, 1983, p. xxxiii)." This is what excites me about education—the opportunity to for each of us, teacher and student alike, to bring our experiences, perspectives, strengths and needs to the table in an environment that encourages critical thought and dialogue. Every classroom is its own poem in the making, and we as educators have a responsibility to examine ourselves, our methods and our motives, to be aware of our own "becoming" in order to shape the process into one that is transformational.

Work Cited

Anzaldua, G. E., & Keating, A. (2002). *This bridge we call home: Radical visions for transformation.* New York, NY: Routledge.

Arc of High Point (Ed.). (2007). *The spirit can still fly: Writing and art that celebrates people first.* United States of America: CaféPress.

Collins, P. H. (1990). *Black Feminist Thought: Knowledge, consciousness, and the politics of empowerment.* New York, NY: Routledge.

Courvant, D. (2002). Speaking of privilege. In G. E. Anzaldua & A. Keating (Eds.), *This bridge we call home: Radical visions for transformation.* New York, NY: Routledge.

Davis, A. Y. (1983). *Women, race [and] class.* New York, NY: Vintage Books.

Denzin, N. (2007). The politics and ethics of performance pedagogy. In P. McLaren & J. Kincheloe (Eds.), *Critical pedagogy: Where are we now?* New York, NY: Peter Lang Publishing.

Giovanni, N. (1999). *Blues: For all the changes: New poems.* New York, NY: William Morrow and Company.

Giovanni, N. (2003). *The prosaic soul of Nikki Giovanni.* New York, NY: Perennial.

Hill, C. P. (1990). *Black feminist thought: Knowledge, consciousness, and the politics of empowerment.* Boston, MA: Unwin Hyman.

hooks, b. (1990). *Yearning: Race, gender, and cultural politics.* Boston, MA: South End Press.

Jackson, A. (1993). *Dark legs and silk kisses: The beatitudes of the spinners.* Evanston, IL: TriQuarterly Books.

Jordan, J. (1998). *Affirmative acts: Political Essays.* New York, NY: Anchor Books.

Kincheloe, J. (2007). Critical pedagogy in the 21st century. In P. McLaren & J. Kincheloe (Eds.), *Critical pedagogy: Where are we now?* New York, NY: Peter Lang Publishing.

Kincheloe, J. (2008). *Knowledge and critical pedagogy: An introduction*. London: Springer.
Leistyna, P. (2012). Maintaining a Vibrant Synergy among theory, qualitative research, and social activism in this ever-changing age of globalization. In S. Steinberg & G. Cannella (Eds.), *Critical qualitative research reader.* New York, NY: Peter Lang Publishing.
Lorde, A. (1994). *Our dead behind us: Poems*. New York, NY: W.W. Norton.
Moraga, C., & Anzaldua, G. (1983). *This bridge called my back: Writings by radical women of color.* New York, NY: Kitchen Table-Women of Color Press.
Sanchez, S. (1984). *Homegirls and handgrenades: A collection of poetry and prose.* New York, NY: Thunder's Mouth Press.
Sensoy, O., & DiAngelo, R. J. (2012). *Is everyone really equal? An introduction to key concepts in social justice education.* New York, NY: Teachers College Press.
Shange, N. (1977). *For Colored Girls Who Have Considered Suicide/When the Rainbow Is Enuf.* New York, NY: Macmillan Publishing
Shange, N. (1978). *Nappy edges*. New York, NY: St. Martin's Press.
Smith, B. (1983). *Home girls: A Black feminist anthology.* New York, NY: Kitchen Table—Women of Color Press.
Smith, P. (1993). *Close to death*. Cambridge, MA: Zoland books.
Steinberg, S. (2012). Critical cultural studies research: Bricolage in action. In S. Steinberg & G. Cannella (Eds.), *Critical qualitative research reader.* New York, NY: Peter Lang Publishing, Inc.
Weiner, E. (2007).Critical pedagogy and the crisis of the imagination. In P. McLaren & J. Kincheloe (Eds.), *Critical pedagogy: Where are we now?* New York, NY: Peter Lang Publishing.

CHAPTER 28

Follow the Yellow Brick Road

Uncovering the Significant Learning Experiences in Southern Colored Schools

Toby S. Jenkins

Introduction: Follow the Yellow Brick Road

In the classic story, The Wizard of Oz, the young character Dorothy, is swept up in a storm and taken away to a foreign and sometimes frightening land. Dorothy spends the length of the movie searching for a sense of belonging, searching for home. Along the way, she meets other abandoned souls—those that have a shortcoming here or there and who are also looking for someone to patch them up. As a collective, they are in search of a wizard to work his magic and meet their unique needs. They are searching for Oz. In many ways, this story mirrors the educational experience for many students of color both historically and today. With the field of education continuing to face serious challenges with issues of satisfaction, retention, and completion of students of color, many wounded learners are in need of alternative places of inclusion and creative educators that can "work their magic" so that these learners are truly engaged and included (Hurtado, 1992; Harper, Patton, & Wooden, 2009; Lambert, Terenzini, & Lattuca, 2007; Lopez, 1993; Rendón, Jalomo, & Nora, 2004). Part of the problem is that in our attempts to "transform" education, we stand still. We continue to examine the same spaces to better understand their faults and problems rather than taking a creative and inspiring journey (the yellow brick road) towards fresh perspectives. We focus on pathology rather than possibility.

Beyond Pathology: The Witch versus the Wizard

There is a substantial amount of well-intentioned and important literature that explores the reasons for the high rates of attrition, dissatisfaction, and lack of inclusion of students of color (Allen, 1992; Ancis, Sedlacek, & Mohr, 2000; Bauman, Bustillos, Bensimon, Brown, & Bartee, 2005; Cabrera et al., 2006; Hurtado, 1992; Harper et al., 2009; Sheu & Sedlacek, 2002). By identifying the individual, institutional and broader social problems that impede educational access and achievement such as poverty, parental involvement, academic preparedness, faculty/staff diversity; and stereotypical beliefs held by peers and educators; this work has provided necessary insight on how institutions must change. This work has broadened the view of the situation by shifting the focus from the individual to the society—from the student to the institution. As, Marilyn Frye (2010) reminds us in her classic essay on oppression, these types of issues require a macroscopic rather than microscopic approach.

> Consider a birdcage. If you look very closely at just one wire in the cage, you cannot see the other wires … you could look at that one wire, up and down the length of it, and be unable to see why a bird would not just fly around the wire any time it wanted to go somewhere … It is only when you step back, stop looking at the wires one by one, microscopically, and take a macroscopic view of the whole cage, that you can see why the bird does not go anywhere. … (p. 2, http://feminsttheoryreadinggroup.wordpress.com/2010/11/23/marilyn-frye-the-politics-of-reality-oppression/)

Much of the problem with access, satisfaction, and retention has little to do with individual student efforts or failures to succeed. Ultimately it is about oppression. And previous research has indeed shed light on the various forms of social oppression that impact educational environments at all levels. To understand the socially oppressive context from which a student enters school provides important insight on why differences continue to persist in educational participation, preparation, and success. In the past, scholars that have sought to understand the reasons for student departure have often associated success with the ability to acculturate into the educational environment (the ways in which the student must change rather than how the institution must change). Rendón (2008) provided a very important critique of previous theories of student departure. They suggest that these theories were similar to research ideologies of the 1960's, which often dissected the behavior of the individual without taking into consideration the broader context of the institutional and social forces that impede success. They also assert that this approach failed to privilege the oppositional cultures and forms of community capital that prove to be valuable in the success of students of color.

> It was believed that minority individuals were engaged in a self-perpetuating cycle of poverty and deprivation and that they could avoid social alienation by becoming fully absorbed (assimilated) or adapted (acculturated) into the dominant culture (Hurtada, 1997). Assimilation required a process of separation, a cultural adaptation that required minority individuals to break away from their traditions, customs, values, language, etc in order to find full membership in the pre-dominantly white American society. However, during the 1970s and 1980s critics contested this perspective, citing problems such as the use of mainstream cultural norms as evaluative criteria, as well as the problematic assumption that minority group norms and cultural patterns were inferior, deviant, and self destructive when compared to those of the majority culture (de Anda, 1984). (Rendón et al., 2004, p. 128)

Though many researchers and education activists have championed the inclusion of students' cultures into the college experience and many resources such as cultural centers, multicultural affairs departments, and ethnic studies departments were established as a result of this work, the overall educational experience is still one that in many ways separates a student from her cultural community. Marable (1998) offers an important explanation of the central role of culture in the lives of oppressed people:

> For the oppressed, the central and overriding question was one of identity: who are we as a people, what is our cultural heritage, what values or ideals can we share with other groups to enrich society as a whole, and what do we have a right to expect from the state and civil society? Within explorations of culture resides the kernel of an oppressed group's consciousness. (p. 43)

One of the foremost scholars on this subject, particularly regarding African American education, was Carter G. Woodson, who originally wrote The Mis-education of the Negro in the early 1900s. Woodson's (1977) scholarship placed a firm focus on how African American students were educated and the impact of the cultural perspectives through which education of any kind took place. Woodson (1977) asserted that the Negro, at that time, lacked the faculties of critical thought about her culture as well as the agency to create positive change within her cultural community because of the culturally oppressive lens through which she was educated. bell hooks offered a present day analysis of the same issue of cultural efficacy. According to hooks (2001), in order for African Americans to truly develop agency for positive, loving and progressive cultural development, the act of decolonizing one's mind must occur. In other words, people of color must recognize, understand, and work to counter act the forms of cultural and racial oppression that Woodson acknowledged years ago. As hooks (2001) states, "The practice of self-love is difficult for everyone in society, but it is even more difficult for black folks, as we must constantly resist the negative perceptions of blackness we are encouraged to embrace by the dominant culture (p. 71)." Both historic scholar Woodson and contemporary scholar hooks, establish a strong value for culturally dedicated venues for education and growth. Their comments on negative stereotyping can apply to many underrepresented ethnic groups, particularly regarding the need to have culturally affirming educational environments. This is an issue of education's role in developing cultural efficacy among traditionally marginalized student communities. In this study, I considered cultural efficacy to be a demonstrated level of cultural capacity or agency [positive feelings about one's culture; strong understanding of the components, values, and structures of one's culture; confidence in one's culture to contribute to the world].

Cultural efficacy is ultimately about valuing the cultural capital that marginalized communities have to offer. Centered in the cultural experience of people of color, Yosso (2005) shares six forms of cultural capital that provide a representative voice for the cultural inheritance that is often deemed valuable by the cultural group regardless of their value to the larger society. These include (1) Aspirational capitol or the ability to achieve hopes and dreams; (2) Linguistic Capital or multiple language skills; (3) Familial capital or family history and memory; (4) Social Capital or support systems in the form of friendship and community networks; (5) Navigational Capital or the skill to navigate through various institutions; and (6) Resistant Capital or the skills developed through behavior that works in opposition to oppression. In light of these factors, Yosso (2005) describes community cultural wealth as the total inheritance of the skills present in these six forms of cultural capitol. In approaching this study, I used Yosso's cultural capital framework to evaluate the cultural learning experience in historic colored schools. To understand the rich cultural heritage with which students enter any educational environment is to truly understand the benefits and personal impact of culture. Transformative practice should be guided by an actual understanding of these cultural structures can be fully included in order to establish a healthy educational environment that will better prepare students to interact with the world.

Remembering Colored Schools: A Visit to Emerald City

The Penn School

Many of the early Freedman schools constructed throughout the South originally sought to acculturate African Americans to European cultural norms. These were schools created by white northern missionaries who supposedly sacrificed the comfort of their northern lives to travel south in order to construct schools in a foreign territory—one largely populated by African Americans. But, Lynn (2006) offers a critical perspective of these early missionary efforts:

> When white missionaries and politicians from the North set out to build dozens of "Black schools" in the South during the Reconstruction period, they were not simply concerned about the welfare of ex-slaves with no skills and no means to support themselves … the missionaries were not benevolent do-gooders who sought to lift the African out of poverty and ignorance. Rather, they were concerned about the impact that a population of physically and mentally free Negroes could have in a white supremacist patriarchy. Eurocentric and patriarchal schools could ensure the continuation of white male domination, even if the Negroes were free. Carter G Woodson's often quoted statement sums it up well: "Taught the same economics, history, philosophy, literature, and religions which have established the present code of morals (oppression), the Negro's mind has been brought under the control of his oppressor. The problem of holding the Negro down therefore is easily solved. When you control a man's thinking you do not have to worry about his actions … he will find his 'proper place' and stay in it." …

> As history shows, this system of education has not served African Americans well. While ex-slaves and their children were taught to read the word within a European culture that denigrated other forms of communication and learning, they were not taught to "read the world." (p. 206)

One such perpetrator of acculturation and cultural oppression was the Penn School situated on St. Helena Island, SC. Originally founded by white northern missionary, Laura Townes of Pennsylvania, the Penn School brought "mainland" culture to the Gullah community in South Carolina. The Gullah had a history of strong cultural roots primarily due to their physical isolation on the islands of South Carolina. The water offered a shield that protected language, customs, folk life, and traditions. The Gullah spoke a language similar to the Caribbean patois or the Southern Creole that was a mix of African and American speech patterns. The Gullah weaved sweet grass baskets, made bateaus to travel across the river; fished to make a living; practiced their own unique forms of spirituality; told folktales; and let loose at Juke Joints (Campbell, 2003). A personal reflection from Emory Campbell (2003) explains:

> The foods we ate, the songs we sang, the spirits we embraced, the noble families in which we were loved, and the language we spoke, I had taken all for granted. Through the years each of us had thought that our lifestyle was as American as lifestyles elsewhere. But as people from elsewhere came to the islands we got inklings that something about "we islanders" was different. Sensing that being different culturally presented difficulty in assimilating with mainlanders many of us would take advantage of every chance to learn new folkways and abandon our own … [many] made concerted efforts to become imitations of mainland Americans and the Penn School was where we learned how to do this. … When my older siblings and other relatives would return after a full year at the Penn School there was no trace of their Gullah speech … The school was teaching them to look and act like European-Americans so that they would be accepted as mainstream Americans. (p. 9)

Though at the most basic level, the intent of the missionaries was a worthy one, the school curriculum was most often Euro-centric and forced a suppression of existing language and culture. This educational approach seemed to be driven by an ethic that placed very little value on African American culture. Students had to be "taught" culture because they assumedly did not have any. The history of the Gullah community in the South is a complex history of how culture is sustained by local communities while being unappreciated by larger society. More than any other regional population of African Americans in the United States, the Gullah people are known for preserving African language and cultural patterns both during and after slavery. Due to the isolation and socialization patterns in the low country of SC, the Gullah community has been able to retain strong cultural legacies born in their native Africa (http://www.penncenter.com/). Emory Campbell explains:

> In a brief word, Gullah is a culture comprising a system of beliefs, customs, art forms, food ways, and language practiced among descendants of West Africans who settled along the coasts of North Carolina, South Carolina, Georgia and Florida from slavery to the present … It is widely believed that the regularity of enslaved Angolians arriving at various coastal ports gave rise to the term "Gola Negroes" which later became Gullah. Until the last half of the 20th Century the coastal communities of South Carolina and Georgia were populated almost entirely by African Americans. The harsh, humid climate and accompanying malaria disease deterred white occupancy during slavery, thus allowing for ethnic purity and development of a hybrid West African culture that would become known as Gullah. (p. 5)

Gullah is a unique sub-culture of the African American experience because of its history of having held on so tightly to West African cultural folkways. Broadly, the history of the Gullah community is relevant to 2nd and 3rd generation immigrants of any origin. But the Gullah history and experience is particularly salient for under-represented immigrant groups such as West Indian, Latino, Middle Eastern, and Asian immigrants that are facing the challenge of maintaining strong cultural ties in a contemporary America. Today, we see Latino populations faced with a negative backlash against their language and the full inclusion of their culture in U.S. schools. Time and again history repeats itself. The cultural story of the Gullah community sheds light on what culture means to a community-why it is important to sustain while all around you society pressures you to change your language, rituals, and religion. Eventually, the Penn School was adopted by the Gullah community and transformed into an educational institution that would become the primary learning center for Gullah history and heritage. But even during those culturally difficult years, many of the alumni reference committed educators at the school and a value for the practical education that they received (carpentry, sewing, cooking, agriculture).

The way in which the Penn Center was eventually re-appropriated by the local community and transformed into a culturally centered institution is reminiscent of the critical work that many colored schools managed to do. As Lynn (2006) states, "Of course Black independent schools and churches have historically played a significant role in providing Blacks with emancipatory forms of education (p. 118)." Not all colored schools have been bad. In fact, many have been exemplary. One of the major and lasting contributions of colored schools to the understanding of critical and engaged pedagogy is they way in which these schools unapologetically tied education to the lived experiences of African American students. I can remember my mother sharing stories of her experiences as a student in colored schools—the ways in which they were taught spirituals, how the home economic students were taught to cook the soul food lunches that were served to the entire school; the ways in which teachers were more than teachers—they were neighbors and friends of parents; the ways in which occupations like agriculture were included to ensure that families continued to survive across generations; and the ways in which blackness was never villainized, demeaned, or unappreciated—it was central to everyone's world—students, teachers and the institution itself.

The Rosenwald Fund

Behind every generous funder, is a dedicated activist with an idea. In the case of the Rosenwald schools, Booker T. Washington, then principal of the Tuskegee Normal and Industrial Institute (now Tuskegee University), had as his goal to provide black children throughout the south with safe, quality, and purposeful education. He clearly understood that collegiate achievement was inextricably bound to the availability of a good foundation deep in the pipeline. Paramount to his goal was galvanizing the funds of philanthropists to build schools that could be turned over to the local community to run. Though African American communities did not have the financial resources to build quality schools they did have the commitment and ability to run quality schools. Washington approached Julius Rosenwald, the President of Sears, Robuck and Company and asked him to extend his existing support of the Tuskegee Institute in order to build a fund for primary education schools (http://www.preservationnation.org/travel-and-sites/sites/southern-region/rosenwald-schools/history/origins-at-tuskegee.html).

> The Rosenwald rural school building program was a major effort to improve the quality of public education for African Americans in the early twentieth-century South. In 1912, Julius Rosenwald gave Booker T. Washington permission to use some of the money he had donated to Tuskegee Institute for the construction of six small schools in rural Alabama, which were constructed and opened in 1913 and 1914. Pleased with the results, Rosenwald then agreed to fund a larger program for schoolhouse construction based at Tuskegee. In 1917 he set up the Julius Rosenwald Fund, a Chicago-based philanthropic foundation, and in 1920 the Rosenwald Fund established an independent office for the school building program in Nashville, Tennessee. By 1928, one in every five rural schools for black students in the South was a Rosenwald school, and these schools housed one third of the region's rural black schoolchildren and teachers. At the program's conclusion in 1932, it had produced 4,977 new schools, 217 teachers' homes, and 163 shop buildings, constructed at a total cost of $28,408,520 to serve 663,615 students in 883 counties of 15 states. (http://www.preservationnation.org/travel-and-sites/sites/southern-region/rosenwald-schools/history/origins-at-tuskegee.html)

Beyond the broad access to education that these schools provided, one of the major differences between the Rosenwald School Project and other "missionary" schools was its requirement of commitment and participation by the local African American community. They clearly saw local community commitment as an essential ingredient to the sustainability of these schools. And in order to keep communities committed, it was important for the community to see the tangible benefits of education (the skill sets being developed by their children, the impact of having teachers present in the community, the sense of confidence being groomed in youth, and the ways in which the schools would create a steady workforce of able graduates to continue the work of building, growing, teaching, and doctoring the community). This created a culture of mutual responsibility.

> Grassroots support was the critical ingredient for the success of the Rosenwald school building program. A shared faith in the power of self-help led Booker T. Washington and Julius Rosenwald to insist on local contributions to match the amount of a Rosenwald grant, rather than insisting on full public or philanthropic funding. They believed that personal sacrifices of hard-earned cash, lumber, and labor would strengthen rural African Americans' commitment to their communities. In practice, the self-help requirement made rural African Americans the driving force behind the Rosenwald program and the arbiters of its meaning for southern communities. Local African American leaders—teachers, principals, school trustees, ministers, and successful farm or business owners—often initiated building campaigns. They wrote to state education departments, Tuskegee Institute, and the Rosenwald Fund for information, lobbied county superintendents and school boards for additional funding, and recruited their fellow citizens' support. To make their matching contribution, school patrons organized themselves into committees to find and buy the land, to cut trees and saw the lumber for the school, and to haul the building materials to the school site, sometimes even to build the school themselves. Those who pledged contributions of money and labor included rural wage earners such as sawmill and domestic workers, farm owners and tenants, and the members of church congregations and fraternal lodges. Some donated a day's pay or the proceeds of an acre of cotton; others sold chickens. School rallies, community picnics, and entertainments brought in cash as well. The result was a school building that stood as a tangible expression of a community's determination to provide a decent education for its children. (http://www.preservationnation.org/travel-and-sites/sites/southern-region/rosenwald-schools/history/rosenwald-schools-students.html)

The African American community has always had a dedication to education. Focusing specifically on the African American community, Henry Louis Gates references it in his book, Finding Oprah's Roots (2007). "The very history of the African American people, starting with the newly freed slaves, is a history of the hardheaded determination of a people to overcome their environment" (p. 91). In the article, "Mr. Nigger: The Challenges of Educating African American Men in America," I share the following historical fact about education in black communities:

> The creation of Negro schools during the post slavery years was often a community commitment. In many cases, the black communities supported in spirit and in funds the creation of schools in their community whenever an educator was available. Booker T. Washington, in his legendary text, Up From Slavery, recounted how the community would engage in the practice of boarding round—that is, each family in the neighborhood would agree to board the school teacher for a few weeks to keep an educated person in the community and the school open (Boyd & Allen, 1995). According to Washington, it was a whole race trying to go to school, whether it be day or night schools, or 50- or 75-year-olds, all sought to attend school with the goal of being able to read the bible before they died. Education was viewed as the means for upward mobility, and Black men often led the inroads to creating educational opportunity for the African American race. However, school desegregation proved to be more complex than merely passing and implementing the law: The racial integration of schools provided black students with the access to the educational resources provided in white schools, when school districts actually implemented the law. However, even in these situations, the prejudiced and stereotypical beliefs of white teachers negatively impacted the learning and development of black students, particularly black males. (hooks, 2001) Even the most well-intentioned White teachers may have lacked the social experience with the black community to effectively reach and engage Black students. (p. 2)

Kmt Shockley (2008), a professor at Morgan State University, has done significant research on culturally centered education. His work focuses specifically on African centered education and at the center of the issue is the failure of contemporary educational institutions to simply educate.

> The inability of the American educational system to properly address the cultural and educational needs of blacks is one of the most perplexing problems in U.S. Society today. Even as the population of blacks and other groups has continued to increase, many scholars have reported that the culture of schools has remained ethnocentrically white (Delpit, 2001; King, 2005; Stedman, 1997; Tharp & Gallimore, 1991). For example, according to the National Center for Education Statistics (NCES, 2004), from 1986 to 2001 the population of blacks, first-language Spanish speakers, and Asians enrolled in U.S. public schools grew from 29.7 percent to 39.5 percent. However, the teaching force remained overwhelmingly white and female, and the academic achievement gap between whites and other groups (such as blacks and Latinos) persisted … African-centered education involves the act of making the education that black children receive relevant and meaningful to the black community. In order to do so, it is necessary for those who teach black children to assume the task of conducting careful historical and cultural studies of Africans (Asante, 1990) … blacks need an education that places them at the core of their own learning.

Off to See the Wizard: Significant Learning and Culture in Educational Practice

Integrating cultural based learning into the educational experience is not easy. As the scholar, W. E. B Dubois (1903) stated in his classic talented tenth essay, "Now the training of men is a difficult and intricate task. Its technique is a matter for educational experts, but its object is for the vision of seers." Undoubtedly, we can grow and cultivate the instruction, scholarship, and management skills of educators, but understanding the larger objective of building a free and educated society; deeply committing to the need to grow students as whole persons and not simply academic achievers; and embracing the concept that learning is a mutual and relational process requires a greater vision and a wider view. Essentially, creating meaningful learning environments requires a deep engagement of practices that underscore what Fink (2003), calls "Significant Learning." According to Fink (2003), significant learning differs from other types of learning because of its utility, urgency, and saliency in students' lives. One of the most defining factors is the way in which the educational experience motivates a change in the student:

> I defined learning in terms of change. For learning to occur, there has to be some kind of change in the learner. No change, no learning. And significant learning requires that there be some kind of lasting change that is important in terms of the learner's life. (Fink, 2003, p. 30)

Fink is not talking about the types of change mentioned earlier such as assimilation and acculturation. In this case, the significant learning taxonomy refers to the ways in which education provides opportunities for students to come to know themselves more deeply, develop important attachments to the process of learning, connect what they learn to their lives, establish a since of caring and commitment about a particular topic, and take action on what they have learned in some meaningful way. Through this work, my primary hypothesis is that by developing significant cultural learning experiences for students of color, educational institutions might see meaningful change occur in the students' sense and appreciation of their culture, commitment to community activism, future aspirations, and overall appreciation for the purpose and experience of school. Colored schools offer a perfect example of this. According to bell hooks (2001), internalized self-hatred is more pronounced now then in the era of segregation. hooks asserts that if cultural pride can help black Americans come out of an intense period of racial apartheid with a strong sense of cultural self, then undoubtedly it may be one of the many keys to establishing healthy multi-racial and multi-cultural educational experiences in a society that continues to struggle at all levels with issues of school desegregation.

And so, by the concept of significant learning, I am referring to experiences that embody a sense of innovation, creativity and value for engaged scholarship through their location within the culture and within the community. In his book, *Scholarship Reconsidered: Priorities of the Professorate*, Boyer (1997) points out the growing need for educational institutions to connect with communities in more meaningful ways:

> The scholarship of engagement means connecting the rich resources of the university to our most pressing social, civic and ethical problems, to our children, to our schools, to our teachers and to our cities. … I have this growing conviction that what's also needed is not just more programs, but a larger purpose, a sense of mission, a larger clarity of direction in the nation's life as we move toward century twenty-one. (Boyer, 1997, p. 64)

The scholarship of engagement recognizes that not only do individual students need school, but communities also need school. They need the resources, talents and skills that reside on a school campus and they need deep and creative thinkers who can work in partnership to help achieve community-based goals. But beyond this, schools need communities. Scholars, researchers, teachers, and students have much to learn from activists, artists, organizers, and elders. There is undoubtedly mutual benefit in the scholarship of engagement. Given this need to explore the value of culture in educational environments and the architecture of truly significant cultural learning experiences, a project of this nature has value in its effort to document and share the benefits of culturally centered education.

Methods

Documenting Folk's Tales: Storytellers as the Keepers of the Culture

Across various ethnic groups, the culture of storytelling has been an important community practice. Once, there was a time when spoken words were the primary currency. And so, Indigenous Americans relied on oral tradition for the maintenance of the health of their tribes (Tracey, 2011). Within Latino and Hispanic cultures, the concepts of Chistes (jokes), Cuentos (legendary tales), Corridos (ballads) frame the shape that cultural stories would take. These tales, songs, and dubious characters would teach important life lessons and convey meaningful cultural history. Within the African Diaspora, African Griots were often a multi-faceted performer, a historian, storyteller, praise singer or musician. Griots were the keepers of the tribe's memories and one of the most respected members of the community. Through singing and reciting long poetic narratives they would tell a tribes history. And during the early re-settlement of America, European explorers, marauders, and colonial servants were Spanish, Dutch, French, & English. Initially, they were tent-dwellers; the first villages were fortified encampments. The newcomers had their traditional stories, jokes, poetry, & songs. These stories were adapted songs and stories that helped these "camp tellers" to remember their homelands.

Even now, we learn to love stories at a very early age. Stories teach moral lessons, share knowledge, and pass on values. They provide us with a context to better understand complex issues or broad concepts. Stories help us to make since of the meanings of life experiences. According to Banks-Wallace (2002), story telling, the interactive process of sharing stories, is a vehicle of preserving culture and passing it on to future generations. Allowing students an opportunity to truly reflect on their experiences—to get at the root of their culture—is an important act of self-understanding and rebellion against negative social ideas. Smiley (2006) points out that storytelling and reflection have a critical role to play in community action and cultural sustainability. He describes reflection as "the deliberate process of taking your actions into account, examining them, learning from them, and then adjusting your future actions in accordance with the lessons learned (p. 62)." This seems to underscore the very idea of culture as a toolkit of experiences, values, and lessons that serve to inform how daily life is approached. The reflection shared through stories helps to sustain a sense of self—a proof of existence and history.

Featherstone (1989) has noted the value of the use of storytelling to inform research. He explains both the richness and complexity of the information gained through story as well as the significant responsibility of the researcher.

> The telling of stories can be a profound form of scholarship moving serious study close to the frontiers of art in the capacity to express complex truth and moral context in intelligible ways … The methodologies are inseparable from the vision. Historians have used narrative as a way in which to make sense of lives and institutions over time, but over years they have grown abashed by its lack of scientific rigor. Now, as we look for ways to explore context and describe the thick textures of lives over time in institutions with a history, we want to reckon with the author's own stance and commitment to the people being written about. Storytelling takes on a fresh importance. (p. 367)

To honor the inherently cultural nature of storytelling several research methods were used that were rooted in story, voice, and counter-narrative. Portraiture was one such method. Portraiture combines science and art to paint a holistic picture of an experience or phenomenon. Lawrence-Lightfoot and Davis (1997) offer the following description:

> Portraiture is a method of qualitative research that blurs the boundaries of aesthetics and empiricism in an effort to capture the complexity, dynamics, and subtlety of human experience and organizational life. Portraits seek to record and interpret the perspectives and experiences of the people they are studying, documenting their voices and their visions—their authority, knowledge, and wisdom. (p. xv)

To understand portraiture, you must first understand phenomenology. Marshall & Rossman (1999) define phenomonology as the study of lived experience and how people understand this experience. It assumes that there is an "essence" to shared experiences that can be articulated through narration (Marshall & Rossman, 1999). Portraiture combines science and art to paint a holistic picture of an experience or phenomenon. Portraiture shares in the traditions and values of phenomonology but it expands the boundaries of phenomonology by combining

> empirical and aesthetic description; in its focus on the convergence of narrative and analysis; in its goal of speaking to broader audiences beyond the academy; in its standard of authenticity rather than reliability and validity; and in its explicit recognition of the use of self as the primary research instrument for documenting and interpreting the perspectives and experiences of the people and the cultures being studied. (Lawrence-Lightfoot & Davis, 1997, p. 13)

Through the art of portraiture, the researcher crosses creative boundaries to blend art and science through written products that share stories and convey meaning in ways that other traditional methods may not allow (Lawrence-Lightfoot & Davis, 1997).

This value for creating space to hear the voices of under-represented communities is also underscored by critical race theory (Banks-Wallace, 2002; Barnes, 1990; Ladson-Billings, 1998; Ladson-Billings & Tate, 1995). Critical race theory was originally developed within legal studies but has since been adapted within educational environments to study the experience of under-represented racial groups. To study the merit of cultural spaces is to challenge what education should look like, where it should reside, whose knowledge is real, and who is taken seriously as intellectual contributors to society. A component of critical race theory that is particularly salient to this study is the concept of cultural nationalism. Cultural nationalism places an inherit value on self-created cultural structures that allow people of color to continue the tradition of raising, teaching, and empowering the cultural orientation of their youth.

As Delgado (1990) argues, people of color may speak from a very different experience. Thus, the concepts of authentic voice, story exchange, and naming one's own reality are essential to the critical race theorist (Delgado, 1990). With this in mind, attention must be paid to the real cultural histories and the meaningful cultural stories that have been created in modest schoolhouses, on country roads, and inside of the African American community.

Telling Our Stories

In this ongoing project, I am collecting the oral histories of African American alumni of colored schools in the south. So far, there have been four schools visited and 24 stories collected. All participants have requested that their real names be used and their identity be disclosed in all written and media publications of this project. It is important to note here the sense of ownership, belonging, and credit that is sought by participants in projects of this nature. The participants made very clear that these are their stories, their lives, their community, and their history. Because of the recent public interest, particularly in Gullah culture, it was important for us to create a mutual agreement of partnership to prevent this from becoming another instance where an external other is given credit for simply reporting an experience that they lived. These stories will be collectively made available in video form on a digital story website that will be created at the conclusion of the project. This website will also feature photographic images of the schools. In this chapter, which shares preliminary insight, I offer two short stories from two of the schools: The Penn School and the Rosenwald School, both on St Helena Island. The stories are written in the words of the interviewees. These two stories are followed by an analysis of themes identified across all 24 stories.

The Penn School
Founded in 1862 by Pennsylvania Missionary, Laura Townes
St Helena Island, SC
Alumnus Name: Ms. Gardenia Simmons-White, 78 years old

I grew up during the time of segregation, but being here on St Helena Island I cant say we even really knew what segregation was. You see there really weren't too many white people on the island. You had a handful that owned the local stores but they were okay. They lived among us. And at the Penn School it was started by white missionaries—Laura Townes was a white woman. And they only had white teachers until 1948. But we interacted with those people—we ate with them, we went to their houses. So we didn't really know this idea of white being separated from black until we went away and came back home.

I attended the Penn School from the first through the 12th grade. I started when I was five years old. And I graduated in 1952 so I had both sides of it. I was there when it was a private school and I was there for 4 years when it became Penn High School. In 1948, it was deemed that there must be education for all children on St Helena Island. Before, there was the Penn School, which was private and not everyone could go. And the rest of the children went to the Rosenwald School, which was in an area where most children could walk to it. These were mainly one-room schools and they only went to the sixth grade. So once a child hit the sixth grade there was no more education. Whereas the Penn School provided a high school education and was really prepping students to go to college. So, the Penn School was turned into a county school. In 1948, this was when we had our first black principal at Penn School. The school became open to more students and the name changed. It actually went through three name changes. First it was Penn School and the premise was to get an education. You see if you got an education you could do more because as slaves you couldn't read or anything. Then in the early 1900s the name changed because this is when you had the debate between Booker T Washington and Dubois on what the purpose of education should be. This is when they incorporated the trade into the Penn curriculum and the name changed to Penn Normal, Industrial and Agricultural School. When students got to high school they had to select a trade. It didn't negate their academics but not everyone was going to go to college. In the very beginning the purpose of the Penn School was teacher training. But everyone didn't go to college so with the trades you could do more. We had carpentry, blacksmiths, shoe making—all of that was a part of the curriculum. They had home economics—how to cook, sew, and entertain.

So when they graduated they would be self sufficient—they could build their house, fix their cars, make their own clothes. They had self-sufficiency and independence.

The other important part of the Penn School was it had boarding options. Students came from Bluffton, Hilton Head, Hartysville because there were no high schools for African Americans in those places so they came to the Penn School. You had dormitories, teacher houses, cafeteria, classrooms, labs, auditorium, and so forth. And when all students got to the eleventh grade they were required to board at the school. They were training us to go to college. They made us have that experience so that when you did go to college you knew how to behave, how to be independent and take care of yourself, and how to be responsible.

I learned everything there. Our curriculum was based on English, math, science, physical education. It was good to have home ec for me because my father raised us and I didn't have a mother for a long time, so having home economics and having a female teacher helped me to grow as a young girl. In those days we took the bags that rice and flour was sold in and we made our skirts from those bags in class. They had a hygiene class and taught us to take care of ourselves—to clean our hair, to wear our clothes neatly. All of the teachers stood out. We had a music and English teacher that I loved. Those teachers were strict. I remember the home economics teacher Ms. Dalton had just came out of college. They expected us to be respectful. They cared about us learning. They taught us not to settle. They taught us not to compromise our integrity. They taught us to be proud of ourselves. The teachers knew our parents—they lived in the community. So if you misbehaved the teacher would just come home and tell your parents. They loved us and we loved them. They were all interested in teaching and for us to get an education. We read a lot. Church was our foundation. It was fun going to school. Today it seems there is no respect across the board—students don't respect teachers and teachers don't respect students—you cant learn in that type of environment. We also didn't have all of the distractions. What entertained us was our culture.

I'm invested in the Penn School because I graduated from there and it never left me. When I graduated, I spent 40 years working in New York. But I came back home every year. When they had dances and community service projects we all still participated. We got a great education. When I got to college I never had to take any remedial courses. Im a nurse—I earned my bachelors degree and I got my masters degree. We did well. But we never forgot about home. Our education at Penn taught us to love our community. It gave us roots here. And so that's why you see so many of us have returned to live on St Helena after having lived many other places. We love it here. We understand that we can get exposure by going out in the world and experiencing different things but this place is always home. At Penn we really learned how important it is to help people. That some people aren't as fortunate and that we needed to get an education to help others. So many people that didn't get the education we got didn't understand this power and responsibility of education. You see when you aren't educated you don't know any better—you don't realize that you can stand your ground. Our education at Penn taught us to be confident and to know that we didn't have to settle for less.

If you could describe the Penn Center in just one word, what would it be?

I would say Penn School can be summed up in three words: history, education and culture. It was a beacon to this community. It made us aware of our heritage—where we've been and where we're going. It was about maintaining our culture and not allowing anyone to take it away from you—its about being proud of who we are.

Rosenwald School
St Helena, SC
Queen Brown Porridge, 70 Years Old

I attended the Ronsenwald school from first grade to sixth grade. It was a two room house. Our teachers were Ms. Janie Dudley and Ms. Jenny Gardner, and Ms. Lucille Manigold was our cook. We would get there about seven in the morning. First thing was devotional service, then health check, then we would have a snack and those that were assigned to help in the kitchen they would go with the cook, and the rest of us would do our lessons. We had two teachers so each teacher would teach like two subjects. We helped a lot in the kitchen. We were assigned duties to help prepare the meals, help serve and help clean up. And we also were exposed to cleanliness because each morning we had health check—to check our nails, check our hair, and make sure our clothes were neat on us. And we had a religious program each morning. We would have devotional service we would sing hymns and have prayer and that's how we started our school day. Most days we would get to school very early before the teachers. Our older brothers and sisters attended the Penn School for high school and so we would just stand out with them as they were waiting on their bus and the high school bus driver would just let us ride and drop us off at the elementary school. But the Rosenwald school didn't have a bus. We would walk about 2 miles home after school but we would get a ride in the morning. So when we hitched a ride on the Penn bus we would get to school way too early. So we would go collect the wood and the chips for the wood stove and start the fire to heat the building. So the school was warm by the time the teachers came. Then we would have so much time on our hands that we would go to the old man's house across the street from the school and get wood and start the fire for him in his house. Some mornings we would pick black berries until the teachers came and then we would take them in once school started and we would make preserves from the blackberries when we helped in the kitchen. We did a lot of things. There was a candy store by the school and the teachers didn't allow us to go there until school was over. And even when we got there before the teachers the man that owned the store, Mr. George Austin, he wouldn't sell us the candy because the teachers at the school had given him instructions.

Most of the parents didn't have a car to get to the school so there were often days when the school was closed and the teachers would go to each home and visit the parents and talk about our progress and just keep them up to date with what was happening at school. And we were required to have a little garden at home and when the teachers came for their home visit they would go out back and look at our little garden to make sure we were doing it right. They made us do the garden at home instead of school because they were teaching us to help our family. Our family could benefit from the food we grew. We also had to make our beds every morning and make sure our room was clean because if we got sick the teachers would bring us home or they would just stop by sometimes and our parents didn't want to be embarrassed.

Our learning experience was very good. During the school day we learned English, writing, reading, and arithmetic. And we enjoyed it. I mean maybe we didn't have all of the best books and supplies that they have today but we really learned a lot from what we had. And those teachers really loved us and made sure we learned. All of them were so loving and patient. They were just like a mother to us. After we left that school in 6th grade we would still give them a hug whenever we saw them around town. I think Ms. Janie Dudley was the last to die—she just died this year. But all of us stayed in touch with her and even helped her as an old lady.

But it wasn't until the Rosenwald schools closed down and the big state run school was built that we had fancier things like a cafeteria. At the Rosenwald school we ate a lot of soups and sandwiches and they were served right there in the classroom. Ms. Dudley was a very strong person telling us about life. She traveled a lot and she would tell us about life and what to expect—not just to read and write. One of the most important things I learned was how to carry myself as a lady—how to act with respect, how to take care of your body, and how to interact with boys. We did a lot of crocheting and basket making. You know basket making is important culturally here in St Helena so they taught us how to do it—a lot of arts and crafts. Education meant a lot to my generation. Today kids are going to school because they have to. It's not a place they really want to be. But we loved our school. It was such a loving environment. We were never bored. They would let us pick berries during recess to take home to our families. The teachers would always go outside and play with us so we were never alone. Our parents didn't go very high in school so they wanted their children to get an education. They were farmers and did odd jobs. And they were really involved to make sure the children got an education. So the Rosenwald school is very dear to me—it was important to the community. They refurbished it several years ago and its now a day care for the Penn Center. A lot of us went to the rededication and supported it as much as we could. We had wonderful memories there.

If you could describe the Rosenwald School in just one word, what would it be?

Exciting

There's No Place Like Home: Insights & Wisdom

Metaphorically, Oz is a space of belonging. It is welcoming—a place where the non-conformists can call home—munchkins and fairies are treated like kings and queens. It is different and a bit unorthodox but it works. We should all be searching for Oz, for places of possibility, creative imagine, and cultural inclusion. I have found several key characteristics shared amongst all of the schools visited so far. First teachers were essentially neighbors and community members. The contemporary national "Live Near Your Work" program then makes sense. A different relationship is developed between teacher and student or teacher and parent when we share the same community space. In higher education, this is why living-learning environments are so effective. When faculty live with students they begin to care about much more than achievement, grades, and passing—they care about the person. In several of my past projects, I call for a greater commitment among educational institutions to more fully include family into the educational experience (Citations removed for blind review). In the past, even when parents could not physically make it to school, the school came to them. Even when parents couldn't read themselves, the school still updated them verbally on their child's progress. To make learning more relevant, the curriculum was tied to real family issues—putting food on the table. When parents were poor and couldn't afford new clothes—students were taught to make clothes at school that they could wear the next day. Several years ago, the rapper Tupac Shakur gave an insightful critique of education:

> I think we got so caught up in school being a tradition that we stopped using it as a learning tool … I'm learning about the basic, but they're not the basic for me … to get us ready for today's world, the present [curriculum] is not helping … that's why the streets have taught me … [in school] they teach you to read and write, then teach you to read and write again and again and again … there should be a class on drugs, a class on sex education, a class on scams, a class on religious cults, on police brutality, on apartheid, and racism and why people are hungry. (Dyson, 2001, pp. 76–77)

Some may find these ideas a bit absurd—a class on drugs? But in fact, Shakur isn't suggesting anything different than the pedagogical approach of these colored schools. They related education to the real issues students were facing—how to take care of themselves and be self sufficient, how to feed their families, how to behave in a hostile and racist public. Essentially the second characteristic of these schools was a value of educating for life. One of the many observations that I have made when reviewing these videos and discussing this work with colleagues, is simply how incredibly good these elders look. My oldest participant was 95 years old. She physically looked about 80. She was coherent and active—offered me food to eat and walked me to my car when I left. But one of the critical tools she and many others learned in school was agriculture. She spent her entire life growing and eating her own food. In today's world of fast food, fast conveniences, frozen meals, and chemical based diets, I'm not sure if most of us will even live to her age much less be that healthy. I am 37 and have already battled cancer and lupus. I wish someone had taught me how to eat and grow healthy food as a child.

The third theme that surfaced from these schools is a value for culture. Across 24 interviews, time and again, elders discussed how they were taught to value and appreciate blackness. They were repeatedly taught the many achievements of their race. And they were taught to see their folkways as valuable practices—basketweaving, sea island cooking, boat making, and farming. In the two interviews shared above, it is clear that the education these women received endeared them to their community—it rooted them in St. Helena. So today, if family, culture and community are so important to students and central to their ability to truly feel included in the world, why do so many seek to get away from their community when they graduate? I argue that society is teaching young people that success resides outside of their community—that their success depends upon how far away you can get from your home community. In recent years, it seems that one of the most popular mantras for young people who come from disenfranchised and disadvantaged backgrounds has been the phrase, "Making it Out." The idea of making it out of the housing project or the impoverished community communicates the larger desire to avoid getting caught up in a cycle of oppression—to experience a new opportunity through school or work and to ultimately elevate oneself up and away from the bottom of society. Making it out represents both physical and philosophical mobility. On a facebook group page titled, "Making it out the ghetto," the following post was on the wall for the description of the group:

> For those of us who: Were brought down by societies prejudices; Were seen as a waste; Grew up around gang violence; Seen, been in or, lost someone to gun violence; Went to a poorly funded grammar and high school; Lived day by day; Used food stamps; Grew up on welfare; Know what "getting jumped" means; were victims of racial profiling; In grammar school would run to get the book wit a front cover & all the pages; know what a RIP shirt is; who seen a mother cry for her murdered son/daughter; survived this war zone and through all this managed to make it farther than what was ever expected from us. (http://www.facebook.com/group.php?gid=2390551946)

Getting away from the oppression that is pervasive in "ghetto" communities (any place where poverty is concentrated) has been a part of our cultural landscape for decades. We have heard of many success stories of young adults that "make it out" through sports, entertainment, and college. Time and again, the idea of success is always wrapped up in the fabulous life that the person that made it out now has. Success is a portrait of self rather than community. And even when those that make it demonstrate a concern for the community it is through a lens of "giving back" which implies a physical separation and departure. Some are becoming more critical of the suggestion that a community should see one person's success as a "win" for all.

> Rags to riches or whatever. Even though you have people like 50 cent, puff daddy and Jay-Z making it out the ghetto and going on to become millionaires and billionaires, the black community is still lacking and falling further and further behind. (http://www.topix.com/forum/afam/T505942502BA81VP3)

As I prepared this article, I posted the following on my Facebook page: "Making it Out of the Ghetto. What does it mean? Should that be the dream?" I wanted to get a sense of how young people are being taught to have this same level of cultural and community commitment as was seen in these colored schools. Below I share a few public responses:

> I think it's telling that everyone is trying to get out of the ghetto, and no one is trying to eliminate the ghetto. When people talk of "escaping" they are saying they have left the poverty … and subsequent ignorance and violence of the ghetto. Very rarely do they say, "I want to pull everyone out of the poverty." Trust me, I understand that's a daunting task. But at some point we have to start saying that its unacceptable for anyone to live that way, and that just certain individuals being blessed or chosen to escape that circumstance isn't enough. (Bomani Armah, African American man)

> I've always struggled with the idea of my "making it out the ghetto." Many people talk about where I come from in a way that separates me from where I come from. … that I am only here because I am smart, amicable, and resourceful. That is not necessarily true. We all have those family members that are very smart but just didn't get the same opportunities we were given. So many good things happened to me during my lifetime, whether it's the teachers I had, the friends I met along the way, or just chance that have allowed me to be where I am today. Perhaps making it "out" should come with less elitism than it carries these days … not that we are one of the "special" blacks, but that we are a member of the community given life changing opportunities. Opportunities that we, who "made it out," should extend to others as well? (Dayo, African woman)

The need persists to explore the role, responsibility, and social impact of educated children from so-called ghetto communities. Are students really aspiring to use their education to raise up the community that raised them or is success seen as their ability to navigate their way away from the community? What makes this a pressing issue is that many community leadership activists and scholars affirm that viable community change most often comes from within the community (Bynoe, 2004).

Conclusion: "You've Always Had the Power My Dear. You Had it All Along"

As I began this work, I used Yosso's cultural capital framework as a guide to understand the cultural tools being used in these schools. I found that these educational spaces provided their students with a significant amount of cultural capital. Below is a brief list of what I found:

(1) Aspirational capitol or the ability to achieve hopes and dreams: This was a central foundation of education for African Americans in the early 1900's. Coming out of a history of enslavement, many elders possessed a strong desire to see the future generations of their family educated. They saw education as a vehicle out of poverty and oppression. At the least, it was viewed as a way to expand your options in life. So this idea of aspiring to be educated, to achieve more, and to become a respectable person was critical.

(2) Linguistic Capital or multiple language skills: Though not explicitly discussed in the interviews above, linguistic capital was central to the Gullah community. After having been deprived of their native language for many years in the Penn School, the community developed a commitment to sustaining the language. Rather than allowing the Penn School to become condemned when it was closed, the community invested in transforming it into a Gullah Cultural Center. It is the primary space where children in St Helena are taught to speak Gullah, make baskets, and appreciate their heritage. They run after school programs and summer camps. Additionally, they offer a teachers institute where educators from across the country can come to study Gullah heritage and incorporate it into their curriculum. A critical component of this institute is an introduction to Gullah language.

(3) Familial capital or family history and memory: Undoubtedly, families were central to these schools. Not only did parents and neighbors give money, labor, and building supplies to build the schools, but they also did what they could to support their child's educational participation. Though parents may not have always understood how to help with homework or how to keep their child in school, they knew for sure that they wanted them to be there. And when education was diverse and included a variety of relevant life lessons, families were able to actively participate by helping with the home garden and other such projects.

(4) Social Capital or support systems in the form of friendship and community networks: Another example of the presence of cultural capital in these schools was the way in which strong relationships were developed between teachers and students; peer connections with classmates, and even neighborhood relationships like the candy store owner and the old man that had the children help him with house hold chores in the morning. In these people, children found mentors, supporters, and cheerleaders. One couple shared that for many years there was no formal high school graduation program at the Penn School. Recently, the city decided to retroactively graduate all alumni of the Penn School. They put out a call for graduates to come back and participate in a mass graduation. Hundreds came. Elders in their 60's and 70's wore cap and gowns for the first time and walked across the stage to receive a diploma. This was how connected they remained to the school network. Almost 50 years later, they were still willing to participate in a school program and commune with their peers.

(5) Navigational Capital or the skill to navigate through various institutions: The Penn School clearly provided a wealthy education in this regard. It offered an intentional education that prepared students to take care of themselves, to obtain a variety of different jobs, and to succeed in college if that was their choice. Going so far as to require the students to board at the school, they espoused an ethic that failure was not an option. Students would be able to succeed across all areas of life and navigate their way within or beyond the St. Helena community.

(6) Resistant Capital or the skills developed through behavior that works in opposition to oppression: As Ms. Simmons-White expressed, a major benefit of the education that she and her classmates received was the confidence in knowing that they did not have to settle—that they could stand up for themselves. They were taught that education provided a level of insight, awareness, and freedom that could be powerful in resisting racism. Many of the graduates of these two schools went into helping professions, partly because of the specific opportunities available to African Americans at that time, but also because they were taught the various ways that their communities needed them. Oppressed and impoverished communities need nurses and teachers. Their communities needed skilled hands to build the community infrastructure so they would not have to rely on external investment in order to have homes in which to live. There are many ways to resist oppression. Sometimes fighting and speaking is necessary. But sometimes being able to build, maintain, live and survive is a powerful way to resist an oppressive society that is structured for you to fail.

Undoubtedly, developing positive cultural efficacy in traditional and static educational environments is difficult and may ultimately be impossible. Educational oppression not only manifests itself as a lack of access or through forms of racial and class based segregation. Oppression is also present in classrooms where student life experience and culture is devalued. But how is it that our music, our streets, our homes, our community experiences, and our folkways continue to successfully pull and attract students in deep and meaningful ways? In my previous study examining how young adults define and interpret the utility of culture in a contemporary world, I found young adults to align culture with family, spirituality, art, a value for education, and interactions with elders (citation removed for blind review). Sound familiar? The same values that were upheld in those historic colored schools still seem to hold weight today. Young people still seek to come home to their culture—they still value it as important. In the colored schools, parents, dedicated neighbors and teachers were able to engineer an experience that many educators today struggle to achieve. These nontraditional spaces of education—two room houses and one room shacks—were in many ways the real world manifestation of the fictional Oz. In fact, at the movie's end, we find the wizard to be a regular guy who simply had stewardship over an incredible place. And we come to understand, that Dorothy always had the ability to return home—she carried it in her heart.

Work Cited

Allen, W. (1992). The color of success: African-American college student outcomes at predominantly white and historically black public colleges and universities. *Harvard Educational Review, 62*(1).

Ancis, J., Sedlacek, W., & Mohr, J. (2000). Student perceptions of campus cultural Climate by race. *Journal of Counseling & Development, 78*(Spring).

Banks-Wallace, J. (2002). Talk that talk: Storytelling and analysis rooted in African-American oral tradition. *Qualitative Health Research, 12*(3), 410–426.

Barnes, R. D. (1990). Race consciousness: The thematic content of racial distinctiveness in critical race scholarship. *Harvard Law Review, 103*(8), 1864–1871.

Bauman, G. L., Bustillos, L. T., Bensimon, E. M., Brown, M. C., & Bartee, R. D. (2005). *Achieving equitable educational outcomes with all students: The institution's roles and responsibilities.* Monograph Commissioned by the Association for American Colleges and Universities.

Boyer, E. (1997). *Scholarship reconsidered: Priorities of the professoriate.* Carnegie Foundation for the Advancement of Teaching. San Francisco, CA: Jossey-Bass

Bynoe, Y. (2004). *Stand and deliver: Political activism, leadership, and hip hop culture.* New York, NY: Soft Skull Press.

Cabrera, A. F., Deil-Amen, R., Prabhu, R., Terenzini, P. T., Lee, C., & Franklin, R. E. (2006). Increasing the college preparedness of at-risk students. *Journal of Latinos and Education, 5*, 79–97.

Campbell, E. (2003). *Gullah cultural legacies: A synopsis of Gullah traditions, customary beliefs, art forms and speech on Hilton Head Island and vicinal sea Islands in South Carolina and Georgia.* Penn Center. Hilton Head, SC.

Delgado, R. (1990). When a story is just a story: Does voice really matter? *Virginia Law Review, 76*(1), 95–111.

Du Bois, W. E. B. (1903). *The Talented Tenth.* Retrieved August 6 2015 from http://teachingamericanhistory.org/library/document/the-talented-tenth/

Dyson, M. (2001). Holler if you hear me: Searching for Tupac Shakur. New York, NY: Basic Civitas Books.

Featherstone, J. (1989). Balm in gilead. *Harvard Educational Review, 59*, 367–378.

Fink, D. L. (2003). *Creating significant learning experiences: An integrated approach to designing college courses.* San Francisco, CA: Jossey-Bass.

Frye, M. (2010). *Oppression.* Retrieved May 21, 2011 from http://feminsttheoryreadinggroup.wordpress.com/2010/11/23/marilyn-frye-the-politics-of-reality-oppression/

Gates, H. (2007). *Finding Oprah's roots: Finding your own.* New York, NY: Crown Publishers.

Harper, S. R., Patton, L. D., & Wooden, O. S. (2009). Access and equity for African American students in higher education: A critical race historical analysis of policy efforts. *Journal of Higher Education, 80*(4), 389–414.

hooks, b. (2001). *Salvation: Black people and love.* New York, NY: Harper Perennial.

Hurtado, S. (1992). The campus racial climate. *The Journal of Higher Education, 63*(5), 539–569.

Lambert, A. D., Terenzini, P. T., & Lattuca, L. R. (2007). More than meets the eye: Curricular and programmatic effects on student learning. *Research in Higher Education, 48*(2), 141–168.

Ladson-Billings, G. (1998). Just what is critical race theory and what is it doing in a *nice* field like education? *Qualitative Studies in Education, 11*(1), 7–24.

Ladson-Billings, G., & Tate, W. (1995). Toward a critical race theory of education. *Teachers College Record, 97*(1), 48–68.

Lawrence-Lightfoot, S., & Davis, J. (1997). *The art and science of portraiture.* San Francisco, CA: Jossey-Bass.

Lopez, G. E. (1993). *The effect of group contact and curriculum on white, Asian American, and African American Students' attitudes.* Ph.D. Dissertation, University of Michigan.

Lynn, M. (2006). Education for the community: Exploring the culturally relevant practices of black male teachers. *Teachers College Press, 108*(12), 2497–2822.

Making It Out of the Hood. (2008). Retrieved from http://www.facebook.com/group.php?gid=2390551946

Marable, M. (1998). *Black leadership.* New York, NY: Columbia University Press.

Marshall, C., & Rossman, G. (1999). *Designing qualitative research.* Thousand Oaks, CA: Sage Publications.

Rendón, L. (2008). *Sentipensante: Sensing/thinking pedagogy.* Sterling, VA: Stylus Press.

Rendón, L., Jalomo, R., & Nora, A. (2004). Theoretical considerations in the study of minority student retention in higher education. In J. M. Braxton (Ed.), *Reworking the student departure puzzle* Nashville, TN: Vanderbilt University Press.

Rodriguez, S. (2001). *Giants among us: First generation college graduates who live activist lives.* Nashville, TN: Vanderbilt University Press.

Sheu, H., & Sedlacek, W. (2002). *Help-seeking attitudes and coping strategies among college students by race.* Presented at the Annual Conference of the American Psychological Association.

Shockley, K. G. (2008). Africentric education leadership: Theory and practice. *International Journal of Education Policy and Leadership, 3*(3). Retrieved August 15, 2011 from http://www.ijepl.org.

Smiley, T. (2006). *The covenant in action.* Carlsbad, CA: Smiley Books.

Woodson, C. G. (1977). *The mis-education of the Negro.* New York, NY: The Associated Publishers.

Yosso, T. (2005). Whose culture has capital? A critical race theory discussion of community cultural wealth. *Race, Ethnicity, and Education, 8*(1), 69–91.

CHAPTER 29

The Queer Poetics of Social Justice

Literacy, Affect(ion), and the Critical Pedagogical Imperative

Robert E. Randolph, Jr.

Introduction

In this chapter, the author explores the importance of literacy to the project of social justice. Through critical analysis and personal insights, the author contextualizes literacy and poetry—as critical discourses of power and resistance, conditions of positionality, and essential curriculum for those engaged in higher education. The author contends that writing is a queer act, precisely because it requires the writer to deviate from normalcy, incorporate differences, and employ a praxis and pedagogy of affect(ion).

mmm girl: a prelude[1]

power is neither good nor bad, just dangerous,
as if cover-ups are double downs
it is true power, the ability to listen
god why didn't you give us any power
to love our double standards

ignorance isn't bliss, it's insensitive
your struggles not my own
alone and making a crossroad vow
and let my living be your inspiration

but, why do I have to be your inspiration
you never truly have power
if you don't care to listen to the insensitivities
of those girls and boys with insidious cover-ups
find the power all around me, vested in me,
and

mmm girl ...
they say
recognizing the sisterhood
in my eyes
circles and circles of sorrow

This chapter grew organically from a Fall 2013 course titled "Social Justice in Higher Education" taught by Dr. C. P. Gause, at my alma mater, the University of North Carolina at Greensboro (UNCG). I took the class because I thought it would supplement my educational and research interests in social justice and advocacy. Quite a bit of my research centers around what I call the "queer poetics of social justice." Fundamentally, I examine ways critical literacy functions as a cogent form of political resistance, an analytic that exposes the workings of oppression and hegemony, and a method(ology) of critical pedagogical inquiry. As a critical bricoleur, as conceptualized by Denzin and Lincoln (1999) and Joe Kincheloe (2001, 2004a, 2004b, 2004c, 2005), I pull together the disparate fields of critical pedagogy, rhetorical studies, and (black) queer studies as the nexus of my critical framework. I contend that writing—especially poetry—is a queer act, precisely because it requires the writer to deviate from normalcy, to incorporate differences, and to employ a praxis and pedagogy of affect(ion). Furthermore, through critical analysis and personal insights, I contextualize poetry and literature as discourses of power and resistance, conditions of positionality, and essential curriculum for those dedicated to the aims of critical pedagogy.

Given these pedagogical imperatives, I was pleasantly delighted to see Dr. Gause incorporate analyses of visual art, music (various genres), and poetry in course curriculum. But the tribulations of that semester and a particular incident that occurred in the course would challenge, yet strengthen, my commitments to the pedagogical promises of poetry. Eva, Bemis, Quist, and Hollands (2013) argue that "Poetry, as one art form, can also be used as a teaching tool for enhancing numerous skills and dispositions, including detailed observation skills, reflective thinking, creativity, inferential thinking, and higher-level cognitive skills such as analysis, evaluation and synthesis" (pp. 63–64). What does it mean to shape my life, indeed my world, with language? This question has been at the crux of my being from my earliest childhood memories to the present moment. As a scholar and educator, I am concerned with how poetry can be dispatched and deployed and serviceable to the ongoing project of social justice. In what ways can my poetry or the poetry of others affect meaningful, substantive change as I struggle to become an educated and lettered black man in the 21st Century?

The Poet's Soul: An Interlude

When I was a child, I expected poems to be honest, but they were (and still are to some extent) deceitful. They told me what I wanted to hear and gave me nothing more than shallow glimpses into the poet's soul but not into my own, at least not the way I wanted to see myself. When I was young, I was naïve enough to expect truth from poems; and I wanted them to spur me to my own truth.

Words that Negotiate Violence

To poetize (here I purposefully use the verb rather than the noun), one must be amenable to the daily changes and challenges of language, open to its dangerous utterances, to be vulnerable in ways that eschew ego, style, essence, or idealism. These skills are rather dynamic and are concerned with the very act of literacy itself. A writer must read the world before she can write it. For instance, Amanda Cobb (2000) argues,

> Literacy is valued, for perhaps different reasons, by those who teach literacy and those who learn literacy. What value literacy has for either party is dependent upon the community and context in which it is used, for literacy is always tied to purpose; it is something to be used, used for something. (p. 11)

My literacy is bound up in survival, and my performance of literacy is both racial and gendered. I am not alone in my understanding of literacy's power to affect change. Indeed, I come from a storied and long line of ancestors who depended on literacy to express the complexities—tribulations and triumphs—of the American experiences from the point-of-view of displaced Africans.

Historically, for African Americans, obtaining literacy was not without peril and progress ravaged by the American slavery regimes. We were not allowed to engage in certain written literacy practices because some slave owners feared the ramifications of literate slaves. Here, Frederick Douglass (1845) describes his master's reasoning and justification:

> Very soon after I went to live with Mr. and Mrs. Auld, she very kindly commenced to teach me the A, B, C. After I had learned this, she assisted me in learning to spell words of three or four letters. Just at this point of my progress, Mr. Auld found out what was going on, and at once forbade Mrs. Auld to instruct me further, telling her, among other things, that it was unlawful, as well as unsafe, to teach a slave to read. To use his own words, further, he said, "If you give a nigger an inch, he will take an ell. A nigger should know nothing but to obey his master—to do as he is told to do. Learning would spoil the best nigger in the world. Now," said he, "if you teach that nigger (speaking of myself) how to read, there would be no keeping him. It would forever unfit him to be a slave. He would at once become unmanageable, and of no value to his master."

And his master's fears were warranted, enslaved people began to appropriate Western notions of literacy as a means of resistance, using their knowledge of the reading and writing to forge bills of sale and "freedom papers," to write their own narratives to aid the abolition movement, to create newspapers, and even to spread word of Lincoln's signing of the Emancipation Proclamation. Like Douglass, I learned at an awfully young age to use my literacy against other classmates (and some adults), to protect myself from their insults, their wiles and oppression.

Let us consider an artifact: I practically cut my teeth on old westerns. I loved the exsanguination of shoot outs at high noon, the hustle and bustle of salons, the spurious and *ad hoc* nature of posses, the incredible hubris of "settlers," the rough manner of cowboys, and the intractable tenacity of the "Indians." The American West was a place of wonders and excitement that no one could tame although everyone was desperately trying to do so. Those westerns, though I was not fully aware of this fact at the time, were my first introduction to what I was expected to become in this society—a man. Men were expected to use guns, violence, and rough talk to subdue and conquer each other. And more important, all of these characteristics were desirable. Manhood depended upon my desire to master violence and mete it out when "appropriate." One had to bigger and better than the other cowboys and especially the Indians. Someone had to win, someone had to lose, and the Indians almost never won. Noted social and cultural critic James Baldwin (2012), participating in a 1965 debate at Oxford University, offered this thoughtful observation to an audience of young white men,

> It comes as a great shock around the age of 5 or 6 or 7, to discover the flag to which you have pledge allegiance, along with everyone else, has not pledge allegiance to you. It comes as quite a shock to discover that Gary Cooper killing off the Indians, when you are a child rooting for Gary Cooper, that the Indians are you.

Even now, the fact that I rooted for my own colonization and oppression strikes me as the bitterest poison I could have swallowed. But the heart of this anecdote illustrates a brooding sense of and ignorance toward difference. This is not to say that I was unaware of difference as a child, but I was aware of it in ways that were not generative or affirmative. For instance, I knew I was different from girls. But this difference was grounded in what I thought was the inferiority of girls. Simply, they couldn't do what we boys did—they could not jump as far, run as fast, hit as hard. Paradoxically, as I began to recognize the difference between myself and my female classmates, I also began to notice, with increasing clarity, that I was *different* from the other boys as well. Because my teachers read this difference as brilliant exceptionality, so I choose to as well. While this difference endeared me to my teachers, the distinction made my presence increasingly dubious to my peers. What I didn't realize, almost until it was too late, was that my performance, both intellectually and socially, began to alienate me from my peers. Johnson (2006) notes that "not being aware of privilege is an aspect of privilege itself, what some call 'the luxury of obliviousness'" (p. 22). I want to believe I was completely oblivious to what was going on, but I was not. I loved when my teachers doted and secretly loved the negative attention I received from other boys because of it. Indeed it was the only time I interacted with them. My alienation from other black males began early, and the gap only increased as I moved through educational institutions.

My Own Self-Making: An Interlude

As a boy, I expected poems to entertain me. As a teenager, I wanted them to make me feel happy again and to pull me out of my sallow moods. In hindsight, now that I am saddled with the question of my own self-making, I always wanted busy poems because I was always so still, loud poems because I was so quiet, and conked poems because I was so nappy. I wanted their theatricality, to bestow upon me some grand notion of life or death, good or evil, black or white. However, poems, now that I am a man and a poet, are too busy for me.

When Word "Nigger" Is Implied yet Unspoken: An Interlude

In January 2013, Kendrick Johnson, a black teenage boy, was found dead in his gymnasium, rolled up in a wrestling mat. His death was deemed "accidental;" and to add to the horror of his death, the morticians who attended to his body stuffed his chest cavity with old newspapers. During the spring, George Zimmerman stood trial for the 2012 slaying of Trayvon Martin. Just before the fall semester started, he was acquitted of second-degree murder and of manslaughter. The litany of black deaths continued and followed me into the semester. My haunting by the dead and dying black men in America was exacerbated by my PhD studies. Because of the sometimes harrowing experiences of schooling process, getting an education can often be described as a dominating and subjugating—essentially a colonizing experience. "[For] a black person to get an education [in America]," Baldwin (2011) stated at UC Berkeley in 1977, "he's got to have a lot of guts … and you risk schizophrenia." More than any other time during my tenure as a Ph.D. student, I have seen Baldwin's words manifest in ways that required me to develop a steely mind and a stealthy resolve.

I enrolled in the "Social Justice in Higher Education" course because I knew it would be immensely rewarding. Based on the course material and topics, I thought it would be a class with like-minded scholars and educators open to the free exchange of dialogue and dedicated to the mores of social justice and advocacy. However, it became clear to me that some of my classmates, people who were training to be student personnel in higher education, were merely there for a course credit. Simply, they had no intention to use the class and the space that it provided to challenge themselves, their privilege, and their dominant ideologies. Roughly 80% of the class members were White students. There were times when I challenged their assumptions and ignorances about race and sexuality, and I was met with a host of micro-aggressions, the least of which were disengaged stares, rolling eyes, and sucking of teeth. I interpreted this behavior as their discontent of my "speaking up" and "talking back." It is worth noting that my professor suggested we read an article on mircroagresions, and I'm sure he did so because he had noticed the behavior toward me, the only black male in the class. I resigned myself to keep moving in the course and tried to not let it effect me. But I was not prepared for an incident that, for a small moment, almost crushed my spirit.

During my presentation on "Seven Steps to Becoming an Ally" (this topic later struck me as ironic), a white-female student made comments about being a feminist. She asserted that feminism was for women only, a notion I took particular umbrage with because I am a black male womanist. I confronted her assessment of feminism, inquiring if she was aware that feminism is also about gender—women and men—citing bell hooks' *Feminism is for Everybody: Passionate Politics* (2000). I asked if she was cognizant of discourses about black feminism, Womanism, or global feminisms. She admitted that she had never heard of these feminisms. I was about to continue with my presentation but was interrupted by another student, a Latina (who by her own admission is perceived as White) accused me of being condescending, arrogant, and sarcastic.

The room was already on edge before this incident. Given the mircoagressions, blatant disrespectful behavior, and willful ignorance of previous weeks, I began my presentation by challenging the notion that my classmates even wanted to be allies to constituents who lacked the privilege we enjoyed. This sentiment had lain heavily on my heart for weeks, but it was not until my presentation that I felt compelled to say. As Audre Lorde (1984) states, "the transformation of silence into language and action is an act of self-revelation, and that always seems fraught with danger" (p. 42). My comment was not meant to scold or chastise, but I wanted them to know that my very presence in the class was because of a member of Student Affairs division at UNCG. Indeed, my connection to Pam Wilson, the former Director of the Office of the Multicultural Affairs, kept me alive. During a turbulent time of my undergraduate career, I fell into a deep, rueful depression, one that threaten to consume me in more ways than one. I had had these bouts of sadness but never anything like that. She encouraged me to seek professional counseling and gave me a personal referral to a local therapist, a black man, who would understand my unique position of being a black man at predominantly white institution.

The student's comment about my arrogance did not surprise me. I had heard similar comments most of my life. It is worth nothing that I was never exposed to the thoughts and opinions that I was condescending, arrogant, pompous, and a know-it-all, until I began my formal schooling. I am a Head-Start baby/child. For those first formative years (pp. 3–5), I was taught by my family and my Black teachers that I was loving, thoughtful, and intelligent. So when I heard this student bark at me with accusations about my temperament and demeanor, they conjured up modes of defense and survival that run deep. I "became the jungle" Toni Morrison speaks of in *Beloved* (1987). I smiled and put this question to her, "Am I being condescending or am I refusing to be the good little nigger you want me to be?" She now appeared to be even more disgusted with me and the situation. I suppose no one expected me to say "nigger" in polite conversation. But by this point, we were not having a polite conversation, and I was not holding my tongue any longer. Implicit in her challenge to me was that I was a nigger and had no right to question white students about their knowledge *or* ignorance, that as a nigger I was lucky to be at a white university. The professor intervened and I finished my presentation.

Although I was not visibly disturbed, this incident shook me to my core. Toward the end of the semester, Dr. Gause invited Patrick Hale to speak to us about concerns of immigrant populations and the difficulties they face to become educated, mainly because of America's rabid xenophobia. At the end of this lecture, Gause asked the class what we thought, and I quickly, perhaps too hastily, responded that I wanted to quit, to give up. I expressed how tired I was of thinking and responding to racism. It occurs to me now that those words were borne out a tired, frustrated semester. I had forgotten number seven on my own list of becoming an ally: *develop spirit-sustaining communities.* These networks are essential for survival and help guard against nagging feelings of hopelessness. I returned to my own writers communities, friends, and my favorite authors. I began writing again, something I had convince myself I could afford to do because of my Ph.D. studies.

I survived and, as apart of my healing, I began writing poetry again. The affect of that horrific experience remains with me still. But that experience is not wasted. I understand more than ever that survival is resistance. Perhaps it is the most spiritual and politically rigorous form of resistance. As a sentiment I try to instill in my students, I am committed to speaking my mind no matter the cost. I cannot remain silent. Audre Lorde (1997) illustrates the dynamics of silence and survival in her poem, "A Litany for Survival" from her collection of poetry title, *The Black Unicorn:*

and when we speak we are afraid
our words will not be heard
nor welcomed
but when we are silent
we are still afraid.

So it is better to speak
remembering
we were never meant to survive. (p. 256)

Educators as Poets as Social Justice Advocates

As a poets, educators, and social justice advocates, we must be impeccable with our word(s) and strive to understand how language is imbued with oppressive machinations. We must be true to ourselves in ways that reconcile the realities we see with the lives and faces of those we teach and advocate for with our own positionalities (Sensoy & DiAngelo, 2012, p. xviii). As a writer and poet, I look to other poets to inform me about how my words are a practice of social justice and activism. For writers, self-definition, world-making, and healing begins and ends with words, with poetry, "a revelatory distillation of experience, not the sterile word play that, too often, the white fathers distorted the word poetry to mean—in order to cover a desperate wish for imagination without insight" (Lorde, 1984, p. 37). In hindsight, I began to write early during my childhood and began to form a visceral appreciation for how words fought back the doldrums of my young life. But these words in and of themselves were inadequate because I kept them secret. And the few poems I chose to share were always hiding some bit of myself I didn't want people to know.

It was not until graduate school that I finally began to write more openly about the complexities of my life's goals and yearnings. Audre Lorde chastises her reader, "My silences had not protected me. Your silence will not protect you" (1984, p. 41). I thought that my silence would keep me from suffering, from losing loved ones and friends, and from the often traumatic experience of explaining my existence. But this was faulty and foolish logic. My silence alienated me further. Audre Lorde muses about silence as a strategy for safety, "… if I were to have been born mute, or had maintained an oath of silence my whole life long for safety, I would still have suffered, and I would still die. It is very good for establishing perspective" (Lorde, p. 43). A poet or social justice advocate cannot truly understand the suffering of others unless she understands her own. What makes all art transformative and transcendental is its ability to force the artist to continually self-reflect. As it relates to social justice advocates, this self-reflection helps "to uncover … socialized blind spots, privilege, and internalized superiority" (Sensoy & DiAngelo, 2012, p. 158). Thus, art offers to fulfill the democratic promise. Poets and social justice workers must constantly work toward their own liberation if we are to free others. Advocacy requires taking risks and rupturing boundaries, and art provides a unique education in this respect.

For example, earlier that semester, Dr. Gause showed our class a video of Richard Blanco reading his poem "One Today," for President Barack Obama's second inauguration. As a class, we noticed Blanco's seemingly stilted performance, almost pedestrian in its presentation. But we also recognized how his multiple identities were played out for a national audience. Phrases like "first immigrant," "first Latino," "first openly gay person," "youngest poet" crawled past the television screen and threatened to distract and detract from the gravitas of the moment. Thinking critically about the phrases, we surmised that this act was a political decision to highlight the progressive and liberal agenda of the Obama administration. In essence, like everything in America, the Obama administration had politicized and commodified Blanco's identity and poem.

A month after the semester began, I coincidently had the pleasure to see Richard Blanco read at North Carolina A&T State University. During the reading, which turned into a lecture about the responsibilities of poets as social activist, he reminded the audience that writers really do write to change the world, to make it anew, to leave it differently than they found it. James Baldwin echoes this sentiment:

> You write in order to change the world, knowing perfectly well that you probably can't, but also knowing that literature is indispensable to the world … The world changes according to the way people see it, and if you alter, even by a millimeter, the way people look at reality, then you can change it. (Watkins, 1979, p. 3)

Richard Blanco stated that writing poetry is like opening "an emotional door" and lamented how many writers cannot quite get to where they want because they do not want to walk through that door. Additionally, he discussed the politics of writing an occasional poem. As a queer man of color, he not only had to navigate the politics of being queer but also a Cuban immigrant. Blanco initially felt a self-imposed pressure to write a politically-charged poem, but he did not want to his identities to subsume the work itself. Underscoring the intersectionality of queer identities, Michael Warner (1993) explains why Blanco did not want what he calls "cultural sexuality" to foreground the political potentiality of the inauguration poem:

> Every person who comes to a queer self-understanding knows in one way or another that her stigmatization is connected with gender, the family, notions of individual freedom, the state, public speech, consumption and desire, nature and culture, maturation, reproductive politics, racial and national fantasy, class identity, trust and trust, censorship, intimate life and social display. terror and violence, health care, and deep cultural norms about the bearing of the body. (p. xiii)

Thus, Blanco's identities were already implicitly political. During his lecture, he also reiterated that, while the poem moved and extended beyond his autobiographical sphere, he also wanted to include an intimate space, a moment of personal vulnerability and reflection. For Blanco, or any poet, to display his life-truths and emotions so honestly and in such a public manner, is nothing less than courageous.

"Poetry is not a luxury," as Audre Lorde (1984) tells us, but is "a vital necessity of our existence [that] forms the quality of the light within which we predicate our hopes and dreams toward survival and change" (p. 37). For Blanco, writing and performing the inaugural poem was like "renewing our vows," a way of reminding the country—lawmaker and citizen alike—of our commitment to our democratic ideals. "I became a channel," Blanco explained. Blanco is what he calls a "working poet," an engineer "obsessed with bridges." On that national and international stage, Blanco scrutinized the truth of what it means to be an American and also shaped the language by which we tell that truth.

Highlighting the awakening of one of his personal truths, Blanco read a poem titled "Queer Theory: According to My Grandmother." The poem provided a long laundry list of observations that confirmed, at least in his grandmother's mind, Blanco's early queer tendencies. I chuckled at the first line ("Never drink soda from a straw—") because I, too, had been advised by my father to avoid drinking from a straw (2012, p. 34). This policing of behavior serves to reify dominant/dominating practices of oppression. While the poem's tone is sarcastic and humorous in its complete absurdity, it nevertheless illustrates how deeply wounding the policing of a young boy's affection can severely damage his psycho-social health:

> Avoid hugging men, but if you must,
> pat them real hard
> on the back, even
> if it's your father. (p. 34)

Sing To Me: An Interlude

Now that I am a man and a poet, poems prick me, pinch me, burn me, bind me, beat me, break me, build me, slap me, shake me, pleasure me, politicize me, portray me, sing to me, look for me, lament me, school me, seize me, to enthrall, enrapture me, rape me, rake me, remind me, remember me.

My Deeply Female and Spiritual Plane: A Postlude

As I stated earlier, a social justice educator must constantly engage in deep reflection. So much of myself I've repressed and beat back strictly for the comfort of others. And before I can realized it, major portions of my psyche, personality, testimony, and energy had slipped away. Of course, the difficult task of reconstituting the fragments that remain began as I read authors who challenged my sense of self and the world. In these fantastical worlds, I could escape the reality of my own existence. Writers like Toni Morrison, James Baldwin, Zora Neale Hurston, Terrance Hayes, and Jericho Brown satiated my curiosity and imagination in ways my teachers and parents could not. My relationship with language continued and grew along with me, as I moved from one grade to another, year after year. But it also began to change. No longer was a reading and writing for escape or exile. I began, in earnest, to engage language that reflected who I was. In her seminal essay "The Uses of The Erotic: The Erotic as Power," Audre Lorde writes, "There are many kinds of power, used and unused, acknowledged or otherwise. The erotic is a resource within each of us that lies in a deeply female and spiritual plane, firmly rooted in the power of our unexpressed or unrecognized feeling" (1984, p. 53). While Lorde addresses women specifically, I include myself as well. I recognized my own "deeply female and spiritual plane," and this revelation situated in how literature works for me and so many others.

Perhaps poetry promises a sense of possibility and existence without binary modalities or the totalizing effects of modern life, society, and culture. Poetry works in so many levels because it does not—in form or as genre—insist on fatalist ways of reading or knowing. And perhaps, alas, this is why people have such a "hard time" with poetry and why they often report it being "confusing." Simply, poetry refuses to yield its pedagogical possibilities if the is committed to binary thinking and hegemonic reading strategies. Inflexibility in the reader coaxes nothing from a poem; indeed, it becomes more recalcitrant. Poetry threatens an individualistic and sometimes collective epistemic ruptures. These ruptures are often affective and helps educators develop "promising tools and technologies for non-dualistic thought and pedagogy" (Sedgwick, 2002, p. 1). The epistemological and ontological concerns of literature are useful to the individual and the collective. Literature has the capacity to alter how teachers and students see the world. And this insight is invaluable to sustain social justice projects.

Lorde taught me, through her essay and poetry, that the sensations I felt when I read and wrote were erotic. Unfortunately, in my community, a little black boy who prefers to read and write rather than play war or football is deemed queer. But I have spent years engaging my own erotic and queer life and how it impacts my scholarship and creative work. Here, queerness signals difference, a deviation from normalcy, without foreclosing dialogue of sexual object choice (Cohen, 1997). Adrienne Rich (1993) tells us, "… most often someone writing a poem believes in, depends on, a delicate, vibrating range of difference, that an 'I' can become a 'we' without extinguishing others, that a partly common language exits to which strangers can bring their own heartbeat, memories, images of strangers." This "delicate, vibrating range of difference" is also what excites me as a teacher and writer. And more importantly, I use my (queerly) erotic life to see beyond the veil, to borrow W. E. B. DuBois' phrase, to stave off the banalities of life, to dare see a future where my own trajectories, transformations, and tendencies inform me about what it means to be a father, a writer, an educator, a scholar, a human being, and a stalwart advocate for social justice.

Note

1. I conceptualize and formatted this chapter as originally conceptualized by Dr. Gause for the final assignment of our "Social Justice in Higher Education" course. He wrote, "Let's look at the assignment from a musical perspective: One of many examples … Prelude: The Poem sets the tone for your journey. Interlude: The events that takes place between the musical events … which should be your writing, the thinking that goes into your writing, and the events that shape your writing. Postlude: The concluding musical piece, final notes, final chapter of the movement … which could be your reflections on this journey towards social justice. You should be able to take the information in the syllabus regarding the Critical Reflective Essay and combine it with your midterm to come up with a final paper that would be worthy of

publication. I employ you to take the opportunity to stretch your thinking and include not only the work, texts, writings, videos, and presentations done by your colleagues. … you should also reflect on other research, scholarly writing, and essayists from various perspectives. Doing this would actually create a book chapter that would be engaging and dynamic" (C. P. Gause, personal communication, October 31, 2013).

Work Cited

Baldwin, J. (2011, February 20). *James Baldwin on education.* Retrieved from http://www.youtube.com/watch?v=piGSgnSqO5E

Baldwin, J. (2012, October 27). *James Baldwin debates William F. Buckley (1965).* Retrieved from http://www.youtube.com/watch?v=oFeoS41xe7w

Blanco, R. (2012). *Looking for the gulf motel.* Pittsburgh, PA: University of Pittsburgh.

Cobb, A. J. (2000). *Listening to our grandmothers' stories: The Bloomfield academy for chickasaw females, 1852–1949.* Lincoln, NE: University of Nebraska Press.

Cohen, C. J. (1997). Punks, Bulldaggers, and welfare queens: The radical potential of queer politics? *GLQ: A Journal of Lesbian and Gay Studies, 5,* 437–465.

Denzin, N. K., & Lincoln, Y. S. (Eds.). (1999). *The SAGE handbook of qualitative research* (3rd ed.). Thousand Oaks, CA: Sage Publications.

Douglass, F. (1845). *Narrative of the life of Frederick Douglass, an American slave.* Written by himself. Retrieved from http://docsouth.unc.edu/neh/douglass/douglass.html

Eva, A. L., Bemis, C. A., Quist, M. F., & Hollands, B. (2013). The Power of the poetic lens: Why teachers need to read poems together. *Journal for the Assembly for Expanded Perspectives on Learning, 19*(1), 62–73.

Johnson, A. G. (2006). *Privilege, power, and difference.* Boston, MA: McGraw-Hill.

Kincheloe, J. L. (2001). Describing the bricolage: Conceptualizing a new rigor in qualitative research. *Qualitative Inquiry, 7*(6), 679–672.

Kincheloe, J. L. (2004a). Introduction: The power of the bricolage: Expanding research methods. In J. L. Kincheloe & K. S. Berry (Eds.), *Rigour and complexity in educational research: Conceptualizing the bricolage* (pp. 1–22). Maidenhead: Open University Press.

Kincheloe, J. L. (2004b). Questions of disciplinarity/interdisciplinarity in a changing world. In J. L. Kincheloe & K. S. Berry (Eds.), *Rigour and complexity in educational research: Conceptualizing the bricolage* (pp. 50–81). Maidenhead: Open University Press.

Kincheloe, J. L. (2004c). Redefining and interpreting the object of study. In J. L. Kincheloe & K. S. Berry (Eds.), *Rigour and complexity in educational research: Conceptualizing the bricolage* (pp. 82–102). Maidenhead: Open University Press.

Kincheloe, J. L. (2005). On to the next level: Continuing the conceptualization of the bricolage. *Qualitative Inquiry, 11*(3), 323–350.

Lorde, A. (1984). *Sister outsider: essays and speeches.* Freedom, CA: Crossing Press.

Lorde, A. (1997). *The collected poems of Audre Lorde.* New York, NY: W. W. Norton & Company.

Rich, A. (1993). Someone is writing a poem. *Poetry Foundation.* Retrieved from http://www.poetryfoundation.org/learning/essay/239326

Sedgwick, E. K. (2002). *Touching feeling: Affect, pedagogy, performativity.* Durham, NC: Duke University Press.

Sensoy, O., & DiAngelo, R. (2012). *Is everyone really equal?: An introduction to key concepts in social justice education.* New York, NY: Teachers College Press.

Warner, M. (Ed). (1993). *Fear of a queer planet: Queer politics and social theory.* Minneapolis, MN: University of Minnesota Press.

Watkins, M. (1979, September, 23). James Baldwin writing and talking. *The New York Times Book Review*, p. 3, 36–37.

CHAPTER 30

Politics of Leading

Melissa A. Odegard-Koester

In consideration of writing reflections on the politics of leading, it seemed paramount to start with a quote from a woman I am impacted by profoundly. bell hooks' message and impact on me regarding her teaching and reflections on race, class, gender in education, and sexuality have prompted my own growth and continued development regarding these issues. Much of my research and writing have focused on reflective pedagogy (Koltz & Odegard, 2012; Odegard & Vereen, 2010; Odegard, Hill, & Vereen, 2009). Because I plan to review leadership through a critical pedagogical lens (Freire, 1970 p. 62), it is imperative that I begin by providing a context from which my current understandings of leadership are derived. I will discuss my contextualization of leadership which includes my personal and professional history. I will also discuss my current context and experiences that have influenced my perspectives regarding leadership. Finally, I will bring to light some of the current perspectives of students and their definitions of leadership. Overall, these contexts provide a rich understand of how I navigate the politics of leading.

Contextualization of Leadership

The sources of information that influence my understanding of leadership are embedded in my own experiences spanning from my early childhood, early adulthood, and adulthood. In order to discuss my reflections on the politics of leading, it is important that I am aware of and be transparent about the experiences that shape my conceptual context (Lincoln & Guba, 1985). My formative experiences influence how I interact with students and colleagues as well as inform my current pedagogy, supervision, and clinical practice. I am aware that my personal interactions as a student, counselor, and colleague have greatly influenced my experience as an educator and life-long learner. I see these experiences as being multi-layered, encompassing a variety of interactions which include a personal history, an influential mentor, being a counselor, and being a counselor educator. All of these experiences serve to fuel my passion and commitment to empowering students to be reflective in their work. This personal element of my conceptual context has facilitated the momentum for me to continue engaging in the journey of challenging students to critically reflect on their role in their professional work as well as their contribution to society. The below excerpts: personal history, an influential mentor, being a counselor, and emerging counselor educator are adapted from "A Grounded Theory of Counselor Educators Integrating Social Justice into their Pedagogy" (Odegard, 2009, pp. 19–24).

Personal History

I recognize that my personal history has impacted how I experience working as an educator. I grew up in a rural town in Minnesota in a family of seven, the eldest of five siblings. My father is a third generation Norwegian who came from a farming family. While I did not grow up on a farm, I lived in a rural setting surrounded by farms, one of which was passed down from my great-grandfather. The farming work-ethic is still alive and well in my family of origin based on this history. My immediate family was working-class while I grew up and I remember thinking in my younger years that I was defined by living in a single-wide trailer and all the "white trash" slurs that go with it. We lived in this trailer, the seven of us, until I was eleven. When I turned twelve, my father built a three-bedroom house on the land his father gave him. My father taught me how to drive a tractor, fix the rear brakes on my car, mow lawns, work on engines, and household appliances. My mother grew up in a large family of thirteen in rural Georgia; she taught me various household tasks, such as doing the laundry, cooking meals, cleaning the house appropriately, and nurturing my younger siblings. During the early years, I was unaware of the impacts of issues such as racism, sexism, heterosexism, classism, ableism, and oppression that how they affect many groups in American society. As I reflect back, I experience some feelings of anger because my family didn't offer me different opportunities to see or experience life outside of my rural town of 3,000 people.

An Influential Mentor

The most influential experience I have had in my education was in my undergraduate program. I reflect on this time as critical to my young adulthood as I was in a position where I was vulnerable, yet willing and open to experience and view the world from differing perspectives. I met a woman, Karen, director of the Youth Ministry program I was enrolled in at Bethel University. She is an individual who empowered me to consider issues related to social justice in my work as a youth pastor and educator with urban adolescents. Through my time at Bethel, she invested in me in such a way that I had not experienced. She invested in me through spending time encouraging me and sharing books that enhanced my awareness of racism, sexism, and classism. She also asked me to facilitate educational simulations that assisted college students to attend to social justice concerns in their work with youth and supported me by attending meaningful events with me. She served as a mentor through some of the most difficult challenges in my undergraduate program. One of the challenges I faced was feeling like I didn't fit in to the mainstream culture of the Bethel student body. Karen facilitated a contextual understanding of my history: coming from a rural working-class family as well as my education being primarily funded through scholarships, grants, work study, and student loans to stay enrolled at Bethel. This experience was in contrast to many of my peer experiences who had the financial means to pay for college.

Karen further shared her own personal experiences with me which fostered a growing connection between us. She disclosed her personal struggles as an African-American woman from a low-income, urban background in a predominantly white male-oriented profession. I was able to relate with her because I shared the experience of being a woman in a male dominated profession, as well as coming from a working-class background. This shared experience and her ability to disclose her own personal struggles from her given context allowed me to feel close to her. This connection facilitated an openness and motivation to learn more about social justice issues, such as oppressive political systems and institutions that limit access to marginalized individuals. This includes those of low socioeconomic status, ethnic minority groups, religious minorities, and those in the lesbian, gay, bisexual, and transgender (LGBT) community. I continued to have experiences in my undergraduate program that challenged my perception of society and the injustices that exist within systems of power, including religious, educational, and political institutions.

Based on these experiences, I further explored my role in becoming an active participant in addressing the social inequities existent in society. I began committing my work as a student, community leader, and mentor to this endeavor. For example, I became involved with co-facilitating simulations: experiential activities designed to enhance student awareness of the –isms present in current society. I also engaged in mentoring relationships with high school students and empowered them to create community service-learning projects where they conducted needs assessments in their communities and implemented social change plans. The passion for addressing social justice began for me in my personal experiences and became more poignant as I was challenged to consider ways in which I could further educate myself as well as facilitate educative moments in the life experiences of urban youth. I attribute this recognition and igniting of passion to integrate critical reflection into my pedagogy to my mentor, co-worker, and friend, Karen. Her intentionality in challenging me, encouraging me, walking along side of me, and seeing things in me that I did not see in myself, are characteristics I hope to model for students as an educator.

Being a Counselor

During and following my internship experience in Minneapolis, Minnesota, I worked at a community mental health agency in Hennepin County to provide mental health and life skills services to children, adolescents, and their families. This agency primarily focused on clinical work and life skills with low-income families from urban settings. I had the opportunity to counsel with a variety of families throughout this time who presented with varying degrees of concerns, such as poverty, coping with life in violent neighborhoods and survival. Most of the families I worked with came from poor neighborhoods in both north and south Minneapolis and the surrounding suburbs. Many of the struggles parents faced were related to survival and examples were paying rent, providing winter clothes for their children, gaining access to resources for their children's education, living in communities rampant with gang violence, earning livable wages, and coping with family members in prison. A number of parents I worked with would discuss their frustrations with "the system" and their continued struggle to obtain social services such as Section Eight housing and Medicaid coverage. I soon realized that the challenge for many of the families I worked with was not how to "self-actualize," but rather it was how they were going to navigate through each day to meet their basic needs for survival.

As I would listen to the stories of struggle that many shared, I became overwhelmed with anger, frustration, and sadness. I wondered how I could balance empathy while helping to enact the social change needed to address the psychological stress oppressive systems have placed on the families with whom I worked. I continued to wonder what it would take, in my role as counselor, to address the broad, systemic problems that impact families every day. As a counselor I asked myself the question, "How can I begin to address the predominant struggles that individuals and families face on both micro and macro levels?" As a counselor in my current mental health setting, I work with clients who experience frustrations with similar issues that were described above. It is imperative that I, as counselor, be aware of the circumstances impacting client contexts while integrating appropriate interventions to address the systemic issues that are presented. I feel that grappling with thoughts and questions such as these are a necessary part of my own developmental process as an educator. These thoughts and questions impact my ability to work with clients who face oppressive systems as well inform my instruction of fulfilling this important role in their clinical practice.

An Emerging Educator

I am currently a counselor educator at a Mid-Western state university and have been teaching full-time for the last six years. Based on the culmination of my experiences, both personal and professional, I am motivated to challenge, support, and expand students' perspectives regarding how they might facilitate change with their clients and on the broader community and societal levels. While I have the freedom to engage a critical reflective pedagogy in the classroom with students, I struggle with how to integrate critical reflection more specifically into the overall counselor training curriculum. This is where the politics of higher education interface with being a critical reflective leader. Let me guide you through an imagery exercise that captures my initial experiences as a pre-tenured faculty.

When I first began my role as a tenure-track faculty member, the message I received was "your opinion matters only when it confirms current faculty consensus." I remember initial program meetings where we were discussing important program concerns and were offered opportunities to provide feedback regarding program improvement. I brought up concerns surrounding ethics with regards to multicultural and social justice counselor competency and the need to fully integrate into the curriculum. The feedback I was given endorsed a common perception regarding curriculum training, "oh, we have a cultural diversity course which covers that." There was another pre-tenured faculty who shared program concerns and possible solutions to some of the program issues that emerged who was given feedback as to why his ideas wouldn't work, "we've tried them before." Under the previous "leadership" my interpretation was that whatever solution or feedback I offered didn't matter unless it was the consensus of the majority faculty who were tenured. Shortly after I received these consistent messages, I internalized them and decided to keep quiet until it was safe to share my feedback. In my mind, I believed it was safe when I was guaranteed promotion and tenure *or* when the leadership shifted. Since then, I have struggled over the years with questions such as: How do I teach students that their voice is important when I am behaving in a way where I don't believe my own is? I'm silenced! How do I navigate a climate which doesn't appear to endorse differing perspectives? I'm oppressed!

Current Climate

I now have a voice!!! Over the last couple of years I've had opportunities which have afforded me greater responsibility at the administrative level. Some of the opportunities came at a time in which there was a significant upper administration shift. To illustrate, two years ago there was a position available in our college's Dean's office that came open and I decided to apply out of curiosity. I was eager! Eager to learn a new role and explore the possibilities. The role was to serve as the Assistant to the Associate Dean and shortly following the application process, I was selected to serve in this role. In this position, I gained a clearer understanding of overall program and curricular development within the college. I engaged in learning about new programs of which I was not previously intimately aware. This opportunity also allowed me the opportunity to develop and nurture important relationships across disciplines within the college. In this role I learned that my voice mattered as well as identified that one of my greatest strengths is my ability build bridges across disciplines and gain trusting relationships to do good work with others who are like minded. What I mean when I say "do good work" is the philosophy I recall being instilled in me at a young age by my dad "leave things better than you found it." The working class mentally has stuck with me in my role as faculty member in addition to serving as the Assistant to the Associate Dean of the college.

In the past year, my role has shifted from assisting in the Dean's office to becoming the coordinator of the counseling programs. This shift didn't occur in a smooth manner as the former coordinator was asked to step down from her role which she had previously for six years. I had to consider the outcome of electing to serve in this new role as it would impact the current dynamics in the department as well as the relationships with the other counseling faculty. After consideration of the possibilities, and a week of deliberation, I accepted the challenge. I am afraid! I knew accepting this challenge and new role would come with difficulty and I wasn't looking forward to the conflict that would inevitably ensue following the disclosure of the transition. As soon as it was disclosed, the decision was met with resistance on behalf of the former coordinator. On the bright side, one of the faculty members who has served the longest as a counseling faculty in the department was enthusiastic regarding the transition and has been a consistent source of encouragement and empowerment to me in my new role throughout this past year.

I live! I am proud to say that the bumps of this past year's journey has allowed me to reflect on the beauty and transformation that evolves through challenges. The light! I also see new transitions giving birth to additional transformative and positive development to me personally and professionally. Fortunately, the additional leadership shifts in our department continue to evolve with the hire of our department chair five short months ago. His leadership and encouragement has motivated me to be better at the work I do. It is empowering to share a vision with a new leadership that breaths equity, justice, new life, and a drive to make programs and people better. I am looking forward to the coming year as I also have the privilege of working with an additional counseling faculty who is committed to social justice, equity, and empowering people to have a voice. Hope is alive!!!

Student Perspectives on Leadership

About mid-semester, I was interested in finding out what some of our current counseling students thought about leadership. In one of my courses I asked them to engage in a reflective activity surrounding the concept of leadership and what it means to them. They were given the prompt: "Many of you have engaged in leadership roles and have experienced those who have provided leadership. From your perspective, what is leadership? How would you define a leader?" I had the students write down their responses. There were four students who responded and there perspectives will be shared below while maintaining confidentiality through the use of pseudonyms. According to Sam,

> Leadership is setting an example and being with a group instead of leading from behind, or at a distance. It also accounts for varying degrees of input from others; some of whom have differing backgrounds, and taking feedback as a way of growth to a goal.

Another student, Sasha, reflected on what leadership means to her and considered leadership as comprising certain characteristics: "Leadership … walking the walk, accountability, integrity, leading by example, living congruently with morals and values." Maria discusses her perspectives on what defines a leader. She shares the following:

> A leader is willing to simply come along side of others and show them the path they took. Or if it is a new journey or issue being willing to walk ahead and look for solutions, weigh all the possibilities, and lead them. I was once told, "you only have to be one step ahead of those you are leading."

According to Jennifer, a leader is someone who motivates others. She states, "Someone who motivates others to be their best by encouragement and example. A leader treats others with respect and expects the best from them." Altogether, I noticed a theme of modeling through being an "example" that emerged through the students' definitions. Sam's definition of leadership probably struck me the most as I resonated with getting "varying degrees of input from others; some of whom have differing backgrounds, and taking feedback as a way of growth to a goal." I believe it is critical when leading to consider a variety of voices as well as feedback from others to influence future growth and change.

Recommendations

In order to illuminate further how I navigate the politics of leading, I provided a context from which my current understandings of leadership are derived. I discussed further my contextualization of leadership which included my personal and professional history. I also shared my current context and experiences that have influenced my perspectives regarding leadership. Lastly, I brought to light some of the current perspectives of students and their definitions of leadership. Overall, these contexts provided a rich understanding of how I navigate the politics of leading which empowers me to share my personal guidelines that I follow in leadership roles:

1. Build relationships. I believe that in order to get any good work done, it is through trusting and respectful relationships with others who have a shared vision. These relationships take time, invest!

2. Know your audience. I believe that through the rapport building process it is possible to become aware of the culture/audience you are working within. In some cases you may need to tailor the delivery of a message based on your audience. I have found, when I do this strategically, it has prompted overall success.

3. Accept challenges. In my experience, the most growth in myself occurs when I say "yes" to a challenge. I often determine this when I experience a little fear or anxiety. This is often the gauge that leads to my choice to accept. When I am able to say "yes," work through the fear, and accomplish a role/task set before me, I am better.

4. Maintain a healthy balance of optimism while attending to critical reflection of situations and contexts. Most individuals aren't interested in working with people who ooze negativity. In the most dire circumstances, work to instill hope in others. In addition, critical reflection can assist in assessing the motivation of others as well as audience, work to do this as objectively as possible.

5. Be well. In order to invest in the lives of others it is imperative that I take care of myself and my family. Without this investment in myself and family it is difficult for me to have the strength to invest in the lives of others and influence positive change. Find out what facilitates your overall health and well-being. Engage in those activities and with the people that matter the most.

Work Cited

Freire, P. (1970/2006). *Pedagogy of the oppressed.* New York, NY: Continuum International Publishing Group.

Koltz, R. L., & Odegard, M. A. (2012). Creative art in group: Pedagogical implications for integration in group counseling courses. In G. R. Walz, J. C. Bleuer, & R. K. Yep (Eds.), *Compelling counseling interventions: Celebrating vistas sixth anniversary.* Online version. American Counseling Association.

Lincoln, Y. S., & Guba, E. G. (1985). *Naturalistic inquiry.* Beverly Hills, CA: Sage.

Marcus, G., & Fischer, M. (1986). Ant

Odegard, M. A. (2009). *A grounded theory of counselor educators integrating social justice into their pedagogy* (Doctoral Dissertation, Idaho State University, 2009). ProQuest, UMI Dissertation Publishing.

Odegard, M., Hill, N., & Vereen, L. (2009). Situating supervision in the context of a social justice paradigm: A convergence of Bernard's discrimination model and social justice. In G. R. Walz, J. C. Bleuer, & R. K. Yep (Eds.), *Compelling counseling interventions: Celebrating vistas sixth anniversary.* Online version. American Counseling Association.

Odegard, M. A., & Vereen, L. (2010). A grounded theory of counselor educators integrating social justice into their pedagogy. *Counselor Education and Supervision. Special Issue. Social Justice: A National Imperative for Counselor Education and Supervision, 50*(2), 130–149.

CHAPTER 31

Learning and Leadership in Higher Education

The Role of Service-Learning

Laura Finley, Victor Romano, Glenn A. Bowen, and Celeste Fraser Delgado

Given the increasing discussions over the cost and benefits of higher education, colleges and universities are grappling with how best to attract and retain students, as well as how to prepare those student to effectively work in an increasingly interconnected world. For example, many institutions have begun to offer or dramatically expand their online learning programs and their study abroad curricula (Felten & Clayton, 2011). Others have developed educational niches that will position them favorably against competing colleges and universities. Service-learning and engaged scholarship initiatives constitute one of these niches that some in higher education believe will both attract students and better prepare them to be leaders in their communities and workplaces upon graduation.

Although the idea of inculcating an ethic of civic service in students has been ever present in American higher education, the actual term *service-learning* first emerged in the 1967 work of Robert Sigmon and William Ramsey (Giles & Eyler, 1994). As a form of experiential learning, service-learning is grounded in large part in the work of John Dewey (1938) and his theory of experience. Dewey believed educators should "give the pupils something to do, not something to learn; and the doing is of such a nature as to demand thinking, or the intentional noting of connections; learning naturally results" (Dewey, 1916, p. 181). Thanks in part to its compatibility with the activism of the civil rights movement and the zeitgeist of the late 1960s and 1970s, the service-learning movement gained popularity across college campuses during this period. This popularity, however, was short lived. Problems with curriculum and mission integration, claims of paternalism, and questions about the effectiveness of both the learning and service being provided led to the termination of many service-learning programs in the late 1970s and early 1980s (Kendall, 1990). By the mid-1980s however, due to advancements in the field and the creation of the service-learning advocacy organizations such as Campus Compact and Campus Outreach Opportunity League, service-learning began to reemerge as a popular pedagogy.

Today, service-learning continues to thrive at colleges and universities across the country. Its best practices and principles have been repeatedly refined, and over time, multiple definitions of service-learning have emerged. According to Felten and Clayton (2011), among the most frequently cited operational definitions of service-learning is the one by Bringle, Hatcher, and McIntosh (2006):

> Service learning is a course-based, credit-bearing educational experience in which students (a) participate in an organized service activity that meets identified community needs and (b) reflect on the service activity in such a way as to gain further understanding of course content, a broader appreciation of the discipline, and an enhanced sense of personal values and civic responsibility. (p. 12)

Notwithstanding the presence of competing definitions, service-learning has coalesced into a field with three core characteristics. Service-learning should (a) strive to achieve both academic and civic goals; (b) be based on reciprocal collaboration among all stakeholders; and (c) include critical reflection and assessment of learning and service outcomes (Felten & Clayton, 2011).

While service-learning as pedagogy continues to hold great promise, it runs the risk of being diluted or commodified as institutions begin leveraging it as a tool for marketing instead of a method of promoting engaged learning and civic responsibility. In this chapter, we discuss service-learning as a method of both attracting students and developing students' civic capacities, including leadership for social change. The chapter begins with a discussion of the benefits and potential limitations of service-learning, particularly in relation to marketing a university or college. Specifically, we address how service-learning fails when it does not fully engage the three key stakeholders: students, faculty, and community partners. Rather than becoming a point of pride and an institutional strength, many fear service-learning will become superfluous if practiced in a superficial manner without a genuine institutional commitment. We respond to this concern by documenting best practices and exemplary service-learning programs, from both scholarly literature and our extensive experiences utilizing the pedagogy. In particular, we share information about two innovative service-learning projects to illustrate creative campus-community partnerships that support community organizations, enhance the reputation of the institution, and enable students to strengthen both their content knowledge and their leadership skills.

Benefits of Service-Learning

Proponents see service-learning as a transformative pedagogical strategy in higher education (e.g., Butin, 2006; Meyers, 2009), connecting classrooms with the real world, the cognitive with the affective, and theory with practice. Service-learning is clearly beneficial to all stakeholders—communities, students, faculty, and the host institution. Communities often derive benefits through the service that students provide in local schools, nonprofit agencies, and community-based organizations. Students contribute their time, talents, and energies to meet community needs, usually in the areas of education, health care, the environment, disaster preparedness, and economic opportunity. The students have an opportunity to engage in problem solving as the service-learning project exposes them to the lived experience of individuals grappling with social problems such as hunger, homelessness, and domestic violence. At the same time, community agencies gain some access to university resources, receive support for program development and service delivery, and are better able to implement solutions to pressing problems affecting clients and community residents.

Service Learning: Students' Participation

A fairly robust body of research has produced evidence of service learning's benefits to students in particular. For example, students participating in service-learning develop a deeper understanding of course content, increased motivation to learn, and the ability to apply what they have learned in class to real-life problems (Astin, Vogelgesang, Ikeda, & Yee, 2000; Eyler, Giles, Stenson, & Gray, 2001; Simons & Cleary, 2006). Through service-learning, students develop increased empathy (Koliba, 2000), enhance their critical analysis and writing skills, better see connections between theory and practice (Alberle-Grasse, 2000; Parker-Gwin, 1996; Roschelle, Turpin, & Elias, 2000), and come to see themselves as part of the broader community beyond the campus. Nevertheless, direct service is obviously overemphasized, perpetuating the idea that students are merely benevolent service providers in needy communities where quick fixes are enough. Service-learning without a social justice orientation denies students the opportunity to take appropriate civic action that supports efforts to redress social issues.

Service Learning: Creating Agents of Social Change

Long-time educator Richard Cone's (2003) observation still rings true: University and college curricula do not offer students enough opportunities to build skills in using the civic tools of petition, redress, and advocacy. In our view, more service-learning projects should be designed intentionally to prepare students for a role as agents of social change. Accordingly, we advocate social justice education aimed at increasing students' awareness of social inequalities, identifying the roles that individuals and institutions play in maintaining such inequalities, and taking corrective action (Meyers, 2009). Social justice education should draw attention to the historical, sociological, cultural, and political contexts of the social issues that students seek to address and should prepare them to embrace community-based opportunities to put their civic knowledge and skills into practice.

Regarding the benefits to faculty, those who engage in effective service-learning practice may find that it helps to renew their love of teaching while supporting their collaborative efforts to address issues in local and global settings (Maas Weigert, 1998). Our experience is that service-learning enlivens teaching and enriches learning while improving faculty-student interactions. Moreover, it creates strong networks for faculty across disciplines and open avenues for scholarly research and creative activities.

A service-learning program redounds to the benefit of the host institution as well. It improves town-gown relations and creates a positive image of the institution, making it attractive to prospective students. When institutions are seen as responsive to community interests and priorities, they will be attractive also to donors.

However, far too many institutions pay lip service to the notion of reciprocity—the mutuality of involvement and benefits that should accrue to campus and community participants in service-learning. If institutions accept that reciprocity should be the hallmark of their relationships with their surrounding communities, they should ensure that community agency voice is distinctive in service-learning program planning and implementation.

Exemplary service-learning projects emphasize reciprocal relationships among university and community participants (Bringle & Hatcher, 2002; Conner, 2010); facilitate student exploration of social justice issues (Mitchell, 2007); foster cultural understanding (Bowen & Hackett, 2010); and promote both personal and social transformation (Meyers, 2009; Simons & Cleary, 2006). Further, exemplary service-learning projects are complemented by critical reflection—a process that should challenge and guide students in (a) connecting their service experience to course content; (b) examining salient issues related to their project; (c) developing civic knowledge, skills, and values; and (d) finding personal relevance in their academic work.

Some scholars and practitioners have criticized the practice of service-learning in some higher education institutions. Eby (1998), for instance, argued that service-learning is often ameliorative rather than oriented toward change of social structures. It puts band aids on deeply rooted problems and gives students a false understanding of need as well as a simplistic understanding of service. At the same time, some administrators and faculty members insist that students should be restricted to providing direct service rather than engage also in social change initiatives. These administrators and faculty worry that social action/social change activities are too "political" (Maas Weigert, 1998, p. 8). Whereas direct service within community agencies is most appropriate for students in some service-learning courses, other courses are well suited to a service-learning component that stresses the importance of social change.

Colleges and universities that make social justice a central element of their mission sometimes make social change-focused student leadership development complementary to service-learning practice. In this regard, many employ a co-curricular strategy based on the social change model of leadership development (Higher Education Research Institute [HERI], 1996)—a purposeful, collaborative, values-based process, which remains a tried-and-true approach to social change. Practitioners use it as a framework for creating student leadership programs that promote self-knowledge and collaboration, service and civic responsibility, social justice and equity (Bowen, 2006). In accordance with the social change model, such programs emphasize that all students, not just those with formal leadership titles, have leadership capabilities that can be developed through service and guided reflection.

Students leaders are expected to develop values consistent with the "seven Cs" offered by The Higher Education Research Institute (HERI, 1996): Consciousness of self, or awareness of one's own thoughts and values; congruence, or thinking and acting with consistency and authenticity; commitment, or intense motivation to act; collaboration, or working with others in a common effort; common purpose, or embracing shared values and purposes; controversy with civility, or the recognition that diverse groups will disagree but must do so civilly; and citizenship, or responsible connectedness with the community. The ultimate goal is change.

Redirecting Drive-By Service-Learning

As noted earlier, there is a tendency for students to perform direct service with community agencies. Direct service might involve picking up litter in a park, painting a community center, collecting canned foods for a homeless shelter, or raising funds for a disaster relief organization. Although direct-service projects are worthwhile, they tend to be based on the charity model, as contrasted with the social change model. Service-learning based on charity does provide students with opportunities to serve less-privileged persons (Lewis, 2004), but it also facilitates benevolence and paternalism. By contrast, service-learning based on social justice engages students in experiences that attempt to redistribute resources, empower communities and create more-equitable institutional arrangements (Lewis, 2004; Marullo & Edwards, 2000).

Furthermore, scholars have recently raised the issue that institutions, in their zeal to adopt service-learning campus-wide, have instead created "McService" or "happy meal community service" (Eby, 1998, p. 2), which are, in reality, watered-down offerings of authentic service-learning. Of particular concern is that, when institutions seek to mainstream service-learning, they may promote "McService," rather than service-learning based on social justice. As noted, institutions may fear that transformative efforts are too political or that they contrast with the wishes of donors and thus are more eager to encourage and provide support for service-learning efforts that are far closer to volunteerism (Sigmon, 1995).

Livingston's (2011) investigation into service-learning programs at an urban research institution revealed that they were generally viewed as "just another commodity to be used by an impersonal discourse driven by the economic motive" (p. 102). It was "relegated as a marketing tool for recruitment and retention rather than established as an effective pedagogy" (p. 102). This tendency is so pervasive that, as Gent (2011) noted, less than one percent of service-learning projects can be considered civic action or justice-advocacy projects.

Service-learning for social change is more time-consuming, as it requires intensive preparation of students, building of relationships with community members, and critical dialogue and reflection throughout (Lewis, 2004). Additionally, true community change should be pursued as an interdisciplinary endeavor, as communities inevitably include multiple philosophical, social, spiritual, economic, and other backgrounds. Yet, faculty at universities often are not accustomed to interdisciplinary work, nor are most allotted ample training or time to work collaboratively (Lewis, 2004). In order to coordinate service-learning that is truly transformational, professors and community organizations must do intensive front-end work. Students must be adequately trained in order to move their service past simple labor (Butin, 2011).

When service-learning students come and go at community agencies, what has been described as the "drive-by" model (Hollander, 2010), they may be more disruptive than helpful to the organization. Many organizations find it cumbersome to train students, some of whom may be resentful that they have to participate in agency- or community-based work. Further, trying to accommodate students' schedules puts a huge burden on organizations. Students sometimes fail to recognize their own privilege and, instead of working out a mutually agreeable schedule for service-learning, demand that organizations accommodate the students' needs.

Yet another issue is that students engaged in service-learning with marginalized populations may see themselves as "liberal saviors." Service-learning has the potential to reinforce stereotypes and subconscious beliefs that those being "served" are incapable of helping themselves (Himley, 2004). In doing so, the service-learning may reify the inequities that it is intended to address (Jones, LaPeau, & Robbins, 2013). Successful service-learning experiences must resist "othering" those who are different from college students (Butin, 2011; Himley, 2004). It is particularly challenging to ensure that students do not see themselves as heroic helpers if they are engaged in the type of short-term service-learning projects that many institutions favor.

In order for students to truly benefit from their service-learning experience, professors must help them see connections between the course material and the service performed. Oftentimes, professors do so only minimally, leaving students confused as to how to process what they experienced (Herzberg, 1994). Many have cautioned against predetermined and repetitive forms of reflection (Mezirow, 1991; Schon, 1983). As Stewart (2011) importantly asked, "what is service-learning saying about the types of knowledge that we expect from service-learners service-learning students when we apparently continue to advocate the same, and arguably traditional, methods of reflection?" (p. 41).

Despite these shortcomings, researchers have identified the short-term service model as perhaps the most common form of service-learning (Tryon et al., 2008). This is the case at Barry University, a Catholic, liberal arts institution in Miami Shores, Florida, where students enrolled in general education courses in sociology and theology are required to complete 10 hours of service over the course of a semester. Students choose from a broad range of service activities, with many students cycling through their service with several community agencies throughout the semester. These are precisely the conditions typical of "McService."

Yet, two long-standing service projects have established practices that redirect the drive-by toward a social justice model of service-learning. These projects have spanned several years, allowing the faculty to establish ongoing relationships with community partners that deepen every semester. Faculty and community partners collaborate across disciplines, drawing from the content of all participating courses and enriching that content with approaches drawn from the arts. In these projects, faculty members direct student activities, taking responsibility for training and scheduling students in response to the needs of community partners.

College Brides Walk

The College Brides Walk (CBW) is a campus-community collaborative campaign to raise awareness about dating and domestic violence, to educate youth about these phenomena, and to mobilize the community in efforts to prevent abuse. The campaign extends the legacy of Josie Ashton, a Miami domestic violence advocate, who started the original Brides Walk in 2001 after she heard about the brutal murder of Gladys Ricart by Ricart's abusive ex-boyfriend. Ricart was murdered on her wedding day, September 26, 1999, while she posed for photos with her family. As is so often the case with domestic, dating, and sexual violence, media coverage placed blame on Gladys Ricart when it belonged on the perpetrator. With permission from the Ricart family, Ashton raised awareness through the media and the public when she wore her own wedding gown and walked from New Jersey to Miami, staying in domestic violence shelters along the way.

Hosted at Barry University with partners representing seven other South Florida colleges and universities, local domestic violence agencies and organizations, activist groups, attorneys, therapists, and women's organizations, this campaign involves more than just a one-day event. Instead, it has been the catalyst for year-round programming on Barry's main campus and includes a peer education program that, to date, has reached more than 1,000 youth in Miami Dade and Broward counties. Additionally, persons involved in CBW are invited to take part in advocacy efforts related to important dating and domestic violence legislation and are encouraged to continue their work by assisting one of the partner agencies.

CBW has included a service-learning component since its inception. It involves community organizing, advocacy, and activism for social justice and human rights. It is intended to (and organizers believe that it does) assist in transforming the community by helping to correct misconceptions about abuse; assisting victims in identifying resources; and in bringing together students, faculty, organizers, professionals, and advocates to promote peace in every relationship.

CBW service opportunities are not one-size-fits-all. A range of activities are available to meet diverse student interests, skills, and commitment levels. A small group of very committed students are invited to participate in the planning of the campaign and thus earn service hours by working with the other organizers in bimonthly meetings and calls. Other students are trained to present workshops about dating and domestic violence to local youth and school groups. These students, then, are working collaboratively to challenge their own assumptions and beliefs and with the common purpose of educating youth (HERI, 1996). Interested service-learning students are enlisted to dress in formal gear and to make presentations to campus and community groups about the campaign so as to encourage attendance. Others help research incidents of abuse to be included in visual displays at the event or conduct research to prepare poster displays on specific facets of abuse, such as male victims, the impact of abuse on children, and working with immigrant victims. Yet another way to complete service-learning hours is through researching relevant bills under consideration, both in the state and in Congress, and preparing information sheets and petitions to be distributed at the event.

Students also fulfill part of the service-learning requirements by helping the youth who attend the event paint t-shirts for the Clothesline Project, a survivor-initiated therapeutic program in which t-shirts, painted as tributes to those who have been harmed or bearing messages of peace, are hung on clotheslines as an ever-growing display. Of course, on the day of the event students also assist with setting up, providing lunch and dinner, moderating workshops, aiding non-profit and community organizations that table at the event, and even completing the 6.5 mile walk.

The long-term nature of the campaign allows for the design of more effective action over time. In 2013, organizers realized the need to begin evaluating the campaign in more than anecdotal ways and thus initiated a community-based research (CBR) project with support from a Barry University Center for Community Service Initiatives (CCSI) mini-grant. Researchers have noted that service-learning and CBR are ideally suited for domestic violence educational programming (Bell et al., 2004; Bowes, 1996; Langan & Morton, 2003; MacDonald, 2003 Students from Barry University and Nova Southeastern University, one of the partner institutions, helped create and disseminate a survey that measured attendees' satisfaction with CBW and assessment of what more needs to be done to educate about dating and domestic violence in the community.

Current assessment plans include enlisting students to help create interview questions and discussion prompts, conduct audio interviews, coordinate an expressive "graffiti-art" project in which attendees can visually express how they've been impacted, and facilitate a written feedback component.

The structure of the CBW, bolstered by the CBR projects, allow for successive generations of students to collaborate in a variety of individual roles with organizers and faculty in the co-construction of the event, outreach to the community, and evaluation of its success. The entire campaign is built on a community-organizing model that brings together diverse constituencies to transform social norms that result in acceptance of abuse. Already, as indicated by the recent assessment, the CBW is equipping students with the skills and knowledge they will need as future leaders (Astin & Astin, 2000), as well as the emotional wisdom and maturity that will be required to create a better, more peaceful world.

Carnival Arts

Founded in 2007, Carnival Arts is an arts learning program originally designed for youth living in crisis shelters across the state of Florida. So far, approximately 80 professional artists have shared Caribbean and Latin American carnival traditions with more than 1,000 youth who have been adjudicated by the court to live in the shelter, or who are experiencing another crisis such as a lapse in foster care, abuse or neglect at home, or exploitation in the sex or drug trade. Since September 2010, more than 350 college students at Barry University also have participated in the program, assisting the artists in sharing these traditions with the youth.

Together, this diverse group of artists, students, and youth spends weeks and sometimes months exploring dance, drum, song, theater, and mask-making traditions from places like Havana, Cuba; Jacmel, Haiti; Port of Spain, Trinidad; San Salvador, El Salvador; Brazil; and Barranquilla, Colombia. Carnival Arts passes on the traditions of celebrating life in a time of crisis created by the indigenous and African peoples who survived genocide and the slave trade in the Americas to low-income youth of color who confront the contemporary crises of poverty, violence, and mass incarceration. The program also allows master artists in these traditions to earn money for practicing their craft and to pass on their skills to new generations. Carnival Artists have produced dozens of carnival celebrations, two films on carnival themes, several music videos, and a major art exhibit showing the youth's masks and costumes at the Miami International Airport. All of these works are posted online for the youth to revisit long after they have left the shelter.

Initially, only students enrolled in a Caribbean literature course participated in this service opportunity, giving them a direct connection between the classroom curriculum and the service-learning experience. Since 2010, the opportunity has been extended to Barry undergraduates enrolled in theology, sociology, and orientation courses fulfilling the same 10-hour service-learning requirement as for the College Brides Walk. The college students play the role of artist's assistant, partnering with the youth to keep them engaged in the day's task. This is especially important for youth in crisis, who are often easily discouraged and likely to give up when they feel their artwork is not up to their own standards. Faculty train students at an orientation at the beginning of each semester and maintain a website where students schedule their participation on a set calendar, shifting the burden of training and scheduling away from the community partner.

Whereas the CBW personalizes the service experience for each student, the Carnival Arts structure takes into account the transient nature of not only the service-learning students, but the participatory youth as well. The average stay at the shelter is 30 days; however, an individual youth may stay there a single night or several months. Carnival is a collective art form, where costumes and masks transform individuals into fantastic, archetypal characters like the black-caped Midnight Robber in Trinidad and the elephant-headed Marimonda in Barranquilla, Colombia. College students and youth alike step in and out of these roles, highlighting the connection of one generation to the next. Carnival Arts transforms the service-learning "drive-by" into a carnival procession.

The ongoing nature of Carnival Arts, offering workshops to the youth one or more times a week over a period of years, allows for a deepening of the relationship between the university and the community partners. The workshops have become a part of the shelter culture, as established residents now frequently teach new arrivals the program's songs, dances, and rituals on their own, in advance of the next workshop. When youth return to the shelter after a repeated crisis, they also return to the workshops as veterans, serving as leaders and the repository of memories from earlier workshops. At every workshop, organizers stress that each participant will always be present as because individual contributions are carried on by the collective.

The long-term nature of the program also has allowed for expansion. It is anticipated that state funding will allow the program to expand to reach youth at local public schools who have been identified as having the same issues with truancy, violence, or drug use that can lead youth to be adjudicated to the shelters. Carnival Arts organizers also have applied for a federal grant to begin an apprenticeship program, where youth who have shown talent in Carnival Arts will be paid to study with master artists, and will eventually earn money teaching in the program themselves. The organizers also are working with Miami-Dade County's juvenile justice authorities to expand the program in partnership with social service agencies that serve the youth after they leave the crisis shelter and return to their own or foster families or age out of the system.

The ultimate goal is to establish a self-sustaining professional arts collective, including master artists and graduates of the apprenticeship program that will continue to educate the youth of the future, while also presenting carnival performances and producing film and video. Individual students and youth may cycle in and out of the program, but the carnival procession dances on.

Conclusion

Creative service-learning projects that utilize established best practices have the potential to transform students, faculty, and communities. Due to the enhanced marketing, community partnerships, and positive publicity that service-learning projects can create, they also provide significant benefits to the educational institutions that offer and host them. Each of us, in various courses and capacities, has debated how best to implement service-learning projects rooted in the values of reciprocity, reflection, and social justice. We believe the two service-learning programs described in this chapter are exemplary of these values.

Furthermore, we feel that sharing these examples of service-learning projects that employ a social justice orientation and prepare students to become agents of social change helps promote the growth of such projects nationally. Although the point of our examples is not replication (since different institutions will need to consider how best to address the needs of their students and local communities, in relation to their mission), we hope they can help spark thinking, debate, and dialogue on the future direction of the field.

We also hope that advocacy for projects of this type will help tip the scales in favor of social justice models of service-learning that are both personally and socially transformative, foster cultural understanding, and help bring about systemic social change. Concomitantly, we eschew the McService style of charity-based service-learning that employ a drive-by model and are simply ameliorative in their aims. In part, this is because McService style service-learning projects typically limit students' ability to develop leadership skills and experience employing civic tools like petition, redress, and advocacy or cultivating the skills emphasized by the social change model of leadership development (HERI, 1996).

While our examples are by no means perfect, they represent a concerted effort by service-learning practitioners to provide service-learning that is ethical, purposeful, and truly enriching to both students and the communities they serve. In the rush to capitalize on the many benefits of service-learning pedagogy, many institutions and practitioners have been shortsighted in their desire to scale-up service-learning projects and programs. However, there is no need to persist in being shortsighted forever.

Work Cited

Alberle-Grasse, M. (2000). The Washington study-service year of Eastern Mennonite University: Reflections on 23 years of service learning. *American Behavioral Scientist, 43,* 848–857.

Astin, A., & Astin, H. (2000). *Leadership reconsidered: Engaging higher education in social change.* Battle Creek, MI: W. K. Kellogg Foundation.

Astin, A. W., Vogelgesang, L. J., Ikeda, E. K., & Yee, J. A. (2000). *How service learning affects students.* Los Angeles, CA: Higher Education Research Institute, University of California.

Bell, H., Busch, N. B., Heffron, L. C., White, B., Engelelli, M. J., & Rivaux, S. (2004). Balancing power through community building: Researchers, survivors, and practitioners set the research agenda on domestic violence and sexual assault. *The Journal of Women in Social Work, 19,* 404–417.

Bowen, G. A. (2006). Exemplary leadership practices and social change: An experiential learning approach. In G. Brewer (Ed.), *Inspiring leadership: Experiential learning and leadership development in education* (pp. 19–24). Ambleside: Brathay.

Bowen, G. A., & Hackett, P. B. (2010). Developing cultural understanding through Spanish-language learning: A service-learning approach. *Journal on Excellence in College Teaching, 21*(2), 29–43.

Bowes, A. (1996). Evaluating an empowering research strategy: Reflections on action-research with South Asian women. *Sociological Research Online, 1*(1). Retrieved January 15, 2013 from www.socresonline.org.uk/socresonline/1/1/1.html.

Bringle, R. G., & Hatcher, J. A. (2002). Campus community partnerships: The terms of engagement. *Journal of Social Issues, 58*(3), 503–516.

Bringle, R. M., Hatcher, J., & McIntosh, R. (2006). Analyzing Morton's typology of service paradigms and integrity. *Michigan Journal of Community Service Learning, 13,* 5–15.

Butin, D. W. (2006). The limits of service-learning in higher education. *The Review of Higher Education, 29*(4), 473–498.

Butin, D. W. (2011). Service-learning as an intellectual movement: The need for an 'academic home' and critique for the community engagement movement. In T. Stewart & N. Webster (Eds.), *Problematizing service learning: Critical reflections for development and action* (pp. 19–35). Charlotte, NC: Information Age.

Cone, R. (2003). Service-learning and civic education: Challenging assumptions. *Peer Review, 5*(3), 12–15.

Conner, J. O. (2010). Building the reciprocal relationship: How students in an affluent private university and low-income public high school became partners in service and learning. *Information for Action: A Journal for Research on Service-Learning for Children and Youth, 3*(2), 1–23.

Dewey, J. (1916). *Democracy and education: An introduction to the philosophy of education.* New York, NY: Macmillan.

Dewey, J. (1938). *Experience and education.* New York, NY: Collier Books.

Eby, J. W. (1998). *Why service-learning is bad.* Retrieved October 19, 2013 from http://www.messiah.edu/external_programs/agape/servicelearning/articles/wrongsvc.pdf

Eyler, J. S., Giles, D. E., Stenson, C. M., & Gray, C. J. (2001). *At a glance: What we know about the effects of service-learning on students, faculty, institutions and communities, 1993–2000* (3rd ed.). Washington, DC: Corporation for National Service (Learn and Serve America) and National Service-Learning Clearinghouse.

Felten, P., & Clayton, P. H. (2011). Service-Learning. *New Directions for Teaching and Learning, 128,* 75–84.

Gent, P. (2011). Service-learning and the culture of ableism. In Stewart, T., & Webster, N. (Eds.), *Problematizing service learning: Critical reflections for development and action* (pp. 223–243). Charlotte, NC: Information Age.

Giles, D. E., & Eyler, J. (1994). The theoretical roots of service-learning in John: Toward a theory of service-learning. *Michigan Journal of Community Service Learning, 1*(1), 77–85.

Herzberg, B. (1994). Community service and critical teaching. *College Composition and Communication, 45,* 307–319.

Higher Education Research Institute. (1996). *A social change model of leadership development* (Guidebook, Version III). Los Angeles, CA: University of California, Los Angeles.

Himley, M. (2004, February). Facing (up to) "the stranger" in community service. *College Composition and Communication, 55*(3), 416–438.

Hollander, E. (2010). Foreword. In Butin, D. W. (Ed.). *Service-learning in theory and practice* (pp. vii–xii). New York, NY: Palgrave Macmillan.

Jones, S., LePeau, L., & Robbins, C. (2013). Exploring the possibilities and limitations of service-learning: A critical analysis of college student narratives about HIV/AIDS. *The Journal of Higher Education, 84*(2), 213–238.

Kendall, J. C. (1990). Combining service and learning: An introduction. In J. C. Kendall (Ed.), *Combining service and learning: A resource book for community and public service* (Vol. 1). Raleigh, NC: National Society for Experiential Education.

Koliba, C. (2000). Moral language and networks of engagement: Service-learning and civic education. *American Behavioral Scientist, 43,* 825–838.

Langan, D., & Morton, M. (2003). Reflecting on community/academic "collaboration:" The challenge of "doing" feminist participatory action research. *Action Research, 7*(2), 165–184.

Lewis, T. (2004). Service learning for social change? Lessons from a liberal arts college. *Teaching Sociology, 32,* 94–108.

Livingston, S. (2011). Virtual adoption of service-learning through controlled discourse. In T. Stewart, & N. Webster (Eds.), *Problematizing service learning: Critical reflections for development and action* (pp. 71–105). Charlotte, NC: Information Age.

Maas Weigert, K. (1998). Academic service learning: Its meaning and relevance. *New Directions for Teaching and Learning, 73,* 3–10.

MacDonald, S. (2003). Answering questions and asking more: Reflections on feminist participatory research. *Resources for Feminist Research, 30*(1/2), 77–95.

Marullo, S., & Edwards, B. (2000). From charity to justice: The potential of university—community collaboration for social change. *American Behavioral Scientist, 43,* 895–912.

Mezirow, J. (1991). *Transformative dimensions in adult learning.* San Francisco, CA: Jossey-Bass.

Mitchell, T. D. (2007). Critical service-learning as social justice education: A case study of the citizen scholars program. *Equity & Excellence in Education, 40*(2), 101–112.

Meyers, S. A. (2009). Service learning as an opportunity for personal and social transformation. *International Journal of Teaching and Learning in Higher Education, 21*(3), 373–381.

Parker-Gwin, R. (1996). Connecting service to learning: How students and communities matter. *Teaching Sociology, 24*, 97–101.

Roschelle, A, Turpin, J, & Elias, R. (2000). Who learns from service learning? *American Behavioral Scientist,* 43, 839–847.

Schon, D. (1983). *The reflective practitioner: How professionals think in action.* New York, NY: Basic Books.

Sigmon, R. (1995). *An organizational journey to service-learning.* Washington, DC: Council of Independent Colleges.

Simons, L., & Cleary, B. (2006). The influence of service learning on students' personal and social development. *College Teaching, 54*(4), 307–319.

Stewart, T. (2011). Opening up service-learning reflection by turning inward: Developing mindful learners through contemplation. In T. Stewart & N. Webster (Eds.), *Problematizing service learning: Critical reflections for development and action* (pp. 37–67). Charlotte, NC: Information Age.

Tryon, E., Stoecker, R., Martin, A., Seblonka, K., Hilgendorf, A., & Nellis, M. (2008). The challenge of short-term service-learning. *Michigan Journal of Community Service Learning,14*(2), 12–26.

CHAPTER 32

Bridging the Divide

Improving Teacher-Student Relations, Teacher Evaluations, and Retention Levels of African American and Minority Faculty

Pearlie Strother-Adams

Introduction

Dressed in jeans, a Tee-shirt and tennis shoes, I prepare to greet my next student appointment, her entry signaled by a light tap upon my office door. A familiar face enters, one of the four Japanese students I am privileged to have in my introductory mass communications course. Honoring her cultural custom and tradition, she bows slightly to show respect for my position of authority as her professor. Suddenly, she steps back, as if caught by surprise. Pausing, she stares as if seeing me for the first time as she exclaims: "You're pretty!" I thank her as both of us break out in ecstatic laughter. "Perfect!" I thought, the moment, the action, so electric, so enlightening and eye opening, so symbolic of exactly what I had hoped to accomplish through my make-shift brand of teacher-student conferences. My hope was to have students see me as a "person," to "humanize" myself for students who, many, sadly, had never had an African-American or other minority teacher or professor, and, in some instances, many who had not experienced African American or other minorities in their living environments, and, therefore, had come to know these groups, for the most part, either through the stereotypical lenses of American media or, through the, oftentimes, judgmental, prejudiced eyes of significant others. I will share briefly an incident that registers as a symbol of the shared struggle between some minority groups. A female Middle Eastern faculty member of East Indian descent who was not retained after receiving poor evaluations and suffering other injustices allegedly perpetrated by an official in her department sought counsel from concerned faculty and staff. Pulling her aside, I remarked that I was shocked to learn that she had been treated this way. I told her, "I, as an African American, have suffered many indignities." She moved close to me and placed her tiny hand next to mine and asked, "What's the difference?" I stared at our hands, both brown. It was a powerful moment. I felt great sorrow as a barrage of confusing images flooded my memory, for I had somehow fantasized my battle to be strangely limited to my ethnic group, forgetting that others also suffer scorn, rejection and ridicule. The incident serves as a connecting metaphor for me, a bridge between African Americans and other minorities.

Thus, it is no mystery that minority faculty on predominately European American college and university campuses often find themselves being treated, and thus find themselves feeling, as if they are in enemy territory. They are often not welcomed or accepted by students. They often battle in the classroom with students finding themselves falling victim to rejection and both overt and passive resistance as authority figures. Likewise, they are often rendered invisible, "other" alien, outsiders by colleagues and are left to make it the best way they can in the face of tremendous odds, devaluation and rejection of research/scholarly efforts, lack of mentoring in environments where there are few or no fellow minorities to show them the ropes and how to prepare and polish themselves for advancement and movement through the system.

This chapter is twofold, first, its purpose is to discuss some of the well defined problems that often plague African American/minority tenure/tenure track faculty within their classrooms and academic departments at predominately European American universities, and to touch upon how individual faculty student conferences and faculty-peer mentoring can make the difference in both retention and overall success of these faculty; however, most "groundbreaking," this chapter introduces educators to the concept of innovative faculty-student conferences and the "power" and possibility it has to help improve relations between minority professors and students, particularly where barriers created by perceptions based on systemic racial stereotypes (Barthes, 1972; Hall, 1997) may be a factor and, consequently, a hindrance to both teaching effectiveness as well as an added professional stumbling block for African American and minority faculty; and equally as important an obstacle to student learning; for, even though it is hard to sometimes discuss in American society, as Cornel West (1994) concludes in his book by the same title, *Race Matters* (1994). Hopefully this work contributes and adds to this body of literature and seeks to answer the following research questions (RQ):

> (1) Does race play a role in many problems that plague minorities and African Americans at tenure/tenure track positions at predominately European American universities? (2) Can peer and same cultural/same race mentoring help to improve retention of minority and African American faculty? (3) Can teacher-student conferences improve rapport between African American and minority faculty and their students and thus improving student–teacher evaluations and inevitably faculty retention?

Review of the Literature

A review of the literature in the area of teacher-student conferences reveals that research on individual conferences in higher education tends to focus primarily on three areas ESL (English as a Second Language students), students with disabilities, and students in English composition courses. Studies in these areas tend to note conferencing being used as a tool to help students adjust to college, arguing that problems encountered by beginning students are due to and common to the first year experience (Kaufka, 2010). Kaufka further argues the focus tends to be on academics, helping students to better understand course content and work. Conferencing is also found to be useful with students with disabilities, particularly in an effort to better find ways of encouraging this group to pursue math and science. Further, research confirms students benefit from individual teacher comments written on composition papers and also in the case of ESL classes (Hyland, 1998); however, as Hyland further offers (1998) more individual or one on one dialogue is needed to lessen the chance of misconception and confusion. Bitchener, Young, and Cameron, (2005) concludes in the case of ESL that it is beneficial to offer corrections of some grammatical aspects of students' work while non beneficial in the case of others; however, it is concluded that corrections paired with conferences is beneficial to students (Hyland, 1998). No research, however, was located that looks at conferencing as a way of building rapport between teachers and students, as a way (Jackson, Kite, & Branscombe, 1996) of breaking down cultural barriers while at the same time being used as a way to further explain and help students to better understand academic material.

Summarily, in reviewing the literature on peer faculty mentoring of African Americans and minorities, it is noted in the literature that faculty benefit greatly from peer mentoring (Williams & Williams, 2006). Jackson et al. (1996) offer Mentoring relationships, in most cases, have been fundamental to aiding learning in the workplace, advancing careers, helping new employees learn workplace culture, and providing developmental and psychological support. However, it is noted in the literature that majority culture faculty tend not to reach out to African American and other minority faculty (Moody, 2004), that African American faculty would benefit from being mentored by others like them that have gone through the ranks (Williams & Williams, 2006), and that African American women may prefer female African American mentors in environments where there are few (Jackson et al., 1996).

Background: Defining and Experiencing Race in the Work Environment

As an educator working in predominately European American settings, I have experienced both passive and aggressive resistance from students. Little did I know at the beginning of my career that such would occur because of my very presence as an African American female or minority, factors, cited often by scholars to be major catalysts for such actions the result of deeply entrenched stereotypical racial and gender myths that run through the American culture that can and do contribute to poor teacher evaluations (Williams & Williams, 2006). Research has shown that when faculty of color are hired at predominantly European American institutions, it is not uncommon for them to find themselves to be the "onlys" in their department, or one of two or three.

Consequently, it is important to look at the benefits of individual teacher-student conferences for both students who need individual help academically and for faculty in need of establishing better rapport with students. Both issues, which, if addressed, can inevitably improve the classroom environment and as a result improve students' perceptions of minority faculty and, thus, positively effect how students evaluate these faculty, thus improving retention rates of these faculty.

More Background: Stories of Student Resistance in a Culture of Fear

Scholars have determined students of all races and genders seem extremely judgmental towards non-white, non-male faculty (Moody, 2004). People of color and white women are often harassed and rebuked by students who have come to see white males in power, in control and as authority figures as the norm (Moody, p. 29).

In an early morning class, a female student sits with her arms folded, staring coldly and defiantly at her female professor. Later at a student union cafe` the student repeats the offense, dishing out to the same professor more of the same. Ironically, both the student and the professor are African American. Interestingly, as Moody offers, even students of color may act out and harass this group because they too have internalized white males in power as the norm (p. 29). Thus, the reaction of this African American female student is not out of character or context. In another class, a male student sits, with his arms folded tightly in defiance, staring down the same professor with a show of disdain and contempt. Across the room, in the same class, another male student sits with his head down on his desk totally ignoring this professor's lecture. On another occasion a male student drops a late paper off to the same professor's office. The assignment is a short essay on the purpose of the early black press, an alternative press, but somehow, totally out of context, the student initiates a conversation with the professor about African American students on campus and gleefully informs that at an earlier time in history he could have owned the students as slaves. All students in the above latter three cases are European American.

I am a female, African American professor who has worked in only predominately European American settings. These short anecdotes are real life personal experiences. Much of this work will involve personal experience for I have often been forced to search deeply within myself for answers to perplexing problems in complicated system.

I would be remiss, however, to neglect sharing that I have witnessed similar stories concerning non–African American minorities. Indeed, in my experiences, I have found, as Moody maintains "Minority professors often have to spend precious time and energy deciphering the complex psychological dynamics unfolding between them and majority students or colleagues" (p. 24).

Theoretical Frame: African Americans and Minorities as "Other"

According to Moody (2004) minority professors in predominately European American academic settings often "struggle against the presumption that they are incompetent" (p. 15) and are often viewed as "outsiders and have to endure extra psychological stresses and the general feeling of not belonging" which can undermine their success (Moody, p. 15).

Stereotypes and Myths Mirrored in Classroom and Work Environments

According to Roland Barthes (1972) myths pass through the culture in the form of stereotypes and metaphors. These myths tell a story about each of us, stories that are highly identifiable in the culture. Thus, we are all aware of this myth because we share an understanding of what they mean (Hall, 1997). Further, Hall (1997) refers to this "shared meaning" as "conceptual" or "cultural maps" that we all carry in our heads as stereotypes. Consequently, these stereotypes that often function to define African Americans and other minorities, including women, negatively, i.e., as not smart and, consequently, as not the norm in positions of power and authority are naturalized in the culture and are therefore the accepted way of seeing and viewing these groups (Hall, 1997). Hence, it is no surprise that even many members of these groups, such as the female African American student mentioned above or European American females, have also fallen prey and victim to these ever present images and ideologies that extend into the classroom from the greater society as a whole. The classroom, thus, mirrors the society on a micro level. For example, it was not surprising that some of Democratic presidential candidate, for nomination, Hillary Clinton's most vocal detractors were European American women. Acknowledging political differences among females, it was still harsh, a bit of a knee jerker, to hear a European American female say during a John McCain rally, "How do we stop the 'bitch'?" Given the struggles of women, one would think there would be a certain amount of respect and refrain or rejection of such misogynistic references, which represent an acceptance and agreement or buying into such ways of labeling women. Thus, African Americans, other minorities and women often, become participants in the victimization of their own and inevitably the victimization and to some degree the demise of themselves. Although Quinton Terintino's character "Steven," a classic tom, played by Samuel Jackson in the movie Django (2012) might be seen as somewhat of an exaggeration, its creation is masterful, for "Steven" represents the ultimate betrayal that a member of a group can visit upon his ethnic/racial group and himself. He embodies the spirit and soul of his slave master, thus, seeing his own race as inferior and their enslavement and the cruelty visited upon them by the slave masters as justified. In short, as far as "Steven" is concerned they, African American slaves, are where they should be and European Americans are where they should be. On one of a few occasions when I was asked to answer to a student's complaints, or for what I now refer to as a student "telling on me" as if I were a child, a suspected criminal, or someone on probation that needed to be watched and monitored, I was promptly told that the student was African American as if this should make a difference and somehow made the criticism not only legitimate but free of any racial bias. I recall the shock on the mediator's face when I said that it was no difference because sadly some African American students had bought into the idea that African American females were not the norm in the classroom or not legitimate authority figures. "They may be from an African American family and community," I said, "but they too have learned that power is reserved for the European American male. They do not see many African Americans in power, particularly females. Thus, this is not their world view," I explained, "even though they see black or brown when they look in the mirror." Thus, it stands to reason that this is why many cannot envision themselves being in a position of authority or being successful for that matter as a professional.

The "Other" v. society's "norm" at European American institutions Williams and Williams (2006) offer present day images of African Americans are filtered through media lenses; thus, the problem that African American faculty face is a historical one, where black men are seen as thugs, pimps, and not as intelligent and articulate. When intelligence and articulateness are revealed, African Americans, the research shows, are often described as "arrogant" or "cocky." Many have been bold enough to even refer to President Barack Obama and First Lady Michelle Obama as "uppity"(Rush Limbaugh after First Lady Obama's appearance at Nasser Race in Florida where she was booed), referencing a term that harkens back to the Jim Crow South that implies a [black] person is socially and maybe economically beyond their designated place. The term is particularly used by some European Americans to reference successful, outspoken African Americans of whom the mark of slavery, in the psyche of some in the dominant culture, set in place a permanent status of inferiority. In this vein, African American females are perceived as even less relevant than African American males and are not valued for their rhetoric or as authority figures. Pittman (2007) argues African American women are outside of the community in which they seek acceptance and have to debunk stereotypes that are carryovers from slavery when they were used by European American males as sexual objects who were paraded about the auction block naked, a forced act which degraded them in such a way that the stain still lingers. Pittman (2007) further argues that this victimization was reversed in that the African American female is seen today as a temptress who somehow tricked the slave master into taking her sexually; thus, the European American male has been able to maintain his dignity and reputation while the African American female, though the real victim, is scarred on many levels. This phenomenon shows itself best in the greater society when we look at the treatment of First Lady Michelle Obama who was hounded during the 2008 presidential campaign after she made a statement indicating she was "really" proud of her country for the first time in her adult life. Thus, she was accused of being anti American and an "angry black woman." Right wing radio host Rush Limbaugh along with other right wingers at Fox News also accused the First Lady of trying to tell the country what to do in reference to healthy eating and even her campaign to get Americans to drink more water was criticized. Limbaugh referred to the First Lady's suggestion as "command and control." Others said the First Lady is saying that she does not trust Americans to know how to feed their children. In the past little has been said about the particular causes that first ladies have taken on, such as Betty Ford taking on alcoholism and creating the Betty Ford Center and Nancy Regan's campaign against drugs and popularizing the slogan, "Just say no." However, First Lady Obama, who chose the least controversial cause, nutrition, has received a flood of criticism from right wing politicians, republicans, and pundits who viciously attack her every word.

Devaluing the Work and Achievements of the "Other"

In a similar vein, it is not uncommon for outstanding efforts of African American males and females to be referred to as "clever," in the way that an animal might be considered clever as if they have managed to pull off a trick, thus, accomplishing a deed, action or feat not common to their group or kind. Generally such accomplishments are not seen as a sign of intelligence or genius and are often dismissed rather quickly so that the achiever gets little or no credit. On the other hand, European American colleagues are generally accepted as "intelligent, smart, bright" (Williams & Williams, 2006). Moreover, minorities, particularly African Americans that are self—assured, confident, may find themselves accused of being arrogant or cocky, akin to "uppity;" whereas European Americans are admired for these qualities and are respected as strong leaders. These attitudes have a direct effect on the promotion and tenure process because such perceptions filter into teacher evaluations. It is difficult for African Americans to step outside of the shadows of American history. The reality is that a system was in place that denied this group's humanity and still has present-day ramifications (Williams & Williams, 2006).

Student-Teacher Evaluations and the Invisible "Other"

During the course of my professional career as an educator, I have taught a variety of students of different ethnic backgrounds and nationalities, as both a high school teacher and a university professor (Hispanics, Mexican, Latinos: Asians, Japanese, Chinese, Koreans, Laotian and, Hmong, European Americans; African Americans). This and other experiences in educational settings proved valuable as I later struggled to make my way through the tenure-track system.

However, as a university professor the majority of my students have tended to be European American. I feel honored when I have two or three African students and maybe an Asian or a Hispanic. Not surprising, one of the biggest problems that minority face at predominately European American universities is low student evaluations, prompting many to feel that such evaluations are not fair, given the fact that the majority of their students are generally European American and, more likely to judge them harshly, given societal trends and negative stereotypes ingrained in the culture about minorities, particularly African Americans. Many of these faculty complain that poor evaluations come despite hard work with students both inside and outside of the classroom. Moody (2004) explains minority professors are often vulnerable to unfair evaluations of their worthiness and their work because of negative stereotypes associated with their gender and racial/ethnic backgrounds. If you are a minority in a majority department, Moody offers, quoting an African American professor, "You spend a lot of time proving that you are competent" (p. 26).

I shall never forget a new black faculty member, complaining during a faculty orientation that "Something needs to be done about student evaluations. Some students evaluate black faculty unfairly," he openly protested. Others agreed. The incident stayed with me because this new faculty member was Ethiopian and had come from another university where he had experienced difficulty with evaluation scores. I remember thinking his accent would not help either since some students tend to complain about professors who do not speak English as a first language. I recall one student complaining to me as she exited a classroom where she had just finished a test that she was not pleased with that the faculty member, who was foreign, had no right to have high expectations of students since, quoting the student, "She can't even speak English." It is common for students to complain about the speech patterns of bi-lingual faculty as if these faculty should automatically speak perfect English. Here, I offer the educational system fails in helping students to better understand at an early age the difficulty of becoming fluent in a second language. Such criticisms might be silenced if students were asked to put themselves in the place of the professor in his/her country and culture.

On one hand, student evaluations are used to give feedback to faculty for instructional improvement; however, this subjective measure can and does place some faculty at a disadvantage and risk since evaluations are also used to determine teacher effectiveness, to help make personnel and administrative decisions such as promotion and to determine tenure merit, and merit of teaching awards (Centra, 1973; Marsh & Roche, 1993; Smith, 2007). While student evaluations are the most commonly used measure of teaching effectiveness, their use as a legitimate indicator of quality teaching is questionable (d'Apollonia & Abrami, 1997; Greenwald & Gilmore, 1997; Smith, 2007). For example, many faculty complain that they do not feel students are qualified to evaluate their work and that some use evaluations to exact revenge on professors when they do not give them the grades they want but have not earned.

Appropriation Not Appreciation of the "Other"

Initially, I naively thought "If I do my best and work hard to help students achieve success, it will show in my evaluations, their assessments of my work." I worked overtime, creating additional handouts, providing study guides for tests, staying after class and after hours. I was also careful to read my syllabi to each class verbatim on the first day of class. Yet, there were still students who indicated on evaluations that I had not gone over syllabi. Admittedly, many students thrived under my system. Others did not seem to connect. Ironically, I noted that sometimes even students who improved, particularly European

American males, were generally reluctant to acknowledge that I played a role in their success. In one classic case, a European American male student who was a very poor writer at the beginning really came into his own after I worked overtime, helping him to revise several papers. Excited for him, I said "You have really improved. I am proud of you." Looking slightly embarrassed, he responded saying that he just had to think back to what he had learned about writing from his high school English teacher. Feeling insulted, I thought, "Perhaps, I should have let him come to this enlightening revelation in absence of my hard work" since he showed no appreciation. His response was a slap in the face. I had spent hours after work time, working side by side with this student. On another occasion, I tutored a European American male student who was having difficulty in a composition class. The student's skill level was very poor. He could not spell simple words and had problems constructing simple sentences. I worked through every paper with him, talking him through each sentence to help him with the simplest technical problems. He received an "A" in the course. When the director of the tutoring program, who was European American, I must acknowledge, asked him to thank me, his face turned a fiery red and he looked at me with anger, showing contempt rather than appreciation for all of my hard work and sacrifice. The psychology of it all is, at times, confusing and too much to fully comprehend; however, I am reminded, as I look back upon it, of how President Barack Obama is treated by those who refuse to accept him as President, how his credentials are questioned, his education, his birth place, how his intelligence, articulateness, and superior rhetorical abilities and skills are often represented as a negative and a deficit instead of a positive. I might add though such positive characteristics are often not viewed with appreciation by some members of the dominant culture, such skills as the President's rhetorical abilities, are likely to be emulated and appropriated once he is no longer in office; however, it will be interesting to see if he will ever be recognized as such and given long overdue credit, or will it stand that he is as Limbaugh has labeled him, "uppity?" Will he be regarded with contempt and scorn as a black man simply because he dares to have all of these qualities rolled into one?

Winning Strategy: Teacher-Student Conferences and Faculty Peer Mentoring

An African American colleague once shared with me that her six year old said she often felt like a spirit in her school where there were very few blacks that no one seemed to really see her. She said her child told her it is as if "I am not there" and that even as she walked down the isle of the school bus she floated to the back where there was a welcoming empty seat for all of the other seats, many occupied by just one person, held books or some other item in the space which should have been open for her to sit. This was sometimes my feeling in my work environment where I smiled, shared a laugh with colleagues here and there, held cordial conversations but was not treated as if I were truly in the club so to speak, not to the degree whereby I was considered for serious matters. However, out of frustration, I decided I had to devise a way of helping my students see me and thus in some cases hear and understand what I wanted to give them as an educator. I had achieved some success in news writing and reporting courses allowing students to rewrite assignments to improve their skills, using possible attainment of a higher grade as incentive. I edited their work closely, and required students to make the changes, read my comments, do any additional work, such as further research, correct grammar and improve style. In addition, I advised them to build a small desk library complete with a dictionary, thesaurus, style book and concise grammar book.

Moreover, it was not uncommon for students to challenge me, sometimes abruptly stating "I don't agree," or interrupting, as I lectured, to ask an unrelated question, perhaps one of the most baffling I have witnessed, "What is my grade in this course?" At such times, I found myself in total shock over the disrespect. One student, an older European American male generally absent from class, would come in about once a month on average to challenge me, telling me that I was wrong about something during lecture or discussion. I finally gathered the courage to tell him that it appeared there was nothing I could teach him and that I did not see the logic in him taking my classes. In the theory courses, I had to finally start telling students at the beginning of the term that the assigned readings were the result of long years of scholarly study and research conducted by people who are experts in their fields. I further informed students that unless they had done the research, they had no plausible argument. In essence, I had to remind them that they were to learn the material from these scholars instead of presenting an uninformed argument. I do not recall any professor having to do this during all my years as a student either at the undergraduate or graduate level. However, save for two or three, the majority of my professors were European American and male so there was no argument no matter what they said or taught.

In short, my evaluations were too often a disappointment. I noted most responded with a high mark for the item that asked if I were knowledgeable about my subject area. The same was true for questions that related to preparedness and concern for students. Ironically, low ratings often came in overall effectiveness after a student had scored me high in most other areas. I was baffled most when students indicated that I did not explain the syllabus, particularly after I, as a rule, deliberately, devote a whole class period to the document, literally reading and explaining each item and asking students to review it carefully and ask questions. Moody offers students too are likely to hold and act out stereotypical views about who is worthy and who is not (p. 29). Subsequently, this social, psychological and political culture forced me to settle in to a hard, cold reality—"Minority professors often have to spend precious time and energy deciphering the complex psychological dynamics unfolding between them and majority students or colleagues" (Moody, p. 24).

However, left on my own with no mentoring, I did not know where to turn when it came to the issue of evaluations. One of the many obstacles facing African Americans as they advance towards tenure is a lack of a senior African American faculty to serve as a mentor, role model or scholar to emulate, a lack of role models who look like them, and who have been down the tenure track in their discipline, others who know what it is like to be black, and in academe (Williams & Williams, 2006). This is no surprise since African American faculty are vastly underrepresented at predominately white institutions (Tillman, 2001).

Further, Moody offers "Exhaustive research" on minority faculty in eight mid-western states underscore majority faculty do not make a habit of reaching out to minority faculty (p. 17). Also, African American women may prefer African American female mentors, but have a difficult time locating such women on predominately European American campuses (Jackson et al., p. 1996). Indeed, I would have found comfort in being mentored by someone with similar research interests, someone familiar with and in touch with my "holistic experience," an experience that is generally different on many levels from that of members of the dominant culture because I am perceived differently in the classroom because society has written African American women into a narrow stereotypical narrative that renders them "other."

Desperate, I talked to faculty outside of my department and I also shared my problems with black educators at conferences from other universities. Most shared similar horror stories. Many faculty maintain that discrepancies in teaching ratings may be the result of external issues or factors outside of the faculty member's control (Smith, 2007). On one occasion, an accomplished African American female scholar remarked, "I think they [European American students] sometimes resent the fact that we are black and are so smart, innovative and accomplished." I pondered this and decided there may be some merit in it given the history of the nation and what appears to be an assumed designated place for African Americans. However, I began to ask myself "What's lacking in my teaching?" Williams and Williams (2006) offered structured mentoring programs were noted as the primary support system that should be in place at the departmental, college and university levels to assist African American faculty through the promotion and tenure process. It was observed that the color of the mentor was not as important as the level of awareness and sensitivity to the issues and concerns that face African American junior faculty. However, it was concluded that it would be helpful if the mentor is African American.

Struggle and Disappointment Yields Innovative Strategic Revelation

Actually, my great revelation came on an occasion after a European American student complained that I was teaching about the representation of minorities in the media in a mass media history class, and that he was not interested in that. I explained to the mediator that it was impossible to teach such a course without including the representation of minorities and African Americans. I said to the mediator, thinking he would agree and be supportive, "I believe students will appreciate having exposure to this information as they mature and move past college and into adulthood." Surprisingly, I was greeted with a disapproving "I don't know about that," which left me feeling weak, numb, lost, out of place and without support. It was a staggering psychological blow that took a toll on me physically as well as emotionally and spiritually. In essence, my efforts were not encouraged. I was treated as if I was the enemy under attack, engaged in a one sided battle. I was left defenseless, untenured, with no weapons of which to fight back. I literally felt weak as if a dagger had assailed my heart. I remember walking out of the office holding my chest, trying to keep the heaviness that had invaded it from somehow revealing itself on my down cast face. Physically and emotionally, I felt old, bent over from the weight of it all, way beyond my years. I concluded that I had been reported on or "told on" by any student who cared to do so, watched as if I were a child, constantly expected to do something wrong, to step out of order as if I were not really a part, a member of the faculty. Disillusioned, I felt my efforts to include minorities as a part of the curriculum was not considered valid and worthy of study. My mind raced back to an earlier incident where a senior faculty member and I, during an earlier conference with this same mediator, had to argue, the logistics and validity of the study of minorities as a research/scholarly venture. Williams and Williams (2006) offer minority respondents expressed a perceived lack of respect for their research and scholarship and that this served as an obstacle to their being able to successfully navigate through the promotion and tenure process.

Similarly, Moody offers Minorities are often unfairly constrained in their scholarly research efforts and face "brown-bagging" (34). In short, Moody argues it is assumed that minorities cannot perform objectively when researching their own group. On the other hand, members of the dominant culture are allowed legitimacy no matter what they research (35). Further, research and topics beyond the mainstream and publishing in outlets beyond select journals may be greeted with lack of acceptance. Consequently, it may take some convincing to bring some older faculty along to a point of acceptance of scholarship and research that is not traditional, such as race and gender issues. Thus, such a negative reaction, confirmed that my problem was bigger than student evaluations. I was up against a system that had counted me and others like me out before we got started. The student evaluations were only a reflection, a residual effect of a rejection that was already set in place,—the student resistance a mere mirror/reflection, a microcosm of the larger reality. As I reflected more deeply upon the mediator's words, words meant to set in stone a designated place for me as an African American woman, a place of invalidation, where my work was not taken seriously, was not legitimate, was not worthy. A frustration rose in me, causing my mind to drift to thoughts of my home, the Jim Crow South, a place where I, as a child, witnessed the horrific brutality of my people, a people labeled not good enough, not quite human, inferior. Thus, here I was in a place of higher learning "up North" decades later, a place that I had thought to be a center of enlightenment, where educated people had, I thought, read and studied the great works of a diverse group of enlightened thinkers and thus wrestled with issues involving social justice, freedom, equality, respect and tolerance.

I found myself hesitant or reluctant to reach out professionally because I felt I always had to prove my worthiness both inside and outside of the classroom. I began to doubt myself and as Moody says to feel as if I were an "imposter" and perhaps did not belong (p. 23). The irony of it all is that I started with so much to give and students who were able to open up and receive what I had to offer testified to receiving much.

Overcoming Invisibility: Drawing upon Pain and Experiences

Moody informs minorities are likely to be treated as invisible, their opinions are ignored (p. 21). Thus, fighting through my pain, during a conference with the mediator, I explained, much to his surprise,

> When many students see me, they do not see what they consider to be the norm. White students see you and they see someone that reminds them of their dad, uncle, brother, cousin. When they see me they see "Other", non person, alien, black woman. They do not see their sister, aunt, mother, cousin. They see someone that they can run to you and "tell on or report on" as if I am a child, or someone that needs to be watched closely, monitored, so I do not offend or commit a crime of some kind because this is the narrative that society created to represent me. In some cases, they don't see me at all. I am invisible. I do not exist and if I do, in their psyche, I am out of place and therefore invalid. I have to try and break through that wall of misconception and misperception each day before I can even begin to teach them,

I said. I left there determined to succeed against all odds. I refused to be the loser in this tortuous game.

According to Stewart and Phelps (2000), when faculty of color attend to things that are in their control, such as class preparation, course content and evaluations are negative, a portion of students' evaluations of teaching may rest in the students' biases, prejudices, misperceptions, and lack of interaction and experience with such faculty.

Thus, I determined I had to devise a system that would allow students to see me outside of the classroom in a different setting, less formal, more revealing of my "just another person like you," more friendly, if that were possible. I had to take them out of the box that long years of living and being immersed in a culture that assured them they were the "one" norm, human, but painted minorities as "the other," alien, different and inferior, thus incapable and not fit to lead, to serve in authoritative positions of power over them, not truly worthy or valid human beings. Given the depth of the history, of these intricately woven and ingrained perceptions of themselves and of minorities, particularly African Americans, I had some understanding for their plight. They too were victims of the system, even if it served to benefit them in many ways while it short changed them in others. I was still the adult and the teacher and mentor and part of my goal, I felt, was to make this a big teachable moment, a huge metaphor representing what I decided should guide my whole teaching career. It had to become my overall goal to help make the world a better, more tolerant place by making each session in my classes a learning experience for my students.

I had a lot to draw from recalling a time when a European American high school student purchased me a copy of U-2's "One Love," which celebrates Dr. Martin Luther King, Jr. I had shown the class the documentary "From Montgomery to Memphis," which focused on King and the civil rights movement of the 1960's. This high school senior's gift brought me to tears because I realized I had given him a gift that made a mark in his life. I had provided him greater context for a rock song sang by a world famous rock group. He now understood that this tribute to King was well deserved and that King was greater than the words of the song could ever express. I believe teachers need to make a difference, even if it is one student at a time. I also recalled the first time I walked into a university classroom. It was a composition course. About twenty pair of curious freshmen eyes greeted me, all European American, save one African American young woman. I can't say I was too nervous, for this was not too far from high school seniors. It was as if I had left the high school setting to be with the same students at college, though I knew none of these students. I remember writing my name and some other information on the black board. A roar of laughter filled the room. I turned around quickly and faced the students. "Don't laugh," I ordered, turning back quickly to conceal my smile and complete my task. Amazingly, the quiet was such that you could have heard a pin drop. I had asserted myself, but I always felt they were laughing at me because I was not suppose to be there. It was an eye opener for me, and a shock to their systems. Most I learned later had come from schools where there were one or two black teachers or maybe none. Some had never had a black teacher or even a black classmate.

Emergence of Teacher-Student Conferences in Friendly, Attractive Atmosphere

Though oppressed and discriminated against in a plethora of ways in their work environments, African Americans [and other minorities] often emerge sound, a testament to their resilience (Alexander & Moore, 2007). Determined to make a difference and succeed, I decided I would create opportunities to do required conferences with my students. I made my office more reflective of me, pictures of key authors and artists, such as writers Toni Morrison, Richard Wright, Langston Hughes and even singers Bob Marley (a real attention grabber) and Miles Davis. I purchased a card table and chairs so I could sit across from students and have them relax as we discuss their individual work. Generally, I require that they rewrite all major articles in writing classes. However, in media history or theory courses, I have them workshop their final paper with me which requires at least two meetings. We discuss the work. I explain the changes and further instruct students on how they can make their work better. Many ask questions that they are too shy to ask in class. I know this because they sometimes apologize for asking in conference. I tell them that this is why I sit in the seat of the professor to answer their questions and that they sit in the seat of the student because they have questions. This puts them at ease and I believe it helps to establish the fact that I know what I am doing and deserve to be where I am. Most students say that they get so much out of these conferences and that they understand the material much better as a result. I have had students say to me in general: “Now I know how to do it,” or “Now I get it.”

I shall never forget the conference with the Japanese student that I began with in the “Introduction” of the chapter. As I said she was one of four Japanese students that I had that semester. I had established a reputation for working hard with students; thus, these students’ academic advisor informed me she deliberately placed these students in my class because other Asian students had told her that I would work hard to help them be successful. However, as I explained this student’s visual picture of me as “pretty” was powerful, a crystal clear metaphor, a symbol from the Heavens that my prayer had been answered. I had devised a system that would allow me and other African American and minority faculty to break through the invisible dark shaded thick plated glass of white supremacy, allowing us to as the great multicultural guru Stuart Hall (1997) said “re-present” ourselves in our own way, somehow navigating our way through and hopefully eventually debunking societal stereotypes and discourse.

For me the conference is a time when I can let my hair down a bit and relax. I cancel class for that period because I spend no less than twenty minutes with each student. Because students come to trust me and see me in very human terms, and as an accomplished, skilled writer, some come during my regular office hours to chat with me or to ask questions about class work, sometimes work in classes other than mine. Some just drop in to see me and some come if they are having personal problems and need an ear and on rare occasions, a shoulder.

In short, student conferences can help minority faculty to establish good relations with their students and thus improve evaluations. Students of many ethnicities credit me with taking them to a higher level of understanding of the world. Some of my students have gone on to graduate school, others work in the journalism profession and elsewhere. Some maintain contact and communicate with me from distant lands, Nigeria, Ghana, China and Japan. One of my European American students has consistently come back each summer with her mother in tow to treat me to dinner. I am now a tenured, full professor, of course. I can say that my evaluations are generally very high. I know some of this has come with my own self-assurance and confidence which are so important in the classroom. However, a faculty mentor, I now reach out to other minority faculty within my immediate work environment as well as to colleagues who teach at other universities. Some come to me when they have problems in the classroom. After they incorporate my brand of conferencing into their program, they too report improvements in their rapport with students and inevitably see improvements in student evaluations. As I shared with a European American male faculty member who, oddly, was having problems in the classroom and was sent to me for help: “I developed this system because I realized that as an African American, I sometimes need to break through a wall to reach my students. I had to find a way to have them see me. You can try it," I told him. "Maybe it will work for you." He later reported improvements. Another faculty member of Middle Eastern dissent also complained about low evaluations. I told her to create situations for having her students come in and share at least one paper with her. I assured her that this would help them to warm up to her. She too has seen great improvement in her evaluations and student rapport. I have had the pleasure of mentoring several Asian and African American and African faculty members and all report improved evaluation scores and better relations with their students that they attribute, at least, in part, to student conferences. Finally, many minority faculties that I encounter at academic conferences have incorporated student conferences into their classes and most report my brand of conferences to be one of the best things that ever happened to them in terms of their teaching careers. Several suggested I get a patent.

Conclusion: Teacher-Student Conferences Introduced During Faculty-Peer Mentoring

My brand of teacher-student conferences is a proven self-aid for faculty in the classroom. If African American and other minority faculty are to be successful at predominately European American educational institutions, they must achieve success in the classroom. Teacher-student conferences should be discussed as part of the mentoring process for African American and minority faculty. If officials at predominately European American institutions are sincere in their efforts to hire and retain African American and minority faculty, mentoring programs that include instructions on how to conduct successful teacher-student conferences can serve as a tremendous plus to the eventual success of these faculty who seem to struggle the most. We cannot change the hearts of all in the work environment who may approach African American, other minorities and even female faculty with prejudice and bias which can and do affect professional movement within an institution; however, it is important to understand that faculty among these groups who adjust in the classroom, work well with their students and foster a good learning environment, as well as gain the trust and respect of their students, will also have a better chance at success at predominately European American institutions. Finally, it is crucial that the connection between the attitudes expressed by many European American students and that are embraced or practiced by minority students as well towards African American, minority and female faculty are connected to the narratives that society has scripted for these groups and that these narratives are played out not only in society and in the classroom but also in institutions of higher learning as a whole to such a degree that the professional growth and status of African American, minority and some female faculty are generally affected in ways that are severely life altering, permanently damaging to their self-esteem and their professional career potential.

Work Cited

Barthes, R. (1972). *Mythologies* (Jonathan Cape Ltd., Trans.). New York, NY: Hill and Wang 1957.

Bitchener, J., Young, S., & Cameron, D. (2005). The effect of different types of corrective feedback on ESL student writing. *Journal of Second Language Writing, 14*(3), 191–205.

Centra, J. A. (1973). Self-ratings of college teachers: A comparison with student ratings. *Journal of Educational Measurement, 10*, 287–295.

d'Apollonia, S., & Abrami, P. C. (1997, November). Navigating student ratings of instruction. *American Psychologist, 52*(11), 1198–1208. doi: 10.1037/0003-066X.52.11.1198

Django Unchained. (2012). Dir. Quentin Tarrantino. Film.

Greenwald and Gilmore. (1997). In Ramedios, R., & Lieberman, D. (2008). I liked your course because you taught me well: the influence of grades, workload, expectations, and goals on students' evaluations of teachering. *British Educational Research Journal, 34*(1), 91–115. Published by William Blackwell from 2013.

Hall, S. (1997). *Media and Representation*. Dir. Sut Jhally. Prod. Sut Jhally. Media Education Foundation Video/Film.

Hyland, F. (1998). The impact of written teacher feedback on individual writers. *Journal of Second Language Writing, 7*, 255–286.

Kaufka, B. (2010). Beyond the classroom: a case study of first-year student perceptions of required student-faculty conferences. *Journal of the Scholarship of Teaching & Learning, 10*(2), 25–33.

Laden, B. V., & Linda, S. H. (2000). Job satisfaction among faculty of color in academe: Individual survivors or institutional transformers? *New Directions for Institutional Research, 2000*(105), 57–66.

Moody, J. A. (2004). *Faculty diversity: Problems and solutions.* New York, NY: Routledge.

Patton, L. D., & Shaun R. H. (2003). Meeting the needs of African American women. In M. F. Howare-Hamilton (Ed.), *New directions for student services* (Vol. 104, pp. 67–78). San Francisco, CA: Jossey-Bass.

Pittman, C. (2007). Black women writers and the problem with ethos. *Rhetoric of Society Quarterly, 37,* 43–70.

Tillman, L. C. (2001). Mentoring African American faculty in predominantly white institutions. *Research in Higher Education, 42,* 295–325. doi: 10.1023/A:1018822006485

West, C. (1994). *Race matters.* Boston, MA: Beacon Press.

Williams, B. N., & Williams, S. M. (2006). Perceptions of African male junior faculty on promotion and tenure: Implications for community building and social capital. *Teachers College Record, 108*(2), 287–385.

CHAPTER 33

That's the Way I See It
Exploring Collaborative Writing and Critical Ethnographic Research with College Students with Intellectual Disabilities

Lalenja Harrington and Remington Brown

Introduction

The principle objective of this chapter is to shed light on a collaborative process involving the development of strategies for exploring desired post-graduation outcomes of students with intellectual disabilities (ID) attending college. Much of the current literature on post-secondary education for students with ID focuses on topics like transition from high school to college, identification and/or review of post-secondary options, and employment. At the time of this writing, there have been few studies that focus on holistic, post-graduate outcomes, and there is a need for research that addresses broader life outcomes using "effective strategies and methods to address the needs of a wider range of learners, so that more individuals with disabilities can benefit from the formation of new values and broader attitudes and, therefore, enjoy a better quality of life" (Hesse-Biber & Piatelli, 2012, p. 51). Through the lens of post-critical, ethnographic research, the authors of this study—the academic director and a student from the course of study, discussed how they collaborated together to structure and conceptualize a pilot study designed to highlight student perspectives on the impact of college on post-graduation outcomes. In the same vein as Participatory Action Research studies, this study serves as a much-needed platform for the voices of students who have historically been relegated to the margin.

Transformative Happenings

Creative transformation is an amazing process. And this collaborative effort represents just that: a true transformation of process and intention. The chapter grew out of an assignment for a research methods class where, initially, there was a desire to utilize critical, ethnographic research methods to explore the perspectives of college students with intellectual disabilities (ID). Another important goal for the chapter was to engage and collaborate with those students in "co-producing knowledge." Time was not a friend however, to what needed to be a deeply engaged and participatory process, and gradually it became apparent that the study was going to have to transform into a pilot. Although this was initially frustrating, that transformation created an opportunity to think differently, as the focus shifted from reporting findings, to describing process—an unexpected boon that has set the stage for a creative mapping of method.

The authors of this chapter are involved in a postsecondary program for students with ID at UNC-Greensboro in North Carolina. Lalenja is the Academic Director responsible for guiding students through the program of study, and Remington is a junior who has been an active advocate and member of the university community, and who was also involved in the pilot study. The concepts for the chapter, the elements and content were discussed, expanded and edited by both authors, and a joint decision was made that Lalenja would be responsible for the overall structure of the chapter and for connecting both of the author's positions to existing literature and theory. The chapter will outline collaborative strategies that the authors used to develop the structure of the pilot study as well as the writing partnership. Recommendations will also be made for future research with a focus on participatory methodology. Both authors are committed to exploring ways that students with ID are invited into the research process, and encouraged to take ownership of knowledge produced about their college experiences.

College Matters

College has not traditionally been an option for students with intellectual disabilities, with the exception of a limited few that were able to gain access to the small number of postsecondary education programs that have been in existence since the 1970s (Neubert, Moon, Grigal, & Redd, 2001). In the past ten years, high school graduates with ID in larger numbers have begun to demand access to opportunities for the personal and professional growth that college offers. This movement towards inclusive higher education calls for a reevaluation of some of the elitist philosophies and exclusive educational practices that have been barriers to a more socially just system of learning. Federal legislation in the form of the Reauthorization of the Higher Education Act of 2008 has served as a spring board for action resulting in an explosion of postsecondary educational programming across the country (Grigal, Hart, & Weir, 2012). Acceptance of this contemporary post-secondary programming by community college and university campuses reflects what I like to call a "pocket of resistance," the "long history in the United States of educators who foreground social justice issues in their work and who argue passionately for their centrality to schooling in a democratic society" (Philip, 2012, p. 8), even in the midst of oppressive educational philosophies and practice. Students with ID and their educational allies are moving the social justice "agenda" forward by demonstrating the importance of self-determination and personal liberation within higher education.

Programming for Students with Intellectual Disabilities

In 2001, Grigal, Neubert and Moon were right on the mark regarding their assessment of the research landscape regarding postsecondary education programs (PSE) for students with intellectual disabilities. Early studies were, as I stated before, much more "practical" in nature, outlining the history of postsecondary education from the 1970s to the present, the status of the current, limited pool of options, as well as the connection to social movements calling for an expansion of those postsecondary options (Grigal, Neubert, & Moon, 2002; Migliore, Butterworth, & Hart, 2009; Neubert et al., 2001).

After the post-Reauthorization of Higher Education Act program development "boom" in 2008, we saw a related increase in research focusing on survey and program descriptions highlighting basic programmatic characteristics, recruitment and admissions, course access, employment strategies, etc. (Grigal et al., 2012). As of 2009, Grigal et al. (2012) had surveyed as many as 149 programs across 39 states, and PSE programs across the nation offered descriptions of their 2-year, and less frequent 4-year certificates at community colleges and universities, identifying themselves as substantially separate, mixed programs, or fully inclusive/individualized programs (Folk, Yamamoto, & Stodden, 2012; Grigal et al., 2012; Hafner, Moffatt, & Kisa, 2011; Hendrickson, Busard, Rodgers & Scheidecker, 2013; May, 2012).

There are currently more than 200 PSE programs available to students with intellectual disabilities in the US, and with the increase in options, there also comes an increased need to look at how programs are evaluating outcomes and the efficacy of their supports/programs. The majority of studies looking at outcomes for college students with intellectual disabilities focus on employment outcomes (Grigal & Hart, 2010, 2013; Migliore et al., 2009). There are limited studies that have used student feedback to identify more comprehensive ideas about outcomes (Folk et al., 2012; Papay & Bambara, 2011), but in general, I am in agreement with Hendrickson et al. (2013) who urge us to expand research because,

> There is a dearth of empirical data on the immediate and long-term outcomes of program components and postsecondary programs in general … There is an urgent need for both qualitative and quantitative research to examine the many questions that must be addressed to guide policy makers, administrators, educational practitioners, and family members/guardians. We strongly encourage individuals and institutions to work together to establish evaluation designs and research agendas in concert with the development of postsecondary education options for students with ID. (p. 196)

Grigal et al. (2012) reflect the same concern in their call for intervention studies that explore the impact of PSE practices on outcomes as well as more longitudinal data on PSE and post-PSE outcomes beyond employment. There is a need however, for caution as we move forward, in making sure that we do not exclude the voices of the very people for whom we are advocating in our attempts to race to the top with our own research agendas—which will require an understanding of theory and methodologies that are participatory and emancipatory in nature.

Theory and Method

A wider expanse of literature that values the "variety of traditions within critical pedagogy" that share the "broad objective" to,

> empower the powerless and transform existing social inequalities and injustices (Hytten and Bettez, 2012, p. 17) is needed to balance the current field of PSE research. Critical disability theory is a key tradition to finding this balance, although with the exception of researchers like Cory, White, and Stuckey (2010), few educators within higher education have explored (disability) as a social construct, a political concern or an experience that warrants a theoretical framework. (Rocco & Delgado, 2011, p. 8)

In their study, Cory et al. used a case study of student activism to examine how disability studies theory can effectively be used to change disability services on campus. Remington is in agreement with their efforts, saying "we can't complain about other stuff if we don't change our own." As PSE programs move to become more deeply and seamlessly integrated within higher education communities, this type of research will become even more crucial in highlighting ideas like Rocco and Delgado's (2011) argument that "people with disabilities have unique voices and experiences, the right to self-determination, the right to escape the 'commodification' of the labor and disability business" (pp. 7–8).

According to Hytten and Bettez (2011) ethnographic writing as that which increases "understandings of personal experience related to difference and discrimination" (p. 16). This focus on the viewpoint of stakeholders provides readers with a more personal way to enter into and respond to the research—it calls for readers to "see injustices and their consequences through the eyes of real people" (Hytten & Bettez, 2011, p. 16).

Collaborative Process

As a researcher who identifies with critical theory and the focus described by Hytten and Bettez, when I (Lalenja) was given the assignment in class, I knew immediately that I wanted to approach Remington about working with me on the chapter. Remington and I have had many conversations about his experience in college, and his belief that access to college is a social justice issue—a perspective that we both share. I brainstormed with Remington about how a qualitative study that focused on student perspectives on college might be structured, and this conversation had a significant impact on the research design. We determined that semi-structured interviews and focus groups would be used to capture student's voices and thoughts about post-college outcomes, and that once themes from the interviews were identified, that they would be shared with participants in a focus group designed to verify analysis. Six students in the Integrative Community Studies Certificate at UNCG were included as participants, including Remington. Poetic analysis was also used to construct "voice poems" as a method for placing the "subjectivity" of each narrator at the center of analysis (Chadwick, 2012).

Remington was involved very early in the development of the research design, and provided essential feedback throughout. For instance, after developing research and interview questions, I asked Remington to review them and provide feedback on their efficacy. Remington made a number of suggestions on ways that consent forms needed to be re-written so that they were more accessible, and how the language of some of the interview questions need to be modified. He also participated in a formal interview so that he could provide further feedback on flow, relevance and connectedness to research questions. After a preliminary analysis of interview responses, I shared themes with Remington and confirmed that we were on the right track before sharing with the focus group, who also provided feedback on themes that they considered to be most important. The themes provided valuable insight into what is important to college students with ID, and both Remington and myself look forward to having the opportunity to share results publicly through an IRB approved study in the future.

One of the most transformative "happenings" that occurred, was the decision to use poetic analysis as a way to bring student voices to the fore in a more engaging, powerful way. For each participant, including Remington, transcripts were "mined" for thoughts relating to the larger themes, which were then structured in poetic formats. Poems only included language directly from transcripts, although basic poetic conventions regarding phrasing, repetition, line breaks, etc. were used to enhance ideas. Remington felt that his poem was indeed representative of his experiences, and after some discussion and a few additions for the purposes of this chapter, we both decided that it would be an effective way to reflect his position as a student researcher.

Remington's Positionality

I am a black american raised by white parents
in my family race didn't matter
I feel like god created me
to change the world
he put me here to be an example of diversity

I would say my dreams and goals would be
to become a professional rock musician
to study disability advocacy
that's why I chose
I chose to come here just like any other college student
I chose and I had the money to come here
I said hey, let me come to college
let me just apply

Its like here
race doesn't matter
disability doesn't matter
you're a person first
I'm a human being
I was put on this world for a reason
I was created to be diverse

I've had experience living on my own before
but I didn't really know exactly what the difference
that the university would be
but I was excited about being here
I was excited
about seeing my friends
about being able to become who I am, you know
who people told me I couldn't become
Transforming
transforming from a less confident guy to the more of the hipster
I have developed into that
there is more than one black culture
blipster, rastafarian, ebonic
they all go hand in hand
people can choose whatever culture they want
some people believe in "talking black"
but there are black people from all over the world
who dont talk that way
it becomes a problem
when people expect you to talk a particular way because of your race

My parents
my parents are kind of stuck in the old high school version of me
One time
I remember I got off the train
and I was dressed more like a hipster
I used to dress more hip hop and ebonic
So when I got off the train
with a little beanie and skinny jeans
my dad made a joke
whats up with the crazy hat style
I told him
I'm more of a hipster now
I'm not really the old school version of me

This certificate
it is just a good education to have
like the advocacy class
where we learned about human rights
and about how jobs can't discriminate
even though they still do it and society says they do it
doesn't make it right
never once did I learn about this stuff in high school
we do not get a good enough education about gender and disability rights
we shouldn't just pick and choose
people want to say that things don't exist
just because they don't feel good about it
Now in college I am learning it
and I am really enjoying it
learning about human rights
learning about equality in the community of unrepresented groups
but I don't see them as unrepresented
I see them as people

I feel that you have the right to go to college period
anyone has the right
any specific group

black americans, women or men, disability
it doesn't matter
I believe that ableism is a bad thing
just like racism or sexism
they are all bad at the same time
whether people like it or not
you should have the right to go to college

What would I change about college?
The main thing is
I think that they shouldn't require SAT's
SAT's aren't really what you are going to be learning
sometimes it is just a way to get in
there should be a human right that they shouldn't require it
I think that public universities should be able to provide access
to people of all abilities and not make it challenging
there should be standards of course
but at the same time
I think that you should be able to have access with the right supports
there shouldn't be unaccess

People with disabilities should be able to have the awareness
that they have the option
that college is an option
some parents that are old school
they are not really used to it you know
they are used to if you are not disabled then you go to school
if you are disabled
the person without the disability is the person ruling
that is ableism
it's a form of bias
like ability power
and no one has power over no one
We are all human

Lalenja's Positionality

Although I initially wrote my positionality statement in what would be considered a more traditional prose approach, I decided to apply the same poetic conventions to my own writing for the purposes of this chapter. I believe that by doing so, I was able to distill out the most essential components of my own position thusly,

critical
emancipatory
research
resonates within me
finding value in the articulation
of that which has previously been
unheard
undervalued
pushed to the margins
product of black, southern family
I know suffocation
family system expectations
of blind obedience
and quiet suffering
woman born

to black mother and white father
I know the feeling
of voice not being counted
because it is not
authentic
or credible enough
to the very community to which you most wish
to belong
mother of black boy growing to man
I know the watching of educators
who try to silence
with labels
child who questions everything
and moves through learning

on all counts
my mother was the catalyst
that helped me find my way
past limitations
her books
her ideas
and her unrelenting expectation
that I question everything
made life
uncomfortable
but out of that discomfort
grew a critical viewpoint
that became my anchor
even when I didn't have the language
to define it
as critical
even in finding my own personhood
beyond her influence
I could still hear her voice in my ear
see her thoughts on the pages of the books I read
even as I discovered myself
in spoken word revelations
she continued to pop up
in my writings
creeping into my metaphors
leaving her mark
like kilroy

my experiences
have molded my view of the world
my belief that the desire for power is at the foundation
of this country's cultural, political and social scaffolding
creating inequities
and pockets of oppression across lines
of race, ethnicity, gender, ability
and so many other
ways to be different
my understanding of truth as it exists
and my relationship to knowledge
will all continue to influence me
guide me with gentle
and not so gentle insistence

as I find my place
within the workings of research
and scholarship

Remington and I decided to use prose to capture shared beliefs and epistemological standpoints in the following section.

"Our" Positionality

Our inherent belief that knowledge and awareness are critical tools for "emancipating the oppressed and improving the human condition" (Lincoln, Lynham, & Guba, 2011, p. 114), informed our research activities, and encouraged us to explore participatory methods where "knowledge is founded in transformation" (Lincoln, Lynham, & Guba, 2011, p. 114) and where that "transformation is based on democratic participation between researcher and subject" (Lincoln, Lynham, & Guba, 2011, p. 102). Having experienced our own personal transformation and "searches for truth" through spoken word and advocacy, we were particularly drawn to research techniques that create opportunities for all participants to do the same—to those techniques that "support social transformation and revolution" (Lincoln, Lynham, & Guba, 2011, p. 106). This belief in the impact of social structures like "freedom and oppression, power and control" also drove our research efforts towards the production of knowledge that can "change existing oppressive structures and remove oppression through empowerment" (Lincoln, Lynham, & Guba, 2011, p. 103).

Whose Truth Do We Seek?

We believe that we are our own experts in our life experiences, and that we must not give someone else power over our "story." How do we, as researchers, ensure that we are not claiming authority over the "stories" of our research participants and partners? How do we structure research so that it helps to "illuminate how theory informs lived experience" and respects the narratives/voices of those being researched? These were critical questions that we wanted to explore through this collaboration.

For our purposes, post-critical ethnography was a natural response to those questions. It provides a space for the lived experiences of oppressed people to be juxtaposed to the post-modernity asserted by critical theorists. This method gave us an opportunity to be a "passionate participants" and co-researchers in a research process that encourages transformation and empowerment.

The Process of Seeking

With our background and positions in mind, we approached our discussion of the pilot study through the lens of post-critical ethnography, where both the "researcher and the researched" will be involved in a learning process that is "fully dialogic, collaborative, and pedagogical" (Hytten, 2004, p. 101). Data collection methods were informed by what Kathy Hytten describes as the post-critical ethnographic traditions of Educative Research and Emancipatory Research, which build from the premises that, respectively, "research subjects have legitimacy and authority to produce socially useful knowledge (p. 101)," and that research should be used to help people "better understand their social situations so that they can be empowered to change them (p. 102)." The research process remained fluid, self-reflective, collaborative, and dialogic, with the aim of challenging educational practices that limit access to a specific segment of the student population, qualities that all situated this study firmly within post-critical ethnographic research.

A Few Words on Poetic Transcription/Analysis

Maynard and Cahnmann-Taylor (2010) assert that there has been experimentation with ethnographic methods since the 1990's, including poetry. After exploring the use of poetry in the pilot study, I am in agreement with their argument that,

> Like poetic ethnographic prose, both free verse and more formal structures in poetry can offer a paradoxical freedom to be honest, more explicit, about one's observations and feelings, whether as an ethnographic outsider, or as a cultural insider who writes from outside oneself. Ethnographic poetry—when crafted within the rigors and opportunities offered by compressed and heightened language—requires the writer to revise and remove excess, highlighting emotions and attitudes, our stance, as well as ideas.

I certainly found that using a poetic approach to highlight essential language and ideas and then compressing them into more purposeful and succinct structures enhanced the data. This method also matched well with the different communication styles and types of language used by study participants, and I would argue that it is a method that could be used to more accurately capture the unique voices of individuals with intellectual disabilities. In his study using poetic transcription Andrew Huddleston (2012) states that "poetry has a way of speaking to people that expository and narrative writing lack" (p. 736). Phipps and Saunders (2009) express this in their work as well, in their statement "poetry can say things and mock things and create things which other ways of working with words cannot" (p. 362).

Remington thought it important to reference the Afro-punk genre here, as an example of a movement in which the participants have "claimed" their space within a genre that has not typically been representative of the black experience. Remington views this as a political act, and I think that his point is a good one. Members of the Afro-punk community, like those with disabilities, have been located at the margins of those cultural groups that have dominant positions, as highlighted here by Ramirez-Sanchez (2008),

> Black punks, male and female, talk about similar experiences of isolation and marginalization. This reality is consistent with the ideology of racism and White supremacy that still imbues U.S. culture, even within co-cultural groups. (p. 96)

Ramirez-Sanchez goes on to point out that "research has been mostly silent about the communicative practices of marginalized groups within a larger marginalized group" (p. 91).

I believe that this is reflective of what has occurred within the disability community as well, particularly for students with ID struggling to find their place on college campuses. One could look at the use of a non-traditional research approach like poetic analysis as a way for students with intellectual disabilities within the world of higher education to also "claim" their space, as a "struggle to speak of the hidden, unjust things felt in the depths" (Phipps & Saunders, 2009, p. 359).

Recommendations for Future Post-critical Ethnographic Studies

Remington and I participated in a number of discussions about what we would like to see in the future regarding research with students with ID. These are the main recommendations that we would like to offer the field, including elements that we were not able to execute ourselves in the pilot study:

- Deeper engagement of participants—students should not only have the opportunity to be interviewed about their experiences, but should also be actively involved in analysis and research design.

- Guidance on research process—to be fully engaged participants and co-researchers, time and resources must be made available to ensure that students understand the research process

- Collaboration on final creative/alternative data—true, post-critical ethnographic research cannot just consist of researchers "doing the creating" based on participant responses; participants themselves should be involved in the creative process and with final authority over the finished product.

- More time to review findings—The research process must therefore include sufficient time for participants to confirm that they are in agreement with the findings, including time for feedback and recommendations.
- Explore collaborative writing options—students should have the opportunity to co-author studies; tools like mixed ink (online collaborative writing tool), shared documents, etc.
- Provide learning opportunities re: advocacy and social change—As a part of the research process, students should be given opportunities to learn more about how they can become agents of change, another critical component of post-critical methodology, as well as their potential role in the social justice movement.
- Find other ways for people to share their experiences—alternative methods beyond photovoice and poetry should be explored to provide students with multiple options for representation and involvement in research.

That's the Way We See It

This chapter represents an outline of possibilities for conducting critical research with students with ID in ways that honor and make space for their voices and agency. Co-authoring this piece with a student was an essential way to ensure that student voice was represented, and the result was that much richer, and reflective of the student viewpoint due to the collaboration. There are any number of research possibilities out there that can be used to co-produce knowledge with members of marginalized groups—we present this example simply as one possibility. We do think that our recommendations are universal however, and could be used as guideposts for the development of research practices that are more socially just and emancipatory. And that is indeed, the way that we see it.

Work Cited

Chadwick, R. J. (2012). Fleshy enough? Notes toward embodied analysis in critical qualitative research. *Gay & Lesbian Issues & Psychology Review, 8*(2), 82–97.

Cory, R., White, J., & Stuckey, Z. (2010). Using disability studies theory to change disability services: A case study in student activism. *Journal of Post-secondary Education and Disability, 23*(1), 28–26.

Folk, E. D. R., Yamamoto, K. K., & Stodden, R. A. (2012). Implementing inclusion and collaborative teaming in a model program of postsecondary education for young adults with intellectual disabilities. *Journal of Policy and Practice in Intellectual Disabilities, 9*(4), 257–269.

Grigal, M., & Hart, D. (2013). Transition and postsecondary education programs for students with intellectual disability: A pathway to employment. *Think college fast facts* (Issue No.4). Boston, MA: University of Massachusetts Boston, Institute for Community Inclusion.

Grigal, M., Hart, D., & Weir, C. (2012). A survey of postsecondary education programs for students with intellectual disabilities in the United States. *Journal of Policy and Practice in Intellectual Disabilities, 9*(4), 223–233.

Grigal, M., Neubert, D. A., & Moon, M. S. (2002). Postsecondary options for students with significant disabilities. *Teaching Exceptional Children, 35*(2), 68–73.

Hafner, D., Moffatt, C., & Kisa, N. (2011). Cutting-Edge: Integrating students with intellectual and developmental disabilities into a 4-year liberal arts college. *Career Development and Transition for Exceptional Individuals, 34*(1), 18–30.

Hart, D., Grigal, M., & Weir, C. (2010). Expanding the paradigm: Postsecondary education options for individuals with autism spectrum disorder and intellectual disabilities. *Focus on Autism and Other Developmental Disabilities, 25*(3), 134–150.

Hendrickson, J., Busard, A., Rodgers, D., & Scheidecker, B. (2013). College students with intellectual disabilities: How are they faring? *The Journal of College and University Student Housing, 40*(1), 186–199.

Hesse-Biber, S., & Piatelli, D. (2012). Holistic reflexivity: The feminist practice of reflexivity. In Hesse-Biber, S. (Ed), *Handbook of feminist research: Theory and praxis* (pp. 493–514). Los Angeles, CA: Sage Publications.

Huddleston, A. (2012). Understanding responses to high school exit exams in literacy: A Bourdieusian analysis of poetric transcriptions. *Journal of Adolescent and Adult Literacy,* May, 734–744.

Hytten, K., & Bettez, S. (2011). Understanding education for social justice. *Educational Foundations, Winter-Spring,* 7–24.

Lincoln, Y. S., Lynham, S. A., & Guba, E. G. (2011). Paradigmatic controversies, contradictions, and emerging confluences, revisited. In N. K. Denzin & Y. S. Lincoln (Eds.), *The SAGE handbook of qualitative research* (4th ed., pp. 97–128). Thousand Oaks, CA: Sage.

May, C. (2012). An investigation of attitude change in inclusive college classes including young adults with an intellectual disability. *Journal of Policy and Practice in Intellectual Disabilities, 9*(4), 240–246.

Maynard, K., & Cahnmann-Taylor, M. (2010). Anthropology at the edge of words where poetry and ethnography meet. *Anthropology and Humanism, 35*(1), pp. 2–19.

Migliore, A., Butterworth, J., & Hart, D. (2009). Postsecondary education and employment outcomes for youth with intellectual disabilities. *Think college fast facts* (Issue No.1). Boston, MA: University of Massachusetts Boston, Institute for Community Inclusion.

Neubert, D. A., Moon, M. S., Grigal, M., & Redd, V. (2001). Post-secondary educational practices for individuals with mental retardation and other significant disabilities: A review of the literature. *Journal of Vocational Rehabilitation, 16*, 155–168.

Papay, C. K., & Bambara, L. M. (2011). Postsecondary education for transition-age students with intellectual and other developmental disabilities: A national survey. *Education and Training in Autism and Developmental Disabilities, 46*(March), 78–93.

Philip, T. M. (2012). Desegregation, the attack on public education, and the inadvertent critiques of social justice educators: Implications for teacher education. *Teacher Education Quarterly, Spring*, 29–41.

Phipps, A., & Saunders, L. (2009). The sound of violets: The ethnographic potency of poetry? *Ethnography and Education, 4*(3), 357–387.

Ramirez-Sanchez, R. (2008). Marginalization from within: Expanding co-cultural theory through the experience off the Afro punk. *The Howard Journal of Communications, 19*, 89–104.

Rocco, T., & Delgado, A. (2011). Shifting lenses: A critical examination of disability in adult education. *New Directions for Adult Continuing Education, 132*(winter), 3–12.

CHAPTER 34

Intellectual Property Rights in the Online Learning Era

Sarah J. Dhilla

Introduction

Online education has sparked a debate between faculty and administrators regarding the ownership of online courses. Longstanding academic president has granted faculty ownership of their scholarly work; however, the emergence of online learning has called that tradition into question. Administrators claim that online courses are distinctly different than their face-to-face counterparts in terms of investment and development and the institution is entitled to course ownership. Faculty argue that they should retain the copyright as the course authors and that institutional ownership is a violation of their academic freedom. Ambiguous legal statues and the absence of institutional online copyright policies have only contributed to the tensions. Today, the issue remains controversial as colleges and universities experiment with different models of ownership.

An analysis of stakeholders' claims and concerns sheds light on the explicit arguments and unspoken motivations that influence the policy development process, while an investigation of changing economic conditions and institutional characteristics illustrates the variety of factors that also affect copyright policy. An overview of potential policy solutions illustrates the variety of approaches to policy development and provides a basis for discussing implications.

The Issue

Faculty and administrators disagree about who should retain the intellectual property rights to online courses. Longstanding academic president has granted faculty ownership of their scholarly works; however, the emergence of online learning has called that tradition into question. Administrators claim that online courses are distinctly different than their face-to-face counterparts in terms of investment and development, therefore the institution is entitled to ownership. Faculty believe that they should retain the rights as the course authors and argue that institutional ownership violates their academic freedom. Ambiguous legal statues and the absence of institutional policies have only contributed to the tensions. Today, the issue remains controversial as institutions experiment with different models of ownership.

The debate over ownership directly impacts the design, development and delivery of online courses, influencing the tone and quality of the student experience. If faculty have control of a course, they are more likely to be invested and engaged, which is crucial to creating a positive online learning experience (Conceição, 2006). Faculty control also ensures that subject matter experts are managing course revisions, making changes that retain the academic fidelity and rigor of the original course (Zhang & Carr-Chellman, 2006). On the other hand, a high degree of faculty control can lead to inconsistent course quality and a subpar learning experience, the worst of which is only magnified by the online medium (Conrad, 2004).

Administrators claim that institutional control of online courses allows them to optimize course scheduling, standardize course quality, increase course offerings and deliver online classes to hundreds of students for little additional cost (Chambers, 1999). But faculty contend that such uniformity creates a sterile learning experience and warn that taking a "big box" approach to online education will hurt the academic quality of such courses. They believe that institutional ownership would destroy academic freedom, compromise the academic integrity of online courses and profoundly change the educational experience for faculty and students. Consequently, policies regarding the intellectual property rights of online courses must balance the academic and economic needs of the administration, faculty and students.

Brief History

Copyright law & the teacher exception. Arguments regarding the ownership of online courses are based upon the Copyright Act of 1976, which grants ownership of a creative work to the author—the person who translated the idea into a tangible expression (DiRamio & Kops, 2004). Owners enjoy exclusive rights to their work, which allow them to reproduce the work, prepare derivations and distribute copies or recordings to the public (Klein, 2004). On the other hand, works-made-for-hire are not owned by the author if they are produced during the course of his/her employment or commissioned to be a contribution to a collective work; instead, such works are owned by the employer (17 U.S.C. Section 101).

Contrary to these policies, persuasive court dicta have upheld a "teacher exception" to the work-for-hire doctrine, giving academics the copyright to the works and publications they create during the course of their employment (Blanchard, 2010; Leslie, 2002; McMichael, Bonner, Pomea, & Kelley, 2002).

Academic tradition. The idea that faculty are entitled to ownership of their scholarly works—while not codified—has become a commonly accepted exception to the work-for-hire doctrine in the eyes of the legal system. Likewise, colleges and universities have acquiesced and granted faculty ownership of their works (DiRamio & Kops, 2004). Faculty publications have traditionally been of little value to colleges and universities because they do not produce significant profits (Leslie, 2002). Given this, administrators have left scholarly works to the faculty and the "teacher exception" has become a de-facto tradition in higher education.

Disruption

The emergence of online learning. This all changed with the introduction of online learning, which first emerged in the 1990s when a small number of universities began experimenting with web-based learning tools. As technology advanced, more schools began to offer online learning modules as part of their curricula, eventually developing full online courses and complete degree programs. The expansion of Internet access and the proliferation of wireless devices further encouraged the development of online programs and, by the end of the decade, the popularity of online courses had exploded. As of January 2014, 7.1 million students were enrolled in an online course at one of the nearly 4,000 US colleges and universities that offer online options (*Grade Change*, 2013; *Online Nation*, 2007).

The emergence of online learning disrupted the longstanding status quo regarding the copyright of academic works. In addition to being highly lucrative, successful online courses enable colleges and universities to promote their institutional brand and allow faculty to publicize their work (Klein, 2004). Thus, both sides have a vested interest in retaining the copyright of online courses and are engaged in a "tug of war" as they fight for ownership and control.

The growing dispute. Many institutions have gone against the traditional "teacher exception" and retained the copyrights to online courses, claiming that the courses are a collaborative work that needs to be protected from competitors (Blanchard, 2010). Faculty have resisted, arguing that institutional control of online courses goes against longstanding tradition and violates their academic freedom (Kranch, 2008). Making matters worse, few colleges or universities had institutional copyright policies in place when they began developing online courses; as arguments emerged between faculty and administrators over course ownership, the lack of institutional guidance and ambiguous legal statues only led to further confusion.

In response to the escalating copyright debate, both the Association of American Universities (AAU) and American Association of University Professors (AAUP) released formal statements outlining frameworks for online course copyright policy development. The AAU model calls for a shift in focus from product to process. In their opinion, online courses are a "collaborative creation" made in an institutional setting, thus "the university should own the intellectual property that is created at the university by faculty, research staff and scientists and with substantial aid of its facilities or its financial supports" (AAU, n.d.).

The AAUP model, on the other hand, proposes an informed allocation of rights between faculty and universities when it comes to the ownership, control, use and compensation for online courses. They classify online course development projects into three categories: (1) works that are considered to be "made-for-hire" (institutional ownership) (2) negotiated contractual transfers (faculty ownership) and (3) jointly-owned works, as defined by the Copyright Act. Regardless of classification, the AAUP believes that faculty should be given the right to future use of any online courses they develop, including right of "first refusal" when making new versions and the right to be consulted about course revision and re-use (AAUP, n.d.). Ownership of online courses is more than a matter of profits, and the AAUP endeavors to "protect the faculty's rights as scholars, researchers, authors, and creators … [because] these rights are essential to ensure their academic freedom and continuous advancement of knowledge through teaching" (AAUP, n.d.).

Current Landscape

Wanting to avoid further conflict, many colleges and universities have begun drafting institutional policies to address copyright of online courses. Today we have a continuum of policies, from total faculty ownership to complete institutional control with a variety of joint-ownership models in between; policies vary widely across higher education and there does not seem to be single policy that is favored according to institution size or type (DiRamio & Kops, 2004).

Despite the varied approaches, the new policies have only created more tension between faculty and administrators. The majority of institutional copyright policies have been created by the administration with little faculty input and, as a result, the faculty feel disenfranchised and alienated. Paradoxically, the policies that were designed to clarify copyright issues and encourage online course development have created a chilling effect, causing faculty to shy away from their institution's online enterprises. This leaves us with pressing questions, such as: how have we gone from a state of longstanding, wide-spread acceptance to such bitter and contentious dissent? Who is involved in the dispute and who stands to be impacted by it? What do they have at stake and how are their concerns taken into account? What contextual factors are influencing their arguments and the overall debate? And, given all this, how can we create policies that satisfy the multiple and varied demands? The following sections analyze these aspects to provide all involved parties with the information they need to successfully advocate and participate in the online copyright policy development process.

Stakeholders

Analyzing stakeholders' claims and concerns regarding online course copyright sheds light on some of the explicit arguments and unspoken motivations that influence the policy development process. Faculty and administrators believe they have a vested interest in retaining the intellectual property rights for online courses and have expressed serious concerns if the other retains control. Both actors play a pivotal role in shaping the policy development process and their interests need to be taken into account.

Faculty Claims

Authorship. Faculty are the content experts when it comes to creating a course and, while they may need assistance with online design and web-based development, they see themselves as the authoritative course creators (Zhang & Carr-Chellman, 2006). Faculty determine the subject matter, course direction and intellectual approach, making each course a distinct academic creation that is thoughtfully and intentionally designed to suit their students' learning needs (Bain, 2004).

Faculty stress that creating a course—whether it is online or face-to-face—is a serious academic undertaking and bristle at the idea of designing standardized course modules to be run systematically without scholarly supervision. A highly standardized approach can limit the breadth and range of learning opportunities and fail to develop key cognitive skills that are difficult to master without individualized attention and coaching. No algorithm can provide the meaningful formative feedback that is needed to help students learn how to analyze, reflect upon and accurate apply new concepts (Rubin, 2013). Given their indispensible role in the design and delivery process, faculty argue that they are the fundamental course creators and are entitled to ownership on the grounds of authorship (Rubin, 2013; Talab, 2007).

Precedent. Despite copyright laws that typically favor the employer, faculty have long enjoyed a "teacher exception" whereby universities grant faculty members the copyright of the scholarly works they create; thus, faculty have come to understand that they own their courses and all materials associated with them. Even when universities have policies that state otherwise (e.g.: the university owns course syllabi), these rules are rarely enforced and most faculty are unaware that such policies even exist (Zhang & Carr-Chellman, 2006). Their claim is further bolstered by the fact that academics own the rights to nearly all of their other intellectual works; thus, faculty feel that they should be able to retain the rights to their online courses as well.[1]

Academic freedom. Faculty argue that institutional ownership of online courses would be an infringement upon their academic freedom (Zhang & Carr-Chellman, 2006). They feel that they should be

> free to chose and pursue areas of study and concentration without interference, to share the results of their intellectual efforts with colleagues and students, to use and disseminate their own creations, and to take their created works with them should they leave. (*Preamble to the Columbia University copyright policy*, 2000)

If institutions retain the copyrights to online courses, administrators would be able to decide where the work is published, to edit and revise it, to produce derivation works (translations, abridgments, etc), and even censor or forbid the dissemination of their work altogether, undermining the core tenants of academic freedom (Talab, 2007). Thus, faculty argue that they must retain course copyrights to maintain the integrity of their courses and preserve their scholarly right to academic freedom.

Faculty Concerns

Mobility. Faculty are becoming increasingly itinerant as they align more with their discipline than a particular institution. If universities claim the copyright of online courses, faculty are concerned that their mobility as scholars will be limited (Zhang & Carr-Chellman, 2006). Strict anti-competition clauses further restrict faculty, prohibiting them from using their works at other institutions or creating new works for other entities. Faculty argue that doing so would be no different than creating a lecture-series to present at another school—something that historically has not been regulated or limited. Given this, faculty feel that such restrictions are unwarranted and unfair.

Control. Faculty are also concerned about control of online courses. If institutions retain the copyright, faculty worry that their courses may be changed without their approval, used far into the future without proper attribution or offered under the direction of unqualified instructors. Faculty contend that institutional control would place courses in the hands of administrators who have more interest in making a profit than maintaining the academic fidelity and integrity of the course (Zhang & Carr-Chellman, 2006). Specifically, they fear that administrators will respond to internal and external market pressures through economies of scale, taking a "big box store approach" that will lead to the denigration of online courses (Talab, 2007). Thus, faculty argue that they need to retain control of their online courses in order to offer high-quality online courses that provide effective and authentic learning experiences.

Job security. Many faculty also worry about the future of their profession. Recent trends in higher education show that tenured faculty are becoming increasingly rare as colleges and universities hire more part-time faculty (Talab, 2007; Weissmann, 2013).

Even if a faculty member has been lucky enough to secure a tenure track position, there has been little change in tenure and promotion policies to accommodate online course development. This is especially concerning given that institutional ownership also reduces faculty mobility—thus, if an institution claims ownership of online courses without incorporating online course development into their tenure and reward processes, faculty are effectively disenfranchised because they are neither adequately rewarded for their online contribution nor allowed to take their work with them if they decide to leave for another institution.

Faculty are afraid institutional ownership of online courses will only exacerbate the declining role of the faculty and further diminish the importance of their work (Talab, 2007). Some faculty question whether they are working themselves out of a job by creating high-caliber online courses and fear that administrators will run their course indefinitely, replacing them with less qualified adjuncts and instructors to keep the course going.

Administrators' Claims

Commitment. First and foremost, administrators argue that faculty are university employees; course development, whether its face-to-face or online, is a normal part of their job duties and they should not expect ownership (Zhang & Carr-Chellman, 2006). From an institutional standpoint, online courses are works-for-hire and are the property of the employer—not the author (DiRamio & Kops, 2004).

Investment. Furthermore, administrators argue that faculty could not create online courses without substantial institutional support. They are much more complex and complicated to develop than face-to-face courses and faculty rely upon specialized staff, services and facilities to create online them (Kranch, 2008). Online courses are also much more labor intensive to create; in fact, studies have found that developing an online course takes twice the amount of time to develop when compared to a face-to-face course (DiRamio & Kops, 2004).

In addition to the extra manpower and labor, online courses require a significant financial investment and are much more expensive to create than traditional courses. Given the significant institutional investment, administrators expect to receive a return on their investment and owning the copyright for online courses allows them to do so by increasing the frequency of course offerings to bring in more tuition revenue (Kranch, 2008; DiRamio & Kops, 2004).

When faculty point to the longstanding precedent of faculty ownership, administrators argue that online courses are inherently different than face-to-face courses because they require such a significant institutional investment and the two cannot be compared; thus, the "teacher exception" does not apply (Kranch, 2008).

Competition. Administrators argue that the university needs to protect itself and its online investments against increasing competition from other institutions (Blanchard, 2010; DiRamio & Kops, 2004; Zhang & Carr-Chellman, 2006). Administrators feel that they need to protect the institutional brand from for-profit schools who seek to lure popular faculty members (and their courses) away from their home institution.

Administrators also want to protect the university against unscrupulous faculty who may be looking to capitalize on the institutional investment by selling their online courses to other entities. When faculty claim ownership on the grounds of authorship and academic freedom and then attempt to sell the course to another institution, not only does it create a conflict of interest but it also grossly misapplies the essence of academic freedom (Blanchard, 2010). Retaining ownership allows administrators to guard their investment, online assets and institutional brand while protecting their stake in the increasingly competitive higher education landscape (Blanchard, 2010). Given these potential new avenues of academic commercialization and the threats associated with them, institutions have a vested interest in retaining the ownership of online courses.

Faculty Concerns

Quality and control. Administrators worry that giving faculty full control of the online courses they create will lead to highly variable outcomes in terms of course quality. While some courses may be brilliantly designed, others may not be. And, while some faculty will carefully prepare the course content ahead of time, others will require multiple revisions, which can be cumbersome and cause confusion among student (Rubin, 2013). When institutions retain the copyright, online courses can be designed to fit a common structure with uniform appearance and naming conventions; this provides a consistent visual brand and simplifies the acclimation process for students who quickly become familiar with the institution's online learning format. Institutional control also means that key decisions are centralized and the majority of the work is standardized, minimizing course development times and costs (Rubin, 2013). Thus, administrators argue that they should retain ownership of online courses because institutional control allows for efficient, effective and economical implementation and provides a better online learning experience.

Cost. The individualized approach to creating online courses favored by the faculty is extremely expensive. It requires intensive training with pedagogical coaches and multiple consultations with course designers in addition to the technological support services that keep the online enterprise running smoothly (Rubin, 2013). Administrators would rather standardize and streamline the course development process, minimize faculty control and, as a result, reduce the need for expensive individualized support services.

Administrators also worry that faculty will constantly request costly revisions because they are overly concerned about the content and are not cognizant of the financial ramifications of their modifications (Zhang & Carr-Chellman, 2006). And administrators are concerned that some faculty may make unnecessary updates simply to earn additional course development money. Ultimately, administrators are worried that a high degree of faculty control will lead to a financially unsustainable online enterprise and, thus, argue that the institution should retain course copyright (Zhang & Carr-Chellman, 2006).

Factors

While faculty and administrators are at the center of the dispute over course copyright, they must be sensitive to the contextual factors that also influence the ownership debate. Changing economic conditions and institutional characteristics have played a not-so-subtle role in shaping how faculty and administrators have perceived and approached the online copyright policy development. The following sections detail those factors and their influence upon the ownership debate.

External Economic Considerations Shrinking budgets. Colleges and universities have seen a steady decline in state and federal funding over the past twenty-five years; in fact, state spending per student is now at its lowest level since 1980 (Hebel, 2014). At the same time, institutional operating costs have increased due to the construction of new physical facilities, the expansion of research activities, an exponential increase in the number of administrative personnel and the implementation of new student support services (Rubin, 2013). To make up the difference, colleges and universities have increased tuition costs and reduced financial aid (Hebel, 2014). But their physical campuses can only accommodate a limited number of students, so institutions have turned to online learning as a way to increase enrollment and raise additional revenue. Online courses enable institutions to enroll many more students for little increased cost, making them a relatively easy source of income for cash-strapped schools (Talab, 2007).

Growing demands and increased competition. Fortunately, the number of online students has rapidly grown in recent years. But the increase in the number of online students has been accompanied by an increase in competition from for-profit and nonprofit institutions alike. And the fight for online students has been especially fierce because it is not restricted by traditional regional constraints. Thus, universities have had to work hard to distinguish themselves among the myriad of online courses providers to attract students away from their competitors.

All of the abovementioned factors place pressure on administrators to grow their online learning enterprises and maximize online enrollments. While this need-to-produce mindset is understandable, administrators must pause and reflect on the ramifications of what they are doing. They should consider: what type of students is our school looking to attract? What are their academic expectations and learning needs? How can faculty help students realize their goals? How can we create policies that are financially stable as well as supportive of faculty and students in their online academic endeavors?

Faculty need to be involved in these discussions as well and they must be cognizant of the demands administrators face so these external economic factors can be acknowledged in the policy development process. Failing to do so will likely produce an online learning enterprise that is financially unsustainable, out of touch with students' needs and unable to stand up to the intense online competition.

Internal Institutional Considerations

Organizational culture. While external aspects play an influential role in policy development, internal institution-specific aspects are equally as important. Policy makers should consider how the faculty-administrator relationship impacts the way each party approaches the policy development process (DiRamio & Kops, 2004). For example: Is there a history of shared governance and academic community on campus? Is the faculty-administrator relationship collegial, collaborative and synergistic? Or is the relationship fractured and combative? Does the administration hand down unilateral decisions and neglect to consult with the faculty? And are the faculty uninvolved, disinterested and recalcitrant when it comes to collaborative institutional activity? (Del Favero, 2002).

Online copyright policy is an area fraught with possibilities for unintended consequences and stakeholder dissatisfaction (DiRamio & Kops, 2004). Thus, it is important to remember that the faculty-institution relationship is symbiotic: faculty rely on colleges and universities as a venue in which to teach and conduct research, and they trust that the university will allow them to disseminate their knowledge throughout the academic community. Likewise, colleges and universities rely on faculty not only to teach but to bring notoriety to the institution via research and scholarship; popular professors also attract high quality students, talented faculty and grants, increasing the institution prestige (Blanchard, 2010).

Restrictive copyright policies are at odds with such a relationship because they inhibit the free flow of knowledge that the faculty-institution relationship depends upon. While some limitations may be necessary, faculty and administrators should aim to enact fair copyright and conflict-of-interest policies that clearly delineate how online courses are treated when it comes to issues regarding ownership and use, encouraging the free flow of knowledge that the academy relies upon (Blanchard, 2010).

Mission. Policy makers should also consider the historical and contemporary goals of the institution and create an online copyright policy that is aligned with these aims (Zhang & Carr-Chellman, 2006).

Faculty and administrative advocates of online learning cite the importance of democratizing the university, opening educational access and, in the case of public land grant universities, furthering the institutional mission of outreach and service as their primary goals (Zhang & Carr-Chellman, 2006). But, while the rhetoric has focused on democracy, the online copyright policies at many institutions have not.

If faculty and administrators are committed to increasing access to higher education and promoting the advancement of knowledge via online learning, their actions ought to align with their beliefs. Administrators should not enact policies that restrict faculty from offering online courses; instead, faculty ought to be able to offer their courses to all interested persons through any available outlets. Nor should faculty try to restrict use of their course materials citing issues of authorship and academic freedom; they ought to openly share them with the academic community.

If faculty and administrators are genuinely committed to expanding access to higher education, they ought to consider open online learning options, like MIT's OpenCourse Ware project. Such an approach makes institutionally funded research and high-quality course materials available to anyone with an Internet connection for free. Not only does this approach support their espoused goal of increasing educational access, but it may also engender much needed public support for higher education institutions, making the entire enterprise much more relevant than it has been in years (Blanchard, 2010; Zhang & Carr-Chellman, 2006).

Arguably, MIT's model does not offer the individualized attention or instructional support that traditional online courses provide; however, their emphasis on open access—not competition and compensation—ought to guide faculty and administrators as they create online learning enterprises that align with the institution's mission.

Solutions

Given the variety of factors that may influence an institution's approach and attitude towards intellectual property rights in the online realm, it is highly unlikely that a single policy will work in all cases (AAUP, n.d.). The following sections outline some of the emerging policy models, modes of implementation and methods of assigning ownership that institutions are experimenting with. Faculty and administrators involved in the policy development process should consider how each model, mode and method of ownership may suit their online learning aims and institutional needs, weighing the advantages and drawbacks of each option.

Different Models of Ownership

Faculty Ownership. Some institutions have implemented online copyright policies that favor the faculty and grant them ownership of the online course they create. This allows them to have complete control in the development process, make updates and revisions as they see fit, and even take their course materials with them if they leave for another institution (DiRamio & Kops, 2004).

This model makes the faculty feel emboldened and encourages them to participate in online learning initiatives; however, there are disadvantages. As mentioned earlier, such policies can lead to inconsistent course quality and leave the institution open to competitors who are looking to poach the best online faculty members (and their courses), reaping the rewards of another institution's investment (Zhang & Carr-Chellman, 2006). Faculty ownership also means that institutions are not entitled to the revenue generated by the online courses they invested in; thus, faculty ownership models tend to be rare.

Institutional Ownership. On the other end of the spectrum, the institutional ownership policy model allows colleges and universities to claim course copyrights carte blanche, giving them complete control over the design, development and delivery process. This model protects their institutional investment and is far more efficient and economical than the faculty ownership approach but, again, there are downsides. Such a standardized and systemized approach can alienate faculty members who want to teach online and lead to a dull and lifeless learning experience for students. Faculty and student dissatisfaction has a perceptible chilling effect on online course development, so many institutions tend to avoid implementing such strict policies (Zhang & Carr-Chellman, 2006).

Joint Ownership. The joint-ownership policy model is the most common approach and assigns ownership according to the level of individual and/or institutional contribution in the course development process (DiRamio & Kops, 2004). Such policies take an un-bundled approach to online learning where the course elements are broken out into separate entities and course-related roles are divided into distinct responsibilities; such divisions help clarify who has a claim to copyright and which components they can make a claim to.

For example, online courses are separated into multiple components, such as: courseware, multimedia, lectures, assignments, exercises, evaluations and other supplemental materials. Likewise, course-related responsibilities are divided into several distinct roles, including: course creators, who are responsible for designing new online courses; instructors, who are responsible for teaching prepackaged online courses; and administrators, who are responsible for the organizational and managerial duties of the online learning enterprise.

Course authors are entitled to the copyrights of certain course materials and, in some cases, can make a claim for joint-ownership of the entire course. These shared-agreements typically follow a textbook model where the university can hire other instructors to teach the course for a period of time, but the author maintains the rights to the course materials. The agreement might be extended for a fee, based upon the number of students who take the course and, if a course proves to be extremely popular or essential to an academic program, the copyright may be purchased outright, giving the institution ownership of the course (Rubin, 2013). Similarly, instructors can claim ownership of any original supporting course materials they create upon negotiation with the institution. Faculty and administrators tend to agree that the joint-ownership policy model is the most equitable option, but it is also the most complicated and requires frequent communication, consultation and a high degree of commitment from all involved parties.

Different Modes of Implementing Ownership

Once faculty and administrators decide upon a particular policy model, they still need to determine how to implement the policy. The sections below describe some of the different contractual arrangements colleges and universities have been experimenting with.

Institutional policies. Broad institutional copyright policies are commonly used to address ownership issues in the university setting. These blanket policies are vague, but they easily allow administrators to collectively cover all types of intellectual property—including copyright, trademarks and patents—at once without much effort.

Some institutions have enacted special subordinate clauses to specifically address copyright issues related to online learning. These policies typically: (1) define what online learning is, (2) focus on specifying the terms of ownership in detail, (3) set a threshold that defines when the institution will retain ownership and when the faculty have the right to make a claim, and (4) define the rights of the author and the institution to reuse the online course or related course materials. This has helped clarify ownership issues upfront and avoid misunderstandings when the work is ready for distribution (McMichael et al., 2002). Administrators who have implemented such policies report that the greater clarity and transparency of these policies has encouraged faculty participation and innovation, leading to a stronger online learning enterprise that is accepted and supported by the entire university community.

But administrators at other institutions worry that such specialty policies will quickly become outmoded due to the rapid pace of technological innovation; also, having multiple copyright policies is difficult to maintain. As a result, most institutions have opted to stick with their standard institutional copyright policies (McMichael et al., 2002).

Individual contracts. Since the majority of colleges and university do not have copyright policies that specifically mention online learning, many faculty feel that online ownership issues are inadequately addresses by the existing institutional policies; thus, separate contracts between individual faculty members and the institution have become more common (McMichael et al., 2002). Not only do they help clarify important issues related to online ownership, but contracts can also alter the standard work-for-hire arrangement to create customized ownership arrangements, providing greater legal protection for both faculty and administrators. Their customizability also offers increased flexibility in the ever-evolving the online learning environment and give institutions greater control over assigning ownership and stipulating future use of online course materials and modules.

While this may allow for greater latitude, some policy experts warn that individual contracts do not serve the best interests of the institution or the faculty. Savvy faculty members can negotiate their way to exceptions, which may hurt the institution or be unfair to the rest of the faculty. Furthermore, they can lead to inconsistent treatment of faculty members, making them more hesitant to enter the online learning arena (Talab, 2013). Individual contracts can also burdensome for administrators, depending on the size of the university's online learning enterprise, and may not be a viable option for all institutions.

Collective Bargaining. In a few instances, faculty and administrators have entered into collective bargaining agreements to establish online copyright policies; however, such agreements tend to be rare. Many institutions do not allow collective bargaining and, if they do, the negotiation process tends to be arduous and time consuming. Thus, while it may be the most democratic approach to assigning ownership, this option is only available to a select few institutions (McMichael et al., 2002).

Assigning Ownership

Once faculty and administrators have settled on a policy model and mode of implementation, they must decide how to assign ownership. Unless they have decided on a strict faculty or institutional-ownership policy model, most colleges and universities rely upon a proportional approach to assigning ownership that evaluates the conditions under which the course was (or will be) developed and awards ownership accordingly (Zhang & Carr-Chellman, 2006). For example, copyright policies commonly assess how much institutional support was used to create the course. In most cases, ownership resides with the author unless a "substantial" amount of institutional resources were used; otherwise, the institution can claim the rights to the course. While this seems straightforward enough, it can be problematic because the term "substantial" it is rarely defined in copyright policies and, when it is included, most definitions are "nebulous" at best (Zhang & Carr-Chellman, 2006).

Further complicating matters, policy makers need to consider questions regarding scope of employment. Does online course creation fall within a faculty member's scope of employment and, thus, would be considered a commissioned work or work-for-hire? If so, ownership would reside with the institution regardless of the amount of resources used (unless the faculty member had an individual contract with the institution that states otherwise).

And was the course an individual or a collaborative creation? If it was a collaborative effort, as most online courses are, who can claim ownership? Do all involved parties have a right to ownership or only the key contributors? Even if a faculty member creates a course on their own, outside the scope of their employment and without substantial institutional support, they still may run aground of their institution's conflict-of-interest clause, which would prevent them from selling their work to another institution. Thus, while a proportional approach to online ownership may seem like the most equitable option, it is the most complicated and the most likely to cause conflict.

If institutions are considering adopting such a model, they may also want to establish a committee to settle copyright disputes. Klien (2004) recommends a three-step arbitration process: the first step would attempt to solve the dispute among the parties claiming ownership. The second step would bring in a standing committee to adjudicate and bring the dispute to a close. If all else fails, the final step would be formal arbitration involving legal counsel.

Considerations and Implications

There is not a one-size-fits-all solution to online course copyright. As institutions contemplate creating their own policies, faculty and administrators should consider the following questions:

- Who has the right to claim the copyright of online courses? And under what circumstances may they do so?
- How are different aspects of an online course defined and delineated? And who owns each part? (For example: who owns the course syllabi, assignment, exercises and exams? Who owns the multimedia or courseware if a third party was involved in the development?)
- Who controls the course once it is created? (For example: Who is in charge of revisions, adaptations, alterations and scheduling subsequent course offerings?)
- Should course authors be given the right of first refusal?
- Who may teach the course?
- Who may use the course materials?
- What type of compensation should course authors receive if other instructors want to use components of their course?
- How are any funds distributed? And whom are they distributed among?
- How will emerging disputes be settled?

Answers to these questions will help faculty and administrators create a copyright policy that is comprehensive and clear, covering the crucial aspects of online course ownership and the rights of each involved party.

Implications. Once the online copyright policy is created, faculty and administrators will have another set of questions to consider as they implement it. How will they assess the effectiveness of the policy? How often will it be measured? And who is responsible for doing so? Furthermore, what steps will be taken if the policy is not meeting expectations?

Faculty and administrators should also be conscious of the effects the new policy has upon the institution's online learning enterprise. Has the policy encouraged online course development or discouraged it? Has the policy affected the content and tone of online courses and, if so, how? What kind of impact has the policy had upon the online teaching experience for faculty? Has it impacted their roles, responsibilities and rights as a professor? And how has the policy impacted the students who take online courses? Are they receiving a high-quality learning experience? Online copyright policies impact how faculty and administrators approach online learning and will undoubtedly have an affect upon an institution's online learning enterprise. The challenge for future researchers will be to determine how to accurately assess the impact of such policies upon the various aspects of the online learning experience. Doing so will be crucial because online learning has become a permanent part of the higher education landscape and institutions have a responsibility to ensure that they are providing the best educational opportunities possible whether they are face-to-face or online.

Conclusion

Online learning has ignited a serious debate within higher education and raised new questions regarding the ownership, control, and reproduction of college courses. Who owns courses that are designed for online delivery? Who is in charge of course revisions? Who is entitled to the revenue online courses generate? Who retains control of a course if the faculty member who designed it decides to leave and teach at another institution? Should faculty be able to take the online course with them or should it remain with the institution? These issues have disrupted established academic traditions and inflamed longstanding disputes regarding authorship, ownership and academic freedom, and the highly-lucrative nature of online courses has only added to the tensions.

Faculty and administrators need to come together to develop institutional copyright policies that address these questions. They need to start by identifying who is involved in the online learning enterprise and understand what they have at stake; and they must examine the external economic influences and internal institution-specific characteristics that impact the policy development process too. With this, faculty and administrators will have the information they need to select an appropriate policy model, mode of implementation and method of assigning ownership and create an effective and equitable online copyright policy that is in keeping with their institutional mission and organizational culture as well as their educational and economic goals.

But their work does not end there; policymakers must be cognizant of how these policies affect the online learning enterprise, the stakeholders, the institution and the higher education industry as a whole to ensure that the policies are having the intended impact. Online learning is quickly becoming a permanent part of the higher education landscape and universities need to act to implement copyright policies that address the intricacies of online courses, address issues related to authorship, ownership and academic freedom, and officially incorporate it incorporate into the academy.

Note

1. The key exception being patents, which are covered by a separate section of intellectual property law that deals with inventions (Lang, 1998).

Work Cited

American Association of University Professors. (n.d.). *Statement on copyright*. Retrieved February 18, 2014, from American Association of University Professors, http://www.aaup.org/report/statement-copyright

Association of American Universities. (n.d.). *AAU intellectual property and new media technologies: A framework for policy development at AAU institutions*. A report to the AAU Digital and Intellectual Property Management Committee by the Intellectual Property Task Force. Retrieved February 18, 2014, from Association of American Universities, http://www.aau.edu/reprots/IPReport.html

Bain, K. (2004). *What the best college teachers do*. Harvard University Press. Cambridge, MA.

Blanchard, J. (2010). The teacher exception under the work for hire doctrine: Safeguard of academic freedom or vehicle for academic free enterprise? *Innovative Higher Education*, *35*(1), 61–69. http://dx.doi.org.ezproxy.bu.edu/10.1007/s10755-009-9124-1

Chambers, G. (1999). Toward shared control of distance education. *The Chronicle of Higher Education*, November 19, B8. Copyright Act of 1976. Public Law 94–553, 17 USC Sec. 101.

Conceição, S. C. O. (2006). Faculty lived experiences in the online environment. *Adult Education Quarterly*, *57*(1), 26–45. doi:10.1177/1059601106292247

Conrad, D. (2004). University instructors' reflections on their first online teaching experiences. *Journal of Asynchronous Learning Networks, 8*(2), 31+.

Del Favero, M. (2002, June). *Faculty—Administrator relationships and responsive decision making systems: New frameworks for study.* Paper presented at Research Forum on Higher Education Governance, Santa Fe, NM.

DiRamio, D. C., & Kops, G. C. (2004). Distance education and digital intellectual property issues. *Planning for Higher Education, 32*(3), 37–46.

Grade Change: Tracking Online Education in the United States. (2013). The Sloan Consortium. Retrieved March 28, 2014, from http://sloanconsortium.org/publications/survey/grade-change-2013

Hays v. Sony Corporation of America. (1988). 847 F.2d 412 (7th Cir.).

Hebel, S. (2014, March 2). From public good to private good. *The Chronicle of Higher Education.* Retrieved from http://chronicle.com/article/From-Public-Good-to-Private/145061

Klein, M. W. (2004). Equitable rule: Copyright ownership of distance-education courses. *The Journal of College and University Law, 31,* 143.

Kranch, D. A. (2008). Who owns online course intellectual property? *Quarterly Review of Distance Education, 9*(4), 349–356, 445.

Lang, S. (1998). Who owns the course? Online composition courses in an era of changing intellectual property policies. *Computers and Composition, 15*(2), 215–228. doi: 10.1016/S8755-4615(98)90055-X

Leslie, L. (2002). Application of the teacher exception doctrine to on-line courses. *Journal of Legislation, 29,* 109.

McMichael, J. S., Bonner, K., Pomea, N., & Kelley, K. B. (2002). Intellectual property, ownership and digital course materials: A study of intellectual property policies at two and four year colleges and universities. *Portal: Libraries and the Academy, 2*(2), 255–266. doi: 10.1353/pla.2002.0035

Online Nation: Five Years of Growth in Online Learning. (2007). Online Learning Consortium. Retrieved November 27, 2014, from http://onlinelearningconsortium.org/survey_report/2007-online-nation-five-years-growth-online-learning/

Preamble to the Columbia University copyright policy. (2000). Retrieved August 21, 2014, from http://www.columbia.edu/cu/provost/docs/copyright.html

Rubin, B. (2013). University business models and online practices: A third way. *Online Journal of Distance Learning Administration, 16*(1). Pp. 1–15

Talab, R. (2007). Faculty distance courseware ownership and the "Wal-Mart" approach to higher education. *TechTrends: Linking Research and Practice to Improve Learning, 51*(4). doi:10.1007/s11528-007-0047-3

Weissmann, J. (2013, April 10). *The ever-shrinking role of tenured college professors* (in 1 Chart). Retrieved November 22, 2014, from http://www.theatlantic.com/business/archive/2013/04/the-ever-shrinking-role-of-tenured-college-professors-in-1-chart/274849/

Zhang, K., & Carr-Chellman, A. A. (2006). Courseware copyright: Whose rights are right? *Journal of Educational Computing Research, 34*(2). Pp. 173–186

CHAPTER 35

"Othering" of English Language Learners in Higher Education

Redefining Literacy and Identity in the Digital Age

John J. Lee

Introduction

In educational institutions, there are many ways students become marginalized or feel "Othered." Some of these categories of marginalization include race, gender, skin color, and sexuality, but one category not often discussed, particularly in higher education, is by language. Each student comes to school with unique background experiences, cultural practices, and even attitudes toward learning. For ELLs (English language learners), one of their academic needs may be specialized language instruction, yet there exists several complications in the way they are placed into their English courses as well as the labeling of these students as they enter postsecondary institutions. Upon entering U.S. colleges and universities—institutions that have historically played a significant role in enforcing policies of monolingualism and English-only movements—many ELLs are viewed in deficit terms and attributed labels such as *difficult*, *underachieving*, and *deficient* (Gaffney, 1999; Harklau, 2000; Yoon, 2008). Ensuingly, ELLs in higher education become viewed as a single monolithic, homogenous group; more importantly, standard academic English continues to be the norm against which the linguistic "Others" are measured.

As the world becomes increasingly more diverse with respect to language and technology, being literate, particularly in today's digital age, requires knowing how to use digital texts (e.g., images, videos, and hyperlinks) for navigating nontraditional spaces. There is an increasing number of students communicating online, each one of them reading and writing thousands of words online each week (Williams, 2008). Notably, the digital literacy practices of today's youths reflect the emerging reality that their social and academic lives are mediated by the ubiquitous presence of SNSs like Facebook, which has over 850 million daily active users on average and 1.35 billion monthly active users. Consequently, digitally-mediated forms of communication have become central to students' lives, and one of the more interesting developments in literacy research has been the ways that students construct and negotiate their identities through digital texts and fully disembodied-text mode that "reveals nothing about their physical characteristics" (Zhao, Grasmuck, & Martin, 2008).

The images, stereotypes, and identities that are manifested through institutional practices and policies can affect how students are socialized and how they negotiate classroom life and achievement. Findings from this study show that the deficit view and discourse of ELLs in higher education is commonly known and shared among ELLs, yet the *hidden curriculum of schooling* (Harklau, 2000) which perpetuates negative societal images of students of minority groups can be negotiated. As literacy practices evolve and shift from the page to the screen and from the classroom to digital space, ELLs have found that they can negotiate their identities through digital texts and different multimodal representations.

The Majority-Minority Nation

Fueled by high immigration levels and higher birth rates among minorities, the United States is undergoing a historic demographic shift. In 2010, the nation's Hispanic population surpassed the 50 million mark, growing 43% and accounting for more than half the national growth from 2000 to 2010. Evidently, Hispanics have become the nation's second largest race or ethnic group, and their population is projected to triple to 133 million and represent approximately 60% of the U.S. population by 2050 (U.S. Census Bureau, 2012). The rise of racial minorities is also reflected by the growing populations of African Americans—the second largest minority group in the U.S.—and Asian Americans—the fastest growing ethnic group in 2012. The burgeoning minority population is indicative of an impending historic shift in which America will become a majority-minority nation.

As the ethnic, racial, and cultural composition of the United States continues to change, it becomes clear that our nation's schools will also experience the increased diversity in our society. One salient indicator of the changing face of American classrooms is the rise of non-native speakers of English. ELLs—students with limited English proficiency and whose primary language is not English—have become the fastest growing segment of the school-age population in the United States (National Clearinghouse for English Language Acquisition, 2002). The ELL student population—also referred to as ESL (English as a second language), LEP (Limited English proficient), and EL (English learner)—are a highly complex group with different levels of immigration status, language proficiency, and educational needs. ELL enrollment in the U.S. is projected to soon reach 10 million, and by 2025, one out of every four public school students will be an ELL (National Education Association, 2008). They have become increasingly present in all U.S. states, and contrary to common assumptions, more than 75% of the elementary school population and more than half of secondary ELLs are native-born U.S. citizens (National Education Association, 2008). The exponential growth of the K-12 ELL population strongly indicates that U.S. colleges and universities will also face the challenges and opportunities presented by a student population with limited English proficiency.

ELLs in Higher Education

Historically, ELLs have always had a presence in U.S. colleges and universities. Between the 1960s and 1980s, thousands of students were admitted into colleges and universities due to open admissions policies and government funding. The influx of students entering postsecondary institutions were students of color and students from low-income and immigrant backgrounds. At the same time, there was a large segment of students entering postsecondary education (PSE) who reported speaking a language other than English at home. In response to the growing linguistic and cultural diversity, educators and policy makers began to address the needs of these students who soon started to demand for U.S. schools, colleges, universities to be reformed and to reflect their "cultures, identities, hopes, and dreams" (Banks, 2009, p. 13). Ensuingly, the social actions of these students were one of the impetuses of the multicultural education movement, and they also helped generate awareness for the effective teaching of ELLs.

Surprisingly, too little is known about ELLs at the postsecondary level. There are very few qualitative and quantitative studies on ELLs' participation and experiences in higher education (Kanno & Grosik, 2012, p. 131). There is, however, a large body of research on ELLs at the secondary level, and these studies exposed serious achievement gaps between ELLs and non-ELLs. ELLs at the secondary level lag behind their English proficient peers in all content areas and are more likely to be taught by teachers without appropriate teaching credentials (Abedi & Gandara, 2006, p. 36). We also know that they are not achieving at the same rates as their English proficient peers and their academic achievement is among the lowest of all students (Wolf, Herman, & Dietel, 2010). But in discussions regarding equity, participation, and access to PSE, ELLs are virtually absent because they have historically been unrecognized as a special population. Many ELLs were confounded with the international students, and there still exists a significant lack of "communication and articulation between secondary and post-secondary institutions in the United States, and colleges are inconsistent in the data they collect and the policies they enact regarding ESL students" (Harklau, 2000, p. 36). It is evident that there needs to be a comprehensive data-collection effort to understand the needs and experiences of ELLs in higher education.

ELLs, like most students, face challenges of balancing academic and social demands of PSE. But ELLs, in particular, face problems that stem from not only socioeconomic factors but also linguistic and cultural differences. For example, they have more difficulties in developing academic literacy, no matter what their level of English proficiency or amount of prior schooling (Walqui, 2000). They are also more likely than native-English-speaking students to come from low-income families and are more likely to have parents with limited formal education (Garcia, Jensen, & Scribner, 2009). We also know that ELLs are commonly disproportionately placed in low-level, undergraduate courses, which in turn can lead to lower academic achievement and reduced opportunities to take college courses (Callahan, Wilkinson, & Muller, 2010). While it is important to continue to examine the socioeconomic disadvantages and linguistic barriers that ELLs face, it is just as important—if not more—to consider the culture and policies of U.S. postsecondary institutions that may inhibit ELLs' access and graduation.

Institutional policies and classroom organization can lead to the creation of certain social structures of a particular population of students. For example, a teacher's sequencing of classroom activities and the classroom seating arrangement can affect how students are socialized and how they negotiate classroom life and achievement. For ELLs, these institutional policies and practices can be particularly problematic. ELLs have more difficulties with speaking up, negotiating, and engaging critically with the conditions of their classrooms due to their language barrier, which can lead to the development and perpetuation of a subordinated social group and social identity. That is, the way schools categorize and position ELLs through classroom curricula, classroom organization, and classroom interactions marginalize the status of ELLs, making them invisible and marking them as the "Others."

"Othering" of ELLs

When the proportion of minority students and students from linguistic minority groups grow, schools need to evolve to accommodate the needs of the new student population. Relatedly, the social, academic, and linguistic norms must also change when a traditionally marginalized group grows significantly (Linton, 2004). To accommodate the fast growing language minority population, policy makers and educators developed procedures to identify students in need of linguistic support. At the secondary level, students are placed into language assistance programs, most commonly referred to ESL courses. At the postsecondary level, they are placed into "remedial" education programs, also referred to as "developmental education" and "college prep."

These placement procedures were created to deal with the unique pedagogical needs of non-native speakers of English, yet Matsuda (2006) argues that these procedures convey the "myth of linguistic homogeneity—the tacit and widespread acceptance of the dominant image of composition students as native speakers of a privileged variety of English."

Through the common use of language proficiency tests, many ELLs are placed into lower level courses, and upon entering college, they are quarantined from the rest of higher education students. According to Matsuda (2006), ELLs are expected to erase the traces of their language differences before they are allowed to enroll in the required composition courses. They are also expected to become socialized into the dominant linguistic practices of U.S. postsecondary institutions. These expectations reflect what Matsuda calls a policy of unidirectional English monolingualism. This policy marginalizes the language diversity in higher education and this practice is also commonly reflected in the discourse of ELLs. That is, ELLs are overwhelmingly viewed as a homogenous group and all ELL students are assumed to possess the same low-level literacy skills. On the contrary, ELLs in U.S. colleges and universities come from diverse cultural and educational backgrounds, which include different levels of oral proficiency and literacy. Their placement into lower-level or ELL-designated courses, then, presents an issue, not simply due to placement concerns, but also because "the term is linked to a student's institutional experience with the term" (Ortmeier-Hooper, 2008, p. 392). That is, schools hold a deficit view of these students, and these differential expectations often lead to differential treatment.

In education, there are many ways students are "Othered" or considered the outsiders. Some ways would be by race, gender, skin color, and sexuality. One way we do not talk about very often is being "Othered" by language. Language permeates students' everyday lives—both inside and outside the classroom—and it is through language that students mediate their relationship with their peers and their social environment. Consequently, it is through language that students gain communicative competence, membership, and legitimacy into a group (Duff, Due to their placement in "remedial" or ELL-designated courses, ELLs have been equated with multiple identity markers like *difficult*, *underachieving*, and *deficient* (Gaffney, 1999; Harklau, 2000; Yoon, 2008). The various meanings associated with the labeling of the *ELL student* impacts not only their PSE experiences but also how they view themselves in higher education.

Beyond Language

Placing ELLs in developmental English programs to help them transition from their native language to English fluency presents a challenge. Learning a new language and teaching ELLs to become effective communicators requires much more than acquiring grammatical and syntactical knowledge. Russian developmental and educational psychologist Lev Vygotsky stated that learning a language requires acquiring new conceptual knowledge and modifying existing knowledge as a way of "re-mediating one's interactions with the world" (Lantolf & Thorne, 2006). Additionally, learning a new language requires mastery of linguistic conventions and the adoption of appropriate ideologies associated with the target group to gain communicative competency, membership, and legitimacy into a new group (Duff, 2007). This lifelong and "lifewide" process, known as language socialization, requires mediation from those who are more knowledgeable and proficient in the language, as well as explicit and implicit socialization through linguistic and social interaction into relevant local communicative practices (Duff, 2007). Consequently, one should not only focus on developing a high level of communicative proficiency while continuing to think in terms of his or her native conceptual system.

The process of acquiring a language is also a part of a much larger process of becoming a person in society. Heller (1987) argued that:

> It is through language that a person negotiates a sense of self within and across different sites at different points in time, and it is through language that a person gains access to—or is denied access to—powerful social networks that give learners the opportunity to speak. (as cited in Peirce, 1995, p. 13)

The goal of language instruction, then, should not only focus on teaching the form of language. We use language to belong, to defend ourselves, and to negotiate our identities. That is, we learn and use language to develop and negotiate the concept of *self*.

Digital Literacy

By the end of the 20th century and in the early years of the 21st century, literacy scholars started to pay more attention to learners' identity construction. Interest in students' identity development rose as a result of several recognitions, including: the growing number of culturally and linguistically diverse students in schools today, a growing interest in foregrounding the actor in social practices, and a growing body of research arguing that literacy education influences and shapes an individual's sense of identity. But what is literacy and how do we define it in today's multicultural and multilingual society?

Literacy is a loaded and evolving term embedded within social, cultural, political, and cognitive contexts. It is a concept that can only be defined in a multiplicity of ways because of its historically transient nature of what it represents to people at different times. A classical view of literacy defines literacy as a cognitive ability, a set of context-neutral and functional skills that involve coding and decoding texts. This *autonomous* model of literacy discards the "social structures within which the concepts and philosophies of specifics cultures are formed" (Street, 1997). From this perspective, literacy is viewed independent of social context and the culture in which it is used. In contrast, the *ideological* model of literacy embraces a much more culturally-sensitive view of literacy. From this perspective, literacy is not limited to a technical definition of just as a set of skills but rather a social practice existing within a social system. "As a cultural, social activity, literacy is something people do" (Sheridan & Rowsell, 2010). Literacy as a social practice is reading the language in contextualized settings and living the language as part of a cultural practice.

Building on the theories of literacy as a social practice, the New London Group wanted to examine and advocate the future of literacy pedagogy. A group of 10 prominent literacy academics came together to discuss the idea that if the mission of education is to ensure students become informed and critical participants in the political realm of their communities and countries, then literacy educators and students must see themselves as designers and makers of social change. "Effective citizenship and productive work now require that we interact effectively using multiple languages, multiple Englishes, and communication patterns that more frequently cross cultural, community, and national boundaries" (The New London Group, 1996). Their work addressed the linguistic and cultural diversity of the changing world and focused on the real-world contexts in which people practice literacy. Ultimately, they argued that the way we communicate has drastically transformed due to the multiplicity of new communication channels and media. Their emphasis on redefining literacy as the ability to understand information however presented gave birth to new representations and labels, like *plurality of literacies*, *multiliteracies*, and *social literacies*.

These new concepts reflected the digitally-mediated literacy practices and the diversity of communication modes, which now include traditional print text and digital text—texts which can include spoken, written, visual, aural, and interactive aspects. Kress (2003) echoed this notion of multimodality, arguing that "we can no longer treat literacy—or "language"—as the sole, the main, let alone the major means for representation and communication." We now live in a digital age where literacy is no longer: a sequence of alphabetic characters, bound to the textbook, and unidirectional. Through the multiplicity and integration of significant modes of meaning-making (Cazden et al., 1996), we are now able to see the imagined realities and identities of others through different multimodal representations.

Digital Identity

As social life blends into a digital world, both researchers and educators are discovering that students are discovering new ways to learn about their world, to express themselves, and to communicate with others (Alvermann, 2002). Notably, the literacy practices of today's adolescents involve engagements such as those with digital technologies and popular culture. Computer-mediated communication has drastically changed the ways young people learn and socialize, yet this change has not affected the national curriculum policies and state learning and assessment standards, which still focus almost exclusively on foundational literacies (Skinner & Hagood, 2008). According to Skinner and Hagood, the literacies required to be "successful" in school include only: decoding and reading comprehension of print-based texts; written composition of academic texts; and, oral fluency with Standard English grammar and vocabulary. However, the digital demands of the 21st century require that students be able to navigate a plurality of text forms to be considered "successful" communicators in digital space.

As the world becomes increasingly more diverse with respect to the interactions of culture, language, and technology, we have moved toward a more complex and multimodal literacy, one that incorporates "multiple semiotic modes into integrative expression" (Vincent, 2006, p. 55). We have moved from the century-long dominance of the medium of books to the medium of screens. Yet regardless of this change, our production and use of language continues to expresses our identity formation and identity display. How the *digital youth* read and write in today's digital age reflect not only their literacy skills and academic performance, but also how they construct their identities in non-traditional and non-academic settings, like social networking sites (SNSs).

SNSs are web-based services that allow individuals to construct a public profile within a bounded system, articulate a list of other users with whom they share a connection, and view their list of connections and those made by others within a system (Boyd & Ellison, 2007). SNSs, like Facebook, are now ubiquitous fixtures among youths. As of September 30, 2013, there were 1.19 billion monthly active users on Facebook, more than 500 million users on Twitter, and 25 million users on MySpace. Studies of social media use in higher education also revealed that more than 90% of college students have profiles on Facebook (Harvard Institute on Politics, 2011). Due to the popularity of SNSs, researchers have examined the factors contributing to Facebook use from multiple theoretical perspectives (Boyd & Ellison, 2007; Snyder, Carpenter, & Slauson, 2006). But few studies have yet to specifically examine the literacy practices that take place in SNSs and how users construct their identities.

Engagement in SNSs means participation in socially recognized ways of communicating and negotiating meaning with others in a space. Becoming socialized into any community—virtually or non-virtually—requires presenting oneself as a particular kind of person, and the advent of SNSs has changed the traditional conditions of identity production. These technologically-mediated environments have created a new mode of identity production for the *digital youth*. They are learning how to enter a community and to socialize with others through their reading and writing. They are achieving this by: recognizing what kind of comments and writing are appropriate for context, establishing a convincing ethos, and understanding general textual convention and the context-specific customers of message and responses (Williams, 2008). Through multimodal compositions, which consist of media-centric forms of engagement, they are learning about social life and creating a *virtual identity*. SNSs, like Facebook and MySpace, allow students to "play" with their identities, which often appear to be highly socially desirable identities individuals aspire to have offline (Zhao, Grasmuck, & Martin, 2008). These digitally produced identities are created through personal pages that display their interests, photographs, movies, videos, and other information that are influenced by culture and popular media. In particular, the digital youth are negotiating their virtual identities in the contexts of social forces and popular media, as stated by Williams (2008):

> Students may not be thinking about how they are portraying themselves in terms of gender or social class when they put together their MySpace pages or post on discussion forums. Yet they are negotiating their identities in these virtual spaces in the contexts of social forces. Their decisions to put images of Orlando Bloom or Jessica Alba on MySpace pages or to list songs by hip-hop artists or teen pop bands shape the identities they perform online and how those identities are read by others. (p. 684)

Examining the literacy practices of the digital youth may teach us about how much they know about traditional literacy concepts, and more importantly, we must examine how they position themselves in "changing cultural contexts and how that influences their ability to communicate with others"

(Williams, 2008, p. 686). As more youths engage in SNSs, researchers need to accept that the traditional view of identity is no longer relevant in today's digital world.

ELLs in Digital Space

Recently, the research on ELLs has focused on development of identity as a fluid construct that shifts over time and as closely tied to the learner's interactions in various social contexts. One of the researchers who contribute to this perspective is Rebecca Black. Black (2006) examined how an ELL student developed English literacy skills and constructed her identity through online sites. Her study demonstrated how popular culture and digital space "converge to provide a context in which adolescent ELLs develop a powerful, transcultural identity." She focused on virtual spaces—particularly fanfiction—as a platform that crosses traditional cultural, linguistic, and geographic borders.

The participant in Black's case study is Nanako, an ELL who emigrated from China to a large Canadian city. She practiced with different genres and forms of writing in English through Fanfiction.net, an online site that archives fanfiction. Fanfiction is a type of fiction that is written using another author's characters from a particular TV series, books, etc. Black's study showed that Nanako was able to use her developing writing skills and interest in Japanese comic books to participate in an online, social environment, which allowed her to develop confidence in her identity as a writer. Her first, fictitious stories reflected her adjustment to life and school in a new country. For example, her early narratives were filled with her daily experiences as an immigrant adolescent. Initially, her focus was to work on her writing by experimenting with and practicing with new genres and forms of writing in English. As readers provided her with "gentle feedback," she became more confident and her writing and language use gradually developed. Over the years, Nanako achieved the identity of a successful and popular author, thus she was not expected to "adhere to the identity of an immigrant, a Canadian, or a native Mandarin Chinese speaker, nor was she forced to choose between the languages in her linguistic repertoire" (Black, 2006, p. 182).

Another study that viewed identity as constantly changing and as socioculturally constructed is a qualitative case study by Jayoung Choi. Choi's (2009) study examined the process of identity construction in an after-school literacy club that used several Asian multicultural literary texts. The four participants in the study, who were adolescent ELLs, responded to several short stories and poems and discussed the readings in face-to-face club meetings. In addition to the meetings, they wrote responses to the books on a private Wiki site, which is an online space where anyone can share his or her work and idea. Engaging with the text through these spoken and written formats to study identity is derived from Rosenblatt's (1938, 2004) transactional theory and model of reading. Rosenblatt argued that reading is a *transaction* between the reader and text, and that text interpretation is contingent upon the reader's connections to personal experiences. That is, textual meaning does not reside in the work or the reader but evolves out of a transactional relationship between the text and the reader. Rosenblatt also suggested that reading literature aesthetically requires readers to make connections to personal experiences (Choi, 2009), which is an important part of identity building. The findings of Choi's study revealed that the literacy club offered opportunities to talk about where the participants positioned themselves academically, socially, ethnically, culturally, and linguistically.

These two studies revealed that there is value in creating spaces for identity negotiations, and for ELLs in particular, establishing a safe and intimate environment can "inspire ELLs to talk about their lives and their feelings, which will in turn foster communicative competence and literacy skills" (Choi, 2009). However, these studies did not show us how the identities made available in digital spaces, specifically SNSs, compare and contrast to the identities made available in academic spaces, specifically in higher education. As classrooms become more diverse and as students' engagement in digital space become more ubiquitous, more research must be conducted on how ELLs negotiate their identities in digital space.

Discussion

Communication now takes place across a diversity of modes, and the pervasive consumption of digitally-mediated texts has led to an increasing amount of research studies devoted to understanding how students participate in online communities. SNSs, like Facebook, have permeated students' academic and social lives, and their participation in online communities has changed how they view themselves and interact with the world. Consequently, the digital literacy practices that have been embedded into students' lives significantly impact their experiences and identity formations not only in the classrooms as learners but also in virtual environments as members of online communities. Scholars in many fields, ranging from psychiatry (Nadkarni & Hofmann, 2012), information science and technology (Nie & Sundar, 2013; Zhang, Jiang, & Carroll, 2010), and sociology (Zhao, Grasmuck, & Martin, 2008), have examined the use of SNSs and the forging of online identities, and these studies have revealed myriad ways that students use digital space for articulating their ideal self-identity, fostering a sense of belonging, and constructing self-presentations. However, there needs to be more research that examines the "offline" or real-world sociocultural influences of the participants and the participants' positionality in institutions and classrooms. Institutional policies, educational institutions, classroom practices, cultural dynamics, and even the classroom organization can play a significant role in the creation and recreation of labels and identities as students grapple with the lifelong question of, "Who am I?" This analysis is particularly significant in today's rapidly-growing multicultural and multicultural society.

Work Cited

Abedi, J., & Gandara, P. (2006). Performance of English language learners as a subgroup in large-scale assessment: Interaction of research and policy. *Educational Measurement: Issues and Practices, 26*(5), 36–46.

Alvermann, D. E. (Ed.). (2002). *Adolescents and literacies in a digital world.* New York, NY: Peter Lang.

Banks, J. A. (2009). Multicultural education: Dimensions and paradigms. In J. A. Banks (Ed.), *The Routledge international companion to multicultural education* (pp. 9–32). New York, NY: Routledge.

Black, R. W. (2006). Language, culture, and identity in online fanfiction. *E-Learning and Digital Media, 3*(2), 170–184.

Boyd, D. M., & Ellison, N. B. (2007). Social network sites: Definition, history, and scholarship. *Journal of Computer-Mediated Communication, 13*(1), 210–230.

Callahan, R. M., Wilkinson, L., & Muller, C. (2010). Academic achievement and course taking in U.S. schools: Effects of ESL placement among language minority students. *Educational Evaluation and Policy Analysis, 32*(1), 84–117.

Cazden, C., Cope, B., Fairclough, N., Gee, J., Kalantzis, M., Kress, G., … Nakata, M. (1996). A pedagogy of multiliteracies: Designing social futures. *Harvard Educational Review, 66*(1), 60–92.

Choi, J. (2009). Asian English language learners' identity construction in an after school literacy site. *Journal of Asian Pacific Communication, 19*(1), 130–161.

Duff, P. (2007). Second language socialization as sociocultural theory: Insights and issues. *Language Teaching, 40*(4), 309–319.

Gaffney, K. S. (1999). Is immersion education appropriate for all students? *University of Minnesota.* Retrieved from http://www.carla.umn.edu/immersion/acie/vol2/Bridge2.2.pdf

Garcia, E. E., Jensen, B. T., & Scribner, K. P. (2009). The demographic imperative. *Educational Leadership, 66*(7), 8–13.

Harklau, L. (2000). From the "good kids" to the "worst": Representations of English language learners across educational settings. *TESOL Quarterly, 34*(1), 35–67.

Harvard Institute on Politics. (2011). *IOP youth polling: Spring 2011 survey.* Cambridge: Harvard University Kennedy School of Government.

Heller, M. (1987). The role of language in the formation of ethnic identity. In J. Phinney & M. Rotheram (Eds.), *Children's ethnic socialization* (pp. 180–200). Newbury Park, CA: Sage.

Kanno, Y., & Grosik, S. A. (2012). Immigrant English learners' transitions to university: Student challenges and institutional policies. In Y. Kanno & L. Harklau (Eds.), *Linguistic minority students go to college: Preparation, access, and persistence* (pp. 130–147). New York, NY: Routledge.

Kress, G. (2003). *Literacy in the new media age.* New York, NY: Routledge.

Lantolf, J. P., & Thorne, S. L. (2006). *Sociocultural theory and the genesis of second language development.* New York, NY: Oxford University Press.

Linton, A. (2004). A critical mass model of bilingualism among US-born Hispanics. *Social Forces, 83*(1), 279–314.

Matsuda, P. K. (2006). The myth of linguistic homogeneity in U.S. college composition. *College English, 68*(6), 637–651.

Nadkarni, A., & Hofmann, S. (2012). Why do people use Facebook? *Personality and Individual Differences, 52*, 243–249.

National Clearinghouse for English Language Acquisition. (2002). *Frequently asked questions: Ask NCELA No. 14.* Retrieved from http://www.ncela.gwu.edu/expert/faq/14shortage.htm

National Education Association (NEA). (2008). *English language learners face unique challenges*. Washington, DC: NEA Policy and Practice Department, NEA Human and Civil Rights Department, and Center for Great Public Schools. Retrieved from http://www.nea.org/assets/docs/HE/ELL_Policy_Brief_Fall_08_(2).pdf

Nie, J., & Sundar, S. S. (2013). Who would pay for Facebook? Self esteem as a predictor of user behavior, identity construction and valuation of virtual possessions. In P. Kotzé et al. (Eds.), *Proceedings of INTERACT 2013*, Part III, LNCS 8119, 726–743.

Ortmeier-Hooper, C. (2008). English may be my second language, but I'm not 'ESL.' *College Composition and Communication, 59*(3), 389–419.

Peirce, B. N. (1995). Social identity, investment, and language learning. *TESOL Quarterly, 29*(1), 9–31.

Rosenblatt, L. M. (1938). *Literature as exploration*. New York, NY: Appleton-Century, Inc.

Rosenblatt, L. M. (2004). The transactional theory of reading and writing. In R. B. Ruddell & N. J. Unrau (Eds.), *Theoretical models and processes of reading* (5th ed., pp. 1363–1398). Newark, DE: International Reading Association.

Sheridan, M. P., & Rowsell, J. (2010). *Design literacies: Learning and innovation in the digital age*. London: Routledge.

Skinner, E. N., & Hagood, M. C. (2008). Developing literate identities with English language learners through digital storytelling. *The Reading Matrix: An International Online Journal, 8*(2), 12–38.

Snyder, J., Carpenter, D., & Slauson, G. J. (2006). Myspace.com: A social networking site and social contract theory. *Proceedings of ISECON 2006*. http://isedj.org/isecon/2006/3333/ISECON.2006.Snyder.pdf

Street, B. (1997). The implications of the "New Literacy Studies" for literacy education. *English in Education, 31*(3), 45–59.

The New London Group. (1996). A pedagogy of multiliteracies: Designing social futures. *Harvard Educational Review, 66*, 60–92.

U.S. Census Bureau. (2012, August 6). *An older and more diverse nation by midcentury*. Retrieved August 15, 2013, from http://www.census.gov/newsroom/releases/archives/facts_for_features_special_editions/cb12-ff19.html

Vincent, J. (2006). Children writing: Multimodality and assessment in the writing classroom. *Literacy, 40*, 51–57.

Walqui, A. (2000). *Access and engagement: Program design and instructional approaches for immigrant students in secondary schools*. McHenry, IL: Delta Systems for the Center of Applied Linguistics.

Williams, B. T. (2008). Tomorrow will not be like today: Literacy and identity in a world of multiliteracies. *Journal of Adolescent & Adult Literacy, 51*, 682–686.

Wolf, M. K., Herman, J. L., & Dietel, R. (2010). Improving the validity of English language learner accountability systems. (*CRESST Policy Brief 10*). National Center for Research on Evaluation, Standards, and Student Testing.

Yoon, B. (2008). Uninvited guests: The influence of teachers' roles and pedagogies on the positioning of English language learners in the regular classroom. *American Educational Research Journal, 45*(2), 495–522.

Zhang, S., Jiang, H., & Carroll, J. M. (2010). Social identity in Facebook community life. *International Journal of Virtual Communities and Social Networking, 2*(4), 66–78.

Zhao, S., Grasmuck, S., & Martin, J. (2008). Identity construction on Facebook: Digital empowerment in anchored relationships. *Computer in Human Behavior, 24*, 1816–1836.

CHAPTER 36

Fresh Prince in a Different World

Brian W. Collier Jr.

Day after Day, channel after channel, cable networks and satellite companies provide hours upon hours of "classic" television shows that are now in syndication. Depending on the network and the cultural context, one has the privilege to ingest hours of classic "black" sitcoms. Although these sitcoms and stations are an anomaly, the images provide a very clear insight into African American culture. These sitcoms are territories where multiple worldviews, stereotypes, and identities have been developed and perpetuated. Candidly speaking, one day while indulging in a sitcom, the researcher in me began to question the intent and the impact of "Black" television. Within this Huey Freeman like moment, I realized that content and the context inextricably go hand in hand. The social reproduction of certain norms and the normalization of hegemonic and oppressive standards was evident but it also subversively challenged the status quo associated with minorities attain higher levels of education. The same can be explicitly recognized and attributed to the educative process and Historically Black Colleges and Universities.

In this essay, the syndicated television shows *The Fresh Prince of Bel-Air* and *A Different World* serve two specific points of reference. These two references were specifically chosen because they explicitly engage spaces that higher education was designed to impact. Inherently education is supposed to promote traditional American ideals. Ideal that are suppose to lead one to success and affluence. The Fresh Prince of Bel-Air is an amalgam of several "American" tropes and ideologies. On the one hand, The Fresh Prince of Bel-Air tells a narrative of the journey of an African American male going through the rigors of growing up in an affluent environment. The "rags to riches" narratives as well as the "bootstraps" narrative are those that many conforming to the norms can of society. One could liken this experience as to an African American male going through college. Navigating black maleness is not an experience that is not novel but it has and continues to be very complex and perplexing. Within the context of The Fresh Prince, the protagonist is forced (prompted by his mother) to leave an environment he is comfortable (understands the nuances of his urban culture) in order to engage in one that fundamentally shifts his previous paradigms. That is not to suggest that his previous "mindsets" were deficient but the exposure and experiences he was privy too changed the way he would now "read" the world. I posit that this transition can be more complicated for males of color because statistically males of color (specifically black males) are still significantly outnumbered by their female counterparts. On the other hand, when examining the sitcom *A Different World*, one must openly recognize that the media texts (particularly those in this analysis) provided American society with an alternative view or counter-narrative of the African American family and community. One specific community that serves as a central theme within this analysis is the Historically Black Colleges and University. These distinguished institutions have historically serviced African Americans and other marginalized groups of people that were incapable of attending predominately white institutions. Within the current context of education, these institutions have been criticized for holding on to "separatist" ideologies and lacking racial diversity. They have also been maligned for not being high academic achieving institutions of higher education. This argument is rhetorically weak and the original intent of these institutions still has merit. The statistics (which social conservative seem to prefer) reflect the number of professionals and terminal degree holding HBCU alumni would clearly have a differing viewpoint.

Throughout this essay, the theoretical framework most suitable and representative within the two televisions shows story lines, images, and narratives are Cultural Studies and Critical Race Theory. Admittedly, many of the themes are similar to my own minus some of the cultural and socioeconomic privileges. This seemingly close relationship identified in both media texts clearly demonstrates the connectivity associated with some of the lived experiences at an HBCU and a PWI. For the purposes of this discussion, the development of this essay's argument way cultivated through the lens of Cultural Studies and Critical Race Theory perspective. A cultural studies framework provides a method of analysis that will help to explain how these two programs/texts have affected "culture" within the HBCU experience and how African American males navigate higher education learning spaces. The usage of Critical Race Theory was utilized because it lends well to telling and affirming counter-narratives. Hip-Hop and Black masculinity can most readily be discussed within this discourse because it the main characters in each ascribe to being groomed and shaped by hip hop culture. Subsequently, this analysis takes into consideration the linguistic limitations of traditional academic research and ways in which "knowledge" has been traditionally conceptualized and created. Both of the television series serve as prime examples of how CRT can expand the narratives surrounding HBCUs and African American Males. Moreover, both theoretical contexts help situate HBCU's and their divergent culture in a space where their analysis and critique is not contextually based on the personifications and experiences of predominately white institutions. These particular institutions must be respected for the original purposes because in many instances the validity of these spaces can be understood and affirmed by statistical data.

In the latter sections of the essay, the conversations surrounding the role of popular culture and the effects it has on society and the educative process will further overlap the discussion of HBCU. After analysis there is an understanding that the media representation of people of color in higher education and the lack there of in current media, does have an effect on the way education is viewed by the masses and in particular marginalized groups of people. Moreover, those specific images have the potential to subconsciously tell society who is worthy of quality education or receiving higher education degrees. There is an age old saying, "you are what you eat". If society continues to consume images of minorities that do not honestly and consistently depict an array of lived experiences, one being minorities successfully traversing higher education, they will continue to thoroughly believe that people of color in college only get their degrees from PWI or online institutions.

Furthermore, this essay uses Hip Hop/R&B lyrics from both theme songs throughout this analysis to gird and give a voice to both African American males and often criticized HBCUs. This is specifically don't because lyrics have been the voice of a culture for decades and there should be some recognition within academic discourses that shows how "knowledge" outside of academia and normalized understanding of curriculum can in fact be birth from the lived experiences of those who were "othered" during formal education or have not pursued higher education.

The two highly recognizable shows were and still can be influential depending on how they are "read" and contextualized. Ultimately, the premise of the two shows can give insight if used as a reflective tool. Because both shows were predicated on adolescent youths navigating life and being transformed by their experiences, the shows, particularly for minorities, provide a substantive reference point and connectivity to their own experiences inside and out of their HBCU experience. It is with these experiences that HBCU's can use to counter the narrative that they are antiquated. One would hope that the narratives provided by the producers of *A Different World* ultimately sought to portray included images that were not only critical and substantive but also provides a counter-narrative that substantiates the statistical data that shows their effectiveness and the importance to the communities they serve.

"No Brotha' Left Behind"

There is a substantial amount of rhetoric in the discourse of educational studies and who actually benefits from the process of education in America. Yet, much of educational research is centered on students that have been historically marginalized or considered special needs. In so many ways, it is subconsciously stated that they are the problems with the education system. Getting past political correctness, it can be asserted that because of race, class, and poverty, the students that fit under these signifiers and are adversely affected by these social constructs are often relegated to a label within education that suggests they are cognitively deficient and incapable achieving what society has superficially suggested is the most valuable entity on earth, an education. When examining this discourse specifically from an African American males context, it can be posited that the discourse of education is one that often seems unattainable and often times not worth the struggle. The value of education does not only seem implausible but a sheer waste of time when considering what one must endure pre and post education attainment.

When discussing the issues of gender, black maleness, and the stigma that surrounds these constructs, this can be easily recognized in *The Fresh Prince of Bel-Air*. Due the fact that the show was based on a young man coming from the "urban jungle" of Philadelphia to the "cultured" subdivision of Bel-Air, California, this is readily recognizable. This struggle was not always as apparent or as easily seen in the show *A Different world*. Albeit this was an underlying issues, the expectation in this show is that if one of the "Huxtable"[1] children could attend college, there must be "others" out there like the "Huxtable's" that sent their children to historically black institutions. From a gender identity standpoint, much of the same issues that were seen in the Fresh Prince of Bel-Air can be said for many of the African Americans males in the Television show A Different World. The major difference in the images depicted in *A Different World*, were that those black males came from urban setting now and were immediately immersed in an education environment where they immediately were able to dispel the myths that society had constructed about black males. Although the shows eventually chose to examine the experiences of an HBCU, its original conceptualization based on following one of the "Huxtables" through college. It was not until the second season that the shows content became more reflective of students of color that came from urban environment. The very discussion of race and social class issues were prevalent in both television shows. The creators and writers of those programs had a few things right when it came to opening the discussion of race, class, and other social constructs. This was evident in the experiences in both student at "Hillman College" and at Bel-Air Academy. The question that must continually be asked within academic research and examined within media today, be it literary or visual, why do our media outlets fail to analyze these issues critically. In addition, considering how critical Dr. Cosby has been of the black community and its generational issues (current legal issues aside),[2] I find it very prophetic in some way that the main cast he put forth over 20 years ago on *A Different World* accurately depicts the gender disparities between African American males and females at HBCU.

Even though there is still a negative stigma that is aligned to attending HBCUs, they still produce the highest amount of undergraduate students of color that continue on to achieve professional and terminal degrees. considering HBCU's do cater to marginalized populations that lack fiscal resources and a certain level of "social capital," it becomes important actively interrogate the negative perceptions that continue to permeate higher education and provide narratives that laud the successes and cultural attributes are rarely discussed. It is paramount that the discussion surrounding African American males and the institutions that help to uplift so many from destitute circumstances allow for both criticism and praise. Inherently, I believe that both contribute to growth and progress in the person and the institutions. Criticism and praise must coexist in order for these institutions to provide the services they have for the past one hundred and seventy-seven years.

Navigating and Understanding a World so Different than the Norm

Academic research discussing the importance and reputation of historically Black colleges can be found several popular media outlets. Most of the research on HBCU's discusses their impact and relevance in a multicultural world that is now heavily promoting diversity and social justice. Although this could be a critique of A different world it is not the focal point of this essay. It must be emphasized that the show "A Different World" was not the only media representation of HBCU's. The creator of the show, Bill Cosby heavily promoted HBCU institutions as he wore sweatshirts of many of the private Black Colleges on his television show. This was a frequent occurrence long before the shows initial airing. Those schools included but were not confined to Spelman College, Hampton University, and Clark Atlanta to name a few. Another film that heavily advocated the HBCU was the Spike Lee Film School Daze. In films that are more recent movies like "Stomp the Yard" and "Drumline" can be labeled as films that attempted to shed light on the importance of HBCU's. "Concomitantly, there was a national rise in historically Black college and university enrollments" due to these films (Brown, 1999; Brown & Bartee, 2007). HBCUs are a unique set of institutions in higher education and each of them are very different from each other.

It is at this point that one must reiterate that historically Black colleges are held to a different standard than other institutions of Higher Education. It cannot be stated enough that their reputation is one that is a "complicated cross-section of culture and public opinion" (Brown, 2013, p. 9). They are not like Harvard in the movie "How High." Their reputation doesn't get tarnished nor are they stereotyped when films of that nature come out. Yet, HBCUs are viewed as institutions that have awesome bands and glorify Greek organization. As stated by Brown

> Reputation is a ubiquitous and amorphous amalgamation of facts and fiction, ambition and reality, ignorance and relationships, as well as social distance or proximal placement. It can be argued that reputation is an intangible instrument of defined constructs employed to promote or delimit power, prestige, or public perception. (p. 9)

These perceptions of HBCUs are damaging and create an image of black institutions that reflect an all-encompassing narrative. However, most research would assert that HBCU are not monolithic despite them servicing a specific population. They are "defined as institutions of higher education whose principal mission is the education of Black Americans" (Brown, 2013, p. 5). Besides the debate over relevancy, some scholars believe that HBCUs are an ever-present reminder of the institution of segregation. These institutions in essence shroud the progress that has been made in race relations. I personally believe this is a myth that needs to be dispelled. What seems to come to the forefront of every discussion surrounding HBCU are their performance levels and the lack their of in some instances. Considering the state in which the institution resides, they still could be facing unconstitutional funding practices. The example alone has the potential to fiscally cripple an institution of higher education where the cost of operating is increasing each year. These levels of performativity need to be contextualized discussed in a way that recognizes the financials and racist hurdles they still endure. Many "states as well the federal government have also placed a renewed focus on accountability, and HBCUs have been criticized for their performance on the metrics used to evaluate all higher education institutions" (Lee & Keys, 2013, p. 5). These statistics are often refuted by the student outcomes. It cannot be stated enough that graduates of HBCU are leaders in their communities and in their professions.

The Impact of Historically Black Colleges and Universities

For those on the outside of the HBCU experience, the educational relevance is unseen and rarely understood. It is unfortunate that every Higher education institution must have the same educational outcomes yet; historically they have never had the same resources or tools. It amazes me that "HBCUs have a national impact on the number of minorities who are ready to enter the workforce and contribute to the American economy," but they do not receive the respect or credit for operating for generation from a disadvantage.

Data would suggest that the narrative of HBCUs is incorrectly told. Moreover, the current narrative about HBCUs is one that needs to be countered at every opportunity. Historically Black universities are the premier agency of African American educational attainment (Allen, 1992; Brown, 1999, 2013; Brown & Freeman, 2004; Fleming, 1984; Freeman, 1998; Garibaldi, 1984; Merisotis and O'Brien, 1998; Thomas, 1981; Willie, Reed, & Garibaldi, 1991). According to Brown, the propensity to focus solely on the academic statistics is dangerous. The cultural experiences and the communal/social support are logical reasons as to why these institutions' value can be calculated. The history and traditions associated with growing up and matriculating through such an institution are just as important as the content taught inside of the classroom. It is the maintenance of these experiences allows HBCUs to continually produce scholars, leaders, and professionals of a high caliber (Brown & Davis, 2001).

HBCUs have historically been responsible for cultivating African American students and awarding college degrees to African Americans in the country (Allen, Epps, & Haniff, 1991; Garibaldi, 1984; Gurin & Epps, 1975; U.S. Department of Education, 1996). According to the National Center for Education Statistics (2004), although historically Black colleges represent only three percent of this country's higher education institutions, they graduate roughly 20% of African Americans who earn undergraduate degrees in this country. In 2011 alone, these institutions continued to produce 4,995 associate's degrees, 32,652 bachelor's degrees, 7,442 master's degrees, 483 doctoral degrees, and 1,717 professional (Lee & Keys, 2013, p. 16). Despite enrolling only 9% of African American undergraduate students, HBCUs produce 17% of all bachelor's degrees, 25% of bachelor's degrees in education, and 22% of bachelor's degrees in STEM fields to African American students. This means that HBCUs overproduce bachelor's degrees to African Americans nationally despite only operating in 19 states and the District of Columbia. HBCUs also award a significant percentage of undergraduate degrees in the sciences to African Americans. According to Clay Phillips (2013), less than 9% of African American college students attend HBCUs, yet these institutions produce a significant percentage of undergraduate degrees earned by African Americans.

This paper has already begun to examine the historical challenges, opportunities, and successful areas for HBCUs. The purpose of this analysis is to again provide a counter-narrative to the debate over HBCU relevancy. Secondly, this was specifically accomplished by using the media texts most popular in the era in which HBCU enrollment was at its highest and discuss why they are relevant especially for African American males. Specifically, this report will focus on the on the cultural intangibles provided by Historically Black Colleges and Universities. The paper was not written nor can one assume that it will remotely be the answers to all of the questions surrounding HBCUs. As any inquiry or analysis, this analysis is to create a dialogue that I believe Dr. Cosby began in the creation of *A Different World.* I will ask questions and seek to validate the experiences that do not show up on statistical data sheets.

The history, contributions, and cultural experiences and traditions of historically Black colleges and universities must be documented. The aforementioned sitcom successfully began that process.

Now, this is a story all about how;
My life got flipped-turned upside down;
And I liked to take a minute Just sit right there …

Listen to Me Theorize

As I sat in my living room watching the television show, I realized I was analyzing it through the aforementioned discourses. The two lenses, Critical Race Theory and Cultural studies, helped me to become "critical" in ways that I hadn't imagined and I began to notice things within written and visual text that I didn't before. Most of the images, sounds, and messages that observed were not as recognizable before reading and beginning to comprehend these two critical discourses. Implicit curriculum became a realization very quickly. In the case of the *A Different World* and *Fresh Prince of Bel-Air,* I noticed that Critical Race Theory was very noticeable. Race was an underlying theme in each. In Fresh Prince, it was rare almost unheard of that a black family lived in Bel-Air with a Butler. As for a different world, its main setting, the HBCU was the cornerstone for black intellectualism. Within CRT these few examples within the media text could be labeled under the concept of "story-telling" and "counter-storytelling". The concept of counter storytelling as defined by Solórzano and Yosso (2002), states that, counter storytelling "as a method of telling the stories of those people whose experience are not often told" (i.e., those on the margins of society) (p. 32). Providing a counter story should be looked at as a tool for exposing, analyzing, and challenging the majoritarian stories of racial privilege. Counter-stories do have the capacity to demystify the norm and challenge the dominant discourse on race. I would argue that both televisions shows could have easily incorporated many of the other concepts within the theory but attempting to explain them could potentially redirect the focus of the essay. From the context of cultural studies, the explanation and analysis of these television programs have admittedly affected "culture" and subsequently my research interests, education aspirations, and future societal contributions. The impact of media can't be underestimated or taken for granted.

Besides being a pop culture television show, I chose the *A Different World* as my main example because it was one of the first primetime T.V shows that examined and portrayed historically Black colleges from multiple contexts and experiences. The premise of this show was predicated on the college experience of underrepresented youth. These youth were from multiple socioeconomic and cultural backgrounds. Some of the characters were from wealthy families, while other were from urban single parent environments. Ultimately, the outcome of the show was for the characters to realize that the "world" they left (home) was not going to be the one they traversed (college experience). It should have also been understood that world they were privilege enough to enter (college) would render or produce a drastically different outlook on the world (home or community) they once knew so well. This was visible for every character. The paradigms they possessed were constantly shifted with each new experience. This was true for both males and females but in this paper, I focus on African American males. This is the rationale for including the show the *Fresh Prince of Bel-Air*. There is a concluding belief that the television show provides an accurate example of how African American males have to transition into experience that is higher education. Reflecting on the premise behind the show, one could easily suggest that the show typified the challenges a young man from "the hood" to one that was totally different from what was "normal" to him. Throughout the show, his subsequent transition into a "higher" class enabled him to many different things, which ultimately challenged his character ideologies, identity (identities) and his representations. Quietly kept, Will Smith's character successfully showed that someone from a different class and "culture" could adapt to the dominant culture, all while seemingly maintaining some sense of his own "identity." From a societal standpoint, Will Smith helped to present

Hip Hop culture, the African American family, and African American males could be viewed in a different light. When one examines Hip Hop for example, it can be recognized that the show provided a view of a specific culture and it was different than the images provided by mainstream society. It provided a view and perspective that allowed for the culture to positively embraced. It became a phenomena where someone or something may be different (dress, music or vernacular), but it doesn't equate to them (the culture) being deficient. Even though some people still viewed it (Hip Hop Culture) as one of society's problems, it also gave some demographics that were not typically targeted or marketed, a new outlook. Furthermore, by (re) presenting the African American family it provided a view that had not been previously viewed on television. Even though none of the family in the show attended an HBCU, it shows a career outcome and lifestyle that promoted education heavily. In addition, the family on The *Fresh Prince of Bel-Air* was nothing like that of the *Cosby Show* or *Good Times.* One reason one might want to take note of this notion is because it recognizes the attempt to address all of the images or stereotypes seen in society. Unlike the other shows mentioned, *The Cosby's* for example, was based on the Black Middle class and many of the images portrayed it. Some of the critiques of his show were that he failed thoroughly reflect the larger African American community. Some would suggest that this show was the "black" version of *Leave it to Beaver*. That is not to take away the cultural impact and counter narrative the show provided but one could question whose interests were being better served with the images projected. On the other hand, one could also suggest that shows like *Good Times* were for those who are/were in the same economic plight. *Good Times* as a show probably seemed more realistic than the *Cosby Show*. This is exactly why *A Different World* becomes so important. The narrative they sought to tell was one that was all encompassing. It was not solely about Greek life or academic opportunities. The show covers the gamut of experiences while attending these particular of a kind institution.

When once again incorporating the CRT, the reappearance of already said concepts became even more noticeable in the storyline of the two-television show used as a reference point. Both *A Different World* and *The Fresh Prince of Bel-Air* had to be the idea of "storytelling" and "Counter-storytelling." One must recognize that before even attempting to understand either of the concepts one must first understand that CRT explains life experiences very differently from many other discourses. "Critical Race theorist have built on everyday experiences with perspective, viewpoint, and the power of stories and persuasion to come to a better understanding of how Americans see race" (Delgado & Stefancic, 2001). Considering this fact alone, one must constantly reflect on and recognize that TV is a construction as well. Clearly, television programs in production must have the elements of a narrative. Ascertaining the counter-narrative is much more important that reiterating the same socially constructed narrative perpetuated by American culture.

In one instance, the narrative told is one about a wealthy African American family living in an upper class neighborhood. In so many instances, this in and of itself is a counter-story. It presents itself as such because their experiences within the environment had to be different from someone in the dominant group. Being Black in Bel-Air while going to a private school while both parents have had very successful careers was a very narrative and image. In an era that now boasts an African American president, this phenomena seems to be the norm but in the early 1990s, this was rare and far from the norm. If one goes back to when *A Different World* began airing, this notion was even more absurd. A counter-story within *A Different world* could have easily been the character Dwayne Wayne. Here you had an African American male from Brooklyn New York, who introduced himself by stating his "perfect SAT" math score and ultimate goal was to be an engineer. Scholar Mark Anthony Neal might call this an "Illegible masculinity." I would consider this to be counter and illegible simply because those are rare images and personifications for African American males. This character's "representation" was one that definitely sought to (re) present his cultural background. Some of the non-verbal images he provided (i.e. looking and dressing what would constitute a nerd), and messages (language and verbal articulation) were all a part of the "counter-story." Logically speaking, one can deduce that this was the rationale for creating such a character, He provided an alternative view of Black maleness in education and constitutes as an attempt to (re) write the narrative on black males and the differences existing in the cultural experiences at an HBCU.

When using the *Fresh Prince of Bel-Air* as an example, one can easily suggest that the family is the quintessential counter narrative. The rationale for labeling the family as the counter-story is in essence directly correlated to of the way they were (re) presented in the televisions show. The family had taken on all of the stereotypical qualities a bourgeois family from Bel-Air California may possess yet they still in very distinct ways possessed the "identity" of African Americans. Although the children within the sitcoms cultural identity were more stereotypical of those who were raised in a privilege living environment, the show constantly returned to this theme of humble beginnings and the main characters, Will Smith was typically at the center of those circumstances. In so many words, their identity was not just their race. It was also how they identified with their past life and experiences. At the same time, it cannot be ignored that they also adopted some practices that would most often be associated with the dominant groups. Yet and still, it was not until a kid from a different background and social status, did some of their behaviors and attitudes change or questioned. Will Smith's character is a walking "counter-story" yet his character could have been consider a "legible masculinity" or a masculinity that is recognizable and accepted by main stream society. This was obvious in so many ways. Everything from his clothes, to the way he spoke was different from his new environment. Once again repositioning this discussion towards Hillman College and the show *A Different World*, one can posit that the HBCUs represent a sort of "legible" institutionalized education. It can and has been asserted that these institutions are failing to confront the changing climate of higher education institutions. One question that must be asked in the process of labeling HBCU has to be are these institutions in their current state truly failing? Depending on the context, some may agree but a reassessment of the institution intangibles must be weighed in conjunction to the academic and statistical outcomes of these institutions.

In closing, the notion of counter-storytelling is the essence of these two sitcoms. Both shows begin with music that has historically been associated with African Americans. These art forms, especially Hip Hop, were deemed counter to the norm. The lyrics in each song told a narrative that spoke of challenges and successes. The lyrics throughout both songs could be recognized as a story that spoke of departure and arrival into a new environment. The original intent within either example was to give a voice to institutions and circumstances that brought a certain amount of social awareness to a group of people that were historically marginalized. For these artist, they used their stories as an outlet for those who were unrepresented. Delgado and Stefancic stated, "powerfully written stories and narratives that may begin a process of adjustment in our system of beliefs and categories by calling attention to neglected evidence and reminding readers of our common humanity" (Delgado & Stefancic, 2001, p. 43). In this paper, the aspects of "Counter-Storytelling" shed light on the connections between the two shows. Moreover, repositions HBCUs so that it reflects their rich history and varying experiences in the American cultures. Those experiences cannot be erased or ignored because they are ultimately what shaped these institutions so that they are capable of producing productive alumni and professionals.

HBCU (Re) presentation through the Lens of Cultural Studies

In the process of reflecting on this two television classics, immediately returning to the lyrics of the theme songs are is important. Both songs immediately returned the conversation to an article by Paul Du Gay and Stuart Hall. The article *Doing Cultural Studies The study of the Sony Walkman* helps to understand the cultural impact of both shows. This article substantiates how Hip Hop and the television programs are valid avenues for analysis. This particular perspective allows for the examination of many facets within both HBCU and Hip Hop culture. Du Gay and Hall call these five essential pieces of culture, "The Circuit of Culture." "Representation" and "Identity" are the two concepts that I intend to focus on with the Circuit of culture but they provide three other concepts. Those concepts are production, consumption, and regulation. Each facet of the "circuit of culture" has a connection and "each part of the circuit is taken up and reappears in the next part" (p. 4). In this conversation, the recognition that or representation is vital. The representations of these two sitcoms have impacted several generations of students. In the case of this analysis, the people and institution in question were African American Males and HBCUs. The questions that constantly arose had to be what are the social implications stemming from some of these representations? Who is regulating the culture and narrative of HBCUs? Has this "subculture" substantiated the way HBCU Alumni identify themselves? Each of these questions gets at the issue of representation and identity.

The concept of "Representation" is like most things, reliant on language and interpretations. Representations connect meaning and language to culture. So when looking at culture, presumably any culture, one can say that culture itself, along with the representations stemming from it, are about "shared meanings." "Language is the privileged medium in which we make sense of things, in which meaning is produced and exchanged" (Hall, 1997). To use Hip Hop as an example, one can say this art form comes in the format of musical lyrics or spoken word. As stated earlier, within the CRT discourse, it looks like a counter-narrative. Within the discourse of cultural studies, this is dictated by language. Depending on the narrative and the language used when discussing HBCU's, the subsequent representation can be one that is accurately reflective of these honorable institutions. Hall might validates my thoughts when he suggests that,

> Language is able to do this because it operates on a *representational system.* In language, we use signs and symbols—whether they are sounds, written words, electronically produced images, musical notes, even objects to stand for or represent to other people our concepts, ideas, and feelings. (Hall, 1997)

When rearticulating this in the contexts of these two television programs, this becomes easily recognizable because its central themes are those that are reliant on visual cues and verbal language.

An immediate question I had to ask myself was, how did this media source approach addressing "representation"? According to cultural studies there are several ways but the three major ways in addressing representation are "the reflective," "the intentional" and "the constructionist" (Hall, 1997). In the Fresh Prince of Bel-Air it seems that all three approaches were used. At the same time, it seems that most T.V. programs do. One caveat when examining cultural studies within this context is the fact if representations are indeed "constructed, themselves", aren't they ultimately meant to be "intentional?" So if one looks at the way masculinity is constructed in these two shows, the way each character was constructed, it would suggest that they were constructed in that way for a reason. From a constructionist perspective, one could suggest that most representations or images are constructed through some form of language. Moreover, this assertion "recognizes the public, social character of language" (Hall, 1997). With that being said, there are a multitude of representations within the episodes of both sitcoms that one could suggest are constructed through language. In the context of *The Fresh Prince of Bel–Air*, the realization that Will Smith's character is constructed and in some instances embellishes certain behaviors and stereotypes associated with Hip Hop, sexual orientation and "whiteness". The same could be said for the characters on *A Different World.* Their example could be extended to define or (re) presenting what it meant to be a Black intellectual, a member of the talented tenth or what it meant to be a "true" gentleman or lady. In many instances, there can be an argument that these representations were to tell a specific story or simply come off as funny. One subsequent outcome, be it intentional or unintentional, it brought attention to some of the pressing issues of that day. Some of those issues included but were not limited to apartheid, racism, the Rodney king trial and the riots that followed. More importantly, in light of the representations, both shows innately challenged some of the ideologies embraced by the American culture. For example, on October 15, 1990, there was an episode where two characters were pulled over for "DWB,"[3] and this immediately became a source of contention and debate. As a young person experiencing this episode live, I can now recall this episode very vividly because my father made a huge deal out of it. This occurrence and the episode aired in 1990, even before the Rodney King incident. *A Different World* would follow up the next year by explicitly discussing the Rodney king case and setting their episode in the middle of the 1992 LA Riots. For many European Americans, these instances have not been the norm or an issue but for African Americans, even those with social and economic success, they still face the fear of being pulled over, abused and discriminated against daily. These were vivid representations of what it means to be black. These were realizations that even for college educated and HBCU graduates that they to still must endure the rigors of the world. These were images of a college life that promoted advocacy and action towards changing the paradigms of race. These were episode where an understanding of maleness and the importance of the HBCU experience are vital. Yet one must ask, what has changed? What is most appalling is that since the airing of these episodes, the political climate of this country has changed but in regards to race relations, one can debate that they have broken down and the legal system has been justifying the murder of African American males. The media is presenting these current representations.

The aforementioned episodes serve only as example to the power of representation. I'm sure the episodes were enlightening for a lot of people. Even to this day, I encounter people outside of my "culture" that do not know or understand this "cultural" language. Yet, this is where I believe lies the HBCUs greatest asset and attributes.

I know my parents love me,
Stand behind me come what may.
I know now that I'm ready,
Because I finally heard them say
It's a different world from where you come from …

Validating the HBCU and African Male Identity

Like the representation section, one must acknowledge that "identity" is socially constructed. When I look at through a cultural studies denotation, I find that "identity", is constructed on the recognition of shared characteristics with another person or group, or with the natural closure of solidarity and allegiance. One can interpret this to mean that identity is constructed with some form of consensus.

For example, when first thinking about an HBCU, one immediately can assert or assume that they are strictly about Bands and Black Greek Letter organizations. These are constructed identities. Yet, historically when examining the culture of HBCUs, this was not the only positive attribute. In the past, they were institutions that produced leading scholars and scientists. They are the institutions that birthed Dr. Martin Luther King Jr., Leontyne Price and W. E. B. DuBois. The identity of these older institutions is inevitably, what gave birth to the "Band" and Greek Letter Organizations but they are rarely examined that way. In this sense, I can agree with how Hall begins to view the construction of identity. From the perspective of the institution, the identities of HBCU have constantly changed despite what some scholar believe. Moreover, his words substantiate the important fact that HBCUs are not monolithic. Each of them is different and should be treated as such. Much of the same should be said of African American males, for they too are not a monolithic construct.

When returning this conversation to the CRT discourse, one might say that it to discusses race in a way that those within the Cultural Studies discourse could relate. One can't deny that there is a clear goal within CRT to challenge the status quo.

> Critical Race theory contains an activist dimensions. It not only tries to understand our social situation, but to change; it sets out not only to ascertain how society organizes itself along racial lines and hierarchies, but to transform it for the better. (Delgado & Stefancic, 2001)

This is also true for cultural studies. "Most work in cultural studies is concerned with investigating and challenging the construction of subaltern, marginalized or dominated identities, although some recent work has begun to explore dominant identities as social constructions" (Hall & Du Guy, 1996). Besides some nuances in the language used it can easily be suggested that the goals within each discourse are similar.

I came to the conclusion that the *Fresh Prince of Bel-Air* in many instances helped to shape the perceptions and identities of a lot of young people. The same can be said for *A Different World* and the images they portrayed. Despite the times they fed into the dominant narrative about maleness and HBCUs, they did give some credence to their potential despite being negatively stigmatized within culture. Hall (1996) said it best,

> identities are about questions of using the resources of history, language, and culture in the process of becoming rather than being: not who we are or where we came from, so much as what we might become, how we have been represented, and how that bears on how we might represent ourselves.

This statement is very plausible when looking at these two texts. One can come to the conclusion that identity is dependent on varying social factors. That would suggest the identity of African American males and HBCU is contingent upon how much they are invested in. Moreover, it supports the idea that no one identity is the same and trying to structure an institution after such a model is detrimental to its success. Therefore the ultimate restructuring of the HBCU identity is reliant not only on people that control the production, consumption and regulation of identity but also those consciously choose stereotype and marginalize these institutions.

I Looked at my kingdom
I was Finally there
To sit on My throne as the prince of Bel-Air

Conclusion: We Must Love Our Past

When examining everything through the context of popular culture, I can't help but admit that almost every word or thought written was initially and in some ways continuously viewed and understood through a socially constructed lens. I openly suggest that "popular culture" is defined in so many ways that it can easily conjoined with Critical Race Theory and Cultural Studies. It very nature has historically been contrary to the norm, which in it case was adult. In *Cultural Theory and Popular Culture*, John Storey goes through several definitions. He first defines popular culture in a specific way as to suggest that popular culture is simply culture which is widely favored and well-liked by many people (Storey, 2006). I don't suggest that that denotation is very critical but it does get to its rudimentary denotation. Some might suggest that the definition oversimplifies popular culture. A professor once told me, "Making things simple makes it simplistic." Popular Culture, CRT, and Cultural Studies are anything but simple. The underlying issues within the media and HBCU are messy. The stereotypes and concerns for African American males are a reality. None of which can be constituted simple. With all sincerity, this is a definition that I would expect the majority of society use. In reality, this is probably what most people constitute as popular culture. As I worked through explaining the different context within both media text, I concluded that popular culture is much closer to John Storiey's latter definition of popular culture. He "contends that popular culture is the culture which originates from 'the people'. It takes issue with any approach which suggest that it is something imposed on the 'the people' from above" (Storey, 2006). This denotation resonate more with these two text and themes because it suggest one, a system of hegemony and two a culture willing to resist and dispel the myths that exists. According to Bennett, "The field of popular culture is structured by the attempt of the ruling class to win hegemony and by forms of opposition to this endeavor" (Storey, 2006). In other words, it systematically sets up oppositional binaries that would always be in some form of conflict. The concept of hegemony successfully produces and allows discursive practices to continue in order to maintain some notion of "power." I contest that that these discourses, Critical Race Theory and Cultural Studies, seek to challenge these dynamics. Popular culture in some ways can operate the same way these other two discourses do.

> Popular culture is a site where the construction of everyday life may be examined. The point of doing this is not only academic—that is, an attempt to understand a process or practice—it is also political, to examine the power relations that constitute this form of everyday life and thus reveal the configurations of interests its construction serves. (2006)

A more in-depth examination of the lyrics and episodic instances inserted through this paper would easily conjure up a number of personal experience and counter narrative stories that would easily validate the idea that popular culture is a social construction. There is countless research that has sought to understand many of these same issues. This again has not been the explicit goal of this analysis. The intentions of this paper were to provide an alternative look at HBCU and African American males that may have not been visible before. My desire was to not elaborate heavily on the statistics around HBCUs or black male involvement/enrollment in these institutions but to examine two diametrically different narratives that hold alternative truths and realities. CRT may label this same idea, "Multiple consciousness." If that is the case, then a new level of consciousness needs to be reached when interrogating these two constructs. American culture needs to embrace these two entities and respect them for their complexities and their contributions.

Notes

1. Huxtable denotes the last name of one of the original main characters in the Television sitcom "A Different World." This character was directly connected to the Cosby Show, which was already in production and also created by Bill Cosby. Denise Huxtable was the daughter of Heathcliff and Claire Huxtable. One could assert that being a "Huxtable" on television was comparable to being one of the Brady Bunch family of the 1970's or the Cleaver family of the 1950's. In so many words, the Huxtable's constituted the typical American family.
2. This essay was written prior to Dr. Cosby's legal matters and the heteronormative behaviors associated with sexual assault and his particular case. While there is a need for further discussion, this essay does not explore those matters.
3. DWB—Driving While Black

Work Cited

Allen, W. R. (1992). The color of success: African American college student outcomes at predominately White and historically Black college and universities. *Harvard Educational Review, 62,* 26–44.

Allen, W. R., Epps, E., & Haniff, N. Z. (Eds.). (1991). College in Black and White: African American students in predominately White and in historically Black public universities. Albany, NY: State University of New York Press.

Allen, W. R., & Jewell, J. O. (2002). A backward glance forward: Past, present, and future perspectives on historically black colleges and universities. *Review of Higher Education, 25*(3), 241–261.

Bartee, R. D., & Brown, M. C. (2007). *School matters: Why African American students need multiple forms of capital.* New York, NY: Peter Lang.

Brown, M. C. (1995). In defense of the public historically Black college and its mission. *The National Honors Report, 16,* 34–40.

Brown, M. C. (1999). *The quest to define collegiate desegregation.* Westport, CT: Bergin and Garvey.

Brown, M. C., & Bartee, R. D. (2007). *Still not equal: Expanding educational opportunity in society.* New York, NY: Peter Lang.

Brown, M. C, & Davis, J. E. (2001). The historically Black college as social contract, social capital, and social equalizer. *Peabody Journal of Education, 76,* 31–49.

Brown, M. C., & Freeman, K. (Eds.). (2002). Research on historically Black colleges. *The Review of Higher Education, 25,* 237–368.

Brown, M. C., & Hendrickson, R. M. (1997). Public historically Black colleges at the crossroads: United States v. Fordice and higher education desegregation. *Journal for a Just and Caring Education, 3,* 95–113.

Brown, M. C., Ricard, R. B., & Donahoo, S. (2004). The changing role of historically Black colleges and universities: Vistas on dual missions, desegregation, and diversity. In M. C. Brown & K. Freeman (Eds.), *Black colleges: New perspectives on policy and practice* (pp. 3–28). Westport, CT: Praeger.

Clay, P. L. (2013). *Historically black colleges and universities facing the future: A fresh look at challenges and opportunities*. Cambridge, MA: Massachusetts Institute of Technology.
Delgado, R., & Stefancic, J. (2001). Critical race theory: An introduction.New York: New York University Press.
National Center for Education Statistics. (2004). *Historically Black colleges and universities, 1976 to 2001 (NCES 2004-062)*. Washington, DC: U.S. Department of Education.
Solórzano, D. G., & Yosso, T. J. (2002). Critical Race Methodology: Counterstorytelling as an Analytical Framework for Educational Research. Qualitative Inquiry, 8(1), 23–44.
Storey, J. (2006). Cultural theory and popular culture. A reader. University of Georgia Press.
Willie, C. V., Reed, W. L., & Garibaldi, A. M. (Eds.). (1991). *The education of African-Americans*. New York, NY: Auburn House.

Contributors

Hans F. Bader is a senior attorney at the Competitive Enterprise Institute in Washington, Columbia.

Glenn A. Bowen is the Director of the Center for Community Service Initiatives at Barry University. His scholarly work has focused on community-driven development, service-learning pedagogy, and the institutionalization of community engagement in higher education.

Remington Brown graduated from Integrative Community Studies at the University of North Carolina Greensboro in 2014. He is a passionate advocate for social justice who has been involved in numerous organizations and activities both in college and beyond that have provided him with a platform to challenge ableism, racism, sexism and other injustices. Remington also uses his music as a channel for his advocacy, as a member of his band Alternative States and as a co-founder of Efland United underground studio.

James H. Campbell is a native of Cincinnati, Ohio. He received his doctorate from Miami University. James has worked in the field of athletics for over 15 years. He has been employed at both the collegiate and professional levels. Dr. Campbell primarily researches black males at Division I institutions who participate in collegiate athletics.

Mary Cannito-Coville is a doctoral student and teaching assistant in Cultural Foundations of Education at Syracuse University where she concentrates in Sociology of Education. Her primary research interests focus on the school-to-prison pipeline trend, educational inequalities, and youth involvement in gangs. Mary also facilitates Intergroup Dialogue workshops for urban high school students in Syracuse, NY. Mary holds a Master of Arts in Spanish Language, Literature and Culture, and a Certificate of Advanced Study in Latin American Studies from Syracuse University. Prior to entering the doctoral program, Mary has worked as a Spanish teacher in a Central New York high school and was awarded a U.S. Fulbright Grant to teach English at the Universidad de Medellín, Colombia.

Nia I. Cantey is a former director of home based services with over ten years working in child welfare services. She is currently an associate professor in the Mid-Tennessee Collaborative-Masters of Social Work Program (MTC-MSW) at Tennessee State University (TSU). Dr. Cantey is Director of the Center for Aging: Research and Education Services (CARES) and is also a WRITE Associate at TSU. She has published peer-reviewed articles and book chapters on issues related to historically black colleges and universities, gender and sexuality studies, and social injustices.

Brian Collier currently serves as a lecturer in the Department of Teacher Education at Northern Kentucky University. Dr. Collier received his Doctor of Philosophy degree in Educational Administration from Miami University of Ohio.

Kelly Concannon is Assistant Professor of Writing at Nova Southeastern University in Ft. Lauderdale Florida. Dr. Concannon encourages global awareness and responsibility, which she situates as central to various literacy practices. She has published work in journals such as the *Journal of the Assembly for Expanded Perspectives on Learning, The Journal of Feminist Scholarship, Academic Exchange Quarterly, the Journal of Advanced Composition, Enculturation, and College Literature.* She participates in various community activist projects and alliances including the South Florida Diversity Alliance, and serves as a Mentor for the Women of Tomorrow Program in Ft Lauderdale, FL. She also serves as a mentor for the *Undergraduate Journal of Service Learning and Community-Based Research.*

Jewell E. Cooper is currently Associate Dean of Academic Affairs and Student Success and an Associate Professor in the Department of Teacher Education and Higher Education at the University of North Carolina-Greensboro, NC. Dr. Cooper's research areas include multicultural education, particularly community-based learning and culturally responsive teaching, secondary school reform, and teacher development. She has published several journal articles in national and international journals such as *Journal of Teacher Education, Teacher Education Quarterly, The New Educator*, and *Issues in Teacher Education.* She has also published book chapters in such publications as *Leadership and Building Professional Communities, Home, School, and Community Collaboration: Supportive Family Involvement Practices*, and *Race, Ethnicity, and Education: The Influence of Racial and Ethnic Identity on Teaching and Learning.* She is co-author of *Developing Critical Cultural Competence: A Guide for 21st Century Educators*, a Corwin Press publication. Dr. Cooper has taught college and university courses in multicultural education and secondary school education. For the past 15 years, her students have participated in community-based learning projects where they explore the educational experiences of their students within their learners' home/community environments. She has also conducted professional development related to diverse learners, culturally responsive teaching, and inclusive practices for both public and private schools.

Joseph N. Cooper joined the Sport Management program at the University of Connecticut in August 2013. Prior to joining the faculty at UConn, Dr. Cooper served as an instructor and graduate teaching assistant at the University of Georgia while completing his doctorate. Dr. Cooper's research agenda focuses on the nexus between sport, education, race, and culture with an emphasis on sport as a catalyst for holistic development and positive changes in society. He is a member of the North American Society for the Sociology of Sport (NASSS), North American Society for Sport Management (NASSM), and the American Educational Research Association (AERA). Dr. Cooper is also the founder of Collective Uplift (CU), an organization designed to educate, empower, and inspire students across racial and ethnic backgrounds at UConn (and the world) to maximize their full potential as holistic individuals both within and beyond athletic contexts

Christopher Cumo is a native of Italy. He is the author of 6 books and numerous encyclopedias, articles, essays, reviews, and short stories, all in print. He has completed a seventh book forthcoming from Arcadia Publishing. He has written extensively about history, science, agriculture, and higher education.

Steven R. Cureton is currently an Associate Professor in the department of Sociology at The University of North Carolina-Greensboro. Research interests remain focused on African-Americans' life chances and life course outcomes relative to economics, justice processing, education, access to opportunities, gangs, street corner politics, norms and ethics governing lifestyle decisions, and the impact of family dynamics on behavioral outcomes. Essentially, his research concerns how the "race variable" impacts the American experience. His book *Black Vanguards and Black Gangsters: From Seeds of Discontent to a Declaration of War* was published in 2011. Another book *Hoover Crips: When Cripin' Becomes a Way of Life* was published in 2008. Dr. Cureton has published in the Journal of Black Masculinity, Journal of Gang Research, Journal of Black Studies, Journal of Criminal Justice, African-American Research Perspectives, and has published book chapters in Gangs in America III, The System in Black and White: Exploring the Connections between race, crime and justice, and a forthcoming chapter in Leadership,

Equity, and Social Justice in American Higher Education. Community service outreach was ignited by participating and graduating from Leadership Greensboro (class of 2013).Dr. Cureton has been a consultant on several capital murder cases involving gang members.

Andrea S. Dauber has lectured for the Department of Sociology at UC San Diego since fall 2012 and the Department of Sociology at University of San Diego since January 2014. She obtained her Doctor philosophiae in Sociology from Johannes Gutenberg University Mainz, Germany in 2010. As a forensic sociologist, she focuses on gender and crime, victimology, the criminal justice system and rehabilitation. She also takes an interest in historical sociology as well as labor markets and social inequality. She is currently evaluating a therapeutic community for the San Diego Sheriff's Department at Las Colinas Detention and Reentry Facility. As Managing Editor of the Sociology program at De Gruyter Open she is responsible for developing the profile of the program and oversees a team of associate and assistant editors.

Celeste Fraser Delgado is a professor of English and humanities in the School of Professional and Career Education at Barry University. She is the founder and director of Carnival Arts, an ongoing community-engaged arts project through which more than 100 artists and 400 college students have collaborated with more than 1000 youth living in crisis shelters across the state of Florida. She is also the founder of the La Paloma Neighborhood Initiative, a campus-community partnership promoting neighborhood health, prosperity, peace, and culture.

Susan Dennison is an Associate Professor in the Department of Social Work at the University of North Carolina at Greensboro. She is the National Consultant for K-12 Schools with expertise in regard to setting up groups for at risk students. She is the president of UNCG AAUP Chapter and was the co-chair of UNCG Equity, Diversity, & Inclusion Committee from 2008–2011.Susan has written numerous peer reviewed articles and books on faculty mentoring in higher education and groups with at risk children and adolescents.

Sarah J. Dhilla is a Doctoral Fellow in the Educational Leadership and Policy Studies program at Boston University's School of Education. Her broader research area is online learning at the postsecondary level, while her dissertation work focuses on expert faculty perceptions of the virtual teaching experience and online faculty development.

Tessly A. Diequez is the senior study abroad advisor at the University of Florida, where she facilitates international experiences for students interested in studying in Spain. She has developed a study abroad re-entry colloquium that includes content on the psychoemotional aspects of returning from study abroad and how to translate study abroad experiences into job skills. She also works closely with study abroad peer advising and publications, and re-entry programs. Tessly holds an MS in Higher Education from Florida State University.

Ty-Ron M. O. Douglas is an Assistant Professor in the Educational Leadership and Policy Analysis Department at the University of Missouri-Columbia. His research explores the intersections between identity, community/geopolitical space, and the socio-cultural foundations of leadership and education, with an emphasis on Black masculinity/families, spirituality, and community-based pedagogical spaces. Dr. Douglas was the recipient of the 2013 Distinguished Dissertation Award by the Critical Educators for Social Justice Special Interest Group of the American Educational Research Association (AERA) and the UNCG School of Education Early Career Alumni Award. His work has appeared in outlets such as *The Urban Review, Educational Studies, Teachers College Record, and Race, Ethnicity, and Education*. He is currently engaging in a study of Black male student-athletes after being awarded a 2015 NCAA Innovations in Research and Practice Grant.

John P. Elia is Professor of Health Education and Interim Associate Dean of the College of Health and Social Sciences at San Francisco State University, California, USA, where he has taught and served in administrative capacities for nearly three decades. He is Editor-in-Chief of the *Journal of Homosexuality*, a landmark, internationally acclaimed, peer reviewed scholarly journal in sexuality studies. He has published a number of scholarly articles, book chapters, and encyclopedia entries on sexuality education, in addition to co-editing a number of books in the areas of sexuality studies, lgbt studies, and queer studies. His most recent research has focused on bisexuality and schooling and school-based sexuality education.

Laura Finley is Associate Professor of Sociology and Criminology at Barry University in Miami Shores, Florida. She is the author, co-author, editor or co-editor of fourteen books as well as numerous journal articles and book chapters and a syndicated columnist with *PeaceVoice*. Additionally, Dr. Finley is co-editor (with Michael Minch) of the Cambridge Scholars book series *Peace Studies: Edges and Innovations* and editor of the ABC-CLIO series *Crime in Popular Culture*. Dr. Finley is also a community activist for peace, social justice and human rights. She serves on the Boards of several local, statewide and national organizations, is co-founder of the College Brides Walk, a dating and domestic violence awareness initiative, and co-founder of the South Florida Consortium for Restorative Justice.

C. P. Gause is Professor and Chair of the Department of Educational Leadership and Counseling at Southeast Missouri State University. He is a former public school teacher, principal, and district administrator. Gause received his PhD in Educational Leadership from Miami University, his Master of Educational Administration from The University of South Carolina-Columbia, his Master of Arts in Teaching-Elementary Education from The Columbia International University, his Bachelor of Science in Human Resource Management and Religious Studies from Trinity International University.

Dr. Gause is an internationally recognized award winning author, teacher, scholar and motivational speaker. He has published numerous books, articles, book chapters, and manuscripts with regards to educational leadership, equity, diversity, and inclusive education. His books, *Integration Matters* and *Keeping the Promise*, received the American Educational Studies Association 2007 and 2009 Critics' Choice Award. He is a prolific writer and poet.

His current book, *"Black Masculinity in America: Can I Get a Witness,"* brings together a collective who give witness to how black masculinity is (re)presented in hip-hop, film and social media. The works in this volume continue to question and interrogate our understanding of how black males are marginalized and disenfranchised in the American public sphere. In 2009, Gause received the National Faculty Mentor Role Model of the Year Award given by Minority Access Inc., a non-profit firm, with support from the U.S. Department of Health and Human Services. His award was inscribed "For Guiding, Mentoring and Leading Others." Dr. Gause believes in the transformational power of teaching and learning and is committed to creating engaging dynamic and equitable learning communities, for all, locally and globally.

Rebecca N. Gigi is a graduate student in the Communication Studies at San Francisco State University. Her research interests include queer theory and media representations of gender and trans identities.

Christopher Gregory is the Assistant Director for Residence Life at the University of North Carolina at Greensboro. He is a doctoral candidate in the Department of Teacher Education and Higher Education. Prior to coming to UNCG, Chris worked at West Virginia University in the Office of the Vice President for Student Affairs, primarily with issues involving athletics and student affairs. Chris earned his M.S. in Industrial Relations and B.A. in Political Science, both from WVU. Chris's interests lie in professional development, and recruitment and training of professional staff members.

Kathy L. Guthrie is an Associate Professor of Higher Education at Florida State University where she coordinates the Undergraduate Certificate in Leadership Studies. Guthrie focuses her research on undergraduate leadership education, civic engagement, and online teaching and learning. She has co-edited a New Directions in Student Services sourcebook titled "Developing Undergraduate Student Leadership Capacity" and recently co-authored "Cultivating Leader Identity and Capacity in Students from Diverse Backgrounds." Currently, Guthrie is the associate editor of the New Directions in Student Leadership series.

Lalenja Harrington is the Academic Director for Integrative Community Studies at University of North Carolina at Greensboro and she is currently a PhD. student within the Educational Studies and Cultural Foundations program at UNCG, with a focus on access to higher education, inclusive pedagogy and community engaged/participatory research. Lalenja considers performance to be one of her passions, and welcomes all opportunities to include creative expression, specifically poetry and music into all aspects of her life-including academic work and research. Lalenja is a graduate of Princeton University with a BA in psychology, and is a graduate of UNC-CH with an MA in Journalism and Mass Communication Studies.

Michael Harris is a professor and the Dean of The College of Public Service and Urban Affairs at Tennessee State University, Nashville, TN. Dr. Harris is an experienced academic leader and scholar. Dr. Harris has published 5 books and close to 40 academic papers. Dr. Harris has been awarded nearly $3.5 million in grants. Among the positions he held: Chancellor of Indiana University Kokomo, and professor of public and environmental affairs, education and business; provost at Kettering University; associate provost at Eastern Michigan University (EMU). Honors and academic recognition include: The Kokomo Perspective named: "2011 Person of the Year." Appointed: "Honorary Wing Commander" for the 434th Air Refueling Wing at Grissom Air Base, IN. Received from the Shin II Educational Foundation Board, Seoul, South Korea an award for "furthering the globalization of education."

Kim Hunt is currently a doctoral research assistant at the University of San Diego's Caster Family Center for Nonprofit and Philanthropic Research and a doctoral student at the University of San Diego's School of Leadership and Education Studies. Prior to joining USD, she worked with non-profits as a business manager, volunteer, communications specialist, and budget analyst throughout the US and Europe with a focus on education and military services. She holds a Master's in Education with an emphasis in Curriculum Development from the University of Phoenix and a Bachelor's Degree from California Polytechnic University, San Luis Obispo in Economics with an emphasis in Developing Nations.

Tara Jabbaar-Gyambrah is currently the Senior Assistant Director of the Honors College at the University at Buffalo, and an Adjunct Professor in the Sociology Department at Niagara University. She has a wide range of leadership experiences including, but not limited to: serving as co-chair of the Middle States Research Group, academic advising, coordinating a peer mentoring program, overseeing a high school to college program, and managing a diversity office. Dr. Tara received her Ph.D. from the University at Buffalo's American Studies program specializing in Women Studies She earned her Ph.D. from the University at Buffalo's, American Studies program specializing in Women's Studies along with an Advanced Certificate in Teaching for Leading Diversity. Her scholarly articles and chapters have been published in the *Journal of College Admissions*, *Journal of Race and Policy*, *NACADA Publications*, *Palgrave*, and *Southwest Journal of Cultures*. Dr. Tara is the contributing editor for *Afro-Americans in New York Life and History*. She has also presented at numerous national conferences and is known for her expertise and extensive field work on the cross-cultural experiences of women in hip-hop and hip-life music industries in America and Ghana. In her spare time, Dr. Tara enjoys spending time with family and friends, traveling, listening to music and poetry.

Toby S. Jenkins is currently an Assistant Professor of Higher Education at Georgia Southern University. Prior to GSU, she served as a Visiting Assistant Professor at the University of Hawaii Manoa and an Assistant Professor of Interdisciplinary Studies at George Mason University. Her professional background includes ten years of experience as a student affairs administrator at Penn State University and the University of Maryland. Her research interests focus on how communities of color use culture as a politic of social survival, a tool of social change, and a medium for transformative education. She is also interested in the ways in which culture influences students' perceptions of the purpose of education and their commitment to community based leadership. From a policy and curriculum perspective, Dr. Jenkins also studies issues related to culturally relevant pedagogy and culturally relevant educational policy.

Elizabeth C. Jodoin is the Associate Director of Counseling Services at the University of South Carolina Upstate. Dr. Jodoin is a Licensed Professional Counselor and received her Doctor of Philosophy in Higher Education from the University of North Carolina-Greensboro.

Brent E. Johnson is a native of Cincinnati, Ohio. Dr. Johnson received his undergraduate degree from Howard University, a graduate degree in School Counseling from Xavier University (Ohio), and a PhD in Educational Leadership from Miami University (Ohio). With almost 20 years working in the field of education, Dr. Johnson researches the inequitable power relationships within and outside of schooling systems and the maintenance of the American Caste System resulting from these relationships. Dr. Johnson currently works as a school counselor at Forest Park High School (Georgia) as well as an adjunct professor at Gordon State College (Georgia).

P. Brandon Johnson is currently Director of the Center for Academic Achievement at Florida Gulf Coast University. Dr. Johnson received his Doctor of Philosophy degree in Higher Education from the University of North Carolina-Greensboro. He previously served as the Assistant Director for Tutoring Services: TRiO Special Support Services at the University of North Carolina-Greensboro. He is interested in creating initiatives that focus on student success both academically and socially.

John J. Lee's research draws on a sociocultural perspective of language and identity for the purpose of understanding the positionality of English language learners' in higher education. His work also examines the literacy and identity practices that occur in digital space and social networking sites. Prior to joining University of Illinois at Chicago's Literacy, Language, and Culture doctoral program, he served as a K-12 literacy specialist, journalist, and non-profit program coordinator that served underprivileged children in urban communities.

Angelo Letizia is an assistant professor of Graduate Education at Newman University in Wichita Kansas. His research interests include the public good, neoliberalism and crucial pedagogy.

Brenda L. H. Marina is an Associate Dean for the Division of Academic Affairs at Baltimore City Community College. She has served as an Associate Professor, teaching graduate courses in Educational Leadership and Higher Education Administration at Georgia Southern University. Additionally, she has served as an affiliate faculty and executive board member for a Women & Gender Studies program. Her scholarship explores Women in Leadership, Mentoring for Leadership, Multicultural Competence in Higher Education, and Global Education Issues from a womanist perspective. Dr. Marina is a board member for the International Mentoring Association (IMA) and a peer reviewer for the International Journal of Mentoring and Coaching in Education. She is the editor of the Georgia Journal for College Student Affairs, a journal sponsored by the Georgia College Personnel Association (GCPA). Dr. Marina has published book chapters related to identity development for female students of color, religiosity and spirituality in leadership programs, managing diversity in workplaces and society, as well as journal articles on cultural competence and the glass ceiling. She recently published a book entitled *Mentoring Away the Glass Ceiling in Academe: A Cultured Critique. Marina* is currently working on a book that articulates a vision for equitable, fair, and just spaces for women faculty of color within academe in the United States.

Melissa A. Odegard-Koester is an Associate Professor and Counseling Program Coordinator with the Counseling Program at Southeast Missouri State University where she has taught for the last six years. She holds a Doctor of Philosophy in Counselor Education and Counseling from Idaho State University. Dr. Odegard-Koester has worked in several private agency settings with children, adolescents, adults, couples and families with a wide array of presenting concerns. She is a licensed professional counselor in the State of Missouri and is also a National Certified Counselor. She has several peer-reviewed publications that focus on clinical supervision, social justice pedagogy, and counselor training. She maintains a number of professional memberships and has given many presentations on the state, regional, and national levels.

Donna-Marie Peters received an undergraduate degree from Middlebury College, an M.A. from The University of Connecticut, and an M.A. and Ph.D. from The New School for Social Research and a Ph.D. in Sociology from the New School for Social Research. Donna-Marie has taught various courses on topics of race and ethnicity since joining the Sociology Department at Temple University in 2003. Dr. Peters has published in numerous journals including *Journal of Women and Aging, Leisure Studies, The Western Journal of Black Studies*, and *The Journal of Pan African Studies.* Her research interests examine areas of race, class, ethnicity, gender, age, family, and address community issues including community building, community incorporation, safe spaces and health. Dr. Peters has received numerous grants and is currently completing a manuscript based on her research of the African American summer community on Martha's Vineyard. Donna-Marie is the creator of ongoing monthly faculty professional development workshops titled Can We Talk that explore best teaching practices for teaching controversial and sensitive topics of race. She is the producer of Global Women's Dialogue discussion groups and events that provide students from diverse racial and ethnic backgrounds (nationally and internationally) to meet to discuss issues and concerns that women share globally. Donna-Marie has conducted teaching workshops at the Lilly Conference on College and University Teaching that address specific issues related to faculty teaching courses on race and diversity at the undergraduate level.

Sonja Peterson-Lewis is an Associate Professor in the Department of African American Studies at Temple University in Philadelphia PA. She earned her doctorate in Social Psychology at the University of Florida. Her major teaching interest is in social research methods, an arena in which she has guided hundreds of empirical projects and created several skill-building games. Her research interests include the effects of popular culture on interpersonal and social behavior and the dramaturgy of race. She is completing an interview- and archival-based study of the quest for formal education among African Americans in a Northeast Florida community, 1865–1965.

Jay Poole is Associate Professor at the University of North Carolina at Greensboro in the Department of Social Work. His career in clinical social work spans over 30 years and currently he is involved with efforts to examine diversity, equity, and inclusion. One of his research interests is identity studies with particular focus on gender and sexuality. His recent work appears in *Men Speak Out: Views on Sex Power and Gender* edited by Shira Tarrant (2008; 2010), and in *Brightlights Film Journal* as well as *Sexualities in Education: A Reader* (2011). Also, look for Dr. Poole's work in *The Journal of Black Masculinity* and in the book *South to Queer Place: An Interdisciplinary Collection of Queer Lives and Southern Sensibilities* (2011). Dr. Poole is currently the Principal Investigator for *The Congregational Social Work Education*

Initiative and *The Partnership to Address Co-Occurring Disorders in Vulnerable Populations*, both funded by the Cone Health Foundation.

Robert E. Randolph currently serves as the Director of the University Writing Center at North Carolina A & T State University. He is currently a doctoral candidate in the Department of Educational Leadership and Cultural Foundations at the University of North Carolina-Greensboro. Mr. Randolph is a well sought after Poet and motivational speaker. His research interests are in the critical aspects of creative writing, black masculinity and popular culture, as well as the public consumption of the black aesthetics.

Tremayne S. Robertson is the Violence Prevention Health Educator at Virginia Commonwealth University's Wellness Resource Center. Tremayne is an industry leader in bringing males into the circle of discussion, prevention, and solutions for violence on campus. Tremayne is a graduate of the University of Virginia and Syracuse University, where he is currently completing a Ph.D.

Cara Robinson is an assistant professor in the Urban Studies Program at Tennessee State University. Dr. Robinson currently teaches undergraduate courses in Urban Studies and Nonprofit Management and Leadership and graduate courses in Public Administration within the College of Public Service & Urban Affairs. She also previously taught courses in Public Policy at the University of Delaware. She is the Coordinator of the TSU Democracy Project and Assistant Director for TSU's Center for Human Capital. Currently, Dr. Robinson also serves as Chair of the Metro Homelessness Commission Data and Cost Savings Workgroup and is a member of the NashvilleNext Housing Resource Team and the Metropolitan Development and Housing Authority Gaps Governance Committee. Dr. Robinson has published research in a variety of public policy areas primarily focused on issues related to poverty, homelessness and social equity.

Dalia Rodriguez is Associate Professor of Cultural Foundations of Education and associated faculty in Women's and Gender Studies at Syracuse University. Her main interests include race, ethnicity, and gender in education. Her teaching and research interests examine race and racism within the United States, critical race theory, and qualitative research methods. She has a special interest in narrative and autobiographical writing. Some of her work includes "The Usual Suspect: Negotiating White Student Resistance and Teacher Authority in a Predominantly White Classroom" (*Cultural Studies/Critical Methodologies*, August 2009), "Storytelling in the field: Race, Method, and the Empowerment of Latina College Students" *Cultural Studies/Critical Methodologies*, April 2010), "Silence as Speech: Meanings of Silence for Students of Color in Predominantly White Classrooms" *International Review of Qualitative Research*, Spring 2011), and "Silent Rage and the Politics of Resistance: Resistance and Empowerment for Women of Color in the Academy" *Qualitative Inquiry*, Summer 2011). She has also collaborated in establishing support groups for students and faculty of color, has presented her research to offices of multicultural affairs as well as Provost offices across the country, as well as written policy reports about the status of students of color in higher education. In addition, she has conducted teaching diversity workshops on college campuses, addressing how intersectionality is central to understanding identity.

Victor Romano is Associate Professor of Sociology and Chair of the Faculty Senate. He earned a BA in Sociology/Anthropology from Florida International University and an MA and Ph.D. from the University of Florida. Dr. Romano teaches courses on race, class, and gender, marriage and the family, and introductory sociology, as well as courses in the university's Honors Program. His scholarly research and writings focus on the areas of racial and ethnic relations, gender stratification, and childlessness. Dr. Romano is Chairperson of the Miami-Dade County Commission on Human Rights and is Board Secretary for Hope, Inc., a non-profit organization committed to combating housing discrimination.

Sabrina N. Ross is an Associate Professor of Curriculum Studies at Georgia Southern University. Her scholarship involves intersections of race, gender, and power within formal and informal educational contexts. She has published articles in *Educational Foundations, The Journal of African American Education, The International Journal of the Scholarship of Teaching and Learning*, and *Teaching in Higher Education.* She guest-edited a special issue of *The Journal of Curriculum Theorizing* (2012, with Ming Fang He) examining narrative of curriculum in the U.S. South. Her forthcoming edited book (with Brenda Marina) is titled *Beyond Retention: Cultivating Spaces of Equity, Justice, and Fairness for Women of Color in U.S. Higher Education.*

Sage E. Russo is a graduate student in the Communication Studies Department at San Francisco State University. Her current interests include critical theory, gender, and sexuality in specific relation to gendered perceptions of sexual behaviors.

Rickie Sanders is Professor of Geography/Urban Studies and former Director of Women's Studies at Temple University and Director of the Greater Philadelphia Women's Studies Consortium. During her tenure at Temple University she has served as both Graduate Chair and Chair of her Department and was a Fellow at the Center for the Humanities at Temple. She also served on the Temple University General Education Executive Committee.

Sanders has published in numerous publications including Women's Studies Quarterly, Revista Artemis XVI, Journal of Geography, Professional Geographer, Gender Place and Culture, Journal of Geography in Higher Education, Antipode, Urban Geography, and a Legislative Atlas for the Commonwealth of Pennsylvania. Her current research focusses on images of the city/photography/visual studies, urban geography, gender on the landscape, and critical pedagogy. Her recent (2012, 2013) work includes "Making INVISIBLE CITIES Visible" a photo essay with Bogdan Jankowski in Journal of Research and Didactics in Geography; Trayvon Martin: The Blogosphere, Racial Profiling, and Social Justice in Antipode Issues Forum; "The Ambiguous Rhetoric of Invisibility and Visibility in Women's Lives" Revista Artemis XVI with Loreley Gomez Garcia; "The Complexities of Teaching Simple Geographic Concepts: A Guide to Connecting Critical Geography to the Classroom" in Geography and Social Justice in the Classroom (Routledge Research in Education Series), Todd Kenreich, Ed.; "The Whitening of the Public University: The Context for Diversifying Geography," The Professional Geographer with Audrey Kobayashi and Victoria Lawson. She presented her work this summer at the meeting of the International Visual Studies Association in Pittsburgh as well as the International Geographers Union in Krakow.She was recently honored by the Association of American Geographers for her success in Enhancing Diversity in the discipline.

Talha Ali Siddiqi hails from Karachi, Pakistan. He received his Master of Science in Technology Management from Southeast Missouri State University. He has expertise in Transportation, Manufacturing, and Industrial Engineering. Talha currently resides in the United States and works in the field of Computer Technology and Engineering.

Pearlie Strother-Adams is a full professor in the Department of Broadcasting and Journalism at Western Illinois University, Macomb. She is both a career educator and journalist. Prior to becoming a professor in higher education, she taught high school English for several years in addition to writing as a freelance journalist. Her most recent articles are narratives of her life in Selma and Birmingham, Alabama as a child of the civil rights movement. She is contributor to groundbreaking scholarly anthology titled *From Uncle Tom's Cabin to the Help* (2014), a collection of theoretical works that look at the representation of blacks in films produced in Hollywood by whites about blacks. Her article is titled "Good Mother, Trickster, tom, Jezebel in Blind Side" (2014), published by Palgrave/Macmillan. She is co-editor as well as a contributing author to two editions of *Dealing With Diversity II: The Anthology* (2001 and 2008), First and Second Editions, both compilations of scholarly works on diversity issues that is used in classrooms throughout the nation. Her research, which has been published broadly and presented nationally, centers on the representation of African Americans in American media. Her passion and concern for social justice, freedom and equality is evident in all of her works. In 2006 she was awarded the prestigious American Society of Newspaper Editor's (ASNE). In 2013, she was awarded Western Illinois University's President's Teacher's Recognition Award for her efforts to teach from a diverse perspective in the classroom and to provide outside learning experiences for students in the areas of politics and social justice. She is presently completing a book on her life and civil rights in the sixties in Selma and Birmingham, Alabama.

Elizabeth L. Sweet is an Assistant Professor Instructional at Temple University in the Department of Geography and Urban Studies. She received her BA from Boston University in Soviet and East European Studies and her Masters in Urban Planning and Policy as well as her PhD in Public Policy Analysis from the University of Illinois Chicago. She is an interdisciplinary critical scholar focusing on the nexus of economies, identity, and violence. Her scholarship examines the role of planning and policy in the production and reproduction of social, economic, and spatial inequalities, particularly in Latino/a and Indigenous communities. She also has a strong, long running interest and publication record on diversity in the academy. Her research has been funded by the National Science Foundation, American Sociological Association, The George Soros Civic Education Project, the Rockefeller Foundation, the Fulbright Scholars Program, the Illinois Department of Human Services, The Center for Democracy in a Multiracial Society, The Institute of Research on Race and Public Policy, Catholic Charities for Human Development, and Temple University, Faculty Senate and Internationalization grants.

Karen M. Turner is an associate professor and director of the broadcast journalism concentration in the Department of Journalism at Temple University. She served as department chair from 2000–2003 and is a founding member of Temple's Academic Center on Research in Diversity (ACCORD). She is currently its director. Karen teaches undergraduate and graduate courses in broadcast journalism, performance and media race studies. She is a 2013 Lindback Foundation Distinguished Teaching Award recipient. She was selected the inaugural recipient of the School of Communications and Theater's Innovative Teaching award in 2004. Her research interests include the integration of new media technologies in race studies and journalism pedagogy; and diversity issues in media. Before joining the Temple faculty in 1992, Karen was the press secretary to former Philadelphia Mayor Edward Rendell. She has extensive experience as a radio journalist and talk radio interviewer having worked in such markets as Philadelphia, Cincinnati and New Brunswick, N. J. Karen has degrees from Dartmouth College, Columbia University Graduate School of Journalism and the Northwestern University School of Law. In 2012 she earned a Certificate in Diversity Leadership through Temple's Graduate School of Education. She has an active social media presence publishing comments through her Facebook page, "Professor Karen's Corner" and her blog www.karenmturner.com. Her twitter hand is @karenmturner

Seneca Vaught has interned at TransAfrica Forum and has been a senior fellow of information and technology at the Africana Cultures and Policy Studies Institute. He has published articles on gender and policy, critical pedagogy, and technological change. His recent work has examined the role of race and Black Studies in higher education and the future of learning.

Paul Watkins has been an educator for over 35 years. He started his career as an eighth grade English teacher, and later became an administrator both at the building and district levels until retirement, when he took a position as a Professional Development Coordinator, serving the Southeast region of

Missouri. He later became a faculty member at Southeast Missouri State University where he works today as the coordinator for the University of Missouri's Statewide Cooperative Ed.D. Program.

Jillian Volpe White serves as a Community Engagement Coordinator at the Center for Leadership & Social Change at Florida State University. Through experiential learning and reflection, White facilitates student development focused on community, identity, and leadership. She also teaches in the Undergraduate Certificate in Leadership Studies. White received her doctor of philosophy degree in Higher Education, master's degree in Higher Education, and undergraduate degree in Mass Media Studies all from Florida State University. Her research interests include reflection, community engagement, leadership, and experiential learning.

Kimmika Williams-Witherspoon is an Associate Professor of Urban Theater and Community Engagement. Recipient of the 2013 Associate Provosts for the Arts Grant; a 2008 Research and Creative Seed Grant Co-recipient, a 2003 Provost's Arts Commission Grant; a 2001 Independence Foundation Theater Communications Group Grant, the 2000 winner of the PEW Charitable Trust fellowship in scriptwriting, and the 1999, winner of the DaimlerChrysler "Spirit of the Word" National Poetry Competition. Author of *Through Smiles and Tears: The History of African American Theater (From Kemet to the Americas)* (Lambert Academic Publishing, 2011); *The Secret Messages in African American Theater: Hidden Meaning Embedded in Public Discourse* (Edwin Mellen Publishing, 2006) she has had over twenty-three of her plays produced. Her stage credits include thirteen productions and she is a contributing poet to twenty-six poetry anthologies. Dr Williams-Witherspoon holds the following degrees: PhD (Cultural Anthropology), MA (Anthropology), MFA (Theater), Graduate Certificate) Women's Studies, BA (Journalism)

Gust A. Yep is Professor of Communication Studies, Graduate Faculty of Sexuality Studies, and Faculty in the Ed. D. Program in Educational Leadership at San Francisco State University. His research examines communication at the intersections of culture, race, class, gender, sexuality, and nation, with a focus on sexual, gender, and ethnic minority communities. In addition to three books, he has authored more than seventy articles in (inter)disciplinary journals and anthologies. He is recipient of numerous academic and community awards including the 2011 San Francisco State University Distinguished Faculty Award for Professional Achievement (Researcher of the Year) and the 2015 Association for Education in Journalism and Mass Communication (AEJMC) Leroy F. Aarons Award for significant contributions to LGBT media education and research.

Index

A

D

P

Q

T

Questions about the Purpose(s) of Colleges and Universities

Norm Denzin,
Shirley R. Steinberg
General Editors

What are the purposes of higher education? When undergraduates "declare their majors," they agree to enter into a world defined by the parameters of a particular academic discourse—a discipline. But who decides those parameters? How do they come about? What are the discussions and proposed outcomes of disciplined inquiry? What should an undergraduate know to be considered educated in a discipline? How does the disciplinary knowledge base inform its pedagogy? Why are there different disciplines? When has a discipline "run its course"? Where do new disciplines come from? Where do old ones go? How does a discipline produce its knowledge? What are the meanings and purposes of disciplinary research and teaching? What are the key questions of disciplined inquiry? What questions are taboo within a discipline? What can the disciplines learn from one another? What might they not want to learn and why?

Once we begin asking these kinds of questions, positionality becomes a key issue. One reason why there aren't many books on the meaning and purpose of higher education is that once such questions are opened for discussion, one's subjectivity becomes an issue with respect to the presumed objective stances of Western higher education. Academics don't have positions because positions are "biased," "subjective," "slanted," and therefore somehow invalid. So the first thing to do is to provide a sense—however broad and general—of what kinds of positionalities will inform the books and chapters on the above questions. Certainly the questions themselves, and any others we might ask, are already suggesting a particular "bent," but as the series takes shape, the authors we engage will no doubt have positions on these questions.

From the stance of interdisciplinary, multidisciplinary, or transdisciplinary practitioners, will the chapters and books we solicit solidify disciplinary discourses, or liquefy them? Depending on who is asked, interdisciplinary inquiry is either a polite collaboration among scholars firmly situated in their own particular discourses, or it is a blurring of the restrictive parameters that define the very notion of disciplinary discourse. So will the series have a stance on the meaning and purpose of interdisciplinary inquiry and teaching? This can possibly be finessed by attracting thinkers from disciplines that are already multidisciplinary, for example, the various kinds of "studies" programs (women's, Islamic, American, cultural, etc.), or the hybrid disciplines like ethnomusicology (musicology, folklore, anthropology). But by including people from these fields (areas? disciplines?) in our series, we are already taking a stand on disciplined inquiry. A question on the comprehensive exam for the Columbia University Ethnomusicology Program was to defend ethnomusicology as a "field" or a "discipline." One's answer determined one's future, at least to the extent that the gatekeepers had a say in such matters. So, in the end, what we are proposing will no doubt involve political struggles.

For additional information about this series or for the submission of manuscripts, please contact Shirley R. Steinberg, msgramsci@gmail.com. To order other books in this series, please contact our Customer Service Department at: (800) 770-LANG (within the U.S.), (212) 647-7706 (outside the U.S.), (212) 647-7707 FAX, or browse online by series at: www.peterlang.com.